Real-Time Data Analysis Exercises

Up-to-date macro data is a great way to engage in and understand the usefulness of macro variables and their impact on the economy. Real-Time Data Analysis exercises communicate directly with the Federal Reserve Bank of St. Louis's FRED site, so every time FRED posts new data, students see new data.

End-of-chapter exercises accompanied by the Real-Time Data Analysis icon 🌐 include Real-Time Data versions in **MyEconLab**.

Select in-text figures labeled **MyEconLab** Real-Time Data update in the electronic version of the text using FRED data.

G: Assignment 3

① ② ③ ④ ▷ ▷▷

RTDA: GDP and the Business Cycle

Score: 0 of 1 pt   Assignment Score: 0% (0 of 4 pts)   0 of 4 complete

al-Time Data Analysis Exercise

following table contains data for nominal GDP, real GDP, and
ntial real GDP from FRED* for the **third quarter of 2012.**

Series	Value (in billions)
Nominal GDP	$15,775.7
Real GDP	$13,616.2
Potential real GDP	$14,474.4

ariable identified as nominal is one that is measured in current dollars.

g the data above, calculate the following: *(Enter your responses rounded
o decimal places)* ❓

GDP deflator is 115.86

tive to potential real GDP, real GDP is 5.93 percent below potential real
.

*Real-time data provided by Federal Reserve Economic Data (FRED), Federal Reserve Bank of Saint Louis.

U.S. GDP Data

Click this icon for a helpful formula.

To compute the GDP deflator, divide nominal GDP by real GDP and multiply the result by 100.

To calculate the percent that real GDP is below real potential GDP, use the following formula:

any number or expression in each of the edit fields, then click Che[ck]

Current News Exercises

Posted weekly, we find the latest microeconomic and macroeconomic news stories, post them, and write auto-graded multi-part exercises that illustrate the economic way of thinking about the news.

Homework: Assignment 3

◁◁ ◁ ① ② ③ ④ ▷ ▷▷

November 2, 2012

Exercise Score: 0 of 1 pt   Assignment Score: 25% (1 of 4 pts)   1 of 4 complete

Phillipines' Credit Rating Boosted by Moody's to Ba1

Source: Yap, Cecilia and Max Estayo. "Phillipines' Credit Rating Boosted by Moody's to Ba1." *Bloomberg.com*, posted 10/29/2012. Click here to read the article.

Moody's Investors Service upgraded Philippines debt to "one step away from investment grade." The move is on the heels of President Aquino's efforts to control deficit spending and take steps to "lure foreign investors." Moody's cited the country's ability to maintain solid tax revenues in the face of declining global output demand. The country has maintained economic growth while keeping inflation in check.

Credit ratings impact the cost of borrowing for countries and firms. A higher credit rating indicates lower credit risk and therefore attracts investors that may have shunned lower rated debt. The higher credit rating will lower the overall cost of borrowing and also signal that the country is politically stable. Foreign investors will not only look more closely at Philippine bonds but also at direct foreign investment in the country.

Analyzing the News

Credit ratings are important to both firms and countries because they are an external assessment of risk. A credit upgrade can be due to a number of factors but it sends the same positive signal to investors. More investors will buy the country's bonds but also invest in other aspects of the Philippine economy.

Thinking Critically Questions

1. A higher bond rating translates to a(n) _____ interest rate.

○ A. lower
○ B. erratic
○ C. stable

Interactive Homework Exercises

Participate in a fun and engaging activity that helps promote active learning and mastery of important economic concepts.

Pearson's experiments program is flexible and easy for instructors and students to use. For a complete list of available experiments, visit *www.myeconlab.com.*

INSTRUCTIONS   EXPERIMENT

Market for Cranberries

Round 1 of 4

●○○○

PLAY   PRINT   EXPORT   ?

KEY: ⊙ Free Market

Click Play to start this round.

WTP: **$12.00**   You are a Buyer

Your Bid: $

Round 1

Your WTP: $12.00
Transaction Price: $11.50
Average Transaction Price: $11.75
Total Transactions: 8

OK

CURRENT BIDS AND ASKS

Your Bid: Highest Bid: $
$11.50   Lowest Ask: $

TOTAL RESULTS

Round	Role	WTP	Cost	Bid	Ask	Price	Gain
1	Buyer	$12.00		$11.50		$11.50	$0.50

Total Gain: $0.50

TIME

Legend: ▶ Lowest Ask ▶ Highest Bid ▶ Sellers ▶ Buyers ◆ Transaction ◆ Your Transaction

Macroeconomics

Second Edition

R. Glenn Hubbard
Columbia University

Anthony Patrick O'Brien
Lehigh University

Matthew Rafferty
Quinnipiac University

Boston Columbus Indianapolis New York San Francisco Upper Saddle River
Amsterdam Cape Town Dubai London Madrid Milan Munich Paris Montreal Toronto
Delhi Mexico City São Paulo Sydney Hong Kong Seoul Singapore Taipei Tokyo

Dedication

For Constance, Raph, and Will
—*R. Glenn Hubbard*

For Lucy
—*Anthony Patrick O'Brien*

For Sacha
—*Matthew Rafferty*

Editor in Chief: Donna Battista
Executive Editor: David Alexander
Executive Development Editor: Lena Buonanno
VP/Director of Development: Stephen Deitmer
Editorial Project Manager: Lindsey Sloan
Director of Marketing: Maggie Moylan
Executive Marketing Manager: Lori DeShazo
Managing Editor: Jeff Holcomb
Senior Production Project Manager: Kathryn Dinovo
Manufacturing Director: Evelyn Beaton
Senior Manufacturing Buyer: Carol Melville
Creative Director: Christy Mahon

Senior Art Director: Jonathan Boylan
Cover Illustration: Nikita Prokhorov
Manager, Rights and Permissions: Michael Joyce
Permissions Specialist, Project Manager: Jill Dougan
Executive Media Producer: Melissa Honig
Content Lead, MyEconLab: Noel Lotz
Full-Service Project Management: PreMediaGlobal
Composition: PreMediaGlobal
Printer/Binder: Von Hoffman dba R.R. Donnelley/Jefferson City
Cover Printer: Lehigh-Phoenix Color/Hagerstown
Text Font: Minion Pro

Credits and acknowledgments of material borrowed from other sources and reproduced, with permission, in this textbook appear on the pages with the respective material.

FRED® is a registered trademark and the FRED® logo and ST. LOUIS FED are trademarks of the Federal Reserve Bank of St. Louis, http://research.stlouisfed.org/fred2/

Many of the designations by manufacturers and sellers to distinguish their products are claimed as trademarks. Where those designations appear in this book, and the publisher was aware of a trademark claim, the designations have been printed in initial caps or all caps.

Library of Congress Cataloging-in-Publication Data
Hubbard, R. Glenn.
  Macroeconomics / R. Glenn Hubbard, Anthony Patrick O'Brien, Matthew Rafferty.—2nd ed.
    p. cm.
  ISBN-13: 978-0-13-299279-4 (hard cover)
  ISBN-10: 0-13-299279-5
  1. Macroeconomics. I. O'Brien, Anthony Patrick. II. Rafferty, Matthew. III. Title.
  HB172.5.H86 2014
  339—dc23
                                                        2012039476

10 9 8 7 6 5 4 3 2 1

PEARSON

ISBN 10: 0-13-299502-6
ISBN 13: 978-0-13-299502-3

About the Authors

Glenn Hubbard, Professor, Researcher, and Policymaker

R. Glenn Hubbard is the dean and Russell L. Carson Professor of Finance and Economics in the Graduate School of Business at Columbia University and professor of economics in Columbia's Faculty of Arts and Sciences. He is also a research associate of the National Bureau of Economic Research and a director of Automatic Data Processing, Black Rock Closed-End Funds, KKR Financial Corporation, and MetLife. Professor Hubbard received his Ph.D. in economics from Harvard University in 1983. From 2001 to 2003, he served as chairman of the White House Council of Economic Advisers and chairman of the OECD Economy Policy Committee, and from 1991 to 1993, he was deputy assistant secretary of the U.S. Treasury Department. He currently serves as co-chair of the nonpartisan Committee on Capital Markets Regulation and the Corporate Boards Study Group. Professor Hubbard is the author of more than 100 articles in leading journals, including *American Economic Review*; *Brookings Papers on Economic Activity*; *Journal of Finance*; *Journal of Financial Economics*; *Journal of Money, Credit, and Banking*; *Journal of Political Economy*; *Journal of Public Economics*; *Quarterly Journal of Economics*; *RAND Journal of Economics*; and *Review of Economics and Statistics*.

Tony O'Brien, Award-Winning Professor and Researcher

Anthony Patrick O'Brien is a professor of economics at Lehigh University. He received a Ph.D. from the University of California, Berkeley, in 1987. He has taught principles of economics, money and banking, and intermediate macroeconomics for more than 20 years, in both large sections and small honors classes. He received the Lehigh University Award for Distinguished Teaching. He was formerly the director of the Diamond Center for Economic Education and was named a Dana Foundation Faculty Fellow and Lehigh Class of 1961 Professor of Economics. He has been a visiting professor at the University of California, Santa Barbara, and at Carnegie Mellon University. Professor O'Brien's research has dealt with such issues as the evolution of the U.S. automobile industry, sources of U.S. economic competitiveness, the development of U.S. trade policy, the causes of the Great Depression, and the causes of black–white income differences. His research has been published in leading journals, including *American Economic Review*; *Quarterly Journal of Economics*; *Journal of Money, Credit, and Banking*; *Industrial Relations*; *Journal of Economic History*; *Explorations in Economic History*; and *Journal of Policy History*.

Matthew Rafferty, Professor and Researcher

Matthew Christopher Rafferty is a professor of economics and department chairperson at Quinnipiac University. He has also been a visiting professor at Union College. He received a Ph.D. from the University of California, Davis, in 1997 and has taught intermediate macroeconomics for 15 years, in both large and small sections. Professor Rafferty's research has focused on university and firm-financed research and development activities. In particular, he is interested in understanding how corporate governance and equity compensation influence firm research and development. His research has been published in leading journals, including the *Journal of Financial and Quantitative Analysis*, *Journal of Corporate Finance*, *Research Policy*, and the *Southern Economic Journal*. He has worked as a consultant for the Connecticut Petroleum Council on issues before the Connecticut state legislature. He has also written op-ed pieces that have appeared in several newspapers, including the *New York Times*.

Brief Contents

Contents

Chapter 4   The Global Financial System   108

Chapter 5   The Standard of Living over Time and Across Countries 147

Chapter 6   Long-Run Economic Growth   176

Chapter 9   Business Cycles   294

Chapter 10 Explaining Aggregate Demand: The *IS–MP* Model

Chapter 14   Aggregate Demand, Aggregate Supply, and Monetary Policy 504

Chapter 15   Fiscal Policy and the Government Budget in the Long Run   543

Chapter 16   Consumption and Investment   573

Preface

The financial crisis and recession of 2007–2009 have changed how students, instructors, and policymakers think about the economy. The first U.S. financial crisis in 75 years showed the importance of the financial system, including "shadow banks," to macroeconomic theory and policy. The global nature of the crisis demonstrated that countries have become more connected economically and financially. In late 2012, the macroeconomic scene remained unsettled: The euro zone grappled with a debt crisis and austerity plans; growth slowed in the United States, China, and Brazil; recession returned to several European countries; and the U.S. Congress and president struggled to come to terms with a ballooning deficit. Many economists view the Great Recession and its aftermath as a watershed in macroeconomics second only to the Great Depression.

The events of the past few years have reinforced the views that inspired us to write the first edition:

1. The financial crisis makes it critical for students to receive more background on the financial system.
2. Short-run macroeconomic policy plays too small a role in many current texts.
3. Students will be interested in macroeconomic models when applied to understanding real-world events and current policies that are in today's news headlines.

New to This Edition

We were gratified by the enthusiastic response of students and instructors who used the first edition. The response confirmed our view that the market needed a text that provided more coverage of the financial system and presented a modern short-run model. In this second edition, we retain the key approach of our first edition while making several changes to address feedback from instructors and students and also to reflect our own classroom experiences. Here is a summary of our key changes. Please see the pages that follow for details about these changes:

- Increased the emphasis on the open economy by adding a new early international chapter—Chapter 4, "The Global Financial System"—and increasing integration of international examples in several chapters
- Streamlined, substantially revised, and reorganized the presentation of economic growth in two chapters: Chapter 5, "The Standard of Living over Time and Across Countries," and Chapter 6, "Long-Run Economic Growth"
- Reorganized and revised the presentation of the *IS–MP* model, which is now covered in two chapters: Chapter 10, "Explaining Aggregate Demand: The *IS–MP* Model," and Chapter 11, "The *IS–MP* Model: Adding Inflation and the Open Economy"
- Added 10 new *Making the Connection* features
- Added 46 new real-time data exercises that students can complete on MyEconLab
- Replaced or updated approximately one-half of the questions and problems at the end of each chapter
- Updated graphs and tables with the latest available data; added 8 new figures; and added 3 new tables

"The book places welcome emphasis on financial markets (both domestic and international)."

Mark Tendall,
Stanford University

"Accessible, current, and relevant . . . students will enjoy the balance between model development and real-world applications. I really enjoyed the integration of the financial crisis, housing crash, oil shock and exchange rates. Wonderful!"

Carlos F. Liard-Muriente,
Central Connecticut
State University

"It is the best textbook to use in an Intermediate Macro course that emphasizes the ongoing financial crisis and its impact on the real economy. The discussion of the sovereign debt crisis in Europe in the second edition is valuable."

Ted Burczak,
Denison University

Increased the emphasis on the open economy by adding a new early international chapter—Chapter 4, "The Global Financial System"—and increasing integration of international examples in several chapters

In 2012, U.S. policymakers, firms, and investors held their breath as Europe grappled with a debt crisis and the possibility of recession. The reaction of the U.S. stock market was an indication that what was happening in Europe could potentially have a major effect on the U.S. economy. Because the international flows of goods and investment have grown so rapidly, we decided to include a new and early chapter on the global financial system: Chapter 4, "The Global Financial System." The chapter provides important background that can help students understand some of the key policy issues facing Congress, the president, and the Federal Reserve. We know, though, that many instructors are pressed for time just covering the short-run and long-run models and macroeconomic policy. So we wrote Chapter 4 in a way that allows instructors to skip it without loss of continuity.

This new chapter opens with a discussion of the economic performance of Brazil and the link between U.S. monetary policy and the value of Brazil's currency, the real. The chapter explores the topics of balance of payments, advantages and disadvantages of different exchange rate policies, factors that determine exchange rates, and the loanable funds model in an open economy. A theme of the text is to aid students' engagement by using each chapter's key features to support the topic presented in the chapter opener. We do so in Chapter 4 with the *Making the Connections* "Brazilian Firms Grapple with an Unstable Exchange Rate" and "Greece Experiences a 'Bank Jog,'" as well as a *Solved Problem* titled "Making a Financial Killing by Buying Brazilian Bonds?"

To complement the early chapter on the global financial system, we have added international examples throughout the text, including the following:

"Why Should the United States Worry About the 'Euro Crisis'?" (Chapter 1, "The Long and Short of Macroeconomics")

"Real Interest Rates and the Global Savings Glut" (Chapter 10, "Explaining Aggregate Demand: The *IS–MP* Model")

"Will the European Financial Crisis Cause a Recession in the United States?" (Chapter 10, "Explaining Aggregate Demand: The *IS–MP* Model")

"Did the Gold Standard Make the Great Depression Worse?" (Chapter 11, "The *IS–MP* Model: Adding Inflation and the Open Economy")

The material on monetary policy and fiscal policy in an open economy that was covered in the first edition's Chapter 15 is now covered in Chapter 12, "Monetary Policy in the Short Run," and Chapter 13, "Fiscal Policy in the Short Run."

Streamlined, substantially revised, and reorganized the presentation of economic growth in Chapter 5, "The Standard of Living over Time and Across Countries," and Chapter 6, "Long-Run Economic Growth"

Chapter 5, "The Standard of Living over Time and Across Countries," provides a complete discussion of how potential GDP is determined. We use the models developed in the chapter to explain why real GDP per capita varies across countries. The chapter provides a thorough enough discussion of potential GDP to allow instructors who want to emphasize short-run policy issues to move directly from Chapter 5 to Chapter 9 and the short-run chapters, while still introducing students to the basic determinants of the standard of living. Chapter 6, "Long-Run Economic Growth," provides a concise step-by-step introduction to the Solow growth model and to endogenous growth models. The chapter explains how policy affects the growth rate of the standard of living. Both chapters integrate information about China, India, and other developing countries to illustrate applications of the models. Chapter 6 includes expanded coverage of endogenous growth models, including *AK* growth models.

Reorganized and revised the presentation of the IS–MP *model, which is now covered in two chapters*

The *IS–MP* model in the first edition received a very favorable response from students and instructors. The model shifts the focus from the central bank's targeting the money supply to the central bank's targeting the bank lending rate. This change results in a more realistic and modern approach that allows students to tie what they learn in class to the discussions they hear on the news. Many students reading texts that use the traditional *IS–LM* model are surprised to learn that the Federal Reserve has no targets for M1 and M2 and that articles in the financial press rarely discuss the money supply. In the first edition, we attempted to cover the *IS–MP* model in a single rather long chapter. We now realize that a slower development of the model across two briefer chapters will aid student understanding.

In light of feedback, we reorganized our discussion of the short-run model as follows:

- Chapter 9, "Business Cycles," remains largely the same as in the first edition, but we added a new section that discusses the basic aggregate demand–aggregate supply (*AD–AS*) model. We added this section in response to feedback that we had not made sufficiently clear that *IS–MP* is a model of aggregate demand. With a review of aggregate demand in Chapter 9, students are now better equipped to understand the discussion of the *IS–MP* model in Chapter 10.
- Chapter 10, "Explaining Aggregate Demand: The *IS–MP* Model," is devoted to building the basic model with increased discussion of the determinants of the *IS* curve.
- Chapter 11, "The *IS–MP* Model: Adding Inflation and the Open Economy," as the title indicates, adds the Phillips curve and open-economy analysis to complete the discussion of the short-run model.

New Making the Connection *features and supporting exercises at the end of each chapter*

Each chapter includes two or more *Making the Connection* features that provide real-world reinforcement of key concepts. The second edition includes the following 10 new *Making the Connections*:

"Why Should the United States Worry About the 'Euro Crisis'?" (Chapter 1, "The Long and Short of Macroeconomics")

"Does the CPI Provide a Good Measure of Inflation for a Family with College Students?" (Chapter 2, "Measuring the Macroeconomy")

"The Controversial World of Subprime Lending" (Chapter 3, "The U.S. Financial System")

"Greece Experiences a 'Bank Jog'" (Chapter 4, "The Global Financial System")

"Making a Financial Killing by Buying Brazilian Bonds?" (Chapter 4, "The Global Financial System")

"Brazilian Firms Grapple with an Unstable Exchange Rate" (Chapter 4, "The Global Financial System")

"Should the Federal Government Invest in Green Energy?" (Chapter 6, "Long-Run Economic Growth")

"How Important Is Housing in the Business Cycle?" (Chapter 9, "Business Cycles")

"Did the 2007–2009 Recession Break Okun's Law?" (Chapter 9, "Business Cycles")

"Lots of Money but Not Much Inflation Following the Recession of 2007–2009" (Chapter 11, "The *IS–MP* Model: Adding Inflation and the Open Economy")

Making the Connections retained from the first edition have been updated with the most recent data.

MyEconLab

MyEconLab is a powerful assessment and tutorial system that works hand-in-hand with *Macroeconomics*. MyEconLab includes comprehensive homework, quiz, test, and tutorial options, allowing instructors to manage all assessment needs in one program. Key innovations in the MyEconLab course for *Macroeconomics*, second edition, include the following:

- Real-time *Data Analysis Exercises*, marked with (icon), allow students and instructors to use the absolute latest data from FRED, the online macroeconomic data bank from the Federal Reserve Bank of St. Louis. By completing the exercises, students become familiar with a key data source, learn how to locate data, and develop skills to interpret data.
- In the eText available in MyEconLab, select figures labeled MyEconLab Real-time data allow students to display a popup graph updated with real-time data from FRED.
- Current News Exercises, new to this edition of the MyEconLab course, provide a turn-key way to assign gradable news-based exercises in MyEconLab. Every week, Pearson scours the news, finds a current article appropriate for the macroeconomics course, creates an exercise around this news article, and then automatically adds it to MyEconLab. Assigning and grading current news-based exercises that deal with the latest macro events and policy issues and has never been more convenient.

Other Changes

- *New Contemporary Opening Cases*

We open each chapter with a real-world example, often drawn from policy debates or from the business world. All chapter openers have been updated. The following six chapter openers are new to this edition:

"Did U.S. Monetary Policy Slow Brazil's Growth?" (Chapter 4, "The Global Financial System")

"Is the Housing Cycle the Business Cycle?" (Chapter 9, "Business Cycles")

"Where's the Inflation?" (Chapter 11, "The *IS–MP* Model: Adding Inflation and the Open Economy")

"Why Didn't the Fed Avoid the Recession of 2007–2009?" (Chapter 12, "Monetary Policy in the Short Run")

"Driving Toward a 'Fiscal Cliff'" (Chapter 13, "Fiscal Policy in the Short Run")

"Drowning in a Sea of Debt?" (Chapter 15, "Fiscal Policy and the Government Budget in the Long Run")

- New *Solved Problems*

Each chapter includes one or more *Solved Problems* that provide students with step-by-step guidance in applying concepts and theories to problems. Students can complete related *Solved Problems* on MyEconLab and receive tutorial help. This edition includes the following new *Solved Problems*:

Solved Problem 5.2, "Calculating the Marginal Product of Labor and the Marginal Product of Capital" (Chapter 5, "The Standard of Living over Time and Across Countries")

Solved Problem 8.1, "Why Don't People Work as Much as They Did Decades Ago?" (Chapter 8, "The Labor Market")

Solved Problem 10.1, "Calculating Equilibrium Real GDP" (Chapter 10, "Explaining Aggregate Demand: The *IS–MP* Model")

- New figures and new tables

We have updated figures and tables using the most recent data, simplified several figures, cut complex or repetitive figures, and added the following new figures and tables:

> *"I appreciate the use of "Data Exercises." Seeing as how Macroanalysis is based so much in "Data Science," I feel that any opportunity that students have to deal with real-world data is a benefit to them."*
>
> Giacomo Santangelo,
> Fordham University

- Finally, we have gone over the text literally line-by-line, tightening the discussion, re-writing any unclear points, and making many other small changes. We are grateful to the students and instructors who made suggestions for improvements in the previous edition. We have done our best to incorporate as many of the suggestions as possible.

Our Approach to Intermediate Macroeconomics

There was a time when it seemed self-evident that policy should be the focus of a course in intermediate macroeconomics. The extraordinary macroeconomic events surrounding the Great Depression, World War II, and the immediate postwar era naturally focused the attention of economists on short-run policy measures. But by the 1970s, the conventional Keynesian–neoclassical synthesis of Samuelson, Hansen, and Hicks had come to seem inadequate to many economists. To summarize briefly the complicated evolution of macroeconomic theory during those years, conventional macroeconomics was seen as being inadequately grounded in microeconomic foundations and as being too neglectful of long-run considerations.

Although macroeconomic theory evolved rapidly during the 1970s and 1980s, intermediate macroeconomic textbooks largely remained unchanged. Only in the 1990s did the first generation of modern intermediate textbooks appear. These new texts dramatically refocused the intermediate course. The result was a welcome emphasis on the long run and on microfoundations. The Solow growth model, rather than the Keynesian IS–LM model, became the linchpin of these texts.

While in many ways we agree with the focus on the long run and on microfoundations, we have found ourselves in our own courses increasingly obliged to supplement existing texts with additional material. Our aim is certainly not to revolutionize the teaching of the intermediate macroeconomics course. Rather, we would like to shift its emphasis. We elaborate on our approach in the next sections.

A Modern Short-Run Model That Is Appropriate for the Intermediate Course (Chapters 10–13)

In the texts of the 1980s and earlier, the IS–LM model held center stage. The IS–LM model provided a useful way for instructors to present the major points of the Keynesian model of how short-run GDP is determined. Investigating the slopes of the IS and LM curves gave students some insights into the policy debates of the 1960s and early 1970s. In 2013, the IS–LM model has two obvious pedagogical shortcomings:

- The Keynesians versus Monetarists debates, while substantively important, are now a part of the history of macroeconomics.
- The assumption of a constant money supply used in constructing the LM curve no longer correctly describes the policy approach of the Fed or the central banks of other

"After developing the theory (i.e., the IS–LM–MP model), they used the model to analyze the 2007–09 recession. . . . I really like this approach. And students? Well, they don't like it, they love it . . . when we apply theory to the checkerboard of real life."

William Hart,
Miami University

"IS–MP is a major innovation."

James Butkiewicz,
University of Delaware

"I absolutely love the IS–MP model, I think it is more realistic and has been a long time coming. Morphs the theory in well with the graphs that are shown. Clear, and I love the tables like Table 10.2."

Nate Perry,
Mesa State College

developed countries. When central banks target interest rates rather than the money stock, the *LM* curve is no longer as useful as it once was in discussing monetary policy.

We do believe that the *IS* curve story provides a good account of the sources of fluctuations in real GDP in the short run, when prices are fixed. But, because the Fed targets interest rates rather than the money stock, we substitute a monetary policy, *MP*, curve for the *LM* curve. The result is similar to the *IS–MP* model first suggested by David Romer. We cover the *IS–MP* model in Chapter 10, "Explaining Aggregate Demand: The *IS–MP* Model," and Chapter 11, "The *IS–MP* Model: Adding Inflation and the Open Economy." We include a full appendix on the *IS–LM* model at the end of Chapter 11 for those who wish to cover that model. We use the *IS–MP* model to analyze monetary policy in Chapter 12, "Monetary Policy in the Short Run," and fiscal policy in the short run in Chapter 13, "Fiscal Policy in the Short Run."

Significant Coverage of Financial Markets, Beginning with Chapter 3

One of the most fundamental observations about conventional monetary policy is that, while the Fed has substantial influence over short-term effect interest rates, long-term real interest rates have a much larger effect on the spending decisions of households and firms. To understand the link between nominal short-term rates and real long-term rates, students need to be introduced to the role of expectations and the term structure of interest rates. We provide a careful, but concise, discussion of the term structure in Chapter 3, "The U.S. Financial System," and follow up this discussion in Chapter 10, "Explaining Aggregate Demand: The *IS–MP* Model," Chapter 11, "*IS–MP* Model: Adding Inflation and the Open Economy," and Chapter 12, "Monetary Policy in the Short Run," by analyzing why the Fed's interest rate targeting may sometimes fail to attain its goals.

The conventional story of a central bank's targeting interest rates or monetary aggregates is told in terms of the commercial banking system, so an overview of commercial banks is included in all texts. The explosion in securitization in the past 20 years has caused tremendous changes in the financial system and, recently, in Fed policy. Although securitization has been an important part of the financial system for years, its significance for Fed policy only became clear with the problems in the markets for mortgage-backed securities that developed during 2007. We provide an overview of securitization in Chapter 3, including a discussion of the increased importance of investment banks and other financial firms that are part of the "shadow banking system." Interest rate targeting is simply no longer the be-all and end-all of Fed policy. The events of 2008 have made it clear that an exclusive focus on commercial banks provides too narrow an overview of the financial system.

Early Discussion of Long-Run Growth (Chapters 5 and 6)

Students need to be able to distinguish the macroeconomic forest—long-run growth—from the macroeconomic trees—short-run fluctuations in real GDP, employment, and inflation. Because many macroeconomic principles texts put a heavy emphasis on the short run, many students enter the intermediate macro course thinking that macroeconomics is *exclusively* concerned with short-run fluctuations. The extraordinary success of the market system in raising the standard of living of the average person in the United States and the other high-income economies comes as surprising news to many students. Students know where we are today, but the economic explanation of how we got here is unfamiliar to many of them.

In addition, we believe that it makes sense for students to first understand both a basic model of long-run growth and the determination of GDP in a flexible-price model before moving on to the discussion of short-run fluctuations and short-run policy. In Chapter 5, "The Standard of Living over Time and Across Countries," we show the determination of GDP in a classical model and also discuss the difference between flexible price models and fixed price models.

Modern Federal Reserve Policy and Its Broadened Emphasis Beyond Interest Rate Targeting

The developments of 2007–2009 have demonstrated that the Fed has moved beyond the focus on interest rate targeting that had dominated policy since the early 1980s. To understand the broader reach of Fed policy, students need to be introduced to material—in particular, the increased importance of investment banking and role of securitization in modern financial markets—that is largely missing from competing texts. In addition, recent Fed policy initiatives require more discussion of issues of moral hazard. While these discussions are common in money and banking texts, they have been largely ignored in intermediate macro texts. We cover these topics in Chapter 7, "Money and Inflation," Chapter 12, "Monetary Policy in the Short Run," and Chapter 14, "Aggregate Demand, Aggregate Supply, and Monetary Policy."

Fourteen Core Chapters

This text consists of 14 core chapters and 2 "extension" chapters. Many instructors subscribe to the idea that fewer topics covered well is better than many topics covered superficially. We achieve brevity in two ways: First, we ignore almost entirely the "dueling schools of thought" approach. We do this for several reasons: Although this approach at one time provided a useful way of organizing textbooks, it no longer represents well the actual views of the profession. Emphasizing differences among economists obscures for students the broad areas of macroeconomics on which a professional consensus exists. Finally, most students find detailed discussions of disagreements among economists to be dull and unhelpful in understanding today's policy issues.

Our second key to achieving brevity in the core presentation is to push all nonessential topics to a separate Part 4, "Extensions," at the end of the text. While the topics covered in Part 4—long-run fiscal challenges (Chapter 15, "Fiscal Policy and the Government Budget in the Long Run") and the microfoundations of consumption and investment decisions (Chapter 16, "Consumption and Investment")—are important (and we typically cover many of them in our own courses), they are not *essential* to the basic macroeconomic story. In our view, it is better for instructors to present students with the key ideas in a relatively brief way with minimum distractions and then consider additional material during the last few weeks of the course when students have mastered the key ideas.

Flexible Chapter Organization

We have written the text to provide instructors with considerable flexibility. Instructors who wish to emphasize the short run can begin by covering Chapters 1–4 (Part 1, "Introduction"), and then jump to Chapters 9–13 (Part 3, "Macroeconomics in the Short Run: Theory and Policy"), before covering Chapters 5–8 (Part 2, "Macroeconomics in the Long Run: Economic Growth"). We have arranged content so that nothing in Chapters 9–13 requires knowledge of the discussion in Chapters 5–8.

Instructors wishing to omit the Solow model of long-run growth can skip Chapters 5 and 6 without loss of continuity.

Special Features

We have developed a number of special features. Some are similar to the features that have proven popular and effective aids to learning in the Hubbard and O'Brien *Economics* textbook and the Hubbard and O'Brien *Money, Banking, and the Financial System* textbook, while others were developed specifically for this book.

"I like the long-run-first arrangement. I appreciate the 'extensions' at the end; do them as time permits in the term. The inclusion of IS–LM as an appendix alongside the more current IS–MP model is an excellent idea. I like the relatively limited number of chapters, it's less daunting to students."

Christopher Burkart, University of West Florida

"I like it. It is good to have the financial system early in the book. I always struggle teaching that section since I find it very important for the development of the course."

Luisa Blanco, Pepperdine University

"I like the use of the "Key Issue and Question." I feel that it is an important tool to keep the student's focus. I find that having a unifying question that runs through the chapter exposes the students to a level of critical thinking that will benefit them and that they may not normally be accustomed to."

Giacomo Santangelo, Fordham University

Continued on next page

Key Issue and Question

Issue: Real GDP has increased substantially over time in the United States and other developed countries.

Question: What are the main factors that determine the growth rate of real GDP per capita?

Answered on page 206

Answering the Key Question

Continued from page 176

At the beginning of this chapter, we asked:

"What are the main factors that determine the growth rate of real GDP per capita?"

In this chapter, we saw that the long-run growth rate is determined by technological change. If we use a broader definition of capital to include human capital and knowledge, then a higher saving rate could lead to faster long-term growth. In addition, policies that result in more resources being devoted to the production of new ideas and technology or that make researchers more productive may also increase the long-run growth rate. However, it is difficult for the government to identify which types of capital goods or technologies will be the most productive so it is difficult for the government to design policies that will increase the long-run rate of growth.

Key Issue-and-Question Approach

To provide a roadmap for the book, we use an issue–question framework that shows why learning macroeconomics gives students the tools they need to analyze intelligently some of the important issues of our time. See pages 20–21 of Chapter 1, "The Long and Short of Macroeconomics," for a complete list of the 15 issues and questions. We start each subsequent chapter with a key issue and key question and end each of those chapters by using the concepts introduced in the chapter to answer the question.

"[This book] is very closely related to the current issues and real world. Students should enjoy reading those examples and stories."

Liaoliao Li,
Kutztown University

"Engages students in macroeconomics with interesting real-life examples and questions."

Fabio Mendez,
University of Arkansas

Contemporary Opening Cases

A common complaint among students is that economics is too dry and abstract. At the intermediate level, students will inevitably have to learn a greater amount of model building and algebra than they encountered in their principles course. Nevertheless, a real-world approach can keep students interested. We open each chapter with a real-world example—drawn from either policy issues in the news or the business world—to help students begin the chapter with a greater understanding that the material to be covered is directly relevant. We revisit the example within the chapter to reinforce the link between macroeconomics and the real world.

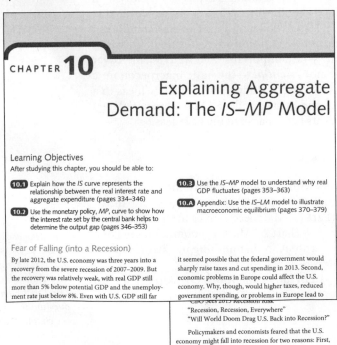

CHAPTER **10**

Explaining Aggregate Demand: The *IS–MP* Model

Learning Objectives

After studying this chapter, you should be able to:

10.1 Explain how the *IS* curve represents the relationship between the real interest rate and aggregate expenditure (pages 334–346)

10.2 Use the monetary policy, *MP*, curve to show how the interest rate set by the central bank helps to determine the output gap (pages 346–353)

10.3 Use the *IS–MP* model to understand why real GDP fluctuates (pages 353–363)

10.A Appendix: Use the *IS–LM* model to illustrate macroeconomic equilibrium (pages 370–379)

Fear of Falling (into a Recession)

By late 2012, the U.S. economy was three years into a recovery from the severe recession of 2007–2009. But the recovery was relatively weak, with real GDP still more than 5% below potential GDP and the unemployment rate just below 8%. Even with U.S. GDP still far

it seemed possible that the federal government would sharply raise taxes and cut spending in 2013. Second, economic problems in Europe could affect the U.S. economy. Why, though, would higher taxes, reduced government spending, or problems in Europe lead to

"Recession, Recession, Everywhere"
"Will World Doom Drag U.S. Back into Recession?"

Policymakers and economists feared that the U.S. economy might fall into recession for two reasons: First,

economy. Why, though, would higher taxes, reduced government spending, or problems in Europe lead to a recession in the United States? Based on our discussion of long-run growth, we can conclude that changes in taxes or government spending will affect the mix of goods and services produced, but will leave the level of *total* production or potential GDP unaffected. Similarly, if economic problems cause Europeans to buy fewer U.S. goods and services, then *in the long run* households in the United States will buy more U.S.-produced goods and services, once again leaving total production and potential GDP unaffected.

Continued on next page

Key Issue and Question

Issue: The U.S. economy has experienced 11 recessions since the end of World War II.

Question: What explains the business cycle?

Answered on page 364

Solved Problem Feature

Including solved problems in the text of each chapter may have been the most popular pedagogical innovation in the Hubbard and O'Brien *Economics* text, now in its fourth edition, and the Hubbard and O'Brien *Money, Banking, and the Financial System* text, now in its second edition. Students have fully learned the concepts and theories only when they are capable of applying them in solving problems. Certainly, most instructors expect students to solve problems on examinations. Our *Solved Problems* highlight one or two important concepts in each chapter and provide students with step-by-step guidance in solving them. Each *Solved Problem* is reinforced by a related problem at the end of the chapter. Students can complete related *Solved Problems* on MyEconLab and receive tutorial help. Here are examples of the *Solved Problems* in the book:

- Solved Problem 2.2A, "Calculating Real GDP" (Chapter 2, "Measuring the Macroeconomy")
- Solved Problem 8.3, "How Many Jobs Does the U.S. Economy Create Every Month?" (Chapter 8, "The Labor Market")
- Solved Problem 11.1, "Fed Policy to Keep Inflation from Increasing" (Chapter 11, "The *IS–MP* Model: Adding Inflation and the Open Economy")

> *"The step-by-step approach to the problem is very clear and makes the material digestible to the students by breaking it down. The tie-in to end-of-chapter exercises is excellent. The student can very quickly see where to go for more practice."*
>
> Francis Mummery, California State University, Fullerton

> *"I appreciate the connection between the solved problem and one of the end-of-chapter problems—this is an excellent idea. Breaking the problem down into small steps seems like a good way to lead students through and develop good problem-solving habits."*
>
> Christopher Burkart, University of West Florida

---

assembling carriages and wagons pulled by horses. Similarly, most workers employed assembling and repairing typewriters eventually lost their jobs following the introduction of personal computers. So, while the analysis in Figure 8.6 allows us to conclude that the real wage in the aggregate labor market will increase following technological change, in the markets for some jobs, the real wage may fall.

Solved Problem 8.1

Why Don't People Work as Much as They Did Decades Ago?

In the early twentieth century, it was common for someone to work 48 to 50 hour per week. Steel workers at some firms worked 12-hour days into the 1920s. Today, 40 hours is the typical workweek, and more people routinely work less than 40 hours than work more. What explains the decline? One clue comes from the work of Douglas Holtz-Eakin of the American Action Forum, David Joulfaian of the U.S. Treasury Department, and Harvey Rosen of Princeton University. They examined the effect of inheritances on labor supply decisions in the United States. They found that the larger the inheritance, the more likely the recipient was to reduce

his or her labor supply. T[...] individuals who receive la[...] funds to purchase goods a[...] the need to work as many[...] individuals but also raises[...] aggregate labor market as[...] From 1950 to 2011, total h[...] States increased from $7 [...] ured in 2005 dollars. Pred[...] wealth had on the equilibri[...] employment. Use a graph t[...]

Solving the Problem

Step 1 Review the chapter material. This problem is about determining the effect of an increase in wealth on the aggregate labor market, so you may want to review the section "Equilibrium in the Labor Market," which begins on page 266.

Step 2 Draw a graph that shows the effect of the increase in wealth on the labor demand and labor supply curves. The labor demand curve shows the relationship between the real wage and the quantity of labor that firms want to hire, holding capital, technology, and the level of efficiency constant. The increase in wealth should not affect the marginal product of labor, so the labor demand curve should not shift. The labor supply curve will shift, however. When wealth increases, individuals can purchase the same quantity of goods and services that they currently buy while working fewer hours. So, we would expect individuals to reduce the quantity of labor supplied at each real wage, which you should show on your graph as the labor supply curve shifting to the left, from S_1 to S_2.

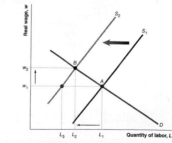

Step 3 Use your graph to explain the effect on the real wage and quantity of labor. The graph shows that at the original real wage of w_1, a shortage of labor exists because the quantity of labor supplied is L_3, and the quantity of labor demanded is L_1. As a result, the equilibrium real wage will rise, while the equilibrium quantity of labor will decrease, from L_1 to L_2.

Over the years, people in high-income countries such as France, Germany, and the United States have spent fewer hours working and more time in leisure. This Solved Problem helps explain why: As wealth has increased, individuals have used the increase in wealth to "purchase" more leisure time, thereby decreasing the number of hours spent working.

Source: Douglas Holtz-Eakin, David Joulfaian, and Harvey Rosen, "The Carnegie Conjecture: Some Empirical Evidence," *Quarterly Journal of Economics*, Vol. 108, No. 2, May 1993, pp. 413–435.

See related problem 1.4 at the end of the chapter.

Making the Connection Feature

Each chapter includes two to four *Making the Connection* features that present real-world reinforcement of key concepts and help students learn how to interpret what they read on the Web and in newspapers. Most *Making the Connection* features use relevant, stimulating, and provocative news stories, many focused on pressing policy issues. Here are some examples:

- "Comparing Research and Development Spending and Labor Productivity in China and the United States" (Chapter 5, "The Standard of Living over Time and Across Countries")
- "What Explains Recent Economic Growth in India?" (Chapter 6, "Long-Run Economic Growth")

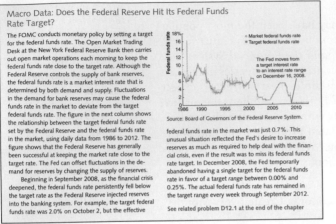

Macro Data: Does the Federal Reserve Hit Its Federal Funds Rate Target?

The FOMC conducts monetary policy by setting a target for the federal funds rate. The Open Market Trading Desk at the New York Federal Reserve Bank then carries out open market operations each morning to keep the federal funds rate close to the target rate. Although the Federal Reserve controls the supply of bank reserves, the federal funds rate is a market interest rate that is determined by both demand and supply. Fluctuations in the demand for bank reserves may cause the federal funds rate in the market to deviate from the target federal funds rate. The figure in the next column shows the relationship between the target federal funds rate set by the Federal Reserve and the federal funds rate in the market, using daily data from 1986 to 2012. The figure shows that the Federal Reserve has generally been successful at keeping the market rate close to the target rate. The Fed can offset fluctuations in the demand for reserves by changing the supply of reserves.

Beginning in September 2008, as the financial crisis deepened, the federal funds rate persistently fell below the target rate as the Federal Reserve injected reserves into the banking system. For example, the target federal funds rate was 2.0% on October 2, but the effective

federal funds rate in the market was just 0.7%. This unusual situation reflected the Fed's desire to increase reserves as much as required to help deal with the financial crisis, even if the result was to miss its federal funds rate target. In December 2008, the Fed temporarily abandoned having a single target for the federal funds rate in favor of a target *range* between 0.00% and 0.25%. The actual federal funds rate has remained in the target range every week through September 2012.

See related problem D12.1 at the end of the chapter

- "Will the European Financial Crisis Cause a Recession in the United States?" (Chapter 10, "Explaining Aggregate Demand: The *IS-MP* Model")
- "Lots of Money but Not Much Inflation Following the Recession of 2007–2009" (Chapter 11, "The *IS-MP* Model: Adding Inflation and the Open Economy")

Macro Data Feature

Most chapters include a *Macro Data* feature that explains the sources of macroeconomic data and often cites recent studies using data. This feature helps students apply data to a recent event. An exercise related to each feature appears at the end of the chapter so instructors can test students' understanding.

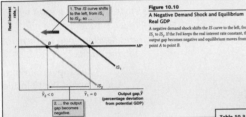

Figure 10.10
A Negative Demand Shock and Equilibrium Real GDP

A negative demand shock shifts the *IS* curve to the left, from *IS₁* to *IS₂*. If the Fed keeps the real interest rate constant, the output gap becomes negative and equilibrium moves from point A to point B.

Graphs and Summary Tables

We use four devices to help students read and interpret graphs:

1. Detailed captions
2. Boxed notes
3. Color-coded curves
4. Summary tables with graphs

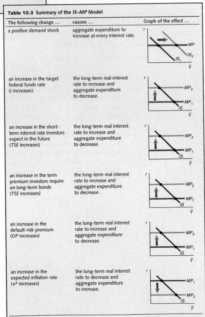

Table 10.3 Summary of the *IS–MP* Model

The following change …	causes …	Graph of the effect …
a positive demand shock	aggregate expenditure to increase at every interest rate.	
an increase in the target federal funds rate (*i* increases)	the long-term real interest rate to increase and aggregate expenditure to decrease.	
an increase in the short-term interest rate investors expect in the future (*TSE* increases)	the long-term real interest rate to increase and aggregate expenditure to decrease.	
an increase in the term premium investors require on long-term bonds (*TSE* increases)	the long-term real interest rate to increase and aggregate expenditure to decrease.	
an increase in the default-risk premium (*DP* increases)	the long-term real interest rate to increase and aggregate expenditure to decrease.	
an increase in the expected inflation rate (*π*ᵉ increases)	the long-term real interest rate to decrease and aggregate expenditure to increase.	

"I like that this book asks students to interpret quotes from policymakers, speeches and from newspaper articles."

George Hall,
Brandeis University

End-of-Chapter Problems Written Around the Award-Winning MyEconLab and Grouped by Learning Objective

Each chapter ends with a *Key Terms* list, *Review Questions*, *Problems and Applications*, and *Data Exercises*. The problems are written to be fully compatible with MyEconLab, an online course management, testing, and tutorial resource. Using MyEconLab, students can complete select end-of-chapter problems online, get tutorial help, and receive instant feedback and assistance on the exercises they answer incorrectly. Instructors can access sample tests, study plan exercises, tutorial resources, and an online Gradebook to keep track of student performance and time spent on the exercises. MyEconLab has been a successful component of the Hubbard and O'Brien *Economics* and *Money, Banking, and the Financial System* texts because it helps students improve their grades and helps instructors manage class time.

The *Review Questions* and *Problems and Applications* are grouped under learning objectives. The goals of this organization are to make it easier for instructors to assign problems based on learning objectives, both in the book and in MyEconLab, and to help students efficiently review material that they find difficult. If students have difficulty with a particular learning objective, an instructor can easily identify which end-of-chapter questions and problems support that objective and assign them as homework or discuss them in class. Select problems that utilize real-time data are marked with 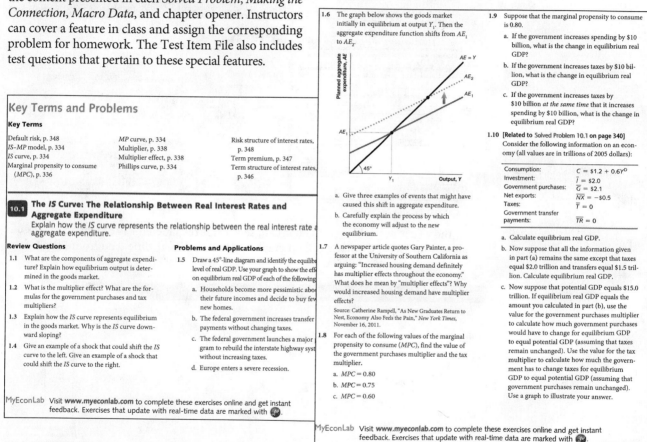.

We include one or more end-of-chapter problems that test students' understanding of the content presented in each *Solved Problem, Making the Connection, Macro Data*, and chapter opener. Instructors can cover a feature in class and assign the corresponding problem for homework. The Test Item File also includes test questions that pertain to these special features.

> *"There are lots of questions and problems for each section and some good data problems also."*
>
> Soma Ghosh,
> Albright College
>
> *"Organizing the problems by topic is a wonderful idea that will help both instructors and students."*
>
> Kevin Sylwester,
> Southern Illinois University

Key Terms and Problems

Key Terms

Default risk, p. 348
IS–MP model, p. 334
IS curve, p. 334
Marginal propensity to consume (*MPC*), p. 336

MP curve, p. 334
Multiplier, p. 338
Multiplier effect, p. 338
Phillips curve, p. 334

Risk structure of interest rates, p. 348
Term premium, p. 347
Term structure of interest rates, p. 346

10.1 The *IS* Curve: The Relationship Between Real Interest Rates and Aggregate Expenditure

Explain how the *IS* curve represents the relationship between the real interest rate and aggregate expenditure.

Review Questions

1.1 What are the components of aggregate expenditure? Explain how equilibrium output is determined in the goods market.

1.2 What is the multiplier effect? What are the formulas for the government purchases and tax multipliers?

1.3 Explain how the *IS* curve represents equilibrium in the goods market. Why is the *IS* curve downward sloping?

1.4 Give an example of a shock that could shift the *IS* curve to the left. Give an example of a shock that could shift the *IS* curve to the right.

Problems and Applications

1.5 Draw a 45°-line diagram and identify the equilibrium level of real GDP. Use your graph to show the effect on equilibrium real GDP of each of the following:

a. Households become more pessimistic about their future incomes and decide to buy fewer new homes.

b. The federal government increases transfer payments without changing taxes.

c. The federal government launches a major program to rebuild the interstate highway system without increasing taxes.

d. Europe enters a severe recession.

1.6 The graph below shows the goods market initially in equilibrium at output Y_1. Then the aggregate expenditure function shifts from AE_1 to AE_2.

a. Give three examples of events that might have caused this shift in aggregate expenditure.

b. Carefully explain the process by which the economy will adjust to the new equilibrium.

1.7 A newspaper article quotes Gary Painter, a professor at the University of Southern California as arguing: "Increased housing demand definitely has multiplier effects throughout the economy." What does he mean by "multiplier effects"? Why would increased housing demand have multiplier effects?

Source: Catherine Rampell, "As New Graduates Return to Nest, Economy Also Feels the Pain," *New York Times*, November 16, 2011.

1.8 For each of the following values of the marginal propensity to consume (*MPC*), find the value of the government purchases multiplier and the tax multiplier.

a. $MPC = 0.80$
b. $MPC = 0.75$
c. $MPC = 0.60$

1.9 Suppose that the marginal propensity to consume is 0.80.

a. If the government increases spending by $10 billion, what is the change in equilibrium real GDP?

b. If the government increases taxes by $10 billion, what is the change in equilibrium real GDP?

c. If the government increases taxes by $10 billion *at the same time* that it increases spending by $10 billion, what is the change in equilibrium real GDP?

1.10 [Related to Solved Problem 10.1 on page 340] Consider the following information on an economy (all values are in trillions of 2005 dollars):

Consumption:	$C = \$1.2 + 0.6Y^D$
Investment:	$\overline{I} = \$2.0$
Government purchases:	$\overline{G} = \$2.1$
Net exports:	$\overline{NX} = -\$0.5$
Taxes:	$\overline{T} = 0$
Government transfer payments:	$\overline{TR} = 0$

a. Calculate equilibrium real GDP.

b. Now suppose that all the information given in part (a) remains the same except that taxes equal $2.0 trillion and transfers equal $1.5 trillion. Calculate equilibrium real GDP.

c. Now suppose that potential GDP equals $15.0 trillion. If equilibrium real GDP equals the amount you calculated in part (b), use the value for the government purchases multiplier to calculate how much government purchases would have to change for equilibrium GDP to equal potential GDP (assuming that taxes remain unchanged). Use the value for the tax multiplier to calculate how much the government has to change taxes for equilibrium GDP to equal potential GDP (assuming that government purchases remain unchanged). Use a graph to illustrate your answer.

Supplements

The authors and Pearson Education have worked together to integrate the text, print, and media resources to make teaching and learning easier.

MyEconLab

MyEconLab is a powerful assessment and tutorial system that works hand-in-hand with *Macroeconomics*. MyEconLab includes comprehensive homework, quiz, test, and tutorial options, allowing instructors to manage all assessment needs in one program. Key innovations in the MyEconLab course for *Macroeconomics*, second edition, include the following:

- Real-time *Data Analysis Exercises*, marked with ⟨⟩ allow students and instructors to use the very latest data from FRED®, the online macroeconomic data bank from the Federal Reserve Bank of St. Louis. By completing the exercises, students become familiar with a key data source, learn how to locate data, and develop skills to interpret data.

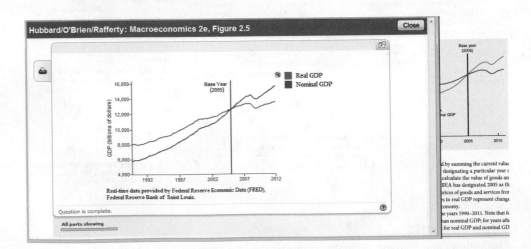

- In the eText available in MyEconLab, select figures labeled MyEconLab Real-time data allow students to display a popup graph updated with real-time data from FRED.

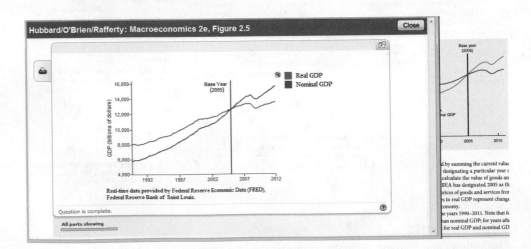

- Current News Exercises, new to this edition of the MyEconLab course, provide a turn-key way to assign gradable news-based exercises in MyEconLab. Every week, Pearson scours the news, finds a current article appropriate for the macroeconomics course, creates an exercise around this news article, and then automatically adds it to MyEconLab. Assigning and grading current news-based exercises that deal with the latest macro events and policy issues and has never been more convenient.

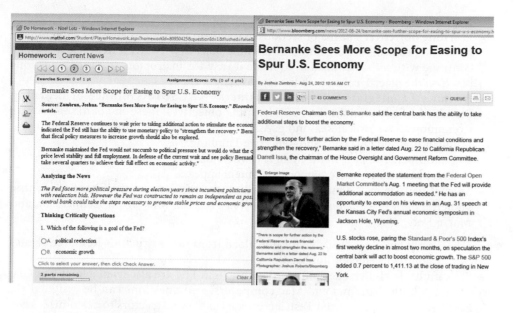

Other features of MyEconLab include:

- All end-of-chapter Questions and Problems, including algorithmic, graphing, and numerical questions and problems, are available for student practice or instructor assignment. Test Item File multiple-choice questions are available for assignment as homework.
- The Custom Exercise Builder allows instructors the flexibility of creating their own problems or modifying existing problems for assignment.
- The powerful Gradebook records each student's performance and time spent on the Tests and Study Plan and generates reports by student or chapter.

A more detailed walk-through of the student benefits and features of MyEconLab can be found at the beginning of this book. Visit **www.myeconlab.com** for more information on and an online demonstration of instructor and student features. MyEconLab content has been created through the efforts of Melissa Honig, executive media producer, and Noel Lotz and Courtney Kamauf, content leads.

Access to MyEconLab can be bundled with your printed text or purchased directly with or without the full eText at **www.myeconlab.com**.

Instructor's Manual

Edward Scahill of the University of Scranton prepared the *Instructor's Manual*, which includes chapter-by-chapter summaries, key term definitions, teaching outlines with teaching tips, and solutions to all review questions and problems in the book. The solutions were prepared by Randy Methenitis of Richland College and the authors. The *Instructor's Manual* is available for download from the Instructor's Resource Center (**www.pearsonhighered.com/hubbard**).

Test Item File

Randy Methenitis of Richland College prepared the Test Item File, which includes more than 1,500 multiple-choice, short-answer, and essay questions. Test questions are annotated with the following information:

- **Difficulty:** 1 for straight recall, 2 for some analysis, and 3 for complex analysis
- **Type:** Multiple-choice, short-answer, and essay

- **Topic:** The term or concept that the question supports
- **Learning objective:** The major sections of the main text and its end-of-chapter questions and problems are organized by learning objective. The Test Item File questions continue with this organization to make it easy for instructors to assign questions based on the objective they wish to emphasize.
- **Advanced Collegiate Schools of Business (AACSB) Assurance of Learning Standards:** Following the AACSB's learning objectives, these standards emphasize Communication; Ethical Reasoning; Analytic Skills; Use of Information Technology; Multicultural and Diversity; and Reflective Thinking.
- **Page number:** The page in the main text where the answer appears allows instructors to direct students to where supporting content appears.
- **Special feature in the main book:** Select questions support the Chapter-opening vignette, the *Key Issue and Question*, *Solved Problem*, *Making the Connection*, and *Macro Data*.

The Test Item File is available for download from the Instructor's Resource Center (**www.pearsonhighered.com/hubbard**).

The multiple-choice questions in the Test Item File are also available in TestGen software for both Windows and Mac computers, and questions can be assigned via MyEconLab. The computerized TestGen package allows instructors to customize, save, and generate classroom tests. The TestGen program permits instructors to edit, add, or delete questions from the Test Item Files; analyze test results; and organize a database of tests and student results. This software allows for extensive flexibility and ease of use. It provides many options for organizing and displaying tests, along with search and sort features. The software and the Test Item Files can be downloaded from the Instructor's Resource Center (**www.pearsonhighered.com/hubbard**).

PowerPoint Lecture Presentation

The PowerPoint slides were prepared by Paul Holmes of State University of New York–Fredonia. Instructors can use the slides for class presentations, and students can use them for lecture preview or review. These slides include all the graphs, tables, and equations from the textbook.

Student versions of the PowerPoint slides are available as PDF files in MyEconLab. These files allow students to print the slides and bring them to class for note taking. Instructors can download these PowerPoint presentations from the Instructor's Resource Center (**www.pearsonhighered.com/hubbard**).

CourseSmart
Learn Smart. Choose Smart.

Instructors CourseSmart goes beyond traditional expectations, providing instant online access to the textbooks and course materials you need at a lower cost to students. And, even as students save money, you can save time and hassle with a digital textbook that allows you to search the most relevant content at the very moment you need it. Whether it's evaluating textbooks or creating lecture notes to help students with difficult concepts, CourseSmart can make life a little easier. See how when you visit **www.coursesmart.com/instructors**.

Students CourseSmart goes beyond traditional expectations, providing instant, online access to the textbooks and course materials students need at lower cost. They can also search, highlight, and take notes anywhere, at any time. See all the benefits to students at **www.coursesmart.com/students**.

Reviewers and Other Contributors

The guidance and recommendations of the following instructors helped us to revise the content and organization of this text. While we could not incorporate every suggestion from every reviewer, we carefully considered each piece of advice we received. We are grateful for the hard work that went into their reviews and truly believe that their feedback was indispensable in revising this text. We appreciate their assistance in making this the best text it could be; they have helped teach a new generation of students about the exciting world of macroeconomics.

Special thanks to Edward Scahill of the University of Scranton for preparing many of the *Making the Connection* features and Randy Methenitis for revising many of the end-of-chapter questions and problems.

We also extend special thanks to Bob Gillette of the University of Kentucky for his extraordinary work accuracy checking these chapters in page proof format and playing a critical role in improving the quality of the final product.

Reviewers and Focus Group Participants

Matthew T. Alford, Southeastern Louisiana University
Lian An, University of North Florida
Syeda Aneeqa Aqeel, Lake Forest College
Mina Baliamoune-Lutz, University of North Florida
Erol Balkan, Hamilton College
Marcelo Bianconi, Tufts University
Ted Burczak, Denison University
James Butkiewicz, University of Delaware
John T. Dalton, Wake Forest University
Roberto Duncan, Ohio University
Todd Fitch, University of California–Berkeley
Hisham Foad, San Diego State University
Jean Gauger, University of Tennessee
Robert Gillette, University of Kentucky
Steven A. Greenlaw, University of Mary Washington
Oskar R. Harmon, University of Connecticut–Stamford
Frank Hefner, College of Charleston
Miren Ivankovic, Anderson University
Parul Jain, Baruch College
Yong-Gook Jung, Wayne State University
Bryce Kanago, University of Northern Iowa
Sherif Khalifa, California State University–Fullerton
Yoonbai Kim, University of Kentucky

Kishore G. Kulkarni, Metropolitan State College of Denver
Ali M. Kutan, Southern Illinois University–Edwardsville
Carlos F. Liard-Muriente, Central Connecticut State University
Kathryn Marshall, California Polytechnic State University
Nivedita Mukherji, Oakland University
John A. Neri, University of Maryland
Nathan Perry, Colorado Mesa University
Van Pham, Salem State University
Jack Russ, San Diego State University
Benjamin Russo, University of North Carolina–Charlotte
Giacomo Santangelo, Fordham University
Amy B. Schmidt, Saint Anselm College
Arun K. Srinivasan, Indiana University–Southeast
James Caleb Stroup, Grinnell College
Edward F. Stuart, Northeastern Illinois University
Mark L. Tendall, Stanford University
Nora Underwood, University of Central Florida
Milos Vulanovic, Western New England University
Parag Waknis, University of Massachusetts–Dartmouth

Accuracy Checkers

Erol Balkan, Hamilton College
Clare Battista, California Polytechnic State University
Shuang Feng, Edinboro University
Robert Gillette, University of Kentucky

Anthony Gyapong, Pennsylvania State University
Kishore G. Kulkarni, Metropolitan State College of Denver
Nathan Perry, Mesa State College
Fernando Quijano, Dickinson State University

First Edition Class Testers

We extend special thanks to both the instructors who class tested manuscript chapters of the first edition and their nearly 200 students for providing recommendations on how to make the chapters engaging and relevant.

Gilad Aharonovitz, Washington State University

Don Coes, University of New Mexico

Kelfala Kallon, University of Northern Colorado

Jeffrey Miller, University of Delaware

Andre Neveu, James Madison University

Walter Park, American University

First Edition Reviewers and Focus Group Participants

We also appreciate the thoughtful comments of our first edition reviewers and focus group participants. They brought home to us once again that there are many ways to teach a macroeconomics class. We hope that we have written a text with sufficient flexibility to meet the needs of most instructors. We carefully read and considered every comment and suggestion we received and incorporated many of them into the text. We believe that our text has been greatly improved as a result of the review process.

Gilad Aharonovitz, Washington State University

Francis Ahking, University of Connecticut–Storrs

Nazneen Ahmad, Weber State University

Mohammed Akacem, Metropolitan State College of Denver

Serife Nuray Akin, University of Miami

Laurence Ales, Carnegie Mellon University

David Altig, University of Chicago

J. J. Arias, Georgia College and State University

Mina Baliamoune, University of North Florida

Erol Balkan, Hamilton College

King Banaian, St. Cloud State University

Cynthia Bansak, St. Lawrence University

Eugene Bempong Nyantakyi, West Virginia University

Doris Bennett, Jacksonville State University

Randall Bennett, Gonzaga University

Charles Scott Benson, Jr., Idaho State University

Paul Blackely, Le Moyne College

Luisa Blanco, Pepperdine University

Joanne M. Blankenship, State Fair Community College

Emma Bojinova, Canisius College

Inoussa Boubacar, University of Wisconsin–Stout

Mark Brady, San Jose State University

David Brasfield, Murray State University

John Brock, University of Colorado, Colorado Springs

Christopher Burkart, University of West Florida

James Butkiewicz, University of Delaware

Colleen Callahan, American University

Douglas Campbell, University of Memphis

Bolong Cao, Ohio University

Matthew Chambers, Towson University

Marcelle Chauvet, University of California, Riverside

Darian Chin, California State University, Los Angeles

Susanne Chuku, Westfield State University

Donald Coes, University of New Mexico

Olivier Coibion, College of William and Mary

Mark Cullivan, University of San Diego

John T. Dalton, Wake Forest University

H. Evren Damar, State University of New York–Brockport

Stephen Davis, Southwest Minnesota State University

Dennis Debrecht, Carroll University

Greg Delemeester, Marietta College

James Devine, Loyola Marymount University

Dennis Edwards, Coastal Carolina University

Ryan Edwards, Queens College, City University of New York

Wayne Edwards, University of Alaska–Anchorage

Noha Emara, Columbia University

Christine Farrell, University of the Ozarks

John Flanders, Central Methodist University

Timothy Ford, California State University, Sacramento

Johanna Francis, Fordham University

Joseph Friedman, Temple University

Timothy Fuerst, Bowling Green State University

William T. Ganley, Buffalo State College

Phillip Garner, Brigham Young University

Doris Geide-Stevenson, Weber State University

Sarah Ghosh, University of Scranton

Satyajit Ghosh, University of Scranton

Soma Ghosh, Albright College

Robert Gillette, University of Kentucky

Tuncer Gocmen, Shepherd University

Robert Godby, University of Wyoming

William Goffe, State University of New York–Oswego

David Gulley, Bentley College

William Hart, Miami University

James Hartley, Mount Holyoke College

Scott Hegerty, Canisius College

Kasthuri Henry, North Park University

Yu Hsing, Southeastern Louisiana University

Kyle Hurst, University of Colorado, Denver

Miren Ivankovic, Anderson University

Aaron Jackson, Bentley University

Louis Johnston, College of Saint Benedict and Saint John's University

Yong-Gook Jung, Wayne State University

Kelfala Kallon, University of Northern Colorado

Lillian Kamal, University of Hartford

Arthur E. Kartman, San Diego State University

John Keating, University of Kansas

Randall Kesselring, Arkansas State University

Yoonbai Kim, University of Kentucky

Sharmila King, University of the Pacific

Janet Koscianski, Shippensburg University

Mikhail Kouliavtsev, Stephen F. Austin State University

Kishore G. Kulkarni, Metropolitan State College of Denver

Gregory Krohn, Bucknell University

Felix Kwan, Maryville University

Elroy M. Leach, Chicago State University

Jim Leady, University of Notre Dame

Eva Leeds, Moravian College

Liaoliao Li, Kutztown University

Carlos F. Liard-Muriente, Central Connecticut State University

Chris Lundblad, University of North Carolina

Guangyi Ma, Texas A&M University

Gabriel Martinez, Ave Maria University

Kenneth McCormick, University of Northern Iowa

Fabio Mendez, University of Arkansas University

Diego Mendez-Carbajo, Illinois Wesleyan

Peter Mikek, Wabash College

Fabio Milani, University of California, Irvine

Jeffrey Miller, University of Delaware

Bruce Mizrach, Rutgers University

Francis Mummery, California State University, Fullerton

Andre R. Neveu, James Madison University

Farrokh Nourzad, Marquette University

Eugene Bempong Nyantakyi, West Virginia University

Ronald Olive, University of Massachusetts–Lowell

Esen Onur, California State University, Sacramento

Walter G. Park, American University

Claudiney Pereira, Tulane University

Nathan Perry, Mesa State College

Stephen Pollard, California State University, Los Angeles

Abe Qastin, Lakeland College

Masha Rahnama, Texas Tech University

Rati Ram, Illinois State University

Reza Ramazani, Saint Michael's College

Malcolm Robinson, Thomas More College

Brian Rosario, California State University, Sacramento

Farhad Saboori, Albright College

Nicole Cornell Sadowski, York College of Pennsylvania

Joseph T. Salerno, Pace University

Subarna Samanta, The College of New Jersey

Shane Sanders, Nicholls State University

Mark Scanlan, Stephen F. Austin State University

Buffie Schmidt, Augusta State University

Gary Shelley, East Tennessee State University

Olga Shurchkov, Wellesley College

Tara Sinclair, George Washington University

Fahlino F. Sjuib, Framingham State College

Julie Smith, Lafayette College

Arun Srinivasan, Indiana University–Southeast

Kellin Stanfield, DePauw University

Herman Stekler, George Washington University

Paul Stock, University of Mary Hardin–Baylor

Leonie Stone, State University of New York–Geneseo

Georg Strasser, Boston College

Gordon Stringer, University of Colorado, Colorado Springs

Peter Summer, Texas Tech University

Kevin Sylwester, Southern Illinois University

Wendine Thompson, Monmouth College

Kwok Ping Tsang, Virginia Tech

Kristin A. Van Gaasbeck, California State University, Sacramento

John Van Huyck, Texas A&M University

David Vera, California State University, Fresno

Rahul Verma, University of Houston, Downtown

Bhavneet Walia, Nicholls State University

Yaqin Wang, Youngstown State University

Robert Whaples, Wake Forest University

Jeffrey Woods, University of Indianapolis

Guy Yamashiro, California State University, Long Beach

Sheng-Ping Yang, Gustavus Adolphus College

Janice Yee, Worcester State University

Wei-Choun Yu, Winona State University

Erik Zemljic, Kent State University

Christian Zimmermann, University of Connecticut

First Edition Accuracy Checkers

In a long and relatively complicated manuscript, accuracy checking is of critical importance. Our thanks go to a dedicated group who provided thorough accuracy checking of both the manuscript and page proof chapters:

Cynthia Bansak, St. Lawrence University
Doris Bennett, Jacksonville State University
Douglas Campbell, University of Memphis
Satyajit Ghosh, University of Scranton
Robert Gillette, University of Kentucky
Robert Godby, University of Wyoming
Anthony Gyapong, Pennsylvania State University

James Moreno, Blinn College
Ronald Olive, University of Massachusetts–Lowell
Nicole L. Cornell Sadowski, York College of Pennsylvania
Robert Whaples, Wake Forest University

Special thanks to Rob Godby of the University of Wyoming and Cynthia Bansak of St. Lawrence University for both commenting on and checking the accuracy of all the chapters of the first edition manuscript.

We are grateful to Fernando Quijano of Dickinson State University and Shelly Tefft for their careful accuracy check of the art program in the first edition. They helped ensure that the graphs are clear, consistent, and accurate.

A Word of Thanks

We benefited greatly from the dedication and professionalism of the Pearson Economics team. Executive Editor David Alexander's energy and support were indispensable. David shares our view that the time has come for a new approach to the macroeconomics textbook. Just as importantly, he provided words of encouragement whenever our energy flagged. Executive Development Editor Lena Buonanno worked tirelessly to ensure that this text was as good as it could be and to coordinate the many moving parts involved in a project of this complexity. We remain astonished at the amount of time, energy, and unfailing good humor she brought to this project. Without Lena, this book would not have been possible.

Director of Key Markets David Theisen provided valuable insight into the changing needs of macroeconomics instructors. We have worked with Executive Marketing Manager Lori DeShazo on all three of our books, and we continue to be amazed at her energy and creativity in promoting the field of economics. We also appreciate the input of Steve Deitmer, Director of Development.

Lindsey Sloan managed the supplement package that accompanies the book. Emily Brodeur managed the review program. Kathryn Dinovo and Jonathan Boylan turned our manuscript pages into a beautiful published book. Tammy Haskins went above and beyond the call of duty to carefully incorporate all the changes we requested while ensuring consistency and accuracy. We are grateful for her flexibility and the care she took in preparing the text.

Fernando Quijano of Dickinson State University created the graphs, ensuring a consistent style. He also diligently accuracy checked the graphs in two rounds of page proofs.

We received excellent and speedy research assistance from Matthew Saboe. We thank Pam Smith, Elena Zeller, and Jennifer Brailsford for their careful proofreading of two rounds of page proofs.

We extend our special thanks to Wilhelmina Sanford of Columbia Business School, whose speedy and accurate typing of multiple drafts is much appreciated.

A good part of the burden of a project of this magnitude is borne by our families, and we appreciate their patience, support, and encouragement.

CHAPTER 1

The Long and Short of Macroeconomics

Learning Objectives

After studying this chapter, you should be able to:

1.1 Become familiar with the focus of macroeconomics (pages 2–14)

1.2 Explain how economists approach macroeconomic questions (pages 14–19)

1.3 Become familiar with key macroeconomic issues and questions (pages 19–21)

When You Enter the Job Market Can Matter a Lot

If you could choose a year to be born, 1983 or 1984 would have been pretty good choices because you might have graduated college and entered the job market in 2005. You would have entered the labor force when the economy was expanding: Sales of houses and cars were strong, Wall Street was booming, and unemployment was low and declining. As stock prices and home prices both soared, many people felt wealthier than ever before.

The year 2008, on the other hand, was *not* a good year to be graduating and entering the job market. Nor were 2009, 2010, or 2011. By 2009, the unemployment rate was higher than it had been in 25 years. By 2011, more people had been out of work for longer than a year than at any other time since the Great Depression of the 1930s. In 2011, a study found that more than 25% of people under age 25 with bachelor's degrees were unemployed and another 25% were stuck in jobs for which they were overqualified.

The U.S. economy endured one of the worst economic downturns in history from 2007 to 2009. During 2008 and 2009, over 600,000 more firms closed than

opened. Sales of houses and cars were at depressed levels. The prices of homes and shares of stock were well below their levels of a few years earlier, which meant that trillions of dollars of wealth had been wiped out. The median wealth for families declined from $126,400 in 2007 to $77,300 in 2010. This decline of almost 40% in just three years brought the wealth of the average family to about the same level as in 1992. Many older workers delayed retirement. Clearly, this was not the best of times to enter the labor force. Even though an economic recovery began in June 2009, the recovery was weak, and the job market remained difficult for new college grads.

The U.S. economy has its ups and downs, and the consequences of the ups and downs can significantly affect people's lives. For instance, a recent study found that college students who graduate during an economic recession have to search longer to find a job and end up accepting jobs that, on average, pay 9% less than the jobs accepted by students who graduate during economic expansions. What's more, students who graduate during recessions will continue to earn less for 8 to 10 years after they graduate. On the other hand, strong expansions result in rising income, profits, and employment. Searching for a job or starting a new business is a lot easier during a strong expansion than during a recession or a weak expansion. Clearly, understanding why the economy experiences periods of recession and expansion is important.

Sources: James R. Hagerty, "Young Adults See Their Pay Decline," *Wall Street Journal*, March 6, 2012; Associated Press, "Half of New Graduates Are Jobless or Underemployed," *USA Today*, April 23, 2012; Lisa Kahn, "The Long-Term Labor Market Consequences of Graduating from College in a Bad Economy," *Labour Economics*, Vol. 17, No. 2, April 2010, pp. 303–316; Jesse Bricker, Arthur B. Kennickell, Kevin B. Moore, and John Sabelhaus, "Changes in U.S. Family Finances from 2007 to 2010: Evidence from the Survey of Consumer Finances," *Federal Reserve Bulletin*, Vol. 98, No. 2, June 2012; and Bureau of Labor Statistics, "Business Employment Dynamics—Third Quarter 2011," May 1, 2012.

Microeconomics The study of how households and firms make choices, how they interact in markets, and how the government attempts to influence their choices.

Macroeconomics The study of the economy as a whole, including topics such as inflation, unemployment, and economic growth.

How can we understand these fluctuations in the economy? By learning *macroeconomics*. Economics is traditionally divided into the fields of microeconomics and macroeconomics. **Microeconomics** is the study of how households and firms make choices, how they interact in markets, and how the government attempts to influence their choices. **Macroeconomics** is the study of the economy as a whole, including topics such as inflation, unemployment, and economic growth. Both microeconomics and macroeconomics study important issues, but the very severe recession of 2007–2009 made macroeconomic issues seem particularly pressing. Although economic theory has the reputation for being dull, there was nothing dull about the events of 2007–2009, which had a major impact on millions of families and thousands of firms.

Many students open an economics textbook and think, "Do I have to memorize all these graphs and equations? How am I going to use this stuff?" Once the final exam is over (at last!) everything learned is quickly forgotten. And it should be forgotten, because economics as an undigested lump of graphs and equations has no value. Graphs and equations are tools; if they are not used for their intended purpose, then they have no more value than a blunt pair of scissors forgotten in the back of a drawer. We have to admit that this textbook has its share of graphs you should know and equations you should memorize. But no more than are necessary. When we present you with a tool, we use it, and we show you how to use it. Our intention is for you to remember these tools long after the final exam, even if this is the last economics course you ever take. With these tools, you can make sense of things that will have a huge effect on your life. Studying macroeconomics will be less of a chore if you keep in mind that *by learning this material you will come to understand how and why economic events affect you, your family, and the well-being of people around the world.*

Learning Objective
Become familiar with the focus of macroeconomics.

What Macroeconomics Is About

In this text, we will analyze the macroeconomics of the U.S. and world economies. This section provides you with an overview of some of the important ideas about macroeconomics. We will discuss these ideas in more detail in the following chapters.

Macroeconomics in the Short Run and in the Long Run

Business cycle
Alternating periods of economic expansion and economic recession.

The key macroeconomic issue of the short run—a period of a few years—is different from the key macroeconomic issue of the long run—a period of decades or more. In the short run, macroeconomic analysis focuses on the **business cycle**, which refers to alternating periods of *economic expansion* and *economic recession* experienced by the U.S. and other economies. The U.S. economy has experienced periods of expanding production and employment followed by periods of recession during which production and employment decline dating back to at least the early nineteenth century. The business cycle is not uniform: Each period of expansion is not the same length, nor is each period of recession, but every period of expansion in U.S. history has been followed by a period of recession, and every period of recession has been followed by a period of expansion.

For the long run, the focus of macroeconomics switches from the business cycle to **long-run economic growth**, which is the process by which increasing productivity raises the average standard of living. A successful economy is capable of increasing production of goods and services faster than the growth in population. Increasing production faster than population growth is the only lasting way that the standard of living of the average person in a country can increase. Achieving this outcome is possible only through increases in *labor productivity*. **Labor productivity** is the quantity of goods and services that can be produced by one worker or by one hour of work. If the quantity of goods and services consumed by the average person is to increase, the quantity of goods and services produced per worker must also increase.

Unfortunately, many economies around the world are not growing at all or are growing very slowly. In some countries in sub-Saharan Africa, living standards are barely higher, or are even lower, than they were 50 years ago. Many people in these countries live in the same grinding poverty as their ancestors did. In the United States and other developed countries, however, living standards are much higher than they were 50 years ago. An important macroeconomic topic is why some countries grow much faster than others.

As we will see, one determinant of economic growth is the ability of firms to expand their operations, buy additional equipment, train workers, and adopt new technologies. To carry out these activities, firms must acquire funds from households, either directly through financial markets—such as the stock and bond markets—or indirectly through financial intermediaries—such as banks. Financial markets and financial intermediaries together comprise the *financial system*. As we will see in later chapters, the financial system has become an increasingly important part of the study of macroeconomics.

The focus of this book is the exploration of these two key aspects of macroeconomics: the long-run growth that has steadily raised living standards in the United States and some other countries and the short-run fluctuations of the business cycle.

Long-Run Growth in the United States

By current standards, nearly everyone in the world was poor not very long ago. For instance, in 1900, although the United States was already enjoying the highest standard of living in the world, the typical American was quite poor by today's standards. In 1900, only 3% of U.S. homes had electricity, only 15% had indoor flush toilets, and only 25% had running water. The lack of running water meant that before people could cook or bathe, they had to pump water from wells and haul it to their homes in buckets—on average about 10,000 gallons per year per family. Not

Long-run economic growth The process by which increasing productivity raises the average standard of living.

Labor productivity The quantity of goods and services that can be produced by one worker or by one hour of work.

surprisingly, water consumption in the United States averaged only about 5 gallons per person per day, compared with about 150 gallons today. The result was that people washed themselves and their clothing only infrequently. A majority of families living in cities had to use outdoor toilets, which they shared with other families. Few families had electric lights, relying instead on candles or lamps that burned kerosene or coal.

Most homes were heated in the winter by burning coal, which was also used as fuel in stoves. In the northern United States, many families saved on winter fuel costs by heating only the kitchen, abandoning their living rooms and relying on clothing and blankets for warmth in their bedrooms. The typical family used more than 7 tons of coal per year just for cooking. Burning so much coal contributed to the severe pollution that fouled the air of most large cities. Poor sanitation and high levels of pollution, along with ineffective medical care, resulted in high rates of illness and premature death. Many Americans became ill or died from diseases such as smallpox, typhus, dysentery, measles, and cholera that are now uncommon in developed nations. Life expectancy in 1900 was about 47 years, compared with 78 years in 2012. In 1900, 5,000 of the 45,000 children born in Chicago died before their first birthday. And, there were, of course, no televisions, radios, computers, air conditioners, washing machines, dishwashers, or refrigerators. Without modern appliances, most women worked inside the home at least 80 hours per week. The typical American homemaker in 1900 baked a half-ton of bread per year.[1]

How did the United States get from the relative poverty of 1900 to the relative affluence of today? Will these increases in living standards continue? Will people living in the United States in 2100 look back on the people of 2013 as having lived in relative poverty? The answer to these questions is that changes in living standards depend on the rate of long-run economic growth. Most people in the United States, Western Europe, Japan, and other developed countries expect that over time, their standard of living will improve. They expect that year after year, firms will introduce new and improved products, new prescription drugs and better surgical techniques will overcome more diseases, and their ability to afford these goods and services will increase. For most people, these are reasonable expectations.

The process of long-run economic growth brought the typical American from the standard of living of 1900 to the standard of living of today and has the potential to bring the typical American of 100 years from now to a standard of living that people today can only imagine. **Real gross domestic product (GDP)**, which is the value of final goods and services, adjusted for changes in the price level, provides a measure of the total level of income in the economy. Accordingly, the best measure of the standard of living is real GDP per person, which is usually referred to as *real GDP per capita*. We typically measure long-run economic growth by increases in real GDP per capita

Real gross domestic product (GDP) The value of final goods and services, adjusted for changes in the price level.

---

[1]Most of the data on economic conditions in the United States in 1900 come from Stanley Lebergott, *Pursuing Happiness: American Consumers in the Twentieth Century*, Princeton, NJ: Princeton University Press, 1993. Data on economic conditions in 2012 come from the U.S. Census Bureau, *The 2012 Statistical Abstract*, www.census.gov/compendia/statab/, and other sources.

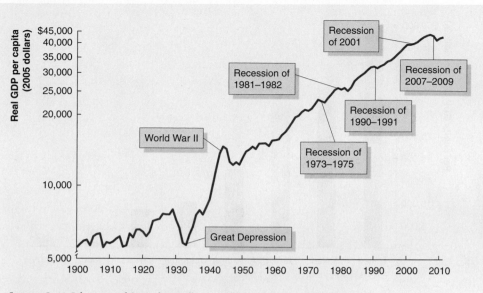

Figure 1.1

The Growth in U.S. Real GDP per Capita, 1900–2011

Measured in 2005 dollars, real GDP per capita in the United States grew from about $5,500 in 1900 to about $42,671 in 2011. The average American in the year 2011 could buy nearly eight times as many goods and services as the average American in the year 1900.

Note: The values in this graph are plotted on a logarithmic scale so that equal distances represent equal percentage increases. For example, the 100% increase from $5,000 to $10,000 is the same distance as the 100% increase from $10,000 to $20,000.

Sources: Louis Johnston and Samuel H. Williamson, "What Was the U.S. GDP Then?" *MeasuringWorth*, 2012, www.measuringworth.org/usgdp/; U.S. Bureau of Economic Analysis; and U.S. Census Bureau.

over long periods of time, generally decades or more. Figure 1.1 shows real GDP per capita in the United States from 1900 to 2011. The figure shows that the long-run trend in real GDP per capita is strongly upward. The figure also shows that real GDP per capita fluctuates in the short run. For instance, real GDP per capita declined significantly during the Great Depression of the 1930s and by smaller amounts during later recessions, including the recession of 2007–2009. But it is the upward trend in real GDP per capita that we focus on when discussing long-run economic growth.

In Chapters 5 and 6, we will explore in detail *why* the U.S. economy has experienced strong growth over the long run, including the role of the financial system in facilitating this growth.

Some Countries Have Not Experienced Significant Long-Run Growth

One of the key macroeconomic puzzles that we will examine is why rates of economic growth have varied so widely across countries. Because countries have experienced such different rates of economic growth, their current levels of GDP per capita are also very different, as Figure 1.2 shows. GDP per capita is higher in the United States than in most other countries because the United States has experienced higher rates of economic growth than have most other countries. Figure 1.2 shows that the gap between U.S. GDP per capita and GDP per capita in other high-income countries, such as the United Kingdom and Japan, is relatively small, but the gap between the high-income countries and the low-income countries is quite large. Although China has recently been experiencing rapid economic growth, this rapid growth began only in the late 1970s, when the Chinese government introduced economic reforms. As a result, GDP per capita in

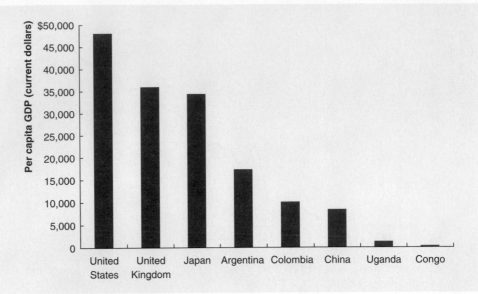

Figure 1.2

Differing Levels of GDP per Capita, 2011

Differing levels of long-run economic growth have resulted in countries today having very different levels of GDP per capita.

Note: Values are GDP per capita, measured in dollars corrected for differences in price levels across countries.

Source: U.S. Central Intelligence Agency, *The World Factbook 2012*, Washington, DC: Central Intelligence Agency, 2012.

the United States is nearly six times greater than GDP per capita in China, which is not much smaller than the gap between real GDP per capita in the United States today and real GDP per capita in the United States in 1900. The gap between the United States and the poorest countries is larger still: U.S. GDP per capita is almost 40 times greater than GDP per capita in the African country of Uganda and a staggering 160 times greater than GDP per capita in the African country of Congo.

Why is average income in the United States so much higher than that in Uganda and China? Why is China closing the gap with the United States, while Uganda falls further behind? What explains the stark differences in income levels across countries? Why has it been so difficult to raise the incomes of the very poorest countries? In Chapters 5 and 6, we will address these important questions.

Aging Populations Pose a Challenge to Governments Around the World

Panel (a) of Figure 1.3 shows that the percentage of the world population over age 65 has been continually expanding. Between 1950 and 2012, the percentage increased by two-thirds and is expected to almost triple between 2012 and the end of the twenty-first century. Panel (b) shows the same pattern for the United States. In 2012, more than 13% of the U.S. population was older than 65. This percentage is expected to double by the end of the century. The aging of the population is the result of lower birthrates and of people living longer. While in 1990 there were only about 7 million people in the United States age 80 and older, by 2010 there were almost 12 million, and by the end of the century there are expected to be more than 50 million.

Some economists and policymakers fear that aging populations may pose a threat to long-run economic growth. A key part of the problem is that governments have

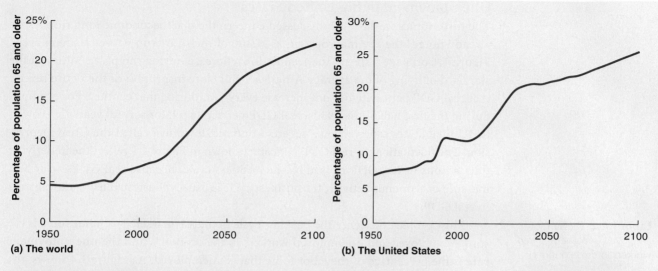

Figure 1.3 The Aging of the Population

Panel (a) shows that low birthrates and increases in life span combined have resulted in an increasing percentage of people 65 and older in the world.

Panel (b) shows that this trend also holds for the United States.

Source: United Nations, Department of Economic and Social Affairs, *World Population Prospects, the 2010 Revision.*

programs to make payments to retired workers and to cover some or all of their health-care costs. For instance, the United States has three programs that fill these roles:

1. *Social Security*, established in 1935 to provide payments to retired workers and the disabled
2. *Medicare*, established in 1965 to provide health care coverage to people age 65 and older
3. *Medicaid*, established in 1965 to provide health care coverage to the poor, including elderly poor in nursing homes and other facilities

Spending on Social Security, Medicare, and Medicaid was about 3% of GDP in 1962 (Medicare and Medicaid did not exist yet), but is projected to grow to nearly 20% of GDP by 2050. In other words, by 2050, the federal government will be spending, as a fraction of GDP, nearly as much on these three programs as it currently does now on all programs. Most of the money for Social Security, Medicare, and Medicaid comes from taxes paid by people currently working. As the population ages, there are fewer workers paying taxes relative to the number of retired people receiving government payments. The result is a funding crisis that countries can solve only by either reducing government payments to retired workers, reducing spending on all other programs, or by raising the taxes paid by current workers.

In some European countries and Japan, birthrates have fallen so low that the total population has already begun to decline, which will make the funding crisis for government retirement programs even worse. How countries deal with the consequences of aging populations will be one of the most important macroeconomic issues of the coming decades.

Unemployment in the United States

The three topics we have just discussed concern the macroeconomic long run. As we already noted, the key macroeconomic issue of the short run is the business cycle. Figure 1.1 on page 5 shows the tremendous increase during the past century in the standard of living of the average American. But close inspection of the figure reveals that real GDP per capita did not increase every year during that century. For example, during the first half of the 1930s, real GDP per capita fell for several years in a row as the United States experienced a severe economic downturn called the Great Depression. The fluctuations in real GDP per capita shown in Figure 1.1 reflect the underlying fluctuations in real GDP caused by the business cycle. Because real GDP is our best measure of economic activity, the business cycle is usually illustrated using movements in real GDP.

Labor force The sum of employed and unemployed workers in the economy.

Unemployment rate The percentage of the labor force that is unemployed.

Most people experience the business cycle in the job market. The **labor force** is the sum of employed and unemployed workers in the economy, and the **unemployment rate** is the percentage of the labor force that is unemployed. As Figure 1.4 shows, the unemployment rate in the United States has risen and fallen with the business cycle. The figure shows that prior to the 1940s, unemployment rates were typically higher during recessions than they have been in the years since. In particular, following the end of the severe 1981–1982 recession, the United States entered into a period of mild business cycles, with relatively low peak unemployment rates. Some economists called this period the *Great Moderation*. The Great Moderation ended in December 2007,

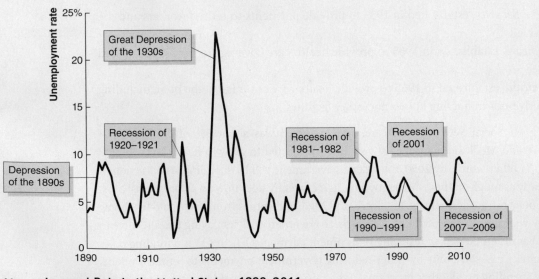

Figure 1.4 Unemployment Rate in the United States, 1890–2011

Unemployment rises and falls with the business cycle.

Sources: Data for 1890–1947 from *Historical Statistics of the United States Millennial Edition Online*, edited by Susan B. Carter, Scott Sigmund Gartner, Michael R. Haines, Alan L. Olmstead, Richard Sutch, and Gavin Wright, Cambridge University Press. Series Ba475; data for 1948–2011 from the Bureau of Labor Statistics.

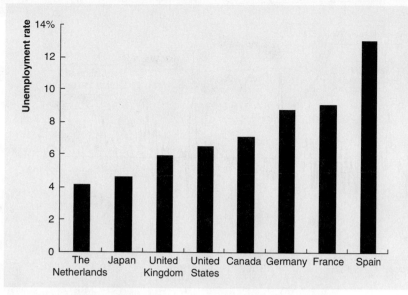

Figure 1.5

Average Unemployment Rates in the United States and Other High-Income Countries, 2002–2011

The average unemployment rate varies significantly across high-income countries. It has been relatively low in the Netherlands, Japan, the United Kingdom, and the United States and relatively high in France, Germany, and Spain. Differences in labor-market policies are the most likely explanation for these differences in unemployment rates.

Sources: U.S. Bureau of Labor Statistics; and International Monetary Fund.

with the start of the 2007–2009 recession. During that recession, the unemployment rate soared from less than 5% to more than 10%—with more than 8.5 million workers losing their jobs.

In later chapters, we will explore why unemployment has been so much higher in some periods than in others. In particular, we will look at why the unemployment rate in the United States was so low during the Great Moderation and so high during the 2007–2009 recession and its aftermath.

Unemployment Rates Differ Across Developed Countries

Figure 1.5 shows the average unemployment over the 10-year period from 2002 to 2011 for the United States and several other high-income countries. The average unemployment rates range from a low of 4.1% in the Netherlands to a high of 13.1% in Spain. These differences indicate that although some swings in unemployment are caused by the business cycle, unemployment has been persistently higher in some countries than in others for reasons not connected to the business cycle. What explains these differences? The varying labor-market policies governments have pursued seem to be the key to explaining these differences in unemployment rates. As we will see, though, economists have not yet reached consensus on which policy differences are most important.

Inflation Rates Fluctuate Over Time and Across Countries

Just as the unemployment rate varies over time in the United States and differs between the United States and other countries, so does the *inflation rate*. Figure 1.6 shows the **inflation rate** in the United States as measured by the percentage change in the average level of prices (here measured by the consumer price index) from one year to the next. The data

Inflation rate The percentage increase in the price level from one year to the next.

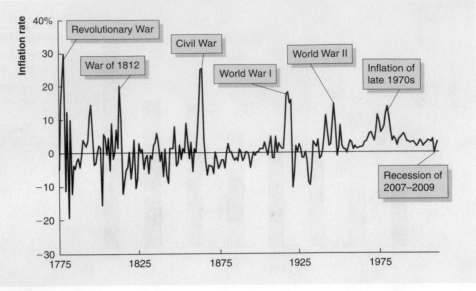

Figure 1.6

Inflation in the United States, 1775–2011

With the exception of the late 1970s and early 1980s, inflation in the United States has generally been high only during wars. Since the 1930s, periods of falling prices, or deflation, have been rare. The inflation rate during the past 25 years has generally been below 5%.

Sources: Data for 1775–2003 from *Historical Statistics of the United States Millennial Edition Online*, Series Cc1; data for 2004–2011 from the Bureau of Labor Statistics.

in this figure stretch back to 1775 to provide a long-run view of how the inflation rate in the United States has varied over time. There are several points to notice about this figure:

1. Most of the periods of very high inflation have occurred during times of war.
2. An important exception to point 1 is the high levels of inflation in the late 1970s and early 1980s.
3. Periods of falling prices, or **deflation**, were relatively common during most of the country's history, but the United States experienced deflation in 2009 for the first time in more than 50 years.
4. The inflation rate during the past 25 years has generally been below 5%.

Deflation A sustained decrease in the price level.

In later chapters, we will discuss what determines the inflation rate, why the United States has rarely experienced deflation during the past 50 years, and why inflation has been relatively low during recent years.

Figure 1.7 shows inflation during 2011 for several countries around the world. Some countries, including Japan, Norway, Germany, and the United States, experienced mild inflation. Many other countries, though, experienced significantly higher inflation rates, as shown by the values in the figure for Pakistan, Vietnam, and Venezuela. In fact, the figure understates how much inflation rates can differ across countries. For instance, the inflation rate in Zimbabwe, not shown in the figure, was an extraordinary 15 billion percent in 2008! By exploring the reasons for the differences in inflation rates across countries, we will gain better insight into what makes prices increase.

Economic Policy Can Help Stabilize the Economy

A basic measure of economic stability is how much real GDP fluctuates from one year to the next. The more GDP fluctuates, the more erratic firms' sales are and the more likely workers are to experience bouts of unemployment. Figure 1.8 shows annual growth rates of real GDP in the United States since 1900. Notice that before 1950, real GDP went through much greater year-to-year fluctuations than it has since that time.

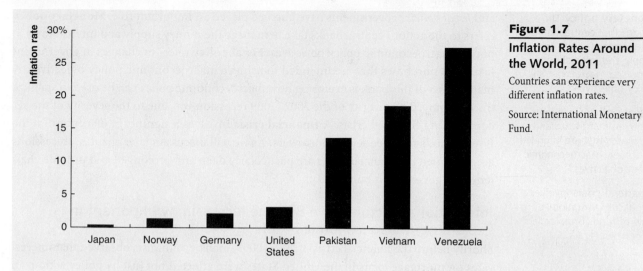

Figure 1.7

Inflation Rates Around the World, 2011

Countries can experience very different inflation rates.

Source: International Monetary Fund.

In particular, during the past 50 years, the U.S. economy has not experienced anything similar to the sharp fluctuations in real GDP that occurred during the 1930s. The increased stability of the economy since 1950 is also indicated by the increased length of business cycle expansions and decreased length of recessions during these years. From 1950 to 2007, the U.S. economy experienced long business cycle expansions, occasionally interrupted by brief recessions. Most other high-income countries have experienced similar increases in economic stability since 1950. As mentioned earlier, the period 1984–2007 was particularly stable, but ended with the severe 2007–2009 recession. How do we explain the increased stability of the post-1950 period and the severity of the recession of 2007–2009?

Although there are a number of reasons the economies of most high-income countries became more stable after 1950, many economists believe that the *monetary policies*

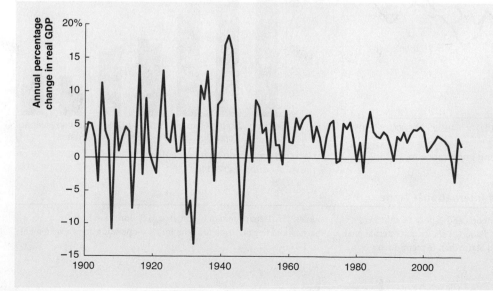

Figure 1.8

Fluctuations in U.S. Real GDP, 1900–2011

Real GDP had much more severe swings in the first half of the twentieth century than in the second half. The severe recession of 2007–2009 interrupted a long period of relative economic stability.

Sources: Louis D. Johnston and Samuel H. Williamson, "What Was the U.S. GDP Then?" *MeasuringWorth*, 2011, www.measuringworth.org/usgdp/; and U.S. Bureau of Economic Analysis.

Monetary policy The actions that central banks take to manage the money supply and interest rates to pursue macroeconomic policy objectives.

Fiscal policy Changes in government taxes and purchases that are intended to achieve macroeconomic policy objectives.

Financial crisis involves a significant disruption in the flow of funds from lenders to borrowers.

and *fiscal policies* governments have pursued played an important role. **Monetary policy** refers to the actions central banks take to manage the money supply and interest rates to pursue macroeconomic policy objectives. **Fiscal policy** refers to changes in government taxes and purchases that are intended to achieve macroeconomic policy objectives. A major focus of this book is exploring how macroeconomic policy can be used to stabilize the economy. The severity of the 2007–2009 recession was due to the severity of the accompanying financial crisis. A **financial crisis** involves a significant disruption in the flow of funds from lenders to borrowers. As we will discuss in later chapters, recessions accompanied by financial crises are particularly deep and prolonged and provide challenges to government policymakers.

International Factors Have Become Increasingly Important in Explaining Macroeconomic Events

Shortly before the financial crisis of 2007–2009, many economists observed that interest rates on mortgage loans in the United States were affected not just by policy actions in Washington, DC, but also by policy actions in China's capital of Beijing. Federal Reserve Chairman Ben Bernanke spoke of a "global savings glut" that had driven down interest rates in the United States. Thirty years ago, the U.S. economy was much more insulated from developments abroad.

International Trade Economists measure the "openness" of an economy in terms of how much it trades with other economies. Panel (a) of Figure 1.9 shows that for the United

MyEconLab Real-time data

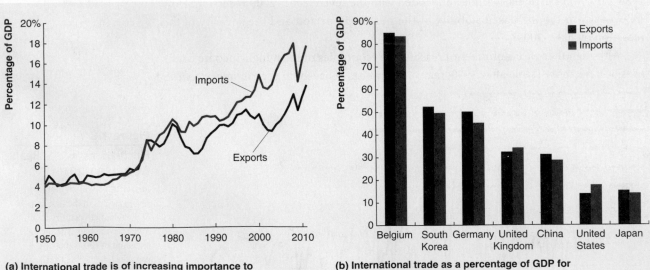

(a) International trade is of increasing importance to the United States

(b) International trade as a percentage of GDP for several countries, 2011

Figure 1.9 The Importance of International Trade

Panel (a) shows that since 1950, both imports and exports have been steadily rising as a fraction of U.S. GDP. Panel (b) shows that international trade is still less important to the United States than to many other countries, with the exception of Japan.

Sources: U.S. Department of Commerce; U.S. Bureau of Economic Analysis; and Organisation for Economic Co-operation and Development.

States, both imports and exports have been growing as a percentage of GDP. Panel (b) shows that even though the openness of the U.S. economy has increased over time, a number of other developed countries are significantly more open than the United States. Some small countries, such as Belgium, export and import more than 80% of GDP because many firms based in those countries concentrate on exporting rather than on producing for the domestic market. Countries such as South Korea and Germany are heavily dependent on international trade, with exports and imports making up more than 50% of GDP. Although China has greatly increased its exports over the past 20 years, in 2011, exports made up about 31% of China's GDP, well below the percentages for Belgium, South Korea, Germany, and a number of other countries not shown in the figure.

Global Financial Markets As markets in goods and services have become more open to international trade, so have the financial markets that help match savers and investors around the world. Over the past 20 years, there has been an explosion in the buying and selling of financial assets, such as stocks and bonds, as well as in the making of loans across national borders. A *stock* is a financial security that represents part ownership in a firm, while a *bond* is a financial security that represents a promise to repay a fixed amount of funds. Figure 1.10 shows the ebb and flow of foreign financial investments in the United States. Between 1995 and the middle of the next decade, a large rise occurred in foreign purchases of stocks and bonds issued by U.S. corporations. The recession of 2007–2009 led to a sharp decline in foreign purchases of U.S. corporate stocks and bonds as foreign investors saw increased risk in holding these securities. Foreign purchases of U.S. government bonds temporarily soared, however, as fears that some European governments might default on their bonds led investors to a *flight to safety*, in which they sold other investments to buy U.S. government bonds.

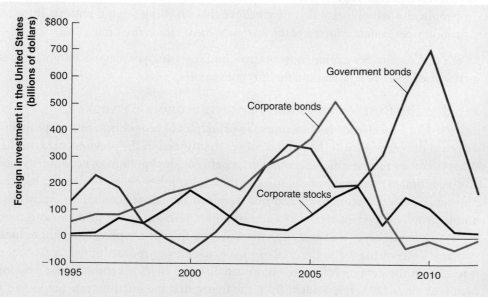

Figure 1.10

Growth of Foreign Financial Investment in the United States

Between 1995 and the middle of the next decade, a large rise occurred in foreign purchases of corporate stocks and bonds. The financial crisis of 2007–2009 resulted in declines in foreign purchases of corporate stocks and bonds and a temporary surge in purchases of bonds issued by the federal government.

Sources: International Monetary Fund, *International Capital Markets*, August 2001; and U.S. Department of the Treasury, *Treasury Bulletin*, June 2012.

U.S. investors have also increased their purchases of foreign financial assets. The increased openness of the U.S. and other economies has raised incomes and improved economic efficiency around the world. But increased openness also means that macroeconomic problems in one economy can have consequences for other economies. For example, the recession of 2007–2009 reduced the demand for China's exports, and the Greek debt crisis of 2011–2012 caused stock prices to decline around the world. Openness can also complicate the attempts of policymakers to stabilize the economy. In this book, we explore the macroeconomic implications of increasing trade and investment among countries, as well as the role of the international financial system.

How Economists Think About Macroeconomics

1.2

Learning Objective

Explain how economists approach macroeconomic questions.

Macroeconomics happens to us all: Over the course of your life, you may be laid off from your job during a recession or you will have friends or relatives who are. You are likely to see a stock market investment soar or collapse, find getting a loan to buy a house or car to be easy or difficult, and experience periods when prices of goods and services rise rapidly or slowly.

We all have opinions about why these things happen, whether or not we are economists or whether or not we have taken even a single course in economics. Here is feedback from the general public on several economic questions:

- "What causes inflation?" The number-one response in a poll of the general public was "corporate greed."
- "How would an increase in inflation affect wages and salaries?" The most popular response was that profits would increase but wages and salaries would stay the same.
- "What causes recessions?" Many people believe that recessions happen only because of mistakes Congress and the president make and will end only if the government implements the correct policies.
- "How do foreign imports affect unemployment rates into the United States?" Many people also tell pollsters that they believe that allowing foreign imports into the country permanently increases the unemployment rate in the United States.

In this section, we explore how macroeconomists analyze macroeconomic issues such as the causes of inflation and the effect of imports.

What Is the Best Way to Analyze Macroeconomic Issues?

Because you have already taken a course in principles of economics, you are probably skeptical of the validity of the poll responses mentioned in the previous paragraphs. What accounts for the differences that exist between the opinions of economists and non-economists? Are economists smarter than most other people? Actually, the key difference between economists and non-economists is that economists study economic problems systematically by gathering data relevant to the problem and then building a *model* capable of analyzing the data. For instance, suppose we want to look systematically at the claim that inflation is caused by corporate greed. A first step is to look at the data on inflation. Figure 1.6 on page 10 shows the inflation rate for each year since 1775. It is evident from the figure that the inflation rate has varied a lot over this long period. For instance, in the most recent 50 years, inflation varied from below 3% in the 1950s and 1960s to well above 10% in the late 1970s and early

1980s, and then it returned to relatively low rates below 4% for most of the years after the early 1980s.

By themselves, these data make the corporate greed explanation of inflation unlikely. If corporate greed were the cause of inflation, then greed would have to be fluctuating over time, with corporate managers having been comparatively less greedy in the 1950s and 1960s, more greedy in the late 1970s and early 1980s, and then less greedy again beginning in the mid-1980s. While a simple examination of the data can often help us to roughly gauge how likely an explanation is, this type of analysis is not completely satisfying for two reasons: First, in many cases, just inspecting the data can give misleading results. Second, rather than just reject an explanation, it is more useful to provide an alternative explanation. That is, we need to build a *macroeconomic model* that will allow us to explain inflation.

Macroeconomic Models

Economists rely on economic theories, or models, to analyze real-world issues, such as the causes of inflation. (We use the words *theory* and *model* interchangeably.) Economic models are simplified versions of reality. By simplifying, it's possible to move beyond the overwhelming complexity of everyday life to focus on the underlying causes of the issue being studied. For instance, rather than use a model, we could analyze inflation by looking at the details of how every firm in the country decides what price to charge. The problem with that approach is that even if we had the time and money to carry it out, we would end up with a huge amount of detailed information that would be impossible to interpret. And we would end up no closer to understanding why inflation has fluctuated over the years. In contrast, by building an economic model of inflation that simplifies reality by focusing on a few key variables, we would be more likely to increase our understanding of inflation. In particular, we would be better able to predict which factors are likely to make inflation higher or lower in the future. (Remember from your principles of economics class that an *economic variable* is something measurable that can have different values, such as the rate of inflation in a particular year.)

Sometimes economists use an existing model to analyze an issue, but in other cases they need to develop a new model. To develop a model, economists generally follow these steps:

1. Decide on the assumptions to be used in developing the model and decide which *endogenous variables* will be explained by the model and which *exogenous variables* will be taken as given.
2. Formulate a testable hypothesis.
3. Use economic data to test the hypothesis.
4. Revise the model if it fails to explain the economic data well.
5. Retain the revised model to help answer similar economic questions in the future.

We further explore the basics of economic model building in the next two sections.

In each chapter of this book, you will see the special feature *Solved Problem*. This feature will increase your understanding of the material by leading you through the steps of solving an applied macroeconomic problem. After reading the problem, you can test your understanding by working the related problem that appears at the end of the chapter. You can also complete related Solved Problems on www.myeconlab.com, which also allows you to access tutorial help.

Solved Problem 1.2

Do Rising Imports Lead to a Permanent Reduction in U.S. Employment?

Opinion polls show that many people believe that imports of foreign goods lead to a reduction in employment in the United States. On the surface, this claim may seem plausible: If U.S. automobile firms use more imported steel, production at U.S. steel firms declines, and U.S. steel firms will lay off workers. Briefly describe how you might evaluate the claim that employment in the United States has been reduced as a result of imports.

Solving the Problem

Step 1 **Review the chapter material.** This problem is about how economists evaluate explanations of macroeconomic events, so you may want to review the section "What Is the Best Way to Analyze Macroeconomic Issues?", which begins on page 14.

Step 2 **Discuss what data you might use in evaluating this claim.** The relevant data are for imports and employment over the years. The U.S. Bureau of Economic Analysis (www.bea.gov) is a good source of data on GDP, including imports, and the U.S. Bureau of Labor Statistics (www.bls.gov) is a good source of data on employment.

Step 3 **Draw a graph that shows total employment and imports as a percentage of GDP.** One way of inspecting whether the data support the claim is to plot the data on a graph. Your graph should look like the one below, which shows for the years 1970 to 2011 imports as a percentage of GDP measured on the left vertical axis and a measure of total employment on the right vertical axis.

MyEconLab Real-time data

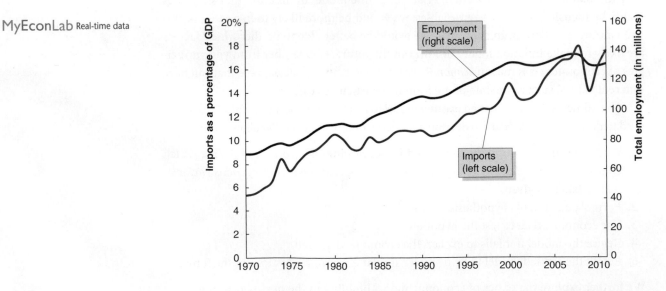

The graph shows that imports and employment have both increased over time, which makes it unlikely that imports have permanently reduced employment.

Step 4 **Discuss what else you might do to evaluate this claim.** Most economists see inspecting the data as only the first step in evaluating a claim about a macroeconomic event. Economists use models to provide systematic explanations. In this case, although the fact that imports and employment have both risen over the past 40 years makes it seem unlikely that rising imports have reduced employment, we can't be entirely sure. It is possible that employment would have risen even more than it did if imports had increased less. In Chapter 8, we will study a model of the labor market to better understand what determines the level of employment in the long run. At that point, it will become more evident that the level of a country's imports has no effect on its level of employment in the long run.

See related problem 2.5 at the end of the chapter.

Assumptions, Endogenous Variables, and Exogenous Variables in Economic Models

Any model is based on making assumptions because models have to be simplified versions of reality in order to be useful. We cannot analyze an economic issue unless we reduce its complexity. For example, economic models make behavioral assumptions about the motives of consumers and firms. Economists assume that consumers will buy the goods and services that will maximize their well-being or satisfaction, or *utility*. Similarly, economists assume that firms act to maximize their profits. These assumptions are simplifications because they do not describe the motives of every consumer and every firm. How can we know if the assumptions in a model are too simplified or too limiting? We discover the validity of assumptions when we form hypotheses based on these assumptions and test the hypotheses using real-world data.

In building a model, we must decide which variables we will attempt to explain with the model and which variables we will take as given. Economists refer to variables that are taken as given as **exogenous variables** and variables that will be explained by the model as **endogenous variables**. For example, suppose we build a macroeconomic model that explores the effect of changes in the money supply on the inflation rate. If we assume that the Federal Reserve determines changes in the money supply, then the money supply is an exogenous variable because we are not using the model to try to explain it. The inflation rate, though, would be an endogenous variable because we are attempting to explain it using the model.

Exogenous variable
A variable that is taken as given and is not explained by an economic model.

Endogenous variable
A variable that is explained by an economic model.

Forming and Testing Hypotheses in Economic Models

A *hypothesis* in an economic model is a statement that may be either correct or incorrect about an economic variable. An example is the statement that the higher the marginal tax rate on income in a country, the higher the country's unemployment rate will be. An economic hypothesis is usually about a *causal relationship*. In this case, the hypothesis states that increases in the marginal tax rate *cause*, or lead to, higher rates of unemployment. A higher marginal tax rate might cause a higher rate of unemployment because the higher the tax rate, the smaller the after-tax wage a person earns from working and the smaller the incentive people have to accept jobs.

To evaluate a hypothesis, we need to test it. To test a hypothesis, we need to analyze statistics on the relevant economic variables. In our example, we might gather statistics on tax rates and unemployment rates for different countries. Testing a hypothesis can be tricky. For example, showing that countries with higher tax rates have higher unemployment rates would not be enough to demonstrate that the higher tax rates *caused* the higher unemployment rates. Just because two things are *correlated*—that is, they happen at the same time—does not mean that one caused the other. For example, suppose that many of the countries with high tax rates also have laws that make it difficult for firms to fire workers. In that case, firms in those countries may be reluctant to hire workers because they would have difficulty firing them if they turned out not to be productive. Perhaps the restrictive laws, rather than the high tax rates, were the cause of the high unemployment rates. Over a period of time, many economic variables change, which complicates testing hypotheses even further. In fact, when economists disagree about a hypothesis, such as the effect of higher tax rates on unemployment rates, it is often because of disagreements over interpreting the statistical analysis used to test the hypothesis.

Note that hypotheses must be statements that could, in principle, turn out to be incorrect. Statements such as "High taxes are good" or "High taxes are bad" are value judgments rather than hypotheses because it is not possible to disprove them. Economists accept and use an economic model if it leads to hypotheses that are confirmed by statistical analysis. In many cases, the acceptance is tentative, however, pending the gathering of new data or further statistical analysis. In fact, economists often refer to a hypothesis having been "not rejected" rather than having been "accepted" by statistical analysis. But what if statistical analysis clearly rejects a hypothesis? Then we need to consider why the hypothesis was rejected. Perhaps the model used to determine the effect of taxes on unemployment assumed that governments in all countries are equally effective in collecting taxes. If some countries with high tax rates do not enforce their tax laws, few individuals and firms end up paying the high tax rates. This fact may explain why our hypothesis was rejected by the data.

Throughout this book, as we build economic models and use them to answer questions, you need to bear in mind the distinction between *positive analysis* and *normative analysis*. **Positive analysis** is concerned with *what is*, and **normative analysis** is concerned with *what ought to be*. Economics is concerned primarily with positive analysis, which measures the costs and benefits of different courses of action.

In each chapter, the *Making the Connection* feature discusses a news story or another application related to the chapter material. The following *Making the Connection* discusses why it is important to understand macroeconomic issues.

Positive analysis Analysis concerned with what is.

Normative analysis Analysis concerned with what ought to be.

Making the Connection

Why Should the United States Worry About the "Euro Crisis"?

The euro zone includes 17 member states of the European Union that adopted the euro as their currency beginning in 2001. Monetary policy for the euro zone is the responsibility of the European Central Bank (ECB). To be granted permission for their states to join the euro zone, government officials agree to limits on their budget deficits and debt. The recession that began in 2007 worsened the debt problems of several euro-zone members as government spending increased and tax receipts fell. Ireland, Portugal, Greece, and Spain petitioned fellow euro-zone members and the International Monetary Fund (IMF) to approve loans that would allow them to avoid defaulting on their government-issued debt.

To secure the loans, government officials had to agree to economic reforms, spending cuts, and tax increases—so-called *austerity policies*. By the spring of 2012, voters in these countries began to resist the austerity policies, and it seemed possible that Greece and perhaps other countries might abandon the euro and resume using their previous currencies.

Although the "euro crisis" threatened Europe's economies, many people in the United States wondered if the crisis would affect them. Exports from the United States could suffer as European consumers tightened their belts, but foreign trade is a relatively small part of U.S. gross domestic product (GDP), and the European share of this trade is even smaller. But since the end of the recession in 2009, U.S. exports have accounted for over 40% of the growth of GDP. Also, the euro crisis could threaten the supply chains of many U.S. manufacturers who rely on European companies for components such as engines and plastic parts. The crisis could also threaten U.S. banks, which at the end of 2011 held over $650 billion worth of euro-zone debt. A decline in the value of the euro in exchange for the U.S. dollar would reduce the value of this debt.

The U.S. economy could also suffer from the euro crisis for reasons that are difficult to measure. Some economists believe Europe's debt problems have contributed to a lack of confidence among business leaders in the United States. This lack of confidence may be one reason for sluggish economic growth in the United States. Shawn DuBravac, chief economist for the Consumer Electronics Association, explained, "A lack of confidence can be very contagious." However the euro crisis is resolved, it is one of many macroeconomic issues that have important implications for consumers, workers, and firms. The purpose of this book is to help you better understand these issues.

Sources: Elena Becatoros, "Greek Radical Left Insists on Canceling Bailout," *Associated Press*, June 12, 2012; "EU Floats Worst-Case Plans for Greek Euro," *Reuters*, June 11, 2012; and Matthew Philips, "How Europe's Contagion May Hit the U.S. Economy," *BloombergBusinessWeek*, June 7, 2012.

See related problem 2.9 at the end of the chapter.

Key Issues and Questions of Macroeconomics

This text discusses a number of important macroeconomic issues and questions. Beginning with Chapter 2, we highlight one key issue and related question at the start of each chapter, and we end each chapter by using the concepts introduced in the chapter to answer the question. This issue–question framework presented in the following list provides a roadmap for the rest of the book and shows why learning macroeconomics gives you the tools to analyze intelligently some of the most important issues of our times.

Learning Objective
Become familiar with key macroeconomic issues and questions.

Chapter 2: Measuring the Macroeconomy

Issue: The unemployment rate can rise even though a recession has ended.

Question: How accurately does the government measure the unemployment rate?

Chapter 3: The U.S. Financial System

Issue: The financial system moves funds from savers to borrowers, which promotes investment and the accumulation of capital goods.

Question: Why did the bursting of the housing bubble that began in 2006 cause the financial system to falter?

Chapter 4: The Global Financial System

Issue: Some governments allow the value of their currency to fluctuate in foreign-exchange markets, while other governments fix the value of their currency.

Question: What are the advantages and disadvantages of floating versus fixed exchange rates?

Chapter 5: The Standard of Living Over Time and Across Countries

Issue: Some countries have experienced rapid rates of long-run economic growth, while other countries have grown slowly, if at all.

Question: Why isn't the whole world rich?

Chapter 6: Long-Run Economic Growth

Issue: Real GDP has increased substantially over time in the United States and other developed countries.

Question: What are the main factors that determine the growth rate of real GDP per capita?

Chapter 7: Money and Inflation

Issue: The Federal Reserve's actions during the financial crisis of 2007–2009 led some economists and policymakers to worry that the inflation rate in the United States would be increasing.

Question: What is the connection between changes in the money supply and the inflation rate?

Chapter 8: The Labor Market

Issue: The unemployment rate in the United States did not fall below 8% until more than three years after the end of the 2007–2009 recession.

Question: Has the natural rate of unemployment increased?

Chapter 9: Business Cycles

Issue: Economies around the world experience a business cycle.

Question: Does the business cycle impose significant costs on the economy?

Chapter 10: Explaining Aggregate Demand: The *IS-MP* Model

Issue: The U.S. economy has experienced 11 recessions since the end of World War II.

Question: What explains the business cycle?

Chapter 11: The *IS-MP* Model: Adding Inflation and the Open Economy

Issue: The recession of 2007–2009 was the worst since the Great Depression of the 1930s.
Question: What explains the severity of the 2007–2009 recession?

Chapter 12: Monetary Policy in the Short Run

Issue: The Federal Reserve undertook unprecedented policy actions in response to the recession of 2007–2009.
Question: Why were traditional Federal Reserve policies ineffective during the 2007–2009 recession?

Chapter 13: Fiscal Policy in the Short Run

Issue: During the 2007–2009 recession, Congress and the president undertook unprecedented fiscal policy actions.
Question: Was the American Recovery and Reinvestment Act of 2009 successful in increasing real GDP and employment?

Chapter 14: Aggregate Demand, Aggregate Supply, and Monetary Policy

Issue: Between the early 1980s and 2007, the U.S. economy experienced a period of macroeconomic stability known as the Great Moderation.
Question: Did discretionary monetary policy kill the Great Moderation?

Chapter 15: Fiscal Policy and the Government Budget in the Long Run

Issue: In 2012, the federal government's budget deficit and the national debt were on course to rise to unsustainable levels.
Question: How should the United States solve its long-run fiscal problem?

Chapter 16: Consumption and Investment

Issue: Households and firms make decisions about how much to consume and invest based on expectations about the future.
Question: How does government tax policy affect the decisions of households and firms?

Key Terms and Problems

Key Terms

Business cycle, p. 2	Inflation rate, p. 9	Monetary policy, p. 12
Deflation, p. 10	Labor force, p. 8	Normative analysis, p. 18
Endogenous variable, p. 17	Labor productivity, p. 3	Positive analysis, p. 18
Exogenous variable, p. 17	Long-run economic growth, p. 3	Real gross domestic product (GDP), p. 4
Financial crisis, p. 12	Macroeconomics, p. 2	
Fiscal policy, p. 12	Microeconomics, p. 2	Unemployment rate, p. 8

1.1 What Macroeconomics Is About

Become familiar with the focus of macroeconomics.

Review Questions

1.1 What is long-run economic growth, and how is it measured? Have all countries experienced about the same amount of long-run economic growth? Briefly explain.

1.2 What is a business cycle? What has happened to the severity of the U.S. business cycle since 1950?

1.3 Describe the average inflation rate in the United States over the past 40 years. Since 1775, when has the United States experienced high inflation? When has the United States experienced deflation? Are inflation rates roughly the same in countries around the world? Briefly explain.

1.4 Why is spending on government retirement programs increasing in the United States and other high-income countries? What problems might this increased spending pose to the economy?

Problems and Applications

1.5 The average rate of growth of U.S. real GDP is approximately 3%, as measured over long periods of time. China has been averaging growth rates that are considerably higher than 3% for much of the past two decades, while some sub-Saharan African countries have experienced growth rates that are considerably lower than 3% or even negative.

a. What is happening to the difference in the level of income between the United States and China?

b. What is happening to the difference in the level of income between the United States and these African countries?

c. In general, for countries to "catch up" to higher-income countries, what must happen in terms of growth rates?

1.6 Consider the following statement: "A country like the United States is more open than a country like Belgium because it is larger and has a higher total value of imports and exports." Do you agree with this statement? Explain.

1.7 According to a January 2012 Gallup poll, "Regardless of income, age, or region, Americans were more optimistic about their future standard of living in December 2011 than they were in December 2008...." What does this poll imply about expectations of real GDP growth rates in coming years?

Source: Dennis Jacobe, "Americans' Standard-of-Living Perceptions Best Since June: Fifty-five Percent of Upper-Income Americans Say Their Standard of Living Is 'Getting Better,'" January 12, 2012, www.gallup.com.

1.8 During the 2007–2009 recession and financial crisis, each of the programs listed below was implemented. Identify whether each of these programs represents monetary policy or fiscal policy.

a. The Federal Reserve decreased interest rates.

b. Congress provided funding for extended payments to unemployed workers.

c. Congress authorized new spending on infrastructure, such as high-speed railway lines.

d. The Federal Reserve took actions that greatly increased the money supply.

1.9 [Related to the Chapter Opener on page 1] According to an economic study, "Increasing evidence suggests that even short [recessions] can have substantial ... effects on workers' careers." Why might graduating when there is a weak labor market have a substantial effect on a college graduate's career even after the economy has recovered and the job market has improved?

Source: Philip Oreopoulos, Till von Wachter, and Andrew Heisz, "The Short- and Long-Term Career Effects of Graduating in a Recession: Hysteresis and Heterogeneity in the Market for College Graduates," IZA Discussion Paper No. 3578, June 2008.

1.2 **How Economists Think About Macroeconomics**
Explain how economists approach macroeconomic questions.

Review Questions

2.1 Why do economists build models? Explain the steps generally used in building an economic model.

2.2 Explain the difference between an endogenous variable and an exogenous variable.

2.3 Why is it customary to say that a hypothesis has "not been rejected" rather than "accepted"?

2.4 What is the difference between normative analysis and positive analysis? Is economics concerned primarily with normative analysis or with positive analysis?

Problems and Applications

2.5 [Related to Solved Problem 1.2 **on page 16**] Many people believe that significant numbers of U.S. jobs have been "outsourced"—that is, firms have relocated operations to countries in which labor is cheaper, so the jobs have moved overseas. Briefly describe how you would analyze the following question: "Has the amount of outsourcing by U.S. companies been significant relative to the size of the U.S. labor market?" What problems might you expect to encounter in carrying out your analysis?

2.6 Explain which of the following statements would make a reasonable hypothesis to test. Use the concepts of normative and positive statements in your answers.

  a. Increases in the duration of unemployment benefits lead to higher rates of unemployment.

  b. Immigration is bad for society.

  c. Increases in the labor force cause output to rise.

  d. Welfare programs make workers lazy.

  e. Higher rates of taxation increase work effort.

2.7 If you were studying the following relationships, which variable would be exogenous and which would be endogenous?

  a. The effect of investment growth on the growth rate of GDP

  b. The relationship between the amount of sunshine and plant growth

  c. The relationship between hours of studying and a student's GPA

2.8 Consider the following statement: "Economic models use many simplifying assumptions. Therefore, they do not apply to the more complex events in the real world." Do you agree or disagree with this statement? Explain your answer.

2.9 [Related to the Making the Connection **on page 18**] Assume that you overheard a student make the following statement in your macroeconomics class:

  The so-called European debt crisis may be important to people who live in Greece or Italy but it has little effect on the economy of the United States. Our economy does not depend on foreign trade as much as the economies of these countries do. And if we can't sell our exports in Europe, we can always sell them in Canada, South America, or Asia.

  Write a response to this student that explains how debt crises in Europe can affect the U.S. economy.

Data Exercises

D1.1: [Excel exercise] The Federal Reserve Bank of St. Louis offers a wide range of economic data at its Web site, called FRED (research.stlouisfed.org/fred2/). Use these data to examine real GDP for the United States from 1929 to the present.

a. Download annual data (GDPCA) on real GDP from 1929 to the present. Calculate the annual growth rates, starting with 1930. Are there years in which real GDP decreased? With what events are these years associated?

b. Calculate the average rate of real GDP growth for the period from 1930 to the most recent year available. Calculate the average annual growth rate from 2009 to 2011. How does the growth rate during this three-year period compare to the average growth rate from 1930 to the present?

D1.2: The Federal Reserve Bank of St. Louis offers a wide range of economic data at its Web site, called FRED (research.stlouisfed.org/fred2/) including data for Japan. We can use these data to compare the behavior of real GDP per capita and inflation in Japan and the United States.

a. Download annual data on real GDP per capita in Japan (JPNRGDPC) and for the United States (USARGDPC) from 1960 to the present. Chart the two data series on the same graph. How does real GDP per capita in Japan compare to real GDP per capita in the United States? Have there been any changes in the relationship over time? Briefly explain.

b. Download annual data on the consumer price index for Japan (JPNCPIALLAINMEI) and the United States (USACPIBLS) from 1955 to the present. For both Japan and the United States calculate the inflation rate as the annual growth rate of the consumer price index. Chart the two data series on the same graph. How does the inflation rate in Japan compare to the inflation rate in the United States? In particular, how do the inflation rates in the two countries compare since 1990? Has either country ever experienced negative inflation rates?

D1.3: [Excel exercise] Use the *MeasuringWorth* data to practice the following Excel skills, which you will need to use in later chapters:

a. Import the data on inflation and wage change in the United States from 1990 to 2012 into Excel.

b. Chart the two series on the same graph. How do they compare with each other?

c. Find average wage change and average inflation for the current year. What is the standard deviation of each series?

d. What is the correlation coefficient for the two series? What does it mean?

CHAPTER 2

Measuring the Macroeconomy

Learning Objectives

After studying this chapter, you should be able to:

2.1 Explain how economists use gross domestic product (GDP) to measure total production and total income (pages 27–37)

2.2 Discuss the difference between real GDP and nominal GDP (pages 37–44)

2.3 Explain how the inflation rate is measured and distinguish between real and nominal interest rates (pages 44–51)

2.4 Understand how to calculate the unemployment rate (pages 51–53)

How Do We Know When We Are in a Recession?

President Harry Truman famously remarked, "A recession is when your neighbor loses his job; a depression is when you lose yours." In fact, governments typically do not formally announce when the economy is in recession. Instead, they leave the dating of recessions to economists. In the United States, most economists—inside and outside the government—accept the dates for business cycle recessions and expansions determined by the Business Cycle Dating Committee of the National Bureau of Economic Research (NBER). For example, the committee determined that the business cycle expansion that began in November 2001 ended in December 2007, and it determined that the following recession ended in June 2009, when the next expansion began.

How does the NBER's Business Cycle Dating Committee determine when a recession begins and ends? The committee defines a recession as "a significant decline in

economic activity [that] spreads across the economy and can last from a few months to more than a year." Deciding whether a particular economic episode fits this definition requires the committee to examine a broad range of data:

> The Committee does not have a fixed definition of economic activity. It examines and compares the behavior of various measures of broad activity: real GDP measured on the product and income sides, economy-wide employment, and real income. The Committee also may consider indicators that do not cover the entire economy, such as real sales and the Federal Reserve's index of industrial production (IP).

> The committee does not focus on any one industry. For example, residential construction fell by 1.4% during 2011, even though it was a year of economic

Continued on next page

Key Issue and Question

Issue: The unemployment rate can rise even though a recession has ended.

Question: How accurately does the government measure the unemployment rate?

Answered on page 53

expansion according to the NBER. The economy was expanding, but it was a difficult recovery for home-builders. The committee also does not rely entirely on the strength of the labor market. The 2007–2009 recession ended in June 2009, when the unemployment rate was 9.5%. Despite the recession's having ended, the unemployment rate kept increasing during the beginning of the following expansion, peaking at 10.0% in October 2009. By September 2012, the unemployment rate was still 7.8%, much higher than the 4.7% unemployment rate just before the beginning of the recession. Although the economy was in an expansion, the expansion was too weak to rapidly bring down the unemployment rate.

The economic data the committee uses are collected primarily by government agencies. Two problems arise in using and interpreting the data: First, there is a lag before the first estimates of production, employment, and other data are released. That is, the data measure economic activity during a period that has already passed. Second, the first estimates by government agencies are based on incomplete information. As the agencies continue to collect additional data and refine their estimates, they issue revised data on production and employment. Revised data continue to be issued over a period of years, with the final estimates often differing substantially from the first estimates. As a result, the NBER committee takes time to consider the revised estimates carefully before announcing that a recession has begun or ended. For example, the committee waited one year—until December 2008—to announce that a recession had begun in December 2007. The committee waited even longer—15 months—to announce that the recession had ended in June 2009.

The Federal Reserve, Congress, and the president of the United States, though, are typically unwilling to wait a year or more to take action when they believe a recession may have begun. Newly issued macroeconomic data—whatever their flaws—guide the actions of these policymakers. Businesses, investors, and households are in a similar position. Businesses often have to make decisions—such as whether to open new stores or factories or introduce new products—that will turn out to be good ideas if the economy is in an expansion and poor ideas if the economy heads into a recession. For example, at the height of the housing boom in 2004, KB Home and Toll Brothers purchased hundreds of acres of land outside Las Vegas. The builders planned to construct 14,500 homes. Then the housing bubble burst, and the economy entered a severe recession in 2007. Only 635 homes were constructed, and the builders suffered heavy losses on the development.

Households are in a similar situation. When they buy houses, cars, or furniture, they may regret the decision if the economy unexpectedly falls into a recession and businesses start laying off workers.

We can conclude that knowledge of key macroeconomic data, including how they are constructed and their possible shortcomings, is important to the study of macroeconomics.

Sources: National Bureau of Economic Research, "Statement of the NBER Business Cycle Dating Committee on the Determination of the Dates of Turning Points in the U.S. Economy," www.nber.org; and Robbie Whelan, "Builders Face a Desert Reckoning," *Wall Street Journal*, January 5, 2011.

Economists believe that the 2007–2009 recession was one of the worst since the Great Depression of the 1930s, but how do they know that? How do they know how many people lost their jobs during the recession or what happened to the inflation rate? The answer is that economists, consumers, firms, and policymakers all rely on economic data gathered by agencies of the federal government. These data allow us to measure key aspects of the economy, including total production, total employment, and the price level. Economists rely on these data not just to measure the economy but also to test hypotheses derived from macroeconomic models of the economy. Macroeconomics is about much more than just describing what has happened. Macroeconomics is also about building models that can help us to understand *why* recessions, periods of high inflation, and other macroeconomic events have happened.

In this chapter, we will focus on the data used in calculating three important measures of the macroeconomic performance of the economy:

1. Gross domestic product (GDP)
2. The inflation rate
3. The unemployment rate

GDP: Measuring Total Production and Total Income

In macroeconomics, we study the economy as a whole, so we need a measure of total production. Economists measure total production by **gross domestic product (GDP)**. GDP is the market value of all final goods and services produced in a country during a period of time. The Bureau of Economic Analysis (BEA) compiles the data needed to calculate GDP and issues reports giving quarterly and annual values for GDP and related statistics. Because these reports provide important information on the state of the economy, economists, business managers, policymakers, and investors on Wall Street watch them closely.

How the Government Calculates GDP

Here are some important facts about the definition of GDP and how the BEA calculates it:

- *GDP is measured using market values, not quantities.* When looking at individual firms or industries, we typically measure output in terms of quantities, such as the number of copies of Windows produced by Microsoft, the number of automobiles produced by Ford, or the number of Big Macs produced by McDonald's. But in measuring total production, we can't just add the quantity of software to the quantity of automobiles to the quantity of hamburgers, and so on because the result would be a meaningless number. Instead, we use market prices and take the *value* in dollar terms of all the goods and services produced. In addition to being convenient, market prices also tell us how much consumers value a particular good or service. If pears sell for $0.50 each and plums sell for $1.00 each, then the market prices tell us that consumers value a plum twice as much as a pear.
- *GDP includes only the market value of final goods and services.* A **final good or service** is one that is purchased by its final user and is not included in the production of any other good or service. Examples of final goods are a hamburger purchased by a consumer and a machine tool purchased by Ford.

   Some goods and services, though, become part of other goods and services; they are **intermediate goods or services**. For example, McDonald's does not produce the buns it uses in making Big Macs. McDonald's purchases the buns from suppliers, so the buns are an intermediate good. In calculating GDP, the BEA includes the value of the Big Mac but not the value of the bun. If they included the bun, they would be *double counting*: The value of the bun would be counted once when McDonald's buys it and again when McDonald's sells the Big Mac to a consumer.
- *GDP measures production within a country, regardless of who does the production.* For example, Toyota is a Japanese automobile company, but it has assembly plants in Indiana, Kentucky, Mississippi, and Texas. The automobiles produced at these plants

Learning Objective

Explain how economists use gross domestic product (GDP) to measure total production and total income.

Gross domestic product (GDP) The market value of all final goods and services produced in a country during a period of time.

Final good or service A good or service purchased by a final user.

Intermediate good or service A good or service that is an input into another good or service, such as a tire on a truck.

count as part of U.S. GDP because, even though Toyota is a Japanese company, the automobiles were produced within the borders of the United States.[1]

- *GDP includes some imputed values.* The BEA uses market values for goods and services in computing GDP, but in some cases where there is no market for a good or service, the value has to be *imputed*, or estimated. For example, the rent paid for an apartment or a house is the value of housing services the apartment or house provides. But many people own their own homes, so there is no rent that can be used to value the housing services they receive. The BEA has to impute a value for the rental services generated by owner-occupied housing. Similarly, many government services, such as police and fire services, do not have a market price. The BEA imputes the value of these services as being equal to the cost of providing them.

- *The BEA does not count some types of production.* The BEA does not attempt to impute values for some goods or services that are produced outside the market, such as the services a homemaker provides to the homemaker's family. The BEA also does not impute a value for goods and services produced in the *underground economy*, which refers to buying and selling that is not recorded either to avoid tax payments or because the goods and services—for example, cocaine or heroin—are illegal. Clearly these market transactions are part of the economy, but information on the underground economy is so imperfect that the BEA does not include estimates of it in the official GDP data. Economists Friedrich Schneider of Johannes Kepler University and Dominik Enste of the University of Cologne have surveyed studies estimating the size of the underground economy in countries around the world.[2] They find that estimates for the size of the underground economy in the United States vary widely, but it is probably less than 10% of GDP, or about $1.5 trillion. In contrast, the underground economy may be 76% of GDP in Nigeria, 40% in Russia, and 20% in Greece and Italy.

  Most economists believe that the BEA's decision not to impute values for some goods and services does not present a problem in using GDP data. Typically, we are most interested in using GDP to measure changes in total production over a relatively brief period of time—say, several years. It is unlikely that the total value of goods and services—such as the services of homemakers or goods and services sold in the underground economy— that are not counted by the BEA changes much over a short period. So, our measures of the *changes* in total production would not be much different, even if the BEA were able to impute values for every good and service.

- *GDP includes only current production during the indicated time period.* For example, the sale of a used car would not be included because the production of the car would have already been counted in an earlier period, when the car was first sold. If we counted the sale of a used car, we would be double counting the car: first when it was initially produced and again when it was resold.

---

[1]As we note later, the value of imported goods is subtracted from GDP. So, the parts in U.S.-assembled Toyotas that are imported from Japan would be subtracted from GDP.

[2]Friedrich Schneider and Dominik H. Enste, "Shadow Economies: Size, Causes, and Consequences," *Journal of Economic Literature*, Vol. 38, No. 1, March 2000, pp. 77–114.

Production and Income

The rules used in calculating GDP are called **national income accounting**. The word *income* in this term indicates that by calculating GDP, the BEA is measuring both total production and total income. Note that nearly all countries around the world use similar rules to produce their *national income accounts*, which is the name given to GDP and other related measures of total production and total income. The BEA refers to the U.S. accounts as the U.S. National Income and Product Accounts (NIPA).

National income accounting reveals that *the value of total production in an economy is equal to the value of total income.* To see why, think about what happens to the money you spend on a single product. For example, if you purchase a Vizio high-definition television from Best Buy for $1,000, all of the $1,000 must end up as someone's income. Vizio and Best Buy will receive some of the $1,000 as profits, workers at Vizio will receive some as wages, the salesperson who sold you the television will receive some as salary, the firms that sell parts to Vizio will receive some as profits, and the workers at those firms will receive some as wages. Every penny must end up as someone's income.[3] So, we can conclude that the revenues firms receive from selling goods and services are completely distributed to the owners of the inputs that are used to make those goods and services. Therefore, if we add up the total value of every good and service sold in the economy, we must get a total that is exactly equal to the value of all the income in the economy.

National income accounting The rules used in calculating GDP and related measures of total production and total income.

The Circular Flow of Income

Figure 2.1 is called a circular-flow diagram, and it uses the flow of spending and money in the economy to illustrate how the total value of spending on goods and services—*total expenditures*—equals the total value of income. Firms sell goods and services to three groups: domestic households and firms, foreign households and firms, and the government. Expenditures by foreign households and firms (shown as the "Rest of the World" in the diagram) on domestically produced goods and services are called *exports*. As we note at the bottom of Figure 2.1, we can measure GDP by adding up the total expenditures of these three groups on goods and services produced in the United States.

Firms use *factors of production* to produce goods and services. A **factor of production** is any input used to produce goods and services. Factors of production are usually divided into three categories: labor, capital, and natural resources. **Capital** refers to physical capital goods, such as machine tools, computers, factories, and office buildings, that are used to produce other goods and services. The term *natural resources* refers to land and raw materials, such as coal or iron ore, that are used to produce goods and services. All factors of production are owned by households. It seems natural to say that households own their labor, but we generally think of the capital and natural resources as being owned by firms. Ultimately, though, every firm is owned by households. Even a very large corporation, such as Microsoft, is owned by its shareholders—the people who have bought stock issued by Microsoft. So, in this sense, we can say that households supply all of the factors of production to firms in exchange for income.

Factor of production Any input used to produce goods and services.

Capital Goods, such as machine tools, computers, factories, and office buildings, that are used to produce other goods and services.

---

[3]Note, though, that any sales tax that Best Buy collects on the television will be sent by the store directly to the government, without ending up as anyone's income.

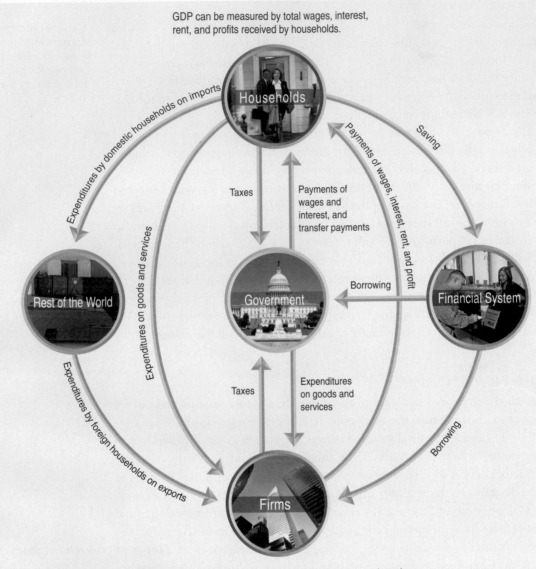

GDP can be measured by total wages, interest, rent, and profits received by households.

GDP can be measured by total expenditures on goods and services by households, firms, government, and the rest of the world.

Figure 2.1 The Circular Flow of Income and the Measurement of GDP

The circular-flow diagram illustrates the flow of spending and money in the economy. Firms sell goods and services to three groups: domestic households and firms, foreign households and firms, and the government. To produce goods and services, firms use factors of production: labor, capital, and natural resources. Households supply the factors of production to firms in exchange for income in the form of wages, interest, profit, and rent. Firms make payments of wages and interest to households in exchange for hiring workers and other factors of production. The sum of wages, interest, rent, and profit is total income in the economy. The diagram also shows that households use their income to purchase goods and services, pay taxes, and save. Firms and the government borrow the funds that flow from households into the financial system. We can measure GDP either by calculating the total value of expenditures on final goods and services or by calculating the value of total income.

We divide income into four categories: wages, interest, rent, and profit. Firms pay wages to households in exchange for labor services, interest for the use of capital, and rent for the use of natural resources. Profit is the income that remains after a firm has paid wages, interest, and rent. Profit is the return to *entrepreneurs* for organizing the factors of production and for bearing the risk of producing and selling goods and services. As Figure 2.1 shows, federal, state, and local governments make payments of wages and interest to households in exchange for hiring workers and other factors of production. The sum of wages, interest, rent, and profit is the total income received by households.

The circular-flow diagram also allows us to trace the ways that households use their income. Households spend some of their income on goods and services. Some of this spending is on domestically produced goods and services, and some is on foreign-produced goods and services, or *imports*. Households also use some of their income to pay taxes to the government. Some of the income households earn is not spent on goods and services or paid in taxes but is deposited in checking or savings accounts in banks, or other *financial intermediaries*, or used to buy financial assets, such as stocks or bonds, in *financial markets*. Financial intermediaries and financial markets together make up the **financial system**. The flow of funds from households into the financial system makes it possible for the government and firms to borrow. As became clear during the 2007–2009 financial crisis, the health of a financial system is vital to an economy. Without the ability to borrow funds through the financial system, firms will have difficulty carrying on their day-to-day operations, much less expanding and adopting new technologies.

Financial system The financial intermediaries and financial markets that together facilitate the flow of funds from lenders to borrowers.

An Example of Measuring GDP

As mentioned earlier in this chapter, the BEA gathers data on quantities and prices of final goods and services, multiplies the quantity of each good or service by its price, and adds up the totals to determine the value of GDP. For example, consider a very simple economy in which only two goods are produced: copies of Windows 8 and McDonald's Big Mac hamburgers. The value of GDP could then be calculated as:

$$\text{GDP} = (\text{Quantity of Windows 8} \times \text{Price of Windows 8})$$
$$+ (\text{Quantity of Big Macs} \times \text{Price of Big Macs}).$$

If 1,000 copies of Windows 8 are sold at a price of $100 per copy, and 10,000 Big Macs are sold at a price of $4 per Big Mac, then the value of GDP is:

$$(1,000 \times \$100) + (10,000 \times \$4) = \$140,000.$$

By using this method for all final goods and services, the BEA can calculate GDP.

National Income Identities and the Components of GDP

The BEA divides its statistics on GDP into four major categories of expenditures:

1. Personal consumption expenditures, or "Consumption" (C)
2. Gross private domestic investment, or "Investment" (I)
3. Government consumption and gross investment, or "Government purchases" (G)
4. Net exports of goods and services, or "Net exports" (NX)

Table 2.1 GDP in 2011

	Billions of dollars		Percentage of GDP	
Consumption	**$10,726.0**		**71.1%**	
Durable goods	1,162.9		7.7	
Nondurable goods	2,483.7		16.5	
Services	7,079.4		46.9	
Investment	**1,916.2**		**12.7**	
Business fixed investment	1,532.5		10.2	
Structures		409.5		2.7
Equipment and software		1,123.0		7.4
Residential investment	337.5		2.2	
Changes in business inventories	46.3		0.3	
Government purchases	**3,030.6**		**20.1**	
Federal	1,232.9		8.2	
National defense		824.9		5.5
Nondefense		407.9		2.7
State and local	1,797.7		11.9	
Net exports	**−578.7**		**−3.8**	
Exports	2,085.5		13.8	
Imports	2,664.2		17.7	
Gross domestic product	**$15,094.0**		**100.0%**	

Source: U.S. Bureau of Economic Analysis.

If we let Y represent GDP, then we have the following *national income identity*:

$$Y = C + I + G + NX.$$

This expression is an identity because the BEA assigns all expenditures on final goods and services into one of the four categories. Table 2.1 shows the values for 2011 of each of the major categories of expenditures, as well as their important subcategories.

We next briefly review some important points about the four categories of expenditures:

Consumption The purchase of new goods and services by households.

- **Consumption** is the purchase of new goods and services by households, regardless of which country the goods or services were originally produced in.[4] The BEA tracks three categories of consumption. *Durable goods* are tangible goods with an average life of three years or more, such as cars, furniture, and televisions. *Nondurable goods* are shorter-lived goods, such as food and clothing. *Services* are consumed at the time and place of purchase, such as haircuts, healthcare, and education. In the United States, as in most other high-income countries, the fraction of services in consumption has risen relative to goods. As people's incomes rise, they tend to buy relatively less food, clothing, and other goods and relatively more healthcare and other services.

[4]Later, we will see that because imports are subtracted out (or netted out), GDP only reflects the consumption of domestic products.

- **Investment** is divided into three categories. *Fixed investment* is spending by firms on new factories, office buildings, and machinery used to produce other goods. *Residential investment* is spending by households or firms on new single-family and multi-family homes. *Changes in business inventories* are also included in investment. *Inventories* are goods that have been produced but not yet sold. For example, if Ford produces 365,000 Mustangs in the United States during 2013 but sells only 350,000, then the BEA counts the 15,000 unsold Mustangs as investment spending by Ford in the changes in business inventories category. In effect, the BEA assumes that Ford purchased the Mustangs from itself.

  Recall that the BEA wants GDP to measure production during a specific time period. Therefore, the BEA includes inventories as a form of investment. To see why, suppose that a Ford Mustang rolls off the assembly line on December 30, 2013. This is finished production that occurs during 2013, so the BEA counts the Mustang as part of 2013 GDP. However, it takes time for Ford to ship the Mustang to a dealer and for the dealer to sell it. As a result, the Mustang may not sell until June 2014, so the BEA records consumption as having increased in that month by the value of the Mustang, and it records inventories as falling by the same amount.

  How does the BEA ensure that the Mustang counts as part of 2013 GDP and not 2014 GDP? The BEA assumes that Ford "purchases" the Mustang from itself to hold as inventory on December 31, 2013. Therefore, the "sale" of the Mustang to Ford occurs in 2013, so the Mustang is counted as part of 2013 GDP. When the dealer sells the Mustang in June 2014, the dealer is not selling a new automobile since Ford previously "purchased" the Mustang at the end of 2013. Therefore, the sale of the Mustang by the dealer is the sale of a used good and so does not count as part of GDP in 2014.

  The key characteristic of investment goods is that they add to the total amount, or *stock*, of capital goods that provide a flow of services into the future. For example, new capital goods include tools and machines that firms will use to produce goods and services in the future. Similarly, residential housing provides housing services for many years, so the production of new residential housing is counted as investment. The BEA classifies inventories as investment because firms plan to sell the inventories in the future.

- **Government purchases** are spending by federal, state, and local governments on newly produced goods and services. Some government purchases represent consumption spending, as when the government pays the salaries of teachers or FBI agents. Other government purchases represent investment spending, as when the government buys new structures, such as bridges and school buildings, or equipment, such as aircraft carriers. Purchases of this type allow the government to provide services—such as education or national defense—in the future.

  It is important to note that *government purchases do not include transfer payments*, which are one of the largest components of the government's budget. **Transfer payments** are payments by the government to individuals for which the government does not receive a new good or service in return. Examples of transfer payments include Social Security payments to retired and disabled people, Medicare payments to provide healthcare services for people 65 years and older, unemployment insurance payments to unemployed workers, and pension payments to retired government workers.

Investment Spending by firms on new factories, office buildings, machinery, and additions to inventories, plus spending by households and firms on new houses.

Government purchases Spending by federal, state, and local governments on newly produced goods and services.

Transfer payments Payments by the government to individuals for which the government does not receive a good or service in return.

MyEconLab Real-time data

Figure 2.2

Government Purchases and Government Expenditures, 1951–2011

Since 1951, transfer payments have become an increasing fraction of government expenditures, as federal spending on Social Security and Medicare and state and local spending on public employee pensions have increased. Government purchases were the same fraction of GDP in 2011 that they were in 1951.

Source: U.S. Bureau of Economic Analysis.

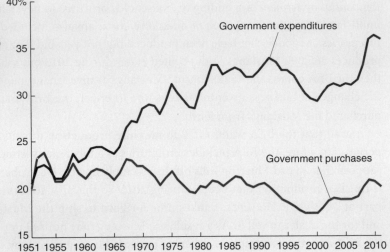

Economists often distinguish between government purchases and *government expenditures*, which include government purchases, government transfer payments, and government interest payments on bonds. As Figure 2.2 shows, since 1951, government expenditures have been growing relative to government purchases, as transfer payments have been increasing relative to government purchases of goods and services. In fact, as a percentage of GDP, government purchases in 2011 were the same percentage of GDP that they were in 1951, while government expenditures were 75% greater in 2011 than they were in 1951.

Net exports The value of all exports minus the value of all imports.

• **Net exports** is the value of all exports of goods and services minus the value of all imports of goods and services. When exports are greater than imports, net exports are positive, and the country runs a trade surplus. When exports are less than imports, net exports are negative, and the country runs a trade deficit. When exports equal imports, net exports are zero, and the trade deficit is zero.

If you purchase a Nintendo Wii for $300 at Best Buy, then U.S. consumption increases by $300. Does this lead to higher U.S. GDP? No. The Nintendo Wii is imported from Japan, so imports increase by $300, causing net exports to decrease by $300.[5] Because consumption increases by $300 and net exports decrease by $300, the change in expenditure is zero, and GDP does not change.

The Relationship Between GDP and GNP

Prior to 1991, the BEA's main measure of total production was gross *national* product rather than gross *domestic* product. The BEA switched its emphasis to GDP to be more consistent with the United Nation's System of Nation Accounts which emphasizes GDP.

---

[5]Technically, GDP would rise by an amount equal to the difference between what Best Buy pays Nintendo for the Wii and the price you paid for it. This difference represents the value of the service Best Buy has performed by importing the Wii from Japan and making it available for you to buy. We ignore this complication here.

In addition, GDP is more closely related to employment, industrial production and other economic variables which do not take the nationality of the firm into account. Writers, particularly non-economists, still sometimes slip and refer to GNP when they should be referring to GDP. **Gross national product (GNP)** is the value of final goods and services produced by residents of a country, even if the production takes place outside that country. GDP measures the production of goods and services within the borders of a country, and GNP measures the production of goods and services by factors of production owned by a country's citizens. For example, the Japanese firm Toyota owns factories in the United States, so the value of the cars produced in those factories is included in U.S. GDP. The profits received by the Japanese owners of Toyota in exchange for the factors of production they supply, however, have to be subtracted from U.S. GNP and added to Japanese GNP. The BEA defines *net factor payments* as equal to the difference between factor payments from other countries and factor payments to other countries.

> **Gross national product (GNP)** The value of final goods and services produced by residents of a country, even if the production takes place outside that country.

So, GDP and GNP are related by the following identity:

$$GDP = GNP + \text{Net factor payments.}$$

In practice, for the United States, net factor payments are small, so the value of GDP is typically within about 1% of the value of GNP. The difference can be quite large for some smaller countries, such as the Netherlands and Ireland, where citizens of other countries own a substantial number of the factories and stores that produce domestic goods and services. For those countries, GDP is a much more accurate measure of the value of total production than is GNP.

GDP Versus GDI

Figure 2.1 on page 30 illustrates a key macroeconomic fact: We can measure the value of total production in the economy either by calculating the value of total expenditure on final goods and services or by calculating the value of total income. The BEA uses the expenditure approach in calculating the familiar GDP and the income approach in calculating the less familiar *gross domestic income (GDI)*. If GDP and GDI were calculated exactly, they would have the same value. In fact, the BEA uses different data sources in calculating GDP and GDI—primarily sources on expenditure for GDP and primarily sources on income for GDI. Because these data sources do not measure production or income exactly, typically the values for GDP and GDI are different. The BEA refers to the difference between the values for GDP and GDI as the *statistical discrepancy*.

Figure 2.3 plots the annualized growth rates in real GDP and real GDI for each quarter beginning with the first quarter of 2005. The figure illustrates that although the two measures move roughly together, there are significant differences between the measures during some quarters.

Does it matter whether economists and policymakers use GDP or GDI? It might. For example, the two measures give different accounts of the period around the recession of 2007–2009. All four quarters of 2007 show positive growth in real GDP, but two quarters show declines in real GDI. The decline in real GDI is greater during the worst of the recession in late 2008 and early 2009 than is the decline in real GDP. Real GDI increases significantly more in late 2009 and early 2010 than does real GDP.

MyEconLab Real-time data

Figure 2.3

Movements in Real GDP and Real GDI, 2005–2012

Although the values of GDP and GDI should be the same, because the BEA constructs them from different data sources, the values usually differ.

Source: U.S. Bureau of Economic Analysis.

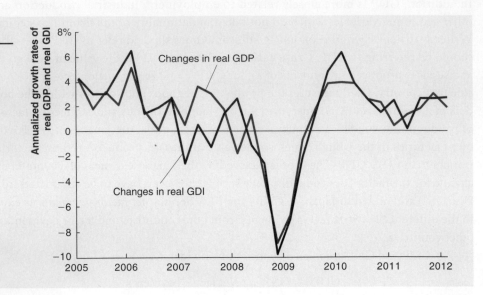

Jeremy Nalewaik, an economist at the Federal Reserve Board, argues that although GDP and GDI move together closely, GDI may be giving a more accurate measure of the state of the economy. He argues that other *business cycle indicators,* such as the unemployment rate, the change in the S&P 500 stock index, surveys of the Institute of Supply Management of manufacturing and services output, and forecasts of output growth by the Survey of Professional Forecasters, are more closely correlated to GDI than to GDP. Nalewaik and some other economists argue that policymakers should pay greater attention to movements in GDI or to an average of movements of GDI and GDP, and less attention to GDP by itself.

One key drawback to GDI is that for the first three quarters of the year, the BEA releases its initial estimate of GDI a month later than it releases its estimate of GDP for that quarter. For the fourth quarter of the year, the BEA releases its estimate of GDI two months after it releases its estimate of GDP. Supporters of greater use of GDI in analyzing the business cycle urge the BEA to take steps to gather data on GDI sooner so that estimates of GDI can be released at the same time as estimates of GDP.

GDP and National Income

We have seen that GDP is a measure of both the value of total production and the value of total income. GNP is also a measure of total production and total income. The BEA publishes data on several other measures of total income in addition to GDP and GNP. In producing goods and services, firms wear out some capital—such as machinery, equipment, and buildings—and have to replace it. *Depreciation* represents the value of worn-out or obsolete capital. In the data published by the BEA, depreciation is referred to as *consumption of fixed capital.* If we subtract this value from GDP, we are left with *national income.* The BEA publishes data on five categories of income: employee compensation, proprietors' income (which is the income earned by businesses that are not corporations), rental income, corporate profits, and net interest payments.

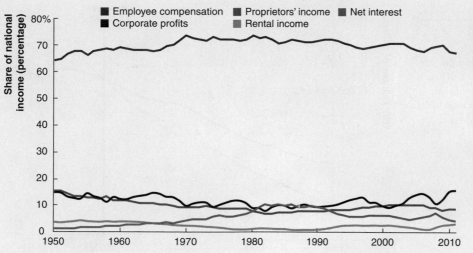

Figure 2.4

Shares of National Income in the United States, 1950–2011

Employee compensation is by far the largest component of national income, averaging 70%. In contrast, corporate profits averaged less than 12%. The compensation of sole proprietors, net interest, and rental income all averaged less than 10% of national income.

Source: U.S. Bureau of Economic Analysis.

Figure 2.4 shows the five categories of income as percentages of national income. Employee compensation—mainly wages, salaries, and fringe benefits, such as employer-provided medical insurance and pension contributions—is by far the largest part of national income. Public opinion polls show that many people believe that corporate profits make up 40% or more of national income. In fact, though, over the past 60 years, while employee compensation has averaged about 70% of national income, corporate profits have averaged less than 12%. The figure shows that, over time, the shares of the different categories of income have remained fairly stable.

The BEA also publishes data on *personal income*, which is income received by households. To calculate personal income, the BEA subtracts from national income the earnings that corporations retain rather than pay to shareholders in the form of dividends. The BEA also adds in household receipts of transfer payments and interest on government bonds. The BEA publishes data on *disposable personal income*, which is equal to personal income minus personal tax payments, such as the federal personal income tax. Disposable personal income is the best measure of the income households have available to spend.

Real GDP, Nominal GDP, and the GDP Deflator

Learning Objective

Discuss the difference between real GDP and nominal GDP.

When your income rises, you may have worked more hours or earned more per hour. For the economy, the *value* of total production as measured by GDP can increase either because the quantity of goods and services increases or because the prices used to value the quantities rise (or because some of both happen). For instance, if the quantities of every good and service remain the same, but all prices double, then the value of GDP will double. Because we are primarily interested in GDP as a measure of production, the BEA separates price changes from quantity changes by calculating a measure of

Figure 2.5

Nominal GDP and Real GDP, 1990–2011

Real GDP is calculated using prices from the base year. For years before the base year, real GDP is greater than nominal GDP. For years after the base year, nominal GDP is greater than real GDP.

Source: U.S. Bureau of Economic Analysis.

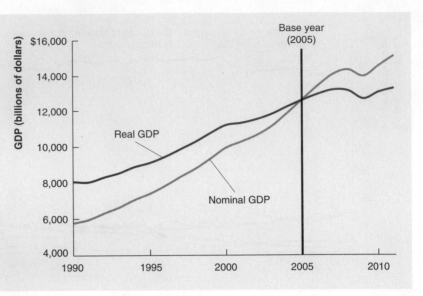

Nominal GDP The value of final goods and services calculated using current-year prices.

Real GDP The value of final goods and services calculated using base-year prices.

production called *real GDP*. **Nominal GDP** is calculated by summing the current values of final goods and services. **Real GDP** is calculated by designating a particular year as the *base year* and then using prices in the base year to calculate the value of goods and services in all other years. For instance, currently the BEA has designated 2005 as the base year. So, real GDP for 2012 is calculated by using prices of goods and services from 2005. By keeping prices constant, we know that changes in real GDP represent changes in the quantity of goods and services produced in the economy.

Figure 2.5 shows nominal GDP and real GDP for the years 1990–2011. Note that for years before the base year of 2005, real GDP is greater than nominal GDP; for years after 2005, nominal GDP is greater than real GDP. The lines for real GDP and nominal GDP cross in the base year.

Solved Problem 2.2A

Calculating Real GDP

Consider a very simple economy that produces only four final goods and services: apples, plums, hamburgers, and teeth whitening. Assume that the base year is 2005. Use the information in the following table to calculate nominal and real GDP for 2005 and 2013:

Product	2005		2013	
	Quantity	Price	Quantity	Price
Apples	200	$ 0.50	220	$ 0.60
Plums	90	0.40	85	0.35
Hamburgers	60	3.00	70	3.25
Teeth whitening	5	50.00	7	52.00

Solving the Problem

Step 1 **Review the chapter material.** This problem asks you to calculate real GDP, so you may want to review the section "Real GDP, Nominal GDP, and the GDP Deflator," which begins on page 37.

Step 2 **Calculate nominal GDP for the two years.** To calculate nominal GDP, we multiply the quantities produced during a year by the prices for that year to obtain the value of production for each good or service. Then, we need to add up the values.

For 2005:

Product	Quantity	Price	Value
Apples	200	$ 0.50	$ 100.00
Plums	90	0.40	36.00
Hamburgers	60	3.00	180.00
Teeth whitening	5	50.00	250.00
Nominal GDP			$ 566.00

For 2013:

Product	Quantity	Price	Value
Apples	220	$ 0.60	$ 132.00
Plums	85	0.35	29.75
Hamburgers	70	3.25	227.50
Teeth whitening	7	52.00	364.00
Nominal GDP			$ 753.25

Step 3 **Calculate real GDP for 2013, using the prices for 2005.** To calculate real GDP for 2013, we need to multiply the quantities produced in 2013 by the prices for those goods and services in the base year 2005:

Product	Quantity (2013)	Price (2005)	Value
Apples	220	$ 0.50	$110.00
Plums	85	0.40	34.00
Hamburgers	70	3.00	210.00
Teeth whitening	7	50.00	350.00
Real GDP			$704.00

Notice that because the prices of three of the four products increased between 2005 and 2013, for 2013 the value of real GDP is significantly less than the value of nominal GDP.

Step 4 **Determine real GDP for 2005.** To calculate real GDP, we multiply current year quantities by base-year prices. Because 2005 is the base year, our calculation of real GDP would be the same as our calculation of nominal GDP. In fact, nominal GDP will always equal real GDP in the base year.

See related problems 2.3, 2.4, and 2.5 at the end of the chapter.

Price Indexes and the GDP Deflator

From year to year, the prices of some goods and services, such as college tuition and health care, have risen, while the prices of other goods and services, such as computers and high-definition televisions, have fallen. To gauge what is happening to prices in the economy as a whole, economists need a measure of the *price level*, which is an average of the prices of goods and services in the economy. Economists measure the price level with a *price index*, which is a measure of the average of the prices of goods and services in one year relative to a base year. We can use values for nominal GDP and real GDP to calculate a price index called the *GDP deflator*, which is also called the *GDP implicit price deflator*. We can calculate the **GDP deflator** by using the following formula:

GDP deflator A measure of the price level, calculated by dividing nominal GDP by real GDP and multiplying by 100; also called the GDP implicit price deflator.

$$\text{GDP deflator} = \frac{\text{Nominal GDP}}{\text{Real GDP}} \times 100.$$

Because nominal GDP equals real GDP in the base year, the GDP deflator equals 100 in the base year.

To see why the GDP deflator is a measure of the price level, think about what would happen if prices of goods and services rose while production remained the same. In that case, nominal GDP would increase, but real GDP would remain constant, so the GDP deflator would increase. In fact, in most years, both prices and production increase, but the more prices increase relative to increases in production, the more nominal GDP increases relative to real GDP, and the greater the value for the GDP deflator. Economists measure the inflation rate as the percentage increase in the price level from one year to the next. By calculating the GDP deflator for two consecutive years, we get a measure of the inflation rate in the second year. In symbols, if P_{t-1} is the price level last year, P_t is the price level this year, and π_t is this year's inflation rate, then:

$$\text{Inflation rate} = \pi_t = \frac{P_t - P_{t-1}}{P_{t-1}} \times 100.$$

Solved Problem 2.2B

Calculating the Inflation Rate

Use the values for nominal GDP and real GDP given in the following table to calculate the inflation rate for 2011:

	2010	2011
Nominal GDP	$14,498.9 billion	$15,075.7 billion
Real GDP	$13,063.0 billion	$13,299.1 billion

Solving the Problem

Step 1 Review the chapter material. This problem asks you to calculate the inflation rate using values for the GDP deflator, so you may want to review the section "Price Indexes and the GDP Deflator," which begins above.

Step 2 Calculate the GDP deflator for each year. To calculate the GDP deflator, you divide nominal GDP by real GDP and multiply by 100:

$$\text{GDP deflator for 2010} = \frac{\$14,498.9 \text{ billion}}{\$13,063.0 \text{ billion}} \times 100 = 111.0$$

$$\text{GDP deflator for 2011} = \frac{\$15,075.7 \text{ billion}}{\$13,299.1 \text{ billion}} \times 100 = 113.4$$

Step 3 Calculate the inflation rate for 2011 and provide an interpretation of it. You can calculate the inflation rate for 2011 as the percentage change in the GDP deflator between 2010 and 2011:

$$\left(\frac{113.4 - 111.0}{111.0}\right) \times 100 = 2.2\%.$$

This calculation tells you that an average of the prices of all final goods and services produced in the United States rose 2.2% between 2010 and 2011.

See related problems 2.6 and 2.7 at the end of the chapter.

The Chain-Weighted Measure of Real GDP

One drawback to calculating real GDP using base-year prices is that over time, prices may change relative to each other. For example, the price of cell phones may fall relative to the price of milk. Because this change in relative prices is not reflected in the fixed prices from the base year, the estimate of real GDP is somewhat distorted. In effect, changes in relative prices reflect changes in consumers' relative valuation of goods and services, and we would like the measure of real GDP to include these changes.

An additional drawback arises because the goods and services that an economy produces change over time, so using prices from 2005 to value output in 2012 is difficult. For example, what was the value of an Apple iPad in 2005? The iPad did not exist in 2005, so we do not have a direct measure of its price in that year.

To address these two drawbacks, in 1996, the BEA switched to using *chain-weighted prices*, and it now publishes statistics on real GDP in "chained (2005) dollars." We do not need to go into the details of calculating real GDP using the chain-weighted price index, but the basic idea is straightforward. Starting with the base year, the BEA takes an average of prices in that year and prices in the following year. It then uses this average to calculate real GDP in the year following the base year. For the next year—in other words, the year that is two years after the base year—the BEA calculates real GDP by taking an average of prices in that year and the previous year. In this way, prices in each year are "chained" to prices from the previous year, and the distortion from changes in relative prices is minimized. The key point to remember is that chain-weighting effectively updates the prices for the base year each year and reduces the errors from changes in relative prices and the introduction of new goods and services.[6]

---

[6]For more detail on chain-type price indexes and other issues relating to the National Income and Product Account, see Bureau of Economic Analysis, "Concepts and Methods of the U.S. National Income and Product Accounts," October 2009, www.bea.gov/national/pdf/NIPAhandbookch1-4.pdf.

Trying to Hit a Moving Target: Forecasting with "Real-Time Data"

We saw at the beginning of the chapter that the Federal Reserve, Congress, and the president rely on GDP data in making policy. Unfortunately for these policymakers, the GDP data the BEA provides are frequently revised, and the revisions can be large enough that the actual state of the economy can be different from what it at first appeared to be.

The BEA's *advance estimate* of a quarter's GDP is not released until about a month after the quarter has ended. This delay can be a problem for policymakers because it means that, for instance, they will not receive an estimate of GDP for the period from January through March until the end of April. Presenting even more difficulty is the fact that the advance estimate will be subject to a number of revisions. The *second estimate* of a quarter's GDP is released about two months after the end of the quarter. The *third estimate* is released about three months after the end of the quarter. Although the BEA used to refer to the third estimate as the "final estimate," in fact, it continues to revise its estimates through the years. For instance, the BEA releases first annual, second annual, and third annual estimates one, two, and three years after the third estimate. Nor is that the end because *benchmark revisions* of the estimates will occur in later years.

Why so many estimates? Because GDP is such a comprehensive measure of output in the economy, collecting the necessary data is very time-consuming. To provide the advance estimate, the BEA relies on surveys carried out by the Commerce Department of retail sales and manufacturing shipments, as well as data from trade organizations, estimates of government spending, and so on. As time passes, these organizations gather additional data, and the BEA is able to refine its estimates.

Do these revisions to the GDP estimates matter? Sometimes they do, as the following example indicates. At the beginning of 2001, there were some indications that the U.S. economy might be headed for recession. The dot-com stock market bubble had burst the previous spring, wiping out trillions of dollars in stockholder wealth. Overbuilding of information technology, particularly fiber optic cables, also weighed on the economy. The advance estimate of the first quarter's real GDP, though, showed a reasonably healthy increase of 2.0% at an annual rate. It seemed as if there was nothing for government policymakers to be worried about. But, as the graph on the next page shows, that estimate of 2.0% was revised a number of times over the years, mostly downward. Currently, BEA data indicate that real GDP actually declined by 1.3% at an annual rate during the first quarter of 2001. This swing of more than 3 percentage points is a large difference—a difference that changes the picture of what happened during the first quarter of 2001 from one of an economy experiencing moderate growth to one of an economy suffering a significant decline. The National Bureau of Economic Research dates the recession of 2001 as having begun in March, but some economists believe it actually began at the end of 2000. The current BEA estimates of GDP provide some support for this view.

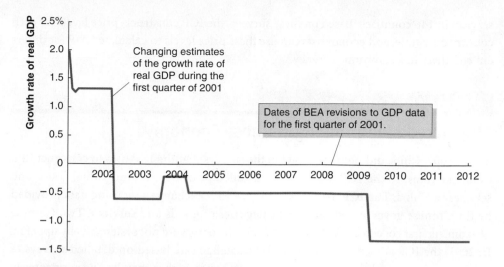

This example shows that in addition to the other problems that the Federal Reserve, Congress, and the president face in successfully conducting macroeconomic policy, they must make decisions using data that may be subject to substantial revisions.

Sources: Federal Reserve Bank of Philadelphia, "Historical Data Files for the Real-Time Data Set," August 24, 2010; and Bruce T. Grimm and Teresa Weadock, "Gross Domestic Product: Revisions and Source Data," *Survey of Current Business*, Vol. 86, No. 2, February 2006, pp. 11–15.

See related problem 2.8 at the end of the chapter.

Comparing GDP Across Countries

Economists often want to know which countries are rich and which are poor so they can determine which policies are most effective at increasing well-being and living standards. To do that, economists must be able to compare economic activity across countries. One way to do this is by comparing levels of GDP. These comparisons are complicated because countries calculate GDP in terms of their own currencies. For example, for 2011, Chinese GDP was 47.2 trillion yuan, Japanese GDP was 468.4 trillion yen, and U.S. GDP was 15.1 trillion dollars. Which economy was the largest?

We could translate these values into a single currency—say, U.S. dollars—by using exchange rates. For example, if Japanese GDP is ¥500 trillion and the exchange rate between the yen and the dollar is ¥100 = $1, then Japanese GDP in dollar terms equals ¥500 trillion/(¥100/$) = $5 trillion. One problem with this approach is that exchange rates tend to fluctuate widely, so our value for Japanese GDP would depend on which day's exchange rate we used. To get around this problem, rather than use the actual exchange rate, economists use the *purchasing power parity (PPP) exchange rate*, which is the number of units of a country's currency required to buy the same amount of goods and services in the country as one U.S. dollar would buy in the United States. Because the purchasing power of a country's currency tends not to change substantially over short periods of time, PPP exchange rates are more stable than actual exchange rates.

The World Bank, an international economic organization, coordinates the International Comparison Program (ICP), which collects data on more than 1,000 goods and services in 146 countries. Based on these surveys, the ICP constructs price levels for each country over time, and economists can use these price levels to calculate GDP for different countries in a common currency.

Making the Connection

The Incredible Shrinking Chinese Economy

Before 2007, China did not participate in the surveys that the ICP uses to construct PPP exchange rates, so the ICP did not have detailed price data on individual goods and services in China. The ICP had to estimate the PPP exchange rate using data provided by the Chinese government on broad categories of goods and services. Two Chinese economists first collected the data in 1986, but the data were not systematically updated. In 2007, the ICP announced the first PPP exchange rate based on detailed surveys of prices and discovered that prices in China were much higher than had been previously estimated. As a result, the previous PPP exchange rates were much too low for China, and the previous estimates for the dollar value of Chinese GDP were much too high.

By how much did the original estimates miss the mark? A lot. Based on the initial data, the ICP estimated that Chinese GDP was $8.8 trillion in 2005, but based on the more detailed data, the ICP estimated that Chinese GDP was actually only $5.3 trillion, or about 40% less. The original estimate indicated that the Chinese economy was 71% as large as the U.S. economy, but the new estimate indicated that the Chinese economy was only 43% as large as the U.S. economy. The adjustment reduced China's share of world GDP from 14% to 10%. In 2011, China's GDP was $11.3 trillion, a 9.2% increase from the previous year. China's GDP in 2011 was about 75% as large as the GDP of the United States, about the same ratio as the initial data erroneously estimated in 2005.

The ICP believes that the new estimates are more accurate, and Eswar Prasad, an economist at Cornell University, has referred to the work involved in gathering them as a "heroic effort." Still, the new price surveys are based on only 11 cities and the surrounding rural areas, so the data may not accurately represent prices in distant rural areas, where a large fraction of the Chinese population lives. As with all macroeconomic data, as time passes, economists refine and improve their estimates. Undoubtedly, future estimates of PPP exchange rates for China will become more accurate. It is unlikely, however, that future changes will have nearly the impact of the one described here.

Sources: World Bank, *International Comparison Program, Preliminary Results*, Washington, DC: World Bank, December 17, 2007; Keith Bradsher, "A Revisionist Tale: Why a Poor China Seems Richer," *New York Times*, December 21, 2007; and "Clipping the Dragon's Wings," *Economist*, December 19, 2007.

See related problem 2.9 at the end of the chapter.

2.3

Learning Objective

Explain how the inflation rate is measured and distinguish between real and nominal interest rates.

Inflation Rates and Interest Rates

We have seen that inflation is measured by the percentage change in the price level from one year to the next. The GDP deflator provides a measure of the price level that allows us to calculate the inflation rate. But for some purposes, the GDP deflator is too broad a measure because it includes the prices of every good and service included in GDP. Economists and policymakers are usually interested in inflation as it affects the prices paid by the typical household. The typical household does not buy large electric generators or 40-story office buildings, among other goods whose prices are included in the GDP deflator. So, economists and policymakers often rely on the *consumer price index*, which includes only goods and services consumed by the typical household. The consumer price index does a better job than the GDP deflator at measuring changes in the *cost of living* as experienced by the typical household. For households, the consumer price index helps assess whether increases in earnings keep pace with the cost of living.

The Consumer Price Index

The **consumer price index (CPI)** is an average of the prices of the goods and services purchased by the typical urban family of four. To obtain this information, the U.S. Bureau of Labor Statistics (BLS) surveys 30,000 households nationwide on their spending habits. The BLS uses the results of this survey to construct a market basket of 211 types of goods and services purchased by the typical family.

Panel (a) of Figure 2.6 shows the goods and services in the market basket, grouped into eight broad categories. Almost three-quarters of the market basket falls into the categories of housing, transportation, and food. Each month, hundreds of BLS employees visit 23,000 stores in 87 cities and record prices of the goods and services in the market basket. Each price in the CPI is given a weight equal to the fraction of the typical family's budget spent on that good or service. The BLS chooses one year as the base year, and the value of the CPI is set equal to 100 for that year. In any year other than the base year, the CPI is equal to the ratio of the dollar amount necessary to buy the market basket of

Consumer price index (CPI) An average of the prices of the goods and services purchased by the typical urban family of four.

MyEconLab Real-time data

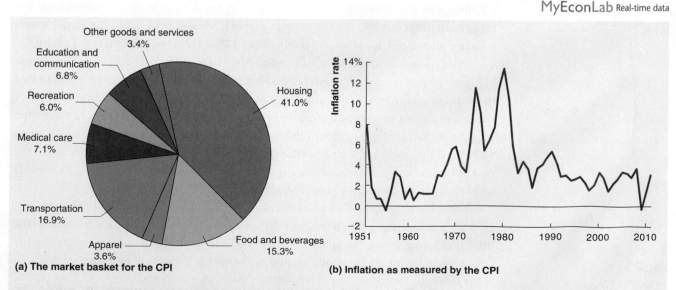

(a) The market basket for the CPI

(b) Inflation as measured by the CPI

Figure 2.6 The Consumer Price Index

Panel (a) shows the market basket the BLS uses to weight the prices included in the CPI. Panel (b) shows the inflation rate as measured by the annual percentage change in the CPI.

Source: U.S. Bureau of Labor Statistics.

goods in that year divided by the dollar amount necessary to buy the market basket of goods in the base year, multiplied by 100.

$$CPI = \frac{\text{cost of current basket}}{\text{cost of basket in base year}} \times 100$$

Panel (b) of Figure 2.6 shows the annual inflation rate from 1951 to 2011, as measured by the CPI. The figure shows that inflation rates were high during the late 1970s and early 1980s—reaching above 10%—and typically below 5% since the early 1980s. The severity of the 2007–2009 recession caused the price level to fall—that is, the economy experienced *deflation* according to the CPI—during 2009.

The CPI is widely used in *indexing*, which involves increasing a dollar value to protect against inflation. For example, each year, the federal government increases the Social Security payments it sends to retired workers by the percentage increase in the CPI during the previous year. If the CPI increases by 3%, then increasing Social Security payments by 3% should keep the purchasing power of the payments from declining. The federal government does not reduce Social Security payments when—as in 2009—the CPI declines during a year. The federal government also indexes the dollar thresholds that determine the federal tax rates individuals pay. Some union wage contracts are also indexed.

Making the Connection

Does the CPI Provide a Good Measure of Inflation for a Family with College Students?

The CPI is an average of the prices of the goods and services purchased by a typical urban family of four. If the family's income increases at the same rate as the CPI, then the purchasing power of the family's income should be unchanged. But what if the family includes one or more college students? The market basket the BLS uses in calculating the CPI puts a weight of only 1.7% on college tuition and fees. Why such a low weight? Because most of the families the BLS surveys do not have college students. But families with college students clearly spend much more than 1.7% of their budgets on college tuition.

The College Board is a nonprofit organization of schools that seeks to expand access to higher education and administers standardized tests. The College Board reported that the average tuition at a public university in 2011–2012 was $8,244. Adding the cost of living and dining on campus drove the cost to $21,447. The College Board estimated that the annual cost for a student living at a typical private college in 2011–2012 was $42,224, almost double the cost of attending a public college. The BLS estimates that the cost of tuition and other school fees rose about 500% from CPI's base year (1982–1984) to 2011, while the overall CPI rose about 125% over the same period.

The 1.7% weight the CPI gives to college tuition means that a tuition increase of 10%, for example, has a much smaller effect on the CPI than would a 10% increase in the price of housing or another spending category that has greater weight in computing the CPI. Although the CPI is a good measure of changes in the cost of living for people who come close to consuming the same market basket of goods and services as the typical consumer, the CPI can be a poor measure for people, such as college students and their families, whose purchases do not match those of the typical consumer. And the burden of paying for a college education often extends beyond the years students spend in college. Students who borrow money to pay for tuition take years to pay off their loans.

Many colleges and universities offer scholarships and other forms of financial aid that reduce the cost of a college education. The rising cost of a college degree has forced colleges and universities to compete for students as any firm in a competitive market would compete for customers, and students and families have learned that it pays to ask for financial assistance. The National Association of College and University Business Officers, a nonprofit organization that assists business managers in higher education, reported that in 2011, 88% of first-year students at private colleges received an average of over $15,000 in scholarships and federal tax benefits. Federal surveys found that 52% of students at four-year public universities received scholarships and grants that significantly reduced the cost of living on campus in 2011–2012. In recent years, the BLS has begun taking into account financial aid when determining the correct price of tuition to include in the CPI.

It is important to understand that the CPI is based on the spending behavior of and prices faced by the average household. The rising cost of a college education shows how much the "average family with college students" differs from other "average families."

Sources: U.S. Bureau of Labor Statistics; Kim Clark, "College Costs Climb, Yet Again," cnnmoney.com, October 29, 2011; and College Board, "Living Expense Budget 2012," professionals.collegeboard.com/data-reports-research/trends/living-expense.

See related problem 3.6 at the end of the chapter.

How Accurate Is the CPI?

Because the CPI is the most widely used measure of the inflation rate, it is important that it be accurate. Most economists believe, however, that there are four reasons the CPI *overstates* the true inflation rate.

First, the CPI suffers from *substitution bias*. In constructing the CPI, the BLS assumes that each month, consumers purchase the same quantity of each product in the market basket. In fact, though, consumers are likely to buy less of the products whose prices increase the most and more of the products whose prices increase the least. For example, if the price of pears increases much more than the price of plums, consumers are likely to buy more plums and fewer pears. Because the BLS assumes that consumers buy fixed quantities of pears and plums, the CPI will overstate the price increase in the market basket that consumers actually buy.

Second, the CPI suffers from a bias due to the *introduction of new goods* because the market basket is updated only every two years. The prices of many new goods, such as smart phones, Blu-ray players, and high-definition televisions, decrease significantly in the months after these goods are introduced, but these price decreases will not be reflected in the CPI if the goods are not included in the market basket.

Third, the *quality of goods and services* changes over time, and these changes are not completely reflected in the CPI. For example, if you spend $2,000 on a high-definition television in 2013, you will get a much better television than if you had spent $2,000 on a high-definition television in 2006, which means that, in effect, the price of a television of constant quality has decreased. The BLS attempts to make adjustments for changes in the quality of products, but doing so is difficult. The failure to fully adjust prices for changes in the quality of products results in an upward bias in the CPI.

Fourth, there is an *outlet bias* in the CPI data. That is, the BLS collects price data primarily from traditional retail outlets such as supermarkets and department stores. However, many households shop at large discount stores such as Costco or BJ's or on the Internet, and these sources are underrepresented in the sample of prices the BLS gathers.

The BLS is working continually to improve the accuracy of the CPI, but many economists still believe that CPI inflation overstates the true inflation rate by 0.5 percentage point to 1 percentage point. That is, when the BLS reports an inflation rate of 2%, the actual inflation rate is probably 1% to 1.5%. Do such small differences matter? They can when compounded over long periods of time. For example, suppose that a Social Security payment starts out at $1,000 in 2012. If over the following 20 years, the CPI indicates that inflation has been 2%, the federal government will have increased the payment to $1,486. If the inflation rate is actually only 1%, then the payment should have grown to $1,220, or about 18% less. Multiplied by millions of Social Security recipients, the effect on the federal government's budget could be substantial.

The Way the Federal Reserve Measures Inflation

Federal Reserve The central bank of the United States; usually referred to as "the Fed."

The **Federal Reserve** (the Fed) is the central bank of the United States. One of the Fed's main policy goals is price stability. To meet this goal, the Fed has an inflation target of 2%. So, the Fed has to consider carefully the best way to measure the inflation rate. Because the CPI suffers from biases that cause it to overstate the true underlying rate of inflation, the Fed announced in 2000 that it would rely more on the **personal consumption expenditures price (PCE) index** than on the CPI in tracking inflation. The PCE is a measure of the price level that is similar to the GDP deflator, except that it includes only the prices of goods from the consumption category of GDP.

Personal consumption expenditures price (PCE) index A price index similar to the GDP deflator, except that it includes only the prices of goods from the consumption category of GDP.

The Fed believes that there are three advantages to using the PCE:

1. The PCE is a chain-type price index, as opposed to the market-basket approach used in constructing the CPI. Because consumers shift the mix of products they buy each year, the market-basket approach causes the CPI to overstate actual inflation. A chain-type price index allows the mix of products to change each year.
2. The PCE includes the prices of more goods and services than the CPI, so it is a broader measure of inflation.
3. Past values of the PCE can be recalculated as better ways of computing price indexes are developed and as new data become available. Much of the survey information that the BEA uses to construct GDP or the PCE comes from firms. The sample of firms that the BEA uses does not include some new firms. Over time, however, the BEA revises its estimates as data from these new firms become available. The BLS is unable to make similar adjustments to the CPI. Therefore, the PCE allows the Fed to better track historical trends in inflation.

Since 2004, the Fed has focused on a subcategory of the PCE—the *core PCE*, which excludes food and energy prices. Prices of food and energy tend to fluctuate up and down for reasons that may not be related to the causes of general inflation and that the Fed cannot easily control. These events include severe weather, such as droughts in farm areas or hurricanes along the Gulf Coast, and political events, such as unrest in oil-producing countries that temporarily disrupts oil production.

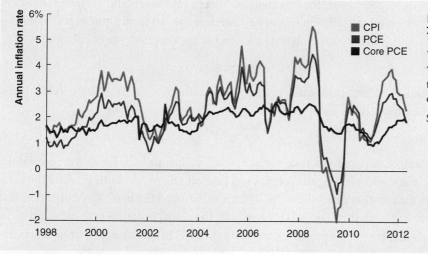

Figure 2.7

The Measures of the Inflation Rate, 1998–2012

The Federal Reserve measures inflation using the core PCE, which is more stable than the CPI or the PCE.

Source: Federal Reserve Bank of St. Louis.

Figure 2.7 shows the inflation rate as measured by the CPI, the PCE, and the core PCE. Although the three measures of inflation move roughly together, the core PCE has been more stable than the other indexes. Note in particular that during most of 2009, when the CPI and the PCE were indicating that the economy was experiencing deflation, the core PCE was still showing moderate inflation of greater than 1.5%. If you want to know what the Fed thinks the current inflation rate is, look at data on the core PCE. The BEA publishes these data monthly.

Interest Rates

The financial crisis and severe recession of 2007–2009 showed that what happens in the financial system can affect the rest of the economy. A key economic variable in understanding the financial system is the interest rate. The **interest rate** is the cost of borrowing funds, usually expressed as a percentage of the amount borrowed. For example, if you borrow $100 and have to pay back $105 in one year, then you have paid $5 in interest, and the interest rate on the loan is 5%: ($5/$100) $\times$ 100 = 5%. Similarly, if you deposit money in a savings account or a certificate of deposit in a bank, the interest rate you earn is the return on your savings.

The **nominal interest rate** is the stated interest rate you pay on a loan or receive on your savings. Inflation reduces the purchasing power of interest payments. For example, suppose that you buy a $1,000 certificate of deposit bond that pays you $50 in interest each year for five years. If the purchasing power of the dollars that you receive declines over time, you are, in effect, losing part of your interest income to inflation. In addition, inflation causes the purchasing power of the $1,000—the *principal*—to decline as well. For example, if inflation is 3% per year, the purchasing power of your $1,000 principal falls by $30 each year. Lenders and borrowers know that inflation reduces the purchasing power of interest income, so they base their decisions not on the nominal interest but on the **real interest rate**, which is the nominal interest rate adjusted for the effects of inflation.

Because borrowers and lenders don't know with certainty what the inflation rate will be during the period of a loan, they don't know what the *actual* real interest rate will be. So,

Interest rate The cost of borrowing funds, usually expressed as a percentage of the amount borrowed.

Nominal interest rate The stated interest rate on a loan.

Real interest rate The nominal interest rate adjusted for the effects of inflation.

they must make borrowing or investing decisions on the basis of what they *expect* the real interest rate to be. To estimate the expected real interest rate, savers and borrowers must decide what they expect the inflation rate to be. Therefore, we can say that the expected real interest rate, r, equals the nominal interest rate, i, minus the expected rate of inflation, π^e, or[7]:

$$r = i - \pi^e.$$

Note that this equation also means that the nominal interest rate equals the real interest rate plus the expected inflation rate:

$$i = r + \pi^e.$$

For example, suppose you take out a car loan from your local bank. You are willing to pay, and the bank is willing to accept, a real interest rate of 3%. Both you and the bank expect that the inflation rate will be 2%. Therefore, you and the bank agree on a nominal interest rate of 5% on the loan. What happens if the actual inflation rate turns out to be 4%, which is higher than you and the bank had expected? In that case, the actual real interest rate that you end up paying (and the bank ends up receiving) equals 5% − 4% = 1%, which is less than the expected real interest rate of 3%. Because the inflation rate turns out to be higher than you and the bank expected, you gain by paying a lower real interest rate, and the bank loses by receiving a lower real interest rate.

We can generalize by noting that the actual real interest rate equals the nominal interest rate minus the actual inflation rate. If the actual inflation rate is greater than the expected inflation rate, the actual real interest rate will be less than the expected real interest rate; in this case, borrowers will gain and lenders will lose. If the actual inflation rate is less than the expected inflation rate, the actual real interest rate will be greater than the expected real interest rate; in this case, borrowers will lose, and lenders will gain.

For the economy as a whole, economists often measure the nominal interest rate as the interest rate on U.S. Treasury bills that mature in three months. In Figure 2.8, we show the nominal interest rate, the actual real interest rate, and the expected real interest rate for the period from the first quarter of 1982 through May 2012. To calculate the actual real interest rate, we used the actual inflation rate as measured by percentage changes in the CPI. To calculate the expected real interest rate, we used the expected percentage change in the CPI, as reported in a survey of professional forecasters conducted by the Federal Reserve Bank of Philadelphia.

Figure 2.8 shows that the nominal and real interest rates tend to rise and fall together. The figure also shows that the actual and expected real interest rates follow each other closely, which is an indication that during most of this period, expectations of the inflation rate were fairly accurate. Note that in some periods, particularly after the beginning of the recession in late 2007, the real interest rate was negative. Finally, note that it is possible for the nominal interest rate to be lower than the real interest rate. For this outcome to occur, the inflation rate has to be negative (deflation).

---

[7]To fully account for the effect of changes in purchasing power on the nominal interest rate, we should use the equation: $(1 + i)/(1 + \pi^e) = 1 + r$. Rearranging terms gives us $1 + i = 1 + r + \pi^e + r\pi^e$, or $r = i - \pi^e - r\pi^e$. This equation is the same as the one in the text except for the term $r\pi^e$. The value of this term is usually quite small. For example, if the real interest rate is 2% and the expected inflation rate is 3%, then $r\pi^e = 0.02 \times 0.03 = 0.0006$. So, as long as the inflation rate and the real interest rate are relatively low, the equation for the real interest rate given in the text is a close approximation.

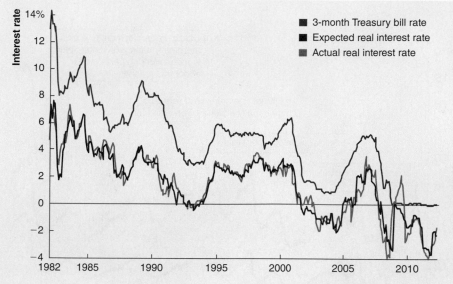

Figure 2.8

Nominal and Real Interest Rates, 1982–2012

In this figure, the nominal interest rate is the interest rate on three-month U.S. Treasury bills. The actual real interest rate is the nominal interest rate minus the actual inflation rate, as measured by changes in the CPI. The expected real interest rate is the nominal interest rate minus the expected rate of inflation, as measured by a survey of professional forecasters. When the U.S. economy experienced deflation during 2009, the real interest rate was greater than the nominal interest rate.

Sources: Federal Reserve Bank of St. Louis; and Federal Reserve Bank of Philadelphia.

Measuring Employment and Unemployment

Learning Objective
Understand how to calculate the unemployment rate.

When most people think about an economic recession, they don't think about declines in GDP as much as they think about problems with finding and keeping a job. In fact, the unemployment rate can have important political implications. In most presidential elections, the incumbent president is reelected if unemployment is falling early in the election year but is defeated if unemployment is rising. Investors also closely monitor the reports the U.S. Department of Labor issues each month on changes in employment and unemployment as the investors try to gauge the health of the economy. The levels of employment and unemployment are key macroeconomic variables, so it is important to have some familiarity with how the federal government measures them.

Each month, the U.S. Bureau of the Census conducts the *Current Population Survey* (often referred to as the *household survey*). The BLS uses the data from this survey to calculate the monthly unemployment rate. People are considered *employed* if they worked during the week before the survey or if they were temporarily away from their jobs because they were ill, on vacation, on strike, or for other reasons. People are considered *unemployed* if they did not work in the previous week but were available for work and had actively looked for work at some time during the previous four weeks. The **labor force** is the sum of employed and unemployed workers. The **unemployment rate** is the percentage of the labor force that is unemployed, or:

Labor force The sum of employed and unemployed workers in the economy.

Unemployment rate The percentage of the labor force that is unemployed.

$$\text{Unemployment rate} = \left(\frac{\text{Number of unemployed}}{\text{Labor force}}\right) \times 100.$$

For example, in September 2012, there were 12,088,000 unemployed workers in a labor force of 155,063,000, so the unemployment rate was (12,088,000/155,063,000) × 100 = 7.8%.

The BLS can have a problem distinguishing between unemployed workers and people who are not in the labor force. The official unemployment rate includes just those workers who have looked for work in the past four weeks. But some *discouraged workers*

MyEconLab Real-time data

Figure 2.9

Alternative Measures of the Unemployment Rate, 1948–2012

Because of the uncertainty about the best way to measure the unemployment rate, the BLS publishes data on alternative measures.

Source: U.S. Bureau of Labor Statistics.

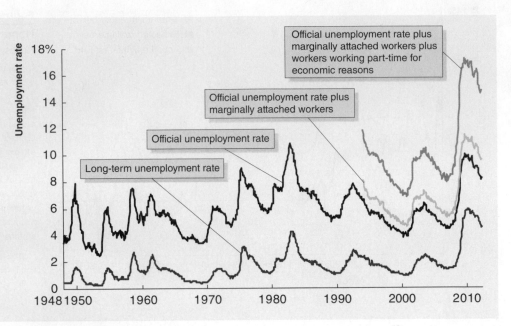

might prefer to have a job but have given up looking because they believe finding a job is too difficult. Because these workers are not actively looking for a job, they are not considered to be in the labor force and so aren't counted as unemployed. Therefore, the unemployment rate as measured by the BLS may understate the true degree of joblessness in the economy. A second problem arises because the BLS also counts people with part-time jobs as being employed, even if they would prefer to hold full-time jobs. Counting as employed a part-time worker who wants to work full time tends to understate the degree of joblessness in the economy and make the employment situation appear better than it is. For example, the official unemployment rate for September 2012 was 7.8%. However, the unemployment rate when including discouraged workers was 8.3%. The unemployment rate when taking into account both discouraged workers and part-time workers who would have preferred to work full time was 14.7%.[8]

As a result of problems with the official unemployment rate measure, the BLS publishes data on several different measures of the unemployment rate. Figure 2.9 shows several of these alternative measures of the unemployment rate. The long-term unemployment rate in the figure shows the percentage of the labor force that has been unemployed for 15 weeks or more. The alternative series are higher than the official unemployment rate—and sometimes substantially higher. These alternative measures of unemployment have been available only since 1994, but the data show that

---

[8]The BLS refers to the official unemployment rate as the U-3 measure of unemployment. The broadest measure of the unemployment rate is the U-6 measure, which includes marginally attached workers and part-time workers who would prefer to work full time. This is the BLS's definition of marginally attached workers: "Persons marginally attached to the labor force are those who currently are neither working nor looking for work but indicate that they want and are available for a job and have looked for work sometime in the past 12 months. Discouraged workers, a subset of the marginally attached, have given a job-market related reason for not currently looking for work."

the alternative measures tend to rise and fall with the official unemployment rate. As a result, changes in the official unemployment rate accurately reflect *changes* in the difficulty of finding a job. Most economists believe that the official unemployment rate is a useful, although not perfect, measure of conditions in the labor market.

In addition to using the household survey, the BLS uses the *establishment survey*, sometimes called the *payroll survey*, to measure total employment in the economy. This monthly survey samples about 300,000 business establishments. The establishment survey provides information on the total number of persons who are employed and on a company payroll. The establishment survey has three drawbacks. First, the survey does not provide information on the number of self-employed persons because they are not on a company payroll. Second, the survey may fail to count some persons as employed at newly opened firms that are not included in the survey. Third, the survey provides no information on unemployment.

Despite these drawbacks, the establishment survey has the advantage of being determined by actual payrolls rather than by unverified answers to survey questions, as is the case with the household survey. In addition, because the BLS gathers data from additional firms over time, the employment data from the establishment survey is updated as the BLS obtains new information. In recent years, some economists have come to rely more on establishment survey data than on household survey data in analyzing current labor market conditions. Some financial analysts who forecast the future state of the economy to help predict stock prices have also begun to rely more on establishment survey data than on household survey data.

Answering the Key Question

Continued from page 25

At the beginning of this chapter, we asked:

"How accurately does the government measure the unemployment rate?"

We have just seen that the BLS faces challenges when measuring the unemployment rate. Clearly, not everyone who doesn't have a job should be counted as unemployed. Some people are full-time homemakers; others suffer from chronic illnesses that leave them unable to work; and some are retired. People in these groups are voluntarily without jobs and so should not be counted as being in the labor force or as being unemployed. There are gray areas. For example, some people responding to the household survey say that they want a job and are available to take one, but they have not actively searched for a job during the previous four weeks. Other people who say that they want a full-time job and are available to take one are part-time workers who can't find full-time jobs. Whether and how to count these people in the unemployment statistics remains open to debate.

In addition, the household survey does not verify the responses of people included in the survey. Some people who claim to be unemployed and actively looking for work may not be actively looking. A person might claim to be actively looking for a job to remain eligible for government payments to the unemployed. In this case, a person who is actually not in the labor force is counted as unemployed. Other people might be employed but engaged in illegal activity—such as drug dealing—or might want to conceal a legitimate job to avoid paying taxes. In these cases, individuals who are actually employed are counted as unemployed.

We can conclude that, although the unemployment rate provides some useful information about the employment situation in the country, it is far from an exact measure of joblessness in the economy.

Key Terms and Problems

Key Terms

Capital, p. 29
Consumer price index (CPI), p. 45
Consumption, p. 32
Factor of production, p. 29
Federal Reserve, p. 48
Final good or service, p. 27
Financial system, p. 31
GDP deflator, p. 40
Government purchases, p. 33

Gross domestic product (GDP),
    p. 27
Gross national product (GNP), p. 35
Interest rate, p. 49
Intermediate good or service, p. 27
Investment, p. 33
Labor force, p. 51
National income accounting, p. 29
Net exports, p. 34

Nominal GDP, p. 38
Nominal interest rate, p. 49
Personal consumption expenditures
    price (PCE) index, p. 48
Real GDP, p. 38
Real interest rate, p. 49
Transfer payments, p. 33
Unemployment rate, p. 51

2.1 ## GDP: Measuring Total Production and Total Income
Explain how economists use gross domestic product (GDP) to measure total production and total income.

Review Questions

1.1 In what sense is GDP both a measure of total production and a measure of total income?

1.2 What is the difference between GDP and GNP? Is the difference between GDP and GNP large for the United States? Briefly explain.

1.3 Explain the differences in the way the BEA calculates GDP and GDI. Because both GDP and GDI measure the value of total production in the economy, does it matter which measure we use to track the level of economic activity? Briefly explain.

1.4 What is the difference between GDP and national income? What is the difference between national income and personal income?

Problems and Applications

1.5 How would each of the following events change measured GDP?

  a. There is an increase in illegal drug sales.

  b. An oil spill causes pollution on beaches in California.

  c. There is a surge in sales of used cars, and there is a decline in sales of new cars.

1.6 By the 1960s, a larger percentage of women were entering the labor force. Because more women were working, their production of services within the home, such as cooking and cleaning, may have fallen. In addition, they may have employed others to do some tasks that they had previously done themselves, including caring for their children.

  a. How did these changes affect GDP as measured by the BEA?

  b. If we define "actual GDP" as GDP measured with the inclusion of such things as household production, illegal goods and services, and other typically excluded variables, how would actual GDP have changed?

1.7 Which of the following goods and services are included in GDP? If the good or service is included in GDP, in which expenditure category is it included? If the good or service is not included in GDP, explain why not.

  a. Cynthia buys some house paint.

  b. Cynthia uses the paint that she purchased to paint her own house.

  c. Bruce hires a painter to paint his house.

MyEconLab Visit **www.myeconlab.com** to complete these exercises online and get instant feedback. Exercises that update with real-time data are marked with .

d. Randy sells the house that he bought 10 years ago and uses the proceeds to purchase a newly constructed condominium.

e. Kishore buys a new Toyota Prius.

f. Kishore buys a 2005 Dodge truck to drive on the weekends.

g. California lawmakers enact a bill that reduces retired teachers' pensions by 15%.

1.8 Suppose that a simple economy produces pizza, video games, and candy. The following table gives quantities and prices for each good in three successive years:

	2011		2012		2013	
	Quantity	Price	Quantity	Price	Quantity	Price
Pizza	100	$0.50	125	$0.50	125	$0.60
Video games	75	1.00	85	1.00	85	1.25
Candy	20	5.00	30	5.00	30	6.00

a. Calculate nominal GDP in 2011, 2012, and 2013.

b. What is the growth rate of nominal GDP between 2011 and 2012? What is the growth rate of nominal GDP between 2012 and 2013?

c. Do the growth rates you calculated in part (b) measure the changes in the quantity of goods produced during these years? Briefly explain.

1.9 [Related to the Chapter Opener on page 25] The chapter opener notes that in dating business cycle expansions and recessions, the National Bureau of Economic Research relies on, among other things, "real GDP measured on the product and income sides." What is the name for real GDP measured on the "product side"? What is the name for real GDP measured on the "income side"? Are the two measures always identical? Are there reasons for the NBER to prefer one measure to the other? Briefly explain.

1.10 Federal Reserve economist Jeremy Nalewaik has noted that:

> Initial GDI growth estimates have tended to predict revisions (typically years later) to initial GDP growth estimates, especially since the mid-1990s. So, if initial GDI growth is above initial GDP growth, GDP growth tends to revise up, and if initial GDI growth is below initial GDP growth, GDP growth tends to revise down.

Do these observations indicate that changes in GDI or changes in GDP are a better measure of economic growth? Briefly explain.

Source: Cardiff Garcia, "The Case for GDI: a Q&A with Jeremy Nalewaik," ft.com, September 26, 2011.

2.2 **Real GDP, Nominal GDP, and the GDP Deflator**
Discuss the difference between real GDP and nominal GDP.

Review Question

2.1 What is the difference between nominal GDP and real GDP? Why do changes in nominal GDP usually overstate changes in total production in the economy? How can values for nominal GDP and real GDP be used to calculate a price index?

Problems and Applications

2.2 In January 2010, the approximate value of U.S. oil imports was $26.5 billion. In January 2011, the approximate value of U.S. oil imports was $35.2 billion.

a. Given the information above, can you conclude that there has been a significant increase in the number of barrels of oil that the United States is importing? Briefly explain.

b. The average price per barrel of crude oil in January 2010 was $75. By January 2011, the price had risen to approximately $91 per barrel. By what percentage had the *quantity* of oil imported changed?

Source: U.S. Department of Energy.

2.3 [Related to Solved Problem 2.2A on page 38] Use the information in the following table to answer the questions. Assume that 2011 is the base year.

	2011		2012		2013	
	Quantity	Price	Quantity	Price	Quantity	Price
Grapes	100	$0.50	125	$0.50	125	$0.60
Raisins	75	1.00	85	$1.00	85	1.25
Oranges	20	5.00	30	$5.00	30	6.00

a. Calculate real GDP in 2011, 2012, and 2013.

b. Did output in the economy grow by more in percentage terms between 2011 and 2012 or between 2012 and 2013? Briefly explain.

2.4 [Related to Solved Problem 2.2A on page 38] Use the information in the following table to calculate nominal and real GDP for 2005 and 2013. Assume that 2005 is the base year.

	2005		2013	
Product	Quantity	Price	Quantity	Price
Oranges	400	$ 0.50	440	$ 0.75
Plums	90	0.50	85	0.60
Haircuts	7	30.00	10	32.00
Pizza	60	8.00	70	8.25

2.5 [Related to Solved Problem 2.2A on page 38] The answer to Solved Problem 2.2A includes the following statement: "Notice that because the prices of three of the four products increased between 2005 and 2013, for 2013 the value of real GDP is significantly less than the value of nominal GDP."

Construct an example similar to the one in Solved Problem 2.2A for an economy with only four products. Show that it is possible to choose prices in 2013 so that although only one price increases, nominal GDP in 2013 is still greater than real GDP.

2.6 [Related to Solved Problem 2.2B on page 40] In the first quarter of 2012, U.S. GDP was $15,478.3 billion. Real GDP for the same quarter was $13,506.4 billion. Based on this information, what was the GDP deflator for the first quarter of 2012?

2.7 [Related to Solved Problem 2.2B on page 40] Use the values for nominal GDP and real GDP given

in the following table to calculate the inflation rate during 1930.

	1929	1930
Nominal GDP	$103.6 billion	$91.2 billion
Real GDP	$977.0 billion	$892.8 billion

2.8 [Related to the Making the Connection on page 42] If policymakers are aware that GDP data is sometimes subject to large revisions, how might this knowledge affect their views about how best to conduct policy?

2.9 [Related to the Making the Connection on page 44] Suppose that the current exchange rate between the Chinese yuan and the U.S. dollar is 10 yuan = $1. Suppose that you can buy more goods and services in China with 1,000 yuan than you can in the United States with $100. Will China's GDP in dollars be greater if the current exchange rate is used to convert yuan to dollars or if the PPP exchange rate it used? Briefly explain.

2.10 In 2010, the World Bank estimated that, at current exchange rates, Kenya's GDP per capita (in U.S. dollars) was $790. For the same year, U.S. GDP per capita was $47,800.

a. The World Bank uses the Atlas method to convert data into U.S. dollars at current exchange rates. The Atlas method uses an average of three years of exchange rates plus adjustments for inflation and other factors. Why would it be desirable to use a method like this?

b. What problems do you see in comparing GDP per capita in the United States to GDP per capita in Kenya using these data?

c. Adjusting for purchasing power parity, the World Bank calculates Kenya's GDP per capita to be $1,700. Why is this estimate so different from the estimate using the Atlas method?

d. How many times larger is GDP per capita in the United States than GDP per capita in Kenya before the purchasing power adjustment? After the adjustment?

Source: The World Bank.

MyEconLab Visit **www.myeconlab.com** to complete these exercises online and get instant feedback. Exercises that update with real-time data are marked with (W).

2.11 The text states, "For years before the base year, real GDP is greater than nominal GDP. For years after the base year, nominal GDP is greater than real GDP." Suppose that the economy experiences *deflation*, with the price level falling. In this case, will the relationship between real GDP and nominal GDP for years before and after the base year still hold? Briefly explain.

2.3 | ## Inflation Rates and Interest Rates
Explain how the inflation rate is measured and distinguish between real and nominal interest rates.

Review Questions

3.1 What biases in the way the CPI is calculated may cause it to overstate the actual inflation rate?

3.2 How is the PCE calculated? What is the difference between the PCE and the GDP deflator? What is the difference between the PCE and the core PCE?

3.3 If the actual inflation rate is greater than the expected inflation rate, do borrowers gain or lose? Briefly explain.

Problems and Applications

3.4 Explain the major difference between the CPI and the PCE deflator. Why does the Federal Reserve prefer to use the core PCE to measure the inflation rate?

3.5 Suppose that a virus wipes out half the apple crop, causing the quantity produced to go down and the price to increase. Other fruits can be substituted for apples in many cases, so some consumers will switch to other items. What would be the effect of this on the CPI? On the PCE deflator? [Hint: In each case, consider how the quantity of apples used in computing the price index does or does not change.]

3.6 [Related to the Making the Connection on page 46] Refer to Figure 2.6 on page 45. Assume that the prices of each of the following categories of spending were to rise by 10%:
i.   Housing
ii. Education and communication
iii. Transportation
iv. Food and beverages
a. Which of these price increases would have the greatest effect on the CPI? Which would have the least effect on the CPI?

b. Which of these price increases would have the greatest effect on your expenditures? Which would have least effect on your expenditures?

3.7 During the 2007–2009 recession and financial crisis, nominal interest rates fell to nearly 0%, while the rate of inflation remained positive.

a. What happened to the real interest rate?

b. How would this movement in the real interest rate affect savers and borrowers?

c. If *nominal* interest rates were negative, what would happen if you put money in a savings account at a bank?

2.4 | ## Measuring Employment and Unemployment
Understand how to calculate the unemployment rate.

Review Questions

4.1 How is the unemployment rate calculated?

4.2 What do economists mean by *discouraged workers*? Explain the effect discouraged workers have on the measured unemployment rate and the degree of joblessness in the economy. Why might the unemployment rate understate the extent of unemployment?

4.3 What is the difference between the household survey and the establishment survey? Why do some economists prefer to use the employment data from the establishment survey?

MyEconLab   Visit **www.myeconlab.com** to complete these exercises online and get instant feedback. Exercises that update with real-time data are marked with ⬤.

Problems and Applications

4.4 For each of the following, state whether the individual is included or not included in the labor force and, if included, whether that person is counted as employed or unemployed.

a. Soma is employed as a chef at a restaurant in Maine.

b. Randy is working part time but is looking for a full-time job.

c. Bruce would like a job but has stopped looking.

d. Jessie won the lottery and quit her job. She is not seeking a new job.

e. Jose is in college.

f. Christina just graduated from college and is applying for jobs.

4.5 During recessions, industries such as construction often cut back on employees. The newly unemployed workers may seek jobs for a while and then become discouraged if they do not find new jobs.

a. If workers are seeking jobs, how does the BLS count those workers?

b. If workers have stopped seeking jobs, how does the BLS count those workers?

c. Use this information to explain why, when the economy begins to recover from a recession, the unemployment rate may initially increase.

4.6 Suppose that all workers in the economy are currently working 40 hours a week.

a. If all employers cut worker hours so that each employee is working 20 hours a week, what would happen to the unemployment rate?

b. What would happen to real GDP?

c. The unemployment rate is sometimes used as a measure of the slack in the economy or how far the economy is below potential GDP. How do parts (a) and (b) of this question suggest that this might be misleading?

4.7 As an effort to further assist workers who found themselves unemployed as a result of the recession of 2007–2009, the federal government extended the maximum duration of unemployment benefits from 79 to 99 weeks. A May 2012 article from *CNNMoney* states, "More than 200,000 long-term jobless Americans will lose their unemployment checks this week," as their extended benefits come to an end. Explain how this policy might affect the four alternative measures of the unemployment rate shown in Figure 2.9 on page 52.

Source: Tami Luhby, "Bye Bye Unemployment Benefits," *CNNMoney*, May 11, 2012.

Data Exercises

D2.1: Using quarterly nation income data from the St. Louis Federal Reserve (FRED) (http://research.stlouisfed.org/fred2/), analyze recent movements in real GDP and inflation for the United States.

a. How has real GDP (GDPC1) changed over the past year?

b. Is the economy currently in a recession or a recovery? [Hint: See www.nber.org for official definitions of business cycle turning points.] Is your answer a surprise given your answer to part (a)?

c. Using the GDP implicit price deflator (GDPDEF), calculate the inflation rate over the past year.

D2.2: Go to the Statistics Canada Web site of the Canadian government (www.statcan.gc.ca).

a. Search for Income and Expenditure Accounts. What percentage of GDP is accounted for by each of the major GDP subcategories in Canada? How do those percentages compare to the percentages for the United States?

b. What do you think are the reasons for the differences between the percentages for Canada and for the United States?

c. Because Canada is closely tied to the United States in terms of trade and proximity, business cycles in Canada are often very similar to those in the United States. How does the trend in Canada's GDP compare with that in the United States?

D2.3: Using data from the St. Louis Federal Reserve (FRED) (http://research.stlouisfed.org/fred2/), analyze personal consumption expenditures.

a. Find the most recent values from FRED for these four variables: (1) Personal Consumption Expenditures (PCEC), (2) Personal Consumption Expenditures: Durable Goods (PCDG), (3) Personal Consumption Expenditures: Nondurable Goods (PCND), and (4) Personal Consumption Expenditures: Services (PCESV).

b. What percentage of total household expenditures is devoted to the consumption of goods (both durable and nondurable goods)?

D2.4: Using data from the St. Louis Federal Reserve (FRED) (http://research.stlouisfed.org/fred2/), analyze aggregate investment expenditures.

a. Find the most recent values from FRED for these three variables: (1) Gross Private Domestic Investment (GPDI), (2) Private Nonresidential Fixed Investment (PNFI), and (3) Private Residential Fixed Investment (PRFI).

b. Using the most recent values, compute the difference between gross private domestic investment and fixed private investment. What component of GDP does the value computed represent?

D2.5: Using data from the St. Louis Federal Reserve (FRED) (http://research.stlouisfed.org/fred2/), analyze real exports and real imports.

a. Find the values for the most recent two years from FRED for Real Exports of Goods and Services (EXPGSCA) and Real Imports of Goods and Services (IMPGSCA).

b. Compute the value of net exports for each of the two most recent years.

D2.6: Using data from the St. Louis Federal Reserve (FRED) (http://research.stlouisfed.org/fred2/), analyze the difference between gross domestic product and gross national product.

a. Find the most recent values from FRED for Gross Domestic Product (GDP) and Gross National Product (GNP).

b. Given the values found above, explain whether or not foreign production by U.S. firms exceeds U.S. production by foreign firms.

c. If countries have a significant fraction of domestic production occurring in foreign-owned facilities, explain whether GDP will be larger or smaller than GNP.

D2.7: Using data from the St. Louis Federal Reserve (FRED) (http://research.stlouisfed.org/fred2/), analyze income and personal income data.

a. Find the most recent values from FRED for these three variables: (1) Personal Income (PINCOME), (2) Disposable Personal Income (DPI), and (3) Personal Consumption Expenditures (PCEC).

b. Using the most recent values, compute the difference between personal income and disposable personal income. What does the difference between personal income and disposable personal income represent?

c. Compute the ratio of personal consumption to disposable income. Use this ratio and the fact that disposable income increases dollar-for-dollar with a tax reduction to forecast the affect of a tax cut on spending by households.

D2.8: Using data from the St. Louis Federal Reserve (FRED) (http://research.stlouisfed.org/fred2/), analyze the GDP deflator and inflation.

a. Find the most recent values and values from one year earlier from FRED for nominal Gross Domestic Product (GDP) and Real Gross Domestic Product (GDPC1).

b. Using the data from above, compute the GDP price deflator for the most recent period and the GDP price deflator for the period one year earlier.

c. Using the two computed GDP price deflators, calculate the year-over-year inflation rate.

d. Referring to Figure 2.5, explain why the nominal and real GDP lines intersect at the base year. What is the value of the GDP deflator at the point where the nominal and real GDP lines intersect?

D2.9: Using data from the St. Louis Federal Reserve (FRED) (http://research.stlouisfed.org/fred2/), analyze real GDP.

a. Find the most recent values and values from one year earlier from FRED for nominal Gross Domestic Product (GDP) and the GDP Implicit Price Deflator (GDPDEF).

b. Using the data from above, compute the real GDP for the most recent period and for the period one year earlier.

c. Growth in the economy is usually measured as growth in real GDP. Using the two computed real GDP values, find the growth rate of the economy from the first period to the second period.

D2.10: Using data from the St. Louis Federal Reserve (FRED) (http://research.stlouisfed.org/fred2/), analyze CPI (the consumer price index) and inflation.

a. Find the most recent values and values from one year earlier from FRED for the Consumer Price Index (CPIAUCSL). Is this data annual, quarterly, or monthly?

b. Using the CPI data for the two periods, calculate the year-over-year inflation rate.

D2.11: [Excel exercise] Using data downloaded from the St. Louis Federal Reserve (FRED) in an Excel format, (http://research.stlouisfed.org/fred2/), and then performing calculations using Excel or some other compatible spreadsheet program such as OpenOffice, analyze CPI (the consumer price index) and inflation.

a. Find the data from FRED for the Consumer Price Index for All Urban Consumers (CPIAUCSL). From the "download data page," change the beginning date to six years prior to the most recent observation. You can leave the ending date as it is. Then click on the "download" button to download the data and save it to your computer. Finally, open the Excel file.

b. Using Excel, calculate the percentage change in CPI from a year ago for each of the observations, beginning with the observation one year later than the first observation.

c. Using Excel, create a time series graph of the percentage change from a year ago.

d. Using the spreadsheet information, which period experienced the highest inflation rate and what was the inflation rate equal to at the time?

D2.12: [Excel exercise] Using data downloaded from the St. Louis Federal Reserve (FRED) in an Excel format, (http://research.stlouisfed.org/fred2/), and then performing calculations using Excel or some other compatible spreadsheet program such as OpenOffice, analyze different price indexes and inflation.

a. Find the data from FRED for the Consumer Price Index for All Urban Consumers (CPIAUCSL) and the Consumer Price Index for All Urban Consumers less Food and Energy (CPILFESL). From the "download data page," change the beginning date to 2006-07-01. You can leave the ending date as it is. Then click on the "download" button to download the data and save it to your computer. Finally, open the Excel file.

b. Using Excel, calculate the percentage change in each CPI index from a year ago for each of the observation, beginning with the observation 2007-07-01.

c. Using Excel, create a time series graph of the percentage change from a year ago for both indexes. Make sure both data lines are on the same graph.

d. Using the spreadsheet information, identify any months where inflation was negative for one CPI measure but was positive for the other CPI measure. Briefly discuss what must have been true during this month or months.

D2.13: Using data from the St. Louis Federal Reserve (FRED) (http://research.stlouisfed.org/fred2/), analyze different categories of the CPI (the consumer price index) and inflation.

a. Find the most recent values and values from the same month in 2010 from FRED for the following categories of the Consumer Price Index: Food and Beverages (CPIFABSL), Apparel (CPIAPPSL), Transportation (CPITRNSL), and Medical Care (CPIMEDSL).

b. Compute the percentage change in prices over the period from 2010 to the present period for each of the four CPI categories.

c. According to your calculations, which category had the lowest inflation and which category had the highest inflation?

D2.14: Using data from the St. Louis Federal Reserve (FRED) (http://research.stlouisfed.org/fred2/), analyze categories of CPI (the consumer price index) and inflation.

a. Find the most recent values from FRED for the Housing Category of CPI (CPIHOSSL) and the Medical Care Category of CPI (CPIMEDSL).

b. Suppose that prices for both housing and medical care increase by 10% from their most recent values. Compute the new value for each index as a result of the increase.

c. If the eight categories comprising the overall CPI (the CPI for *All Items*) were weighted equally, the values computed above would make equal contributions to the overall index. However, the BLS gives housing a more significant weight than medical care. More specifically, the BLS weights housing at 41.0% while medical care is weighted at only 7.1%. Calculate the contribution each of the increases computed above actually makes to the overall CPI.

d. Explain whether the overall CPI and, therefore, the inflation rate will rise by a larger or smaller amount when prices rise rapidly in a category that carries a relatively large weight.

D2.15: Using data from the St. Louis Federal Reserve (FRED) (http://research.stlouisfed.org/fred2/), analyze the labor force and unemployment.

a. Find the most recent values from FRED for these three variables: (1) Unemployed (UNEMPLOY), (2) Civilian Labor Force (CLF16OV), and (3) Employment Level – Part-Time for Economic Reasons,

Slack Work or Business Conditions (LNS12032195). Are the data reported annually, quarterly, or monthly? What units are the values for these variables reported in?

b. Using the most recent values, compute the civilian unemployment rate and the civilian unemployment rate including persons who are underemployed (part-time for economic reasons).

D2.16: Using data from the St. Louis Federal Reserve (FRED) (http://research.stlouisfed.org/fred2/), analyze the labor force and unemployment.

a. Find the most recent values from FRED for these four variables: (1) Unemployment Level - Men (LNS13000001), (2) Unemployment Level - Women (LNS13000002), (3) Civilian Labor Force Level - Men (LNS11000001), and (4) Civilian Labor Force Level - Women (LNS11000002). Are the data reported annually, quarterly, or monthly? What units are the values for these variables reported in?

b. Using the most recent values, compute the unemployment rate for men and the unemployment rate for women.

c. Explain why some individuals would be considered discouraged workers and explain what will happen to the unemployment rate if there is an increase in discouraged workers.

D2.17: Using data from the St. Louis Federal Reserve (FRED) (http://research.stlouisfed.org/fred2/), analyze the labor force and employment.

a. Find the most recent values from FRED for these three variables: (1) Unemployed (UNEMPLOY), (2) Civilian Employment (CE16OV), and (3) Not in Labor Force (LNS15000000).

b. Using the most recent values, compute the working-age population (in thousands) and the employment-population ratio.

c. All else constant, what would you expect to happen to the employment-population ratio if the economy enters a recession?

D2.18: Using data from the St. Louis Federal Reserve (FRED) (http://research.stlouisfed.org/fred2/), analyze the labor force and unemployment.

a. Find the most recent values from FRED for these four variables: (1) Unemployed (UNEMPLOY), (2) Civilian Employment (CE16OV), (3) Employment Level – Part-Time for Economic Reasons, All Industries (LNS12032194), and (4) Not in Labor Force, Searched for Work and Available (LNU05026642).

b. Using the most recent values, compute the official unemployment rate.

c. It has been argued that the official unemployment rate understates the degree of joblessness because of the narrow definition of who is counted as unemployed. A broader measure, which includes as unemployed those who work part-time for economic reasons and those who were available for work but not actively searching, is also computed by the BLS. Using data from above, compute this broader rate of unemployment.

d. The difference between the official rate and the broader rate changes over the course of the business cycle. Explain what would be expected to happen to this difference during recessions as opposed to expansions.

D2.19: Using data from the St. Louis Federal Reserve (FRED) (http://research.stlouisfed.org/fred2/), analyze real and nominal interest rates.

a. Find the most recent values from FRED for the following four variables: (1) 30-Year Conventional Mortgage Rate (MORTG), (2) Moody's Seasoned Aaa Corporate Bond Yield (AAA), the 3-Month Treasury Bill: (3) Secondary Market Rate (TB3MS), the 10-Year Treasury Constant Maturity Rate (GS10), and (4)University of Michigan Inflation Expectation (MICH).

b. Using the the most recent expected inflation rate, compute the expected real interest rate for each of the above borrowing rates: (the 30-Year Conventional Mortgage Rate; Moody's Seasoned Aaa Corporate Bond Yield; the 3-Month Treasury Bill: Secondary Market Rate; and the 10-Year Treasury Constant Maturity Rate).

c. Suppose the actual inflation rate is greater than the expected inflation rate. Will borrowers or lenders be made better off? Briefly explain.

CHAPTER 3

The U.S. Financial System

Learning Objectives

After studying this chapter, you should be able to:

3.1 Describe the financial system and explain the role it plays in the economy (pages 65–74)

3.2 Understand the role of the central bank in stabilizing the financial system (pages 74–87)

3.3 Explain how interest rates are determined in the money market and understand the risk structure and the term structure of interest rates (pages 87–99)

3.A Appendix: Understand the term structure of interest rates (pages 106–107)

The Wonderful World of Credit

In 2012, a curious thing happened: Consumers substantially increased their purchases of cars and other goods, even though their incomes were rising by less than the inflation rate. Normally, car sales rise rapidly only when employment and income are increasing, but in mid-2012, the unemployment rate was still above 8%, and household income was growing by less than the inflation rate. The key reason car sales were rising was that households had an easier time borrowing money.

Most people have to borrow to buy a car, and during the financial crisis that accompanied the recession of 2007–2009, many people found it difficult to borrow money—not because banks had raised interest rates on car loans but because they had tightened their requirements for obtaining loans. People who could

have borrowed money to purchase a car in 2007 could not do so in 2009. The difficulty of obtaining a loan added to the effects of falling employment and income in causing car sales to plummet. But by mid-2012, consumer borrowing, apart from borrowing using credit cards, had increased by more than $150 billion from its low point after the recession. Only when banks became more willing to make loans did car sales revive.

Car buyers aren't the only ones dependent on bank loans to finance spending. Most small businesses have to finance their operations either through the profits they earn or by borrowing from banks. As banks tightened their lending requirements following the financial crisis, many small businesses found themselves strapped for the funds needed to meet their payrolls, pay their

Continued on next page

Key Issue and Question

Issue: The financial system moves funds from savers to borrowers, which promotes investment and the accumulation of capital goods.

Question: Why did the bursting of the housing bubble that began in 2006 cause the financial system to falter?

Answered on page 99

suppliers, and cover their other expenses. Not surprisingly, these small businesses had to cut back their purchases from suppliers and lay off workers to avoid bankruptcy. During the worst period of the financial crisis—from the last quarter of 2008 through the last quarter of 2009—businesses employing fewer than 50 workers laid off a staggering 17 *million* workers. By comparison, firms that employed more than 250 workers laid off only 10 million workers, even though these larger firms employed twice as many workers.[1]

The difficulty that car buyers and small businesses had in securing loans is an indication of why the recession of 2007–2009 was so severe: It was accompanied by the worst financial crisis since the Great Depression of the 1930s. No modern economy can prosper without a well-functioning financial system facilitating the flow of funds from savers to borrowers. A significant disruption in that flow invites economic disaster, as the world learned again during the financial crisis.

Sources: Alan Zibel and Jeffrey Sparshott, "Banks Ease Rules on Some Lending," *Wall Street Journal*, April 30, 2012; Mike Ramsey and Neal E. Boudettte, "U.S. Auto Sales Sizzle," *Wall Street Journal*, April 4, 2012; and Board of Governors of the Federal Reserve System, *Consumer Credit*, Release G.19; data on employment by firm size are from U.S. Bureau of the Census, *2007 Economic Census*; data on employment losses by firm size are from U.S. Bureau of Labor Statistics, "Business Employment Dynamics."

The financial system channels funds from those who want to save to those who want to borrow. Households borrow for many reasons, including buying cars and houses, or attending college. Firms such as the Ford Motor Company use the financial system to obtain funds to expand and modernize factories and to meet payrolls, among other purposes. Most governments, including state, local, and federal governments in the United States, use the financial system to obtain funds to build new roads and bridges and to finance gaps between the taxes they collect and their spending.

When the financial system operates well, funds move smoothly from savers to borrowers, thereby enhancing economic activity. When the financial system does not operate well, the economy can experience a recession. In extreme cases, the recession can be severe, as with the Great Depression of the 1930s and the 2007–2009 recession.

In this chapter, we describe how the financial system works and explore some of the problems that can occur if the flow of funds through the system is disrupted. Understanding how the financial system works will help you understand the material in later chapters on long-run economic growth, the business cycle, and fiscal and monetary policy. This chapter focuses on the U.S. financial system. (In the following chapter, we expand the focus to the global financial system.)

An Overview of the Financial System

The **financial system** is the network of banks, stock and bond markets, and other financial markets and institutions that make it possible for funds to flow from lenders to borrowers. Households and firms depend heavily on the financial system to attain their goals. For instance, consider how the financial system works for you. When you begin your career, you will probably want to save some of your income to buy a car or a house. Through the financial system, you can save in many ways, including putting funds in a savings account in a bank or buying stocks or bonds.

3.1

Learning Objective
Describe the financial system and explain the role it plays in the economy.

Financial system The financial intermediaries and financial markets that together facilitate the flow of funds from lenders to borrowers.

---

[1]These numbers are *gross* layoffs, which means they do not take into account any hiring of workers that these firms may have done during this period.

At certain points in your life, you are also likely to be a borrower. You may have borrowed money to pay for college. If you need to buy a car without saving enough to pay for it completely, you are likely to borrow the funds from a bank. If you start a business, you probably will not be able to finance the startup costs for the business out of your savings, so once again, you are likely to borrow funds from a bank. Large businesses are often in a similar situation. To find the money they need to expand and grow, large businesses either borrow from banks or sell stocks and bonds directly to savers. In fact, without a well-functioning financial system, economic growth is difficult because firms will be unable to expand and adopt new technologies. History shows that only countries with well-developed financial systems have been able to sustain high levels of economic growth.

Financial Markets and Financial Intermediaries

The financial system consists of *financial markets* and *financial intermediaries*. An **asset** is anything of value owned by a person or a firm. If you own a laptop or a car, those are assets. For a firm, the buildings and equipment it owns are assets. A **financial asset** is a financial claim, which means that if you own a financial asset, you have a claim on someone else to pay you money. For instance, a bank checking account is a financial asset because it represents a claim you have against the bank to pay you an amount of money equal to the dollar value of your account.

Financial securities are *tradable* financial assets, which means they can be bought and sold. Stocks, bonds, and other financial securities are bought and sold in **financial markets**, such as the New York Stock Exchange. **Stocks** are financial securities that represent partial ownership of a firm. If you buy one share of stock in General Electric (GE), you become one of millions of owners of that firm, and you have a legal claim to your portion of anything GE owns and to its profits. Firms typically pay *dividends* to their stockholders. **Bonds** are financial securities that represent promises to repay a fixed amount of funds. When GE sells a bond, the firm promises to pay the purchaser of the bond an interest payment each year for the term of the bond, as well as a final payment equal to the face value of the bond. The interest payments that issuers of bonds pay to bondholders are called *coupon payments*. In a financial market, borrowers can obtain money directly from lenders, as when GE sells a bond to someone who wants to invest by purchasing the bond. Both private firms and governments issue bonds.[2]

Economists make a distinction between primary markets and secondary markets. A *primary market* is a financial market in which stocks, bonds, and other securities are sold for the first time. In 2012, when Facebook first sold stock, which is called an initial public offering (IPO), the stock was sold in the primary market. A *secondary market* is a financial market in which investors buy and sell already existing securities. If you were to buy or sell shares of Facebook's stock today, you would be doing so in the secondary market.

Primary and secondary markets can be in the same physical—or virtual—location. For example, a firm may issue new shares of stock on the New York Stock Exchange

---

[2]A brief note on terminology: In this chapter, when we refer to *investors*, we mean households and financial firms who buy stocks, bonds, and other securities as financial investments. It is important not to confuse financial investment with the macroeconomic term *investment*, which refers to spending by households and firms on *investment goods*, such as houses, factories, machinery, and equipment.

Asset Anything of value owned by a person or a firm.

Financial asset A financial claim.

Financial market A place or channel for buying or selling stocks, bonds, or other financial securities.

Stock A financial security that represents a legal claim on a share in the profits and assets of a firm.

Bond A financial security issued by a corporation or government that represents a promise to repay a fixed amount of funds.

while billions of shares of existing stock are being bought and sold. Some financial assets—such as checking accounts or savings accounts in banks—are not financial securities because they cannot be resold in a financial market. In other words, there is no secondary market for these assets.

A **financial intermediary** is a firm that borrows funds from savers and lends them to borrowers. The most important financial intermediaries are commercial banks. Other financial intermediaries include investment banks, mutual funds, hedge funds, pension funds, and insurance companies. See Table 3.1 for brief descriptions of several important financial intermediaries. In effect, financial intermediaries act as go-betweens for borrowers and savers by borrowing funds from savers and lending them to borrowers. For example, suppose Cindy wants to open a café. Although you may be reluctant to lend money directly to Cindy, you may end up doing so indirectly: You deposit money in a bank, which then combines your deposit with money from other depositors to make a loan to Cindy. Financial intermediaries pool the funds of many small savers and lend the funds to many individual borrowers. The intermediaries earn a profit by paying savers less for the use of their funds than the intermediaries receive from borrowers. For

Financial intermediary A firm, such as a commercial bank, that borrows funds from savers and lends them to borrowers.

Table 3.1 Important Financial Intermediaries

Type of financial intermediary	Description	Examples
Commercial bank	A company that takes in deposits and makes loans to households and firms.	Bank of America Wells Fargo
Investment bank	A company that provides advice to firms issuing new securities, underwrites the issuing of securities, and develops new securities.	Goldman Sachs Morgan Stanley
Mutual fund	A company that sells shares to investors and uses the funds to buy stocks, bonds, or other financial securities.	Vanguard Fidelity
Hedge fund	A company that is similar to a mutual fund but that obtains funds primarily from wealthy investors and uses the funds to make complicated—and often risky—investments.	Bridgewater Paulson & Co.
Pension fund	An institution that receives contributions from workers and uses the funds received to invest in financial securities to fund retirement benefits.	California Public Employees' Retirement System Federal Retirement Thrift
Insurance company	A company that sells insurance policies to households and firms and uses the funds received to invest in financial securities.	MetLife The Hartford Aetna

example, a bank might pay you as a depositor a 2% interest rate, while it lends money to Cindy's Café at a 6% interest rate.

Some financial intermediaries, such as mutual funds, hedge funds, pension funds, and insurance companies, make investments in stocks and bonds on behalf of savers. For example, mutual funds sell shares to savers and then use the funds to buy a *portfolio* of stocks, bonds, mortgage loans, and other financial securities. Most mutual funds issue shares that the funds will buy back—or *redeem*—at a price that represents the underlying value of the financial securities owned by the fund. Large mutual fund companies, such as Fidelity and Vanguard, offer many alternative stock and bond funds. Over the past 30 years, the role of mutual funds in the financial system has increased dramatically. By 2013, competition among hundreds of mutual fund firms gave investors thousands of funds from which to choose.

Financial intermediaries play a key role in the economy because they are the main source of loans to households and small businesses. Households and small firms usually cannot borrow money directly from savers, so they have to do so indirectly by getting loans from banks. Therefore, when banks decide to tighten their requirements for loans, many consumers are unable to obtain the credit they need to buy cars and houses, and small businesses have trouble financing their operations.

Making the Connection

The Controversial World of Subprime Lending

If you apply for a loan at a bank, the bank will check your *credit history* in order to judge whether you are likely to repay the loan. Included in your credit history is information on whether you have made payments on other loans on time, how much debt you have, and how long a history you have of making payments on debts. Lenders often combine the information from your credit history into a *credit score*. For example, the FICO company provides banks and other lenders with a credit score that ranges from 300 (bad credit) to 850 (good credit). The more likely a borrower is to *default*, or stop making payments on a loan, the higher the interest rate a lender will charge on the loan. The higher interest rate compensates the lender for the increased default risk. For instance, if you have a credit score of 650, you might have to pay 1% more on a car loan than would a borrower with a credit score of 800.

Some borrowers with credit scores below 600 have difficulty finding any lenders willing to make loans to them. Often referred to as *subprime borrowers*, these people typically have seriously flawed credit histories that may include failure to make payments on credit cards or on car loans or they may have declared personal bankruptcy in the recent past. Prior to the mid-1990s, many banks and other lenders avoided making loans to subprime borrowers rather than charging them very high interest rates to compensate for the high default risk. The lenders reasoned that the only borrowers who would take out loans at very high rates were people almost certain to default on their loans. Analysts at some banks began to argue, however, that data on loans made to subprime borrowers showed that the higher interest rates these borrowers paid more than compensated for the higher default risk. In other words, subprime loans were actually more profitable than loans made to borrowers with higher credit scores.

During the housing boom of the mid-2000s, many lenders made residential mortgage loans to subprime homebuyers, typically charging them initially low interest rates that would rise after a period of several years to very high rates. During the recession that began in 2007, many of these subprime borrowers defaulted on their loans, causing lenders to suffer heavy losses. As a result of this experience, most lenders tightened their lending standards and subprime borrowers found that once again they had difficulty obtaining loans.

By mid-2012, however, some lenders began again to make loans to subprime borrowers. Although most lenders were still unwilling to make mortgage loans to subprime borrowers, lenders did believe they could profitably make other types of loans to these borrowers. For example, banks began increasing the number of prepaid debit cards, low-limit credit cards, and short-term loans they offered to subprime borrowers, many of whom have low incomes. Prepaid debit cards have a fixed amount of money on them and come with high fees. For example, U.S. Bank charges $3 to issue a card, a maintenance fee of $3 per month, and $3 for each visit to a bank teller. First Premier Bank offers subprime borrowers a credit card with a $400 credit limit that requires the borrower to pay up to $100 in fees. Short-term loans, sometimes referred to as "payday loans," also come with high fees and high interest rates.

Some policymakers and advocates for low-income people have been critical of these ways of extending credit to subprime borrowers. These critics argue that low-income borrowers often do not understand the terms of the borrowings, failing to realize, for example, how much they will be paying in fees. Banks and many economists argue, though, that subprime borrowers have high risks of default, so banks have to charge them high fees and high interest rates in order to make a profit. Restricting the fees and interest rates that banks charge would likely result in banks no longer being willing to provide credit to subprime borrowers. Financial analyst Meredith Whitney has argued, "Excluding millions of Americans from traditional banking services is not an efficient means of commerce and will result in long-term negative consequences for our economy." Policymakers and financial regulators are faced with a difficult balancing act as they try to ensure that subprime borrowers retain access to credit.

Sources: Andrew R. Johnson and Robin Sidel, "Chase Pitches New Plastic," *Wall Street Journal*, May 8, 2012; Jessica Silver-Greenberg and Ben Protess, "Chasing Fees, Banks Court Low-Income Customers," *New York Times*, April 25, 2012; Jessica Silver-Greenberg and Tara Siegel Bernard, "Lenders Again Dealing Credit to Risky Borrowers," *New York Times*, April 10, 2012; Maya Jackson Randall, "Consumer Watchdog Retreats on 'Fee-Harvester' Cards," *Wall Street Journal*, April 12, 2012; and Meredith Whitney, "America's 'Unbanked' Masses," *Wall Street Journal*, February 24, 2012.

See related problem 1.10 at the end of the chapter.

Stocks, Bonds, and Stock Market Indexes Buying stock gives you the opportunity to be a part owner of a firm. Granted, if you are buying a few shares of stock in Apple, you own only a very small piece of the firm. But that ownership allows you to participate in any of the growth and increased profits the firm may experience. For reasons we will discuss later in this chapter, only a relatively small number of U.S. firms—about 5,100 out of the millions of firms in the United States—are *publicly traded companies* that sell stock on one of the U.S. stock markets.

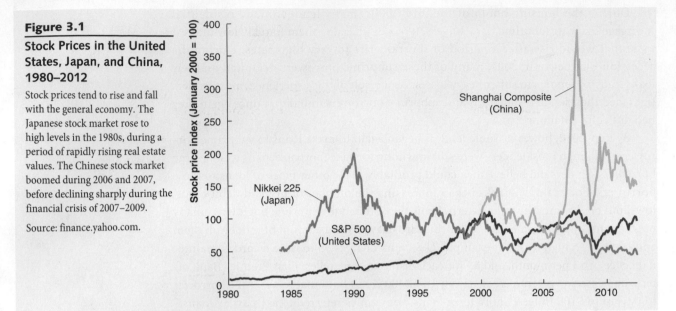

Figure 3.1

Stock Prices in the United States, Japan, and China, 1980–2012

Stock prices tend to rise and fall with the general economy. The Japanese stock market rose to high levels in the 1980s, during a period of rapidly rising real estate values. The Chinese stock market boomed during 2006 and 2007, before declining sharply during the financial crisis of 2007–2009.

Source: finance.yahoo.com.

When many people think of the "stock market," they think of the New York Stock Exchange (NYSE) building located on Wall Street in New York City. Many of the largest and oldest U.S. corporations, such as General Electric, IBM, and ExxonMobil, are listed on the NYSE's Big Board. Although in recent years trading at the NYSE has become increasingly electronic, some buying and selling still takes place on the floor of the exchange. By contrast, the NASDAQ stock market, which is named for the National Association of Securities Dealers, is entirely electronic. As an "over-the-counter" market, buying and selling on NASDAQ is carried out between dealers who are linked together by computer. High-tech firms such as Apple, Microsoft, and Google dominate the listings on NASDAQ.

The performance of the U.S. stock market is often measured using stock market indexes. Like other indexes, stock market indexes are weighted averages of stock prices, with the index set equal to 100 for the base year. Figure 3.1 shows movements from 1980 to 2012 in three stock indexes: the U.S. Standard & Poor's (S&P) 500, the Japanese Nikkei 225, and (beginning in 2000) the Chinese Shanghai Composite.

Stock prices usually mirror what is happening in the economy. When an economy is expanding, firms' profits and expected future profits rise, causing stock prices to increase. During an economic recession, the opposite occurs. Notice in Figure 3.1 that all three stock market indexes peaked at about the same time in 2000 and then again in 2007. These common movements in stock prices suggest that the forces affecting the business cycle and financial markets can be global in nature. In addition, factors specific to each economy can cause movements in stock prices. For example, during the 1980s, Japan experienced a surge in the value of real estate and stocks before both markets crashed. The increase in stock prices in China during 2006 and 2007 was particularly large, reflecting the optimism many investors had about the future growth of the Chinese economy.

Making the Connection

Investing in the Worldwide Stock Market

Suppose you decide to invest in stocks. How would you go about it? Traditionally, an investor would establish an account with a stockbroker, such as Merrill Lynch, who would purchase the stock for the investor in exchange for a payment or commission. Today, many investors who want to buy the stocks of individual companies use online brokerage firms, such as E*Trade or TD Ameritrade, which typically charge much lower commissions than traditional brokerage firms but also do not offer personal investment advice and other services offered by traditional brokers.

Investors can also purchase shares in mutual funds, which invest in a portfolio of stocks. For instance, the Vanguard mutual fund company offers the Index 500 fund, which buys shares in the 500 firms represented in the S&P 500. Buying mutual funds allows savers with small amounts of money to reduce their risk by spreading their savings across the stocks of the many firms included in the fund. So-called no-load mutual funds also allow investors to avoid the commissions they would have to pay to buy individual stocks using brokers. In recent years, many investors have purchased *exchange-traded funds (ETFs)*. ETFs are very similar to mutual funds, except that while mutual funds can only be bought from or sold to the investment firm that issues the funds, ETFs can be bought from and sold to other investors, just as if they were stocks.

What about investing in firms headquartered outside the United States? The 5,100 publicly traded U.S. firms represent only about 10% of all the firms listed on stock exchanges worldwide. The following figure lists world stock markets, by total value of the shares of the listed firms at the end of 2011.

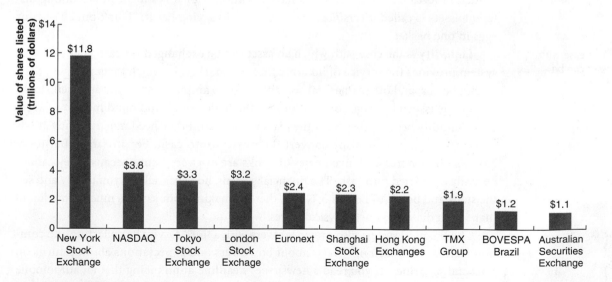

Source: www.world-exchanges.org.

Although the New York Stock Exchange remains the world's largest stock market, foreign stock markets have been rapidly increasing in size. The shares of the largest foreign firms, such as Sony, Toyota, and Nokia, do trade indirectly on the New York Stock

Exchange in the form of American Depository Receipts, which are receipts for shares of stock held in a foreign country. Some mutual funds also invest in the stock of foreign firms. It is possible to buy individual stocks listed on foreign stock exchanges by setting up an account with a local brokerage firm in the foreign country. Although at one time only wealthy people invested directly in foreign stock markets, the Internet has made it much easier for people of more moderate income to establish foreign brokerage accounts and to research foreign companies.

See related problem 1.11 at the end of the chapter.

Services Provided by the Financial System In addition to matching households that have funds to lend with households and firms that want to borrow funds, the financial system provides three key services to savers and borrowers:

1. Risk sharing
2. Liquidity
3. Information

Risk The chance that the value of a financial security will change relative to what you expect.

In financial markets, **risk** is the chance that the value of a financial security will change relative to what you expect. For example, you may buy a share of stock in Apple at a price of $600, only to have the price fall to $300. Most individual savers prefer to avoid risk and seek a steady return on their savings rather than experience erratic swings between high and low earnings. The financial system provides *risk sharing* by allowing savers to spread their money among many financial investments. For example, you can divide your money among a bank savings account, individual bonds, and a mutual fund to reduce the risk you face. Dividing your investment funds among different assets is called *diversification*, or, as the old saying has it, "Don't put all of your eggs in one basket."

Liquidity The ease with which an asset can be exchanged for cash.

Liquidity is the ease with which an asset can be exchanged for cash. The financial system provides the service of liquidity through markets in which savers can sell their stocks, bonds, and other financial securities. For example, savers can easily sell stocks and bonds issued by large corporations on the major stock and bond markets. Savers value liquidity because they want the reassurance that if they need money to buy goods and services, they can easily convert their assets into cash. For instance, Barnes & Noble's retail stores and inventories of books are not very liquid because they cannot be easily converted into cash. The financial system, however, allows you to buy and sell the stock and bonds of Barnes & Noble, thereby making your savings much more liquid than if you directly owned physical stores.

The financial system also provides savers with a third service by collecting and communicating *information*, or facts about borrowers and expectations about returns on financial securities. If you read a newspaper headline announcing that an automobile firm has invented a car with an engine that runs on water, how would you determine the effect of this discovery on the firm's profits? Financial markets do that job for you by incorporating information into the prices of stocks, bonds, and other financial securities. In this example, expectation of higher future profits would boost the prices of the automobile firm's stock and bonds.

Banking and Securitization

Typically, when we refer to "banks," we are thinking of commercial banks, which are financial firms that take in deposits and make loans to households and firms. Today, many financial firms engage not just in commercial banking but also in *investment banking,* which typically involves two key activities: Providing advice to firms issuing stocks and bonds or considering mergers with other firms and *underwriting* new issues of stocks and bonds. In underwriting, banks charge firms a fee to guarantee a certain price for the stocks and bonds the firms issue.

Beginning in the 1990s, investment banks became heavily involved in *securitization.* **Securitization** involves creating secondary markets for financial assets that previously could not be bought and sold and so were not considered financial securities. Until about 1970, most loans made by banks were financial assets to the banks, but they were not securities because they could not be sold in a market. For instance, when a bank granted a car loan, it would keep the loan and collect the payments until the loan *matured* when the borrower made the last payment. Today, many bank loans are bundled together into securities that are resold to investors. When loans are securitized, the banks that make the loans collect the payments from borrowers and send those payments to the investors who have bought the securities based on the loans. This change in financial structure means that there is a good chance that when you take out a car loan at a local bank, you will write a check to the bank each month as payment on your loan, but someone else who bought a security backed by your loan will ultimately receive your payment.

Securitization has been particularly important in the market for mortgage loans taken out by households to buy new and existing homes. Securitization allows banks to make more loans. When a bank sells a mortgage, the bank receives funds that allow it to make additional loans. So, securitization has made it easier for banks to expand the number of loans they make and to earn larger profits.

Securitization The process of converting loans and other financial assets that are not tradable into securities.

Asymmetric Information and Principal–Agent Problems in Financial Markets

Securitization was at the heart of the financial crisis of 2007–2009. In this section, we describe key difficulties that investors encounter in financial markets and how those difficulties led to the financial crisis.

Asymmetric Information Many financial transactions, including loans, are subject to the problem of **asymmetric information**, a situation in which one party to an economic transaction has better information than does the other party. For example, households and firms that want to borrow money know more about their true financial condition than do lenders. A firm wanting to borrow money to avoid bankruptcy has a strong incentive to conceal its shaky financial condition from potential lenders. Similarly, an investment bank that wants to sell a security has an incentive to make the security appear less risky than it is.

Asymmetric information leads to two key problems: *adverse selection* and *moral hazard.* **Adverse selection** refers to a situation in which one party to a transaction takes advantage of knowing more than the other party. For example, adverse selection results in the people who most want to borrow money often being the people lenders would least want to loan money to if they had full information on the borrowers' true financial

Asymmetric information A situation in which one party to an economic transaction has better information than does the other party.

Adverse selection A situation in which one party to a transaction takes advantage of knowing more than the other party.

Asymmetric selection: 1. moral hazard 2. adverse selection

Moral hazard Actions people take after they have entered into a transaction that make the other party to the transaction worse off.

condition. **Moral hazard** refers to actions people take after they have entered into a transaction that make the other party to the transaction worse off. For instance, once a firm or household has borrowed money, what will it do with the funds? The owner of a small firm may have told the bank that she would use a loan to expand her business, but it is possible that, in fact, she intends to visit Las Vegas and gamble with the money. Lenders encounter the adverse selection problem before a loan is made as they attempt to distinguish borrowers who are likely to pay back loans from borrowers who are unlikely to pay back loans. Lenders encounter the moral hazard problem after they have made a loan as they deal with the possibility that borrowers will misuse borrowed funds.

Principal–Agent Problems In many large corporations, moral hazard results in a *principal–agent problem*. Although the shareholders actually own a large corporation, top managers control the day-to-day operations of the firm. Because top managers do not own the firm, they may be more interested in increasing their own pay than in maximizing the profits of the firm. This separation of ownership of the firm from control of the firm can lead to a principal–agent problem because the agents—the firm's top management—pursue their own interests rather than the interests of the principals to whom they are ultimately responsible—the shareholders of the corporation.

Some economists believe that principal–agent problems were at the heart of the financial meltdown of 2007–2009. Top managers of many financial firms, particularly investment banks, received large salaries and bonuses from creating, buying, and selling securities. Because these managers did not own the firms, they were less concerned with the degree of risk involved with securities backed by subprime mortgages. In fact, when the value of these securities declined, the shareholders of many banks and other financial firms who had invested in the securities suffered large losses.

By 2008, increased awareness of principal–agent problems led many investors to realize that some securities were riskier than they had previously believed. As investors became more reluctant to invest in any but the safest securities, many financial firms found it difficult to raise the funds necessary to carry out their role of financial intermediation.

As problems in the financial system increased during 2007–2009, the attempts of the Federal Reserve—the central bank of the United States—to increase financial stability became the focus of economists and policymakers. Many economists believe that the Federal Reserve (the "Fed") may be the most powerful organization in the U.S. economy; perhaps even more powerful economically than Congress or the president. In the next section, we briefly explore the role of central banks in dealing with financial crises.

3.2

do not confuse central bank & commercial bank!

Learning Objective

Understand the role of the central bank in stabilizing the financial system.

Financial Crises, Government Policy, and the Financial System

A central bank is an institution established by the government to operate as a "banker's bank" rather than as a bank for households and firms. Central banks, such as the Federal Reserve in the United States, the Bank of Japan in Japan, and the European Central Bank in Europe, have the following policy responsibilities:

- Regulating the money supply
- Acting as a lender of last resort to the banking system

Assets		Liabilities	
Reserves	$ 200	Deposits	$2,000
Loans	$1,400		
Securities	$ 600	Net worth (capital)	$ 200
Total assets	$2,200	Total liabilities + net worth (capital)	$2,200

Figure 3.2

Simplified Balance Sheet of a Commercial Bank

The items of greatest economic importance on a bank's balance sheet are its reserves, loans, securities, and deposits. Notice that the difference between the value of this bank's total assets and its total liabilities is equal to its net worth. Therefore, the left side of the balance sheet is always equal to the right side.

- Acting as the government's bank by playing a role in the collection and disbursement of government funds
- Facilitating the payment system by providing banks with check-clearing and other services

This list refers to the routine, year-in, year-out policy responsibilities of a central bank. Sometimes, though, a central bank is faced with a *financial crisis* that requires it to take unusual policy actions. A **financial crisis** involves a significant disruption in the flow of funds from lenders to borrowers. Historically, most financial crises in the United States have involved the commercial banking system, but during 2007–2009, the Federal Reserve was faced with a financial crisis that involved other types of financial intermediaries as well. To understand financial crises, we start by looking briefly at the operations of commercial banks and at the important economic concept of *leverage*.

Financial crisis A significant disruption in the flow of funds from lenders to borrowers.

Financial Intermediaries and Leverage

Consider the situation a typical commercial bank faces. Figure 3.2 shows the *balance sheet* of a commercial bank, such as Wells Fargo. A firm's balance sheet sums up its financial position on a particular day, usually the end of a quarter or a year. A firm's assets are shown on the left side of its balance sheet, and its liabilities are shown on the right side. In the simplified balance sheet shown in Figure 3.2, we include only a few of a typical bank's assets and liabilities and, for convenience, use very small dollar amounts. The bank's assets are its *reserves*, its loans, and its securities, such as Treasury bills or securitized loans. A bank's reserves are funds physically present in the bank or on deposit with the Federal Reserve. The bank's liabilities are its deposits.

Subtracting the value of a firm's liabilities from the value of its assets leaves its *net worth*, which is shown on the right side of the balance sheet. For a public firm, net worth is called shareholder's equity; for a bank, net worth is often referred to as the bank's *capital*.[3] The value of the assets on the left side of the balance sheet must always equal the sum of the value of the liabilities plus net worth shown on the right side. This equality holds because net worth is defined as the difference between the value of the firm's assets and the value of the firm's liabilities. Note that anything that reduces the value of a bank's assets without affecting the value of its liabilities will cause the bank's net worth to decline.

---

[3]Technically, under banking regulations, "Tier 1 capital" equals a bank's shareholder's equity, with some minor adjustments.

Leverage A measure of how much debt an investor takes on in making an investment.

Leverage is a measure of how much debt an investor takes on in making an investment. You probably don't think of yourself as lending to a bank when you deposit money into your checking account, but, in effect, you are. Because banks make most of their loans and other investments using borrowed money in the form of deposits, banks are highly *leveraged*. What difference does leverage make and what is the appeal of making leveraged investments? To answer these questions, consider the situation of a large group of leveraged investors: homeowners.

Traditionally, most people taking out a mortgage loan to buy a house made a down payment equal to 20% of the price of the house and borrowed the other 80%, making their house a leveraged investment. During the housing boom of the early to mid-2000s, many people purchased houses with down payments of 5% or less. So these borrowers were even more highly leveraged.

To see how leverage works in the housing market, consider the following example, illustrated in Table 3.2: Suppose you buy a $200,000 house on January 1, 2014. On January 1, 2015, the price of the house—if you decide to sell it—has risen to $220,000. What return have you earned on your investment in the house? The answer depends on how much you invested when you bought the house. For example:

- If you paid $200,000 in cash for the house, your return on that $200,000 investment is the $20,000 increase in the price of the house divided by your $200,000 investment, or 10%.
- If you made a down payment of 20%, or $40,000, and borrowed the rest by taking out a mortgage loan of $160,000, the return on your investment in the house is the $20,000 increase in the price of the house divided by your $40,000 investment, or 50%.
- If you made a down payment of less than 20%, the return on your investment will be greater than 50%.

The second column in Table 3.2 illustrates how the return on your investment increases as your down payment decreases. As this example shows, the larger the fraction of an investment financed by borrowing, the greater the degree of leverage in the investment, and the greater the potential return. But as the third column in the table shows, the reverse is also true: The greater the leverage, the greater the potential loss. To see why, consider once again that you buy a house for $200,000, except that in this case, after one year, the price of the house *falls* to $180,000. If you paid $200,000 in cash for the house—so your leverage was zero—the $20,000 decline in the price of the house represents a loss of 10% of your investment. But if you made a down payment of only

Table 3.2 Leverage in the Housing Market

Down payment	Return on your investment from . . .	
	a 10% increase in the price of your house	a 10% decrease in the price of your house
100%	10%	−10%
20%	50%	−50%
10%	100%	−100%
5%	200%	−200%

$10,000 and borrowed the remaining $190,000, then the $20,000 decline in the price of the house represents a loss of 200% of your investment. In fact, the house is now worth $10,000 less than the amount of your mortgage loan. The *equity* in your house is the difference between the market price of the house and the amount you owe on a loan, If the amount you owe is greater than the price of the house, you have negative equity. A homeowner who has negative equity is also said to be "upside down" or "underwater" on his or her mortgage.

EQUITY

From this example, we can conclude that: *The more leveraged an investment, the greater the potential gain* and *the greater the potential loss*. Or, put another way, increased leverage results in increased risk.

Let's return to the discussion of commercial banks. Because banks finance most of their assets—loans and securities—with deposits, the more assets the banks have relative to their capital, the greater their leverage. If banks suffer losses on their assets—for instance, if the value of their security holdings declines—they can find themselves in the same position as the homeowner in our example: Just as a highly leveraged homeowner can have the equity in her house wiped out by a relatively small decline in the price of her house, a highly leveraged bank can have its net worth, or capital, wiped out by a relatively small decline in the prices of its assets.

The government regulates a bank's *leverage ratio*, which is the value of its capital relative to the value of its assets. The government regulates bank leverage because regulators believe that a bank's managers may otherwise become more highly leveraged in an attempt to earn high returns on the bank's investments. Bank managers are particularly likely to take on more risk than shareholders would prefer if the managers do not own significant stock in the bank and if the managers' salaries depend on how profitable the bank is. In other words, banks and other financial intermediaries can experience significant principal–agent problems.

Although government regulations limit the leverage of commercial banks, other financial intermediaries are also highly leveraged but face less regulation. For instance, investment banks often borrow short term from other financial firms and use the funds to make investments. Money market mutual funds borrow funds by selling shares to investors and use the funds to buy Treasury bills and other short-term securities. Like commercial banks, these other financial intermediaries are subject to sharp declines in their net worth if the value of their investments falls.

Bank Panics

The financial crisis of 2007–2009 was the most severe the United States experienced since the 1930s. The crisis of the 1930s and several financial crises that occurred prior to the 1930s involved the commercial banking system. Government policy responded to the bank panic of the 1930s in ways that put an end to panics originating in the commercial banking system. These policies were not sufficient, however, to avoid the financial crisis of 2007–2009. As we will see, the federal government has responded to this financial crisis with new regulations.

To understand how problems in the commercial banking system can cause a financial crisis, we begin by noting that the United States, like nearly all other countries, has a fractional reserve banking system where banks keep less than 100% of deposits as reserves. When people deposit money in a bank, the bank uses most of the money to make loans or to invest in securities, holding relatively little as reserves. For example, in Figure 3.2, the bank has $2,000 in deposits but only $200 in reserves. While the deposits may be withdrawn at any time, the loans are typically long term, with the bank having to wait months or years before being fully paid back. If depositors want their money back, banks are faced with the problem of having loaned or invested most of the depositors' money without being able to easily get it back.

In practice, withdrawals are usually not a problem for banks because on a typical day about as much money is deposited as is withdrawn. Sometimes, though, depositors lose confidence in a bank if the bank's assets—such as loans and securities—lose value. When many depositors simultaneously decide to withdraw their money from a bank, there is a **bank run**. If many banks experience runs at the same time, the result is a **bank panic**. It is possible for one bank to handle a run by borrowing from other banks to pay off depositors, but if many banks simultaneously experience runs, the banking system may be in trouble. When banks experience a run, they face *liquidity problems* because their loans cannot be easily sold to provide funds to pay off depositors. In other words, the banks do not have enough liquid assets to pay off all the depositors who want their deposits back.

Since 1934, the Federal Deposit Insurance Corporation (FDIC) has insured deposits in commercial banks, initially up to $2,500 per account and currently up to $250,000. Prior to 1934, if depositors suspected that a bank had made bad loans or other investments, the depositors had a strong incentive to rush to the bank to withdraw their money. Depositors knew that the bank would only have enough cash and other liquid assets available to pay off a fraction of the bank's depositors. Once the bank's liquid assets were exhausted, the bank would have to shut its doors, at least temporarily, until it could raise additional funds. A bank that was forced to raise cash by selling illiquid assets at sharply discounted prices might become *insolvent* and permanently close its doors. A bank or other firm is **insolvent** if the value of its assets declines to less than the value of its liabilities, with the result that the firm has negative net worth. Depositors of a failed bank were likely to receive only some of their money back and then usually only after a long delay.

Imagine being a depositor in a bank during this period. If you suspected that your bank was having financial problems, you would want to be one of the first in line to withdraw your money. Even if you were convinced that your bank was well managed and its loans and investments were in good shape, if you believed the bank's other depositors thought there was a problem, you would still want to withdraw your money before the other depositors arrived and forced the bank to close. In other words, in the absence of deposit insurance, the stability of a bank depends on the confidence of its depositors. In such a situation, if bad news—or even false rumors—shakes that confidence, a bank will experience a run.

Moreover, without a system of government deposit insurance, bad news about one bank can snowball and affect other banks in a process called **contagion**. Once one bank has experienced a run, depositors of other banks may become concerned that their banks might also have problems. These depositors have an incentive to withdraw their money from their banks to avoid losing it should their banks be forced to close. These other banks will be forced to sell loans and securities to raise money to pay off depositors. A key point is that if multiple banks have to sell the same assets—for example, securitized

Bank run The process by which depositors who have lost confidence in a bank simultaneously withdraw their money.

Bank panic A situation in which many banks simultaneously experience runs.

Insolvent The situation in which the value of the assets held by a bank or another firm declines to less than the value of its liabilities, leaving the bank with negative net worth.

Contagion The process by which a run on one financial institution spreads to other financial institutions, resulting in a financial crisis.

loans in the modern banking system—the prices of these assets are likely to decline. As asset prices fall, a process called *asset deflation*, the net worth of banks is undermined and some banks may even be pushed to insolvency. A bank panic feeds on a self-fulfilling perception: If depositors believe that their banks are in trouble, the banks are in trouble.

Government Policies to Deal with Bank Panics

The failure of financially healthy banks due to liquidity problems hurts the ability of households and small- and medium-sized firms to obtain loans, which may reduce their spending and bring on an economic recession. A recession caused by a bank panic can lead to further problems for banks as households and firms default on loans and security values fall further. Additional bank failures make it even harder for households and firms to obtain loans, which further reduces spending and makes the decline in output even larger. A downward spiral of this type helps explain why the bank panic of the early 1930s contributed to the Great Depression being the worst economic downturn in U.S. history.

Governments have two main ways they can attempt to avoid bank panics: (1) a central bank can act as a *lender of last resort*, and (2) the government can insure deposits. In the United States, Congress reacted to the bank panics of the late nineteenth and early twentieth centuries by establishing the Federal Reserve System in 1913. Policymakers and economists argued that the banking industry needed a "banker's bank," or lender of last resort. By making *discount loans* to banks experiencing liquidity problems, the Fed would be an ultimate source of credit to which banks could turn for loans during a panic. The Fed would make loans to solvent banks, using the banks' good, but illiquid, loans as collateral. Policymakers expected the Fed to make loans only to solvent banks, allowing insolvent banks to fail.

In the early 1930s, the Fed failed to make loans to enough of the banks experiencing runs to stop the bank panic. The Fed's failure led Congress to create the FDIC in 1934. By reassuring depositors that they would receive their money back even if their bank failed, deposit insurance effectively ended the era of bank panics in the United States. The FDIC was also given the power to take over insolvent banks and either close them or merge them with financially stronger banks. Figure 3.3 illustrates the causes and consequences of bank panics and the feedback loops that cause a panic to become self-reinforcing. Ultimately, government intervention is needed to end the downward spiral illustrated in the figure.

The Financial Crisis of 2007–2009

The government policies enacted in the 1930s effectively put an end to bank panics in the United States. These policies, however, did not extend to nonbank financial intermediaries, such as investment banks or mutual funds. Over time, these nonbank financial intermediaries had become an increasingly important source of funds to many firms. By 2007, then Federal Reserve Bank of New York president Timothy Geithner labeled nonbank financial intermediaries the *shadow banking system*, and he noted that the total value of their assets was greater than the total value of the assets of the commercial banking system. Lenders to nonbanks lacked the federal insurance available on commercial bank deposits and nonbanks lacked a lender of last resort, so the shadow

Figure 3.3

The Feedback Loop During a Bank Panic

Bank runs can cause good banks, as well as bad banks, to fail. Bank failures are costly because they reduce credit availability to households and firms. Once a panic starts, falling income, employment, and asset prices can cause more bank failures. This feedback loop can cause a panic to continue, unless the government intervenes.

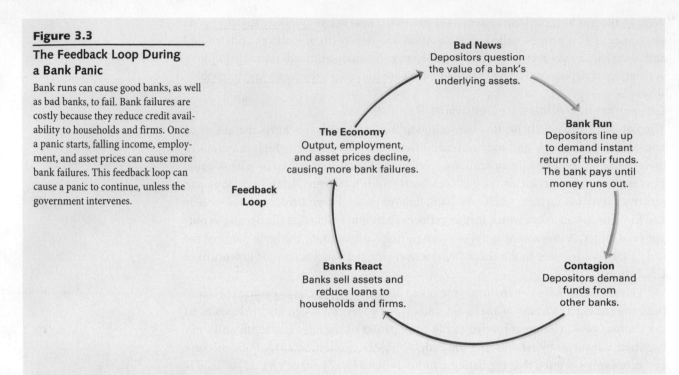

Bad News Depositors question the value of a bank's underlying assets.

Bank Run Depositors line up to demand instant return of their funds. The bank pays until money runs out.

The Economy Output, employment, and asset prices decline, causing more bank failures.

Feedback Loop

Banks React Banks sell assets and reduce loans to households and firms.

Contagion Depositors demand funds from other banks.

banking system was vulnerable to runs in much the same way the commercial banking system had been prior to 1934.

Most economists and policymakers did not recognize that the shadow banking system was vulnerable to runs. However, runs did occur in response to the collapse of the housing bubble that began in 2006. To understand the housing bubble, we need to briefly consider changes that took place over time in the market for residential mortgage loans.

The Mortgage Market and the Subprime Lending Disaster

We discussed earlier the process of securitizing loans. Securitizing mortgages began when Congress created the *Federal National Mortgage Association* (nicknamed "Fannie Mae") in 1938 to stand between investors and commercial banks granting mortgages. Congress created the *Federal Home Loan Mortgage Corporation* (nicknamed "Freddie Mac") in 1970 to further develop the secondary market in mortgages. The goal of Congress in creating Fannie Mae and Freddie Mac was to increase homeownership in the United States by reducing the risks to financial firms of issuing mortgages and by increasing the funds available to be lent as mortgages.

Fannie Mae and Freddie Mac sell bonds to investors and use the funds to purchase mortgages from banks and savings and loans. By the 1990s, a large secondary market existed in mortgages, with funds flowing from investors through Fannie Mae and Freddie Mac to banks and savings and loans and, ultimately, to individuals and families borrowing money to buy houses.

By the 2000s, investment banks began buying mortgages, bundling large numbers of them together as bonds known as *mortgage-backed securities*, and reselling them to investors. Mortgage-backed securities became very popular with investors because they often paid higher interest rates than other securities that appeared to have comparable risk. Mortgage-backed securities helped to increase the funds available to banks and other lenders making mortgage loans. Partly as a result, in the mid-2000s, the U.S. economy underwent a *housing bubble* during which the number of new homes constructed and the prices of homes increased sharply in most parts of the country.

A **bubble** occurs when the price of an asset rises significantly above the asset's fundamental value. The fundamental value of an asset depends on the total expected future returns buyers expect to receive from owning the asset. The owner of stock receives a dividend, which is a payment a firm makes out of its profits. The fundamental value of a stock should reflect the value of the dividends investors expect to receive from buying the stock. When the prices of stocks rise above their fundamental value, as happened with the stocks of many Internet companies during the late 1990s, the stock market experiences a bubble. Typically, bubbles form when investors become overly optimistic about the returns they are likely to receive from owning an asset. Once a bubble begins, investors may buy assets not to hold them but to resell them quickly at a profit, even if the investors know that the prices are greater than the assets' fundamental values.

The fundamental value of a house reflects the housing services the homeowner receives. We can measure the value of these services by looking at the rent of a comparable house. After 2003, housing prices in many cities increased rapidly until they were far above the fundamental values implied by rents on comparable houses.

Bubbles typically end when some investors begin to doubt that prices will rise any higher and decide to sell. This selling causes prices to fall. As prices fall, more investors sell, which causes prices to decline further, which causes more investors to sell, and so on. As a bubble collapses, prices can fall as quickly as they rose when the bubble was inflating.

At the height of the housing bubble in 2005 and early 2006, banks and other lenders had greatly loosened the standards for obtaining a mortgage loan. By 2006, more than 40% of mortgages were being issued to subprime borrowers with flawed credit histories or to "Alt-A borrowers" who did not document their incomes with copies of pay stubs and tax returns. Many buyers made down payments that were smaller than what had been the customary 20% of the price of the house. Some buyers made no down payment at all. These buyers were making highly leveraged investments in their houses. In addition, lenders created new types of mortgages that, rather than charging a fixed interest rate for the life of the loan, allowed borrowers to pay a very low interest rate for the first few years of the mortgage before paying a higher rate in later years. Many borrowers expected that housing prices would rise, and they would be able to take out a new loan—or "refinance" their existing loan at a lower interest rate—before the time came to pay the higher interest rates.

As we saw earlier, with a highly leveraged investment, a small decline in the price of the asset—in this case, a house—can lead to a large loss. By 2006, some buyers, including buyers who had bought houses as investments rather than to live in, became convinced that prices would not rise higher. As these buyers sold their houses, prices began to fall. Falling prices led highly leveraged buyers to sell before their losses became too large. Some subprime and Alt-A buyers stopped making payments on their mortgage loans. By 2006, the housing bubble was collapsing. Rising default rates made investors less likely to purchase mortgage-backed securities, so the prices of the securities declined. Because many

Bubble The situation in which the price of an asset rises significantly above the asset's fundamental value; an unsustainable increase in the price of a class of assets.

commercial and investment banks owned these mortgage-backed securities, the decline in their value caused the banks to suffer losses, amounting to billions of dollars for the largest banks. The decline in the value of mortgage-backed securities and the large losses suffered by commercial and investment banks caused turmoil in the financial system.

Runs on the Shadow Banking System

The first strong indication that a financial crisis might be approaching came in August 2007, when the French bank BNP Paribas announced that it would not allow investors in three of its investment funds to redeem their shares. The funds had held large amounts of mortgage-backed securities. Because trading in these securities had dried up, it had become difficult to determine the securities' market prices and, therefore, the value of shares in the funds. During the fall of 2007 and the spring of 2008, credit conditions worsened and the financial crisis unfolded in a process similar to what had happened during pre-1934 bank panics.

Just as prior to 1934 depositors who were worried about the financial health of commercial banks withdrew their deposits, many lenders during 2007–2009 became reluctant to lend to nonbank financial firms for more than very short terms, and they often insisted on government bonds as collateral. Unlike depositors in the modern commercial banking system, lenders—who are typically financial firms—in the shadow banking system lack any insurance to protect them from loss if the borrower becomes insolvent. Some investment banks had funded long-term investments with short-term borrowing from commercial banks and other financial firms. These investment banks were subject to runs if lenders declined to renew the banks' short-term loans. The investment bank Bear Stearns experienced a run in March 2008, as lenders became concerned that Bear's investments in mortgage-backed securities had declined in value to the extent that the firm was insolvent. With aid from the Federal Reserve, Bear was saved from bankruptcy when JPMorgan Chase acquired it at a price of $10 per share. One year earlier, Bear's shares had sold for $170.

By August 2008, the crisis was deepening, as nearly 25% of subprime mortgages were at least 30 days past due. On September 15, the investment bank Lehman Brothers filed for bankruptcy protection after the Treasury and Federal Reserve declined to commit the funds necessary to attract a private buyer to purchase the firm. At the same time, the investment bank Merrill Lynch agreed to sell itself to Bank of America. The bankruptcy of Lehman Brothers marked a turning point in the crisis. On September 16, Reserve Primary Fund, a large money market mutual fund, announced that because it had suffered heavy losses on its holdings of Lehman Brothers securities, it would "break the buck" by allowing the value of shares in the fund to fall below the usual price of $1 per share. This announcement led to a run on money market mutual funds as investors cashed in their shares. Many parts of the financial system became frozen as trading in securitized loans largely stopped, and large firms as well as small ones had difficulty arranging for even short-term loans. Once again, there were echoes of the 1930s, as the selling of assets by some financial intermediaries reduced the prices of those assets and, therefore, the net worth of the firms that owned the assets. And also as in the 1930s, the financial crisis led to a severe recession, which in turn resulted in households and firms defaulting on loans, further undermining the net worth of financial intermediaries.

Government Policies to Deal with the Financial Crisis of 2007–2009

The federal government responded to the financial crisis of 2007–2009 with new policies, just as it had following the bank panic of the 1930s. Although the details of the steps taken during the crisis itself are too complex to go into here, we can briefly list several key actions:

- In March 2008, the Fed extended its role as a lender of last resort to investment banks by allowing them to receive discount loans, which had been previously available only to commercial banks.
- In September 2008, the Fed began lending to non-financial corporations—such as General Electric and IBM—for the first time since the Great Depression by buying commercial paper issued by those firms. Commercial paper is a security that is the corporate equivalent of a U.S. Treasury bill.
- The U.S. Treasury and the Fed took steps to help a number of financial firms—including Bear Stearns in March 2008 and AIG, the country's largest insurance company, in September 2008—by lending to them or by arranging for them to be merged with other firms.
- In October 2008, Congress passed the *Troubled Asset Relief Program (TARP)*, under which the U.S. Treasury purchased stock in a large number of banks, thereby providing them with new capital in order to increase their stability and making them more likely to make loans to households and firms.

In addition to these temporary policies during the crisis itself, Congress attempted more permanent reform by passing in July 2010 the Wall Street Reform and Consumer Protection Act, often referred to as the *Dodd-Frank Act*. The act reflected the views of some economists and policymakers that the financial crisis had three main causes:

1. Insufficient federal regulation of the shadow banking system
2. Adverse consequences from the failure of large financial firms, sometimes called the *too-big-to-fail problem*
3. Excessive risk taking by commercial banks and other financial intermediaries

Accordingly, the Dodd-Frank Act was intended to increase regulatory control over the shadow banking system and, more generally, to reduce financial risk taking. Some key provisions of the act are:

- Creation of the Consumer Financial Protection Bureau, housed in the Federal Reserve, which has the authority to write rules intended to protect consumers in their borrowing and investing activities.
- Establishment of the Financial Stability Oversight Council, which includes representatives from all the major federal financial regulatory bodies, including the Fed and the FDIC. The council is intended to identify and act on significant risks to the financial system.
- Granting the FDIC authority to close insolvent shadow banks, similar to the authority it already possessed to close insolvent commercial banks.
- Requiring that certain complex financial securities known as financial derivatives be traded on exchanges, such as the Chicago Board of Trade, rather than privately between financial firms.
- Implementing the "Volcker Rule" to restrict most trading of securities by commercial banks.

Government Policy Toward Failing Financial Firms: "Bailouts" and Moral Hazard
Should government policymakers worry about the failure of a large financial firm? If you open a car dealership, restaurant, or hardware store, you accept the risk of losing your investment if the business fails, just as you will gain the profits if the business succeeds. In the United States, many businesses fail—and many new businesses are started—every day. But at least since the founding of the Federal Reserve in 1913, the government has decided that allowing commercial banks to fail may sometimes cause wider problems in the economy and that intervening to save a bank that would otherwise fail may be justified.

When Congress established the FDIC in 1934, it reduced the likelihood that deposit withdrawals would set off a series of commercial bank runs and lead to asset deflation and bank failures. Congress did not extend government insurance, like that offered by the FDIC, to other financial firms. As a result, financial firms such as the investment banks Bear Stearns and Lehman Brothers remained vulnerable to the equivalent of a bank run if lenders decided not to renew their short-term loans to these firms. During 2008, as prices of securities backed by subprime mortgages declined, many financial firms had difficulties. The federal government was left with the policy dilemma of either helping these firms, thereby limiting the cycle of asset deflation and averting a financial crisis, or allowing them to fail, with the owners and investors in these firms bearing the full consequences of the decisions made by the firms' managers.

Some economists argued that helping financial firms is the equivalent of insuring them against losses. Moral hazard is a common problem with insurance because once people are insured, they often change their behavior in a way that makes the insured event more likely to occur. For example, a business that has a fire insurance policy may decide not to install an expensive fire sprinkler system in its warehouse. But not having a sprinkler system increases the chances of a disastrous fire. Or with a generous flood insurance policy, you might decide to build the beach house you always wanted in a hurricane-prone area. Similarly, if the result of bad investment decisions is bankruptcy, managers of financial firms may be more cautious than if they believe the federal government has effectively insured them against bankruptcy. If the federal government's policies increase moral hazard and lead to more risk taking, the financial system may become less stable.

Policymakers continue to struggle with the trade-off between increasing moral hazard and accepting the consequences of allowing large financial firms to fail.

Making the Connection

Fed Policy During Panics, Then and Now: The Collapse of the Bank of United States in 1930 and the Collapse of Lehman Brothers in 2008

Although the Federal Reserve was established in 1913 to stop bank panics, in fact, the worst bank panic in U.S. history occurred during the early 1930s, and the Fed did little to stop it. The panic occurred during the Great Depression, which began in August 1929. By the fall of 1930, many commercial banks found that their assets had declined significantly in value, as both households and firms had difficulty repaying loans. In October 1930, the Bank of United States, a private commercial bank in New York City, experienced a bank run. It appealed to the Fed for loans that would allow it to survive the liquidity crisis caused by deposit withdrawals. The term moral hazard had not yet been coined, but Fed officials were clearly familiar with the concept because they declined to save the Bank of United States on the grounds that the bank's managers had made risky mortgage loans to borrowers investing in apartment houses and other commercial property in New York City. The Fed believed that saving the Bank of United States would reward the poor business decisions of the bank's managers. The Fed also doubted that if the bank's assets were sold, the amount raised would be sufficient to pay off depositors.

Although the Fed's reasons for failing to save the Bank of United States were legitimate, there were adverse financial consequences for the entire economy. When the bank failed, the faith of depositors in the commercial banking system was shaken. Because deposit insurance did not yet exist, depositors were afraid that if they delayed withdrawing their money and their bank failed, they would receive only part of their money back—and only after a delay. Further waves of bank failures took place over the next few years, culminating in the "bank holiday" of 1933, when President Franklin Roosevelt ordered every bank in the country shut down for a week so that emergency measures could be taken to restore the banking system. Although the Fed's actions during the bank panic had avoided the moral hazard problem, they resulted in a catastrophic meltdown of the U.S. financial system, which most economists believe significantly worsened and lengthened the Great Depression.

The figure below shows for each year from 1920 through 1939 the number of banks that were forced to temporarily or permanently suspend allowing depositors to withdraw funds. The figure reveals that bank runs in the United States went from being fairly common in the 1920s, to reaching very high levels in the early 1930s, to practically disappearing after the FDIC was established in 1934. In fact, the Fed acted as a lender of last resort infrequently over the next 75 years.

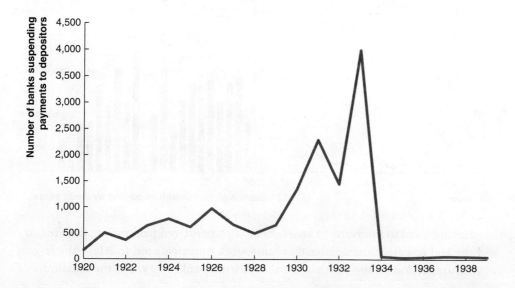

In 2008, the Fed was once again confronted with the dilemma of how to deal with the failure of a large financial firm. In the spring, Bear Stearns, a large investment bank, ran into difficulty because the declining prices for many of the mortgage-backed securities it held made other financial firms reluctant to lend it money. The Fed and the U.S. Treasury responded by arranging for JPMorgan Chase, a commercial bank, to purchase Bear Stearns for a very low price. That fall, though, fear of increasing moral hazard led the Fed and the Treasury to allow Lehman Brothers, also a large investment bank, to declare bankruptcy.

The Lehman Brothers bankruptcy had an immediate negative effect on financial markets, as the graphs below illustrate. Panel (a) shows the difference between the three-month London Interbank Offered Rate (LIBOR), which is the interest rate at which banks can borrow from each other, and the interest rate on three-month Treasury bills. The difference in these two interest rates is called the TED spread and provides a measure of how risky banks consider loans to each other compared with loans to the U.S. government. After fluctuating in a narrow range around 0.5 percentage point during 2005, 2006, and the first half of 2007, the TED spread rose as problems in financial markets began in the second half of 2007, and then it soared to record levels immediately following the failure of Lehman Brothers. Panel (b) shows the decline in issuing of securities backed by credit card debt. Issuance of these securities plummeted to zero in the last quarter of 2008. Because banks could not sell new credit card loans, they became reluctant to issue new credit cards or increase credit limits on existing accounts. These measures made it more difficult for households to finance their spending. Many on Wall Street saw the bankruptcy of Lehman Brothers as such a watershed in the financial crisis that they began to refer to events as having happened either "before Lehman" (declared bankruptcy) or "after Lehman."

MyEconLab Real-time data

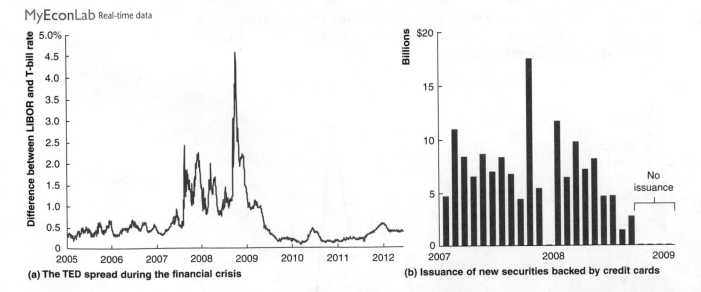

(a) The TED spread during the financial crisis

(b) Issuance of new securities backed by credit cards

Having failed to intervene to save Lehman Brothers from bankruptcy, the Treasury and the Fed reversed course later that same week to provide aid to AIG—the largest U.S. insurance company—that saved the firm from bankruptcy. For the remainder of

2008 and into 2009, the Treasury and the Fed appeared to have set aside concerns about moral hazard as they gave no indication that they would allow another large financial firm to fail. It remains to be seen whether the failure of Lehman Brothers will be viewed as being as significant an event in the 2007–2009 financial crisis as the failure of the Bank of United States was in the 1929–1933 crisis.

Sources: TED spread: Authors' calculations from British Bankers' Association data and Federal Reserve data; credit card securitization: Peter Eavis, "The Fed Goes for Brokerage," *Wall Street Journal*, March 4, 2009; and U.S. Federal Reserve System, Board of Governors, "Bank Suspensions, 1921–1936," *Federal Reserve Bulletin*, Vol. 23, September 1937, p. 907.

See related problem 2.8 at the end of the chapter.

The Money Market and the Risk Structure and Term Structure of Interest Rates

3.3

Learning Objective

Explain how interest rates are determined in the money market and understand the risk structure and the term structure of interest rates.

The interest rate is a key economic variable in the financial system. You encounter interest rates on your savings accounts, your credit card payments, and your student loans. In this section, we first look at interest rates using the *money market model* (which is also called the *liquidity preference model*). To better understand interest rates, we then look more closely at how to calculate one key set of interest rates: the interest rates on bonds.

The Demand and Supply of Money

The money market model focuses on how the interaction of the demand and supply for money determines the short-term nominal interest rate.[4] Recall that the nominal interest rate is the stated interest rate on a loan or bond, without correction for inflation. Short term means that the loan or bond will mature, or be paid off, in one year or less. Figure 3.4 shows the demand curve for money. The nominal interest rate is on the vertical axis, and the quantity of money is on the horizontal axis. Here we are using the M1 definition of money, which equals currency in circulation plus checking account deposits.

To understand why the demand curve for money in Figure 3.4 is downward sloping, consider that households and firms have a choice between holding money and holding other financial assets, such as U.S. Treasury bills. Money has one particularly desirable characteristic: It is perfectly liquid, so you can use it to buy goods, services, or financial assets. Money also has one undesirable characteristic: The currency in your wallet earns no interest, and the money in your checking account earns either no interest or very little interest. Alternatives to money, such as U.S. Treasury bills, pay interest, but you have to sell them if you want to use the funds to buy goods or services. When nominal interest rates rise on financial assets such as U.S. Treasury bills, the amount of interest that households and firms lose by holding money increases. When nominal interest rates fall, the amount of interest households and firms lose by holding money decreases.

---

[4]The money market model was first discussed by the British economist John Maynard Keynes in his book *The General Theory of Employment, Interest, and Money*, which was published in 1936. Keynes referred to the model as the "liquidity preference model," a term that some economists still use. Note one possible source of confusion: Economists sometimes also use the phrase "money market" to refer to the market for bonds, such as Treasury bills, that mature in one year or less.

Figure 3.4

The Demand for Money

The money demand curve slopes downward because lower nominal interest rates cause households and firms to switch from financial assets such as U.S. Treasury bills to money. All other things being equal, a fall in the interest rate from 4% to 3% will increase the quantity of money demanded from $900 billion to $950 billion. An increase in the interest rate will decrease the quantity of money demanded.

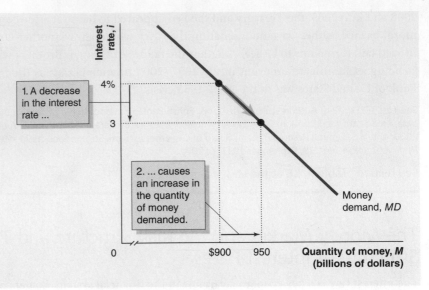

Remember that *opportunity cost* is what you have to forgo to engage in an activity. The nominal interest rate is the opportunity cost of holding money.

We now have an explanation for why the demand curve for money slopes downward: When nominal interest rates on Treasury bills and other financial assets are low, the opportunity cost of holding money is low, so the quantity of money demanded by households and firms will be high. When interest rates are high, the opportunity cost of holding money will be high, so the quantity of money demanded will be low. In Figure 3.4, a decrease in interest rates from 4% to 3% causes the quantity of money demanded by households and firms to rise from $900 billion to $950 billion.

Shifts in the Money Demand Curve

You know from your principles of economics course that the demand curve for a good is drawn holding constant all variables, other than the price, that affect the willingness of consumers to buy the good. Changes in variables other than the price cause the demand curve to shift. Similarly, the demand curve for money is drawn holding constant all variables, other than the interest rate, that affect the willingness of households and firms to hold money. Changes in variables other than the interest rate cause the demand curve to shift. The two most important variables that cause the money demand curve to shift are:

1. Real GDP
2. The price level

An increase in real GDP means that the amount of buying and selling of goods and services will increase. Households and firms need more money to conduct these transactions, so the quantity of money households and firms want to hold increases at each interest rate, shifting the money demand curve to the right. A decrease in real GDP decreases the quantity of money demanded at each interest rate, shifting the money demand curve to the left. A higher price level increases the quantity of money required for a given amount of buying and selling. Eighty years ago, for example, when the price level was much lower, a salary of $30 per week put you in the middle class, and you

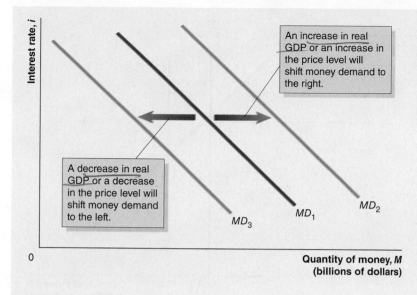

Figure 3.5

Shifts in the Money Demand Curve

Changes in real GDP or the price level cause the money demand curve to shift. An increase in real GDP or an increase in the price level will cause the money demand curve to shift to the right, from MD_1 to MD_2. A decrease in real GDP or a decrease in the price level will cause the money demand curve to shift to the left, from MD_1 to MD_3.

could purchase a new car for $500. As a result, the quantity of money demanded by households and firms was much lower than it is today, even adjusting for the effect of the lower real GDP and the smaller population of those years. An increase in the price level increases the quantity of money demanded at each interest rate, shifting the money demand curve to the right. A decrease in the price level decreases the quantity of money demanded at each interest rate, shifting the money demand curve to the left.

Figure 3.5 illustrates shifts in the money demand curve. An increase in real GDP or an increase in the price level will cause the money demand curve to shift to the right, from MD_1 to MD_2. A decrease in real GDP or a decrease in the price level will cause the money demand curve to shift to the left, from MD_1 to MD_3.

Equilibrium in the Money Market

Even though central banks, including the U.S. Federal Reserve, do not have complete control of the supply of money (see Chapter 12), at this point, we assume that the Federal Reserve is able to set the supply of money at whatever level it chooses. Therefore, the money supply curve is a vertical line, and changes in the nominal interest rate have no effect on the quantity of money supplied. Figure 3.6 includes both the money demand and money supply curves to show how the equilibrium nominal interest rate is determined in the money market. Just as in other markets, equilibrium in the money market occurs where the money demand curve crosses the money supply curve. If the Fed increases the money supply, the money supply curve will shift to the right, and the equilibrium interest rate will fall. Figure 3.6 shows that when the Fed increases the money supply from $900 billion to $950 billion, the money supply curve shifts to the right, from MS_1 to MS_2, and the equilibrium interest rate falls from 4% to 3%.

In the money market, the adjustment from one equilibrium to another equilibrium is a little different from the adjustment in the market for a good. In Figure 3.6, the money

Figure 3.6

The Effect on the Interest Rate When the Fed Increases the Money Supply

When the Fed increases the money supply from $900 billion to $950 billion, the money supply curve shifts to the right from MS_1 to MS_2, and the equilibrium nominal interest rate falls from 4% to 3%.

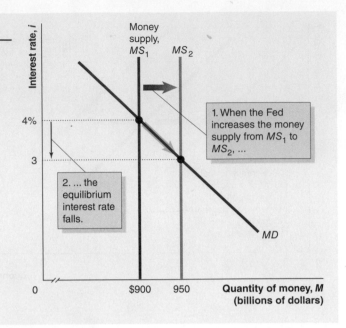

1. When the Fed increases the money supply from MS_1 to MS_2, ...

2. ... the equilibrium interest rate falls.

review

market is initially in equilibrium, with an interest rate of 4% and a money supply of $900 billion. When the Fed increases the money supply by $50 billion, households and firms have more money than they want to hold at an interest rate of 4%. What do households and firms do with the extra $50 billion? They are most likely to use the money to buy short-term financial assets, such as Treasury bills. Short-term financial assets have maturities of one year or less. By buying short-term assets, households and firms drive up their prices and drive down their interest rates. We will discuss this inverse relationship between the prices of financial assets and interest rates in more detail in the next section. Table 3.3 summarizes the key factors that cause shifts in the demand and supply of money.

Calculating Bond Interest Rates and the Concept of Present Value

Because interest rates on bonds are particularly important in the financial system, we spend the remainder of this chapter discussing the most important aspects of bond interest rates. In particular, we look at the relationship between bond prices and interest rates.

The relationship between bond prices and interest rates depends on an important concept called **present value**, which is the value today of funds that will be received in the future. Most people value funds they already have more highly than funds they will not receive until sometime in the future. Consider the following situation: You make a $1,000 loan to a friend who promises to pay back the money in one year. There are three key facts you need to take into account when deciding how much interest to charge him: (1) by the time your friend pays you back, prices are likely to have risen, so you will be able to buy fewer goods and services than you could have if you had spent the money rather than lending it; (2) your friend might not pay you back—in other words, he might default on the loan; and (3) during the period of the loan, your friend can use your money, and you can't. If he uses the money to buy a computer, he gets the use of the computer for a

Present value The value today of funds that will be received in the future.

Table 3.3 Summary of the Money Market Model

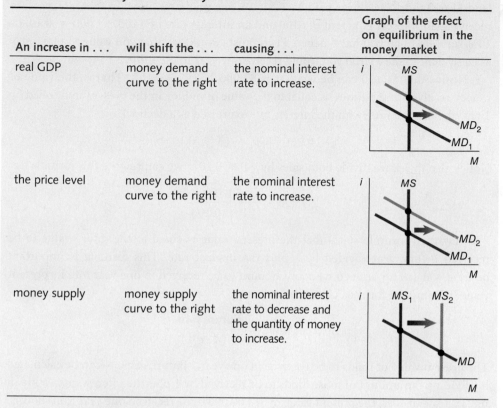

An increase in . . .	will shift the . . .	causing . . .	Graph of the effect on equilibrium in the money market
real GDP	money demand curve to the right	the nominal interest rate to increase.	
the price level	money demand curve to the right	the nominal interest rate to increase.	
money supply	money supply curve to the right	the nominal interest rate to decrease and the quantity of money to increase.	

year, while you wait for him to pay you back. In other words, lending your money involves the *opportunity cost* of not being able to spend it on goods and services today.

So, we can think of the interest you charge on the loan as being the result of:

1. Compensation for inflation
2. Compensation for default risk—the chance that the borrower will not pay back the loan
3. Compensation for the opportunity cost of waiting to spend your money

Notice two things about this list. First, even if lenders are convinced that there will be no inflation during the period of the loan and even if they believe there is no chance the borrower will default, lenders will still charge interest to compensate them for waiting for their money to be paid back. Second, these three factors vary from person to person and from loan to loan. For instance, during periods when lenders believe that inflation will be high, they will charge more interest. Lenders will also charge more interest to borrowers who seem more likely to default. The reward that lenders require for waiting to be repaid can also vary across time and across lenders.

The longer you have to wait to receive a payment, the less value it will have for you: $1,000 you will receive in one year is worth less to you than $1,000 you already have, and $1,000 you will not receive for two years is worth less to you than $1,000 you will receive in one year.

Let's apply the concept of present value to a loan. Suppose that you are willing to lend $1,000 today if you are paid back $1,100 one year from now. In this case, you are receiving an interest payment of $100 and an interest rate of $100/$1,000 = 0.10, or 10%, on the $1,000 you have loaned. Economists would say that you value $1,000 today as equivalent to the $1,100 you would receive one year in the future.

Notice that $1,100 can be written as $1,000 × (1 + 0.10). That is, the value of money received in the future is equal to the value of money in the present multiplied by 1 plus the interest rate, with the interest rate expressed as a decimal, or:

$$\$1,100 = 1,000 \times (1 + 0.10).$$

Notice also that if we divide both sides by (1 + 0.10), we can rewrite this formula as:

$$\$1,000 = \frac{\$1,100}{(1 + 0.10)}.$$

The rewritten formula states that the present value is equal to the future value to be received in one year divided by 1 plus the interest rate. This formula is important because you can use it to convert any amount to be received in one year into its present value. Writing the formula generally, we have:

$$\text{Present value} = \frac{\text{Future value}_1}{(1 + i)}.$$

The present value of funds to be received in one year—Future value$_1$—can be calculated by dividing the amount of those funds to be received by 1 plus the interest rate. With an interest rate of 10%, the present value of $1,000,000 to be received one year from now is:

$$\frac{\$1,000,000}{(1 + 0.10)} = \$909,090.91.$$

This is a very useful way of calculating the value today of funds that will be received in one year. But bonds often involve promises to pay funds over many years.

Present Value and the Prices of Stocks and Bonds

It is easy to expand the present value formula to cover multiple years. Suppose, for example, that you are willing to loan money for two years if you receive 10% interest in each of the two years. That is, you are lending $1,000, which at 10% interest will grow to $1,100 after one year, and you are agreeing to loan that $1,100 out for a second year at 10% interest. So, after two years, you will be paid back $1,100 × (1 + 0.10), or $1,210. Or:

$$\$1,210 = \$1,000 \times (1 + 0.10) \times (1 + 0.10),$$

or:

$$\$1,210 = \$1,000 \times (1 + 0.10)^2.$$

This formula can be rewritten as:

$$\$1,000 = \frac{\$1,210}{(1 + 0.10)^2}.$$

To put this formula in words, the $1,210 you receive two years from now has a present value equal to $1,210 divided by the quantity 1 plus the interest rate squared. We can generalize the concept to say that the present value of funds to be received n years in the future—whether n is 1, 20, or 85 does not matter—equals the amount of the funds to be received divided by the quantity 1 plus the interest rate raised to the nth power. For instance, with an interest rate of 10%, the present value of $1,000,000 to be received 25 years in the future is:

$$\text{Present value} = \frac{\$1,000,000}{(1 + 0.10)^{25}} = \$92,296.$$

Or, more generally:

$$\text{Present value} = \frac{\text{Future value}_n}{(1 + i)^n},$$

where Future value$_n$ represents funds that will be received in n years. Economists use the term **time value of money** to refer to the fact that the value of a payment changes depending on when the payment is received.

Time value of money
The way the value of a payment changes depending on when the payment is received.

Notice that present value depends on the interest rate used. If we change the interest rate from 10% to 5%, the present value of $1,000,000 to be received 25 years in the future changes to:

$$\text{Present value} = \frac{\$1,000,000}{(1 + 0.05)^{25}} = \$295,303.$$

high risk

This example illustrates an important fact: *The higher the interest rate, the lower the present value of a future payment, and the lower the interest rate, the higher the present value of a future payment.*

low risk

Anyone who buys a financial asset, such as a share of stock or a bond, is really buying a promise to receive certain payments in the future. Investors receive the interest on a bond in the form of a coupon, which is a flat dollar amount that is paid each year and that does not change during the life of the bond. Similarly, investors receive a dividend payment from a firm when they buy a firm's stock. The price investors are willing to pay for a bond or a stock (or another financial asset) should be equal to the value of the payments they will receive as a result of owning the bond or stock. Because most of the coupon payments on a bond or dividend payments on a stock will be received in the future, it is the present value of the payments that matters. In other words: *The price of a financial asset should equal the present value of the payments an investor expects to receive from owning that asset.*

Take the case of a five-year coupon bond that pays an annual coupon of $60 and has a face value of $1,000, which the owner of the bond will receive when the bond matures in five years. The expression for the price, P, of the bond is the sum of the present values of the six payments the investor will receive:

$$P = \frac{\$60}{(1 + i)} + \frac{\$60}{(1 + i)^2} + \frac{\$60}{(1 + i)^3} + \frac{\$60}{(1 + i)^4} + \frac{\$60}{(1 + i)^5} + \frac{\$1,000}{(1 + i)^5}.$$

We can use this reasoning to arrive at a general expression for the price of a bond that makes coupon payments, C, has a face value, FV, and matures in n years:

$$P = \frac{C}{(1 + i)} + \frac{C}{(1 + i)^2} + \frac{C}{(1 + i)^3} + \cdots + \frac{C}{(1 + i)^n} + \frac{FV}{(1 + i)^n}.$$

The dots indicate that we have omitted the terms representing the years between the third year and the nth year—which could be the tenth, twentieth, thirtieth, or other, year.

Because the present value of a payment depends on the interest rate used to calculate it, we can say that: *An increase in interest rates reduces the prices of existing financial assets, and a decrease in interest rates increases the prices of existing financial assets.* Consider a simple example: U.S. Treasury bills are discount bonds, which means they do not pay a coupon but are sold at a discount to their face value. Suppose, for instance, that you pay a price of $961.54 for a $1,000 face value one-year Treasury bill. So, in exchange for your investment of $961.54, you will receive $1,000 from the U.S. Treasury in one year. The interest rate, i, on the Treasury bill is equal to the $38.46 $(= \$1,000 - \$961.54)$ in interest you will receive divided by the price you paid (multiplied by 100):

$$i = \left(\frac{\$1,000 - \$961.54}{\$961.54}\right) \times 100 = 4\%.$$

Suppose that the day after you purchase your Treasury bill, investors decide they will only buy one-year Treasury bills if they receive an interest rate of 5% on their investment. Why might investors increase the interest rate they require on Treasury bills? Possibly, new information might convince investors that inflation will be higher during the year than they had previously expected. With a higher inflation rate, the nominal interest rate must rise to keep the real interest rate unchanged. If the interest rate rises to 5%, how will that affect the price at which you could sell your Treasury bill to another investor? The price will have to fall enough so that another investor would receive an interest rate of 5% from buying your bond. We can calculate that price by noting that the new price will be the present value of $1,000 to be received in one year with an interest rate of 5%[5]:

$$\text{Price} = \frac{\$1,000}{(1 + 0.05)} = \$952.38.$$

As a result of the market interest rate for Treasury bills having risen from 4% to 5%, the price of your Treasury bill—should you decide to sell it—has fallen from $961.54 to $952.38. If the price of an asset increases, the increase is a *capital gain*. If the price of an asset decreases, the decrease is a *capital loss*. In this case, you have suffered a capital loss of $9.16. If the market interest rate for Treasury bills had fallen, say, to 3%, then the price of your Treasury bill would have risen, and you would have received a capital gain.

---

[5]Technically, we should take into account that one day has passed since you bought your Treasury bill, which means that anyone buying your Treasury bill will have to wait only 364 days to receive the $1,000 payment from the Treasury. Because making this adjustment would have only a tiny effect on the result, we ignore it in the calculation.

Solved Problem 3.3

Interest Rates and Treasury Bond Prices

The U.S. Treasury issues a variety of securities, including Treasury notes, which have maturities from 2 years to 10 years, and Treasury bonds, which have maturities of 30 years. Suppose that a Treasury bond was issued 28 years ago, so it will mature in 2 years.

If the bond pays a coupon of $45 per year and will make a final par value, or face value, payment of $1,000 at maturity, what is its price if the relevant market interest rate is 5%? What is its price if the relevant market interest rate is 10%?

Solving the Problem

Step 1 **Review the chapter material.** This problem is about the relationship between interest rates and bond prices, so you may want to review the section "Present Value and the Prices of Stocks and Bonds," which begins on page 92.

Step 2 **Explain what determines the price of a Treasury bond.** The price of a financial asset should equal the present value of the payments to be received from owning that asset. So, the price of the Treasury bond we are considering here should be equal to the present value of the two coupon payments and the face value payment that the owner of the bond would receive.

Step 3 **Determine the price of the Treasury bond if the interest rate is 5%.** To determine the price of the bond, calculate the sum of the present values of the three payments an owner of the bond would receive:

$$\text{Bond Price} = \frac{\$45}{(1 + 0.05)} + \frac{\$45}{(1 + 0.05)^2} + \frac{\$1,000}{(1 + 0.05)^2}$$

$$= \$990.70.$$

Step 4 **Determine the price of the Treasury bond if the interest rate is 10%.** Substituting 10% for 5% in the expression in step 3, we have:

$$\text{Bond Price} = \frac{\$45}{(1 + 0.10)} + \frac{\$45}{(1 + 0.10)^2} + \frac{\$1,000}{(1 + 0.10)^2}$$

$$= \$904.55.$$

Notice that increasing the interest rate reduces the price of the bond. This result confirms the general point that an increase in interest rates reduces the prices of existing financial assets.

See related problem 3.6 at the end of the chapter.

The Economy's Many Interest Rates

For simplicity, economists refer to "the" interest rate in the economy, as if there were only one interest rate. In fact, of course, there are many interest rates. In the lobby of your local bank, you will probably find one poster showing the interest rate you will receive if you put money in a certificate of deposit and another poster showing the (higher) interest rate you will pay if you take out a car loan. We have already seen that the interest rates firms and governments pay (and investors receive) on bonds play an important role in the economy. In this section, we explore why the interest rates on some bonds are very different from the interest rates on other bonds.

Panel (a) of Figure 3.7 shows the interest rates that prevailed on July 20, 2012, for four bonds that all mature in 2017. Economists refer to the relationship among interest rates on bonds that all mature at the same time, such as those shown in panel (a), as the **risk structure of interest rates**. The relationship among interest rates on bonds that have the same characteristics except for having different maturities is called the **term structure of interest rates**. A common way to analyze the term structure is by looking at the *Treasury yield curve*, which is the relationship on a particular day among the interest rates on U.S. Treasury bonds with different maturities.

Panel (b) of Figure 3.7 shows the interest rates on July 20, 2012, for Treasury bonds of different maturities. This yield curve shows the typical relationship, with the shorter-maturity bonds having lower interest rates than the longer maturity bonds. The interest rates on the Treasury bonds shown are very low compared with earlier periods. For example, the interest rate on the 30-year bond is only 2.55% compared with an interest rate of more than 13.5% in 1984 and 5.25% in 2007. The low interest rates in 2012 reflected the severity of the 2007–2009 recession, the relative weakness of the expansion that followed the recession, and the steps the Fed had taken to drive down long-term interest rates.

In the next sections, we look more closely at the risk structure and the term structure of interest rates.

The Risk Structure of Interest Rates Investors naturally prefer a higher rate of return on their investments to a lower rate of return. So, everything else being equal, when considering bonds with the same maturity, investors will prefer bonds with higher interest

Risk structure of interest rates The relationship among interest rates on bonds that have different characteristics but the same maturity.

Term structure of interest rates The relationship among the interest rates on bonds that are otherwise similar but that have different maturities.

MyEconLab Real-time data

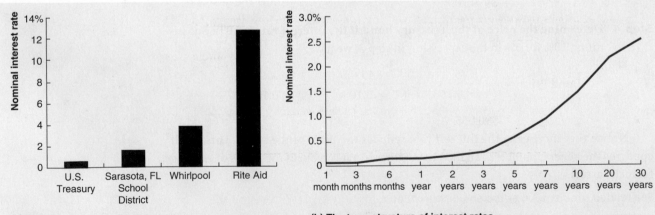

(a) The risk structure of interest rates

(b) The term structure of interest rates

Figure 3.7 The Term Structure and the Risk Structure of Interest Rates

Panel (a) shows an example of the risk structure of interest rates, which is the relationship among interest rates on bonds that all mature at the same time.

Panel (b) shows an example of the term structure of interest rates, which is the relationship among interest rates on bonds that have the same characteristics except for having different maturities.

Sources: Panel (a): Yahoo.com, bond screener; panel (b): U.S. Department of the Treasury, "Daily Treasury Yield Curve Rates."

rates to bonds with lower interest rates. But everything else is usually not equal, because bonds differ in important characteristics. In particular, investors are interested in the following characteristics of bonds:

- *Default risk.* Default risk refers to the chance that the firm or government issuing the bond will declare bankruptcy and stop paying interest on the bond at some time before it matures. Because the bond issued by Rite Aid pharmacy shown in panel (a) of Figure 3.7 has a relatively high default risk, it also has a high interest rate. The Treasury bond shown in panel (a) has a very low default risk, which is one reason it has a low interest rate. The bond issued by Whirlpool has a lower default risk than the Rite Aid bond, but a higher default risk than the Treasury bond.
- *Liquidity.* As we have seen, investors can buy and sell bonds in secondary markets. The more buyers and sellers there are in a market for a bond, the easier it is for an investor to sell the bond and the more liquid the bond is. Another reason Treasury bonds have low interest rates is that they are very liquid.
- *Tax treatment of interest.* The interest you earn from owning a bond is usually counted as part of your taxable income. But the government does not treat all interest the same. For example, the interest on bonds issued by state and local governments, called *municipal bonds*, is usually not taxed. Because the interest on the bond issued by the Sarasota, Florida school district shown in panel (a) of Figure 3.7 is not subject to tax, the interest rate on the bond is low.

Investors prefer to receive a high interest rate on a bond, but they also prefer the bond to have low default risk, high liquidity, and favorable tax treatment. In general, bonds with unfavorable characteristics—for example, higher default risk—have higher interest rates to compensate investors for these unfavorable characteristics. Bonds with favorable characteristics have lower interest rates.

The Term Structure of Interest Rates Panel (b) of Figure 3.7 illustrates the term structure of interest rates by showing the interest rates on bonds issued by the Treasury. One mystery of the term structure is why an investor would be willing to buy a one-month Treasury bill with an interest rate of only 0.07% when the investor could have purchased a 30-year Treasury bond with an interest rate of 2.55%. To understand why an investor might be perfectly rational in making this decision, consider the following simple example. Suppose you intend to invest $1,000 for two years. You are weighing two options:

Option 1. Buying a bond that matures in two years—a two-year bond
Option 2. Buying a one-year bond, and when it matures in one year, investing your money in another one-year bond

According to the *expectations theory* of the term structure of interest rates, the relationship between the interest rate on the one-year bond and the interest rate on the two-year bond should be such that the *average* of the interest rate on the current one-year bond and the interest *expected* on a one-year bond one year from now should equal the interest rate on the two-year bond. For example, the following information would be consistent with the expectations theory:

1. Interest rate on the one-year bond today: 4%
2. Interest rate investors expect on the one-year bond one year from now: 6%

3. Interest rate (per year) on the two-year bond today:

$$5\% = \left(\frac{4\% + 6\%}{2}\right).$$

The logic of the expectations theory is straightforward: If an investor intends to invest over a period of years, the investor has the choice of buying one bond with a maturity equal to the desired period of investment or a sequence of shorter-term bonds. The expectations theory holds that because investors have no reason to prefer buying a long-term bond to buying a series of short-term bonds, competition among investors will ensure that they receive the same expected return either way they invest. To see why the expected returns must be equal, consider what would happen if, for example, investors expected to receive a higher return from Option 2 (buying two one-year bonds). In that case, investors would increase their demand for one-year bonds. This increased demand would drive up the price of one-year bonds, and—because bond prices and interest rates move in opposite directions—drive down their interest rate. Eventually, the interest rate on the one-year bond would fall to the point where investors would expect to receive the same return from pursuing either strategy.

We now have an explanation for why investors would buy a one-month Treasury bill with an interest rate of 0.07% when they could buy a 30-year Treasury bond with an interest rate of 2.55%: When interest rates on long-term bonds are higher than interest rates on short-term bonds, investors must be expecting that interest rates on short-term bonds will be higher in the future. In other words, an *upward-sloping yield curve*, such as the one shown in panel (b) of Figure 3.7, reflects the expectations of investors that short-term interest rates will be higher in the future. Similarly, if the yield curve was downward-sloping—with interest rates on short-term bonds being *higher* than interest rates on long-term bonds—investors must be expecting short-term interest rates will be lower in the future.

The expectations theory does not completely explain the term structure of interest rates because it fails to take into account the important fact that long-term bonds are riskier than short-term bonds. The risk involved here is not default risk but *interest-rate risk*. **Interest-rate risk** refers to the risk that the price of a financial asset will fluctuate in response to changes in market interest rates. For instance, if you own a Treasury bond with an interest rate of 4% and new Treasury bonds are issued with the same maturity but with an interest rate of 6%, the price at which you could sell your bond to other investors will fall. This fall in price would be necessary to compensate investors for buying a bond with a lower interest rate than newly issued bonds.

Although all bonds are subject to interest-rate risk, the longer the term of the bond, the greater the risk. We explain more completely why the extent of interest-rate risk varies with the maturity of a bond in the appendix to this chapter, but we can offer a basic explanation here: If you own a 30-year bond with an interest rate of 4%, and newly issued 30-year bonds have interest rates of 6%, then any investor you sold your bond to would be receiving a lower-than-market interest rate for 30 years. An investor would be willing to do this only if you offered to sell the bond at a significantly lower price. But if you sold a one-year bond, the buyer would be receiving a lower-than-market interest rate for only one year and would be willing to buy the bond with a proportionally smaller price cut.

We can conclude that investors are exposed to greater interest-rate risk when they buy long-term bonds than when they buy short-term bonds. So, we expect that investors will be willing to buy long-term bonds issued by the Treasury—or anyone else—only

Interest-rate risk The risk that the price of a financial asset will fluctuate in response to changes in market interest rates.

if the interest rate is higher than on a short-term bond. The **term premium** is the additional interest investors require in order to be willing to buy a long-term bond rather than a comparable sequence of short-term bonds.

We now have a more complete explanation for the term structure of interest rates. (This more complete explanation is often referred to as the *liquidity premium theory*.) Long-term interest rates are the average of expected short-term interest rates *plus* a term premium. For example, assume that the term premium for a two-year bond is 0.25%. If the interest rate on the current one-year bond is 4%, and the expected interest rate on the one-year bond next year is 6%, then the interest rate on the two-year bond will be 5.25%. Or:

Term premium The additional interest investors require in order to be willing to buy a long-term bond rather than a comparable sequence of short-term bonds.

Interest rate on two-year bond

$$= \left(\frac{\text{Interest rate on one-year bond today } + \text{ Interest rate expected on one-year bond next year}}{2} \right)$$

$+$ Term premium,

or:

$$5.25\% = \left(\frac{4\% + 6\%}{2} \right) + 0.25\%.$$

The term premium explains why the yield curve is typically upward sloping, like the one in panel (b) of Figure 3.7: Because investors require a term premium to buy long-term bonds, the interest rates on long-term bonds will be above the interest rates on short-term bonds not only when investors expect future short-term rates to be higher, but also when investors expect future short-term rates to be constant or even when they expect them to be somewhat lower than current short-term rates. The yield curve will be downward sloping only when investors expect future short-term rates to be significantly lower than current short-term rates.

Both the term structure and the risk structure of interest rates play important roles in the Federal Reserve's attempts to use monetary policy to affect the levels of real GDP, employment, and prices (see Chapter 12).

Answering the Key Question

Continued from page 64

At the beginning of the chapter, we asked:

"Why did the bursting of the housing bubble that began in 2006 cause the financial system to falter?"

When housing prices began to fall in 2006, home buyers, particularly subprime borrowers, who had bought when prices were near their peak, began to default on their mortgage loans. At first, many economists and policymakers did not think that the defaults would have an effect outside of the housing market. However, it soon became clear that many financial firms had significant investments in mortgage-backed securities that contained subprime mortgages.

As the prices of mortgage-backed securities declined rapidly, many financial firms suffered heavy losses and some were forced into bankruptcy. The problems at these financial firms led to a decline in the flow of funds through the financial system. The Federal Reserve took steps to contain these problems, but it was more than a year before the financial crisis ended. The effects of the financial crisis on the economy continued for several more years.

Key Terms and Problems

Key Terms

3.1 An Overview of the Financial System
Describe the financial system and explain the role it plays in the economy.

Review Questions

1.1 What purpose does the financial system serve?

1.2 What is a financial intermediary? Give three examples of financial intermediaries. What are the three key services that financial intermediaries perform for savers and borrowers?

1.3 Explain the process of securitization. What benefits does securitization of mortgage loans provide for banks? What benefits does securitization provide for people who want to buy a home?

1.4 What are adverse selection and moral hazard? What problems can they cause for the financial system?

Problems and Applications

1.5 For each of the following transactions, identify whether it occurs in a financial market or through a financial intermediary. If the transaction occurs in a financial market, state whether it occurs in a primary or secondary market:

a. A bank makes a mortgage loan to a home buyer.

b. A bank sells a mortgage loan to Fannie Mae.

c. A startup company obtains financing by selling shares of stock to investors.

d. One of the investors in a startup company resells her holding of the company's stock to someone else.

e. The federal government sells Treasury bills at a weekly auction, where they are purchased by a pension fund.

f. A pension fund resells some of its holdings of Treasury bills to a bank.

g. An investor purchases 1,000 shares of Microsoft stock on the NASDAQ stock market.

h. Microsoft issues new stock, which it sells on the NASDAQ.

1.6 For each of the following cases, explain what service the financial intermediary is providing to savers or borrowers: risk sharing, liquidity, or information.

a. A mutual fund allows savers to purchase shares in a large number of firms.

b. A bank takes in small deposits and makes mortgage loans.

c. A life insurance company offers consumers life insurance, auto insurance, and fire insurance.

d. A firm deducts money from its workers' paychecks and contributes the money to a pension fund.

e. An investment bank underwrites a new issue of stock.

1.7 An *Annual Report* for the Federal Reserve Bank of Dallas contained the following observation: "For the most part, we take the financial system's routine workings for granted—until the machinery blows a gasket. Then we scramble to fix it, so the economy can return to the fast lane." Why might most people, including most policymakers, tend to take the workings of the financial system for granted? Why can't the economy run in the "fast lane" if the financial system has "blown a gasket"?
Source: Federal Reserve Bank of Dallas, *Annual Report, 2011*, p. 7.

1.8 Banks typically pay low interest rates on certificates of deposit and other savings accounts. Banks use the funds from certificates of deposit to make car loans and mortgage loans on which they charge much higher rates than they pay on checking accounts. Why do people put their funds in certificates of deposit rather than earning a higher interest rate by lending directly to people who want to buy houses or cars?

1.9 Some low-income countries have no stock market and only a few banks. What would you expect the effect to be on growth in these countries?

1.10 [Related to the Making the Connection on page 68] In 2012, writing in the *Wall Street Journal*, financial analyst Meredith Whitney argued, "Fewer Americans have access to traditional banking services such as checking accounts, consumer loans and credit cards than they did five years ago." Assuming that Whitney is correct, what would be the consequences for individuals and for the economy as a whole of fewer people having access to banking services?
Source: Meredith Whitney, "America's 'Unbanked' Masses," *Wall Street Journal*, February 24, 2012.

1.11 [Related to the Making the Connection on page 71] How does the globalization of financial markets improve the ability of the financial system to provide risk sharing, information, and liquidity?

3.2 **Financial Crises, Government Policy, and the Financial System**
Understand the role of the central bank in stabilizing the financial system.

Review Questions

2.1 What are the main functions performed by a central bank?

2.2 What is a bank run? Are only commercial banks subject to runs? Briefly explain a central bank's role as a lender of last resort in dealing with runs.

2.3 In what sense did the federal government "bail out" financial firms during the 2007–2009 financial crisis? How did the federal government's actions affect the extent of moral hazard in the financial system?

Problems and Applications

2.4 Suppose you purchase a new home for $150,000, making a down payment of 30% and taking out a mortgage on the balance.

a. What is the return on your investment in your home if one year later the price of the home increases by 20%?

b. What is your return if the price of the home decreases by 20%?

c. How would your answers to parts (a) and (b) change if your down payment is only 15%? Explain why the return on your investment changes with the size of your down payment.

2.5 In 2011, Deutsche Bank AG, headquartered in Germany, became the largest bank in Europe by increasing its asset holdings at a time when other European banks were reducing their assets. As a result, Deutsche Bank's leverage increased. A *Bloomberg* article quoted a German banker as saying: "It's understandable: The higher your leverage, the higher the returns when times are good." But the article also noted that: "The higher leverage also makes Deutsche Bank's earnings more volatile and dependent on market swings." Explain why higher leverage results in higher returns "when times are good" and why it also makes "earnings more volatile and dependent on market swings."

Source: Aaron Kirchfeld, Elena Logutenkova, and Nicholas Comfort, "Deutsche Bank No. 1 in Europe as Leverage Hits Valuation," *Bloomberg*, March 27, 2012.

2.6 Checking accounts and savings accounts at banks are insured by the FDIC, up to at least $250,000.

a. Some economists argue that the existence of the FDIC increases the extent of moral hazard in the financial system. Briefly explain whether you agree with this argument.

b. If the FDIC does increase moral hazard, why did Congress set up this agency? How else might the federal government have dealt with the problem of bank panics?

2.7 Nassim Nicholas Taleb, an economist at New York University, argued that employees of financial firms that might be bailed out by the federal government during a financial crisis should not be allowed to receive bonuses. According to Taleb, bankers receive "a bonus if they make short-term profits and a bailout if they go bust." He argues that banning bonuses will reduce the principal–agent problem that affects large financial firms.

a. What is the principal–agent problem?

b. When considering the situation of a large financial firm that might be bailed out by the federal taxpayers, who is the principal, and who is the agent?

c. If Taleb's analysis is correct, how might banning paying bonuses reduce the principal–agent problem?

Source: Nassim Nicholas Taleb, "End Bonuses for Bankers," *New York Times*, November 7, 2011.

2.8 [**Related to the** Making the Connection **on page 84**] Why did the Federal Reserve allow the Bank of United States to fail in 1930? Why did the Federal Reserve allow Lehman Brothers to fail in 2008? Contrast the Fed's actions following the failure of the Bank of United States with its actions following the failure of Lehman Brothers.

2.9 An article in the *New York Times* states:

In the last year and a half, the largest financial institutions have only grown bigger, mainly as a result of government-brokered mergers. They now enjoy borrowing at significantly lower rates than their smaller competitors, a result of the bond markets' implicit assumption that the giant banks are "too big to fail."

a. Why are large banks able to borrow at lower rates than smaller banks?

b. Why does the bond market assume that these banks are too big to fail?

c. What are some of the possible consequences for the banking industry if the too-big-to-fail policy continues?

Source: David M. Herszenhorn and Sewell Chan, "Financial Debate Renews Scrutiny on Banks' Size," *New York Times*, April 21, 2010.

2.10 [**Related to the** Chapter Opener **on page 64**] An article in the *New York Times* in mid-2012 quoted an economist as saying, "The improvement in domestic credit conditions provides a further boost to the outlook for the economic recovery."

a. What are "domestic credit conditions"? What does an improvement in domestic credit conditions mean?

b. Why would an improvement in domestic credit conditions provide a boost for the economy?

Source: Alan Zibel and Jeffrey Sparshott, "Banks Ease Rules on Some Lending," *Wall Street Journal*, April 30, 2012.

3.3 **The Money Market and the Risk Structure and Term Structure of Interest Rates**
Explain how interest rates are determined in the money market and understand the risk structure and the term structure of interest rates.

Review Questions

3.1 Why is the demand for money curve downward sloping? Draw a money demand and supply graph that shows how the Federal Reserve can decrease the short-run nominal interest rate.

3.2 Why is $100 you will receive in one year worth more to you than $100 you will receive in five years? What do economists mean by the "time value of money"?

3.3 What is the difference between the risk structure of interest rates and the term structure of interest rates?

Problems and Applications

3.4 Draw a graph of the money market. Show the effect on the money demand curve, the money supply curve, and the equilibrium nominal interest rate of each of the following:
a. The Fed decreases the money supply.
b. A recession causes real GDP to fall.
c. The price level increases.
d. The Fed increases the money supply at the same time that the price level falls.

3.5 Assume that the interest rate is 10%. Would you prefer to receive: (a) $75 one year from now, (b) $85 two years from now, or (c) $90 three years from now? Would your answer change if the interest rate is 20%?

3.6 [Related to Solved Problem 3.3 on page 95] Suppose that a Treasury bond was issued 27 years ago, so it will mature in three years. If the bond pays a coupon of $50 per year and will make a final face value payment of $1,000 at maturity, what is its price if the relevant market interest rate is 5%? What is its price if the relevant market interest rate is 10%?

3.7 Bonds and loans have interest rates that vary according to how many years until they mature, their risk, their liquidity, and other factors. For each of the following pairs of loans and bonds, explain which would be likely to have the higher interest rate:
a. A balance on a credit card and a car loan
b. A 10-year Treasury bond and a 10-year bond issued by the Ford Motor Company
c. A 1-year U.S. Treasury bill and a 10-year U.S. Treasury note
d. A 1-year personal loan you make to a friend and a 1-year corporate bond

3.8 If you buy a bond issued by your state or local government, you will ordinarily not have to pay tax on the interest payments you receive. Suppose that the federal government decides to raise the tax rate on bonds issued by the Treasury and by corporations. How would this higher tax rate affect the interest rate on municipal bonds as investors buy and sell these bonds in the secondary market?

3.9 The following are data on the Treasury yield curve for July 17, 2012:

Time to maturity	Interest rate
6 months	0.15%
1 year	0.18
2 years	0.25
5 years	0.62
10 years	1.53
30 years	2.59

Given these data, why would an investor have been willing to buy a one-year Treasury bill with an interest rate of only 0.18% when the investor could have bought a 30-year Treasury bond with an interest rate of 2.59%?

Source: U.S. Department of the Treasury, "Daily Treasury Yield Curve Rates," July 17, 2012.

3.10 Suppose that today you observe the following interest rates on bonds with differing times to maturity:

Years to maturity	Interest rate
1 year	1.0%
2 years	3.0
3 years	3.5

a. Assume that the expectations theory is correct, so that there is no term premium for a two-year bond or a three-year bond. Use the information above to calculate the expected interest rate on a one-year bond one year from now and the interest rate on a one-year bond two years from now.

b. Now assume that the liquidity premium theory is correct and that the term premium on the two-year bond is 0.25% and the term premium on the three-year bond is 0.50%. Now calculate the interest rate on a one-year bond one year from now and the interest rate on a one-year bond two years from now.

3.11 Yield curves generally slope upward. A downward-sloping, or "inverted," yield curve is often thought to signal a future recession. Why might this observation be true?

3.12 With a zero-coupon bond, the buyer receives only the face value of the bond at maturity; the bond pays no coupons. Suppose that for a price of $675, you buy a 10-year, zero-coupon bond with a $1,000 face value.

a. What interest rate will you receive over the life of the bond if you hold the bond to maturity?

b. Now suppose that the interest rate on equivalent bonds has risen to 10% after one year. If you decide to sell the bond, what price can you sell it for?

Data Exercises

D3.1: At the Treasury Web site (www.treasury.gov), go to the Resources tab and find Data and Charts Center. Then locate the Daily Treasury Yield Curve Rates.

a. For the most recent date, graph the yield curve. Then explain how yield changes with the maturity of the Treasury security.

b. This site gives about two weeks of data. Is the yield curve changing? How? Can you infer anything about the current state of the economy?

D3.2: Go to www.bloomberg.com. In the Market Data menu towards the top of the page, under Rates and Bonds, find Government Bonds. This section gives yields and the yield curves for the United States, Australia, Brazil, Germany, Hong Kong, Japan, and the United Kingdom. How do the yield curves of the different countries vary?

D3.3: Go to http://www.treasury.gov/initiatives/financial-stability/Pages/default.aspx to find information about the Emergency Economic Stabilization Act of 2008 (EESA). The Troubled Asset Relief Program (TARP) is the best-known so-called government bailout program.

a. How did TARP work?

b. Original estimates of the cost of TARP have fallen as financial institutions have repaid funds. Can you find current figures on the cost of TARP?

c. Do you think that TARP created moral hazard problems for the future? Briefly explain.

D3.4: [Excel exercise] The Federal Reserve Bank of St. Louis offers a wide range of economic data at its Web site, called FRED (research.stlouisfed.org/fred2/). Find the data for U.S. three-month and one-year Treasury bill rates from 1990 to the most recent date available and download these data into an Excel file.

a. What is the average interest rate on each type of Treasury bill over this period?

b. What is the standard deviation? Which series is more volatile?

c. Graph the data. Do the rates move together?

d. Calculate the mean and standard deviation again, but end the series at 2006 rather than the current date. How does this change the mean and standard deviation? Briefly explain.

D3.5: Using data from the St. Louis Federal Reserve (FRED) (http://research.stlouisfed.org/fred2/), analyze nominal interest rates.

a. Find the most recent values from FRED for the following four variables: (1) Moody's Seasoned Aaa Corporate Bond Yield (AAA), the (2) Moody's Seasoned Baa Corporate Bond Yield (BAA), (3) the 3-Month Treasury Bill: Secondary Market Rate (TB3MS), and (4) the 10-Year Treasury Constant Maturity Rate (GS10).

b. Explain whether the relationships among these interest rates are what economic theory would predict.

D3.6: Using data from the St. Louis Federal Reserve (FRED) (http://research.stlouisfed.org/fred2/), analyze changes in mortgage interest rates and interest rates on 10-Year Treasury bond.

a. Find the most recent values and the values from the same month 6 years and 10 years earlier from FRED for the 30-Year Conventional Mortgage Rate (MORTG) and the 10-Year Treasury Constant Maturity Rate (GS10).

b. Using these data, describe what has happened to these long-run interest rates over these periods.

D3.7: Using data from the St. Louis Federal Reserve (FRED) (http://research.stlouisfed.org/fred2/), analyze short-term interest rates and the prime loan rate.

a. Find the most recent values and the values from the same month 6 years and 10 years earlier from FRED for the Bank Prime Loan Rate (MPRIME), the Effective Fed Funds Rate (FEDFUNDS), and the 3-Month Treasury Bill: Secondary Market Rate (TB3MS).

b. Using the data found above, describe what has happened to these short-run interest rates over these periods.

D3.8: Using data from the St. Louis Federal Reserve (FRED) (http://research.stlouisfed.org/fred2/), analyze bond prices and interest rates.

a. Find the most recent values and the values from the same month 1 year and 2 years earlier from FRED for the 1-Year Treasury Bill: Secondary Market Rate (TB1YR).

b. Suppose the 1-Year Treasury bill has a face value of $2,000. Using the interest rates found above, calculate the price of a 1-Year Treasury Bill for each of the 3 periods.

c. From the previous computations, what can you determine about the relationship between bond yields and bond prices?

D3.9: Using data from the St. Louis Federal Reserve (FRED) (http://research.stlouisfed.org/fred2/), analyze interest rates and the yield curve.

a. Find the most recent values from FRED for the following six variables: (1) the 1-Year Treasury Constant Maturity Rate (GS1), (2) the 3-Year Treasury Constant Maturity Rate (GS3), (3) the 5-Year Treasury Constant Maturity Rate (GS5), (4) the 10-Year Treasury Constant Maturity Rate (GS10), (5) the 20-Year Treasury Constant Maturity Rate (GS20), and (6) the 30-Year Treasury Constant Maturity Rate (GS30).

b. Using the data found above, draw the yield curve, explain why it has the shape it does, and describe what is expected to happen to interest rates in the future.

MyEconLab Visit **www.myeconlab.com** to complete these exercises online and get instant feedback. Exercises that update with real-time data are marked with ⦿.

Appendix

More on the Term Structure of Interest Rates

3.A

Learning Objective

Understand the term structure of interest rates.

As we saw in the chapter, the term structure of interest rates is the relationship among interest rates on bonds of different maturities. Because the term structure of interest rates plays an important role in monetary policy, it is useful to look at it more closely. First, consider again the situation you face if you want to invest funds over a two-year period and you are considering whether to pursue a strategy of buying a two-year bond or a strategy of buying a one-year bond today and another one-year bond one year from now. To work out the arithmetic, let's use the following notation, where time t is the present and time $t + 1$ is one year from now:

$$i_{1t} = \text{interest rate on a one-year bond at time } t$$
$$i_{2t} = \text{interest rate (per year) on a two-year bond at time } t$$
$$i_{1t+1}^{e} = \text{interest rate that investors expect on a one-year bond at time } t + 1$$

To take a simple example, let's assume that you are investing \$1. What are the expected returns on a \$1 investment after two years for each strategy? If you buy a two-year bond, your \$1 is worth $\$1 \times (1 + i_{2t})$ after the first year and $\$1 \times (1 + i_{2t}) \times (1 + i_{2t})$ after two years. If you buy two one-year bonds, your \$1 is worth $\$1 \times (1 + i_{1t})$ after the first year, and you expect it will be worth $\$1 \times (1 + i_{1t}) \times (1 + i_{1t+1}^{e})$ after two years. According to the expectations theory, investors in the bond market expect the return from the two strategies to be the same. Therefore, we can equate the two returns:

$$\$1(1 + i_{2t})(1 + i_{2t}) = \$1(1 + i_{1t})(1 + i_{1t+1}^{e}).$$

Simplifying the expression, we get:

$$2i_{2t} + i_{2t}^{2} = i_{1t} + i_{1t+1}^{e} + i_{1t}(i_{1t+1}^{e}).$$

Because the product of two interest rates is very small—for instance, $0.02 \times 0.04 = 0.0008$—we can ignore the products on each side of the equation without significantly affecting the result. We are then left with:

$$i_{2t} = \frac{i_{1t} + i_{1t+1}^{e}}{2}.$$

We again see the result of the expectations theory: The interest rate on a two-year bond should equal the average of the interest rate on a one-year bond that can be purchased today and the expected interest rate on a one-year bond that can be purchased one year from now. We could easily extend this reasoning to demonstrate that the interest rate on a bond that matures after n years—an n-year bond—is the average of the expected one-year interest rates over the life of the bond. So, for instance, the interest rate on a 10-year bond should equal the average of the interest rate on the one-year bond today and the expected interest rates on the other nine one-year bonds during this 10-year period.

We saw in the chapter, though, that the liquidity premium theory argues that because investors are subject to greater interest-rate risk on a long-term bond than on a short-term bond, they require a term premium to buy the long-term bond. We can look more closely at why investors require a term premium. Consider the following example: Suppose you purchased a one-year bond for $1,000 that has a $100 coupon and a principal, or face value, of $1,000. The interest rate on this bond, then, will be $100/$1,000 = 0.10, or 10%. Now suppose that immediately after you purchase this bond, new bonds are issued that are otherwise identical, except they have coupons of $150, so buyers of these bonds will receive an interest rate of $150/$1,000 = 0.15, or 15%. What will happen to the price of your bond? If you sell your bond, buyers will only pay a price that will give them a 15% interest rate because that is the interest rate they could receive if they were to buy a newly issued bond rather than your bond. Therefore, the price of your bond will fall to:

$$\text{Price} = \frac{\$100}{(1 + 0.15)} + \frac{\$1,000}{(1 + 0.15)} = \$956.52.$$

So, you will have suffered a loss of $1,000 − $956.52 = $43.48 on your investment. As a percentage of your investment, your loss equals −$43.48/$1,000 = −0.043, or −4.3%.

Now, suppose that instead of buying a one-year bond with a 10% interest rate, you buy a two-year bond with a 10% interest rate, and, once again, immediately after you buy your bond, new bonds are issued with 15% interest rates. In this case, what will happen to the price of your bond? Once again, we can calculate that the price must fall enough so that potential buyers would receive a 15% interest rate from buying your bond:

$$\text{Price} = \frac{\$100}{(1 + 0.15)} + \frac{\$100}{(1 + 0.15)^2} + \frac{\$1,000}{(1 + 0.15)^2} = \$918.71.$$

So, now you have suffered a capital loss of $1,000 − $918.71 = $81.29 on your investment. In percentage terms, your loss equals −$81.29/$1,000 = −0.081, or −8.1%. Your loss from an increase in interest rates is significantly greater if you hold a two-year bond than if you hold a one-year bond. Because investors know this fact, they will buy a two-year bond only if they receive a higher interest rate—the term premium—than they expect to receive from holding two one-year bonds during those two years.

If we denote the term premium on a two-year bond at time t as i_{2t}^{TP}, then we have the following expression for the yield on a two-year bond:

$$i_{2t} = \frac{i_{1t} + i_{1t+1}^e}{2} + i_{2t}^{TP}.$$

Once again, we could extend this analysis to show that according to the liquidity premium theory, the interest rate on an n-year bond is the average of the expected short-term interest rates over the life of the bond plus the term premium for an n-year bond at time t.

CHAPTER 4

The Global Financial System

Learning Objectives

After studying this chapter, you should be able to:

 4.1 Explain how to calculate the balance of payments (pages 109–114)

4.2 Understand the advantages and disadvantages of different exchange rate policies (pages 115–123)

4.3 Discuss what factors determine exchange rates (pages 124–130)

4.4 Use the loanable funds model to analyze the international capital market (pages 130–139)

Did U.S. Monetary Policy Slow Brazil's Growth?

Brazil has made tremendous economic progress during the past decade. By 2011, Brazil had passed the United Kingdom, becoming the sixth-largest economy in the world, as measured by GDP. In 2012, however, economic growth in Brazil had begun to slow. In meetings in Washington, DC, with President Barack Obama, Brazilian President Dilma Rousseff argued that policies of the U.S. Federal Reserve were partly to blame.

Brazilian firms, such as steelmaker CSN and private jet maker Embraer, argued that the high value of the Brazilian currency, the real, relative to the dollar made it difficult for them to sell their products in other countries. When firms pay most of their costs in their domestic currency but receive a significant part of their revenues in other countries' currencies, the firms are vulnerable to fluctuations in *exchange rates* among currencies.

But what does Federal Reserve policy have to do with the value of the U.S. dollar versus the Brazilian real? When most people think of the global economic system, they think of trade in goods: The United States exporting software and wheat, Japan exporting televisions and Blu-ray players, Brazil exporting steel and private jets, and so on. To finance this trade, firms have to buy and sell the currencies of other countries in the *foreign exchange market*. Most of the buying and selling of currency, however, is not motivated by the need to finance international trade. Instead, the bulk of currency trading occurs because people want to engage in international financial investments. For example, a mutual fund manager in the United States who wants to invest in corporate bonds issued by firms in Germany must exchange

Continued on next page

Key Issue and Question

Issue: Some governments allow the value of their currency to fluctuate in foreign-exchange markets, while other governments fix the value of their currency.

Question: What are the advantages and disadvantages of floating versus fixed exchange rates?

Answered on page 139

U.S. dollars for euros, the common currency of most European countries.

When managers at financial institutions such as commercial banks, investment banks, and mutual funds invest, they look for the highest returns, given the amount of risk involved with those investments. Usually, the higher the current interest rate on a bond or similar investment, the higher the return investors expect to receive. Beginning in 2007, a financial crisis and recession began in the United States. The Federal Reserve responded by driving down interest rates. Given the severity of the recession and the weakness of the economic recovery following it, the Fed persisted in a policy of maintaining very low interest rates. By 2012, the Fed had announced that the policy would continue through at least mid-2015.

Because interest rates in the United States were so low, many investors turned to investments in other countries, particularly developing countries such as Brazil, where interest rates were much higher. As investors sold dollars and bought reals, the value of the real rose against the dollar. By April 2012, the *Economist* magazine referred to Brazil as having "the most overvalued currency of any big economy." The increasing value of the real meant that the prices of Brazilian exports were also increasing in terms of dollars and other foreign currencies.

The potential effect of U.S. monetary policies on foreign companies is just one example of how interconnected countries are financially. The days are long gone when policymakers in each country could ignore the effects of their actions on other countries.

Sources: John Lyons and Tom Barkley, "Brazil Leader Slams U.S. Money Policy," *Wall Street Journal*, April 9, 2012; Luciana Magalhaes, "Currency Volatility Poses Risk for Brazilian Companies," *Wall Street Journal*, May 6, 2012; and "Our Friends in the South," *Economist*, April 7, 2012.

One of the most important economic developments of the past 40 years is that countries have become more connected through increased trade and increased investment. International trade has become increasingly important to most countries, including the United States. In addition, firms and governments now have a much greater ability to borrow from investors in other countries, and investors have the ability to spread their investments across bonds and other securities issued in many countries. We begin our discussion of the global financial system with the balance of payments, which shows the links between the U.S. economy and foreign economies.

The Balance of Payments

4.1

Learning Objective
Explain how to calculate the balance of payments.

Every household and every firm in the United States participates in the global economy. Even if you only buy products sold by firms based in the United States, you are participating in the global economy. For example, nearly all of the parts included in Apple's iPhone are made outside the United States, and all iPhones are assembled in China. More parts of the Ford Mustang are made outside the United States than inside the United States. A local restaurant may seem to be far removed from the global economy, but it is likely to serve wine from France and fruits and vegetables grown in Latin American countries, and it probably uses tables, chairs, and plates manufactured in China or elsewhere.

When Chinese firms export goods to the United States, they receive U.S. dollars in exchange. The Chinese recipients of these dollars have to do something with them. The recipients can use the dollars to purchase U.S. goods and services; purchase U.S. financial assets such as stock in U.S. companies or U.S. Treasury bonds; exchange the dollars for other currencies; or simply hold on to the dollars. While China exported $399 billion in goods and services to the United States during 2011, China imported only $104 billion in goods and services from the United States, so China acquired $295 billion that it either had to use to purchase U.S. assets or exchange for other currencies. This flow of goods, services, currencies, and financial investments between China and the United States also occurs between many other countries.

Most people don't have trouble understanding the significance of data on the unemployment and inflation rates or on the growth rate of GDP. But data on the international economy are more difficult to understand. What does it mean if the United States runs a trade deficit? Is it always bad news? What is a current account deficit? In this section, we explain how to measure the trade and financial flows among countries.

Consumers, firms, and investors in one country routinely interact with consumers, firms, and investors in other countries. A consumer in the United States may use a keyboard assembled in China, a consumer in China may use an iPad designed by Apple in the United States, and a consumer in France may watch a television made in South Korea and wear a sweater made in Italy. A firm in India may sell its software in dozens of countries around the world. An investor in London may sell a U.S. Treasury bond to an investor in Mexico City. Nearly all economies are *open economies* and have extensive interactions in trade or finance with other countries. In an **open economy**, households, firms, and governments borrow, lend, and trade internationally. In a **closed economy**, households, firms, and governments do not borrow, lend, or trade internationally. No economy today is completely closed, although a few countries, such as North Korea, have very limited economic interactions with other countries.

There are different ways to measure how open an economy is. One way is to measure the value of exports and imports relative to GDP. Figure 4.1 shows that measured this way, the world economy has become significantly more open. Exports plus imports increased from 24% of world GDP in 1960 to 57% of world GDP in 2007. The global

Open economy An economy in which households, firms, and governments borrow, lend, and trade internationally.

Closed economy An economy in which households, firms, and governments do not borrow, lend, or trade internationally.

Figure 4.1

Trade as a Percentage of GDP, 1960–2010

Global trade has been growing in importance since 1960. Exports plus imports rose from 24% of world GDP in 1960 to 56% of world GDP in 2010. Exports plus imports are generally a smaller percentage of GDP for large economies such as the United States, where trade was 29% of GDP in 2010.

Source: World Bank, *World Development Indicators*.

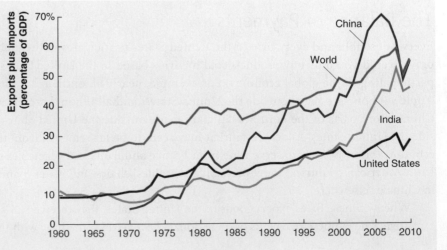

recession and the global financial crisis that reduced incomes worldwide also reduced international trade, but international trade had rebounded to 56% of world GDP in 2010. Note, though, the severe effect of the recession on China's trade.

In addition to international trade in goods and services, there are significant flows of financial assets, such as stocks and bonds, among countries. By being more open to financial flows, countries typically increase their opportunities for economic growth. Firms can borrow funds from investors in other countries, and investors have the opportunity to receive higher returns than if they were only able to invest in their own country. One measure of economic openness to financial flows is the sum of financial assets and financial liabilities as a percentage of GDP. For most countries, this measure of openness to financial flows has increased significantly over the past 40 years. This fact is illustrated in Figure 4.2, which shows the sum of financial assets and liabilities as a percentage of GDP for several countries. Note that the increase in this measure has been particularly large for high-income countries, such as Germany and the United States. The increase has also been large for developing countries that have achieved rapid economic growth, such as China. Low-income countries, such as Kenya, where economic growth has been slow, have typically not experienced as large an increase in financial flows.

Just as economists have a system of accounting for measuring economic activity within a country, they also have a system of accounting for measuring economic interactions among countries. Economists call this system the **balance of payments**, which is a record of a country's trade with other countries in goods, services, and assets. The Bureau of Economic Analysis, which gathers data on GDP and other macroeconomic variables for the domestic economy, also gathers the data included in the balance of payments.

Balance of payments A record of a country's trade with other countries in goods, services, and assets.

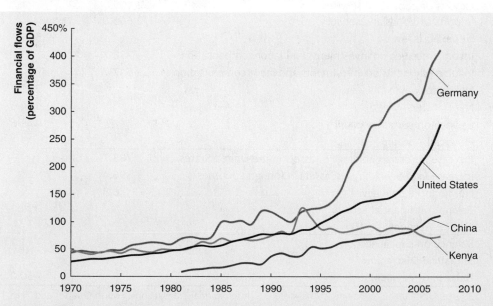

Figure 4.2

Financial Flows as a Percentage of GDP, 1970–2007

Financial flows among countries have increased substantially since 1970, particularly in high-income countries, such as Germany, Japan, and the United States. The increase in financial flows has been smaller in low-income countries, such as Kenya, that have been experiencing slow economic growth.

Note: 2007 is the most recent year for which data are available. Data for China are only available beginning in 1981.

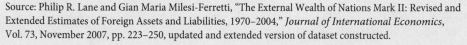

Source: Philip R. Lane and Gian Maria Milesi-Ferretti, "The External Wealth of Nations Mark II: Revised and Extended Estimates of Foreign Assets and Liabilities, 1970–2004," *Journal of International Economics*, Vol. 73, November 2007, pp. 223–250, updated and extended version of dataset constructed.

Current account The part of the balance of payments that records a country's net exports, net investment income, and net transfers.

Financial account The part of the balance of payments that records purchases of assets a country has made abroad and foreign purchases of assets in the country.

Capital account The part of the balance of payments that records (generally) minor transactions, such as migrants' transfers, and sales and purchases of non-produced, non-financial assets.

As Table 4.1 illustrates, the balance of payments has three parts:

1. The **current account** records a country's net exports, net investment income, and net transfers.
2. The **financial account** records purchases of assets a country has made abroad and foreign purchases of assets in the country.
3. The **capital account** records (generally) minor transactions such as migrants' transfers, and sales and purchases of non-produced, non-financial assets, such as copyrights, patents, trademarks, and rights to natural resources.

The Current Account

The current account in the balance of payments records the following three items:

1. *Net exports*, which are the exports and imports of goods and services between the United States and other countries. In 2011, the United States exported $2,105 billion worth of goods and services to other countries and imported about $2,665 billion worth of goods and services from other countries. As a result, net exports were −$560 billion during 2011, which means that the United States ran a *trade deficit*.
2. *Net factor payments*, which are the income U.S. households and firms receive on investments in other countries minus the income foreign households and firms

Table 4.1 Balance of Payments for the United States, 2011 (billions of dollars)

Current Account		
Exports of goods and services	$2,105.0	
Imports of goods and services	−2,665.0	
Net exports		−560.0
Income received on investments and labor compensation	738.7	
Income payments on investments and labor compensation	−517.7	
Net factor payments		221.0
Net transfers		−134.6
Balance on current account		−473.6
Financial Account		
Increase in foreign holdings of assets in the United States	783.7	
Increase in U.S. holdings of assets in foreign countries	−396.4	
Net financial derivatives	6.8	
Balance on financial account		394.1
Capital Account		
Balance on capital account		−1.1
Statistical Discrepancy	80.6	
Balance of payments		$0.0

Source: U.S. Bureau of Economic Analysis, "U.S. International Transactions, Fourth Quarter and Year 2011," March 14, 2012.

Note: The balance on current account does not equal the sum of the listed components because of rounding.

receive on investments in the United States. Many U.S. firms do business overseas through foreign subsidiaries. When these subsidiaries earn a profit or pay dividends, income flows from other countries to the United States. For example, although General Electric is a U.S. firm, with headquarters in Fairfield, Connecticut, it owns several foreign subsidiaries. When these subsidiaries earn profits and pay them to General Electric, net factor payments to the United States increase.

3. *Transfers*, which are the difference between transfer payments made by U.S. residents to residents of other countries and the transfer payments residents of other countries make to residents of the United States. For example, donations by U.S. residents to the victims of the 2011 earthquake in Japan or the 2010 earthquake in Haiti would count as transfers from the United States to the residents of those countries.

If the current account balance is negative, then the country runs a *current account deficit*. A current account deficit indicates that a country is consuming more than its current income, which can happen only if the country borrows from residents of other countries or sells assets to them. For example, we know from Table 4.1 that the United States ran a current account deficit of $473 billion in 2011. So, U.S. residents, including the government, must have (1) sold assets, such as factories or shares of stock, or (2) borrowed by selling bonds or taking out loans, by that same amount. A current account surplus indicates that a country is consuming less than its current income, so it must be lending to the rest of the world or buying assets from the rest of the world.

Table 4.1 shows that in 2011, two categories of the current account—net exports and net transfers—were negative, while net factor payments were positive, indicating that U.S. capital and labor abroad earned more than foreign capital and labor in the United States.

Since the early 1980s, the United States has consistently run large current account deficits. As a result, foreigners have been accumulating Treasury bonds and other U.S. assets. China, like many large emerging economies, has run current account surpluses during recent years. Part of the reason for these surpluses is that the domestic financial systems in such economies are not well developed, which makes investing in them difficult and risky. As a result, funds have flowed from investors in these economies to developed economies such as the United States and Western Europe.

The Financial Account

The financial account records the flow of funds into and out of a country. There is a *capital outflow* from the United States when a U.S. firm builds a factory in another country or when an investor in the United States purchases financial assets, such as bonds, of foreign firms or governments. For example, if Ford builds a factory in Brazil or if U.S. households use their retirement accounts to purchase stocks and bonds in Brazil, there is a capital outflow from the United States to Brazil.

There is a *capital inflow* into the United States when a foreign firm builds a factory in the United States or when a foreign investor purchases financial assets. For example, when the Chinese government purchases U.S. Treasury bonds or when Toyota builds a factory in Mississippi, there is a financial inflow into the United States.

Notice that we are using the word *capital* to refer not only to physical capital goods, such as factories, but also to financial assets, such as stocks and bonds. When firms build factories or buy physical capital goods in foreign countries, they are engaging in *foreign direct investment*. When investors buy stocks or bonds issued in another country, they are engaging in *foreign portfolio investment*. **Net capital outflows** are equal to capital outflows minus capital inflows.

Net capital outflows
Capital outflows minus capital inflows.

The Capital Account

The capital account is the third and least important part of the balance of payments. This account records generally minor transactions such as (1) migrants' transfers, which consist of goods and financial assets people take with them when they leave or enter a country and (2) sales and purchases of non-produced, non-financial assets, which include copyrights, patents, trademarks, or rights to natural resources.

The definitions of the financial account and the capital account are sometimes misunderstood because, prior to 1999, the capital account recorded all the transactions included now in both the financial account and the capital account. In other words, capital account transactions went from being a very important part of the balance of payments to being a relatively unimportant part. Because the balance on what is now called the capital account is so small, for simplicity, we will ignore it in the remainder of the chapter.

The Bureau of Economic Analysis follows international accounting conventions by setting up the balance of payments so that when one item changes in the accounts, there is an offsetting change in another part of the accounts. As a consequence, the balance of payments is zero, apart from minor statistical discrepancies. Table 4.1 shows the balance of payments in 2011 for the United States. The balance on the current account was −$473.4 billion, so $473.4 billion more flowed out of the United States than flowed into the United States due to trade in goods and services and income flows. What happens to the $473.4 billion? The funds did not just disappear. Either foreigners decided to hold onto the dollars, or they decided to purchase assets, such as land, buildings, or financial securities, in the United States. Dollars that are held by foreigners are *official reserves*, and changes in foreign holdings of dollars are *official reserve transactions*. Both a decision to hold the dollars and a decision to use the dollars to purchase assets in the United States show up as positive transactions in the financial account. Therefore, a current account deficit is exactly offset by a financial account surplus, leaving the balance of payments at zero. Occasionally, journalists or commentators will refer to the United States running a balance of payments deficit. Typically, they are mistaking a balance of trade deficit or a current account deficit for a balance of payments deficit.

Countries that run current account surpluses must also run financial account deficits. For example, in 2011, Japan had a current account surplus of $147 billion, so Japan must also have had a financial account deficit of $147 billion. Therefore, households and firms in Japan must have purchased $147 billion more of non-Japanese assets such as U.S. Treasury bonds than households and firms in other countries purchased of Japanese assets.

Exchange Rates and Exchange Rate Policy

A firm, such as a local restaurant or hardware store, that operates entirely within the United States will price its products in dollars and will use dollars to pay its suppliers' invoices, wages and salaries to its workers, interest to its bondholders, and dividends to its shareholders.

A multinational corporation such as Apple, in contrast, may sell its products in many different countries and receive payments in many different currencies. Its suppliers and workers may also be spread around the world and may have to be paid in local currencies. Corporations may also use the international financial system to borrow in a foreign currency. For example, in 2012, many Brazilian firms had received large loans from foreign banks or had sold bonds to foreign investors. Many of these loans and bonds were *denominated* in dollars. When firms make extensive use of foreign currencies, they must deal with fluctuations in the exchange rate.

In this section, we explore exchange rates, how they affect imports and exports, and the exchange rate policies of different countries.

Nominal Exchange Rates

The **nominal exchange rate** (also called simply the exchange rate) is the price of one currency in terms of another country's currency. By convention, we typically express the nominal exchange rate as units of foreign currency per unit of domestic currency, as in 80 Japanese yen per U.S. dollar. In Japan, of course, we would express the exchange rate as dollars per yen.

Fluctuations in exchange rates can have an important effect on the ability of firms to sell their goods in other countries and on the prices that consumers pay for imported goods. For example, suppose a Brazilian grower is exporting coffee to the United States. A bag of coffee with a price of 250 reals in Brazil will have a U.S. dollar price of $100 if the exchange rate is 2.5 reals = $1. But if the value of the real rises against the dollar so that the exchange rate becomes 2.0 reals = $1, the dollar price of the bag of coffee increases to 250 reals/2.0 per dollar = $125. Even though the price of the coffee in Brazil is unchanged, such a sharp increase in the dollar price would cause the firm to lose sales in the United States.

Similarly, as the value of the yen increased against the dollar by more than 25% between 2008 and 2012, many Japanese car companies faced declining sales of their exports to the United States. To avoid the risk involved with selling cars for dollars while incurring production costs in yen, Toyota, Honda, and Nissan relocated more of their production from Japan to the United States.

Because exports have become a larger fraction of GDP for most countries, fluctuations in exchange rates have an increased effect on domestic economies. A sharp rise in the exchange rate that results in a significant decline in exports can lead domestic firms to cut back production and lay off workers. Not surprisingly, the *Wall Street Journal* and other business publications report data on exchange rates and frequently print articles about the effects of exchange rate movements on U.S. firms. Economists and policymakers closely monitor movements in exchange rates because of the effect these movements can have on the economy.

An immediate exchange of one currency for another currency is carried out at the current exchange rate, or *spot exchange rate*. Buyers and sellers of currency can also agree today to exchange currency at some future date at the *forward exchange rate*.

Learning Objective

Understand the advantages and disadvantages of different exchange rate policies.

Nominal exchange rate
The price of one country's currency in terms of another country's currency.

The agreements to exchange currency at some future date are called *forward exchange contracts* or *future exchange contracts*. Forward contracts are typically negotiated between two financial firms—typically, commercial banks. For example, Bank of America might agree today with Deutsche Bank that in 90 days, they will exchange $100 million for euros, at an exchange rate of $1.30 = 1 euro. Unlike forward contracts, futures contracts are exchange products, which means that like stocks and bonds, they are publicly traded on financial exchanges, such as the Chicago Board of Trade or the New York Mercantile Exchange. The details of futures contracts, such as the amounts of currency involved per contract and the dates on which the contract will expire, are established by the exchange. The existence of forward contracts and futures contracts allows firms to *hedge*, or reduce the risk of losses from fluctuations in exchange rates.

For example, Brazilian private jet maker Embraer may suffer losses if the value of the Brazilian real increases against the U.S. dollar. Suppose, for example, that Embraer has sold a jet to a U.S. firm for $50 million, which the U.S. firm will pay in six months, when the plane is delivered. Embraer faces the risk, known as *exchange-rate risk*, that in the six months between when it sells the plane and when it receives the payment, the value of the real will rise against the dollar. If the value of the real rises, Embraer will receive fewer reals in exchange for the $50 million payment made by the U.S. firm. By entering into a forward contract at the time it sells the jet, Embraer can fix the exchange rate at which it can exchange dollars for reals in six months, thereby reducing its exchange-rate risk. Typically, firms do not buy and sell forward contracts themselves; instead, they rely on banks to provide them with this service.

Each currency has a spot exchange rate versus every other individual currency, sometimes called a *bilateral exchange rate*. Economists and policymakers also find it useful to look at a country's *multilateral exchange rate*, which shows how the value of a country's currency is changing relative to a group of other countries' currencies. For example, Figure 4.3 shows the value of the U.S. dollar, as measured against a basket of seven major currencies, where each currency is weighted by the volume of trade between

MyEconLab Real-time data

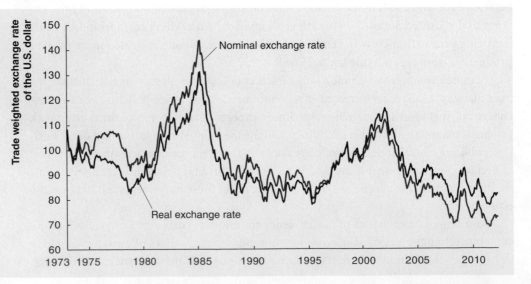

Figure 4.3

The Trade-Weighted Exchange Rate of the U.S. Dollar Against an Index of Major Currencies, 1973–2012

The nominal and real exchange rates for the U.S. dollar have fluctuated widely since 1973.

Source: Board of Governors of the Federal Reserve System.

that country and the United States. The exchange rate is shown as an index number, with its value on the arbitrary date of March 1973 set equal to 100. As with any other index, what matters are movements in the multilateral exchange rate over time rather than its value in a particular month.

The exchange value of the U.S. dollar has fluctuated significantly since 1973. For example, as Figure 4.3 shows, during the 1980s, the dollar experienced a **currency appreciation**, which occurs when the exchange value of a country's currency increases relative to the value of another country's currency. During these years, many U.S. firms had great difficulty exporting their products. Since 2001, the dollar has experienced a **currency depreciation** relative to other major currencies, which occurs when the exchange value of a country's currency decreases relative to the value of another country's currency. Exports of U.S. firms increased as a result of this depreciation.

Currency appreciation
An increase in the market value of one country's currency relative to another country's currency.

Currency depreciation
A decrease in the market value of one country's currency relative to another country's currency.

Real Exchange Rates

Note that in Figure 4.3 we display both the nominal exchange rate of the U.S. dollar and the *real exchange rate*. The nominal exchange rate tells us how much foreign currency we can receive in exchange for one unit of domestic currency—such as how many Brazilian reals we receive for one U.S. dollar. But for some purposes, economists and policymakers are more interested in the prices of foreign goods and services relative to U.S. goods and services. In other words, they are interested in the *terms of trade*, or the rate at which domestic goods can be exchanged for foreign goods. The **real exchange rate** is the rate at which goods and services in one country can be exchanged for goods and services in another country. Just as real GDP gives a better measure of the growth of an economy than does nominal GDP, the real exchange rate gives a better measure of changes in the prices of U.S. goods relative to the prices of foreign goods than does the nominal exchange rate. So when economists and policymakers want to gauge the effect of a change in exchange rates on U.S. exports and imports, they rely on the real exchange rate rather than on the nominal exchange rate.

Real exchange rate The rate at which goods and services in one country can be exchanged for goods and services in another country.

Measuring the Real Exchange Rate with a Single Good: The McDonald's Big Mac Index
We can use the McDonald's Big Mac to illustrate calculating the real exchange rate. The *Economist* magazine keeps track of the prices of Big Macs around the world. In January 2012, the *Economist* reported that the price of a Big Mac was $4.20 in the United States and 10.25 reals in Brazil. At that time, the nominal exchange rate between the Brazilian real and the U. S. dollar was 1.81 reals per dollar. To calculate the real exchange rate in terms of Big Macs, we need to determine how many Brazilian Big Macs we can receive in exchange for one U.S. Big Mac. We can carry out this calculation in two steps. First, we can use the nominal exchange rate to convert the price of a Big Mac in the United States into Brazilian reals. Second, we can divide by the price of a Big Mac in reals to arrive at how many Brazilian Big Macs we can receive in exchange for one U.S. Big Mac. Following these steps, we have:

Real exchange rate = (1.81 Brazilian reals per dollar × $4.20 price of Big Macs in the United States)/(10.25 reals price of Big Macs in Brazil)

or,

Real exchange rate = 0.74 Big Macs in Brazil per Big Mac in the United States

So, 1 Big Mac in the United States, given prices in each country and the nominal exchange rate, can purchase 0.74 Big Mac in Brazil. Notice that because the real exchange rate tells us how many goods in a foreign country a good in the domestic country can purchase, we measure the real exchange rate in terms of goods rather than in terms of currency.

Measuring the Real Exchange Rate Using Price Levels Typically, we don't measure the real exchange rate in terms of the price of a single good, such as the Big Mac, but in terms of average prices, or the price level, in each country. Recall that we can measure the price level by using a price index, such as the consumer price index or the GDP deflator. If we let E stand for the nominal exchange rate, e stand for the real exchange rate, $P^{Domestic}$ stand for the domestic price level, and $P^{Foreign}$ stand for the foreign price level, we have the following general expression for the real exchange rate:

$$e = E \times \left(\frac{P^{Domestic}}{P^{Foreign}} \right).$$

For example, if the real exchange rate between the Brazilian real and the U.S. dollar were 2, then this value would indicate that the average good or service produced in the United States can purchase two of the average good or service in Brazil.

Figure 4.3 on page 116 shows movements in the real exchange rate of the U.S. dollar from 1973 to 2012, calculated using a weighted price level for the seven major currencies included in this multilateral exchange rate. We can see that movements in the real exchange rate closely follow movements in the nominal exchange rate. The equation for the real exchange rate tells us that the nominal exchange rate and the real exchange rate will move together only if the ratio of the domestic price level to the foreign price level is roughly constant. The fact that the nominal and real exchange rates have moved together tells us that the relative prices of goods and services in the United States and in these other countries has been fairly stable. That is, the price level in the United States has risen at about the same rate during this period as have the price levels in these other countries.

The Foreign-Exchange Market

To finance international trade and international financial transactions, banks and other financial firms around the world trade nearly $4 trillion worth of currency each day on the foreign-exchange market. That amount represents nearly $600 for every person in the world each day. The foreign-exchange market is global, and trades occur 24 hours a day.

Typically, rather than actual physical currency, banks trade bank deposits. So, a U.S.-based bank might exchange a bank account denominated in dollars to a German bank in exchange for a bank account denominated in euros. The foreign-exchange market is, in effect, virtual (or what economists call *over-the-counter*), in that most trading takes place between large banks that are linked by computer, rather than on a physical exchange. Although the volume of transactions is large, transactions are concentrated in just a few locations and among just a small number of currencies. More than half of all foreign-exchange transactions involve financial firms in the United States or the United Kingdom. About 85% of all trades involve the U.S. dollar, while 39% involve the euro, 19% involve the yen, and 13% involve the British pound.[1]

---

[1]Bank for International Settlements, "Triennial Central Bank Survey," September 2010.

Exchange Rate Policy

Countries follow different exchange rate policies. Some countries, such as the United States and Canada, allow the exchange rate to be determined in the foreign-exchange market, just as the prices for most goods are determined in markets. A country that follows this approach has a *floating exchange rate*. Some countries prefer a *fixed exchange* rate, also called an *exchange rate peg*, between their currency and another currency. For example, the Chinese government followed a policy of keeping constant the exchange rate between its currency, the yuan, and the U.S. dollar from 1994 to 2005, after which it allowed the exchange rate to move within limited bounds. When countries agree on an exchange rate policy, economists say that there is an **exchange rate system**, or an *exchange rate regime*. Countries have typically used three major types of exchange rate systems:

1. A fixed exchange rate system
2. A floating exchange rate system
3. A managed float exchange rate system

In a **fixed exchange rate system**, exchange rates are set at levels determined and maintained by governments. Historically, the two most important fixed exchange rate systems were the *gold standard* and the *Bretton Woods system*. Under the gold standard, which lasted from the nineteenth century to the 1930s, a country's currency consisted of gold coins and paper currency that the government was committed to redeem for gold. The gold standard was a fixed exchange rate system because exchange rates were determined by the amount of gold in each country's currency. Under the gold standard, the size of a country's money supply depended on the amount of gold available. To expand its currency rapidly during a war or an economic depression, a country would need to abandon the gold standard.

During the Great Depression of the 1930s, many countries, including the United States, decided to abandon the gold standard in order to increase the flexibility of their exchange rates and gain greater control of their money supplies. A few policymakers, such as 2012 presidential candidate Ron Paul, have advocated a return to the gold standard, largely because they believed that the domestic money supply should be based on something—gold—that is not directly controlled by the government. There has been no serious attempt to return to the gold standard, however, for a number of reasons, including the significant constraints the gold standard places on using monetary policy to fight recessions.

Near the end of World War II, many economists and policymakers argued that a return to a fixed exchange rate system would help the world economy recover from more than 15 years of depression and war. The result was a conference held in Bretton Woods, New Hampshire, in 1944 that set up an exchange rate system where the United States pledged to buy or sell gold at a fixed rate of $35 per ounce. The central banks of all other countries that joined the Bretton Woods system pledged to buy and sell their countries' currencies at a fixed rate against the dollar. By fixing their exchange rates against the dollar, these counties were fixing the exchange rates among their currencies as well. Unlike under the gold standard, neither the United States nor any other country was willing to redeem its paper currency for gold domestically. The United States would redeem dollars for gold only if the dollars were presented by a foreign central bank. Fixed exchange rate systems can run into difficulty because

Exchange rate system
An agreement among countries about how exchange rates should be determined.

Fixed exchange rate system A system in which exchange rates are set at levels determined and maintained by governments.

exchange rates are not free to adjust quickly to changes in demand for currencies. By the early 1970s, the difficulty of keeping exchange rates fixed led to the end of the Bretton Woods system.

Following the collapse of the Bretton Woods system, most countries allowed their currencies to *float*, which means that exchange rates were determined by the buying and selling of currencies in the foreign exchange market. Some countries found that the resulting **floating exchange rate system** led to too much instability in their exchange rates. As a result, some central banks intervened occasionally to influence their exchange rates by buying and selling currencies in the foreign exchange market.

The U.S. Federal Reserve rarely intervenes in foreign exchange markets to affect the exchange rate of the dollar. Because other central banks do intervene occasionally, however, the current exchange rate system is called a *managed float exchange rate system*. Under a **managed float exchange rate system**, private buyers and sellers in the foreign exchange market determine the value of currencies most of the time, with occasional government intervention. Many economists question, though, how effective exchange rate interventions by governments are for widely traded currencies. For example, the Bank of Japan can attempt to affect the exchange rate between the U.S. dollar and yen by buying or selling dollars or yen. But the Bank of Japan's purchases or sales will be very small relative to the total amount of buying and selling of these currencies in the foreign exchange market. So it is unlikely that a central bank intervention can affect the exchange rate of a widely traded currency for more than a brief period.

Policy Choices and the Current Exchange Rate Systems

The current exchange rate system reflects three key policy choices:

1. The United States allows the dollar to float against other major currencies.
2. Seventeen countries in Europe have adopted the euro as their common currency.
3. Some developing countries have pegged their exchange rates against the dollar or another major currency.

As noted earlier, since the collapse of the Bretton Woods system, the United States has rarely intervened in the foreign exchange market to try to affect the value of the dollar. The result, as shown in Figure 4.3 on page 116, has been substantial fluctuations in the exchange value of the dollar over time. As noted in the chapter opener, countries such as Brazil that export to the United States sometimes argue that U.S. monetary policy has made the dollar exchange rate artificially low. As we will see, though, the Federal Reserve does not specifically target a particular value for the exchange rate.

What eventually became the European Union (EU) began when six Western European countries signed the Treaty of Rome in 1957, in an attempt to more closely integrate their economies. By 2012, the EU had grown to 27 countries, including several formerly Communist countries in Eastern Europe. In 1999, the EU made the decision to move to a common currency, and on January 1, 2002, euro currency was introduced. By 2012, 17 members of the EU, including all of the largest economies with the exception of the United Kingdom, had adopted the euro. The European Central Bank (ECB) was also established in 1998. Although the central banks of the member countries continue to operate, the ECB has assumed responsibility for monetary policy and for issuing

Floating exchange rate system A system in which the foreign-exchange value of currency is determined in the foreign exchange market.

Managed float exchange rate system A system in which private buyers and sellers in the foreign exchange market determine the value of currencies most of the time, with occasional government intervention.

currency. The ultimate fate of the euro, however, was unclear in late 2012, as the fallout from the financial crisis left several countries, notably Greece, unable to pay all of their government debt. It appeared possible that Greece might decide to drop the euro and return to using its own currency.

Making the Connection

Greece Experiences a "Bank Jog"

Before the United States enacted federal deposit insurance in 1934, commercial banks were subject to bank runs. In a bank run, depositors withdrew their funds because they were afraid that if their bank closed, they would not get back all the money in their accounts. Typically, once a run on a bank began, the bank was quickly forced to close because large numbers of its depositors demanded their money back. In 2012, Greek banks also experienced something like a bank run, but in this case, depositors withdrew their money at a relatively slow pace, so some journalists described Greek banks as undergoing a "bank jog" rather than a bank run.

After June 2002, all countries participating in the euro, including Greece, had removed their individual currencies from circulation. After that date, all deposits in Greek banks were in euros, rather than in drachmas, the previous Greek currency. The period from 2001 until the beginning of the global economic recession and financial crisis in 2007 was one of relative economic stability in most of Europe. With low interest rates, low inflation rates, and expanding employment and production, the advantages of the euro seemed obvious. The countries using the euro no longer had to deal with problems caused by fluctuating exchange rates. Having a common currency also makes it easier for consumers and firms to buy and sell across borders.

The recession and financial crisis resulted in falling real GDP and higher unemployment. A sovereign debt crisis that developed in 2010 made the problems worse. *Sovereign debt* refers to bonds issued by governments. The recession caused large increases in government spending and reductions in tax revenues as incomes and profits declined. Governments in a number of European countries, particularly Greece, Ireland, Spain, Portugal, and Italy, paid for the resulting budget deficits by selling bonds. By the spring of 2010, many investors began to doubt the ability of some countries, particularly Greece, to make the interest payments on the bonds. If Greece defaulted, investors would be likely to stop buying bonds issued by several other European governments, and the continuation of the euro would be called into question.

The ECB helped Greece avoid a default by directly buying its bonds. The bank extended similar help to Spain, Ireland, and Italy. The International Monetary Fund and the European Union put together aid packages meant to keep Greece and other countries from defaulting. In exchange for the aid, these countries were required to adopt an *austerity policy* of cutting government spending and raising taxes even though doing so resulted in significant protests from unions, students, and other groups.

In 2012, unhappiness over spending cuts and higher taxes, along with continuing high unemployment, led Greek voters to elect politicians who vowed to reverse the austerity policy. As a result, speculation increased that Greece would abandon the euro. Many Greeks were afraid that the government might decide to exchange their euro bank deposits for drachmas at a rate of one for one. If the drachma then depreciated—as was widely expected—bank depositors would suffer heavy losses. In response, beginning in May, Greek banks began to lose deposits. Depositors either held their withdrawals as cash or deposited them in foreign banks. Unlike with a normal bank run, however, Greek depositors believed that they had ample time to withdraw their money because the ECB was willing to provide euro currency to Greek banks to meet withdrawals and because it was unclear whether Greece actually would stop using the euro.

The Greek bank jog indicated a potential new source of instability in the global financial system: Not only might depositors in euro countries lose faith in banks because of actions by the banks—for instance, making bad loans—depositors could also become concerned that their country might leave the euro or that the ECB would not be willing to supply an unlimited number of euros to local banks.

Sources: David Enrich, Sara Schaefer Muñoz, and Charles Forelle, "Europe Bank Fear Flight of Deposits," *Wall Street Journal*, May 20, 2012; Matthew O'Brien, "End of the Marathon: The Meaning of Greece's 'Bank Jog,'" *Atlantic*, May 17, 2012; and Damien McElroy, "Greeks Withdraw Savings in National 'Bank Jog,'" (UK) *Telegraph*, May 20, 2012.

See related problems 2.9 and 2.10 at the end of the chapter.

Some developing countries have attempted to keep their exchange rates fixed, or pegged, against the U.S. dollar or another major currency. Having a fixed exchange rate can provide important advantages for a country that has extensive trade with another country. When the exchange rate is fixed, business planning becomes much easier. For instance, if the South Korean won increases in value relative to the dollar, Hyundai, a Korean car manufacturer, may have to raise the dollar price of cars it exports to the United States, thereby reducing sales. If the exchange rate between the Korean won and the dollar is fixed, Hyundai's planning is much easier.

In the 1980s and 1990s, there was an additional reason for countries to have fixed exchange rates. During those decades, the flow of foreign investment funds to developing countries, particularly those in East Asia, increased substantially. It became possible for firms in countries such as Korea, Thailand, Malaysia, and Indonesia to borrow dollars directly from foreign investors or indirectly from foreign banks. For example, a Thai firm might borrow U.S. dollars from a Japanese bank. If the Thai firm wants to build a new factory in Thailand with the borrowed dollars, it has to exchange the dollars for the equivalent amount of Thai currency, the baht. When the factory opens and production begins, the Thai firm will be earning the additional baht it needs to exchange for dollars to make the interest payments on the loan.

A problem arises if the value of the baht falls against the dollar. Suppose that the exchange rate is 25 baht per dollar when the firm takes out the loan. A Thai firm making an interest payment of $100,000 per month on a dollar loan could buy the necessary dollars for 2.5 million baht. But if the value of the baht declines to 50 baht to the dollar, it would take 5 million baht to buy the dollars necessary to make the interest payment. These increased payments might be a crushing burden for the Thai firm. The government of Thailand would have a strong incentive to avoid this problem by keeping the exchange rate between the baht and the dollar fixed.

In the 1980s and 1990s, some countries also feared the inflationary consequences of a floating exchange rate. When the value of a currency falls, the prices of imports rise. If imports are a significant fraction of the goods consumers buy, a fall in the value of the currency may significantly increase the inflation rate. A fixed exchange rate limits this cause of inflation. During the 1990s, an important part of Brazil's and Argentina's anti-inflation policies was a fixed exchange rate against the dollar. As we noted earlier, however, there are difficulties with following a fixed exchange rate policy because a country's central bank must stand ready to buy or sell its currency in exchange for the dollar or other currency at the fixed rate.

Suppose, for example, the Bank of Korea has pegged the Korean won against the dollar, as it did during the 1990s. If there are more traders in the foreign exchange market who want to sell won for dollars at the pegged exchange rate than there are traders who want to buy won for dollars, the Korean central bank must buy the surplus won with dollars. In the reverse case, the Korean central bank must buy surplus dollars in exchange for won. In practice, central banks have often found it difficult to maintain a pegged exchange rate over long periods because they eventually run low on foreign currency. Another drawback to a fixed exchange rate is that it eliminates one means by which countries can recover from a recession. During a recession, if a country has a flexible exchange rate, the exchange rate can decline, thereby increasing the country's exports. Over the past 20 years, a number of countries, including several in East Asia, along with Brazil and Argentina, have established fixed exchange rates, only to eventually abandon them.

Table 4.2 summarizes the advantages and disadvantages of different exchange rate policies.

Table 4.2 Advantages and Disadvantages of Various Exchange Rate Policies

Exchange rate system	Advantages	Disadvantages
Fixed exchange rate system	Easier for businesses to plan and to borrow in other currencies. Easier for central banks to control inflation.	Difficult to maintain. Eliminates possibility of depreciation during a recession.
Floating exchange rate system	No need for government intervention. Allows exchange rate to reflect demand and supply in the market.	Can make business planning difficult. Can worsen inflation if domestic prices of imports rise quickly.
Managed float exchange rate system	Allows greater exchange rate stability than in a floating system.	Central bank interventions are likely to be ineffective with a widely traded currency.

4.3

Learning Objective

Discuss what factors determine exchange rates.

What Factors Determine Exchange Rates?

Our earlier discussion of the real exchange rate measured in terms of Big Macs raises an interesting question: Why isn't the real exchange rate always one for one? That is, why shouldn't you be able to exchange 1 U.S. Big Mac for 1 Brazilian Big Mac rather than for only 0.74 Big Mac? According to the *law of one price*, identical products should sell for the same price everywhere, including in different countries. If the law of one price doesn't hold, then arbitrage should be possible. *Arbitrage* refers to buying a product in one market and reselling it in another market at a higher price. The profits received from engaging in arbitrage are called *arbitrage profits*.

Purchasing Power Parity

Purchasing power parity
The theory that, in the long run, nominal exchange rates adjust to equalize the purchasing power of different currencies.

Consider applying arbitrage to the values in our Big Mac example. Because the prices of Big Macs are not the same in the United States and Brazil, you should be able to earn arbitrage profits. For example, you could buy a Big Mac in the United States for $4.20 and sell it in Brazil for 10.25 reals. Then you could exchange the reals for $5.66 (10.25 reals ÷ 1.81 reals per dollar = $5.66). You would have made a profit of $1.46 on your initial investment of $4.20, which is a return of 35%. If this process works for one Big Mac, why not try it for millions of Big Macs and become very wealthy? The problem is that if this path to easy riches is obvious to you, it will be obvious to many people. Many people will demand dollars in order to buy low-priced U.S. Big Macs. This increased demand should cause the dollar to appreciate until the exchange rate reaches 2.44 reals per dollar. At that exchange rate, arbitrage profits are eliminated, and 1 U.S. Big Mac exchanges for 1 Brazilian Big Mac, so the real exchange rate equals 1. (In the next section, we explain why in practice we do not see the prices of Big Macs equalized across countries.)

The reasoning we have just gone through leads to the theory of **purchasing power parity**, which states that, in the long run, nominal exchange rates adjust to equalize the purchasing power of different currencies. That is, in the long run, the real exchange rate should equal 1. This theory should hold because, if it doesn't, then opportunities for arbitrage profits exist. In the long run, by buying and selling currencies in the foreign exchange market, individuals pursuing profit opportunities should cause the nominal exchange to adjust so that the real exchange rate equals 1, and purchasing power parity holds.

We can use the theory of purchasing power parity to analyze the effect on nominal exchange rates of differences in inflation rates among countries. Here we use a handy mathematical rule that states that an equation where variables are multiplied together is approximately equal to an equation where percentage changes in those variables are *added* together. Similarly, we can approximate the division of two variables by subtracting their percentage changes. Remember that the percentage change in the price level is the same thing as the inflation rate. The expression for the real exchange rate is:

$$e = E \times \left(\frac{P^{\text{Domestic}}}{P^{\text{Foreign}}} \right).$$

If we let π^{Domestic} stand for the domestic inflation rate and π^{Foreign} stand for the foreign inflation rate, then we can convert the above equation into growth rates as:

$$\% \text{ change in } e = \% \text{ change in } E + \pi^{\text{Domestic}} - \pi^{\text{Foreign}}.$$

If the theory of purchasing power is correct, then in the long run e, the real exchange rate, equals 1. Therefore, the percentage change in the real exchange rate is zero and we can rewrite the previous expression as:

$$\% \text{ change in } E = \pi^{\text{Foreign}} - \pi^{\text{Domestic}}.$$

This last equation tells us that the percentage change in the nominal exchange rate is equal to the difference between the foreign and domestic inflation rates. For example, if the inflation rate in Japan is higher than the inflation rate in the United States, we would expect the value of the dollar to increase relative to the value of the yen; that is, the nominal exchange rate would appreciate.

Why Purchasing Power Parity Doesn't Hold Exactly

The theory of purchasing power parity offers an explanation of movements in nominal exchange rates in the long run. Even in the long run, though, we wouldn't expect purchasing power parity to hold exactly for three main reasons.

First, not all goods and services are traded internationally. For example, a Big Mac is perishable, and so despite the assumptions in our earlier example, the search for arbitrage profits would not force the real exchange rate expressed in terms of Big Macs to equal 1. Similarly, services such as doctor visits are not traded internationally. Nontradable goods and services are a large component of GDP, so purchasing power parity will not hold exactly, even in the long run.

Second, countries impose barriers to trade such as *tariffs*, which are taxes on imports, and *quotas*, which are limits on the quantities of goods that can be imported. For example, the U.S. government limits imports of sugar, so the price of sugar in the United States is much higher than it is outside the United States. Because of the quota, it is not possible for individuals to purchase low-priced sugar in the world market and sell it for a profit inside the United States. By legally limiting the pursuit of arbitrage profit, barriers to trade prevent purchasing power parity from holding exactly.

Third, products differ across countries as firms adapt products to local tastes. Because the ingredients in Big Macs may vary across countries, Brazilian consumers may not be willing to pay 10.25 reals for a U.S. Big Mac even if one could be shipped from the United States without becoming a soggy mess. These differences in products prevent purchasing power parity from holding exactly.

So, purchasing power parity gives a reasonable, if not exact, guide to movements in nominal exchange rates in the long run. In particular, countries that have relatively high inflation rates usually see the value of their currencies depreciate and countries that have relatively low inflation rates usually see the value of their currencies appreciate. In the short run, though, purchasing power parity does a poor job in explaining movements in nominal exchange rates. A key reason for this failure is that purchasing power parity focuses on the demand for goods and services in different countries to explain movements in nominal exchange rates. As we noted in the chapter opener, however, in the short run most of the buying and selling of currency is not motivated by the need to finance international trade, but by the desire to engage in international financial investments.

The Interest Parity Condition

The huge demand for foreign exchange for purposes of financial investment reflects the increase in *international capital mobility* in recent decades. Policymakers in many countries have removed regulations that once hindered financial investments across national borders. The Internet allows investors in one country to easily access information about firms in other countries. The Internet also makes it easier for investors to connect with financial firms, particularly brokerage firms, to make investments in foreign firms for them. In this section, we explore how international capital mobility affects exchange rates.

Suppose that you intend to invest $1,000 in one-year government bonds. You are looking for the highest return on your investment, and you don't care which country you invest in. Also suppose that one-year U.S. Treasury bills currently have an interest rate of 3%, while one-year Japanese government bonds currently have an interest rate of 5%. (These interest rates are far above their current values, but we use them here for convenience.) To keep the example simple, assume that you consider the two bonds to be identical except for their interest rates. That is, you believe they have the same default risk, liquidity, information costs, and other characteristics. Which bonds should you purchase? The answer seems obvious: 5% is greater than 3%, so you should purchase the Japanese government bonds. But as a U.S. resident, you want your investment return to be in U.S. dollars. If you invest in the Japanese bond, you first have to exchange dollars for yen at the beginning of the year, and then at the end of the year, you have to exchange yen for dollars. You might receive less than a 5% return on your investment if during the time your funds are invested in Japanese bonds, the value of the yen declines relative to the dollar.

For example, suppose that you exchange your $1,000 for yen when the exchange rate is ¥100 = $1. After one year, you receive the 5% interest rate on the Japanese bond, but you need to exchange the yen for dollars. Suppose that the exchange rate is now ¥104 = $1, which means that the yen has *depreciated* by 4% against the dollar or—another way of saying the same thing—the dollar has *appreciated* by 4% against the yen. So, your investment resulted in your receiving 5% more yen ... but in exchanging the yen for dollars, you lost 4%, leaving your dollar return on your investment in Japanese bonds at just 1%, which is less than the 3% you would have received by investing in U.S. Treasury bills.

If the exchange rate after one year had been ¥98 = $1, you would have gained another 2% from the appreciation of the yen (depreciation of the dollar) that occurred while your funds were invested in yen. In this case, your dollar return on your investment in Japanese bonds would be 7% (= 5% + 2%), which would be well above the 3% you would have received by investing in U.S. Treasury bills.

We can summarize this result: *The return that a domestic investor receives on a foreign investment is equal to the interest rate on the foreign investment minus the rate of appreciation of the domestic currency.* Applying this result to the two examples given above, we have:

Example 1: Return to U.S. investor on Japanese bond = 5% − 4% = 1%

Example 2: Return to U.S. investor on Japanese bond = 5% + 2% = 7%

Therefore, whether you should invest in U.S. Treasury bills or in similar Japanese government bonds depends on what you believe the exchange rate will be one year from now. We would expect that as investors buy and sell bonds in the global financial market, the difference in interest rates among bonds in different countries would equal the expected change in exchange rates. Economists call this result the **interest parity condition**.

If:

i^D = domestic interest rate
i^F = foreign interest rate
E_t = nominal exchange rate today
E_{t+1}^e = expected nominal exchange rate one year from now

then the interest parity condition is:

$$i^D = i^F - \frac{E_{t+1}^e - E_t}{E_t},$$

or:

Interest rate on a domestic bond = Interest rate on a foreign bond − Expected rate of appreciation of the domestic currency.

Interest parity condition
The proposition that differences in interest rates on similar bonds in different countries reflect investors' expectations of future changes in exchange rates.

Solved Problem 4.3

Making a Financial Killing by Buying Brazilian Bonds?

When President Obama and Brazilian President Rousseff met in 2012, the interest rate on a one-year U.S. Treasury bill was just 0.2%, while the interest rate on a comparable one-year Brazilian government bond was 7.8%. With the gap between these interest rates so large, it was easy for an investor to make a high return by borrowing money at the low U.S. interest rate and investing it at the much higher Brazilian interest rate. Or was it? Evaluate this investment strategy.

Solving the Problem

Step 1   Review the chapter material. This problem is about the role exchange rates play in explaining differences in interest rates across countries, so you may want to review the section "The Interest Parity Condition," which begins on page 126.

Step 2   Answer the question by using the interest parity condition to explain the relationship between expected changes in exchange rates and differences in interest rates across countries. If the interest parity condition holds, then a 7.6-percentage-point gap between the interest rate on a U.S. Treasury bill and the interest rate on a similar Brazilian government bond means that investors must be expecting that the value of the dollar will appreciate against the real by 7.6%: 0.2% = 7.8 − (7.6%). Therefore, the expected return on a U.S. investment and a Brazilian investment should be the same. A U.S. investor who borrows money at 0.2% in the United States and invests it at 7.8% in Brazil will not gain anything if the dollar appreciates by 7.6% because the true dollar return on the investment will be 0.2% rather than 7.8%.

We can also mention a few real-world complications: Although the U.S. government can borrow money for one year at 0.2%, a private investor would have to pay a significantly higher interest rate to compensate lenders for the investor's higher default risk. Similarly, the interest parity condition holds only when investors see the two bonds being compared as having the same characteristics. In fact, investors will see the Brazilian bond as having higher default risk and lower liquidity than the U.S. Treasury bill. So, part of the gap between the two interest rates represents compensation for these characteristics of the Brazilian bond rather than expectations of future changes in the exchange rate. In addition, by investing in Brazil, a U.S. investor will be taking on exchange-rate risk because the dollar could appreciate by more than the difference between the U.S. and Brazilian interest rates, which would cause the investor to suffer a loss.

See related problems 3.8 and 3.9 at the end of the chapter.

Does the interest parity condition always hold? Although the interest parity condition provides important insight into movements in exchange rates, in practice, differences in interest rates on similar bonds depend on several factors. First, investors typically see even similar bonds as having important differences in default risk and liquidity. Second, typically, the costs of purchasing foreign financial assets—the *transactions costs*—are higher than for domestic assets. For instance, brokerage firms may charge an investor higher commissions to buy a foreign firm's bonds than they would charge to buy a domestic firm's bonds. Finally, the interest parity condition, as we have stated it, does not take into account the exchange-rate risk from investing in a foreign asset.

The interest parity condition provides some insight into what happens to the exchange rate when a country's interest rate increases or decreases relative to interest rates in another country. For example, suppose that the interest rate on a one-year U.S. Treasury bill is currently 2%, the interest rate on a comparable French one-year government bond is 4%, and the dollar is expected to appreciate by 2% against the euro. If the Federal Reserve takes actions that lead to the Treasury bill rate decreasing from 2% to 1%, we would expect the demand for dollars to decrease as investors exchange dollars for euros in order to invest in French bonds because the interest rate on those bonds is now higher relative to U.S. Treasury bills. A decrease in demand for dollars will cause the exchange rate to decrease: In the new equilibrium, more dollars will be required to buy a euro.

This result of lower U.S. interest rates leading to a lower exchange rate is consistent with the interest parity condition. If the exchange rate expected between the euro and the dollar one year from now remains the same, then a decrease in the exchange rate now—the spot exchange rate—means that the rate of appreciation will be higher. In this example, a decrease in the U.S. interest rate of 1%, with the French interest rate remaining unchanged, means that the expected rate of appreciation of the dollar will increase from 2% to 3% so that interest parity is maintained: $1\% = 4\% - 3\%$.

Making the Connection

Brazilian Firms Grapple with an Unstable Exchange Rate

We saw in the chapter opener that some Brazilian firms were upset with the effects of the U.S. Federal Reserve's interest rate policy. As our discussion of the interest parity condition shows, when the Fed pursues a monetary policy of low interest rates, the exchange rate between the dollar and other currencies will tend to fall. Brazilian firms believed that as the value of the dollar declined relative to the value of the Brazilian real, they would have difficulty selling their goods in the United States at the higher dollar prices. As the figure below shows, though, a larger problem for Brazilian firms is the instability of the real versus the dollar. (The exchange between the real and other major currencies followed a similar pattern.)

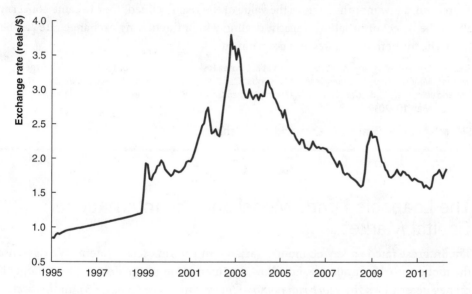

MyEconLab Real-time data

Large Brazilian firms not only have significant exports to other countries, they also sell bonds and take out loans in other currencies, particularly the dollar. Instability in the exchange rate makes it difficult for Brazilian exporters to plan because the foreign currency prices of their products will rise and fall, thereby affecting their sales and profits. In addition, firms that borrow in other currencies will face swings in the domestic currency price of their debt payments.

For example, consider a firm that has to make monthly interest payments of $100,000 to a U.S. bank. Initially, the exchange rate is 1.5 reals = 1 U.S. dollar, so the firm can exchange 150,000 reals for the dollars needed to make the interest payment. If the real depreciates to 2 reals = 1 U.S. dollar, then the firm needs to exchange 200,000 reals to receive the $100,000 it needs—a whopping 50% increase in the interest payment it is making when measured in reals. Even Brazilian firms that export significant amounts of their output will still typically earn most of their revenue in reals. So exchanging reals for dollars at a possibly less favorable exchange rate is necessary to make their debt payments. As the figure on the previous page shows, the real-dollar exchange rate has experienced swings of 50% or more a number of times over the past 20 years.

Notice that movements in exchange rates in either direction result in both good news and bad news for Brazilian firms. A depreciation helps firms that are exporting goods but hurts firms that have borrowed in foreign currencies. An appreciation hurts firms that are exporting goods but helps firms that have borrowed in foreign currencies. In either case, though, exchange rate fluctuations increase uncertainty and make it more difficult for firms to plan. As we discussed earlier, firms have some ability to hedge, or reduce the risk from exchange rate fluctuations, by using forward currency contracts. Such hedging can reduce exchange-rate risk but cannot eliminate it.

Finally, when the real depreciates, the prices of imports increase, which increases the Brazilian inflation rate. Even though as we saw in the chapter opener, Brazilian policymakers in early 2012 complained that actions by the Fed had caused the real to appreciate, a few months later, as the value of the real declined, they became concerned about the threat of inflation. Clearly, dealing with a fluctuating exchange rate can be a headache for both businesses and governments.

Sources: Luciana Magalhaes, "Currency Volatility Poses Risk for Brazilian Companies," *Wall Street Journal*, May 6, 2012; Michael Casey, "FX Global Call," *Wall Street Journal*, May 21, 2012; and Rogerio Jelmayer, "Inflation Woes May Prompt Brazil Central Bank U-Turn on Forex," *Wall Street Journal*, May 10, 2012.

See related problem 3.11 at the end of the chapter.

Learning Objective

Use the loanable funds model to analyze the international capital market.

The Loanable Funds Model and the International Capital Market

The interest rate is a key economic variable in the financial system. We have used the money market model to show how the interaction of the demand and supply for money determines the *short-run nominal interest rate* (see Chapter 3). In this section, we will use the loanable funds model to analyze the determinants of the *long-run real interest rate*. Recall that the nominal interest rate is the stated interest rate on a loan, while the real interest rate is the nominal interest rate adjusted for the effects of inflation. The long-run real interest rate is most relevant to households and firms making decisions about whether to invest in long-lived assets, such as houses or factories. In addition, the loanable funds model is useful when looking at the flow of funds between the U.S. and foreign financial markets.

We begin our discussion of the loanable funds model by noting that the financial system is composed of the many markets through which funds flow from lenders to borrowers: the market for certificates of deposit at banks, the market for stocks, the market for bonds, the market for mutual fund shares, and so on. For simplicity, we combine these markets into a single market for loanable funds. In the loanable funds model, the interaction of borrowers and lenders determines the market real interest rate and the quantity of loanable funds exchanged, as illustrated in Figure 4.4.

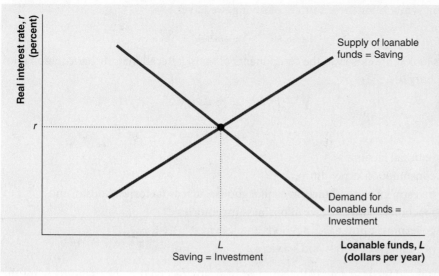

Figure 4.4

The Market for Loanable Funds

The supply of loanable funds is determined by (1) the willingness of households to save, (2) the extent of government saving, and (3) the extent of foreign saving that is invested in U.S. financial markets.

The demand for loanable funds is determined by the willingness of firms to borrow money to engage in new investment projects.

Equilibrium in the market for loanable funds determines the real interest rate and the quantity of loanable funds exchanged. At equilibrium in the loanable funds market, the total quantity of saving must equal the total quantity of investment.

Saving and Supply in the Loanable Funds Market

Let's first focus on the loanable funds market in a single economy. The supply of loanable funds is equal to the supply of saving in the economy. The supply of saving represents the total flow of funds into financial markets from all sources. It's useful to divide total saving into three sources:

1. *Saving from households* ($S_{\text{Households}}$), which equals the funds households have left from their incomes (including transfer payments received from the government) after buying goods and services and paying taxes to the government.

2. *Saving from the government* ($S_{\text{Government}}$), which equals the difference between the government's tax receipts and its spending on goods and services and on transfer payments to households. When a government spends more than it receives in taxes, government saving is negative.

3. *Saving from the foreign sector* (S_{Foreign}), which equals net exports, or the difference between exports and imports, but with the opposite sign. (Or, saving from the foreign sector $= -1 \times$ net exports.) To see why foreign saving equals the negative of net exports, consider that if the United States imports more than it exports, more dollars flow out of the country to purchase imports than flow back in as foreign firms and foreign households buy U.S. exports. These extra dollars held by households and firms outside the United States are available to be reinvested back into U.S. financial markets. So, for instance, in 2011, U.S. net exports equaled $-\$560$ billion. As a consequence, in 2011, households and firms outside the United States had an additional $560 billion available to invest in U.S. financial markets.[2] Saving from the foreign sector is referred to as a *net capital inflow*.

---

[2]We are simplifying here by ignoring items in the current account other than net exports, but this simplification does not significantly affect the main point.

Using symbols for these sources of saving, we have:

$$S = S_{\text{Households}} + S_{\text{Government}} + S_{\text{Foreign}}.$$

Let's look more closely at the components of saving. Recall that the basic national income identity is:

$$Y = C + I + G + NX,$$

where:

$Y =$ national income

$C =$ consumption expenditure

$I =$ investment expenditure on capital goods, such as factories, houses, and machinery, and changes in business inventories

$G =$ government purchases of goods and services

$NX =$ net exports of goods and services

Household income equals the amount of funds received by households from the sale of goods and services (Y), plus what is received from the government as transfer payments (TR) such as Social Security payments or unemployment insurance payments. Using these definitions and letting T stand for households' tax payments to government, we have the following expressions for the three sources of saving:

$$S_{\text{Households}} = (Y + TR - T) - C$$

$$S_{\text{Government}} = T - (G + TR)$$

$$S_{\text{Foreign}} = -NX$$

In Figure 4.4, we show the supply of loanable funds, or saving, as an upward-sloping line. The quantity of saving supplied increases as the interest rate increases for two reasons:

1. When households save, they reduce the amount of goods and services they can consume and enjoy today. The willingness of households to save rather than consume their incomes today will be determined in part by the interest rate they receive when they lend their savings. The higher the interest rate, the greater the reward to saving and the larger the quantity of funds households will save.

2. Foreign saving depends on the size of net exports. When the U.S. interest rate rises, foreign investors increase their demand for dollars in order to buy U.S. financial assets, such as Treasury bills. An increased demand for dollars increases the foreign exchange value of the dollar, reducing U.S. exports and increasing U.S. imports. A fall in exports and a rise in imports makes net exports a larger negative number, which increases the dollars available for people outside the United States to invest in U.S. financial markets. So, the higher the interest rate, the greater the quantity of foreign saving.

Investment and the Demand for Loanable Funds

The demand for loanable funds is determined by the willingness of firms to borrow money to engage in new investment projects, such as building new factories or carrying out research and development of new products, and by the demand by households for new houses.[3] In determining whether to borrow funds, firms compare the real return (that is, the return accounting for inflation) they expect to make on an investment with the real interest rate they must pay to borrow the necessary funds. For example, suppose that Home Depot is considering opening several new stores and expects to earn a real return of 8% on its investment. That investment will be profitable if Home Depot can borrow the funds at a real interest rate of 6% but will not be profitable if the real interest rate is 10%.

In Figure 4.4, the demand for loanable funds is downward sloping because the lower the real interest rate, the more investment projects firms can profitably undertake, and the greater the quantity of loanable funds they will demand.

Explaining Movements in Saving, Investment, and the Real Interest Rate

Equilibrium in the market for loanable funds determines the quantity of loanable funds that will flow from lenders to borrowers each period. Equilibrium also determines the real interest rate that lenders will receive and that borrowers must pay. Notice that because the supply of loanable funds represents saving, and the demand for loanable funds represents investment, in equilibrium, the value of saving equals the value of investment.

We draw the demand curve for loanable funds by holding constant all factors, other than the interest rate, that affect the willingness of borrowers to demand funds. For example, we have assumed that risk, taxes on businesses, and expectations about the profitability of investment projects are constant. We draw the supply curve by holding constant all factors, other than the real interest rate, that affect the willingness of lenders to supply funds. For example, we have assumed that taxes on households, government expenditure, and the desire for households to consume today relative to consuming in the future are constant. We have also assumed that the level of national income or GDP remains constant. A shift in either the demand curve or the supply curve will change the equilibrium interest rate and the equilibrium quantity of loanable funds.

For example, Figure 4.5 shows that if firms expect higher profits in the future, the real interest rate, national saving, and the level of investment will all change. The higher expected profits shift the investment demand curve to the right, which increases the real interest rate from r_1 to r_2 and the equilibrium quantity of loanable funds from L_1 to L_2. Notice that the increase in the quantity of loanable funds means that both the quantity of saving and the quantity of investment has increased.

We can also use the market for loanable funds to examine the effect of a government budget surplus or deficit. When the government's tax receipts exceed its spending, the government's budget is in surplus, and the total amount of saving in the economy is increased. In the more common situation where the government's spending exceeds its tax receipts, the budget is in deficit, and the total amount of saving in the economy is reduced. In 2012, the federal government's budget deficit was $1.3 trillion.

---

[3]Once again, be alert to the important difference between *financial investment* in stock, bonds, and other securities and *investment expenditure* on houses, factories, machinery, equipment, and inventories.

Figure 4.5

An Increase in the Demand of Loanable Funds

An increase in the demand of loanable funds increases the equilibrium real interest rate from r_1 to r_2 and increases the equilibrium quantity of loanable funds from L_1 to L_2. As a result, saving and investment expenditure both increase.

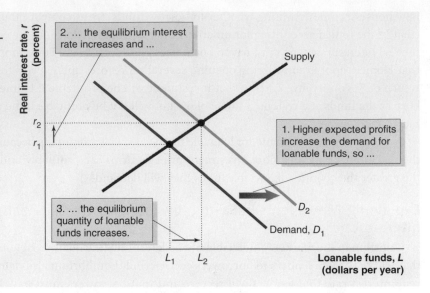

Holding constant other factors that affect the demand and supply of loanable funds, Figure 4.6 shows the effects of a budget deficit as a shift to the left in the supply of loanable funds, from S_1 to S_2. In the new equilibrium, the real interest rate is higher and the equilibrium quantity of loanable funds is lower. Running a deficit has reduced the level of total saving in the economy and, by increasing the interest rate, it has also reduced the level of investment by firms. By borrowing to finance its budget deficit, the government will have crowded out some firms that would otherwise have been able to borrow to finance investment. **Crowding out** refers to the reduction in private investment that results from an increase in government purchases. Figure 4.6 shows the decline in investment due to crowding out by the movement from L_1 to L_2 on the demand for loanable funds curve.

Crowding out The reduction in private investment that results from an increase in government purchases.

Figure 4.6

The Effect of a Budget Deficit on the Market for Loanable Funds

When the government runs a budget deficit, the supply of loanable funds shifts to the left. The equilibrium real interest rate increases from r_1 to r_2, and the equilibrium quantity of loanable funds falls from L_1 to L_2. As a result, saving and investment both decline.

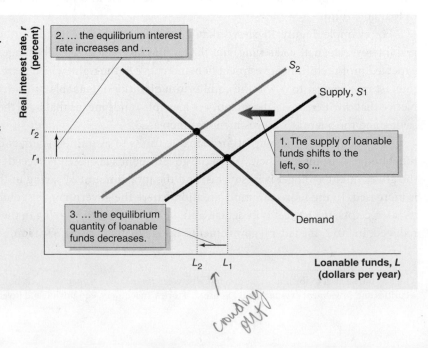

Figure 4.6 shows that an increase in the budget deficit will reduce national saving, leading to higher real interest rates and lower investment. In addition to budget deficits, other government policies can affect national saving. For example, the government gives special tax incentives for savings, such as 401(k) retirement accounts. These accounts allow individuals to delay paying taxes on income put into retirement accounts until they actually retire. The delay in paying taxes increases the after-tax return to saving, so the policy encourages individuals to save.

Table 4.3 on the next page summarizes the key factors that cause shifts in the demand and supply of loanable funds.

The International Capital Market and the Interest Rate

The foreign sector affects the domestic interest rate and the quantity of funds available in the domestic economy. Foreign households, firms, and governments may lend funds to borrowers in the United States if the expected returns are higher than in other countries. Similarly, if opportunities are more profitable outside the United States, loanable funds will be drawn away from U.S. markets to investments abroad. In this section, we expand the loanable funds model to analyze the interaction between U.S. and foreign bond markets.

Borrowing and lending take place in the *international capital market*, where households, firms, and governments borrow and lend across national borders. The *world real interest rate*, r_w, is the interest rate that is determined in the international capital market. The quantity of loanable funds that is supplied in an open economy can be used to fund projects in the domestic economy or abroad. In thinking of the international economy, it is useful to make a distinction between *small open economies* and *large open economies*. Shifts in the supply or demand for loanable funds in small open economies, such as the economies of the Netherlands and Belgium, do not have much effect on the world real interest rate. However, changes in the behavior of lenders and borrowers in large open economies, such as the economies of Germany and the United States, do affect the world real interest rate. In the following sections, we consider interest rate determination in each case.

Small Open Economy

In a closed economy, the equilibrium domestic interest rate is determined by the intersection of the demand curve and supply curve for loanable funds in the country, and we ignore the world interest rate. In an open economy, the world real interest rate is determined in the international capital market. In the case of a small open economy, the quantity of loanable funds supplied or demanded is too small to affect the world real interest rate. So, a small open economy's domestic real interest rate equals the world real interest rate, as determined in the international capital market. For example, if the small country of Monaco, located in the south of France, had a large increase in domestic wealth, the resulting increase in loanable funds would have only a trivial effect on the total amount of loanable funds in the world and, therefore, a trivial effect on the world interest rate.

Why must the domestic interest rate in a small open economy equal the world interest rate? Suppose that the world real interest rate is 4%, but the domestic real

Table 4.3 Summary of the Loanable Funds Model

An increase in ...	will shift the ...	causing ...	Graph of the effect on equilibrium in the loanable funds market
the government's budget deficit	supply of loanable funds curve to the left	the real interest rate to increase and investment to decrease.	
net exports	supply of loanable funds curve to the left	the real interest rate to increase and investment to decrease.	
the desire of households to consume today	supply of loanable funds curve to the left	the real interest rate to increase and investment to decrease.	
tax benefits for saving, such as 401(k) retirement accounts, which increases the incentive to save	supply of loanable funds curve to the right	the real interest rate to decrease and investment to increase.	
expected future profits	demand of loanable funds curve to the right	the real interest rate and the level of investment to increase.	
corporate taxes	demand of loanable funds curve to the left	the real interest rate and the level of investment to decrease.	

interest rate in Monaco is 3%. A lender in Monaco would not accept an interest rate less than 4% because we assume that the lender could easily buy foreign bonds with a 4% interest rate. So, domestic borrowers would have to pay the world real interest rate of 4%, or they would be unable to borrow. Similarly, if the world real interest rate were 4%, but the domestic real interest rate in Monaco were 5%, borrowers in Monaco would borrow at the world rate of 4%. So, domestic lenders would have to lend at the world rate of 4%, or they would be unable to find anyone to lend to. This reasoning indicates why for a small open economy, the domestic and world real interest rates must be the same.

Figure 4.7 shows the supply and demand curves for loanable funds for a small open economy. If the world real interest rate, r_w, is 3%, the quantity of loanable funds supplied and demanded domestically are equal (point E), and the country neither lends nor borrows funds in the international capital market. Suppose instead that the world real interest rate is 5%. In this case, the quantity of loanable funds supplied domestically (point C) is greater than the quantity of funds demanded domestically (point B). What happens to the excess supply of loanable funds? Those funds are loaned on the international capital market at the world real interest rate of 5%. Because the country is small, the amount of funds it has to lend is small relative to the world market, so lenders in the country have no trouble finding borrowers in other countries. As our earlier discussion of the balance of payments indicates, this international lending represents a current account surplus.

Now suppose that the world real interest rate is 1%. As Figure 4.7 shows, the quantity of loanable funds demanded domestically (point A) now exceeds the quantity of funds supplied domestically (point D). How is this excess demand for funds satisfied? By

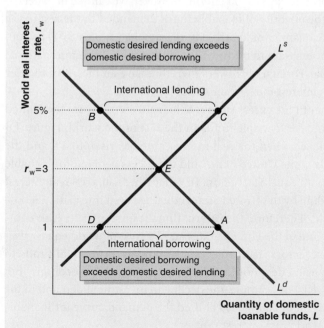

Figure 4.7

Determining the Real Interest Rate in a Small Open Economy

The domestic real interest rate in a small open economy is the world real interest rate, r_w, which in this case is 3%. If the world real interest rate were greater than 3%, the country would lend internationally. If the world real interest rate were less than 3%, the country would borrow internationally.

borrowing on the international capital market. Because the country is small, the amount of funds it wants to borrow is small relative to the world market, so borrowers in the country have no trouble finding lenders in other countries. As our earlier discussion of the balance of payments indicates, this international borrowing represents a current account deficit.

To summarize: The real interest rate in a small open economy is the same as the interest rate in the international capital market. If the quantity of loanable funds supplied domestically exceeds the quantity of funds demanded domestically at that interest rate, the country invests some of its loanable funds abroad. If the quantity of loanable funds demanded domestically exceeds the quantity of funds supplied domestically at that interest rate, the country finances some of its domestic borrowing needs with funds from abroad.

Large Open Economy

Shifts in the demand and supply of loanable funds in some countries—such as the United States, China, Japan, and Germany—are sufficiently large that they affect the world real interest rate, so these countries are considered large open economies.

Suppose to simplify the discussion we think of the world as two large open economies: the economy of the United States and the economy of the rest of the world. Then the real interest rate in the international capital market equates desired international lending by the United States with desired international borrowing by the rest of the world. Using this assumption, Figure 4.8 illustrates how interest rates are determined in a large open economy. The figure presents a loanable funds graph for the United States in panel (a) and a loanable funds graph for the rest of the world in panel (b). In panel (a), if the world real interest rate is 3%, the quantity of loanable funds demanded and supplied in the United States are both equal to $300 billion. However, we can see in panel (b) that at an interest rate of 3%, the quantity of loanable funds demanded in the rest of the world is $800 billion, while the quantity of loanable funds supplied is only $700 billion. This tells us that foreign borrowers want to borrow $100 billion more from international capital markets than is available. Foreign borrowers therefore have an incentive to offer lenders in the United States an interest rate greater than 3%.

The interest rate will rise until the excess supply of loanable funds from the United States equals the excess demand for loanable funds in the rest of the world. Figure 4.8 shows that this equality is reached when the real interest rate has risen to 4% and the excess supply of loanable funds in the United States and the excess demand for loanable funds in the rest of the world both equal $50 billion. In other words, at a 4% real interest rate, desired international lending by the United States equals desired international borrowing by the rest of the world. Therefore, the international capital market is in equilibrium when the real interest rate in the United States and the rest of world equals 4%.

It's important to note that factors that cause the demand and supply of funds to shift in a large open economy will affect not just the interest rate in that economy but the world real interest rate as well. For example, the decline in investment demand in the United States during the recession of 2007–2009 shifted the demand curve for loanable funds to the left, lowering the world real interest rate.

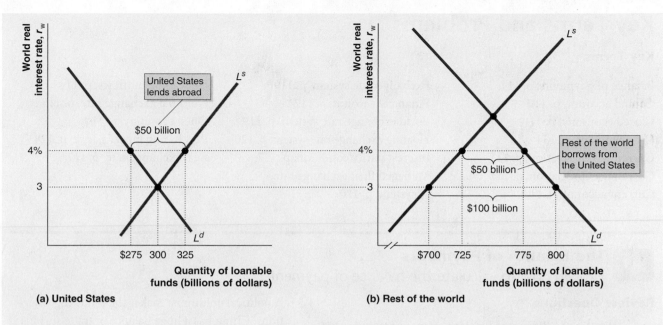

Figure 4.8

Determining the Real Interest Rate in a Large Open Economy

Saving and investment shifts in a large open economy can affect the world real interest rate. The world real interest rate adjusts to equalize desired international borrowing and desired international lending. At a world real interest rate of 4%, desired international lending by the domestic economy equals desired international borrowing by the rest of the world.

Answering the Key Question

Continued from page 108

At the beginning of this chapter, we asked:

"What are the advantages and disadvantages of floating versus fixed exchange rates?"

A fixed exchange rate policy makes it easier for firms that do business internationally to make plans and also makes it easier for the central bank to control inflation. But fixed exchange rate systems are often difficult to maintain because exchange rates are not free to adjust quickly to changes in demand for currencies and because they require the central bank to maintain large reserves of foreign currency. A fixed exchange rate also eliminates the possibility that the central bank can depreciate the currency to stimulate the economy during a recession.

A floating exchange rate policy lets demand and supply determine the exchange rate, so there is no need for government intervention. But exchange rate fluctuations make planning difficult for firms and can worsen inflation if the prices of imported goods rise rapidly.

A managed floating exchange rate policy allows for greater flexibility than a fixed exchange rate system. However, it is unlikely to be effective for large economies because a central bank's purchases or sales will be very small relative to the total amount of buying and selling of its currency in the foreign exchange market.

Key Terms and Problems

Key Terms

Balance of payments, p. 111
Capital account, p. 112
Closed economy, p. 110
Crowding out, p. 134
Currency appreciation, p. 117
Currency depreciation, p. 117
Current account, p. 112

Exchange rate system, p. 119
Financial account, p. 112
Fixed exchange rate system, p. 119
Floating exchange rate system, p. 120
Interest parity condition, p. 127
Managed float exchange rate
    system, p. 120

Net capital outflows, p. 114
Nominal exchange rate, p. 115
Open economy, p. 110
Purchasing power parity, p. 124
Real exchange rate, p. 117

4.1 The Balance of Payments
Explain how to calculate the balance of payments.

Review Questions

1.1 What is the difference between an open economy and a closed economy?

1.2 What is the purpose of the balance of payments? Briefly discuss the components of the current account, the capital account, and the financial account.

1.3 What are a trade deficit, a current account deficit, and a financial account deficit? Is it possible for a country to run a balance of payments deficit?

Problems and Applications

1.4 Briefly explain in which of the three balance of payments accounts each of the following transactions would occur:

  a. An export of goods

  b. A purchase of bonds

  c. A gift to someone in another country

  d. A dividend paid on stock owned in another country

1.5 A political columnist makes the following assertion: "China has a huge balance of trade surplus with the rest of the world. In addition, the rest of the world is investing huge amounts in China, which is the main way that China is able to fund investments in new factories." Use your knowledge of the balance of payments accounts to analyze the columnist's argument.

1.6 An article in the *Economist* magazine states: "India aims to fund its current-account deficit mainly by attracting … flows of FDI [foreign direct investment]." What is foreign direct investment? In what sense can foreign direct investment fund a country's current account deficit?
Source: "Travellers Checked," *Economist*, May 19, 2012.

1.7 Consider the following statement: "Because the percentage of U.S. GDP accounted for by trade is much less than for many other countries, trade is not very important to the United States." Briefly explain whether you agree with this statement.

1.8 The table below represents the balance of payments for a small nation in 2012.
All values are in millions of U.S. dollars. Calculate the missing values in the table
and briefly explain how you arrived at your answers.

Current Account		
Exports of goods and services	$6,525	
Imports of goods and services	_____	
Net exports		1,223
Income received on investments and labor compensation	1,108	
Income payments on investments and labor compensation	−640	
Net factor payments		_____
Net transfers		−303
Balance on current account		_____
Financial Account		
Increase in foreign holdings of assets in the United States	_____	
Increase in U.S. holdings of assets in foreign countries	−2,469	
Net financial derivatives	17	
Balance on financial account		−1,436
Capital Account		
Balance on capital account		−5
Statistical discrepancy	_____	
Balance of payments		_____

4.2	**Exchange Rates and Exchange Rate Policy**

Understand the advantages and disadvantages of different exchange rate policies.

Review Questions

2.1 Most people in the United States rarely exchange
U.S. dollars for another currency. So why do
economists and policymakers worry about
fluctuations in exchange rates?

2.2 Briefly explain the difference between each of the
following:

a. A nominal exchange rate and a real exchange rate

b. A bilateral exchange rate and a multilateral
exchange rate

c. A currency appreciation and a currency
depreciation

d. A fixed exchange rate system and a floating
exchange rate system

2.3 Briefly explain the similarities and the differences between the gold standard and the Bretton
Woods systems.

2.4 Briefly discuss the policy choices reflected in current exchange rate systems.

Problems and Applications

2.5 According to an article in the *Wall Street Journal,* "Japan's three largest auto makers are signaling plans to shift more production overseas to deal with the strong yen."

a. What does the article mean by a "strong yen"?

b. What problem does a strong yen cause for Japanese automobile companies?

c. How would moving production overseas help Japanese automobile companies deal with a strong yen?

Source: "Japan's Big Car Makers Grapple with Strong Yen," *Wall Street Journal*, June 26, 2012.

2.6 In each of the following cases, calculate the real exchange rate:

a. A bottle of wine sells for $16 in the United States and €10 in France, and the nominal exchange rate is $1 = €1.3.

b. A book sells for $10 in the United States and ¥950 in Japan, and the nominal exchange rate is $1 = ¥100.

c. A shirt sells for $45 in the United States and £30 in the United Kingdom, and the nominal exchange rate is $1 = £1.5.

2.7 If you were a U.S. firm whose business mainly involves importing or exporting goods, why might you prefer an exchange rate system like Bretton Woods to the current system?

2.8 Some countries with fixed exchange rates have attempted to overvalue their currencies—that is, they have tried to keep the exchange rate above the market rate.

a. How can a country overvalue its currency?

b. Why would a country want to maintain an overvalued currency?

c. Why is it difficult to maintain an overvalued currency for a long period of time?

2.9 [Related to Making the Connection **on page 121**] In mid-2012, as Greece considered leaving the euro, the *Wall Street Journal* published an article that included this observation: "The Continent's financial system remains vulnerable to the prospect that stampedes of customers could yank their deposits from [banks] perceived as shaky." Were bank depositors afraid that banks were likely to fail? If not, what were they afraid of? Would depositors in U.S. banks be likely to have similar fears about U.S. banks? Briefly explain.

Source: David Enrich, Sara Schaefer Muñoz, and Charles Forelle, "Europe Bank Fear Flight of Deposits," *Wall Street Journal*, May 20, 2012.

2.10 [Related to the Making the Connection **on page 121**] In 2012, as the chances of Greece abandoning the euro increased, a Greek government official was quoted as saying: "Potential investors in Greek assets just don't want to be wrong-footed by investing in euros and getting paid out in drachmas." What did the official mean by potential investors being "wrong-footed"? Why would investing in euros and getting paid in drachmas be bad for investors?

Source: Damien McElroy, "Greeks Withdraw Savings in National 'Bank Jog,'" *Atlantic*, May 20, 2012.

4.3 **What Factors Determine Exchange Rates?**
Discuss what factors determine exchange rates.

Review Questions

3.1 What is purchasing power parity? Why doesn't purchasing power parity hold exactly?

3.2 Assuming that purchasing power parity holds, write an equation that expresses the relationship among the percentage change in the nominal exchange rate, the domestic inflation rate, and the foreign inflation rate. Briefly explain this equation.

3.3 What is the interest parity condition?

3.4 What problems can exchange rate fluctuations cause for firms?

MyEconLab Visit **www.myeconlab.com** to complete these exercises online and get instant feedback. Exercises that update with real-time data are marked with 🌐.

Problems and Applications

3.5 If the euro appreciates, how will this affect your purchases of U.S. and German goods? Explain.

3.6 Suppose that you are planning to study abroad in Mexico for a semester. In planning for your trip, you calculate what you spend in a semester in the United States. Then you check to see what the current exchange rate is.

    a. If you spend $2,000 per semester on food, entertainment, and other incidental expenses in Mexico, and if the current exchange rate is $1 = 12 pesos, how many pesos do you need if your expenses are identical?

    b. Assuming that you consume the same amount of food and other goods no matter where you are in Mexico, do you think that the method you used in part (a) will correctly calculate the number of pesos you need for your trip? Briefly explain.

3.7 Suppose that the inflation rate in the United States is 5%, and the inflation rate in the United Kingdom is 8%. Use purchasing power parity to predict what is likely to happen to the exchange rate between the pound and the dollar.

3.8 [Related to Solved Problem 4.3 **on page 127**] According to an article in the *Wall Street Journal*, in mid-2012, "investors are borrowing money in yen, where [interest] rates are low, and exchanging it for currencies in countries where [interest] rates are high—such as Australia, Canada and Mexico—profiting from the difference." Is it certain that investors actually are profiting from this difference in interest rates? Briefly explain.

Source: Erin McCarthy, "Yen Play Is Blast from the Past," *Wall Street Journal*, May 20, 2012.

3.9 [Related to Solved Problem 4.3 **on page 127**] According to an article in the *Wall Street Journal*, "Revenue U.S. companies generate in Brazil increasingly stays in banks there, where the central bank's interest rate is nearly 10%. That same cash earns almost nothing in the U.S., where the Federal Reserve has said it will hold interest rates near zero into 2014." Do U.S. firms run any risks by adopting this strategy of leaving funds in Brazilian banks rather than bringing the funds back to the United States? Briefly explain.

Source: Chana R. Schoenberger, "Companies Parking Cash in Brazil to Garner High Yields," *Wall Street Journal*, March 12, 2012.

3.10 [Related to the Chapter Opener **on page 108**] In a meeting with President Obama, Brazilian President Dilma Rousseff argued that the monetary policy of the United States was "impairing growth ... in emerging countries." Explain her reasoning.

Source: John Lyons and Tom Barkley, "Brazil Leader Slams U.S. Money Policy," *Wall Street Journal*, April 9, 2012.

3.11 [Related to the Making the Connection **on page 129**] According to an article in the *Wall Street Journal* on the effects of fluctuations in the exchange value of the real on Brazilian firms, "Companies most at risk are those with large amounts of foreign currency debt."

    a. What is foreign currency debt?

    b. Why would firms in Brazil have foreign currency debt?

    c. Why would having foreign currency debt make firms in Brazil more vulnerable to fluctuations in the exchange value of the real? Would these firms be equally hurt by an appreciation of the real as by a depreciation of the real? Briefly explain.

Source: Luciana Magalhaes, "Currency Volatility Poses Risk for Brazilian Companies," *Wall Street Journal*, May 6, 2012.

4.4 **The Loanable Funds Model and the International Capital Market**
Use the loanable funds model to analyze the international capital market.

Review Questions

4.1 What determines the supply of loanable funds? What determines the demand for loanable funds?

4.2 In the loanable funds model, why is the demand curve downward sloping? Why is the supply curve upward sloping?

MyEconLab   Visit **www.myeconlab.com** to complete these exercises online and get instant feedback. Exercises that update with real-time data are marked with ⬤.

4.3 Briefly explain what happens to the world real interest rate if the government of Monaco runs a large government budget deficit.

Problems and Applications

4.4 Suppose this graph represents the demand and supply of loanable funds in the United States. Use the graph to answer the following questions.

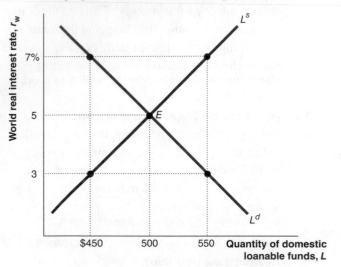

a. If the world real interest rate is 5%, explain what would give foreign borrowers an incentive to offer lenders in the United States an interest rate greater than 5%.

b. If the world real interest rate is 5%, explain what would give foreign lenders an incentive to offer borrowers in the United States an interest rate less than 5%.

4.5 Draw a graph of the market for loanable funds in a closed economy. Show the effect on the equilibrium real interest rate and quantity of funds loaned and borrowed of each of the following events:

a. Consumers decide to spend less.

b. The government decreases its spending.

c. Businesses become pessimistic about future profitability.

d. The government's budget deficit increases, and at the same time, investment in new capital goods becomes more profitable.

4.6 Suppose that in a small open economy, the domestic quantity of loanable funds supplied equals the domestic quantity of loanable funds demanded. In other words, there is no foreign lending or borrowing. If the government budget deficit increases, what will happen in the market for loanable funds? Will the country lend or borrow internationally? Briefly explain.

4.7 Suppose that in a large open economy, the quantity of loanable funds supplied domestically is initially equal to the quantity of funds demanded domestically. Then an increase in business taxes discourages investment. Draw a graph of the loanable funds market to show how this change affects the quantity of loanable funds and the world real interest rate. Does the economy now borrow or lend internationally?

4.8 In a small open economy, how would each of the following events affect the equilibrium interest rate and the amount of international lending or borrowing that the country engages in?

a. A natural disaster causes extensive damage to homes, bridges, and highways, leading to increased investment spending to repair the damaged infrastructure.

b. Taxes on businesses are expected to be increased in the future.

c. The World Cup soccer matches are being televised, and many people stay home to watch them, reducing consumption spending.

d. The government proposes a new tax on saving, based on the value of people's investments as of December 31 each year.

4.9 Repeat problem 4.8 for a large open economy.

4.10 An article in the *Economist* magazine refers to the United Kingdom as a "small open economy." If this statement is correct, will the U.K. economy experience crowding out if the government runs a budget deficit? Briefly explain.

Source: "Austerity Is Pain. So Is Tight Money," *Economist*, January 19, 2012.

Data Exercises

D4.1: Using data from the St. Louis Federal Reserve (FRED) (http://research.stlouisfed.org/fred2/), analyze the trade-weighted value of the U.S. dollar.

  a. Download monthly data on the trade-weighted exchange rate for the U.S. dollar against major currencies (TWEXMMTH) from 1973 to the present.

  b. What has been the long-term trend in the exchange value of the dollar? What effect should changes in the exchange rate have had on U.S. net exports? Briefly explain.

  c. What has been the trend in the exchange value of the dollar over the last year? What effect should changes in the exchange rate have had on U.S. net exports? Briefly explain.

D4.2: Using data from the St. Louis Federal Reserve (FRED) (http://research.stlouisfed.org/fred2/), analyze the current account.

  a. Download quarterly data on the nominal current (NETFI) and on nominal potential GDP (NGDPPOT) from 1973 to the present. Calculate the current account as a percentage of potential GDP.

  b. Download monthly data on the trade-weighted exchange rate for the U.S. dollar against major currencies (TWEXMMTH) from 1973 to the present. How do the current account movements correspond with exchange-rate movements?

D4.3: The U.S. Treasury publishes data on capital flows. Treasury International Capital Flows can be found at www.treasury.gov/resource-center/data-chart-center/tic/Pages/index.aspx. Go to U.S. Transactions in Long-Term Securities.

  a. Look at recent net purchases of long-term securities. How has the volume of purchases changed over the past five years?

  b. Now look at gross purchases of long-term securities. Which countries hold the most U.S.

securities? How have foreign holdings of U.S. securities changed over time?

D4.4: [Excel exercise] The Bank for International Settlements (BIS) publishes data on real effective exchange rates and indexes of nominal effective exchange rates (www.bis.org/statistics/eer/index.htm). These indexes attempt to measure competitiveness.

  a. Find and download the real and nominal effective exchange rate for the Chinese yuan for the past five years.

  b. Plot the two series against each other.

  c. The nominal effective exchange rate of the yuan changes little because it has been a fixed rate. What accounts for the differences between the two exchange rates? [Hint: It may be helpful to read the BIS's explanation of its indexes of competitiveness.]

D4.5: Using data from the St. Louis Federal Reserve (FRED) (http://research.stlouisfed.org/fred2/), analyze foreign exchange rates.

  a. Find the most recent values from FRED for the Japan/U.S. Foreign Exchange Rate (DEXJPUS), China/U.S. Foreign Exchange Rate (DEXCHUS), and the Mexico/U.S. Foreign Exchange Rate (DEXMXUS).

  b. Explain whether the exchange rates are quoted as U.S. dollars per unit of foreign currency or Units of foreign currency per U.S. dollar.

  c. Suppose a Big Mac sells for 300 yen in Japan, 14 yuan in China, and 34 pesos in Mexico. What is the price of a Big Mac in each country in terms of U.S. dollars?

  d. Assuming no transportation costs, explain in which county you would want to purchase a Big Mac and in which country you would want to sell the same Big Mac in order to make the highest profit possible.

MyEconLab   Visit **www.myeconlab.com** to complete these exercises online and get instant feedback. Exercises that update with real-time data are marked with .

D4.6: Using data from the St. Louis Federal Reserve (FRED) (http://research.stlouisfed.org/fred2/), analyze foreign exchange rates.

   a. Find the two most recent values from FRED for the Japan/U.S. Foreign Exchange Rate (DEXJPUS) and for U.S. Exports of Goods to Japan, f.a.s basis (EXPJP).

   b. Given the change in the exchange rate between the two periods, explain if the U.S. exports to Japan change in the direction that economic theory would predict.

D4.7: Using data from the St. Louis Federal Reserve (FRED) (http://research.stlouisfed.org/fred2/), analyze foreign exchange rates.

   a. Find the two most recent values from FRED for the Japan/U.S. Foreign Exchange Rate (DEXJPUS) and the U.S. Imports of Goods from Japan, Custom Basis (IMPJP).

   b. Given the change in the exchange rate between the two periods, explain if the U.S. imports from Japan change in the direction that economic theory would predict.

D4.8: Using data from the St. Louis Federal Reserve (FRED) (http://research.stlouisfed.org/fred2/), analyze foreign exchange rates.

   a. Find the most recent value and the value from the same month one year earlier from FRED for the U.S./Euro Foreign Exchange Rate (EXUSEU).

   b. Using the values found above, compute the percentage change in the euro's value.

   c. Explain whether the dollar appreciated or depreciated against the euro.

D4.9: Using data from the St. Louis Federal Reserve (FRED) (http://research.stlouisfed.org/fred2/), analyze savings and investment.

   a. Find the most recent values and the values from the same quarter three years earlier from FRED for Gross Private Saving (GPSAVE) and Gross Government Saving (GGSAVE).

   b. Using the values found above, compute the total gross saving in the economy for each period.

   c. Draw a graph to show the loanable funds market in equilibrium. Explain which curve represents total gross saving.

   d. On the graph drawn in part (c), show the effect on the loanable funds market from the change in total gross saving between the two periods in part (a).

D4.10: Using data from the St. Louis Federal Reserve (FRED) (http://research.stlouisfed.org/fred2/), analyze savings and investment.

   a. Find the most recent value and the value from the same quarter four years earlier from FRED for Gross Government Saving (GGSAVE).

   b. Total gross saving in the economy is composed of gross private saving and gross government saving. What does gross government saving represent?

   c. Using the values found above, explain whether the government budget is balanced, in a surplus, or in a deficit. From the first period to the most recent period, has government saving increased, decreased, or remained constant?

   d. Draw a graph to show the loanable funds market in equilibrium. Show the effect on the loanable funds market from the change in gross government saving you calculated in part (a). Explain what will happen to the level of investment in the economy.

The Standard of Living over Time and Across Countries

Learning Objectives

After studying this chapter, you should be able to:

5.1 Describe the aggregate production function (pages 148–155)

5.2 Explain how real GDP is determined in the long run (pages 155–161)

5.3 Understand why the standard of living varies across countries (pages 161–164)

5.4 Understand why labor productivity varies across countries (pages 164–170)

Who Is Number One?

What is the leading economy in the world today? In ranking the economic performance of countries, economists generally use two related measures: GDP and GDP per capita. The following table shows the top 10 economies in 2011, based on these two measures (only countries having a population of at least 1 million are included):

Rank	GDP	GDP per capita
1	United States	Qatar
2	China	Singapore
3	India	Norway
4	Japan	Hong Kong
5	Germany	United Arab Emirates
6	Russia	United States
7	Brazil	Switzerland
8	United Kingdom	Netherlands
9	France	Austria
10	Italy	Australia

Both of these measures have some value. The sheer size of an economy, as measured by GDP, can help a country's firms achieve economies of scale, and a large economy may be better able to support a large military, thereby increasing the country's political influence in the world. From the point of view of the average person living in a country, however, GDP per capita is the most important measure. GDP per capita measures the quantity of goods and services available to the average person in the country and, therefore, is a good measure of the standard of living of the typical person. A country can have a large economy, as measured by GDP, but a low standard of living, as measured by GDP per capita. Notice, for instance, that China has the second-largest economy and India has the third-largest economy, as measured by GDP, but as the following table shows, in

Continued on next page

Key Issue and Question

Issue: Some countries have experienced rapid rates of long-run economic growth, while other countries have grown slowly, if at all.

Question: Why isn't the whole world rich?

Answered on page 170

2011, both countries lagged far behind the United States in GDP per capita:

Country	GDP	GDP per capita
United States	$15.0 trillion	$48,100
China	11.3 trillion	8,400
India	4.5 trillion	3,700

While in 2011, GDP in the United States was only about 33% higher than in China, the standard of living of the typical person in the United States was almost six times higher than the standard of living of the typical person in China. The difference in GDP per capita actually understates the true difference in living standards between the two countries. For example, the average person in the United States lives longer, has more years of education, is much less likely to die in infancy or during childbirth, and is much less likely to suffer serious medical problems because of pollution than is the average person in China.

Is the United States likely to maintain its current economic lead over China? Since the Chinese government first introduced market-oriented reforms in 1978, the Chinese economy has grown more rapidly than the U.S. economy. So, part of the gap between the two economies has already closed. The projected growth rate of real GDP in China is nearly three times greater than the growth rate of real GDP in the United States. If those projections are accurate, Chinese real GDP should be larger than U.S. real GDP by 2018. Closing the gap in real GDP per capita will be much more difficult for China. Long-range growth forecasts can be inaccurate because the factors that determine economic growth can change in ways that are difficult to predict. But a recent forecast by the consulting firm PricewaterhouseCoopers indicated that by 2050, Chinese real GDP per capita will still be only about 50% of U.S. real GDP per capita.

Sources: U.S. Central Intelligence Agency, *The* World Factbook *2011*; United Nations Development Program, *Human Development Report, 2011*, New York: Palgrave Macmillan, November 2010; "GDP per Person, Forecasts," *Economist*, January 13, 2011; and authors' calculations.

Real GDP per capita is a key economic concept because it helps determine the standard of living of the average person in a country. Although the United States, Japan, Western Europe, and certain other countries have attained high standards of living, billions of people remain stuck in grinding poverty. In fact, the standard of living in some countries in Asia, Africa, and Latin America has increased relatively little in hundreds of years. Why are some countries rich and others poor? In this chapter, we begin building a model that can help answer that question.

Learning Objective

Describe the aggregate production function.

The Aggregate Production Function

When discussing the standard of living, we are most interested in real GDP *per capita* because that is the best measure of the quantity of goods and services available per person. We begin, though, by developing a model to explain real GDP and then adjust the model to explain real GDP per capita.

To understand how real GDP gets produced, we can think first about how an individual firm combines land, labor, natural resources, and capital—such as machinery, equipment, factories, and office buildings—to produce goods and services. The relationship between the inputs employed by a firm and the maximum output it can produce with those inputs is called the firm's *production function*. A firm's *technology* is the process it uses to turn inputs into outputs of goods and services. Notice that this economic definition of technology is broader than the everyday definition. When we use the word *technology* in everyday language, we usually refer only to the development of new products, such as iPads. In the economic sense, a firm's technology depends on many factors, such as the skills of its managers, the training of its workers, and the speed and efficiency of its machinery and equipment. The technology of pizza production, for example, includes not only the capacity of the restaurant's pizza ovens and how well the ovens bake the pizza but also the skill of the workers in preparing the pizza, how well the manager motivates the workers, and how well the manager has arranged the facilities to allow the cooks to quickly prepare the pizzas and get them in the ovens. Because a firm's technology is the process it uses to turn inputs into output, the production function represents the firm's technology.

The production function is a microeconomic concept when we apply it to an individual firm, but on a macroeconomic level, we can think about how an economy turns the total available inputs into goods and services. So, we can say that the **aggregate production function** is an equation that shows the relationship between the inputs employed by firms and the maximum output firms can produce with those inputs. At the macroeconomic level, we measure output as real GDP, and we include only labor and capital as inputs because land and natural resources are relatively minor components of production in advanced economies such as the United States, Japan, and Germany.

Aggregate production function An equation that shows the relationship between the inputs employed by firms and the maximum output firms can produce with those inputs.

We can write a general version of the aggregate production function as:

$$Y = A \times F(K, L), \text{ or } Y = AF(K, L),$$

where:
Y = real GDP
K = quantity of capital goods available to firms, or the *capital stock*
L = quantity of labor
A = index of how efficiently the economy transforms capital and labor into real GDP

The higher the level of the index, A, the more efficient is the economy and the higher is real GDP. Some of the factors that can affect the value of A include technology, government regulations and institutions, the quality of the labor force, and a nation's geography. In fact, A measures the effect of any factor that determines real GDP other than the quantities of capital and labor. For the sake of simplicity, in the rest of this book, we will refer to the aggregate production function simply as the *production function*.

The Cobb–Douglas Production Function

Economists often analyze the factors that determine real GDP by using a specific production function known as the **Cobb–Douglas production function**. This production function was first developed in the 1920s by Paul Douglas, an economist at the University of Chicago who later became a senator from Illinois, and Charles Cobb, a mathematician at Amherst College. The Cobb–Douglas production function is usually written as:

$$Y = AK^{\alpha}L^{1-\alpha}.$$

Cobb–Douglas production function A widely used macroeconomic production function that takes the form $Y = AK^{\alpha}L^{1-\alpha}$.

Note that in this case the sum of the coefficients on the capital and labor terms is 1. Let's look at an example using values similar to those for the United States:

K = \$40,000 billion
L = 140 million (or 0.140 billion) workers
A = 1,627

$$\alpha = 1/3$$
$$1 - \alpha = 2/3$$

Given these values, according to the Cobb–Douglas production function, the level of real GDP for the year will be:

$$Y = 1{,}627 \times (\$40{,}000 \text{ billion})^{1/3} \times (0.140 \text{ billion workers})^{2/3} = \$15{,}002 \text{ billion}.$$

The Cobb–Douglas production function is relatively simple, and economists have continued to use it for more than 90 years because it does a good job of explaining changes in real GDP over time within a country and differences in levels of real GDP among countries.

There are several important characteristics of the Cobb–Douglas production function we are using here:

1. The function exhibits *constant returns to scale*.
2. The function exhibits *diminishing returns*.
3. Capital and labor both earn shares of total income equal to the value of their exponents in the production function.

We consider the first two characteristics of the Cobb–Douglas production function here and the last one later in the chapter.

Constant returns to scale A property of a production function such that if all inputs increase by the same percentage, real GDP increases by the same percentage.

Constant Returns to Scale A production function has **constant returns to scale** if increasing all inputs by the same percentage increases real GDP by that percentage. For example, under constant returns to scale, if the quantity of capital and the quantity of labor both double, then real GDP will also double. Or:

$$2Y = AF(2K, 2L).$$

As a simple example, suppose a pizza parlor uses 20 workers and 2 pizza ovens to produce 200 pizzas per day. If the owner of pizza parlor expands her business to using 40 workers and 4 pizza ovens and her production function has constant returns to scale, she will now be able to produce 400 pizzas. As we will see, at the macroeconomic level, assuming that the production function has constant returns to scale results in an important conclusion about how total income in the economy is divided up between workers and the owners of capital.

The Cobb–Douglas production function we are using here has constant returns to scale because the exponents (α and $1 - \alpha$) on the capital and labor terms sum to 1. For example, if we increase K and L by 5, we have:

$$A(5K)^{1/3}(5L)^{2/3} = 5^{(1/3+2/3)}AK^{1/3}L^{2/3} = 5AK^{1/3}L^{2/3}.$$

Because the expression on the right side of the equation equals $5Y$, we have shown that multiplying K and L by 5 increases Y by 5. Substituting any other number for 5 gives us a similar result.

Diminishing Marginal Returns Figure 5.1 graphs a Cobb–Douglas production function. Panel (a) shows a graph of the aggregate production function, with the level of real GDP (Y) on the vertical axis and the value of the capital stock (K) on the horizontal axis. In this panel, we hold the values for A and L constant and illustrate how real GDP increases as the capital stock increases. Panel (b) of Figure 5.1 is an alternative way of showing the production function. In this panel, we show the value for labor on the horizontal axis while holding the values for

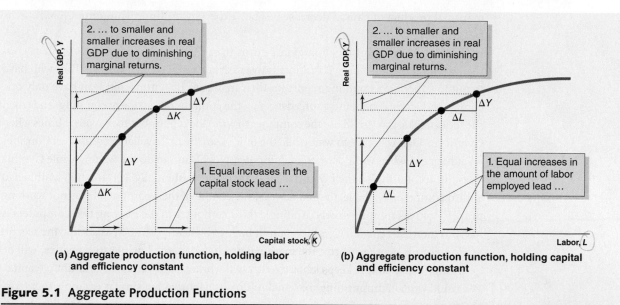

(a) Aggregate production function, holding labor and efficiency constant

(b) Aggregate production function, holding capital and efficiency constant

Figure 5.1 Aggregate Production Functions

Panel (a) shows the aggregate production function, holding labor and efficiency constant while allowing the capital stock to vary. Panel (b) shows the aggregate production function, holding the capital stock and efficiency constant while allowing labor to vary. The production functions in panels (a) and (b) are two different ways of showing the same relationship.

A and K constant. As the quantity of labor increases, real GDP increases. The production functions in panels (a) and (b) are two different ways of showing the same relationship.

The amount by which output increases as a result of a one-unit increase in capital is the **marginal product of capital** (**MPK**). Similarly, the amount by which output increases as a result of a one-unit increase in labor is the **marginal product of labor** (**MPL**). In symbols, we have:

$$MPK = \frac{\Delta Y}{\Delta K},$$

and:

$$MPL = \frac{\Delta Y}{\Delta L}.$$

Notice that the MPK is the slope of the production function, as shown in panel (a) of Figure 5.1, and the MPL is the slope of the production function, as shown in panel (b). The panels in the figure show that for equal increases in either K or L, we get progressively smaller increases in Y. In other words, a Cobb–Douglas production function exhibits *diminishing marginal returns* to both capital and labor. Diminishing marginal returns to capital means that, holding labor and efficiency (A) constant, the marginal product of capital decreases as the capital stock increases. Similarly, diminishing marginal returns to labor means that, holding capital and efficiency constant, the marginal product of labor decreases as the amount of labor employed increases.

Capital experiences diminishing marginal returns because labor and efficiency are fixed, so as the economy adds more capital goods, there are fewer workers per machine. With fewer workers per machine, the machines are not used as efficiently, so the

Marginal product of capital (MPK) The extra output a firm receives from adding one more unit of capital, holding all other inputs and efficiency constant.

Marginal product of labor (MPL) The extra output a firm receives from adding one more unit of labor, holding all other inputs and efficiency constant.

marginal product of capital decreases. Labor experiences diminishing marginal returns for similar reasons.

To illustrate diminishing marginal returns to capital in a microeconomic context, consider a simple example of two administrative assistants named Cynthia and Dan who have to put together an accounting report for their manager. If Cynthia and Dan have only one computer, Cynthia could use a spreadsheet on the computer to do the accounting, and when she took breaks, Dan could use the computer to write the report. But there will be times when Cynthia or Dan will have to wait while the other uses the one available computer. Consider what happens when we add a second computer. Now Dan can do the writing while Cynthia does the accounting, so their output should increase substantially. If Dan and Cynthia had a third computer available, they could use it when one of their computers was not working properly or was running slowly. Adding a third computer to the existing two computers is likely to increase Dan and Cynthia's output but not by nearly as much as adding the second computer did. In other words, the marginal product of capital, while still positive, will be declining. This example keeps labor fixed at two workers and varies the amount of capital. We could explain diminishing marginal returns to labor with a similar example that fixed capital at one computer and varied the amount of labor using the one computer. Extrapolating these examples to the economy as a whole helps us understand why the Cobb–Douglas production function has diminishing returns to both capital and labor.

[handwritten margin note: holds one variable constant]

The Demand for Labor and the Demand for Capital

Panels (a) and (b) of Figure 5.2 show the marginal product of capital and marginal product of labor curves. The marginal product of capital is always positive, but it decreases as the capital stock increases. Similarly, the marginal product of labor is always positive, but it decreases as the labor stock increases. All countries have downward-sloping marginal product of capital and marginal product of labor curves because diminishing returns apply to all types of capital and labor. Notice that these curves slope downward

[handwritten note: first derivative]

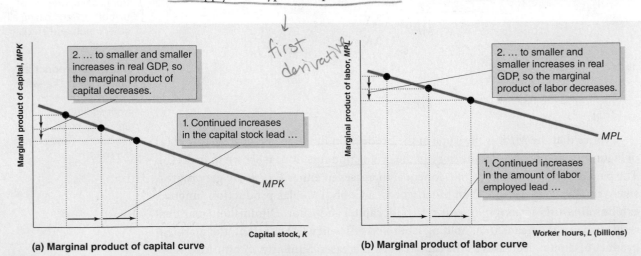

(a) **Marginal product of capital curve**

1. Continued increases in the capital stock lead …

2. … to smaller and smaller increases in real GDP, so the marginal product of capital decreases.

MPK

Capital stock, *K*

(b) **Marginal product of labor curve**

1. Continued increases in the amount of labor employed lead …

2. … to smaller and smaller increases in real GDP, so the marginal product of labor decreases.

MPL

Worker hours, *L* (billions)

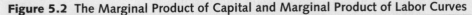

Figure 5.2 The Marginal Product of Capital and Marginal Product of Labor Curves

In panel (a), the marginal product of capital is always positive, but it decreases as the capital stock increases. Similarly, in panel (b), the marginal product of labor decreases as the quantity of labor increases. The downward slope for the marginal product of capital and marginal product of labor curves is the result of diminishing marginal returns. All countries have similarly shaped marginal product of capital and marginal product of labor curves.

very much like demand curves do. In fact, the marginal product of capital *is* the demand curve for capital, and the marginal product of labor *is* the demand curve for labor. We explain why the marginal product curves are also demand curves in the next section.

Changes in Capital, Labor, and Total Factor Productivity

To this point, we have been referring to A in the Cobb–Douglas production function as "efficiency" or, more specifically, as an index of the overall level of efficiency of transforming capital and labor into real GDP. A is intended to capture increases in output that result from factors other than increases in the amount of capital and labor. Because these other factors must have their effect on output by increasing the ability of labor or capital to produce more output, A is also called **total factor productivity (*TFP*)**.

The production function in panel (a) of Figure 5.1 on page 151 shows that an increase in the capital stock will increase real GDP, holding labor and total factor productivity constant. But what happens if either labor or total factor productivity increases? If labor or total factor productivity increases, the production function shifts up, and real GDP increases. Figure 5.3 shows how shifting up the aggregate production function increases real GDP.

Panel (a) shows that if labor increases from, say, 100 million workers to 101 million workers, real GDP will increase from Y_1 to Y_2. If labor increases from 101 million workers to 102 million workers, real GDP will increase from Y_2 to Y_3, which is a smaller amount due to diminishing marginal returns to labor. Panel (b) shows that if total factor productivity (A) increases from, say, 1,000 to 2,000, real GDP will increase from Y_1 to Y_2. If total factor productivity increases from 2,000 to 3,000, real GDP will increase from

> **Total factor productivity (*TFP*)** An index of the overall level of efficiency of transforming capital and labor into real GDP.

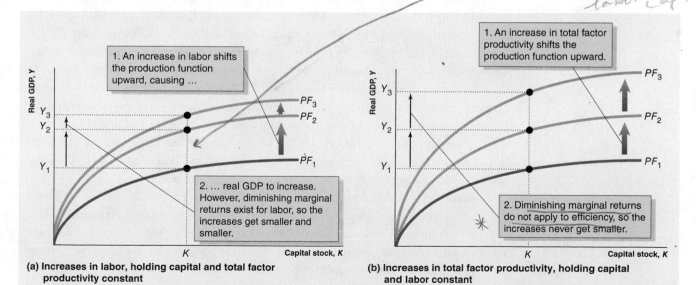

Figure 5.3 The Effect of an Increase in Labor and Total Factor Productivity in the Aggregate Production Function

In panel (a), an increase in workers will shift the production function up and increase real GDP, but labor experiences diminishing marginal returns. As a result, further increases in the number of workers will lead to smaller and smaller increases in real GDP.

In panel (b), an increase in total factor productivity will shift the production function up and increase real GDP. In contrast to labor, total factor productivity does not experience diminishing marginal returns, so the increases in real GDP do not get smaller.

Y_2 to Y_3. The increases will be the same size because diminishing marginal returns do not exist for total factor productivity. This point is important because, as we will see, it helps explain why increases in total factor productivity, rather than increases in labor or capital, are the key to sustained economic growth.

Making the Connection

Foreign Direct Investment Increases Real GDP in China

In 2011, the purchase or building of capital goods by foreign firms in China—*foreign direct investment (FDI)*—reached $116 billion. This news was good for China because investment in manufacturing plants by foreign firms such as PepsiCo Inc. and AU Optronics Corp. increases China's stock of capital goods. The increase in the Chinese capital stock causes a movement along China's production function. Because new capital goods are subject to diminishing marginal returns, however, we know that the rapid growth the Chinese economy has experienced in recent years must be due to more than the accumulation of capital goods. As panel (b) of Figure 5.3 shows, increases in total factor productivity are not subject to diminishing marginal returns. U.S. companies such as Google, General Electric, Intel, and Hewlett-Packard have invested billions of dollars in China. Some of this investment has been used to establish modern research facilities that develop new technology. When these foreign firms build new factories in China, those factories typically embody new technology. Technology is an important component of total factor productivity, so the transfer of technology from other countries to China is an important means of increasing China's total factor productivity.

Despite the recent growth in FDI, there are signs that some U.S. companies are reconsidering investing in China. Much of the increase in FDI in China in 2011 was from firms in Asian countries such as Hong Kong, Taiwan, and Japan, while investment by U.S. companies plunged by over 25% from the previous year. Sluggish economic growth in the United States was one reason for the decline in spending. Another reason was restrictions the Chinese government imposed on FDI. China has pledged to protect the intellectual property rights of foreign companies, but executives of many U.S. firms have expressed frustration regarding the Chinese government's policies on the theft of intellectual property, censorship, and nontariff barriers that favor Chinese firms at the expense of foreign firms. Many U.S. software firms, for example, complain that Chinese users often download updates of software that they are not recorded as having purchased.

Increases in total factor productivity have played a large part in the increase in China's real GDP in recent years. Much of the GDP growth has been fueled by investments by U.S. companies eager to become established in an economy with over 400 million Internet users and 700 million mobile phone subscribers. But for this growth to continue, the Chinese government may have to reconsider its policies on intellectual property and other issues.

Sources: Zhou Xin and Nick Edwards, "China 2011 FDI Stutters to Record $116 Bln," *Reuters*, January 18, 2012; Loretta Chao, "China Issued a Record Number of Patents in 2009," *Wall Street Journal*, February 4, 2010; Chinmei Sung, Zheng Lifei, and Li Yanping, "Foreign Direct Investment in China in 2010 Rises to Record $105.7 Billion," *Bloomberg News*, January 17, 2011; and John Boudreau and Brandon Bailey, "Doing Business in China Getting Tougher for U.S. Companies," *Mercury News*, March 27, 2010.

See related problem 1.7 at the end of the chapter.

Table 5.1 Summary of an Aggregate Production Function Graph with Capital on the Horizontal Axis

Increases in . . .	will . . .	and lead to an increase in real GDP by . . .	Graph of effect on an aggregate production function
the capital stock	cause a movement along the production function	smaller and smaller amounts due to diminishing marginal returns.	
the number of workers	shift the aggregate production function up	smaller and smaller amounts due to diminishing marginal returns.	
total factor productivity	shift the aggregate production function up	the same amount because increases in total factor productivity are not subject to diminishing marginal returns.	

Table 5.1 summarizes movements along and shifts of an aggregate production function graph drawn with capital on the horizontal axis. In Figure 5.3, we drew a production function with capital on the horizontal axis because we will be focusing on the effects of changes in capital on real GDP. If we had put labor on the horizontal axis, the results would have been very similar.

A Model of Real GDP in the Long Run

To fully explain how real GDP is determined, we need to explain how firms choose the quantity of capital goods to purchase and the quantity of labor to hire. To begin, we assume firms maximize **profit**, which equals the total revenue received by a firm minus the total cost a firm pays to produce output. The level of real GDP results from the profit-maximizing decisions of the many individual firms in the economy. In what follows, we make these four assumptions:

1. Firms purchase capital and hire labor only if doing so maximizes profits.
2. Firms operate in *perfectly competitive markets*, so each firm is a *price taker*—that is, each firm is small relative to the market and takes the market price of the goods and services it sells as given, or fixed.
3. Firms take the prices of capital goods and labor as given.
4. Firms decide how much capital and labor to hire and how much output to produce using the available technology, based on the prices of output and inputs.

5.2

Learning Objective
Explain how real GDP is determined in the long run.

Profit Total revenue minus total cost.

A model that describes the behavior of every single firm in the economy would be too complex to work with, so instead we use a simplified model. We consider the behavior of a single representative firm and assume that all firms behave the same as that firm. The firm produces output, Y, and sells it at the perfectly competitive price, P. In addition, the firm takes the *nominal wage rate*, W, and the *nominal rental cost of capital*, R, as given. We measure the cost of capital using the rental cost rather than the purchase price because the rental cost represents the use of capital services for a given period, just as the wage represents the cost of labor services. If firms do not own capital, they can rent it and *pay* the rental cost. If they currently own capital, they could have chosen to rent it out and *receive* the rental cost. So the rental cost is the opportunity cost to the firm of using its own capital. For example, suppose that you own a hardware store and need a small warehouse to hold some of your inventory. If you don't own a warehouse, you could rent one. If you do own a warehouse, by using it in your own business, you are passing up the opportunity to rent it to someone else. Therefore, the rent you could have received is the cost to your business of using that capital, even though you do not have to make a cash payment for using it.

The firm receives revenue by selling output, so total revenue is PY. The firm has to hire labor and rent capital to produce output, so total cost is $WL + RK$. Profits are therefore:

$$\text{Profit} = \text{Revenue} - \text{Cost},$$

or:

$$\text{Profit} = PY - (WL + RK),$$

or:

$$\text{Profit} = PY - WL - RK.$$

The Markets for Capital and Labor

Firms hire capital and labor in markets, so we can use the model of demand and supply to explain the quantities of capital and labor firms hire. At any particular time, there are a given quantity of capital goods and number of workers available, so we treat the supply of capital and labor as fixed and unresponsive to market prices. (Over time, of course, the quantities of capital and labor will change.)

Because we are assuming that the firm is small relative to the market, it cannot influence the price of output, the wage, or the rental cost of capital. If the firm hires one more worker, it can produce more output, so the revenue from hiring one more worker equals the price of output multiplied by the extra output from hiring the worker, which is the marginal product of labor (MPL). To hire that worker, the firm must pay the nominal wage of W. Therefore, the change in profit from hiring one more worker is the difference between the additional revenue earned and the additional cost paid:

$$\Delta\text{Profit} = P \times MPL - W.$$

The firm maximizes profit, so it will hire labor as long as the change in profit is greater than zero, which implies that:

$$P \times MPL > W.$$

The *real wage, w,* is the nominal wage, *W,* divided by the price of output. So, we can say that the firm will hire additional workers as long as the marginal product of labor is greater than the real wage:

$$MPL > (W/P).$$

Because of diminishing returns, the marginal product of labor declines as the firm hires more workers. Eventually, the marginal product of labor will decline to where it is just equal to the real wage. So the profit-maximizing quantity of labor for the firm occurs when:

$$MPL = (W/P).$$

If the real wage decreases, the firm will hire additional workers until the marginal product of labor falls enough to restore the above equality. If the real wage increases, the firm will lay off workers until the marginal product of labor rises enough to restore the equality. *Therefore, the marginal product of labor curve is the demand curve for labor.*

We can make a similar argument about a firm renting capital. The change in profit from adding one more unit of capital, holding the quantity of labor constant, is:

$$\Delta\text{Profit} = P \times MPK - R.$$

The firm maximizes profit, so it will add capital goods as long as the change in profit is greater than zero, which implies that:

$$P \times MPK > R.$$

The *real rental price of capital, r,* is the nominal rental price, *R,* divided by the price of output. The firm maximizes profit, so the firm will add capital goods whenever:

$$MPK > (R/P).$$

Because of diminishing returns, the marginal product of capital declines as the firm adds more capital. Eventually, the marginal product of capital will decline to where it is just equal to the real rental price of capital. So the profit-maximizing quantity of capital for the firm occurs when:

$$MPK = (R/P).$$

If the real rental cost of capital decreases, the firm will add more units of capital until the marginal product of capital falls enough to again equal the real rental cost, and if the real rental cost rises, the firm will sell capital or let its capital stock wear out, or depreciate, until the marginal product of capital rises enough to again equal the real rental cost. *Therefore, the marginal product of capital curve is the demand curve for capital goods.*

We make the simplifying assumption that everything we have discussed so far about a single firm holds true for every firm in the economy. So we can refer to the *aggregate capital market* and the *aggregate labor market.* Figure 5.4 shows these two markets. The real rental cost of capital is *r,* and the real wage rate is *w.* The demand curves slope downward, reflecting diminishing marginal returns to capital and labor. The supply curves for capital and labor are vertical lines, reflecting our assumption that at any particular time, the quantity of capital and labor supplied does not respond to changes in price. The intersections of the demand and supply curves determine the equilibrium quantities of capital and labor. In the next section, we substitute those quantities into the aggregate production function to determine real GDP.

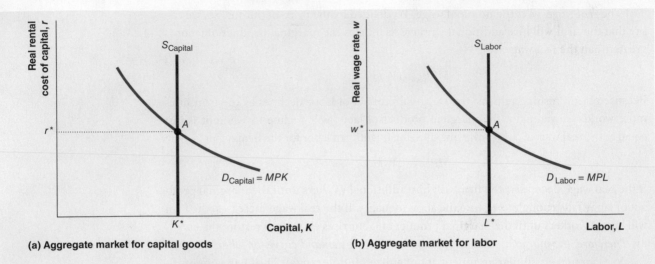

Figure 5.4 Aggregate Capital and Labor Markets

Panel (a) shows the aggregate market for capital goods, and panel (b) shows the aggregate market for labor. The demand curves slope downward, reflecting diminishing marginal returns to capital and labor. The supply curves for capital and labor are vertical lines, reflecting the assumption that the quantity supplied does not respond to changes in prices. The intersections of the demand and supply curves determine the equilibrium quantities of capital and labor.

Combining the Factor Markets with the Aggregate Production Function

Factor markets determine the equilibrium prices and quantities of capital and labor. We can combine the equilibrium quantities of capital and labor with the aggregate production function to determine the equilibrium level of real GDP. Panel (a) in Figure 5.5 shows how real GDP is determined when we measure the capital stock on the horizontal axis and we assume that capital's share of income is one third, so labor's share of income is two thirds. In this case, the quantity of labor is assumed to be fixed at L^*, while the equilibrium quantity and rental cost of capital are determined in the aggregate capital market. Once the equilibrium quantity of capital is determined, we can use that quantity to determine real GDP. Panel (b) shows how real GDP is determined when we measure the quantity of labor on the horizontal axis. In this case, we assume that the capital stock is fixed at K^*, while the equilibrium quantity and real wage are determined in the aggregate labor market. Once the equilibrium quantity of labor is determined, we can use that quantity to determine real GDP.

The Division of Total Income

The Cobb–Douglas production function provides an interesting answer to the question: What determines how much of total income labor receives and how much capital receives? To understand the answer, consider first the total amount of income received by labor and by capital. We saw earlier that, in equilibrium, firms pay and workers receive the real wage, w. Similarly, in equilibrium, firms pay and owners of capital receive the real rental price of capital, r. Therefore, the *total* income received by labor equals wL and the *total* income received by capital equals rK. Because the marginal

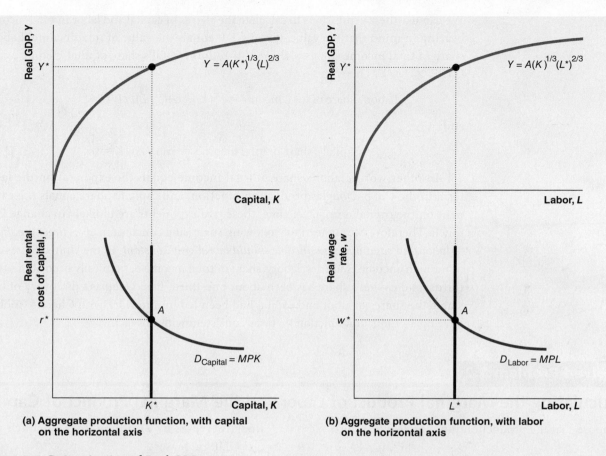

Figure 5.5 Determination of Real GDP

Panel (a) shows how potential real GDP is determined when we measure the capital stock on the horizontal axis. Panel (b) shows how potential real GDP is determined when we measure the quantity of labor on the horizontal axis.

In the lower graph in each panel, we show how the equilibrium quantity (of capital or labor) is determined. The upper panels use the production function and the level of each input to determine the level of real GDP.

product of labor equals the real wage and the marginal product of capital equals the real rental price of capital, we can say that:

$$\text{Total labor income} = MPL \times L,$$

and:

$$\text{Total capital income} = MPK \times K.$$

With a Cobb–Douglas production function of the form $Y = AK^{\alpha}L^{1-\alpha}$, the marginal product of labor and the marginal product of capital equal the following:

$$MPL = (1 - \alpha)(Y/L),$$

and:

$$MPK = \alpha(Y/K).^{1}$$

---

[1] We can derive these expressions using calculus. The marginal product of labor represents how output changes as a result of changes in labor, holding other determinants of output constant, or in symbols, $\frac{\partial Y}{\partial L}$. Calculating this partial derivative gives us: $\frac{\partial Y}{\partial L} = (1 - \alpha)AK^{\alpha}L^{(1-\alpha)-1}$. Rearranging terms give us: $MPL = (1 - \alpha)(Y/L)$. A similar procedure gives us an expression for MPK.

We can use these expressions to calculate the shares of capital and labor in total income, bearing in mind that the value of real GDP equals the value of total income. Labor's share of total income equals $(MPL \times L)/Y$, and capital's share of total income equals $(MPK \times K)/Y$. Therefore:

$$\text{Labor's share of total income} = [(1 - \alpha)(Y/L)]/L = (1 - \alpha),$$

and:

$$\text{Capital's share of total income} = \alpha(Y/K)/K = \alpha.$$

In other words, labor's share of total income equals the exponent on the labor term in the Cobb–Douglas production function, and capital's share equals the exponent on the capital term. Over time, these two exponents are unlikely to change very much. Therefore, we come to the following surprising conclusion: *Over time, the shares of labor and capital in total income should be roughly constant.* In the United States and other high-income countries, labor's share of total income has typically been about two-thirds, and capital's share has been about one-third. Paul Douglas's discovery of how stable the shares of labor and capital had been led him to work with Charles Cobb to develop a production function that was consistent with this fact.

Solved Problem 5.2

Calculating the Marginal Product of Labor and the Marginal Product of Capital

Suppose that the production function for the economy is:

$$Y = AK^{1/2}L^{1/2}.$$

Assume that real GDP is $12,000 billion, the capital stock is $40,000 billion, and the labor supply is 150 million (or 0.150 billion) workers.

a. Calculate the value of the marginal product of capital. Given this value, if the capital stock increases by $1 billion, by how much will real GDP increase?

b. Calculate the value for the marginal product of labor. Given this value, if the labor supply increases by one worker, by how much will real GDP increase?

c. What fraction of total income is received by labor, and what fraction is received by capital?

Solving the Problem

Step 1 Review the chapter material. This problem is about calculating values for the marginal products of capital and labor, so you may want to review the section "The Division of Total Income," which begins on page 158.

Step 2 Answer part (a) by calculating the value of the marginal product of capital and use the value to determine how much real GDP will increase if the capital stock increases by $1 billion. We know that the marginal product of capital for a Cobb–Douglas production function is equal to the exponent on the capital term multiplied by (Y/K). Or, in this case:

$$MPK = (1/2)(Y/K).$$

Substituting the given values, we have:

$$MPK = (1/2)\,(\$12{,}000\text{ billion}/\$40{,}000\text{ billion})$$
$$= \$0.15\text{ billion per dollar of capital.}$$

So, in this case, an increase of $1 billion in the capital stock would increase real GDP by $0.15 billion.

Step 3 **Answer part (b) by calculating the value of the marginal product of labor and use the value to determine how much real GDP will increase if the labor supply increases by one worker.** We know that the marginal product of labor for a Cobb–Douglas production function is equal to the exponent on the labor term multiplied by (Y/L). Or, in this case:

$$MPL = (1/2)\,(Y/L).$$

Substituting the given values, we have:

$$MPL = (1/2)\,(\$12{,}000\text{ billion}/0.150\text{ billion workers})$$
$$= \$40{,}000\text{ per worker.}$$

So, in this case, one additional worker would increase real GDP by $40,000.

Step 4 **Answer part (c) by determining labor and capital's shares of total income.** We can answer this part with an observation rather than a calculation. Because the production function in this problem is a Cobb–Douglas production function, the shares of labor and capital in total income both equal the value of their exponents, which is 1/2.

See related problems 2.5 and 2.6 at the end of the chapter.

What Determines Levels of Real GDP Across Countries?

Countries such as the United States, China, and India have high levels of real GDP because they have large quantities of capital and labor or because they have high levels of total factor productivity. China has the world's largest labor force, India the world's second largest, and the United States the world's third largest. So it is not surprising that these countries produce high levels of real GDP. However, of the three countries, only the United States also has a high level of real GDP per capita. Why? While the size of the labor force is an important determinant of real GDP, *labor productivity* is the critical determinant of real GDP per capita. The United States has a much higher level of labor productivity than do China or India, so the United States also has a higher level of real GDP per capita. We now turn to explaining why labor productivity varies across countries.

Why Real GDP per Worker Varies Among Countries

In the previous section, we used the aggregate production function to show that real GDP is determined by the capital stock, the labor force, and the level of total factor productivity. In this section, we explain why differences in total factor productivity are the most important determinant of differences in real GDP per capita.

5.3

Learning Objective
Understand why the standard of living varies across countries.

The per Worker Production Function

To explain labor productivity, we work with a modified version of the Cobb–Douglas production function called the *per worker production function*. The per worker production function shows the relationship between real GDP per worker and capital per worker. Because the Cobb–Douglas production function we have been using has constant returns to scale, we know that if we multiply both K and L by $(1/L)$, the value of Y will change to Y/L:

$$Y/L = AF(K/L, L/L) = AF(K/L, 1).$$

Output per worker, Y/L, is also a measure of labor productivity. We can define capital per worker, or the **capital–labor ratio**, as $k = K/L$. If we define $f(k) = F(k, 1)$, we have an expression for the per worker production function:

$$y = Af(k).$$

Capital–labor ratio The dollar value of capital goods per unit of labor; measured as the dollar value of capital divided by the total number of workers.

This equation tells us that labor productivity depends on total factor productivity and the capital–labor ratio. We graph this relationship in Figure 5.6.

The per worker production function looks like the production function in Figure 5.1 on page 151 except that the capital–labor ratio is on the horizontal axis, and real GDP per worker (labor productivity) is on the vertical axis. Along the per worker production function in Figure 5.6, as the capital–labor ratio increases, increases in output per worker become progressively smaller, so this production function also exhibits diminishing marginal returns. That is, increases in the capital–labor ratio holding total factor productivity constant lead to smaller and smaller increases in labor productivity. This outcome is not surprising because we already discussed that when we increase the quantity of capital relative to the number of workers, we eventually reach a point where there are not enough workers to efficiently operate the capital goods. Because we hold total factor productivity constant when we draw the per worker production function, increases in total factor productivity will shift the entire production function up, just as we saw with the production function in Figure 5.3 on page 153.

Figure 5.6

The per Worker Production Function

The per worker production function is very similar to the production function we used earlier except that the capital–labor ratio is on the horizontal axis, and real GDP per worker is on the vertical axis. Because the production function gets flatter and flatter as the capital–labor ratio increases, the per-worker production function also exhibits diminishing marginal returns.

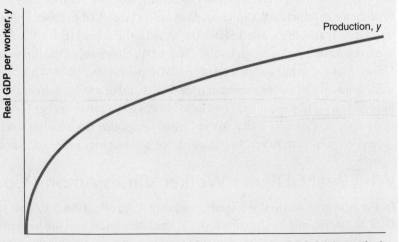

What Determines Labor Productivity?

The per worker production function shows that the capital–labor ratio and total factor productivity combine to determine the level of real GDP per worker. But which of the two is more important?

The key to answering this question is to recognize the importance of diminishing marginal returns. As you can see with Figure 5.6, the production function displays diminishing marginal returns for the capital–labor ratio when total factor productivity is held constant. At some point, providing workers with more capital will not increase real GDP per worker. Therefore, increases in the capital–labor ratio, by themselves, cannot explain most of the differences in real GDP per worker over time within a single country or across countries.

In contrast, diminishing marginal returns do not apply to total factor productivity. This fact means that there is no limit to how high improvements in total factor productivity can push real GDP per worker. When we want to know why labor productivity is higher in one country than in another country, differences in total factor productivity are often more important than differences in the capital–labor ratio. We explain differences in total factor productivity in the next section.

Macro Data: How Well do International Capital Markets Allocate Capital?

If there are no barriers to capital mobility and capital markets are functioning well, capital should move to the countries with the highest rates of return until the rates of return on capital are equal in all countries. The marginal product of capital is the real rental cost of capital, so the marginal product of capital is also the rate of return to capital. When rates of return to capital are not equal, world real GDP will increase if capital moves from countries with low rates of return to countries with high rates of return. When differences in rates of return to capital are large enough, the flow of capital from high-income to low-income countries has the potential to substantially increase world real GDP.

However, Francesco Caselli and James Feyrer found that the rate of return to capital varies much less than economists had believed. So, reallocating capital from low- to high-rate-of-return countries would increase real GDP per worker in the world by just 0.1%. Therefore, international capital markets appear to do a good job of allocating capital across countries.

This finding by Caselli and Feyrer is important because it tells us something about why some countries have persistently low levels of real GDP per worker. Poor countries with profitable investment opportunities are generally able to attract the funds to pursue those opportunities. However, there tend to be relatively few good investment opportunities in poor countries because total factor productivity is lower than in rich countries. The following figure illustrates this point by showing that high-income countries also have high marginal products of capital.

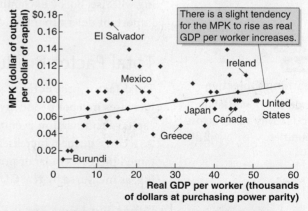

To understand why some countries have persistently lower levels of real GDP per worker, we need to understand why total factor productivity is lower in those countries. We address this issue in the next section.

Source: Francesco Caselli and James Feyrer, "The Marginal Product of Capital," *Quarterly Journal of Economics*, Vol. 122, No. 2, May 2007, pp. 535–568.

See related problem 3.7 at the end of the chapter.

What Determines Real GDP per Capita?

Labor productivity measures how much output, or real GDP, the economy can produce per worker:

$$\frac{\text{Real GDP}}{\text{Workers}}.$$

Because the standard of living in an economy can be measured as real GDP per capita, we can relate the standard of living to labor productivity as follows:

$$\text{Real GDP per capita} = \text{Labor productivity} \times \text{Labor input}$$

or:

$$\left(\frac{\text{Real GDP}}{\text{Population}}\right) = \left(\frac{\text{Real GDP}}{\text{Workers}}\right) \times \left(\frac{\text{Workers}}{\text{Population}}\right).$$

Both labor productivity and the labor input (the fraction of the population working) affect real GDP per capita, but labor productivity is the more important determinant. This conclusion is true because while there is a limit to the labor input, there is no limit to how much labor productivity can increase. The labor input in the population depends on the fraction of the population that works, which cannot rise above 100% and in practice is unlikely to rise above 65%. Some people are too young, too old, or too ill to work, and some choose not to work or to devote their time to childcare or other activities outside of the paid labor force. As a result, there is a limit to how much increases in labor inputs can increase real GDP per capita. In contrast, there is no limit to how much increases in labor productivity can increase real GDP per capita. As long as labor productivity increases, real GDP per capita will also increase, and the standard of living will rise. So, by explaining what determines labor productivity, we explain the most important determinant of real GDP per capita and the standard of living.

5.4 Total Factor Productivity and Labor Productivity

Learning Objective
Understand why labor productivity varies across countries.

Total factor productivity growth and capital accumulation are the two sources of increases in labor productivity. We have seen that increases in labor productivity from capital accumulation eventually decrease to zero due to diminishing marginal returns. As a consequence, increases in total factor productivity are the ultimate source of sustained increases in labor productivity and, therefore, of increases in the standard of living, as measured by real GDP per capita.

What Explains Total Factor Productivity?

Growth in total factor productivity is the key factor in determining growth in labor productivity, but what determines total factor productivity? Although no single theory has emerged, economists have identified several important factors, which we discuss next.

Research and Development and the Level of Technology As we mentioned earlier, total factor productivity measures the overall efficiency of an economy in transforming inputs into real GDP. Two of the most important factors determining total factor productivity are the stock of knowledge that the world possesses and the associated level of technology. For example, the invention of computers made workers more productive by giving them new and better types of capital goods to work with. Word processing software allows one administrative assistant today to do work that would have required several administrative assistants in 1950. Assembly-line workers in automobile plants now operate and oversee robots rather than doing much of the manual labor themselves. As a result, one worker today can produce many more automobiles than could a team of workers in 1950. In both examples, the new capital goods have made labor more productive.

New capital goods do not just appear out of thin air. Private firms and the government devote significant resources to research and development (R&D) activities to develop new capital goods. The United States spent about $405 billion on R&D in 2011, with the private sector responsible for roughly three-quarters of that amount.[2] The United States spends more on R&D than either China or India, which helps make the United States more productive and leads to its higher level of real GDP per capita.

Making the Connection

Comparing Research and Development Spending and Labor Productivity in China and the United States

China's population and labor force are much larger than the U.S. population and labor force. But as we have seen, the key to a high standard of living is not the number of workers a country has but how productive those workers are. Because labor productivity is higher in the United States, U.S. real GDP per capita is larger than China's and, correspondingly, the United States is able to maintain a higher standard of living than China. A key reason the United State has higher labor productivity is that it devotes more resources than China to developing new technology and to accumulating human capital. For example, in 2011, the United States devoted 2.7% of GDP to research and development, while China devoted just 1.6%. And, as recently as 1996, China devoted just 0.6% of GDP to research and development. The higher level of investment in new technology in the United States helps increase knowledge and total factor productivity, so U.S. workers are more productive.

Why doesn't the Chinese government do more to encourage private businesses to devote additional resources to research and development? Part of the explanation is that with the government still controlling important areas of the economy, firms have less incentive than they do in the United States to develop new products or new ways of producing existing products. Despite the strides China has made toward liberalizing its economy since the 1970s, the Heritage Foundation's *2012 Index of Economic Freedom* ranked China only 138th out of 179 countries in economic freedom. This index is used to evaluate countries on the basis of 10 criteria, including protection of property rights, business and investment freedom, and freedom from corruption. China scores low because the Chinese Communist Party maintains tight controls on political expression and heavily influences business decision making. The government decides which

_____

[2]Battelle, *2011 Global R&D Funding Forecast*, December 2010.

businesses receive loans based on political as well as economic criteria. Efforts to enact additional economic reforms have stalled in recent years. Although a number of foreign companies, such as BP, ExxonMobil, General Motors, and Alcoa, have invested heavily in China, the Chinese government has not allowed the companies to exercise full control of their operations, despite the capital, technology, and management skills the companies bring with them.

China has had some success in freeing manufacturing industries from government control, and private firms now produce about two-thirds of the country's manufacturing output. But state-owned enterprises still control much of the banking, telecommunications, and energy industries. Even in the agricultural sector, where China has been given credit for dismantling communes and allowing farmers to raise grain prices, much land remains collectively owned and is only leased to individual households.

Since the 1970s, China has made remarkable progress in moving toward greater economic liberalization, but the extent to which the government still exercises control over the economy has hindered investment in research and development. The result is that labor productivity in China remains relatively low.

Sources: The Heritage Foundation, *2012 Index of Economic Freedom*, www.heritage.org/index/; "The Second Long March," *Economist*, December 11, 2008; "Even Harder Than It Looks," *Economist*, September 16, 2010; and Martin Grueber and Tim Studt, "2012 Global R&D Funding Forecast: China's R&D Momentum," *Advantage Business Media*, December 16, 2011.

See related problem 4.4 at the end of the chapter.

Human capital The accumulated knowledge and skills that workers acquire from education and training or from life experiences.

Quality of Labor The quality of labor, like the quality of capital goods, can change over time. Workers become more productive as they acquire **human capital**, which is the accumulated knowledge and skills that workers acquire from education and training or from life experiences. There are two basic ways for workers to acquire human capital.

First, a worker can attend school for formal training to gain skills that are useful in the workplace. Students learn science, math, English, and other subjects that make them more productive workers. The United States devotes more resources to educating its children than either China or India. Economists Robert Barro and Jong-Wha Lee find that the average person who was over age 25 in the United States in the year 2010 has received 13.3 years of education, and nearly 32% of the population has college degrees. The average person in China has received just 7.5 years of education, and only 4% of the population has college degrees, and the comparable numbers in India are 4.4 years and 4%.[3] While China and India have larger populations and larger labor forces, the average worker in the United States receives much more education, which helps make U.S. workers more productive.

Second, as Nobel Laureate Kenneth Arrow of Stanford University has argued, workers can accumulate skills through *learning by doing*.[4] Arrow noted that the

---

[3]Robert Barro and Jong-Wha Lee, Barro-Lee Educational Attainment Dataset, available at www.barrolee.com.

[4]Kenneth J. Arrow, "Economic Implications of Learning by Doing," *Review of Economic Studies*, Vol. 29, No. 3, June 1962, pp. 155–173.

more often workers perform a task, the more quickly they perform the task—thereby improving their productivity. Arrow cited evidence from engineering studies showing that the amount of time it takes to build an airplane decreases as workers build more airplanes. This relationship emerges because the workers have acquired knowledge and skills through building the previous airplanes, which make them more productive.

Government and Social Institutions Nobel Laureate Douglass North of the Hoover Institution and Robert Paul Thomas of the University of Washington have emphasized the importance of government and social institutions in explaining differences in labor productivity and the standard of living across countries.[5] North and Thomas, along with many other economists, believe that in addition to markets, secure property rights are necessary for sustained economic growth. Individuals and firms are unlikely to risk their own funds, and investors are unlikely to lend them funds, unless the profits from risky investment projects are safe from being seized by the government or by criminals. In other words, property rights must be secure to encourage investment and capital accumulation. In some countries, property rights are not secure, so individuals are reluctant to devote the resources required to develop new goods and services or expand existing businesses.

The case of North and South Korea provides a good example of the importance of government institutions. Japan occupied the whole Korean peninsula from 1905 until Japan's surrender to the Allies at the end of World War II in 1945. At that time, Soviet troops occupied what would become North Korea, while U.S. troops occupied what would become South Korea. North Korea was a Communist dictatorship without strong markets or secure property rights, while South Korea had strong markets and secure property rights. Although economic data for North Korea are unreliable because its government does not make official data available, in 2011, real GDP per capita for South Korea is estimated as being more than 17 times greater than in North Korea.

Economists Daron Acemoglu and Simon Johnson of Massachusetts Institute of Technology and James Robinson of the University of California at Berkeley have analyzed the effects of government and social institutions in explaining differences in levels of real GDP per capita.[6] European countries colonized large regions of the world between the 1600s and the 1800s. In countries such as the United States, Australia, and New Zealand, Europeans came as settlers and established institutions that enforced the rule of law. These favorable institutions encouraged investment, which led to faster economic growth and higher real GDP per capita. In Africa and other areas, Europeans came primarily to extract natural resources and so did not establish government institutions that favored investment. Acemoglu, Johnson, and Robinson find that the areas of the world in which the Europeans established strong property rights are

[5]Douglass North and Robert Paul Thomas, *The Rise of the Western World: A New Economic History*, New York: Cambridge University Press, 1973.

[6]Daron Acemoglu, Simon Johnson, and James Robinson, "The Colonial Origins of Comparative Development: An Empirical Investigation," *American Economic Review*, Vol. 91, No. 5, December 2001, pp. 1369–1401.

generally rich today, while the regions in which Europeans did not establish strong property rights are generally poor.

The experiences of Korea and the former European colonies have reinforced the view of many economists that government institutions play a critical role in explaining differences among countries in real GDP per capita.

Geography Some economists argue that geography plays an important role in explaining the standard of living. In fact, since as long ago as Adam Smith's 1776 book *An Inquiry into the Nature and Causes of the Wealth of Nations*, economists have pointed out that geography affects a country's potential to achieve a high standard of living. For example, access to navigable rivers and having a coastline makes trade easier and should increase labor productivity and the standard of living. The United States has a long coastline and extensive navigable rivers, while countries such as Bolivia and Niger are landlocked and mountainous, so transportation is difficult. Jeffrey Sachs of Columbia University argues that geography affects the standard of living for another reason. Sachs, along with economists Andrew Mellinger of Harvard and John Gallup of Portland State University, argues that tropical climates experience higher rates of infectious disease such as malaria.[7] Many countries that are poor today have had high rates of infectious disease in the past. Infectious disease affects health, especially that of infants and young children, and these health problems can affect labor productivity later in life. For example, children with serious illnesses often grow up to be shorter than healthy children. Workers who are shorter because they suffered from illness or malnutrition as children are often less productive in agricultural or manufacturing jobs that require strength. This adverse link between geography and health may explain why agricultural productivity is lower in tropical areas, such as Burundi, Malawi, Uganda, and Zambia. Low agricultural productivity increases the likelihood of famines and has a further negative effect on health, labor productivity, and the standard of living.

Making the Connection

How Important Were the Chinese Economic Reforms of 1978?

For much of its history, China was ruled by hereditary dynasties. The last of these, the Qing Dynasty, ended in 1911, at which time the Republic of China was established. The Republic of China had difficulty extending its authority over the whole of the country, and by the 1930s, the government had become involved in a civil war with the Communist Party, led by Mao Zedong. The Communists eventually won the civil war and established the People's Republic of China in 1949. The government under Mao created a socialist economy based on state ownership of major industries. Without a system of

---

[7]Jeffrey Sachs, Andrew Mellinger, and John Gallup, "Climate, Coastal Proximity, and Development," in *Oxford Handbook of Economic Geography*, New York: Oxford University Press, 2000.

secure property rights, markets in China were limited and unimportant. For example, rather than selling their crops in the market, farmers had to turn over their crops to the Chinese government. The Chinese government allowed few foreign firms or individuals to purchase financial or physical assets in the country. In 1958, Mao launched what he called the Great Leap Forward, which forced Chinese peasants to move from their farms into cities to build roads and other infrastructure projects. The result was a decline in agricultural output and widespread famine. Mao started another movement, the Cultural Revolution, in 1966 to further advance socialism and rid China, often by violent means, of those who were suspected of advocating free market capitalism.

After Mao's death in 1976, a power struggle resulted in Deng Xiaoping becoming the leader of the Communist Party in 1978. Under Deng's leadership, China instituted many economic reforms, including allowing private ownership of farms and businesses and the establishment of special economic zones that foreign investors could use to establish joint venture enterprises with Chinese firms. The standard of living in China increased rapidly after the country instituted major economic reforms after the 1970s, including opening the country to international trade and investment. This reform allowed foreign technology to flow into the country more easily. China also started allowing agricultural workers to sell some of their crops in markets and keep the proceeds from the sales. This reform provided agricultural workers with a financial incentive to work harder. The reforms accelerated in the 1980s and 1990s to allow a greater role for the market.

The reforms that began in the 1970s allowed total factor productivity and real GDP per capita to increase rapidly in China. Despite the strides it has made toward liberalizing its economy since the 1970s, we saw earlier that China has not ranked highly on the Heritage Foundation's *Index of Economic Freedom*. China's scores on property rights, investment freedom, and financial freedom were all actually lower in 2012 than in 1996, the first year the *Index of Economic Freedom* was published. Another index published by the Fraser Institute measures the degree to which the policies and institutions of countries are supportive of economic freedom. The index uses 42 categories to measure economic freedom in five areas: government expenditures and taxes, property rights, soundness of the money supply, international trade, and government regulation. China ranked only 88th in 1980, the first year the index was published, but even lower—92nd—in 2011. While China has more economic freedom today than it had in 1978, its economic freedom appears to have decreased relative to other countries in recent years. A failure to move toward greater economic freedom could slow China's economic growth in the future.

Sources: Mark Williams, "Foreign Investment in China: Will the Anti-Monopoly Law Be a Barrier or a Facilitator?" *Texas International Law Journal*, Vol. 45, No. 1, Fall 2009, pp. 127–155; "The Second Long March," *Economist*, December 11, 2008; Heritage Foundation, *2011 Index of Economic Freedom*, www.heritage.org/index/; and James Gwartney, Robert Lawson, and Joshua Hall, *Economic Freedom of the World: 2011 Annual Report*, Vancouver: Fraser Institute, 2011.

See related problem 4.9 at the end of the chapter.

The Financial System The financial system allocates resources by matching borrowers with lenders. When the financial system works well, households and firms that want to borrow to finance the accumulation of physical or human capital can find lenders. To the extent that firms and the government pay for R&D with funds obtained through the financial system, a well-functioning financial system can also lead to more investment in R&D. The financial system can also affect total factor productivity by improving the efficiency of the economy. The financial system allocates funds to the firms who are willing to pay the most to obtain the funds. These firms are typically those whose investment projects have the best likelihood of success. Therefore, a good financial system ensures that resources flow to their most productive uses, and total factor productivity for the economy increases. As a consequence, labor productivity and the standard of living are higher.

Research by Thorsten Beck of the World Bank, Ross Levine of the University of Minnesota, and Norman Loayza of the Central Bank of Chile has shown that the financial system has a significant effect on total factor productivity.[8] It is not just banks that matter for economic growth; Ross Levine and Sara Zervos of the World Bank have found that stock market liquidity also affects productivity and capital accumulation.[9] The more liquid a stock market, the easier it is for investors to sell stocks. Investors are more likely to purchase stocks that they know are easy to sell. As a consequence, stock prices are higher, and it is less costly for firms to issue new stock to pay for investment projects. This research tells us that the development of financial markets plays an important role in improving the allocation of funds to those individuals and firms with the most productive investment opportunities. As a result, the economy has a larger capital stock, is more efficient, and has a higher level of labor productivity and a higher standard of living.

Answering the Key Question

Continued from page 147

At the beginning of this chapter, we asked:

"Why isn't the whole world rich?"

In this chapter, we saw that a model based on the aggregate production function for the economy helps us understand why some countries have a low standard of living. Countries with a low standard of living have low levels of total factor productivity due to a combination of (1) lack of investment in R&D; (2) low quality of labor from low investment in education; (3) government institutions that do not protect private property and that discourage investment; (4) geography that makes trade difficult or makes diseases more prevalent; and (5) a lack of financial institutions that allow funds to flow to firms with profitable investment projects.

---

[8]Thorsten Beck, Ross Levine, and Norman Loayza, "Finance and the Sources of Growth," *Journal of Financial Economics*, Vol. 58, No. 1–2, October–November 2000, pp. 261–300.

[9]Ross Levine and Sara Zervos, "Stock Markets, Banks, and Economic Growth," *American Economic Review*, Vol. 88, No. 3, June 1998, pp. 537–558.

Key Terms and Problems

Key Terms

Aggregate production function, p. 149

Capital–labor ratio, p. 162

Cobb–Douglas production function, p. 149

Constant returns to scale, p. 150

Human capital, p. 166

Marginal product of capital (*MPK*), p. 151

Marginal product of labor (*MPL*), p. 151

Profit, p. 155

Total factor productivity (*TFP*), p. 153

5.1 **The Aggregate Production Function**
Describe the aggregate production function.

Review Questions

1.1 What are the distinguishing characteristics of a Cobb–Douglass production function?

1.2 With the Cobb-Douglas production function, $Y = AK^{1/4}L^{3/4}$, if both capital and labor increase by 30%, what will happen to real GDP?

Problems and Applications

1.3 Briefly explain whether the following Cobb-Douglas production function exhibits constant returns to scale: $Y = AK^{1/2}L^{3/4}$.

1.4 Draw a graph of the aggregate production function with capital, K, on the horizontal axis.

a. Why does the graph have the shape that you have drawn?

b. Indicate on the graph the effect of an increase in the capital stock.

c. Indicate on the graph the effect of an increase in the productivity of labor.

1.5 Assume that the labor force is 140 million workers, the capital stock is $50,000 billion, and real GDP is $6,500 billion to answer the following questions:

a. If the production function is $Y = AK^{1/2}L^{1/2}$, what is total factor productivity?

b. If the production function is $Y = AK^{1/4}L^{3/4}$, what is total factor productivity?

1.6 Assume that the labor force is 100 million workers, the capital stock is $25,000 billion, and total factor productivity is 5.

a. If the production function is $Y = AK^{1/3}L^{2/3}$, what is real GDP?

b. If the labor force increases to 110 million workers, what will happen to real GDP?

c. If total factor productivity doubles, what will happen to real GDP?

d. Graph the production function, with capital on the horizontal axis, and use your graph to explain the different effects of a doubling of the labor force and a doubling of total factor productivity.

1.7 [Related to the Making the Connection on page 154] In the 1950s, China had a very rapid population growth rate, which it was able to reduce dramatically over the next half century. During the past two decades, China has experienced rapid growth in both the overall level of economic efficiency and the capital stock.

a. Draw a graph of China's aggregate production function. Put labor on the horizontal axis. Show the effect of increases in labor on real GDP.

b. Draw a graph to show the effect of increases in total factor productivity on real GDP. Are increases in labor or increases in total factor productivity likely to result in larger increases in Chinese real GDP in the long run? Briefly explain.

MyEconLab Visit **www.myeconlab.com** to complete these exercises online and get instant feedback. Exercises that update with real-time data are marked with ⓦ.

5.2 A Model of Real GDP in the Long Run
Explain how real GDP is determined in the long run.

Review Questions

2.1 Explain how firms choose the profit-maximizing quantities of capital and labor.

2.2 How do individual markets for capital and labor relate to aggregate capital and labor markets?

2.3 What determines the shares of labor and capital in total income? How are these shares related to the production function?

Problems and Applications

2.4 The graphs below shows the production function and the labor market. Assume that the labor market is currently in equilibrium at point A.

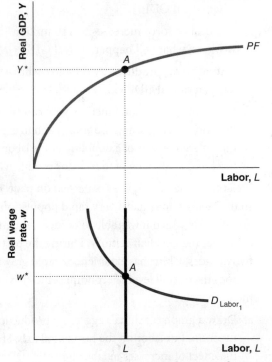

Suppose that total factor productivity decreases.

a. Use the graphs to show the effect on the real wage rate and on real GDP.

b. Now suppose that, at the same time, there is an increase in the labor force. Use the graphs to show the effects. Briefly explain your results.

c. Why is the effect on output different in these two cases?

2.5 [**Related to** Solved Problem 5.2 **on page 160**]

Suppose that the production function is $Y = A K^{1/4} L^{3/4}$.

a. What is the marginal product of labor (MPL)?

b. What is the marginal product of capital (MPK)?

c. Graph the approximate shapes of the MPL and MPK curves.

d. What are the shares of labor and capital in total income?

2.6 [**Related to** Solved Problem 5.2 **on page 160**]

Suppose that the production function is $Y = AK^{1/4}L^{3/4}$. Assume that $A = 1,000$, the current level of the capital stock is $16,000 billion, and the labor force is 200 million workers.

a. Find the marginal product of labor.

b. Graph the marginal product of labor.

c. Graph the production function, putting labor on the horizontal axis and assuming that capital is constant.

d. Now assume that the capital stock increases to $20,000 billion. Show the effect of this increase on your graph of the production function. What effect did the increase in the capital stock have on the marginal product of labor?

2.7 Suppose that the production function is given by $Y = AK^{1/5}L^{4/5}$.

a. If $A = 2,000$, $K = \$10,000$ billion, and $L = 50$ million workers, what is real GDP?

b. Find the real wage.

c. Find the real rental cost of capital.

d. Graph the relationship between the production function and the labor and capital markets.

2.8 Consider the economy described in problem 2.7. Briefly explain the likely changes in real GDP, the real wage, and the real rental cost of capital under each of the following scenarios. Include a graph with your answers:

   a. There are breakthroughs in technology that improve the productivity of all factors of production, causing A to increase to 2,100.

   b. A devastating earthquake causes the capital stock to decrease to $5,000 billion.

   c. A wave of immigration causes the labor force to increase to 60 million workers.

2.9 The productivity of labor is usually a function of at least three factors: the technology available, the amount of capital available, and the human capital (skills) of the workforce. Compare the likely real wages in the following pairs of countries, assuming that all other factors are identical. Draw a graph to support your answer to each part.

   a. Country A is more technologically advanced than Country B.

   b. Country C has a larger labor force than Country D.

   c. Country E has more skilled workers than Country F.

2.10 Some firms produce in both China and the United States. Assume that the labor and capital markets in the two countries are not currently in equilibrium. Suppose that the marginal product of capital in the United States is $100 per dollar of capital, and the real rental cost of capital is $50. Assume further that the marginal product of capital in China is $20 per dollar of capital, and the real rental rate on capital is $5.

   a. All other things being equal and assuming that labor cannot be moved from one country to another, should firms move production from the United States to China or vice versa? Explain your answer in terms of profit-maximizing employment decisions for firms.

   b. What would happen to the marginal product of capital in each country if this reallocation occurred? What would happen to real wages?

5.3 **Why Real GDP per Worker Varies Among Countries**
Understand why the standard of living varies across countries.

Review Questions

3.1 What is the per worker production function? What is the equation for the per worker production function?

3.2 Which two factors determine labor productivity? Which of the two is more important? Briefly explain.

3.3 Why does the standard of living ultimately depend on labor productivity?

Problems and Applications

3.4 Suppose that $y = Ak^{1/4}$, the capital-labor ratio is $20,000 per worker, the level of total factor productivity is 500, 60% of the population works, and there are 60 million workers. What are real GDP per worker and real GDP per capita?

3.5 Assume that total factor productivity is constant.

   a. Use the per worker production function to show the effect of a decrease in the capital-labor ratio. What happens to the marginal product of labor? Briefly explain.

   b. What happens to real GDP per capita?

   c. What happens to the marginal product of capital?

3.6 Assume that the capital–labor ratio is constant.

   a. Use the per worker production function to show the effect of an increase in total factor productivity. What happens to the marginal product of labor? Briefly explain.

   b. What happens to real GDP per capita?

   c. What happens to the marginal product of capital?

3.7 **[Related to the** Macro Data feature **on page 163]**

Capital's share of total income is about 10% in both Colombia and Costa Rica. The capital–labor ratio is $15.25 thousand per worker in Colombia and $23.12 thousand per worker in Costa Rica.

Real GDP per worker is $12.18 thousand in Colombia and $13.31 thousand in Costa Rica. Predict what will happen to the capital stocks in the two countries over time. How will this change affect real GDP per worker in the two countries?

5.4 Total Factor Productivity and Labor Productivity
Understand why labor productivity varies across countries.

Review Questions

4.1 How do increases in total factor productivity increase the standard of living?

4.2 What factors cause total factor productivity to change?

4.3 What is human capital? How does the acquisition of human capital improve the quality of labor? What are the two basic ways in which workers can acquire human capital?

Problems and Applications

4.4 **[Related to the** Making the Connection **on page 165]**

According to an article in the *New York Times*, "A recent study by the Battelle Memorial Institute, a research firm, predicts that China's spending [on research and development] will match ours around 2022." Why might China have an incentive to increase its spending on research and development? Is this increase in spending on research and development likely to raise real GDP per capita in China to the level of real GDP per capita in the United States? Briefly explain.

Source: Adam Davidson, "Will China Outsmart the United States?" *New York Times*, December 28, 2011.

4.5 Consider the following policies aimed at increasing economic growth: 1) Increasing spending on health care in order to reduce communicable diseases; 2) increasing student loans to increase college enrollments; 3) providing tax subsidies to firms to increase spending on physical capital; and 4) providing tax breaks to increase spending on research and development. Briefly discuss which of these four policies would be most effective for each of the following countries: the United States, China, and Uganda.

4.6 **[Related to the** Chapter Opener **on page 147]**

A 2012 Gallup poll states that while Brazil, Russia, China, India, and South Africa are all experiencing economic growth, only Brazil and China have a majority of citizens who believe they are experiencing an improvement in their standard of living. The poll states, "It is uncertain how long high growth rates will last for emerging-market countries. To continue to spur high growth rates and allow gains across income levels, leaders must implement sustainable policies."

What is meant by "sustainable policies"? What are some examples of sustainable policies that policymakers could implement in these countries? How might the implementation of these policies help raise standards of living and continue current high growth rates?

Source: Krista Hoff, "Emerging Economies Struggle to Improve Standard of Living: In Brazil, China Majorities See Their Standard of Living Improving," *GALLUP World*, April 9, 2012.

4.7 According to an article in the *Economist* magazine, the cost of eliminating deaths from malaria in sub-Saharan Africa would be about $6.7 billion for bed nets, diagnostic tests, medicines, and so on. The total economic benefit would be between $231 billion and $311 billion "in lives saved and malaria cases averted, if you factor in productivity gains and savings in the cost of treatment."

MyEconLab Visit **www.myeconlab.com** to complete these exercises online and get instant feedback. Exercises that update with real-time data are marked with (🌐).

The article refers to the required expenditure as "a brilliant investment." With the return so high relative to the cost, is it likely that private firms would make this investment in eliminating deaths from malaria? Briefly explain.

Source: "Net Benefit," *Economist*, July 14, 2012.

4.8 Consider the following statement: "Without a well-functioning financial system, it is not possible for an economy to reach its full potential for real GDP per capita." Is it more likely that a strong banking system or strong stock and bond markets would be more important in facilitating economic growth in a developing economy? Briefly explain.

4.9 **[Related to the** Making the Connection **on page 168]** Most countries that have high levels of real GDP per capita have economies that can roughly be characterized as free market. China's economy is one of the most rapidly growing in the world, yet parts of that economy are state controlled.

a. How did the 1978 economic reforms change the structure of the Chinese economy?

b. What advantages might state control of some parts of the economy have in increasing real GDP per capita? Are these advantages likely to persist in the long run?

Data Exercises

D5.1: Using data from the St. Louis Federal Reserve (FRED) (http://research.stlouisfed.org/fred2/), analyze the relationship between labor productivity in the manufacturing sector and in the non-farm business sector as a whole.

a. Download data on output per hour of all persons in the manufacturing sector (OPHMFG) and in the non-farm business sector (OPHNFB).

b. Which has increased more since 1987, labor productivity in manufacturing or in the non-farm business sector?

c. The manufacturing sector has been shrinking relative to the size of the economy in the United States and other advanced economies. What do your results imply about future labor productivity growth in advanced economies?

D5.2: Using data from the St. Louis Federal Reserve (FRED) (http://research.stlouisfed.org/fred2/), analyze differences in labor productivity among the China, India, and the United States.

a. From 1952 to the present, download data for real GDP per worker for China (RGDPL2CNA627NUPN), India (RGDPLWINA627NUPN), and the United States (RGDPLWUSA627NUPN). Chart the series on a graph.

b. Calculate the relative productivity of workers in China and the United States, measured by U.S. labor productivity divided by China's labor productivity. Describe the change in this measure of relative productivity since 1952.

c. Repeat part (b) for the United States and India.

D5.3: **[Excel exercise]** Using data from the St. Louis Federal Reserve (FRED) (http://research.stlouisfed.org/fred2/), analyze the relationship between compensation and labor productivity for the United States.

a. Download quarterly data from 1947 to the present for real compensation per hour (COMPRNFB) and output per hour of all persons (OPHNFB) as a measure of labor productivity. Chart the two data series on the same graph.

b. Calculate the annual growth rate of real compensation as the percentage change from the same quarter in the previous year. Do the same labor productivity. Calculate the correlation between the two data series.

c. Are your results in parts (a) and (b) consistent with the model of the labor market in the chapter? Briefly explain.

MyEconLab   Visit **www.myeconlab.com** to complete these exercises online and get instant feedback. Exercises that update with real-time data are marked with ⬤.

CHAPTER 6

Long-Run Economic Growth

Learning Objectives

After studying this chapter, you should be able to:

6.1 Understand the effect of capital accumulation on labor productivity (pages 177–186)

6.2 Understand the effect of labor force growth on labor productivity (pages 186–190)

6.3 Understand the effect of technological change on labor productivity and the standard of living (pages 190–193)

6.4 Explain balanced growth, convergence, and long-run equilibrium (pages 193–197)

6.5 Explain the determinants of technological change using the endogenous growth model (pages 197–206)

6.A Appendix: Discuss the contributions of capital, labor, and efficiency to the growth rate of real GDP (pages 212–215)

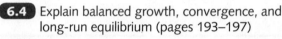

The Surprising Economic Rise of India

When you have a computer problem and need technical support, the person who takes your call may well be in India. This is one indication of how Indian information technology firms have been expanding relative to U.S.-based firms. The largest steel company in the world, ArcelorMittal, although now headquartered in Luxembourg, was founded in India by the Mittal family. In 2012, *Forbes* magazine listed Lakshmi Mittal, ArcelorMittal's chairman and CEO, as the twenty-first-richest person in the world. The nineteenth-richest is Mukesh Ambani, the CEO of Reliance Industries, an oil firm, based in Mumbai, India. Tata Motors, India's largest automobile company, made headlines when it introduced the Nano car, which it sold in India for

only $2,200. Tata also owns Jaguar and Land Rover. Increasingly, U.S. consumers find themselves buying Indian goods and services, and U.S. firms find themselves competing against Indian firms.

The rapid economic rise of India surprised people in many countries, including the United States. In 1950, India was desperately poor. India's real GDP per capita in 1950 was less than $1,000 measured in 2012 dollars, or less than 7% of 1950 U.S. real GDP per capita. Twenty-five years later, India had fallen even further behind the United States, with GDP per capita only 5.5% of U.S. GDP per capita. Recent years tell a much different story. Between 1993 and 2011, real GDP per capita in India grew at an average annual rate of 5.5%,

Continued on next page

Key Issue and Question

Issue: Real GDP has increased substantially over time in the United States and other developed countries.

Question: What are the main factors that determine the growth rate of real GDP per capita?

Answered on page 206

well above the average growth rate of 1.5% experienced by the United States. Consulting firm Pricewaterhouse-Coopers has projected that between 2010 and 2050, the Indian economy will grow three times as fast as the U.S. economy. After centuries of extreme poverty, India has finally begun to close the gap between its standard of living and the standard of living in high-income countries such as the United States and the countries of Western Europe.

India remains a very poor country, however. It has a population of 1.2 billion, more than half of which is employed in agriculture and, in many cases, produce barely enough to feed themselves. Infant mortality remains high, and as many as half of all adult women and one-quarter of adult men are unable to read and write. Still, the rapid economic growth that began in the early 1990s provides hope for a better life for India's population.

What explains the higher growth rates in India during the past 20 years? Clearly, an increase in growth was not inevitable. Prior to 1947, India was part of the colony of British India, which also included the modern countries of Pakistan and Bangladesh. In 1950, real GDP per capita was about the same in all three countries. By 2011, however, as India experienced much faster economic growth, real GDP per capita in Pakistan was 25% lower than in India, and real GDP per capita in Bangladesh was 50% lower.

So, countries that are geographically close and share the same colonial history can have very different experiences with economic growth. In this chapter, we begin explaining economic growth by focusing on a few key ideas that explain what determines the growth rate of real GDP per capita in the long run.

Sources: "Business in India," *Economist*, September 30, 2010; Angus Maddison, *Contours of the World Economy*, New York: Oxford University Press, 2007; "The World's Billionaires," forbes.com, April 24, 2012; "GDP per Person Forecasts," *Economist*, January 13, 2011; and www.cia.gov/library/publications/the-world-factbook/index.html.

In Chapter 5, we saw that capital per worker and the level of efficiency, as measured by total factor productivity (TFP), are the key determinants of the *level* of labor productivity at a particular time. In this chapter, we explain why the rate of technological change and the growth rate of the labor force determine the long-run *growth rate* of the economy. Just as the economy can have an equilibrium level of real GDP or real GDP per capita at a particular time, it can have an equilibrium growth rate of real GDP or real GDP per capita. Economists call the equilibrium growth rate the *steady state growth rate*. Because the economy moves automatically towards its steady state, understanding the factors that affect the steady state is important.

The Solow Growth Model

Labor productivity is the key determinant of real GDP per capita and, therefore, of the standard of living in a country. In this section, we use a model first developed in the 1950s by Nobel Laureate Robert Solow of the Massachusetts Institute of Technology. The **Solow growth model** has become the foundation for how economists think about economic growth.[1] The model can help us understand the key factors that determine why some countries have experienced rapid economic growth while others have stagnated and remain desperately poor. Policies to spur growth have the potential to raise incomes and reduce the poverty and suffering experienced by hundreds of millions of people in low-income countries.

6.1

Learning Objective
Understand the effect of capital accumulation on labor productivity.

Solow growth model A model that explains how the long-run growth rate of the economy depends on saving, population growth, and technological change.

[1]Robert Solow, "A Contribution to the Theory of Economic Growth," *Quarterly Journal of Economics*, Vol. 70, No. 1, February 1956, pp. 65–94.

In fact, Nobel Laureate Robert Lucas has remarked, "The consequences for human welfare involved in questions [about policies to increase economic growth] are simply staggering: once one starts to think about them, it is hard to think about anything else."[2]

The Solow model begins with the aggregate production function for real GDP per worker (see Chapter 5), where y is real GDP per worker, k is capital per worker, or the capital–labor ratio, and A measures the overall level of economic efficiency, or *total factor productivity*:

$$y = Af(k).$$

For simplicity, in this section and the next, we will assume that total factor productivity is constant and equal to 1, so the production function is:

$$y = f(k).$$

We assume that increases in capital are subject to diminishing marginal returns. As we will see in Section 6.3, diminishing marginal returns to capital imply that the steady-state growth rate of real GDP per capita is determined by the rate of technological change.

Capital Accumulation

Because the capital stock plays a key role in determining how real GDP grows over time, it's important to consider carefully *capital accumulation*, or the change over time in the capital stock. At any given time, the capital stock is increasing because of investment in new capital, but it also is decreasing because of *depreciation*, as existing machinery, equipment, and other capital wears out or becomes obsolete.

To begin the discussion, we make the simplifying assumption of a closed economy with no government sector, so net exports, taxes, and government expenditures are zero. With this assumption, all output is either consumed or invested in new capital goods. Therefore, real GDP per worker, y, can be divided into consumption per worker, c, and investment per worker, i:

$$y = c + i.$$

Investment The capital–labor ratio, k, increases when the stock of machines, computers, buildings, and other investment goods increases faster than the increase in the number of workers. We assume for simplicity that s, the faction of total output that is saved, or the *national saving rate*, is a constant fraction of real GDP per worker, y. So, if the saving rate is 10%, then s equals 0.10; if the saving rate is 20%, then s equals 0.20; and so on. The loanable funds model shows that financial markets operate to ensure that saving equals investment (see Chapter 3). Because saving and investment are equal, investment per worker, i, equals:

$$i = sy.$$

[2]Robert E. Lucas, Jr., "On the Mechanics of Economic Development," *Journal of Monetary Economics*, Vol. 22, No. 1, July 1988, pp. 3–42.

Substituting this expression into the equation $y = c + i$ and rearranging terms gives us an expression for consumption per worker:

$$c = (1 - s)y.$$

Substituting the production function into the above expression for investment, we have the following *investment function*:

$$i = sf(k).$$

Figure 6.1 shows the relationship between the production function and the investment function. The figure shows how investment per worker increases as the capital–labor ratio, k, increases. Notice that the investment function has the same general shape as the production function. This similarity occurs because we have assumed a constant saving rate for the economy. As the capital–labor ratio increases, real GDP per worker also increases, causing investment per worker to increase. Because of diminishing marginal returns, increasing the capital–labor ratio causes smaller and smaller increases in real GDP per worker. Investment per worker equals the constant saving rate multiplied by real GDP per worker, so the increase in investment per worker also gets smaller and smaller as the capital–labor ratio increases.

Depreciation Depreciation refers to the reduction in the capital stock that occurs either because machinery, equipment, and other capital goods become worn out by use or because they become obsolete. For instance, a business may find its computers are obsolete if they are too slow or have too little memory to be used with new software programs. We assume that the **depreciation rate**, d, is a constant fraction of the capital–labor ratio and that the depreciation rate, expressed as a decimal, is between zero and one, so:

$$\text{Depreciation} = dk.$$

Depreciation rate The rate at which the capital stock declines due to either capital goods becoming worn out by use or becoming obsolete.

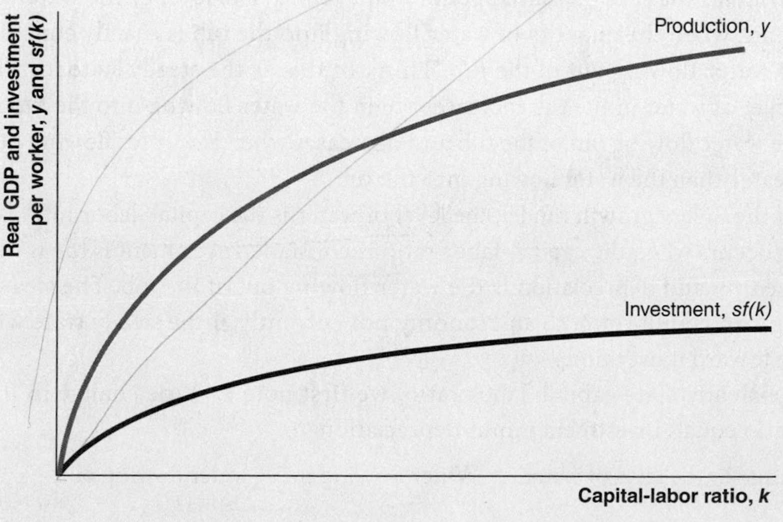

Figure 6.1

Investment per Worker, Real GDP per Worker, and the Capital–Labor Ratio

The production function shows that as the capital–labor ratio increases, real GDP per worker also increases, and that causes investment per worker to increase. Because of diminishing marginal returns, the increase in investment per worker gets smaller and smaller as the capital–labor ratio increases.

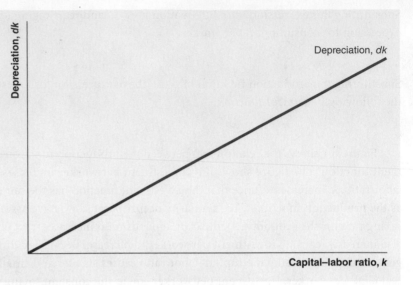

Figure 6.2

Depreciation and the Capital–Labor Ratio

The depreciation line has a slope equal to the depreciation rate. The depreciation line is steeper the higher the depreciation rate, and it is flatter the lower the depreciation.

When we graph depreciation in Figure 6.2, we see that it is a straight line with a positive slope equal to d. The depreciation line is steeper the higher the depreciation rate, and it is flatter the lower the depreciation rate.

The Steady State

In the Solow growth model, equilibrium occurs when the capital–labor ratio is constant because with a constant capital–labor ratio, real GDP per worker is also constant. In this equilibrium, called a **steady state**, capital, labor, and real GDP are all growing. Because these variables are growing at the same rate, though, their ratios—k and y—are constant. One way to think about the steady state is with an analogy to a bathtub. Figure 6.3 shows a bathtub with water flowing into the tub through the faucet and water flowing out through the drain. The level of water is a *stock variable* because we measure it *at a point in time*, while the quantities of water flowing into and out of the tub are *flow variables* that are measured *per period of time*. The level of the water in the tub is constant when the quantity of water flowing into the tub is exactly equal to the quantity of water flowing out of the tub. Think of this as the steady state for the bathtub. The level of water in the tub increases when the water flowing into the tub is greater than the water flowing out of the tub and decreases when the water flowing out of the tub is greater than the water flowing into the tub.

In terms of the Solow growth model, the level of water is the capital–labor ratio, so the steady state occurs when the capital–labor ratio is constant. Investment is the water flowing into the tub, and depreciation is the water flowing out of the tub. The steady state is the long-run equilibrium, so an economy not currently at the steady state will gradually move toward it over time.

To find the steady-state capital–labor ratio, we first note that the change in the capital–labor ratio equals investment minus depreciation:

Change in the level of water = Water flowing in − water flowing out,

so,

Change in the capital-labor ratio = Investment − depreciation.

Steady state An equilibrium in the Solow growth model in which the capital–labor ratio and real GDP per worker are constant but capital, labor, and output are growing.

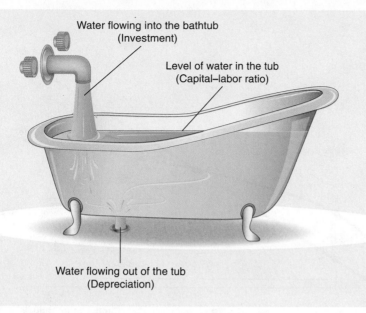

Figure 6.3

The Steady State and the Bathtub Analogy

Investment per worker is like the water flowing into a bathtub, and depreciation is like the water flowing out of the tub. The level of water in the tub is the capital–labor ratio. When the level of water is constant, the tub is in a steady state.

We can express the relationship for a change in the capital–labor ratio as:

$$\Delta k = i - dk,$$

where Δk is the change in the capital–labor ratio. Because i equals $sf(k)$, we can rewrite the above equation as:

$$\Delta k = sf(k) - dk.$$

This equation is a key one for the Solow growth model because it tells us how the capital–labor ratio changes over time and allows us to determine the steady state. We know that in the steady state, the capital–labor ratio is constant, so in the steady state, $\Delta k = 0$.

Figure 6.4 shows the investment function and the depreciation line. The steady state occurs where the investment function intersects the depreciation line because at that point, investment equals depreciation. The steady state is stable because if the economy is not currently at the steady state, it will automatically move toward it. For example, suppose that the initial capital–labor ratio is k_1 in Figure 6.4. At that ratio, the level of investment, $sf(k_1)$, is greater than depreciation, dk_1, so $\Delta k > 0$, and the capital–labor ratio increases toward the steady-state capital–labor ratio, k^*. The increase in the capital–labor ratio is the vertical distance between the investment function and the depreciation line. Notice that this vertical distance decreases as the capital–labor ratio increases. Why? As the economy accumulates more capital goods per worker, capital goods become less productive because of diminishing marginal returns; that is, the marginal product of capital decreases. As a result, the extra output and investment that the economy receives from additional capital decreases as the economy accumulates more capital. The increase in the capital–labor ratio continues until $\Delta k = 0$, which occurs when the capital–labor ratio equals k^*.

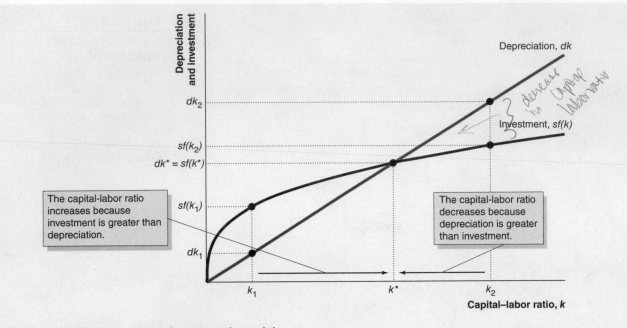

Figure 6.4 Equilibrium in the Solow Growth Model

In the steady state, the capital–labor ratio is constant, so the change in the capital–labor ratio is zero. The steady state occurs where the investment function intersects the depreciation line. If the capital–labor ratio is below the steady-state value, investment per worker, $sf(k_1)$, is greater than depreciation, dk_1, so the capital–labor ratio increases toward the steady-state capital–labor ratio, k^*. If the capital–labor ratio is above the steady-state value, investment per worker, $sf(k_2)$ is less than depreciation, dk_2, so the capital–labor ratio decreases toward the steady-state capital–labor ratio, k^*.

Now suppose that in Figure 6.4 the initial capital–labor ratio is k_2. At that capital–labor ratio, the level of investment, $sf(k_2)$, is less than depreciation, dk_2, so $\Delta k < 0$, and the capital–labor ratio decreases toward the steady-state capital–labor ratio, k^*. The decrease in the capital–labor ratio is the vertical distance between the investment function and the depreciation line. The decrease in the capital–labor ratio continues until $\Delta k = 0$, which occurs when the capital–labor ratio equals k^*.

Transition to the Steady State

Table 6.1 gives an example of the transition to the steady state when an economy starts off with less than the steady-state capital–labor ratio. To illustrate this transition, we assume that capital's share of income and, therefore, the coefficient on the capital–labor ratio, is one-third, so:

$$y = k^{1/3}.$$

We continue to assume that total factor productivity is constant and equal to 1. We also assume that the economy saves 45% of output, so $s = 0.45$; that the depreciation rate is 5%, so $d = 0.05$; and that the initial capital–labor ratio is $8 of capital per worker, so $k = 8$.

BE FAMILIAR W/ ALL VARIABLES!

Table 6.1 An Example of Transition to the Steady State

Year	k	y	c	i	dk	Δk
1	8.000	2.000	1.100	0.900	0.400	0.500
2	8.500	2.041	1.122	0.918	0.425	0.493
3	8.993	2.080	1.144	0.936	0.450	0.486
4	9.480	2.116	1.164	0.952	0.474	0.478
5	9.958	2.151	1.183	0.968	0.498	0.470
⋮						
50	22.817	2.836	1.560	1.276	1.141	0.135
⋮						
100	26.214	2.971	1.634	1.337	1.311	0.026
⋮						
∞	27	3	1.65	1.35	1.35	0

(handwritten: $c = y - i$; $c = 2 - .9 = 1.1$)

At the beginning of year 1, the economy starts with $8 of capital per worker. To find *(handwritten: $y = k^{1/3}$)* out what happens to the capital–labor ratio during the year, we can follow these steps:

1. Given the production function, $8 of capital per worker will produce $2 of real GDP per worker. *(handwritten: $y = 8^{1/3} = 2 = y$)*

2. The economy saves 45% of output and saving equals investment, so $i = 0.90$ and $c = 1.10$. *(handwritten: $i = sy, = .45 \times 2 = .9$)*

3. We know that 5% of the capital stock depreciates each year, so $dk = 0.40$. *(handwritten: $d = 0.05, k = 8, dk = 0.40$)*

4. Because investment is 0.90 and depreciation is 0.40, the change in the capital stock is 0.50. *(handwritten: Δ capital stock = investment − depreciation)*

As a result, the economy begins year 2 with a capital–labor ratio of $8.50 of capital per worker. Following similar calculations, the final column in Table 6.1 shows that the change in the capital–labor ratio is 0.493 in year 2, 0.486 in year 3, and so on. The table shows that each year, the change in the capital stock is becoming smaller. When the change in the capital–labor ratio is 0, the economy has reached its steady state, with the following values:

(handwritten: $c = (.55) \, y$; $c = (0.55)2$)

(handwritten: Steady State values)

The capital–labor ratio is $27 of capital per worker.
Real GDP per worker is $3.
Consumption per worker is $1.65.
Investment per worker is $1.35.

A more direct way to find the steady-state values of k and y is to use the expression for the change in the capital–labor ratio:

$$\Delta k = sf(k) - dk.$$

(handwritten: what exactly is this function defined by?)

When the economy is in the steady state and the capital–labor ratio is equal to its steady-state value, k^*, the change in the capital–labor ratio is 0, so:

$$0 = sf(k^*) - dk^*,$$

(handwritten: $dk^* = s f(k^*)$)

which we can rewrite as:

$$\frac{k^*}{f(k^*)} = \frac{s}{d}.$$

(handwritten:
$0 = 0.45 f(k^*) - .05 \times 8$
$0 = 0.45 f(k^*) - .40$
$f(k^*) = \frac{.40}{.45} = \frac{.8}{.9}$
WHY WRONG)

Using the actual production function and assuming that the level of total factor productivity is 1, we have:

$$\frac{k^*}{(k^*)^{1/3}} = \frac{0.45}{0.05}.$$

We can simplify this to:

$$(k^*)^{2/3} = 9.$$

So:

$$k^* = (9)^{3/2} = 27.$$

Therefore, the steady-state capital–labor ratio is $27 per worker, which is the same result that we see in Table 6.1.

Saving Rates and Growth Rates

We have just seen how the steady-state capital–labor ratio and the level of real GDP per worker are determined. Now we can determine what causes steady state values to differ across countries. For example, can differences among national saving rates explain differences in the steady-state growth rates of countries such as the United States, India, and Bangladesh? Figure 6.5 shows that an increase in the saving rate from s_1 to s_2 causes the investment function to shift up.

Because the investment function has shifted up, the economy is producing more investment goods for any given level of the capital–labor ratio. The level of investment is

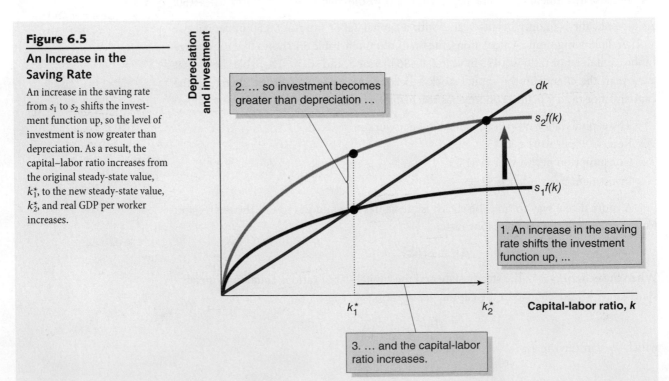

Figure 6.5

An Increase in the Saving Rate

An increase in the saving rate from s_1 to s_2 shifts the investment function up, so the level of investment is now greater than depreciation. As a result, the capital–labor ratio increases from the original steady-state value, k_1^*, to the new steady-state value, k_2^*, and real GDP per worker increases.

Depreciation and investment

2. ... so investment becomes greater than depreciation ...

dk

$s_2f(k)$

$s_1f(k)$

1. An increase in the saving rate shifts the investment function up, ...

k_1^*　　k_2^*　　**Capital-labor ratio, k**

3. ... and the capital-labor ratio increases.

now greater than depreciation, so the capital–labor ratio rises from the original steady-state value of k_1^* to the new steady-state value of k_2^*. An increase in the saving rate increases the steady-state level of the capital-labor ratio and real GDP per worker. *But there is nothing in our analysis so far to indicate that an increase in the saving rate will affect the steady-state growth rate of real GDP per worker.* Following an increase in the saving rate, the level of real GDP per worker will increase to a new, higher steady-state level, but then it will stay at that level. Because the standard of living as measured by real GDP per capita depends on real GDP per worker, we can also say that changes in the saving rate affect only the steady-state level of the standard of living. One conclusion from this analysis is that government policies that change the saving rate have a *level effect*—they can raise real GDP per capita and the standard of living to a higher level—but do not have a *growth effect*—they will *not* result in a sustained increase in the standard of living over time. Only policies that change the steady-state growth rate of real GDP per worker

Macro Data: Do High Rates of Saving and Investment Lead to High Levels of Income?

The Solow growth model predicts that in equilibrium, the higher the saving rate, the higher the level of real GDP per worker. This prediction seems reasonable because a high saving rate results in a high investment rate and a higher capital–labor ratio. A higher capital–labor ratio makes it possible to produce more output per worker. But how well does this prediction hold up when we look at real-world data? The figure below plots the level of real GDP per capita in 2009 and the rate of investment between 1971 and 2009 for 120 countries, with each point representing one country. (Recall that there is a close relationship between real GDP per worker and real GDP per capita.)

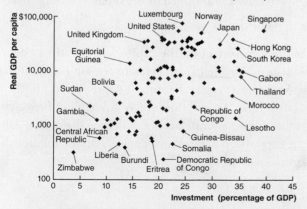

The graph shows that, although the relationship is not exact, the Solow model's prediction is confirmed: Countries with high investment rates have higher levels

of real GDP per capita than do countries with low investment rates. The fact that the Solow model does a reasonably good job of explaining the actual experiences of countries around the world is a key reason economists have widely accepted the model.

There are two important points to bear in mind, though: First, as we will discuss later, the basic Solow model explains some, but not all, of the key facts about economic growth. For this reason, the model needs to be extended. Second, when looking at data, we need to remember the important distinction between *correlation* and *causality*. The graph shows that investment rates and levels of real GDP per capita are correlated—that is, they tend to occur together—but the graph does not provide direct evidence that higher investment rates cause economies to have higher levels of real GDP per capita. It is possible that we are observing a case of *reverse causality*—that is, having a high level of real GDP per capita may cause high investment rates. Most economists, though, believe that the data in the graph confirm the prediction of the Solow model that high investment rates cause high levels of real GDP per capita.

Source: Penn World Tables version 7.0: http://pwt.econ.upenn.edu/.

See related problem 1.4 at the end of the chapter.

have a *growth effect* that will bring about sustained increases in the standard of living. We discuss policies that increase economic growth in Section 6.5.

This result is important because it rules out one potential explanation for differences in growth rates among countries. The United States has experienced sustained increases in the standard of living over the past 200 years, while countries such as Bangladesh have experienced little growth, and countries such as China and India began experiencing significant growth only comparatively recently. The Solow growth model tells us that differences in national saving rates do not explain the differences in steady-state growth rates. To understand these differences, we must consider other factors.

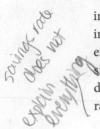
saving rate does not explain everything

Learning Objective

Understand the effect of labor force growth on labor productivity.

Labor Force Growth and the Solow Growth Model

In the previous section, we showed that differences in national saving rates can help explain differences in the level of real GDP per capita across countries but cannot explain differences in *growth rates* of real GDP per capita. In reaching this result, we assumed that the labor force and the level of total factor productivity are constant. In this section, we analyze the effects of a growing labor force on the steady-state values of the capital–labor ratio and real GDP per worker. However, we still assume that total factor productivity is constant and equal to one. In the next section, we consider the effects of technological change.

Labor Force Growth and the Steady State

As we saw in the previous section, the capital–labor ratio increases if investment is greater than depreciation, and it decreases if investment is less than depreciation. Investment and depreciation affect the capital stock, which is in the numerator of the capital–labor ratio. Changes in the labor force affect the denominator of the capital–labor ratio. If the labor force grows faster than the capital stock, the capital–labor ratio will fall, and if the labor force grows more slowly than the capital stock, the capital–labor ratio will rise. We can think of the effect of the labor force increasing faster than the capital stock as spreading out, or *diluting*, the capital stock over more workers. The amount of dilution equals the labor force growth rate, n, multiplied by the capital–labor ratio, k:

★ Dilution

$$\text{Dilution} = nk.^3$$

Conceptually, dilution has the same effect on the capital–labor ratio as depreciation did in our previous discussion. For the capital stock to remain constant, taking into account dilution, investment must equal the sum of depreciation plus labor force growth: $i = dk + nk = (d + n)k$. We call this level of investment *break-even investment* because it represents the investment rate necessary to keep the capital–labor ratio constant. The change in the capital–labor ratio now depends on the relationship between investment and break-even investment:

$$\Delta k = i - (d + n)k.$$

---

[3]To understand why dilution equals nk, keep in mind that $k = K/L$ and n is the growth rate of L. So if L grows by 3% (that is, $n = 3\%$), then K also has to grow by 3% in order to keep k constant.

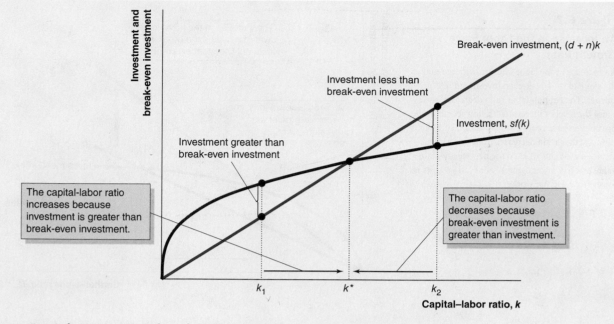

Figure 6.6 Labor Force Growth in the Solow Model

When labor force growth is not zero, the slope of the break-even investment line is $d + n$. To keep the capital–labor ratio constant, the economy must now invest enough to replace capital goods that wear out due to depreciation and to provide new workers with the steady-state amount of capital. The steady-state capital–labor ratio occurs where investment equals the break-even level of investment, which keeps the capital–labor ratio constant.

Or, substituting $sf(k)$ for i as we did previously:

$$\Delta k = sf(k) - (d + n)k.$$

Figure 6.6 analyzes the steady state in the Solow growth model, taking growth in the labor force into account. Figure 6.6 is very similar to Figure 6.4 on page 182. The only difference is that the line labeled "Depreciation" in Figure 6.4 is now labeled "Break-even investment," and the slope of the line has changed from d to $d + n$. As before, k^* is the steady-state capital–labor ratio. If the economy is below this level at k_1, investment is greater than break-even investment, and the capital–labor ratio increases until it reaches k^*. If the economy is at k_2, investment is less than break-even investment, and the capital–labor ratio decreases until it reaches k^*.

The Effect of an Increase in the Labor Force Growth Rate

Economists use the Solow growth model to help explain why the standard of living is higher in some countries than in others. Incorporating the growth rate of the labor force into the model brings us closer to this objective. Figure 6.7 shows what happens when the growth rate of the labor force increases. The break-even investment line becomes steeper, which causes the steady-state capital–labor ratio to decline from k_1^* to k_2^*. A lower capital–labor ratio results in a lower level of real GDP per worker and, therefore, a lower level of real GDP per capita. So, the Solow growth model predicts that a higher labor force growth rate will lead to a lower standard of living.

Figure 6.7

An Increase in the Labor Force Growth Rate

An increase in the labor force growth rate makes the slope of the break-even investment line steeper. The capital–labor ratio decreases because the level of investment is now less than the break-even level of investment. As a result, the capital–labor ratio decreases from the original steady-state value of k_1^* to the new steady-state value of k_2^*. A lower capital–labor ratio results in lower real GDP per worker.

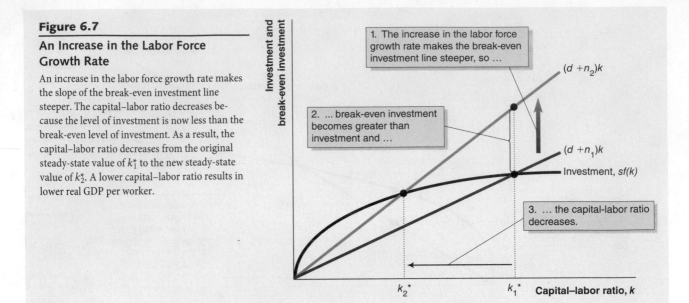

Notice that the growth rate of the labor force and the depreciation rate both affect the slope of the break-even investment line in the same way. Therefore, the Solow growth model predicts that a higher depreciation rate will also lead to a lower capital–labor ratio and a lower standard of living.

An increase in the labor force growth rate will reduce the steady-state level of real GDP per worker but *not* the steady-state growth rate of real GDP per worker. Just as we saw that changes in the saving rate affect the level, but not the growth rate, of the steady-state capital–labor ratio, the same is true of changes in the labor force growth rate. Therefore, differences in labor force growth rates (and, accordingly, population growth rates) cannot explain differences in steady-state growth rates across countries. We have to look elsewhere for an explanation of why the United States has experienced significant steady-state growth in real GDP per capita, while countries such as Bangladesh have not.

Solved Problem 6.2

The Effect of a Decrease in the Labor Force Growth Rate on Real GDP per Worker

According to the United Nations's Population Division, the world's population growth rate averaged 1.7% per year between 1950 and 2010. The following table shows the Population Division's forecasts for the population growth rates for different regions in the world:

Period	Africa	Asia	Europe	North America	South America	World
1950–2010	2.5	1.8	0.5	1.2	2.1	1.7
2010–2100	1.4	0.1	−0.1	0.5	0.2	0.4
Change in the population growth rate	−1.1%	−1.7%	−0.6%	−0.7%	−1.9%	−1.3%

Sources: United Nations, Population Division; and calculations based on the median variant forecast.

In every region, the forecast is for slower population growth. The slower population growth should reduce the growth rate of the labor force. What effect does the Solow growth model predict this reduction will have on the standard of living in the world?

Solving the Problem

Step 1   **Review the chapter material.** The problem asks you to determine the effect of a decrease in the labor force growth rate on the standard of living, so you may want to review the section "The Effect of an Increase in the Labor Force Growth Rate," which begins on page 187.

Step 2   **Use a graph to determine the effects of a decrease in the labor force growth rate in the Solow model.** In Section 6.2, we saw that in the Solow growth model, the break-even investment line is $(d + n)k$. So the slope of the break-even investment line depends on the depreciation rate and the labor force growth rate. When the labor force growth rate decreases, the slope of the break-even investment line will decrease so it becomes less steep. The labor force growth rate does not affect the investment function. Your graph showing the effect of the decrease in the labor force growth rate should look like this:

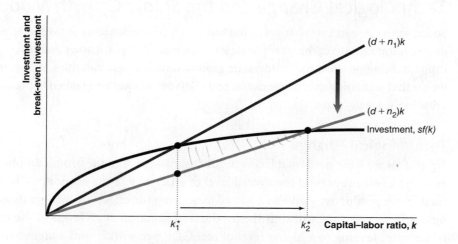

Step 3   **Determine the effect on the capital–labor ratio.** The break-even investment line becomes less steep, so at the initial capital–labor ratio, k_1^*, the level of investment is now greater than the new level of break-even investment. As a result, the capital–labor ratio begins to increase toward the new steady-state capital–labor ratio, k_2^*. The change in the capital–labor ratio is the vertical distance between the investment curve and the new break-even investment line. The vertical distance gets smaller as the capital–labor ratio increases due to diminishing marginal returns, so the increase in the capital–labor ratio gets smaller and smaller as the economy approaches the new steady state. Growth stops when the economy reaches the new steady state, where the new capital–labor ratio is k_2^*.

Step 4 **Determine the effect of the capital–labor ratio on the standard of living.** Because labor productivity has increased, the effect of the decrease in the population growth rate is to increase the standard of living of the average person. The United Nations predicts that the population growth rate will decrease during the 2010–2100 period for all regions of the world, although the decrease in the population growth rate will vary across regions. The largest decrease in the population growth rate is expected to occur in Asia and South America, so, all else being equal, you should expect that the increase in the standard of living that results from slower labor force growth rates will be highest on these continents. The Solow growth model predicts that a decrease in the growth rate of the population will increase the standard of living. However, more recent models suggest that a decrease in the growth rate of the population may decrease the standard of living. We discuss these models later in the chapter.

See related problem 2.3 at the end of the chapter.

Learning Objective

Understand the effect of technological change on labor productivity and the standard of living.

Technological Change and the Solow Growth Model

So far, we have seen that changes in the saving rate, the labor force growth rate, and the depreciation rate affect the steady-state levels of real GDP per worker and real GDP per capita but do not affect the steady-state growth rates of these variables. In this section, we see that technological change causes real GDP per worker and real GDP per capita to grow in the steady state.

Technological Change

Up to now we have used total factor productivity—the A in the production function, $y = Af(k)$—to represent the overall level of efficiency in the economy. Changes in total factor productivity give us a way of measuring the effects of changes in technology. An increase in A will shift the production function at all levels of the capital–labor ratio, leading to a higher level of real GDP per worker and a higher standard of living.

But focusing just on changes in total factor productivity assumes that improvements in technology or efficiency affect capital and labor equally. Some changes in technology, however, are *labor augmenting*. **Labor-augmenting technological change** involve improvements in economic efficiency that increase the productivity of labor but that do not directly make capital goods more efficient. For example, when robots were introduced into automobile factories in the 1970s, they increased the number of automobiles that could be assembled by a given number of workers.

We begin our analysis of labor-augmenting technological change by using the production function expressed in terms of levels of variables (see Chapter 5) rather than the per-worker production function we have been using in this chapter. We make one

Labor-augmenting technological change

Improvements in economic efficiency that increase the productivity of labor but that do not directly make capital goods more efficient.

change to the production function: We measure the labor input in *effective units*, $L \times E$, where E represents the efficiency of labor. So, the production function is:

$$Y = F(K, L \times E).$$

New technology, new methods of organizing production, and improvements in the skill level of the labor force make workers more productive and so increase the efficiency of labor. The labor input in the production function can increase if the number of workers increases or if the efficiency of the existing workers improves, so we can think of the term $L \times E$ as measuring *effective workers*. If better training or access to better technology makes workers on average 3% more productive this year than last year, then in effect, the labor force has increased in the same way as if the economy had 3% more workers. For example, the population and labor force of Brazil are about the same size as the population and labor force of Pakistan. But workers in Brazil are more highly trained and have access to better technology on their jobs. If the E in Brazil is twice the level of E in Pakistan, then the effective labor supply in Brazil is double the effective labor supply in Pakistan.

A simple assumption is that labor-augmenting technological change grows at a rate g. There are, then, two sources of growth in the effective labor force: Growth in the number of workers, n, and growth in the effectiveness of workers, g. Therefore, the growth rate of the effective labor force is $n + g$.

Technological Change and the Steady State

We have introduced technological change by focusing on technology, such as computers or manufacturing robots, that augments labor. Because this type of technological change has the same effect on the labor input as an increase in the labor force, we can use the same analysis as in the previous section.

To incorporate technological change into the model, we focus on capital per *effective* worker and output per *effective* worker. We define output per effective worker as $y = Y/(E \times L)$ and capital per effective worker as $k = K/(E \times L)$. In the previous section, break-even investment consisted of the amount of investment necessary to replace depreciation, dk, plus the amount of dilution of the capital stock due to labor force growth, nk. With labor-augmenting technological change, break-even investment now also has to include the dilution from effective labor growth, gk. Therefore, the break-even level of investment now equals $(dk + nk + gk) = (d + n + g)k$, so the expression for the change in k becomes:

$$\Delta k = sf(k) - (d + n + g)k.$$

Figure 6.8 shows equilibrium in the Solow growth model with labor-augmenting technological change.

Steady-State Growth Rates

While the Solow growth model in this section looks very similar to the model from the earlier sections, it is different in one very important way. In the previous sections, capital per worker was constant in the steady state, so real GDP per worker and, therefore,

Figure 6.8

Equilibrium with Technological Change

With labor-augmenting technological change increasing at rate g, the break-even rate of investment becomes $(d + n + g)k$. The steady-state level of k, the ratio of capital to effective labor, is determined by the intersection of the investment function and the break-even investment line.

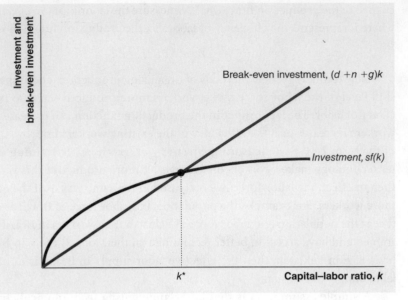

the standard of living were also constant in the steady state. As a result, the Solow growth model could not explain why the standard of living would grow in the steady state, as it has in the United States, France, Germany, Canada, and other high-income countries.

In the steady state, we know that real GDP per effective worker, y, is constant, so the growth rate of y is zero. However, real GDP per worker, $Y/L = y \times E$, will grow when the economy is in the steady state. Even though y is constant in the steady state, the efficiency of labor, E, grows at rate g, so the growth rate of real GDP per worker in the steady state is g. Similar reasoning shows that real GDP, $Y = y \times (E \times L)$, will also grow in the steady state. The efficiency of labor grows at rate g and the labor force grows at rate n, so the growth rate of real GDP equals $n + g$.

What about the standard of living, which we measure as real GDP per capita? The relationship between real GDP per capita and real GDP per worker is:

$$(Y/\text{Population}) = (Y/L) \times (L/\text{Population}).$$

If we make the reasonable assumption that a constant share of the population is working, then in the steady state, both real GDP per worker and real GDP per capita grow at rate g. Changes in the saving rate, labor force growth rate, and depreciation rate will affect the steady-state level of real GDP per capita but not the steady-state growth rate. *Only changes in the underlying rate of labor-augmenting technological change will affect the steady-state growth rate of the standard of living.* The Solow growth model has allowed us to reach an important conclusion: Countries that have experienced sustained increases in their standard of living have achieved them because of sustained technological change, not because of other variables such as higher rates of saving and investment or higher rates of population growth.

Table 6.2 Steady-State Growth Rates of Key Variables in the Solow Growth Model

Variable	Symbol	Steady-State Growth Rate
Capital per effective worker	$k = K/(E \times L)$	0
Real GDP per effective worker	$y = Y/(E \times L)$	0
Real GDP per worker	$Y/L = y \times E$	g
Real GDP per capita	$(Y/\text{Population}) = y \times E \times (L/\text{Population})$	g
Real GDP	$Y = y \times E \times L$	$n + g$

Table 6.2 summarizes the steady-state growth rates of the key variables in the Solow growth model.

Balanced Growth, Convergence, and Long-Run Equilibrium

The steady state is the equilibrium for the economy; however, it is an equilibrium in which the key economic quantities such as the capital–labor ratio and real GDP per worker are growing. **Balanced growth** occurs when the capital–labor ratio and real GDP per worker grow at the same constant rate. Table 6.2 summarizes the steady-state growth rates of key variables in the Solow model. The *balanced growth path* can be illustrated on a graph that shows how real GDP per worker grows over time while the economy is in the steady state. We can think of the balanced growth path as the equilibrium time path for real GDP per worker.

Convergence to the Balanced Growth Path

Just as the steady state is the equilibrium for the economy at a point in time, the balanced growth path is the equilibrium for the economy over time.

The experiences of Germany and Japan after World War II provide good examples of how an economy that is off its balanced growth path eventually converges back to that path. By the end of World War II in 1945, both Germany and Japan had experienced large decreases in their capital–labor ratios as the United States and its allies bombed factories, bridges, and transportation networks in both countries. The decrease in the capital–labor ratio resulted in declines in real GDP per worker and real GDP per capita. Figure 6.9 shows real GDP per capita over time for Germany and Japan. As expected, both countries experienced a large decrease in real GDP per capita at the end of World War II, while in the years immediately after the war, both countries grew much more rapidly than they did before the war. Germany grew rapidly from the end of the war until about 1960, after which it appears to have grown at the same rate as it did prior to the war. In fact, Germany appears to have been on the same growth path since 1960 that it was on before World War II. Japan had a somewhat different experience. The country grew rapidly from the end of the war until the mid-1970s, when it appears to have moved to a higher balanced growth path compared to the one it was on before the war. We can conclude that Japan's steady-state capital–labor ratio and real GDP per worker increased.

6.4

Learning Objective

Explain balanced growth, convergence, and long-run equilibrium.

Balanced growth A situation in which the capital–labor ratio and real GDP per worker grow at the same constant rate.

Figure 6.9

Post–World War II Convergence in Germany and Japan

Germany and Japan experienced a large decrease in real GDP per capita at the end of World War II due to destruction of their capital stock. Germany grew rapidly from the end of the war until about 1960. After 1960, Germany appears to have grown at the same rate as it did prior to the war. Japan grew rapidly from the end of the war until the mid-1970s, but it appears to have moved to a higher balanced growth path compared to the one it was on before the war.

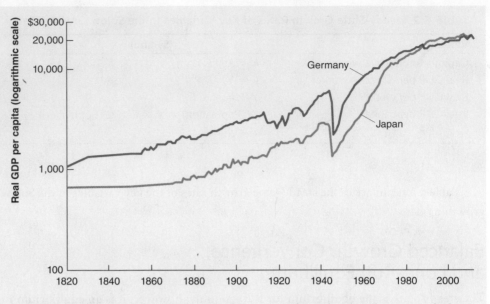

Source: The Conference Board, *Total Economy Database*, www.conference-board.org/data/economydatabase/, Angus Maddison, Statistics on World Population, GDP and Per Capita GDP, 1-2008, http://www.ggdc.net/MADDISON/oriindex.htm

What economic forces cause countries to return to their balanced growth path? We can use the Solow growth model and the experiences of Germany and Japan to explain the process. Assume that in 1939, before World War II, the German economy was in steady state and on its balanced growth path. In that case, according to Table 6.2 on page 193, the capital–labor ratio and real GDP per worker were both growing at a rate of g. By the end of the war, large portions of Germany's capital stock had been destroyed, which decreased real GDP per worker and real GDP per capita. After the war ended, labor-augmenting technological change continued to occur, which caused real GDP per worker and real GDP per capita to grow. However, because the capital–labor ratio had fallen, the German economy grew for an additional reason: It accumulated capital more quickly than it had along the balanced growth path.

From 1945 to 1960, the capital–labor ratio in Germany increased for two reasons. First, labor-augmenting technological change was positive, so the growth rate of the capital–labor ratio along the balanced growth path was positive. Second, Germany was *converging* from the artificially low capital–labor ratio of 1945 toward the steady-state capital–labor ratio. Because the growth rate of the capital–labor ratio helps determine the growth rate of real GDP per worker, the growth rate of real GDP per worker during these years was also the result of both labor-augmenting technological change and convergence toward the steady state. In general, we can think of the growth rate of real GDP per worker as the result of these two factors: steady-state growth and convergence to the steady state.

As long as the capital–labor ratio is less than its steady-state value, growth from convergence is positive, so from 1945 to 1960, the German economy was growing more

rapidly than it did along the balanced growth path. As real GDP per worker converged toward its steady-state value, real GDP per capita converged toward the balanced growth path.

Figure 6.9 on page 194 shows that Japan experienced a similar decrease in real GDP per capita at the end of the war and then rapid growth after the war.

Making the Connection

Will China's Standard of Living Ever Exceed that of the United States?

In 2011, GDP per capita in the United States was nearly six times higher than GDP per capita in China. However, the growth rate of real GDP per capita in the United States has averaged only 1.9% per year since 1980 compared to China's average rate of 8.9% per year over the same time period. Because China's standard of living is growing more rapidly than that of the United States, we could predict that China's standard of living will exceed the U.S. standard of living in the year 2038. However, for China to maintain its high rates of growth that of real GDP per capita, it would have to maintain high rates of technological change, which is unlikely for four key reasons.

First, the United States invests more in activities, such as research and development, that result in new technologies. Second, much of China's growth is likely due to the transition from a centrally planned economy to a market economy, so China's growth rate is likely to decrease as the transition is completed. We can think of the transition to a market economy as moving China's balanced growth path to a higher level of real GDP per capita. Third, much of China's economic growth has been fueled by moving workers from agriculture, where their productivity was low, to manufacturing jobs in the city, where their productivity is much higher. The large supply of low-wage agricultural workers helped keep manufacturing wages low and provided China with a cost advantage in manufacturing goods compared with the United States and other high-income countries. China has exhausted much of its supply of low-wage agricultural workers, so manufacturing wages have begun to rise, eroding China's cost advantage. The high rates of growth in real GDP per capita are due to convergence to the higher balanced growth path. As China approaches the new higher balanced growth path, we would expect its growth rate to decrease significantly.

Another looming problem is demographic. Because of China's low birthrate, it will soon experience a decline in its labor force. Over the next two decades, the population of men and women between 15 and 29 years will fall by about 100 million, or roughly 30%. China will also experience a large increase in older workers, a group that will likely be less educated and less healthy than younger workers. Given current trends, the U.S. Census Bureau projects fewer people under age 50 in China in 2030 than today, with many more in their 60s and older. More ominous is that China has no national public pension system. China still has potential sources for enhancing productivity, including the migration of rural workers to more productive urban jobs and wider application of technical know-how. These factors can fuel future growth, but at some point, China's demographic problems could slow growth.

There already is evidence that the factors that led to China's rapid growth rate are changing. The cost advantage that drove many U.S. manufacturers to relocate production to China is diminishing. More than one-third of 106 U.S.-based executives at companies with annual sales of over $1 billion surveyed by the Boston Consulting Group (BCG) stated that they were actively considering bringing production back to the United States. The survey results led the BCG to predict that productivity-increasing measures taken by U.S. firms in recent years and rising costs in China, a by-product of the country's rapid growth rate, could lead to a significant shift in production from China back to the United States—called *reshoring*—by 2020. The U.S.-based firms that have already reshored include Otis Elevator, Peerless Industries, and Caterpillar, Inc. Executives of the firms cite improved U.S. competitiveness and rising costs in China as the main reasons for their relocation decisions.

The experience of Japan in the past two decades offers a sobering lesson for China: Throughout the 1970s, Japan grew faster than the United States, and there was much discussion about when Japan would surpass the United States in real GDP per capita. But in the 1990s, Japan's average annual growth rate of per capita GDP was only 0.5%, well below the growth rate of the United States, and Japan experienced a decrease in the growth rate of total factor productivity. Although growth in Japan increased during the early 2000s, the country has never approached the growth rates of the years before 1990. Whether China will also suffer a rapid decline in growth rates remains to be seen.

Sources: Nicholas Eberstadt, "The Demographic Future," *Foreign Affairs*, Vol. 89, No. 6, November/December 2010, pp. 54–64; Fumio Hayashi and Edward C. Prescott, "The 1990s in Japan: A Lost Decade," www.minneapolisfed.org/research/wp/wp607.pdf; "More Than a Third of Large Manufacturers Are Considering Reshoring from China to the U.S.," bcgperspectives.com, April 20, 2012; and Eric Markowitz, "Made in USA (Again): Why Manufacturing Is Coming Home," Inc.com, March 23, 2012.

See related problem 4.5 at the end of the chapter.

Table 6.3 provides a summary of adjustments to the steady state.

Do All Countries Converge to the Same Steady State?

Our discussion so far suggests that countries eventually converge to their steady state. But does this mean that all countries converge to the *same* steady state and the same level of real GDP per capita? That seems unlikely because real GDP per capita varies

Table 6.3 Summary of Adjustments to the Steady State

If . . .	the capital–labor ratio . . .	so growth from convergence is . . .	and the growth rate of the economy . . .
$k = k^*$	equals the steady-state value	zero	equals the balanced growth rate, and the economy remains on the balanced growth path.
$k > k^*$	is greater than the steady-state value	negative	is less than the balanced growth rate, so the economy converges to the balanced growth path.
$k < k^*$	is less than the steady-state value	positive	is greater than the balanced growth rate, so the economy converges to the balanced growth path.

dramatically across countries. In 2011, real GDP per capita for the average country in the world was $9,500. Real GDP per capita in the United States was $48,100. The country with the lowest real GDP per capita was the Democratic Republic of the Congo, at $300, so the average person in the United States had an income 160 times that of the average person in the Congo! Economists have closely studied the extent to which poor countries such as the Congo are closing the gap in the level of real GDP per capita between themselves and high-income countries such as the United States. Economists use the term *convergence* to describe the process of low-income countries catching up to the real GDP per capita of high-income countries. For convergence to take place, we should see an inverse relationship between current levels of real GDP per capita and future growth rates of real GDP per capita. In other words, low-income countries should have higher growth rates than high-income countries.

We do see some evidence of convergence. When looking at Japan, the United States, and Western European countries, we see that the countries with low real GDP per capita in 1960 have grown more rapidly just as the Solow growth model would predict. Similarly, the U.S. states and the Japanese prefectures that had lower incomes per person 50 years ago have grown faster than the states and prefectures with higher incomes 50 years ago.[4] But as the huge gap between the United States and the Congo indicates, many low-income countries have not been converging on the levels of real GDP per capita of the high-income countries. In fact, many low-income countries have had growth rates that were lower, not higher, than the growth rates of high-income countries.

What explains the mixed evidence on whether convergence is taking place? The Solow growth model predicts that countries will converge *provided* that they have the same steady state. Steady states can differ among countries, however, as a result of differences in saving rates, labor force growth rates, or the rates of labor-augmenting technological change. Instead of convergence, countries exhibit *conditional convergence*, where each country converges to its own steady state. Research indicates that once we have taken into account differences in their steady states, countries do converge to the steady state at a rate of about 2% a year.[5] Moreover, if low-income countries do not increase their saving rates, increase human capital, or take other measures to increase total factor productivity, the gap in real GDP per capita between high-income and low-income countries is unlikely to disappear.

conditional convergence more likely (handwritten margin note)

Endogenous Growth Theory

6.5

Learning Objective
Explain the determinants of technological change using the endogenous growth model.

As we have seen, in the Solow model, technological change is the cause of sustained increases in real GDP per worker and the standard of living. Therefore, countries experiencing slow rates of technological change cannot hope to experience sustained high growth rates in their standard of living. Given the importance of technological change in explaining economic growth, a shortcoming of the Solow model is that it does not explain

[4]Robert Barro and Xavier Sala-i-Martin, "Convergence Across States and Regions," *Brookings Papers on Economic Activity*, Vol. 1991, No. 1, 1991, pp. 107–182.

[5]N. Gregory Marnkiw, David Romer, and David N. Weil, "A Contribution to the Empirics of Economic Growth," *Quarterly Journal of Economics*, Vol. 107, No. 2, May 1992, pp. 407–437.

*Solow
model assumes
A is exogenous*

Endogenous growth theory A theory of economic growth that tries to explain the growth rate of technological change.

why the rate of technological change differs over time and across countries. Instead, the Solow model assumes that technological change is determined *exogenously*, or outside the model.

In recent years, some economists have addressed this limitation of the Solow model by developing new models that explain technological change. These models are known as **endogenous growth theories** because they explain technological change within the model, or *endogenously*. There are many different endogenous growth models, but in this section, we focus on two general approaches. The first approach is to argue that, contrary to what we have been assuming to this point, capital is not subject to diminishing marginal returns. The second approach assumes that research firms produce new technology and ideas much the same way that other firms produce automobiles or clothing.

AK Growth Models: Reconsidering Diminishing Returns

Is it possible that capital is not subject to diminishing returns? Earlier, we gave a strong argument that capital as conventionally thought of—machinery, computers, buildings, and other physical capital—*is* subject to diminishing returns. Increases in physical capital increase output, but by increasingly smaller amounts. Endogenous growth theory takes a broader view of capital, including both **human capital** and *knowledge*. Neither of these types of capital may be subject to diminishing returns. If an economy accumulates physical and human capital at the same rate, the ratio of physical to human capital remains constant, and the marginal product of capital may not decline. As physical capital increases, a country becomes richer, and the country may invest more in education and devote more resources to on-the-job training. Increased education and on-the-job training, in turn, should both lead to more human capital. In addition, as an economy accumulates more capital goods of a given type, *learning by doing* occurs, so the existing workers become more proficient at using the capital goods. The more highly skilled workers can keep the marginal product of capital from declining. Firms also have an incentive to increase on-the-job training as they install new capital. For example, as personal computers became widespread, firms invested in training office workers in using them. Similarly, when computer-aided robots became widely used in manufacturing, automobile firms and other manufacturers invested heavily in retraining workers.

Human capital The accumulated knowledge and skill that workers acquire from education and training or from life experiences.

There are also good reasons to argue that knowledge is not subject to diminishing returns. As the stock of knowledge increases, the economy can produce new and better types of capital goods and, as a consequence, the marginal product of capital may not decline. In addition, as real GDP grows, firms may have both the resources—from the additional revenues they earn—and the incentive to increase their spending on *research and development (R&D)*. The additional R&D will produce additional knowledge that may further increase the productivity of capital. In fact, some economists have argued that knowledge is subject to *increasing* returns.

Most economists continue to believe that capital experiences diminishing marginal returns. Nevertheless, relaxing the assumption of diminishing marginal returns can provide useful insights into understanding economic growth. So, we next consider a model in which capital is not subject to diminishing returns.

Think about the following production function, where capital is not subject to diminishing returns (for simplicity, we assume that the value of the labor input is fixed at 1):

$$Y = AK.$$

As usual, Y equals real GDP, and A is a constant. We can rewrite the equation to show that $A = Y/K$, or output per unit of capital. Recall that the marginal product of capital is $\Delta Y/\Delta K$. In this model, the marginal product of capital is always equal to the constant A rather than declining as K increases, so capital is not subject to diminishing returns. Note that because we have assumed that the labor force is fixed at the value of 1, there is essentially no difference between real GDP, real GDP per worker, and real GDP per capita. Therefore, the model in this section is not only a model of the determinants of real GDP but also of the standard of living, as measured by real GDP per capita. These models are called *AK growth models*, after the form of the production function that they use.

To see the consequences of using these models to explain economic growth, think again of the bathtub analogy in Figure 6.3 on page 181. Given our aggregate production function, we now have:

$$\text{Water flowing into the bathtub} = sY = sAK.$$

We have assumed a constant labor force, so the growth rate of the labor force, n, equals 0, so we now have:

$$\text{Water flowing out of the bathtub} = dK.$$

Therefore, the change in the level of water in the bathtub, ΔK, equals:

$$\Delta K = sAK - dK.$$

We can divide each side of the equation by the capital stock to find an expression for the growth rate of the capital stock:

$$\frac{\Delta K}{K} = sA - d.$$

Given the new production function and using a little algebra, we have the following expression for the growth rate of real GDP:

$$\frac{\Delta Y}{Y} = sA - d.$$

Because we have assumed a constant labor force, this equation also tells us the long-run growth rate of real GDP per worker and the standard of living, as measured by real GDP per capita. In the Solow growth model, the growth rate of real GDP per worker depends on the rate of labor-augmenting technological change. This endogenous growth equation, however, tells us that *the growth rate of real GDP per worker depends on the national saving rate*, so the national saving rate emerges as an important determinant of the growth rate of real GDP per worker and the standard of living. In contrast with the Solow model's conclusion that the saving rate is irrelevant in explaining long-run growth, this endogenous growth model indicates that countries with high saving rates experience high growth rates, and countries with low saving rates experience low growth rates. The *AK* growth model depends on the assumption that capital does not experience diminishing marginal returns. Many economists are not happy with this assumption. As a result, economists have developed other types of endogenous growth models that still assume diminishing marginal returns to capital.

Two-Sector Growth Model: The Production of Knowledge

An alternative approach to modeling endogenous growth, pioneered by Paul Romer of New York University, looks explicitly at the production of knowledge.[6] In Romer's model, the economy has two sectors. The first sector consists of manufacturing firms, such as Whirlpool or Caterpillar, that use technology to produce consumption and investment goods for households and other firms. The second sector consists of firms that produce ideas and new technology, E, that are useful in producing manufacturing goods. We call these firms *research firms* or *research universities*. In reality, many large firms such as General Electric both produce goods and services and devote substantial resources to research. As a result, the distinction between manufacturing firms and research firms is a bit artificial, but it does provide important insights.

In this model, the labor supply, L, is divided between the manufacturing and research sectors. A constant fraction, p, of the labor force works in the research sector, so pL is the quantity of labor devoted to the research sector and the remaining quantity of labor, $(1 - p)L$, is devoted to the manufacturing sector. Therefore, we can write the production function for manufacturing goods as:

$$Y = F[K, (1 - p)EL],$$

where $(1 - p)EL$ represents the effective quantity of labor in the manufacturing sector. Notice that this is the same production function we used with the Solow model when discussing labor-augmenting technological change except that we now allow for the fact that only $1 - p$ of the labor force is devoted to manufacturing goods. We assume that the production function has constant returns to scale, so if, for instance, we double the available amount of capital and labor, real GDP will also double.

Because we are not using an AK production function, increased saving and capital accumulation do not cause long-run economic growth. In the two-sector growth models, endogenous growth arises from the research sector, where new ideas and technology are produced. We model the production of new ideas as:

$$\Delta E = zpEL,$$

where pEL is the quantity of effective labor employed in the research sector, and z measures the productivity of researchers in producing new ideas and technology.

The last equation for these two-sector growth models is the equation for capital accumulation, which we write as:

$$\Delta K = sY - dK.$$

This equation is the same as the one for the Solow growth model, as we saw earlier in the chapter. The innovation with the two-sector growth models is that technological change

---

[6]Paul Romer, "Endogenous Technological Change," *Journal of Political Economy*, Vol. 98, No. 5, Part 2, October 1990, pp. S71–S102.

is not exogenous; it is produced by the resources that society devotes to the discovery of new technology and ideas.

If we have $\Delta E/E = g$, we can rewrite the production function for new ideas and technology in terms of the growth rate of technology:

$$\Delta E/E = g = zpL.$$

This equation shows that the growth rate of labor-augmenting technological change depends on the size of the labor force, L, the proportion of the labor force devoted to research, p, and the productivity of researchers, z. Therefore, policies that make researchers more productive, that increase the proportion of the labor force devoted to research, or that increase the labor force will lead to higher rates of labor-augmenting technological change.

Policies to Promote Economic Growth

The AK growth models and the two-sector models are important because they can give us further insight into policies that may increase living standards in the long run.

Increasing the National Saving Rate The AK growth model shows that the national saving rate is an important determinant of the steady-state growth rate. Therefore, if this model is accurate, government policies that either increase or decrease the saving rate may be important determinants of the standard of living in the long run. For example, *budget deficits*, such as those the United States has run since 2001, reduce the national saving rate and so may reduce the steady-state growth rate. In contrast, *budget surpluses*, such as those the United States ran in the late 1990s, increase the national saving rate and the steady-state growth rate. Apart from its budget, the government can affect the national saving rate in a variety of ways. The government allows households to save tax-free through retirement programs such as Individual Retirement Accounts (IRAs) and employer-sponsored 401(k) plans. These programs encourage households to save more and should increase the funds available to finance the capital accumulation that generates endogenous growth in the AK growth models. In addition, taxes on corporate income and capital gains reduce the incentive for firms to accumulate capital and therefore reduce the steady-state growth rate. Economic research is not yet clear on how much IRAs, 401(k) plans, and taxes affect capital accumulation, so economists cannot yet determine the extent to which policies to increase the saving rate might increase economic growth.

Making the Connection

What Explains Recent Economic Growth in India?

Economists Barry Bosworth of the Brookings Institution and Susan Collins of the University of Michigan used a growth accounting procedure to explain recent economic growth in India (See the appendix to this chapter for more on growth accounting.). They showed that the growth rate of real GDP per worker increased from 2.4% per year between 1978 and 1993 to 4.6% per year between 1993 and 2004. Bosworth and Collins report that total factor productivity growth increased from

1.4% per year before 1993 to 2.7% per year after 1993. This observation means that 1.3 percentage points of the increase in labor productivity (over half the increase) was due to faster total factor productivity growth. The rest came from an increase in the growth rate of the capital stock. Since 2004, total factor productivity growth has slowed. A report by The Conference Board, a business research firm, found that from 2005 to 2010, "India's transition to a higher growth path had been . . . resource-consuming and . . . constrained by a continuing need for reforms." Although Bosworth and Collins believe that the future prospects for India's economy are good, they point out that the country has devoted much of its high level of private saving to financing a large government debt. Bosworth and Collins also note that without an expansion of India's production of goods—rather than services—the country will have difficulty absorbing a large number of underemployed and undereducated workers.

Another obstacle to growth is the difficulty India has had investing in infrastructure, such as airports, highways, and the electrical system. Critics complain that approval for land acquisition and environmental clearances severely impedes spending on infrastructure investment, as do widespread corruption and government inefficiency. Approval for some projects, such as a new airport in Mumbai, has been delayed for years. In 2012, a weak monsoon season, which reduced the water necessary for hydroelectric power, combined with infrastructure problems resulted in a blackout affecting over 600 million people. Coal has also been in short supply for India's power plants. The economic growth that has benefited the upper and middle classes in India has not resulted in an equivalent amount of political power; politicians often favor measures that benefit hundreds of millions of rural peasants, who earn near subsistence wages, rather than investment projects.

Nicholas Eberstadt, of the American Enterprise Institute, has pointed to another area of concern for India's economy. Although population growth is projected to be positive and will result in a relatively large working-age population, population growth rates are very different in the northern and southern parts of the country. Fertility rates are relatively high in the northern part of India, while fertility rates are much lower in the south. Unfortunately, most of the future prospects for economic growth are in the south. In addition, about one-third of the working-age population has no education at all. Policymakers in India must meet these demographic and educational challenges if the country is to continue its high growth rates.

Sources: Barry Bosworth and Susan Collins, "Accounting for Growth: Comparing China and India," *Journal of Economic Perspectives*, Vol. 22, No. 1, Winter 2008, pp. 45–66; Sudeshna Sen, "India, China, Top Global Labor Productivity," *Economic Times of India*, January 19, 2011; Nicholas Eberstadt, "The Demographic Future," *Foreign Affairs*, Vol. 89, No. 6, November/December 2010, pp. 54–64; Prasenjit Bhattacharya "Why Singh's Infrastructure Pitch May Fall on Deaf Ears," June 8, 2012, wsj.com/indiarealtime/; and Jim Yardley, "In India, Dynamism Wrestles with Dysfunction," *New York Times*, June 8, 2011; Biman Mukherji, Saurabh Chatuvedi, and Santanu Choudhury, *The Wall Street Journal Asia*, August 3, 2012 p. 3.

See related problem 5.10 at the end of the chapter.

Promoting Research and Development In the two-sector growth model, the growth rate of technological change depends on the resources that an economy devotes to creating knowledge. Governments have adopted a number of policies to increase the resources devoted to research and development (R&D). For example:

- The U.S. government has provided special tax credits for spending on R&D to increase the returns firms receive from R&D spending. Paul Romer has argued that without tax credits, firms will devote too few resources to R&D. The creation of knowledge has *spillover benefits* because firms cannot typically capture all the profits to be made from creating the knowledge. For instance, researchers at Texas Instruments (TI) developed the first integrated circuit, which was a necessary component in pocket calculators and other products on which TI earned substantial profits. But the profits TI earned from developing the integrated circuit were tiny compared with the total profits earned by the many firms selling products using integrated circuits. Tax credits help reduce the gap between the private return firms earn from R&D and the total *social return* to the economy.
- Governments also grant individuals and corporations *patents* on new technologies that give inventors the exclusive right to sell the new technology. Patents greatly increase the profitability of R&D. For example, if other firms had been free to copy and sell the Windows operating system software immediately after Microsoft introduced it, Microsoft is unlikely to have incurred the costs involved in developing it.
- Governments fund many research activities through grants to university and private researchers and also directly conduct some research. For example, the forerunner to the Internet was the Advanced Research Project Agency Network (ARPANET), developed by the U.S. Defense Department to help defense researchers at universities around the country.

We can think of these policies as increasing the proportion of the labor force devoted to research, p, in the production function for new ideas and technology.

Making the Connection

Should the Federal Government Invest in Green Energy?

Alan Greenspan, former chairman of the Federal Reserve Board, used the phrase *irrational exuberance* to describe asset prices that appear to rise well in excess of the assets' fundamental values. Although Greenspan made his comment in 1996, irrational exuberance seemed to explain the "dot-com bubble," the period from the mid-1990s to 2000 during which the stock prices of many new companies that offered to sell goods and services online (*e-commerce*) initially soared but later plunged as they failed to achieve expected profits. In hindsight, what seems irrational to critics is that many of the dot-com failures were able to raise revenue from private investors despite the absence of sound business plans or without earning profits. For each firm, such as L.L.Bean and Amazon, that successfully marketed its products and services online, there were many failures—including Pets.com, FreeRide, Kiko, Kibu, Go.com, MVP.com, and eToys.

Although analysts criticized dot-com investors for bankrolling companies without seriously questioning their long-term viability, at least the investors risked their own money. This is not the case when governments use tax revenue to subsidize business ventures. For example, the Obama administration was criticized after Solyndra, a startup company that manufactured solar energy panels, declared bankruptcy in 2011, after having received over $500 million in loan guarantees from the federal government. Critics of the Solyndra loan guarantee asked why, if solar energy was a good investment, would private venture capital firms not fund the firm. But government has provided financial support for private business many times in the past; examples include subsidies and tax breaks for railroads, the petroleum industry, nuclear energy, and aviation. Economists agree that less than the economically efficient quantity of a good or service will be produced in private markets where there are social benefits, or *positive externalities*. Proponents of subsidies for solar power and other forms of "green energy" argue that the social benefits of this spending—lower health costs, reduced effect on global warming, and so on—are received by all households, not just the customers of the firms that provide the energy. Supporters of this policy argue that most of the $16 billion in subsidies for green energy went to successful firms. Another argument in favor of the subsidies is that energy firms, such as electric utilities, operate in regulated markets where there is less incentive for firms to invest in research and development.

Despite the arguments in favor of subsidies, they benefited a relatively small number of firms. This aspect of the program led critics to charge that the government was picking "winners" and "losers." Some of the government investments, such as Solyndra, were losers. If these firms go bankrupt, U.S. taxpayers lose. In contrast, when private financial markets allocate too much investment to Internet firms, private investors suffer the losses. Economists can use positive economic analysis to measure the costs and benefits of subsidies for private businesses, but they cannot state whether the subsidies *should* be made. Policy decisions of this type require normative analysis because they are questions of what "ought to be." Voters and policymakers must make these choices.

Sources: Jamie Walters, "Why Dot-Coms Failed (and What You Can Learn from Them)," *Inc.com*, September 24, 2001; Eric Lipton and Clifford Krauss, "A Gold Rush of Subsidies in Clean Energy Search," *New York Times*, November 11, 2001; Robert J. Shiller, "Definition of Irrational Exuberance," www.irrationalexuberance.com/definition.htm; and James Surowiecki, "A Waste of Energy?" *New Yorker*, October 10, 2011.

See related problem 5.11 at the end of the chapter.

Increasing Human Capital Governments provide the majority of the primary school, high school, and college education in most countries. Education can provide workers with the knowledge and skills that make them more productive at either producing goods or new ideas and technology. By reducing the price of education, the government encourages households to accumulate more skills and become more productive. These policies increase K in the AK growth models or increase z in the production function for new ideas in the two-sector growth model. In either case, increases in human capital can increase the steady-state growth rate of real GDP per capita.

Increasing Population Growth The larger the population of a country, the more researchers it will have. The more research that occurs, the more new ideas and technology the country will develop. In the production function for new ideas and technology in the two-sector growth model, an increase in the labor force, L, will increase the growth rate of technological change.

What is the evidence for the claim that a higher population leads to faster technological change? Michael Kremer of Harvard University examined the relationship between population and technological change across countries.[7] He found that over the very long run, regions of the world with larger populations have typically experienced greater technological change and faster rates of economic growth. This research suggests that as the world's population increases, we should expect the rate of technological change to increase. But the issue of population growth is a complex one. As we saw when discussing the Solow growth model, an increase in the population growth rate can reduce the steady-state value of real GDP per capita. And some economists have argued that rapid population growth has been a barrier to economic growth in certain developing countries.

Reducing Income Tax Rates When people choose to devote more hours to leisure than to work, they are giving up the income that they could have earned had they chosen to work. Therefore, the wage rate is the opportunity cost of engaging in an hour of leisure. The higher the *after-tax* wage rate, the greater the opportunity cost of an additional hour of leisure, so the less leisure and the more work a person is likely to do. The higher the tax rate, the lower the after-tax wage and the fewer the hours that households will devote to working. We would expect, then, that a higher tax rate will decrease L and the growth rate of new ideas. We should note that the tax rate that maximizes economic growth is difficult to determine. In addition, a tax rate that is too low may make it difficult for governments to fund necessary activities, including building the infrastructure that is important for growth.

Reforming the Political Process and Establishing the Rule of Law In many developing countries, the political process is dominated by a small elite that is concerned primarily with its own financial interests. Not surprisingly, in these countries, policies that might spur economic growth are rarely implemented. Even in democratic countries, *property rights* and the *rule of law* may not be well enforced. For entrepreneurs in a market economy to succeed, the government must guarantee private property rights and enforce contracts. Unless entrepreneurs feel secure in their property, they will not risk starting a business. It is also difficult for businesses to operate successfully in a market economy unless they can use an independent court system to enforce contracts. The rule of law refers to the ability of a government to enforce the laws of the country, particularly with respect to protecting private property and enforcing contracts. The failure of many developing countries to guarantee private property rights and to enforce contracts has hindered their economic growth.

---

[7]Michael Kremer, "Population Growth and Technological Change: One Million B.C. to 1990," *Quarterly Journal of Economics*, Vol. 108, No. 3, August 1993, pp. 681–716.

Answering the Key Question

Continued from page 176

At the beginning of this chapter, we asked:

"What are the main factors that determine the growth rate of real GDP per capita?"

In this chapter, we saw that the long-run growth rate is determined by technological change. If we use a broader definition of capital to include human capital and knowledge, then a higher saving rate could lead to faster long-term growth. In addition, policies that result in more resources being devoted to the production of new ideas and technology or that make researchers more productive may also increase the long-run growth rate. However, it is difficult for the government to identify which types of capital goods or technologies will be the most productive so it is difficult for the government to design policies that will increase the long-run rate of growth.

Key Terms and Problems

Key Terms

Balanced growth, p. 193

Depreciation rate, p. 179

Endogenous growth theory, p. 198

Human capital, p. 198

Labor-augmenting technological change, p. 190

Solow growth model, p. 177

Steady state, p. 180

6.1 The Solow Growth Model
Understand the effect of capital accumulation on labor productivity.

Review Questions

1.1 What does it mean to say that an economy is "accumulating capital"? Why does the marginal product of capital decrease as capital is accumulated?

1.2 What is the difference between a stock variable and a flow variable?

1.3 What is depreciation? Explain what happens to the depreciation line when the rate of depreciation increases and when it decreases.

Problems and Applications

1.4 [Related to the Macro Data feature on page 185] An article in the *Economist* argues, "As China's capital accumulates, its population ages and its villages empty, saving will grow less abundant and good investment opportunities will become scarcer."

a. Why might an aging population lead to a lower saving rate? Why might China's saving rate fall as it accumulates more capital?

b. Discuss the likely consequences of these trends for China's steady-state value of real GDP per capita.

Source: "Beyond Growth," *Economist*, May 26, 2012.

1.5 Use a graph to show the effect of an increase in the depreciation rate on the steady-state level of the capital–labor ratio and level of real GDP per worker.

1.6 Suppose that the production function for an economy is given by $y = k^{1/4}$. The depreciation rate is 10%, and the saving rate is 20%.

a. Find the steady-state capital–labor ratio for this economy.

b. Find the steady-state real GDP per worker for this economy.

c. Find the steady-state levels of investment per worker and consumption per worker.

1.7 Suppose that the economy described in problem 1.6 is at the steady-state capital–labor ratio. A change in preferences causes the saving rate to decrease to 10%.

 a. Describe the forces that will move the economy to the new steady state.

 b. Find the new steady-state capital–labor ratio, level of real GDP per worker, level of

investment per worker, and level of consumption per worker.

1.8 The former Soviet Union, a planned economy, was able to maintain consistently high rates of investment for decades. Use the Solow growth model to explain the limitations of growth through high rates of saving and investment.

6.2 **Labor Force Growth and the Solow Growth Model**
Understand the effect of labor force growth on labor productivity.

Review Questions

2.1 What is break-even investment? What happens to the break-even level of investment when the growth rate of the labor force decreases?

2.2 Explain the effect on the steady-state level of the standard of living of an increase in the growth rate of the labor force and of a decrease in the growth rate of the labor force.

Problems and Applications

2.3 [Related to Solved Problem 6.2 **on page 188**] Following World War II, many countries, including the United States, experienced a baby boom—an increase in the growth rate of the population.

 a. Use a Solow model graph to demonstrate the effect of a baby boom on the steady-state capital–labor ratio.

 b. Explain the effect of the baby boom on real GDP and on the standard of living.

 c. The U.S. economy experienced strong growth in real GDP per capita during the years of the baby boom. Reconcile this fact with your answer to part (b).

2.4 Some countries experiencing low birthrates are offering women incentives to have children, such as income subsidies and other benefits. Does the analysis in this section suggest that a decline in the birthrate is bad for the standard of living?

2.5 Suppose that the production function for an economy is given by $y = k^{1/3}$. The depreciation rate is 10%, the saving rate is 24%, and the growth rate of the labor force is 2%.

 a. Find the steady-state capital–labor ratio for this economy.

 b. Find the steady-state level of real GDP per worker for this economy.

2.6 Suppose that the economy described in problem 2.5 is at the steady-state capital–labor ratio. A change in preferences causes the growth rate of the labor force to decrease to 1%.

 a. Describe the forces that will move the economy to the new steady state.

 b. Find the new steady-state capital–labor ratio and level of real GDP per worker.

6.3 **Technological Change and the Solow Growth Model**
Understand the effect of technological change on labor productivity and the standard of living.

Review Questions

3.1 What is labor-augmenting technological change, and how is it different from total factor productivity?

3.2 What is the difference between real GDP per worker and real GDP per effective worker?

3.3 Assume that the economy is currently in the steady state. How will each of the following affect

MyEconLab Visit **www.myeconlab.com** to complete these exercises online and get instant feedback. Exercises that update with real-time data are marked with 🌐 .

the steady-state growth rate of the standard of living?

a. A decrease in the depreciation rate

b. An increase in the saving rate

c. A decrease in the growth rate of labor-augmenting technological change

Problems and Applications

3.4 Suppose that there is an increase in the growth rate of labor-augmenting technological change. The per-worker form of the production function for an economy is given by $y = 10k^{1/4}$. The depreciation rate is 10%, the investment rate is 20%, and the growth rate of the labor force is 2%.

a. What happens to the steady-state level of real GDP per effective worker?

b. What happens to the steady-state level of real GDP per worker?

c. Why are your answers to parts (a) and (b) different?

3.5 Suppose that the production function for an economy is given by $y = k^{1/3}$. The depreciation rate is 5%, the saving rate is 16%, the growth rate of the labor force is 2%, and the growth rate of labor-augmenting technological change is 1%.

a. Find the steady-state level of capital per effective worker.

b. Find the steady-state real GDP per effective worker.

3.6 Suppose that the labor force growth rate increases.

a. What is the effect on the steady-state growth rate of real GDP per worker?

b. What is the effect on the steady-state growth rate of real GDP?

c. Why are your answers to parts (a) and (b) different?

3.7 A report on the differences in the labor force growth rate in the United States and Latin America contains the following statement: "A long-term slowing of labor force growth could reduce the pace of overall economic growth." Assuming no change in the capital stock, use the Solow growth model to explain whether you agree with this statement. Draw a graph to support your answer. Are there factors not taken into account in the Solow model that might change your assessment of the statement? Briefly explain.

Source: "U.S. Behind Latin America in Growth of Labor Force," www.metlife.com, May 24, 2012.

6.4 **The Balanced Growth Path, Convergence, and Long-Run Equilibrium**
Explain balanced growth, convergence, and long-run equilibrium.

Review Questions

4.1 What is a balanced growth path?

4.2 Why did Germany diverge from a balanced growth path at the end of World War II? Why did it return?

4.3 What happens to growth from convergence and to the overall growth rate of the economy if the actual capital–labor ratio is:

a. greater than the steady-state capital–labor ratio.

b. less than the steady-state capital–labor ratio.

c. equal to the steady-state capital–labor ratio.

Problems and Applications

4.4 Consider the following statement: "If the economy is at the steady state, it must not be growing." Is this statement true, false, or uncertain? Briefly explain.

4.5 [Related to the Making the Connection **on page 195**] Suppose that all economies have the same value for capital's share of income. A developed country has a saving rate of 28% and a population growth rate of 1% per year. A less-developed country has a saving rate of 10% and a population growth rate of 4% per year. In both countries, the rate of labor-augmenting technological change is 2% per year, and capital depreciates at 4% per year. Use this information and the Solow model to explain the following.

a. Are the countries likely to converge to the same *level* of real GDP per capita?

b. Are the countries likely to converge to the same *growth rate* of real GDP per capita?

4.6 Suppose that an economy is growing at its steady-state rate of 4% per year when a natural disaster destroys one-quarter of its capital stock, leaving all other factors of production unchanged.

a. What will be the immediate effect on the capital–labor ratio and real GDP per worker?

b. After the disaster, will the economy grow at the same 4% rate in the short run? Explain.

c. What will be the long-run growth rate of the economy?

4.7 How would your answer to problem 4.6 change if, in addition to the loss of capital stock, the natural disaster also caused a permanent reduction in the rate of labor-augmenting technological change?

4.8 **[Related to the** Chapter Opener **on page 176]** In 2011, the growth rate of the United States was about 1.5%, and real GDP per capita was about $48,100. The growth rate in India was 7.2%, and real GDP per capita was about $3,700. The growth rate in Kenya was 6.1%, and real GDP per capita was about $1,700. Is it possible that the levels of real GDP per capita in these countries will converge to the U.S. level of real GDP per capita, given enough time? Briefly explain.

Source: U.S. Central Intelligence Agency, *World Factbook.*

6.5 Endogenous Growth Theory

Explain the determinants of technological change using the endogenous growth model.

Review Questions

5.1 Why does growth occur in *AK* growth models?

5.2 Why does growth occur in two-sector growth models?

Problems and Applications

5.3 Suppose the government decides to impose a tax on consumption, which discourages consumption and encourages saving. Use the *AK* growth model to explain the likely effect on the balanced growth path.

5.4 The government allows households to save tax-free for retirement through IRAs and 401(k) plans. Suppose that these plans increase the national saving rate. Use the *AK* growth model to answer the following questions:

a. What effect would these plans have on the growth rate of the standard of living?

b. Suppose that these plans also reduce government revenue and government saving. How would this assumption affect your answer to part (a)?

5.5 Which is more likely to increase the growth rate of the standard of living: a decrease in income tax rates or a tax cut targeted at corporate spending on research and development? Briefly explain.

5.6 The world's population growth rate is expected to decrease during the twenty-first century. Use the two-sector growth model to explain how this will affect the growth rate of the standard of living in the world.

5.7 An article in the *Economist* about economic growth in Africa contains the following statement:

One [of the big drivers of Africa's growth] is the application of technology. Mobile phones have penetrated deep into the bush. More than 600m Africans have one; perhaps 10% of those have access to mobile-internet services. The phones make boons like savings accounts and information on crop prices ever more available.

Use the *AK* growth model to explain how this technological change will affect the growth rate of real GDP per capita in Africa.

Source: "The Sun Shines Bright: The Continent's Impressive Growth Looks Likely to Continue," *Economist*, December 3, 2011.

5.8 Some studies have projected that Brazil's informal, or underground, economy may be as large as 40% of the country's GDP. An article about Brazil's informal economy states:

> Companies that operate outside the law save money by avoiding tax and welfare payments, allowing them to compete despite being inefficient, but informality also denies them the possibility of accessing markets for capital and technology that would improve their productivity.

Use your knowledge of endogenous growth theory to explain the implications for economic growth in Brazil if these companies operating in the informal economy are denied access to capital and technology.

Source: Brian Asher, "Study: Brazil's Informal Economy Stifling Productivity Growth," *Wall Street Journal*, July 5, 2012.

5.9 What effect would each of the following government actions have on the steady-state growth rate of the standard of living?

a. A growing budget surplus

b. A decreased incentive for individuals to invest in IRAs

c. The elimination of the capital gains tax

d. A cut in funding for research and development at public universities

e. An increase in income tax rates

5.10 **[Related to the** Making the Connection **on page 201]** The *AK* growth model highlights the importance of private capital accumulation in generating economic growth. India has devoted a substantial portion of its high level of private saving to finance government debt. Use the *AK* growth model to show the effect on India's growth rate of the standard of living if India's private saving were available to finance private investment. What type of private investment projects are likely to have the largest effect on economic growth.

5.11 **[Related to the** Making the Connection **on page 203]** The two-sector growth model developed by Paul Romer shows that the rate of labor-augmenting technological change depends on the proportion of the labor force devoted to research and development and on the productivity of researchers.

a. Suppose that government subsidies for green energy lead to a larger fraction of the labor force devoted to research and development. Use the two-sector growth model to explain the effect on the growth rates of labor-augmenting technological change and the standard of living.

b. Now suppose that government subsidies for green energy do not increase the fraction of the labor force devoted to research and development. Instead, the subsidies simply cause existing researchers to move from other areas into green energy. What would have to be true about the productivity of researchers in green energy for the subsidy to still increase the growth rates of labor-augmenting technology and the standard of living?

Data Exercises

D6.1: The U.S. Central Intelligence Agency's *World Factbook* (https://www.cia.gov/library/publications/the-world-factbook/index.html) offers many comparative tables of world data. Go to this site and find the following:

a. The countries with the highest and lowest real GDPs

MyEconLab Visit **www.myeconlab.com** to complete these exercises online and get instant feedback. Exercises that update with real-time data are marked with Ⓜ.

b. The countries with the highest and lowest per capita real GDPs, adjusted for purchasing power

c. The countries with the most equal and least equal income distributions

d. The countries with the highest and lowest real GDP growth rates

e. Where does the United States rank in these categories?

D6.2: One determinant of the productivity of labor is the human capital, or the skills and education of the labor force. Use the CIA *World Factbook* Web site (https://www.cia.gov/library/publications/the-world-factbook/) to look up education expenditures as a percentage of GDP. Which countries spend the most on education? The least? Are there any general relationships between the level of real GDP per capita and the amount spent on education?

D6.3: A 2007 World Bank development report titled "Development and the Next Generation" suggests that countries with rapidly growing populations could achieve higher rates of economic growth by investing in education and health care for their 15- to 24-year-old populations.

a. Find the press release related to this report on the World Bank's Web site (www.worldbank.org).

b. What does the report mean when it calls these young populations a "development dividend"?

Is it also possible that these populations could be a drag on economic growth? Briefly explain.

D6.4: Go to the World Bank's Web site (www.worldbank.org) and look up the most recent *World Development Report*. What are the current challenges for global growth? At what rate is the world expected to grow? How are growth rates different in different regions?

D6.5: [Excel exercise] Using data from the St. Louis Federal Reserve (FRED) (http://research.stlouisfed.org/fred2/), analyze the long-run growth rate of the United States.

a. Download quarterly data on real GDP (GDPC1) from 1947 to the present. Calculate the growth rate of real GDP as the percentage change from the same quarter during the previous year. Graph your results. Calculate the long-run growth trend by calculating the average growth rate over this time period.

b. What is the standard deviation of quarterly real GDP growth?

c. What happened to the economy in 2001? Did the economy return to its long-run growth trend after this period?

d. Has the economy returned to its long run growth path since the 2007–2009 financial crisis?

Appendix

Growth Accounting

6.A

Learning Objective

Discuss the contributions of capital, labor, and efficiency to the growth rate of real GDP.

Technology, labor, and capital all contribute to the growth of real GDP. Nobel Laureate Robert Solow of MIT developed a procedure known as *growth accounting* that allows us to determine how much of the growth rate of real GDP is due to each of these three factors.[8] In this appendix, we use growth accounting to show that total factor productivity has been the most important determinant of economic growth.

The Growth Accounting Equation for Real GDP

Growth accounting starts with the Cobb–Douglas production function (see Chapter 5), where real GDP depends on capital, labor, and total factor productivity:

$$Y = AK^{\alpha}L^{1-\alpha}.$$

Therefore, there are three sources of growth: capital accumulation, labor force growth, and growth in total factor productivity. We know that the extra output from an additional unit of capital is:

$$\Delta Y = MPK \times \Delta K.$$

Because the marginal product of capital is $\alpha(Y/K)$, we can rewrite this equation as:

$$\Delta Y = \alpha(Y/K) \times \Delta K,$$

or:

$$\Delta Y/Y = \alpha(\Delta K/K).$$

This equation tells us that if the capital stock grows and all other inputs remain constant, the growth rate of real GDP equals capital's share of income multiplied by the growth rate of the capital stock.

Similarly, we can show that if the labor force grows and all other inputs remain constant, the growth rate of real GDP equals labor's share of income multiplied by the growth rate of the labor force:

$$\Delta Y/Y = (1 - \alpha)(\Delta L/L).$$

If capital and labor both grow, we have:

$$\Delta Y/Y = \alpha(\Delta K/K) + (1 - \alpha)(\Delta L/L).$$

Real GDP can also grow if total factor productivity grows. If capital and labor are constant, but total factor productivity grows, we have:

$$\Delta Y/Y = \Delta A/A.$$

---

[8]Robert Solow, "Technical Change and the Aggregate Production Function," *Review of Economics and Statistics*, Vol. 39, No. 3, August 1957, pp. 312–320.

where $\Delta A/A$ is the growth rate of total factor productivity. Putting all this together, we can write the growth rate of real GDP as:

$$\Delta Y/Y = \alpha(\Delta K/K) + (1-\alpha)(\Delta L/L) + (\Delta A/A).$$

(Real GDP Growth) = (Contribution from capital) + (Contribution from labor) + (Contribution from total factor productivity)

We can observe everything in this equation except total factor productivity, so we measure the contribution of total factor productivity as the *residual* after all directly observable sources of growth have been accounted for. In fact, the growth rate of total factor productivity is also known as the *Solow residual*.

Growth Accounting for the United States

Capital's share of income has averaged about one-third in the United States. From 1948 to 2010, real GDP grew by 3.3% a year, while the capital stock grew at 3.3% per year, and the labor force grew at 1.7% per year. We can use this information to determine the contributions of capital, labor, and total factor productivity to the growth rate of real GDP, which we do in Table 6A.1.

The table shows that capital, labor, and total factor productivity have contributed about equally to economic growth. However, capital and labor are both subject to diminishing marginal returns so the ultimate source of economic growth is total factor productivity growth.

Total Factor Productivity as the Ultimate Source of Growth

Is it possible for a government to spur rapid economic growth by encouraging the accumulation of physical capital goods, such as factories and machines? Yes, but only for a period of time. Capital accumulation is subject to diminishing marginal returns, so growth driven by the addition of more factories and machines eventually diminishes to zero. For economic growth to be sustainable, it must be driven by increases in total factor productivity. We can illustrate this point with an important historical example: the Soviet Union.

Table 6A.2 uses data from Nicholas Crafts of the University of Warwick to show what growth accounting can tell us about one of the most striking events of the twentieth

Table 6A.1 Sources of Growth for the United States, 1949–2010

Source of Growth	Symbol	Average Annual Growth Rate 1950–2010
Real GDP Growth	$\Delta Y/Y$	3.3%
Contribution of Capital	$\alpha(\Delta K/K)$	1.1
Contribution of Labor	$(1-\alpha)(\Delta L/L)$	1.2
Contribution of Total Factor Productivity	$\Delta A/A$	1.0

Source: Bureau of Economic Analysis and Bureau of Labor Statistics.

Table 6A.2 Accounting for Labor Productivity Growth in the Soviet Union, 1920–1985

	Labor Productivity Growth $\Delta y/y$	Contribution from Capital $\alpha(\Delta k/k)$	Contribution from Total Factor Productivity $\Delta A/A$
1928–1940	2.5%	2.0%	0.5%
1940–1950	1.5	–0.1	1.6
1950–1970	4.0	2.6	1.4
1970–1985	1.6	2.0	–0.4

Source: Nicholas Crafts, "Solow and Growth Accounting: A Perspective from Quantitative Economic History," *History of Political Economy*, Vol. 41, Supplement 1, 2009, pp. 200–220.

century: the economic collapse of the Soviet Union.[9] To obtain his results, Crafts used a growth accounting equation for real GDP per worker similar to:

$$\Delta y/y = \alpha(\Delta k/k) + (\Delta A/A),$$

where y is real GDP per worker or labor productivity and k is the capital–labor ratio.

The Soviet Union was formed from the old Russian Empire following the Communist Revolution of 1917. Under Communism, the Soviet Union was a centrally planned economy, where the government owned nearly every business and made all production and pricing decisions. In 1960, Nikita Khrushchev, the leader of the Soviet Union, addressed the United Nations in New York City. He declared to the United States and the other democracies, "We will bury you. Your grandchildren will live under Communism."

Many people at the time took Khrushchev's boast seriously. After all, labor productivity growth in the Soviet Union was extremely rapid following World War II, averaging 4.0% per year during the 1950–1970 period when Khrushchev made his boast. This growth rate far exceeded that of the United States and many other Western countries and caused some economists in the Union States to predict incorrectly that the Soviet economy would someday surpass the U.S. economy. But if you look closely at the data in Table 6A.2, you can see that Soviet labor productivity growth was driven primarily by capital accumulation. The Soviet economic system was quite good at accumulating more and more capital goods, such as factories. Unfortunately for the Soviets, though, diminishing returns to capital meant that the additional factories the Soviet Union was building resulted in smaller and smaller increases in real GDP per worker. To keep labor productivity growth high, the Soviet Union had to devote more and more resources to accumulating capital goods, which meant diverting resources away from private consumption.

The Soviet Union did experience increases in total factor productivity, but for a 15-year period leading up to its collapse, total factor productivity *decreased* by 0.4% per

---

[9]Nicholas Crafts, "Solow and Growth Accounting: A Perspective from Quantitative Economic History," *History of Political Economy*, Vol. 41, Supplement 1, 2009, pp. 200–220.

year. Why did the Soviet Union fail the crucial requirement for growth: developing new ways to make the economy efficient? The key reason is that in a centrally planned economy, the persons in charge of running most businesses are government employees and not entrepreneurs or independent businesspeople, as is the case in market economies. Soviet managers had little incentive to adopt new ways of doing things. Their pay depended on producing the quantity of output specified in the government's economic plan, not on discovering new, better, and lower-cost ways to produce goods. In addition, these managers did not have to worry about competition from either domestic or foreign firms.

Entrepreneurs and managers of firms in the United States, by contrast, are under intense competitive pressure from other firms. They must constantly search for better ways of producing the goods and services they sell. Developing and using new technologies is an important way to gain a competitive edge and higher profits. The drive for profit provides an incentive for technological change that centrally planned economies are unable to duplicate. In market economies, entrepreneurs and managers who have their own money on the line are the ones who make decisions about which investments to make and which technologies to adopt. In the Soviet system, these decisions were usually made by salaried bureaucrats trying to fulfill a plan formulated in Moscow. Nothing concentrates the mind like having your own funds at risk.

In hindsight, it is clear that a centrally planned economy, such as the Soviet Union's, could not, over the long run, grow faster than a market economy. The Soviet Union collapsed in 1991, and contemporary Russia now has a more market-oriented system, although the government continues to play a much larger role in the economy than does the government in the United States.

CHAPTER 7

Money and Inflation

Learning Objectives

After studying this chapter, you should be able to:

7.1 Define money and explain its functions (pages 217–223)

7.2 Explain how the Federal Reserve changes the money supply (pages 224–227)

7.3 Describe the quantity theory of money and use it to explain the connection between changes in the money supply and the inflation rate (pages 227–232)

7.4 Discuss the relationships among the growth rate of money, inflation, and nominal interest rates (pages 232–236)

7.5 Explain the costs of a monetary policy that allows inflation to be greater than zero (pages 236–243)

7.6 Explain the causes of hyperinflation (pages 243–245)

7.A Appendix: Explain how to derive the formula for the money multiplier (pages 255–259)

What Can You Buy With $100 Trillion?

In Germany in 1923, people burned paper currency rather than wood or coal. In Zimbabwe in 2012, people were washing the currency they used because it was so scarce. Why was it scarce? Because people in Zimbabwe were using foreign paper money—the U.S. dollar—as their currency. Burning paper money and using another country's paper money in place of your own are signs that a country's money has become worthless.

People in most countries are used to some inflation. Even a moderate inflation rate of 2% or 3% per year will gradually reduce the purchasing power of money. For example, if the United States experiences an inflation rate that averages only 3% per year over the next 30 years, it will take more than $24,000 to buy the same amount of goods and services 30 years from now that $10,000 can buy today. Germany and Zimbabwe experienced the much higher inflation rates known as *hyperinflation*, which is defined as rates of inflation reaching 50% or more per month.

Continued on next page

Key Issue and Question

Issue: The Federal Reserve's actions during the financial crisis of 2007–2009 led some economists and policymakers to worry that the inflation rate in the United States would be increasing.

Question: What is the connection between changes in the money supply and the inflation rate?

Answered on page 245

The inflation rates suffered by these two countries were extreme, even by the standards of hyperinflations: The consumer price index in Germany, which had been 100 in 1914, rose to 1,440 in January 1922, and then to 126,160,000,000,000 by December 1923. The German mark became nearly worthless. In Zimbabwe, the inflation rate reached 15 billion percent by 2008. A U.S. tourist visiting the Victoria Falls Hotel in Zimbabwe during the summer of 2008 ordered dinner, two beers, and a mineral water. He received a bill for $1,243,255,000.00 in Zimbabwean dollars. Prices rose so much in Zimbabwe that you could be a billionaire in terms of the local currency and still be starving. By 2009, Zimbabwe was printing currency denominated as $100 trillion Zimbabwe dollars.

Countries suffer from hyperinflations when their governments allow the money supply to grow too rapidly. Between 1999 and 2008, the Reserve Bank of Zimbabwe, the central bank for Zimbabwe, increased the money supply by more than 7,500% per year. In Germany, the money supply rose from 115 million marks in January 1922 to 1.3 billion in January 1923 and to 497 billion billion—or 497,000,000,000,000,000,000,000—in December 1923. Eventually these hyperinflations were brought to an end. In the case of Germany, a new currency was issued and the government committed to protecting the value of the currency. In 2009, the government of Zimbabwe abandoned its own currency and began using the U.S. dollar in its place. But why would a government create so much money in the first place, when it knows that doing so will destroy the money's purchasing power? In this chapter, we will explore this and other issues involving the relationship between money and prices.

Sources: Patrick McGroarty and Farai Mutsaka, "Hanging on to Dollars in Zimbabwe," *Wall Street Journal*, March 26, 2012; Steven D. Levitt and Stephen J. Dubner, "Freak Shots: $1 Billion Dinners and Other African Pricing Problems," *New York Times*, June 2, 2008; Federal Reserve Bank of Dallas, "Hyperinflation in Zimbabwe," *Globalization and Monetary Policy Institute, 2011 Annual Report*: Thomas Sargent, "The Ends of Four Big Inflations," in Robert E. Hall, ed., *Inflation: Causes and Effects*, Chicago: University of Chicago Press, 1982; and "What Can You Do with a Zimbabwean Dollar?" *Economist*, July 26, 2010.

In the previous chapters, we focused on real GDP and real GDP per worker. These are real variables because they are corrected for the effects of price changes. In this chapter, we focus on nominal variables such as the price level, the inflation rate, and the nominal interest rate. In the long run, there is a separation between nominal variables and real variables that economists call the **classical dichotomy**.[1] According to the classical dichotomy, changes in nominal variables such as the price level or the money supply cannot cause changes in real variables such as real GDP, the real interest rate, or the real wage. One implication of the classical dichotomy is *money neutrality*, or the assertion that in the long run, changes in the money supply have no effect on real variables. Today, most economists believe that the classical dichotomy is true in the long run when real GDP equals potential GDP, but not in the short run when changes in the money supply can cause changes in real GDP. We begin our discussion of money and inflation with a discussion of the basic role that money plays in the economy and a review of how the Federal Reserve measures the money supply.

Classical dichotomy The assertion that in the long run, nominal variables, such as the money supply or the price level, do not affect real variables, such as the levels of employment and real GDP.

What Is Money, and Why Do We Need It?

In everyday conversation, we often describe someone such as Bill Gates or Warren Buffet, who are the second- and third-wealthiest men in the world, as "having a lot of money." But, when economists use the word *money*, they are not referring to wealth or

Learning Objective

Define money and explain its functions.

---

[1] In macroeconomics, "classical" refers to theories that were widely accepted before the Great Depression of the 1930s. Economists first discussed the classical dichotomy during that period.

income. Instead, when economists refer to money, they usually mean the total amount of paper currency, coins, and checking account deposits available to households and firms. Governments typically give control of the country's money supply to the country's central bank. In the United States, the Federal Reserve has responsibility for managing the money supply. A major objective of central banks is to control the inflation rate. As we will see, in the long run, the inflation rate is determined by the growth rate of the money supply.

A preliminary question, though, is why do we need money? To understand the answer to this question, we consider the functions of money.

The Functions of Money

Economies can function without money. In the early stages of an economy's development, individuals often exchange goods and services by trading output directly with each other. This type of exchange is called *barter*. For example, on the frontier in colonial America, a farmer whose cow died might trade several pigs to a neighboring farmer in exchange for one of the neighbor's cows. In principle, people in a barter economy could satisfy all their needs by trading for goods and services, in which case they would not need money. In practice, though, barter economies are inefficient because each person must want what the other person has available to trade. That is, there must be a *double coincidence of wants*. Because of the time and effort spent searching for trading partners in a barter economy, there are high *transactions costs*—or the costs in time or other resources of making a trade or an exchange. As a result, a barter economy will devote a significant amount of resources to conducting exchanges rather than to producing goods and services, so real GDP will be lower.

To improve on barter, people had an incentive to identify a specific product that most people would accept in an exchange. In other words, they had a strong incentive to invent money. For example, in colonial times, animal skins were very useful in making clothing, so many people were willing to accept them in exchange for goods and services. A good, such as animal skins, that is used as money while also having value independent of its use as money is called a **commodity money**. Historically, once a good became widely accepted as money, people who did not have an immediate use for it were still willing to accept it. A colonial farmer might not want a deerskin for his own use, but as long as he knew he could use it to buy other goods and services, he would be willing to accept it in exchange for what he had to sell.

Once money is invented—as it has been many times and in many places around the world—transactions costs are greatly reduced, as are the other inefficiencies of barter. People can take advantage of *specialization*, producing the good or service for which they have relatively the best ability. The high income levels in modern economies are based on the specialization that money makes possible. So, the answer to the question "Do we need money?" is "Yes, because money allows for specialization, higher productivity, and higher incomes."

Money has four functions in the economy:

1. It acts as a medium of exchange.
2. It is a unit of account.
3. It is a store of value.
4. It offers a standard of deferred payment.

Commodity money A good used as money that has value independent of its use as money.

Medium of Exchange If you are a teacher or an accountant, you are paid money for your services. You then use that money to buy goods and services. You essentially exchange your teaching or accounting services for food, clothing, rent, and other goods and services. But unlike with barter, where goods and services are exchanged directly for other goods and services, the exchanges you participate in involve money. Money acts as a **medium of exchange**. That is, money is the medium through which exchange takes place. Because, by definition, money is generally accepted as payment for goods and services or as payment for debts, you know that the money your employer pays you will be accepted at the stores where you purchase food, clothing, and other goods and services. In other words, you can specialize in producing teaching or accounting services without having to worry about directly producing the other goods and services you require to meet your needs, as you would in a barter economy.

Medium of exchange Something that is generally accepted as payment for goods and services; a function of money.

Unit of Account Money serves as a **unit of account**, which means it is a way of measuring the value of goods and services in an economy. For example, when you purchase an iPad, the Apple store posts a price in terms of dollars rather than shares of Apple stock or ounces of gold. Having an agreed-upon unit of account makes an economy more efficient because goods and services have a single price rather than many prices.

Unit of account A way of measuring value in an economy in terms of money; a function of money.

Store of Value Money provides a **store of value** by allowing for the accumulation of wealth that can be used to buy goods and services in the future. For example, suppose you want to purchase an iPad next year that has a price of $500. If you have $500 in currency, you can put it aside and purchase the iPad in one year. Note, though, that if prices in an economy rise rapidly over time, as happened recently in Zimbabwe, the quantity of goods and services a given amount of money can purchase declines, and money's usefulness as a store of value is reduced. In that case, you would need more than $500 to purchase the iPad. Of course, money is only one of many assets that can be used to store value. In fact, any asset—shares of Apple stock, Treasury bonds, real estate, or Renoir paintings, for example—represents a store of value. Money, though, has the advantage of being perfectly liquid. When you exchange other assets for money, you incur transactions costs. For example, when you sell bonds or shares of stock, you pay a fee, or commission, either online or to your broker. To avoid such transactions costs, people are willing to hold some money, even though other assets offer a greater return as a store of value.

Store of value The accumulation of wealth by holding dollars or other assets that can be used to buy goods and services in the future; a function of money.

Standard of Deferred Payment Money acts as a medium of exchange to facilitate exchange at a point in time and also as a **standard of deferred payment** to facilitate exchange over time. For example, if you purchase an iPad for $500 today, the store may allow you several months to pay that amount. For money to fulfill this function, its value must be stable over time—or changes in its value must be predictable.

Standard of deferred payment An asset that facilitates transactions over time; a function of money.

Commodity Money Versus Fiat Money

To be considered money, an asset must fulfill the four functions that we described in the previous sections. Because the function of a medium of exchange is so important, we will examine that further. An asset can be used as a medium of exchange if it is:

- *Acceptable* to most people.
- *Standardized in terms of quality*, so that any two units are identical.
- *Durable*, so its value is not quickly lost due to wear and tear.

- *Valuable* relative to its weight, so that amounts large enough to be useful in trade can be easily transported.
- *Divisible*, because prices of goods and services vary.

There are two types of assets with these five characteristics: commodity money and fiat money. Throughout history, gold has been a common form of commodity money. The value of gold depends on its purity, however. If you mix gold with a metal of lesser value, you could make a profit by deceiving others into accepting impure gold as payment for goods and services. Therefore, anyone accepting gold would need to verify its purity. In addition, the supply of gold fluctuates with unpredictable discoveries of gold and changes in the technology for extracting gold from existing mines. Gold also has the disadvantage that large quantities can be heavy and, therefore, difficult to transport.

Because of its convenience and because it meets all five characteristics of money, paper currency has been widely used as money during the past 200 years. **Fiat money** is money, such as paper currency, that has no value apart from its use as money. In most countries, including the United States, during the late nineteenth and early twentieth centuries, paper currency could be redeemed for gold or silver. Today, however, paper currency is not backed by gold, silver, or anything else of value. In the modern economy, people are generally willing to accept paper currency for two reasons.

First, fiat currency is *legal tender*. If you look at a U.S. dollar, you will see the words "This note is legal tender for all debts, public and private." This expression means that the federal government requires that cash or checks denominated in dollars be used in payment of taxes and that dollars must be accepted in private payments of debt. Private businesses, though, are not legally obliged to accept dollars in exchange for goods and services, although most businesses do so most of the time.

Second, households and firms have confidence that if they accept paper dollars in exchange for goods and services, then the dollars will not lose much value during the time they hold them. Without this confidence, dollar bills would not serve as a medium of exchange or fulfill the other functions of money. As we saw at the beginning of the chapter, in Germany and Zimbabwe, paper currency lost its value so quickly during periods of **hyperinflation** that it ceased to function as money. Hyperinflation occurs when the inflation rate becomes extremely high, exceeding 50% per month.

Fiat money Money, such as paper currency, that has no value apart from its use as money.

Hyperinflation Extremely high rates of inflation, exceeding 50% per month.

Making the Connection

When Money Is No Longer Money: Hyperinflation in Zimbabwe

At the time of its independence from Great Britain in 1980, Zimbabwe was poor by the standards of the high-income countries, but it was relatively well off by the standards of sub-Saharan Africa. Zimbabwe's GDP per capita was 35% higher than that of Kenya and 20% higher than that of Nigeria. The following three decades were not good for Zimbabwe, however, as its real GDP per capita declined by 45%. By 2011, real GDP per capita was only about $500, one of the lowest in the world. In that year, the level of real GDP per capita was five times higher in Nigeria than in Zimbabwe and it was three times higher in Kenya. What happened to Zimbabwe's economy?

Zimbabwe has suffered from a long period of economic mismanagement and, in recent years, political strife as long-time president Robert Mugabe has attempted to maintain power in the face of widespread opposition and declining health. Beginning in 2004, hyperinflation made the country's problems much more acute. As noted in the chapter opener, the Zimbabwean central bank, the Reserve Bank of Zimbabwe (RBZ), caused the money supply to increase at an annual rate of 7,500%. The result was an increase in the inflation rate from an already high 130% to more than 15 billion percent in 2008. The exchange rate between the Zimbabwean dollar and the U.S. dollar changed from about 1,000 Zimbabwean dollars per U.S. dollar at the beginning of 2004 to 10,000,000,000,000,000 Zimbabwean dollars by the end of 2009.

As the Zimbabwean dollar lost nearly all of its value, the economy reverted to barter or used as money the limited amounts of foreign currency that were available. Because exchanging Zimbabwean dollars for foreign currency was so difficult, imports plunged, and shortages of food and other basic goods became widespread. Reliable statistics on Zimbabwe's economy are difficult to find, but in 2008, one journalist described a situation bordering on economic collapse: "Zimbabwe is in the midst of a dire economic crisis with unemployment at almost 80%, most manufacturing at a halt and basic foods in short supply." Some estimates put the unemployment rate as high as 95%. Nearly the entire labor force had to scratch out a subsistence living as best they could. Many unemployed Zimbabweans were reported as surviving only by growing vegetables in vacant lots or along roads.

Why would the RBZ allow such high rates of growth in the money supply if the result was a ruinous hyperinflation? The answer is that the RBZ was not independent of the rest of the Zimbabwean government. When the Zimbabwean government decided in the early 2000s to greatly increase its spending, primarily to support the efforts of Robert Mugabe to retain power, it did so not by raising taxes or borrowing by selling government bonds to investors but by having the RBZ increase the money supply.

In early 2009, a new government in Zimbabwe took the drastic step of abandoning its own currency and making the U.S. dollar the country's official currency. By 2011, the economy was showing signs of recovery as the inflation rate declined to less than 3%. Real GDP rose by 4% in 2010 and 6% in 2011. Still, the country faced severe structural problems, the political situation remained uncertain, and many Zimbabweans did not trust the government to control the money supply responsibly.

Sources: "Zimbabwe's Independence: Thirty Years On," *Economist*, April 20, 2010; Angus Maddison, *Contours of the World Economy*, New York: Oxford University Press, 2007; "Zimbabwe Inflation Rockets Higher," news.bbc.co.uk, August 19, 2008; "What a Full-Fledged Economic Collapse Looks Like," *Economist*, May 6, 2009; Michael Hartnack, "Zimbabwe Inflation Tops 1,000 Percent," Associated Press, May 13, 2006; International Monetary Fund, "Statement of the IMF's Mission to Zimbabwe," Press Release No. 10/420, November 8, 2010; and "Move Over, Mugabe," *Economist*, April 14, 2012.

See related problem 1.7 at the end of the chapter.

How Is Money Measured?

Households, firms, and policymakers are all interested in measuring money because, as we will see, changes in the quantity of money are associated with changes in nominal interest rates and prices. If the only function of money were to serve as a medium of exchange, then money should include only currency, checking account deposits, and traveler's checks because households and firms can easily use these assets to buy goods and services. But many other assets can be used as a medium of exchange, even though they are not as liquid as cash or checking account deposits. For example, you can easily convert your savings account at a bank into cash. Likewise, if you own shares in a *money market mutual fund*—which is a mutual fund that invests exclusively in short-term bonds, such as Treasury bills—you can write checks against the value of your shares. So, assets such as savings accounts and money market mutual fund shares can plausibly be considered part of the medium of exchange.

As part of its responsibility to regulate the quantity of money in the United States, the Federal Reserve publishes data on two different measures of the money supply: *M1* and *M2*. These measures are referred to as *monetary aggregates*. Figure 7.1 shows both these measures graphically. **M1** is a narrow measure of the money supply: It is the sum of currency in circulation, checking account deposits, and holdings of traveler's checks. M1 comes closest to the role of money as a medium of exchange. **M2** is a broad measure of the money supply than M1 and includes accounts that many households treat as short-term investments. Households can easily convert these accounts into currency,

M1 A narrow measure of the money supply: The sum of currency in circulation, checking account deposits, and holdings of traveler's checks.

M2 A broad measure of the money supply: All the assets that are included in M1, as well as time deposits with a value of less than $100,000, savings accounts, money market deposit accounts at banks, and noninstitutional money market mutual fund shares.

MyEconLab Real-time data

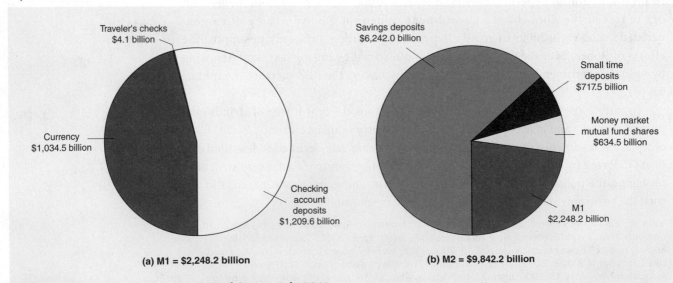

Figure 7.1 M1 and M2 in the United States, July 2012

The Federal Reserve uses two different measures of the money supply: M1 and M2. M1 includes currency, checking account deposits, and traveler's checks. M2 includes all the assets in M1, as well as the additional assets shown in panel (b). Savings deposits include money market deposit accounts.

Source: Board of Governors of the Federal Reserve System, *Federal Reserve Statistical Release, H6,* August 30, 2012.

although not as easily as the components of M1. As shown in panel (b) of Figure 7.1, in addition to the assets included in M1, M2 includes:

- Time deposits with a value of less than $100,000, primarily certificates of deposits in banks.
- Savings accounts and money market deposit accounts at banks.
- Noninstitutional money market mutual fund shares. *Noninstitutional* means that the money market fund shares are owned by individual investors rather than by institutional investors, such as pension funds. Noninstitutional is also sometimes referred to as *retail*.

Which Measure of the Money Supply Should We Use?

Which measure of the money supply is most useful is still an open question among economists. Figure 7.2 shows that M1 and M2 have similar growth rates most of the time, although significant differences in their growth rates occur during certain periods. For example, M2 grew much more rapidly than M1 for much of the 1970s; during the 1990s, the growth rate of M1 fell, while the growth rate of M2 increased.

At one time, fluctuations in the money supply were a major source of discussion among macroeconomists, investment analysts, and policymakers. This interest arose because, for most of the post–World War II period, there had been a stable short-run relationship between M1 and M2 and economic variables such as inflation, interest rates, and real GDP. Whether this relationship was stronger for M1 or for M2 was the subject of considerable debate. However, beginning in 1980, the emergence of new financial assets, such as checking accounts that pay interest and money market deposit accounts, provided households and firms with alternatives to traditional checking accounts. As a result, the relationship between M1 and M2 and many economic variables became unreliable. More importantly, the experience of the 1980s suggests that as banks and other financial firms respond to the demands of households and firms by developing new assets, the relationship between whatever we define as *money* and economic variables may break down. Since the early 1990s, the Fed has therefore deemphasized the roles of M1 and M2 in monetary policymaking.

MyEconLab Real-time data

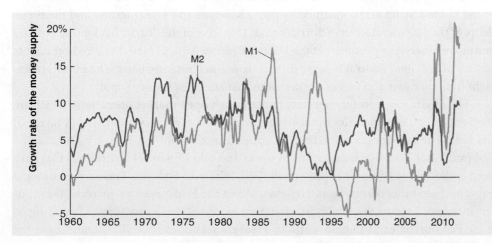

Figure 7.2

Growth Rates of M1 and M2 in the United States, 1960–2012

M1 and M2 have similar growth rates much of the time, but significant differences can emerge during some short periods.

Source: Board of Governors of the Federal Reserve System.

7.2

Learning Objective

Explain how the Federal Reserve changes the money supply

The Federal Reserve and the Money Supply

To understand how the Federal Reserve controls the money supply, we need to describe the *monetary base* and then investigate how it is linked to the money supply. We present a simple model of how the money supply is determined that includes the behavior of three actors:

1. The Federal Reserve, which is responsible for controlling the money supply and regulating the banking system.
2. The banking system, which creates the checking accounts that are an important component of the M1 measure of the money supply.
3. The nonbank public, which refers to all households and firms. The nonbank public decides the form in which they wish to hold money (for instance, as currency or as checking accounts).

Monetary base (or high-powered money)
The sum of currency in circulation and bank reserves.

The process of determining the money supply begins with the **monetary base** (also called **high-powered money**), which is equal to the amount of currency in circulation plus the reserves of the banking system:

$$\text{Monetary base} = \text{Currency in circulation} + \text{Reserves}.$$

Reserves A bank asset consisting of vault cash plus bank deposits with the Federal Reserve.

Reserves are an asset to banks and consist of vault cash plus banks' deposits with the Federal Reserve. The Fed requires banks to hold a fraction of their checking account deposits as reserves. Since the financial crisis of 2007–2009, banks have held reserves far in excess of the required amount. The link between the monetary base and money supply is called the **money multiplier**, which tells us how much the money supply increases when the monetary base increases by $1:

Money multiplier
A number that indicates how much the money supply increases when the monetary base increases by $1.

$$\text{Money supply} = \text{Money multiplier} \times \text{Monetary base}.$$

How the Fed Changes the Monetary Base

By controlling the reserves in the banking system, the Fed is able to control the monetary base and, therefore, the money supply. The Federal Open Market Committee (FOMC) is the Fed's decision-making body for monetary policy. The FOMC is comprised of the seven members of the Board of Governors (who are chosen by the president of the United States and confirmed by the U.S. Senate to 14-year terms) and the presidents of the 12 Federal Reserve district banks. Only five of the district bank presidents are voting members: the president of the Federal Reserve Bank of New York and presidents of four of the other Federal Reserve district banks on a rotating basis. The FOMC meets eight times per year and makes key decisions that affect the money supply.

Open market operations
The Federal Reserve's purchases and sales of securities, usually U.S. Treasury securities, in financial markets.

The FOMC controls the monetary base through **open market operations**, which are the Fed's purchases and sales of securities, usually U.S. Treasury securities, in financial markets. The Fed does not purchase securities directly from the Treasury. Instead, the Fed purchases Treasury securities from banks and other financial institutions that have been authorized to trade securities with the Fed. When the Fed buys Treasury securities, it pays for them by increasing banks' reserves. When the banks' reserves increase, they usually increase the loans they make, which in turn increases the money supply. For example, if the Fed purchases $1 million worth of Treasury securities from JPMorgan Chase, the bank's reserves increase by $1 million. JPMorgan Chase may then, if it chooses, increase the loans it makes to households and firms. If JPMorgan makes new loans, the funds it lends out end up either as currency or as deposits in checking accounts. In either case, a component of the money supply increases. If the Fed sells $1 million of Treasury securities to JPMorgan Chase, the bank pays for the securities by decreasing its reserves and reducing its loans to households and firms. As a result, either the amount of currency in circulation or deposits in checking accounts decrease—so the money supply decreases.

The Process of Money Creation

Because an open market purchase increases either currency or bank reserves by the amount of the purchase, the Fed controls the monetary base. As we indicated above, an increase in the monetary base usually results in an increase in the money supply, and a decrease in the monetary base usually results in a decrease in the money supply. For example, if the Fed decides to increase the monetary base by $1 million, it can achieve its objective by carrying out a $1 million open market purchase.

To know the effect of the open market purchase on the money supply, the Fed needs to know the value of the money multiplier. What follows is a brief description of how banks and the nonbank public also affect the money supply through the money multiplier. We provide a more detailed explanation of the money multiplier in the appendix to this chapter.

If we let M stand for the money supply, MB stand for the monetary base, and m stand for the money multiplier, we can rewrite the equation for the money supply as:

$$M = m \times MB,$$

and, rearranging this equation, we can see that the money multiplier is the ratio of the money supply to the monetary base:

$$m = \frac{M}{MB}.$$

If we use the M1 definition of the money supply, then M is the sum of currency in circulation, C, and checking account deposits, D, (for simplicity, we are ignoring traveler's checks) while the monetary base is the sum of currency in circulation and bank reserves, R. Reserves consist of required reserves, RR, that the Fed requires banks to hold, and excess reserves, ER, that banks hold above the required amount. So, we can expand the expression for the money multiplier to:

$$m = \frac{C + D}{C + RR + ER}.$$

The nonbank public—households and firms—determines how much currency they wish to hold relative to checking account deposits. We can take into account both the nonbank public's desire to hold currency relative to checking account deposits and the desire of banks to hold excess reserves relative to checking account deposits in the expression for the money multiplier. To do so, we want to include the currency-to-deposit ratio (C/D), which measures the nonbank public's holdings of currency relative to its holdings of checking account deposits, and the excess reserves-to-deposit ratio (ER/D), which measures banks' holdings of excess reserves relative to their checking account deposits. To include these ratios in the expression for the money multiplier, we can rely on the basic rule of arithmetic that multiplying the numerator and denominator of a fraction by the same variable preserves the value of the fraction. So, we can introduce the deposit ratios into our expression for the money multiplier this way:

$$m = \left(\frac{C + D}{C + RR + ER}\right) \times \frac{(1/D)}{(1/D)} = \frac{(C/D) + 1}{(C/D) + (RR/D) + (ER/D)}.$$

The Fed calls the ratio of required reserves to checking account deposits the *required reserve ratio*, rr_D. We can use this fact to arrive at our final expression for the money multiplier:

$$m = \frac{(C/D) + 1}{(C/D) + rr_D + (ER/D)}.$$

So, we can say that because:

$$\text{Money supply} = \text{Money multiplier} \times \text{Monetary base},$$

then:

$$M = \left(\frac{(C/D) + 1}{(C/D) + rr_D + (ER/D)}\right) \times MB.$$

For example, if the value of the monetary base is $1 trillion and the money multiplier is 2, the value of the money supply will be $2 trillion.

There are several points to note about the expression linking the money supply to the monetary base:

1. The money supply will increase if either the monetary base or the money multiplier increases in value, and it will decrease if either the monetary base or the money multiplier decreases in value.

2. An increase in the currency-to-deposit ratio (C/D) causes the value of the money multiplier to decline and, if the monetary base is unchanged, it also causes the value of the money supply to decline. This result makes economic sense: If households and firms increase their holdings of currency relative to their holdings of checking account deposits, banks will have a relatively smaller amount of funds they can lend out, which reduces the money multiplier.

3. An increase in the required reserve ratio, rr_D, causes the value of the money multiplier to decline and, if the monetary base is unchanged, it also causes the value of the money supply to decline. An increase in rr_D means that for any increase in reserves banks receive, a larger fraction must be held as required reserves and these funds, therefore, are not available to be loaned, which reduces the multiplier.

4. An increase in the excess reserves-to-deposit ratio (ER/D) causes the value of the money multiplier to decline and, if the monetary base is unchanged, it also causes the value of the money supply to decline. An increase in *ER/D* means that banks are holding relatively more excess reserves, so they are not using these funds to make loans, which reduces the multiplier.

MyEconLab Real-time data

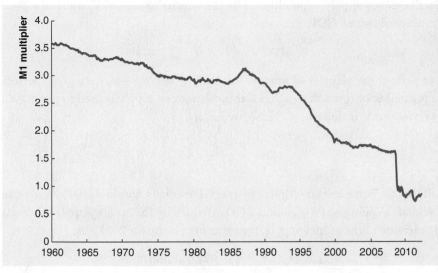

Figure 7.3

The M1 Multiplier for the United States, 1960–2012

There has been a long-term downward trend in the M1 multiplier, as households and firms have begun to rely on financial assets other than cash and checking accounts to conduct market transactions. However, there was a very steep drop in the value of the multiplier during 2008, when the financial crisis caused banks to become reluctant to lend to households and firms.

Source: Board of Governors of the Federal Reserve System.

Figure 7.3 shows values of the money multiplier for M1 since the 1960s. There has been a long-term downward trend in the M1 multiplier, as households and firms have begun to rely on financial assets other than currency and checking accounts in buying and selling. During the financial crisis of 2007–2009, banks tightened the guidelines for households and firms to qualify for loans to avoid having customers default on them. Banks had become concerned about the quality of the loans they had made in the mid-2000s, and they wanted to keep extra reserves to help protect themselves in case households and firms did not repay their current loans. As a result, *ER/D* soared, and the value of the money multiplier decreased dramatically.

[handwritten: not able to lend out the money]

The Quantity Theory of Money and Inflation

When Federal Reserve Chairman Ben Bernanke testified before Congress in July 2012, several members asked that the Fed take no further actions that would increase the money supply. These members were afraid that increasing the money supply would increase the inflation rate. Chairman Bernanke argued that in fact the inflation rate was close to the Fed's target of 2%, and he doubted that it was likely to increase much during future years. Still, economists and policymakers debated whether the Fed's actions to increase the money supply were in fact risking higher inflation, and the issue played a role in the 2012 presidential election.

Writers dating back at least as far as the Greek philosopher Aristotle in the fourth century B.C. have discussed the connection between increases in the money supply and increases in the price level. During the sixteenth century, the Spanish conquest of Mexico and Peru resulted in huge quantities of gold and silver being exported to Europe, where they were minted into coins. Many writers noted that this sharp increase in the money supply had resulted in an increase in inflation. In the early twentieth century, Yale economist Irving Fisher formalized the relationship between money and prices by

7.3

Learning Objective

Describe the quantity theory of money and use it to explain the connection between changes in the money supply and the inflation rate.

Quantity equation (or equation of exchange) An identity that states that the money supply multiplied by the velocity of money equals the price level multiplied by real GDP.

Velocity of money For a given period, the average number of times that each dollar in the money supply is used to purchase a good or service that is included in GDP.

using the **quantity equation** (also called the **equation of exchange**), an identity that states that the money supply, M, multiplied by the *velocity of money*, V, equals the price level, P, multiplied by real GDP, Y:

$$M \times V = P \times Y.$$

Fisher defined the **velocity of money**—or, simply, *velocity*—as, for a given period, the average number of times that each dollar in the money supply is used to purchase a good or service that is included in GDP. So, we have:

$$V = \frac{P \times Y}{M}.$$

Recall that the price level multiplied by real GDP equals nominal GDP. So, we can think of velocity as being equal to nominal GDP divided by the money supply. If we use M1 as the measure of the money supply, the value of velocity for 2011 was:

$$V = \frac{\text{Nominal GDP}}{\text{M1}} = \frac{\$15,094.0 \text{ billion}}{\$2,006.1 \text{ billion}} = 7.5.$$

This result tells us that during 2011, on average, each dollar of M1 was spent 7.5 times on goods and services included in GDP.

The quantity equation tells us that the total amount of spending in the economy ($M \times V$) equals nominal GDP ($P \times Y$). Therefore, the money supply and the velocity of money together determine the level of nominal GDP. As we will see, the central bank determines the money supply in the long run, which means the central bank can also determine the level of nominal GDP in the long run.

The Quantity Theory of Money

Because Fisher defined velocity to be equal to $(P \times Y)/M$, the quantity equation is an identity that must always be true: The left side of the equation must always be equal to the right side. A theory is a statement about the world that could be either true or false. The quantity *equation* is always true, so it does not qualify as a theory. Irving Fisher turned the quantity equation into the **quantity theory of money** by assuming that velocity is constant. Fisher argued that the average number of times a dollar is spent depends on factors that do not change very often, such as how often people get paid, how often they go grocery shopping, and how often businesses mail bills. Because this assertion that velocity is constant may be either true or false, the quantity theory of money is a theory. As we will see, even if velocity is not constant, the quantity theory may still prove to be useful in predicting future inflation rates.

Quantity theory of money A theory about the connection between money and prices that assumes that the velocity of money is constant.

The Quantity Theory Explanation of Inflation

We can use a handy mathematical rule that states that an equation where variables are multiplied together is equivalent to an equation where the *percentage changes* in the variables are added together to rewrite the quantity equation as:

% Change in M + % Change in V = % Change in P + % Change in Y.

The quantity theory assumes that velocity is constant, so the percentage change in $V = 0$. The percentage change in the price level is the inflation rate, which we represent by π. Therefore, we can rewrite the quantity equation as:

$$\% \text{ Change in } M = \pi + \% \text{ Change in } Y.$$

So, this equation tells us that the growth rate of the money supply equals the inflation rate plus the growth rate of real GDP. Rewriting it, we have:

$$\pi = \% \text{ Change in } M - \% \text{ Change in } Y.$$

We now have an important conclusion from the quantity theory: *Inflation results from the money supply growing faster than real GDP.* For example, if the money supply grows by 5%, while real GDP grows by 3%, the inflation rate will be 2%. If the Fed were to increase the growth rate of the money supply from 5% to 6%, the quantity theory predicts that the inflation rate would increase from 2% to 3%. In other words, the quantity theory predicts that, holding the growth rate of real GDP constant, a 1-percentage-point increase in the growth rate of the money supply will cause a 1-percentage-point increase in the inflation rate.

Note that this conclusion about the source of inflation depends on the assumption that velocity is constant. Fluctuations in velocity, particularly in the short run, can break the link between changes in the rate of growth of the money supply and the inflation rate. In the long run, though, most economists believe that the quantity theory accurately predicts changes in the inflation rate. As a result, most economists agree that the central bank, by controlling the growth rate of the money supply, determines the inflation rate in the long run.

Making the Connection

Is the Inflation Rate Around the World Going to Increase in the Near Future?

Through 2012, central banks increased bank reserves to help their economies recover from the financial crisis. In addition, the European Central Bank (ECB) bought bonds to support financial markets after governments in some European countries had difficulty selling bonds to private investors. The resulting increase in bank reserves *necessarily* increased the monetary base, which *can* lead to an increase in the money supply and higher prices, but not necessarily. The ECB's actions surprised some observers who had become accustomed to the central bank's anti-inflation stance. "The sovereign [debt] crisis has pushed the ECB into flooding the system with even more liquidity," wrote Morgan Stanley economist Joachim Fels. "Global excess liquidity should grow by even more, lifting the prices of commodities and other risky assets and adding to global inflation pressures." By mid-2012, the euro-zone inflation rate rose to 2.4%. Though this was above the ECB's target rate of 2%, some analysts predicted that weakness in euro-zone economies would reduce future inflation rates.

There was less evidence of higher inflation in the United States. During 2008, the Fed reduced the short-term nominal interest rate to near 0% and started a new policy of purchasing long-term bonds, a process known as *quantitative easing*, in an attempt to improve the performance of the economy. Quantitative easing resulted in a large increase in the monetary base and could have been inflationary. Because the U.S. economy was slow to recover from the 2007–2009 recession, the Fed embarked on a new round of bond buying in late 2010 and 2011 called *Quantitative Easing II*. Weak economic growth, stubbornly high unemployment, and an inflation rate less than the Fed's 2% target in mid-2012 led some analysts to call for a third round of quantitative easing.

The increase in the monetary base did not lead to proportionally larger increases in the money supply in either the United States or Europe because many banks held on to most of their new reserves. Therefore, although the monetary base increased, the money multiplier decreased. When the economies of the United States and Europe begin to recover, however, banks will be more willing to loan out their new reserves, which will increase the possibility of a sudden rapid rise in the money supply. The quantity equation tells us that in the long run, a sustained increase in the money supply will cause an increase in the inflation rate. In 2012, though, some economists and policymakers were more worried about slow growth than about inflation. John Williams, president of the Federal Reserve Bank of San Francisco, explained, "Some commentators have sounded an alarm that this massive expansion of the monetary base will inexorably lead to high inflation. . . . Despite these dire predictions, inflation in the United States has been the dog that didn't bark."

Sources: Kevin Hall, "Bernanke Unveils Plan to Unwind Fed's Massive Asset Purchases," *McClatchy—Tribune Business News*, February 10, 2010; Neil Shah and Katie Martin, "Europe's Newest Risk: Inflation," *Wall Street Journal*, May 14, 2010; Dave Kansas, "Whiffs of Inflation from Europe," *Wall Street Journal*, January 4, 2011; John Hilsenrath, "Weak Report Lifts Chance of Fed Action," *Wall Street Journal*, July 6, 2012; and Rahul Karunakar, "Euro Zone Price Pressures at 26-Month Low in May: ECRI," *Reuters*, July 6, 2012.

See related problem 3.4 at the end of the chapter.

Solved Problem 7.3

The Effect of a Decrease in the Growth Rate of the Money Supply

The average annual growth rate of real GDP for the United States since World War II has been about 3%. Suppose that the growth rate of velocity is 0%. What happens to the inflation rate if the money supply growth rate decreases from 5% to 2%? Assume that the growth rate of velocity remains 0% and that changes in the growth rate of the money supply do not affect the growth rate of real GDP.

Solving the Problem

Step 1 **Review the chapter material.** The problem asks you to determine the effect of a decrease in the growth rate of the money supply on the inflation rate, so you may want to review the section "The Quantity Theory Explanation of Inflation," which begins on page 228.

Step 2 **Calculate the initial inflation rate.** The quantity equation tells us that:

$$\text{\% Change in } M + \text{\% Change in } V = \text{\% Change in } P + \text{\% Change in } Y,$$

so if the growth rate of velocity is 0%, we have:

$$\text{\% Change in } M = \pi_1 + \text{\% Change in } Y,$$

where $\pi_1 =$ the initial inflation rate. We already know that the growth rate of real GDP is 3%, so the % Change in Y = 3%.

We also know that the growth rate of the money supply is initially 5%, so the % Change in M = 5%. We can plug these two values into the above equation to get:

$$5\% = \pi_1 + 3\%,$$

or:

$$\pi_1 = 5\% - 3\% = 2\%.$$

Step 3 **Calculate the new inflation rate.** If the growth rate of the money supply decreases from 5% to 2%, then, given that velocity is unchanged, the inflation rate will also decrease. We assume that changing the growth rate of the money supply does not change the growth rate of real GDP, which, therefore, remains 3%. The quantity equation tells us:

$$\% \text{ Change in } M = \pi_2 + \% \text{ Change in } Y,$$

where the % Change in M is now 2%, and π_2 is the new inflation rate.

We can solve for the new inflation rate:

$$2\% = \pi_2 + 3\%$$

$$\pi_2 = 2\% - 3\% = -1\%.$$

The 3-percentage-point decrease in the growth rate of the money supply led to a 3-percentage-point decrease in the inflation rate. In this case, the inflation rate is negative, so the price level is decreasing. In other words, deflation occurs. Note that there can be substantial changes in velocity in the short run, so the connection between changes in the rate of growth of the money supply and changes in the inflation rate are usually not as close as in this problem.

See related problem 3.8 at the end of the chapter.

Can the Quantity Theory Accurately Predict the Inflation Rate?

Velocity does not have to be constant in order for an increase in the growth rate of the money supply to cause an increase in the inflation rate. As long as velocity grows at a constant rate, there will be a close relationship between increases in the money supply and increases in the inflation rate. However, when the growth rate of velocity fluctuates, it is difficult for the central bank to predict how changes in the growth rate of the money supply will affect the inflation rate. For instance, an increase in the growth rate of the money supply might be offset by a decline in velocity, leaving the inflation rate unaffected.

What can we conclude, then, about the link between the growth rate of the money supply and the inflation rate? Because velocity sometimes moves erratically over short periods, we would not expect the quantity equation to provide good forecasts of inflation in the short run. Over the long run and across countries, there is evidence of a strong link between the growth rate of the money supply and the inflation rate. Panel (a) of Figure 7.4 shows the relationship between the growth rate of the M2 measure of the money supply and the inflation rate by decade in the United States. (We use M2 here

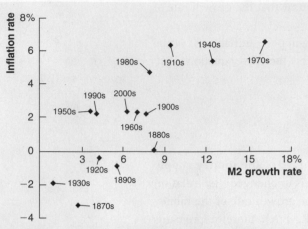

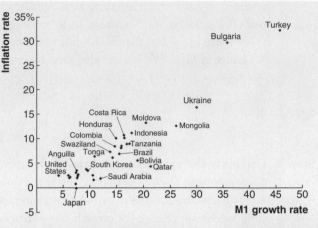

(a) Inflation and money supply growth in the United States, 1870s–2000s

(b) Inflation and money supply growth in 36 countries, 1995–2011

Figure 7.4 The Relationship Between Money Growth and Inflation Over Time and Around the World

Panel (a) shows the relationship between the growth rate of M2 and the inflation rate for the United States from the 1870s to the 2000s. Panel (b) shows the relationship between the growth rate of M1 and inflation for 36 countries during the 1995–2011 period. In both panels, high money growth rates are associated with higher inflation rates.

Source: Panel (a): for 1870s to 1960s, Milton Friedman and Anna J. Schwartz, *Monetary Trends in the United States and United Kingdom: Their Relation to Income, Prices, and Interest Rates, 1867–1975*, Chicago: University of Chicago Press, 1982, Table 4.8; for the 1970s to 2000s: Federal Reserve Board of Governors and U.S. Bureau of Economic Analysis; panel (b): International Monetary Fund, *International Financial Statistics*.

because data for M2 are available for a longer period of time than for M1.) Because of variations in the rate of growth of real GDP and in velocity, there is not an exact relationship between the growth rate of M2 and the inflation rate. But there is a clear pattern that decades with higher growth rates in the money supply were also decades with higher inflation rates. In other words, most of the variation in inflation rates across decades can be explained by variation in the rates of growth of the money supply.

Panel (b) provides further evidence consistent with the quantity theory by looking at rates of growth of the money supply and rates of inflation for 36 countries between 1995 and 2011. Although there is not an exact relationship between rates of growth of the money supply and rates of inflation across countries, panel (b) shows that countries where the money supply grew rapidly tended to have high inflation rates, while countries where the money supply grew more slowly tended to have much lower inflation rates.

We can conclude that the basic prediction of the quantity theory is one of the most reliable relationships in macroeconomics: *If the central bank increases the growth rate of the money supply, then in the long run, this increase will lead to a higher inflation rate.*

Learning Objective

Discuss the relationships among the growth rate of money, inflation, and nominal interest rates.

The Relationships Among the Growth Rate of Money, Inflation, and the Nominal Interest Rate

We have seen that interest rates are critical for allocating resources in the economy (see Chapters 3 and 4). In this section, we discuss how the central bank can affect the inflation rate and interest rates.

Real Interest Rates and Expected Real Interest Rates

Recall that the real interest rate is the nominal interest rate minus the inflation rate:

$$r = i - \pi.$$

The **expected real interest rate** is the real interest rate borrowers and lenders expect at the time that a loan is made. The *expected* real interest rate, r^e, on a loan equals the nominal interest rate minus the *expected* inflation rate, π^e:

$$r^e = i - \pi^e.$$

Expected real interest rate The nominal interest rate minus the expected inflation rate.

If the inflation rate and the expected inflation rate are equal, the actual real interest rate—the real interest rate that borrowers actually pay and lenders actually receive—and the expected real interest rate are also equal. But if, as is frequently the case, the inflation rate does not equal the expected inflation rate, then the real interest rate will be higher or lower than the expected real interest rate. Because the real interest rate is the cost of borrowing, when the real interest rate is less than the expected real interest rate, borrowers benefit because they pay less in real terms for the loan than they had originally expected. By the same token, lenders lose because when the borrower pays less than expected in real terms, the lender receives less.

For example, if you take out a mortgage loan with a nominal interest rate of 6% when you and your bank expect the inflation rate to be 2%, then you expect to pay (and the bank expects to receive) a real interest rate of 6% − 2% = 4%. If the inflation rate turns out to be 0%, then the real interest rate equals 6%, which is higher than you expected. You end up losing by paying a higher-than-expected real rate, and the bank gains. However, if the inflation rate turns out to be 5%, then the real interest rate is 6% − 5% = 1%. In this case, the real interest rate is less than the expected real interest rate. You end up gaining by paying a lower-than-expected rate, and the bank loses.

We can generalize by noting that if the inflation rate is greater than the expected inflation rate, the real interest rate will be less than the expected real interest rate; in this case, borrowers will gain, and lenders will lose. If the inflation rate is less than the expected inflation rate, the real interest rate will be greater than the expected real interest rate; in this case, borrowers will lose, and lenders will gain. Table 7.1 summarizes the important relationships among nominal interest rates, expected real interest rates, and real interest rates.

Table 7.1 The Relationship Between the Expected Real Interest Rate and the Real Interest Rate

If the inflation rate ...	then the real interest rate ...	so ...
is greater than the expected inflation rate	will be less than the expected real interest rate	borrowers will gain and lenders will lose.
is less than the expected inflation rate	will be greater than the expected real interest rate	borrowers will lose and lenders will gain.

The Fisher Effect

In the mortgage interest rate example, the nominal mortgage interest rate was fixed, so we could see what happens to the real interest rate when the inflation rate rises above or falls below the expected inflation rate. However, the mortgage interest rate, as with other interest rates, is fixed only when the borrower signs a mortgage contract. Before the borrower and lender agree on an interest rate, they are free to negotiate an interest rate based on their assessments of market conditions, including the expected inflation rate over the duration of the loan. To determine what nominal interest rate will be acceptable to borrowers and lenders, we can rearrange the expression for the expected real interest rate as follows:

$$i = r^e + \pi^e.$$

This equation states that the nominal interest rate is the sum of the expected real interest rate and the expected inflation rate. It is called the *Fisher equation*, after the same Irving Fisher who developed the quantity theory of money. The **Fisher equation** states that the nominal interest rate is the sum of the expected real interest rate and the expected inflation rate. Therefore, the nominal interest rate changes when the expected real interest rate changes or when the expected inflation rate changes.

There are many different real interest rates in the economy. If we think of the market for Treasury securities, then *r* is the real interest rate that the Treasury must pay to borrow funds. This real interest rate is determined in the market for loanable funds. That is, factors such as the willingness of households to save and the government's spending and taxing decisions affect the real interest rate. For example, if a budget deficit results from the federal government raising expenditures or cutting taxes, the government finances this deficit by borrowing. So, the supply of loanable funds will decrease, causing the real interest rate to increase. According to the Fisher equation, the nominal interest rate will also rise, as long as the expected inflation rate doesn't change.

With the expected real interest rate determined in the market for loanable funds, the Fisher equation tells us that the nominal interest rate changes when the expected inflation rate changes. For example, assume that the real interest rate in the market for loanable funds is 4%, and the expected inflation rate is 2%. In that case, the nominal interest rate on a loan is 4% + 2% = 6%. If the expected inflation rate rises from 2% to 3%, the nominal interest rate will also rise by 1%, to 7%. This adjustment of the nominal interest rate to changes in the expected inflation rate is called the *Fisher effect*. The **Fisher effect** holds that the nominal interest rate rises or falls point-for-point with changes in the expected inflation rate.

Do the data support the Fisher effect? Figure 7.5 shows the relationship between the inflation rate and the nominal interest rate for 56 countries over the period 1995–2011. There is a clear positive relationship between inflation and nominal interest rates, with nominal interest rates being higher in countries with higher inflation rates. Although the figure does not show nominal interest rates rising point-for-point with increases in inflation rates, the Fisher equation still provides a reasonable approximation of how inflation rates affect nominal interest rates around the world.

Fisher equation The equation stating that the nominal interest rate is the sum of the expected real interest rate and the expected inflation rate.

Fisher effect The assertion by Irving Fisher that the nominal interest rate rises or falls point-for-point with changes in the expected inflation rate.

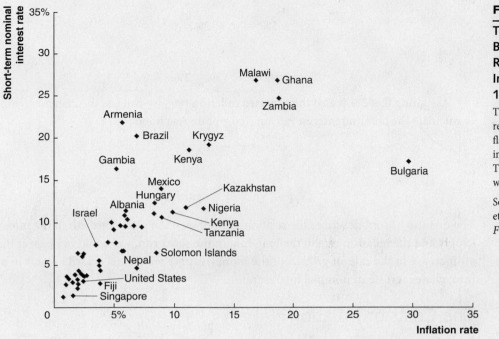

Figure 7.5

The Relationship Between the Inflation Rate and the Nominal Interest Rate, 1995–2011

The figure shows a positive relationship between the inflation rate and the nominal interest rate for 56 countries. This relationship is consistent with the Fisher effect.

Source: International Monetary Fund, *International Financial Statistics*.

Money Growth and the Nominal Interest Rate

If we combine the quantity theory of money with the Fisher effect, we have an important relationship: In the long run, an increase in the growth rate of the money supply causes the inflation rate to increase, which then causes the nominal interest rate to increase. We can conclude that because the inflation rate varies across time and countries as a result of changes in the growth rate of the money supply, nominal interest rates will also vary across time and countries.

Consider the United States. From 1919 to 2011, the growth rate of M2 velocity was approximately 0%, the growth rate of real GDP was 3%, and the expected real interest rate on Aaa corporate bonds averaged 2.8%.[2] Suppose that the Fed sets the growth rate of the money supply at 5%. According to the Fisher equation, what should be the nominal interest rate on a Aaa corporate bond? To answer this question, we must first calculate the expected inflation rate. For simplicity, we will assume that the actual and expected inflation rates are the same. So, we can use the growth rates version of the quantity equation to find the inflation rate. The growth rate of the price level is the inflation rate, and we are assuming that the growth rate of velocity is zero, so:

$$\% \text{ Change in } M = \pi + \% \text{ Change in } Y,$$

---

[2]We measure the expected real interest rate as the nominal interest rate minus the inflation rate during the previous year. The inflation rate is calculated as the growth rate of the consumer price index.

Practice Problems

or:

$$5\% = \pi + 3\%,$$

so that:

$$\pi = 5\% - 3\% = 2\%.$$

Assuming that 2% is also the expected inflation rate, we can use the Fisher equation to calculate the nominal interest rate on a corporate Aaa bond as:

$$i = r^e + \pi^e,$$

or:

$$i = 2.8 + 2 = 4.8\%.$$

The quantity theory describes the relationship between the rate of growth of the money supply and the inflation rate in the long run. In the short run, we would not expect that an increase in the rate of growth of the money supply would necessarily result in an immediate increase in nominal interest rates.

The Costs of Inflation

7.5

Learning Objective

Explain the costs of a monetary policy that allows inflation to be greater than zero.

In the previous sections, we discussed the quantity theory of money, the inflation rate, and nominal interest rates. We now consider how inflation affects households and firms and explore the benefits to society of reducing inflation. As it turns out, the costs of inflation depend on whether the inflation is expected or unexpected. The costs arise partly because inflation interferes with the ability of money to serve its four functions.

Costs of Expected Inflation

There are four costs of expected inflation:

1. Seigniorage
2. Shoe-leather costs
3. Tax distortions
4. Menu costs

Seigniorage The government's profit from issuing fiat money; also called inflation tax.

Seigniorage Governments make a profit from issuing money because it is usually produced using paper or low-value metals that cost far less than the face value of the money. For example, it costs only about 4 cents to manufacture a $20 bill. The government's profit from issuing money is called **seigniorage**. We have seen that, at least in the long run, an increase in the rate of growth of the money supply increases the inflation rate. Inflation causes the purchasing power of money to decrease. Suppose you want to purchase an iPad next year. The current price of the iPad is $500, and you decide to keep $500 in your checking account for one year and then purchase the device. If as a result of the central bank increasing the money supply the inflation rate is 10% for the year, then the price of the iPad will rise to $550. Your $500 can no longer purchase the iPad, so the purchasing power of your money has decreased. Governments are sometimes motivated to increase the money supply to pay for spending that is not paid for by taxes—in other words, to finance a budget deficit. In these circumstances, inflation acts like a transfer of wealth from the holders of money to the government. What the government gains in revenues as a result of increasing the money supply, the holders of money lose because of inflation, so seigniorage is sometimes referred to as an *inflation tax*.

Shoe-Leather Costs Households and firms change their behavior to avoid the inflation tax by choosing to hold less of their wealth as money. The nominal interest rate on money is 0%, so if the expected inflation rate is 3%, the expected real interest rate on money is 0% minus 3%, or −3%. Other assets, such as savings accounts, certificates of deposit, and bonds, have a nominal interest rate greater than zero. To protect themselves from the inflation tax, households and firms transfer their wealth from money to interest-bearing assets. Unfortunately, these other assets are less liquid than money. When people want to use their wealth to purchase goods and services, they must first transfer their wealth from the less liquid interest-bearing assets into money. This transfer takes time and effort, so it is costly. Economists use the term **shoe-leather costs** to refer to the costs of inflation to households and firms from holding less money and making more frequent trips to the bank.

Tax Distortion Expected inflation also creates inefficiencies in the tax system by distorting individual behavior. In addition to taxing income, the federal government also taxes *capital gains*. A capital gain is the increase in the price of an asset. If you buy a share of Apple stock for $100 and sell it 10 years later for $600, you are taxed on the whole $500 gain, even though part of the increase in the price of Apple stock may be due to inflation. The failure to adjust the value of capital gains for inflation increases the tax burden on investors and may reduce the level of saving in the economy. In addition, the tax code fails to adjust for inflation the values of inventories and the tax allowances businesses are allowed to take for the depreciation of buildings, machinery, and other assets. This failure makes the economy less efficient by increasing the real value of the tax payments corporations make, thereby reducing their real profits. Reduced profits may result in corporations making fewer investments in new factories and equipment. This tax burden is particularly large during periods of high inflation.

Expected inflation can also distort financial decisions because lenders pay taxes on nominal rather than real returns. Suppose that expected inflation is 4% and that an investor faces a tax rate of 30%. On an investment with a nominal interest rate of 8%, the investor realizes a *real after-tax return* of:

$$(1 - 0.30) \times (8\%) - 4\% = 1.6\%.$$

Suppose that the expected inflation rate rises to 8% and that the nominal interest rate rises by the same amount, to 12%. The investor's real after-tax return falls to:

$$(1 - 0.30) \times (12\%) - 8\% = 0.4\%.$$

The lower after-tax return to investors discourages saving and capital formation. There are, however, winners as well as losers during a period of high inflation. Borrowers such as corporations and individual homebuyers benefit from expected inflation because borrowers deduct nominal interest payments (*not* real interest payments) in calculating their income tax liabilities. Changes in expected inflation can change the real after-tax cost of borrowing. For example, with high expected inflation, corporations find selling bonds or taking out loans more attractive because nominal interest payments are

Shoe-leather costs
The costs of inflation to households and firms from holding less money and making more frequent trips to the bank; costs related to expected inflation.

deductible. Households find housing investment more attractive relative to investing in stocks because home mortgage interest is tax deductible. Economists continue to debate the net effect on the economy of the tax distortions arising from inflation.

Menu Costs When you go to a restaurant, you see the menu with prices printed on it. When you go to a retail store, you see prices on shelves or on individual items. **Menu costs** are the costs to firms of changing prices due to reprinting price lists, informing customers, and angering customers by frequent price changes. The higher the inflation rate, the more frequently firms change prices and the greater the menu costs. In addition, not all firms have the same menu costs, so when expected inflation occurs, some firms will change prices and others will not. For example, restaurants often have to pay to have new menus printed up, so the menu costs for restaurants are high, and restaurants therefore do not change prices frequently. By contrast, the price of a gallon of gas can change every day because it is relatively cheap and easy for gasoline stations to change posted prices. Therefore, gasoline prices often respond quickly to inflation, while prices at restaurants do not respond quickly. Firms with low menu costs are likely to adjust their prices to the desired level quickly, but firms with high menu costs will not. As a result, the relative prices of goods and services can change, making markets less efficient because the price changes do not reflect underlying changes in demand or in production costs.

Menu costs The costs to firms of changing prices due to reprinting price lists, informing customers, and angering customers; costs related to expected inflation.

How Large Are the Costs of Expected Inflation?

Inflation has averaged around 2% in the United States for the past 20 years. That inflation rate is low, but the rate is still positive, so the average price of goods and services rises over time. Martin Feldstein of Harvard University has argued that there would be substantial benefit to the economy of going from 2% to 0% inflation.[3] Feldstein believes that even at a 2% inflation rate, the welfare costs from inflation range from 0.6% to 1.0% of GDP. According to these estimates, in 2011 the welfare costs of 2% inflation ranged from $90.5 billion to $301.5 billion per year. And these costs are paid every year, which makes the present value of the welfare gain of going from 2% to 0% inflation equal to 35% of GDP, or more than $5.3 trillion in 2011 dollars.

The welfare costs are large because the distortions caused by inflation persist into the future. When inflation combines with the tax code to reduce the incentive for firms to invest, the capital stock falls over time. In addition, if individuals save less because inflation lowers returns to saving, the supply of loanable funds falls. This decline will raise real interest rates and reduce investment. This further reduction in the capital stock depresses economic activity today and into the future. Even a 1% welfare loss is very large in an economy the size of the U.S. economy.

---

[3]Martin Feldstein, "The Costs and Benefits of Going from Low Inflation to Price Stability," in Christina Romer and David Romer (eds.), *Reducing Inflation: Motivation and Strategy*, Chicago: University of Chicago Press, 1997. See also Darrel Cohen, Kevin Hassett, and R. Glenn Hubbard, "Inflation and the User Cost of Capital: Does Inflation Still Matter?" in Martin Feldstein (ed.), *The Costs and Benefits of Price Stability*, Chicago: University of Chicago Press, 1999.

Costs of Unexpected Inflation

When the inflation rate turns out to be higher or lower than expected, wealth is redistributed. For example, suppose you borrowed $500 to purchase an iPad instead of paying cash for it. The bank charges you a nominal interest rate of 10%, and you repay the loan after one year. That is, you pay the bank $550 at the end of the year in exchange for the bank lending you $500 at the beginning of the year. If the expected inflation rate for the year is 4%, then the expected real interest rate is 10% − 4% = 6%. That means you expect to pay—and the bank expects to receive—a 6% real interest rate. The nominal compensation to the bank for the loan is $50, but the real compensation is $30. What happens if the inflation rate turns out to be 8%? In that case, the actual real interest rate is 10% − 8% = 2%. While the nominal compensation to the bank remains $50, the real compensation is just $10. You gain, and the bank loses. As we saw in Table 7.1 on page 233, when actual inflation is higher than expected, borrowers gain, and lenders lose.

MyEconLab Real-time data

Macro Data: What Is the Expected Inflation Rate?

The expected inflation rate is clearly important. Although we cannot directly observe a person's expectations, we can estimate the inflation rate that investors in financial markets expect.

In 1997, the U.S. government started issuing Treasury Inflation-Protected Securities (TIPS). Most Treasury securities have a fixed nominal face value, so when the Treasury sells these securities in auctions, we learn the nominal interest rate. In contrast, TIPS have a fixed real face value that increases with the inflation rate, so when they are sold, we learn the expected real interest rate.

The Fisher equation states:

$$i = r^e + \pi^e.$$

We can use this relationship to determine the expected inflation rate. When the Treasury auctions standard securities, i is determined by demand and supply in the bond market; when the Treasury auctions TIPS, expected r is determined by demand and supply in the bond market. The difference between these two market interest rates is an estimate of the inflation rate that investors in the bond market expect. For example, on July 19, 2012, the nominal interest rate on a standard 10-year Treasury bond was 1.50%, and the expected real interest rate on a 10-year TIPS Treasury bond was −0.65%. We can conclude that investors in the bond market were expecting the average annual expected inflation rate over the next 10 years to be 1.50% − (−0.65%) = 2.15%.

The following figure shows the expected inflation rate over the following 5 years and 10 years, calculated using the interest rates on standard 5-year and 10-year Treasury notes and TIPS with the same maturities. Inflationary expectations were stable from 2003 through the fall of 2008, then as a result of the worsening of the financial crisis, expected inflation plummeted and actually became negative before rebounding to previous levels.

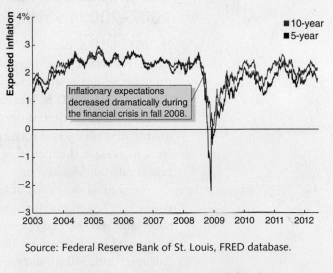

Source: Federal Reserve Bank of St. Louis, FRED database.

See related problem D7.4 at the end of the chapter.

Some people are better able to adjust to unexpectedly high or low inflation than are other people. For example, the financial crisis of 2007–2009 helped cause inflation rates to fall well below what households, firms, and investors had expected them to be. The low inflation rates contributed to the very low nominal interest rates that prevailed after 2008. By 2012, interest rates on home mortgages fell below 4%—the lowest on record. Some homeowners refinanced their mortgages to take advantage of these low interest rates. A homeowner with a $200,000 mortgage who had been paying a 6% nominal interest rate could save $300 per month on his or her mortgage payment by getting a new mortgage with a 4% nominal interest rate. Some homeowners were unable to take advantage of these low interest rates, however, either because their credit scores were too low to meet the higher lending standards imposed by banks after the crisis or because they had no equity in their homes. In this case and others, an unexpected change in the inflation rate helped some people but not others.

In general, if inflation is higher than households and firms expected, there is a redistribution of wealth from lenders, such as banks, to borrowers. The total wealth in the economy does not change, but unexpected inflation can nevertheless generate true costs for the economy. First, both lenders and borrowers devote resources to forecasting inflation and avoiding the costs of unexpectedly high or low inflation. These resources could be used elsewhere to produce goods and services. Second, lenders and borrowers can avoid the costs associated with unexpected inflation by not borrowing or lending. Unexpected inflation can therefore reduce economic activity—investment activity in particular.

Making the Connection

Did the Fed's Actions During the Financial Crisis of 2007–2009 Increase the Expected Inflation Rate?

In 2008, the U.S. economy was in a financial crisis and the worst recession since the 1930s. Federal Reserve officials believed they should take bold action by undertaking a program known as *quantitative easing*. Under this program, the Fed purchased more than $1 trillion of U.S. Treasury bonds and mortgaged-backed securities in order to reduce long-term interest rates and increase real GDP and employment. The result of quantitative easing was a substantial increase in the monetary base. Normally, such a large increase in the monetary base would spark fears among investors that the future rate of inflation would rise.

To combat the threat of increased inflation, the Federal Reserve announced that it would take actions to reduce the monetary base as the economy recovered. How successful was the Fed in convincing households and firms that inflation would not accelerate? The figure from the *Macro Data* box on the previous page helps us answer this question. Inflationary expectations did increase during the latter part of the 2007–2009 recession. For example, the five-year expected inflation rate rose from a low of −2.2% on November 28, 2008, to 2.0% on April 6, 2010—an increase of more than 4 percentage points in under 18 months—but this increase only returned expected inflation to its pre-crisis level. And in June 2012, the expected inflation rate was only 1.8%. The actual rate of inflation, as measured by the consumer price index, increased to about 3% in 2011, but the rate fell to less than 2% in the first half of 2012.

Although Fed policy during the financial crisis led to large increases in the monetary base, the economy remained weak into 2012, with real GDP still barely above its pre-recessionary levels and the unemployment rate over 8%. As the economy was recovering, banks were increasing their loans, and the new lending had the potential to result in increases in the money supply and, potentially, an increase in the expected inflation rate. Overall, though, the fact that the expected inflation rate remained low indicated that investors, households, and firms expected that the Federal Reserve would be able to take action quickly enough to prevent inflation from increasing significantly.

Sources: Board of Governors of the Federal Reserve System; Ben S. Bernanke, "Aiding the Economy: What the Fed Did and Why," *Washington Post*, November 4, 2010; Sudeep Reddy, "Unanimous Fed Keeps Buying Bonds," *Wall Street Journal*, January 27, 2011; and Bureau of Labor Statistics.

See related problem 5.4 at the end of the chapter.

Inflation Uncertainty

Relative prices play an important role in allocating resources. For example, suppose that the price of a new residential house is $300,000, and the price of a new retail store is also $300,000. Then the relative price of residential housing is one retail store. If the population increases because many young families move into an area, the price of residential housing is likely to rise relative to the price of retail stores. Suppose the price of residential housing doubles to $600,000, while the price of a retail store remains $300,000. As a result, the relative price of residential housing is now two retail stores. Building residential housing becomes more profitable relative to building retail stores, so resources will flow into the construction of residential housing. The change in the relative price plays a critical role in allocating resources to the construction of residential housing to satisfy the increased demand. In a market economy, relative prices help guide resources to their most efficient use.

When the inflation rate fluctuates significantly from year to year, relative prices become distorted and can send misleading signals to households and firms. As we discussed earlier, when inflation occurs, not all prices rise by the same amount, so relative prices can change, and markets may misallocate resources. Consider the previous example of residential housing and retail stores. Suppose there is no increase in the number of young families in the area, but inflation occurs. We traditionally think of menu costs as the dollar cost of changing prices, but the term is actually much broader than that. When a firm increases prices, it runs the risk of losing customers to its competitors. This loss is also a cost of increasing prices, so it is a menu cost. When builders increase prices, they run the risk of losing customers to their competitors. Menu costs may be higher in constructing retail stores than in constructing residential housing because firms are often not tied to one city and may choose to locate a store in a different area if faced with a higher price of construction. Households are less mobile because many people want to live near where they work. As a result, the builders of retail stores may increase prices more slowly than will the builders of residential housing. Assume, for instance, that the price of residential housing rises to $600,000 while the price of retail stores remains at $300,000. The relative price of residential housing has again risen to two, so resources will flow into the construction of residential housing. But relative prices have not changed as a result of changes in the number of young families, so the new residential housing does not satisfy increased demand from consumers. In this situation, the economy's resources have been misallocated because too few retail stores have been built relative to residential housing.

The more the inflation rate changes from year to year, the more likely it is to distort relative prices. We can measure the volatility of inflation using the statistical measure, standard deviation. Figure 7.6 shows the relationship between the average inflation rate and the volatility of the inflation rate for countries around the world. There is a clear tendency for the volatility of inflation to increase as the average annual inflation rate increases. Therefore, as the inflation rate increases, it becomes less predictable. In this situation, the ability of market prices to help households and firms allocate resources is reduced.

Benefits of Inflation

So far, we have emphasized the costs of inflation. However, some economists believe that there are benefits to low inflation because it can allow for adjustments in relative prices in situations where nominal prices are sticky. For example, it is the real wage—the nominal wage divided by the price level—that determines how many workers a firm will hire. In a situation where the real wage needs to decrease to restore equilibrium in a labor

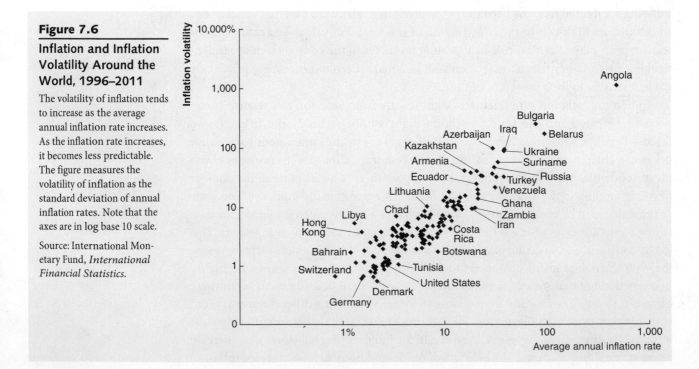

Figure 7.6

Inflation and Inflation Volatility Around the World, 1996–2011

The volatility of inflation tends to increase as the average annual inflation rate increases. As the inflation rate increases, it becomes less predictable. The figure measures the volatility of inflation as the standard deviation of annual inflation rates. Note that the axes are in log base 10 scale.

Source: International Monetary Fund, *International Financial Statistics*.

market, this decrease can happen either by cutting the nominal wage or by keeping the nominal wage constant while inflation causes the real wage to decline.

Workers are often more reluctant to see their nominal wages cut than they are to see their real wages fall as a result of inflation, even though in the end the result can be equivalent. For example, in 2010, the Dr Pepper Snapple Group tried to cut the nominal wages of its workers by $1.50 per hour, or about $3,000 per year for the typical worker at a plant producing Mott's apple juice near Rochester, New York. The company argued that workers at the plant were overpaid compared to similar workers in the Rochester area. The workers went on strike to resist the nominal wage cuts. In September 2010, the company and the union agreed not to cut nominal wages but did agree to freeze nominal wages for three years. During the three years that the nominal wages are frozen, inflation will reduce the real wages of the workers and bring them closer to those of similar workers in the Rochester area. As the real wage falls at the Mott's plant, the Dr Pepper Snapple Group should become more willing to hire additional workers and make the labor market in the Rochester area operate more efficiently.[5] Economists sometimes refer to the situation where nominal wages are rigid but real wages fall as a result of inflation as *greasing the wheels of the labor market.*

Hyperinflation and Its Causes

7.6

Learning Objective
Explain the causes of hyperinflation.

Hyperinflation occurs when the inflation rate is extremely high. At extremely high rates of inflation, the volatility of inflation is also typically high, making it difficult for households and firms to determine relative prices of goods and services, which can result in a severe misallocation of resources. For example, rising prices may lead firms to think that the demand for their products has increased, when, in fact, the demand for their products is unchanged and the rising prices they observe are solely due to inflation. When a country experiences hyperinflation, its currency will eventually cease to function as money, which is what happened in Germany in 1923 and more recently in Zimbabwe.

Prices rise rapidly during a hyperinflation, so households and firms try to minimize how much currency they hold, and firms must pay employees frequently. Employees must spend money quickly or convert it to more stable foreign currencies before prices increase further. Merchants raise prices as quickly as possible. The ability of government to collect taxes diminishes significantly during a hyperinflation. Because tax bills typically are fixed in nominal terms, households and firms have an incentive to delay their payments to reduce their real tax burden.

Causes of Hyperinflation

Hyperinflations begin when governments rapidly increase the growth rate of the money supply, and hyperinflations end when governments reverse course and reduce the growth rate of the money supply. While hyperinflations are caused by rapid increases in the money supply, ultimately, hyperinflations are typically due to persistently large budget deficits. To

---

[5]Debra Groom, "Mott's Strike Ends in Williamson as Union Approves Contract," *The (Syracuse) Post-Standard*, September 13, 2010; and Steven Greenhouse, "In Mott's Strike, More Than Pay at Stake," *New York Times*, August 18, 2010.

understand why large budget deficits cause hyperinflations, first look at the *government's budget constraint*. Governments purchase goods and services, *G*, and make transfer payments, *TR*. A government must raise the funds for these expenditures by collecting taxes, *T*; borrowing by selling more bonds, *B*; or printing money, *M*. So, in any given year:

$$G + TR = T + \text{Change in } B + \text{Change in } M.$$

The government's budget deficit is the difference between its expenditure, *G* + *TR*, and its tax revenue, *T*. We can therefore rewrite the above equation with the government's budget deficit on the left side as:

$$G + TR - T = \text{Change in } B + \text{Change in } M.$$

A government can finance a large budget deficit either by issuing bonds or by printing money. Some governments, however, may have trouble selling bonds because investors believe that the government may not pay them back. If investors won't buy the government's bonds and the government is unable or unwilling to raise taxes or cut spending, the government can finance the budget deficit only by printing money. In these circumstances, to finance a large budget deficit, the growth rate of the money supply will have to increase dramatically, leading to higher inflation.

German Hyperinflation After World War I

At the end of World War I, the German government was unable to find the political support necessary to balance its budget by raising taxes or cutting expenditures. Once inflation began to accelerate, the structure of the tax system made the government's budget deficit worse. Taxes were levied in nominal terms, and there were lags between when the government levied a tax and when it collected the tax revenue. In addition, the government consistently underestimated the inflation rate, and individuals had a strong incentive to delay paying taxes, so real tax revenues lagged behind real government expenditures. As a result, the government was forced to print money to finance the budget deficit, until eventually it was financing nearly 100% of its expenditures by printing money.

By the time the hyperinflation ended in Germany, the price level was *50 billion times higher* than before the hyperinflation. The inflation rate reached 41% *per day* during October 1923, so prices doubled every two days. A similar hyperinflation today in the United States would cause a pack of gum to go from a price of $1.50 to nearly $3 *billion* after just two months! Such rapid increases in the price level make currency almost worthless.

The hyperinflation ended in November 1923, after the German government made the following policy changes:

- Established a new central bank in October 1923 called the Rentenbank to control a new currency, the Rentenmark, which was worth 1 trillion of the old German marks. Just a few months after the establishment of the Rentenbank, the German government stopped borrowing from the central bank, the government balanced its budget, and the hyperinflation ended.
- Limited the ability of the Rentenbank to issue new currency to just 3.2 billion Rentenmarks.

- Limited the ability of the Rentenbank to extend loans to the German government to only 1.2 billion Rentenmarks.
- Cut the number of its employees by 25% in October 1923 and by another 10% in January 1924.
- Negotiated relief from the reparation payments it was making to France and the United Kingdom as part of the treaty to end World War I.

These steps were enough to bring the hyperinflation to an end—but not before the savings of anyone holding the old German currency had been wiped out. Most middle-income Germans were extremely resentful of this outcome. Many historians believe that the hyperinflation greatly reduced the allegiance of many Germans to the Weimar Republic, the government at that time, and may have helped pave the way for Adolf Hitler and the Nazis to seize power 10 years later.

Answering the Key Question

Continued from page 216

At the beginning of the chapter, we asked:

"What is the connection between changes in the money supply and the inflation rate?"

In this chapter, we saw how the growth rate of the money supply determines the inflation rate in the long run. The quantity theory tells us that the inflation rate should equal the rate of growth of the money supply minus the rate of growth of real GDP. This result, though, holds exactly only if velocity is constant. In the short run, velocity can fluctuate, so the relationship between the rate of the growth of the money supply and the inflation rate can be unstable. During and after the recession of 2007–2009, the money supply grew rapidly, but the inflation rate remained low.

Key Terms and Problems

Key Terms

7.1 What Is Money, and Why Do We Need It?
Define money and explain its functions.

Review Questions

1.1 Briefly describe the four functions of money.

1.2 Describe the five characteristics needed for an asset to be used as a medium of exchange. Identify two types of assets that have these five characteristics.

1.3 Explain why the Federal Reserve publishes data on the M2 money supply even though currency, checking account deposits, and traveler's checks, which are the most liquid of assets, are already measured in M1.

Problems and Applications

1.4 Each of the following has been used as money at some time in the past. Briefly discuss how well each fulfills the four functions of money.

   a. Gold or silver

   b. Cigarettes

   c. Salt

   d. Native American beads

1.5 People living in Yap, an island group in the Pacific, at one time used as money large stone disks known as Rai. These disks can be up to 12 feet in diameter and were made of a stone that is not native to the islands, so they had to be transported by canoe with great difficulty and risk. The stones were valued both due to their scarcity and because of the history of their acquisition.

   a. How well do large stones fulfill the functions of money?

   b. In 1874, a Western immigrant to the islands used ships to transport more stones to Yap. While these stones were larger, they did not have the history of risk and hardship associated with them.

   i. What effect would the introduction of these new stones have on Yap's money supply and on the overall value of stones?

   ii. How does what happened to Yap's money illustrate a central problem of commodity monies?

   iii. How would you expect old stones to be valued relative to new stones? Briefly explain.

1.6 A June 2012 investment newsletter reported, "Investors are falling over themselves to buy U.S. dollars. The popular trade is to buy dollars and Treasury bonds and sell everything else. Sell stocks ... sell high-yield bonds ... sell hard assets like gold and silver." What does this newsletter mean by "hard assets"? Why is the dollar not a hard asset?

Source: Brett Eversole, "The 'Long-Dollar, Short-Everything-Else' Trade Ends Now," *Daily Wealth*, June 7, 2012.

1.7 [Related to the Making the Connection **on page 220**]

After the French Revolution in 1789, France experienced a hyperinflation similar to Zimbabwe's. At one point, the French currency was worth so little that people used it for fuel rather than to purchase goods and services.

   a. What function(s) of money did the French currency fail to fulfill during the hyperinflation?

   b. Eventually, France issued a new currency, backed by gold. Why might the French government have believed that it needed to back the new currency with gold?

1.8 On January 1, 2002, Germany officially adopted the euro as its currency, and the deutsche mark stopped being legal tender. According to an article in the *Wall Street Journal*, many Germans continued using the deutsche mark, and many stores in Germany continued to accept it. Briefly explain how it is possible for a currency to continue to be used when the government that issued it has replaced it with another currency.

Source: Vanessa Fuhrmans, "Who Needs the Euro When You Can Pay with Deutsche Marks?" *Wall Street Journal*, July 18, 2012.

7.2 The Federal Reserve and the Money Supply
Explain how the Federal Reserve changes the money supply.

Review Questions

2.1 Why does the Fed have greater control over the monetary base than over the money supply?

2.2 What three actions by households and firms, banks, or the Federal Reserve will cause the value of the money multiplier to decline? Which of these actions is primarily responsible for the drop in value of the money multiplier during the financial crisis of 2007–2009?

Problems and Applications

2.3 In July 2012, the money supply, as measured by M1, was approximately $2,248 billion. The monetary base was approximately $2,605 billion.

   a. What was the value of the money multiplier?

   b. Why is the value of the money multiplier typically greater than 1? What is the key reason that it was less than 1 in 2012?

   Source: Federal Reserve Bank of St. Louis.

2.4 As of mid-2012, banks continued to hold large amounts of excess reserves, leading to concern that potential increases in lending activity could increase the money supply and the inflation rate. Use the money multiplier to explain how a reduction in excess reserves could lead to an increase in the money supply.

2.5 Consider the following statement: "Only the central bank can print money. Therefore, the central bank has complete control over the money supply." Do you agree with this statement? Briefly explain.

2.6 Briefly explain why the monetary base is often called "high-powered money."

2.7 Suppose that the required reserve ratio is 8%, banks hold 5% of checking account deposits as excess reserves, and the currency-to-deposit ratio is 2.

   a. What is the value of the money multiplier?

   b. If the Fed conducts open market operations and buys $100 million in Treasury bonds from banks, what will happen to the money supply?

   c. How would your answer to part (b) change if banks become concerned about the risk involved in making loans and now choose to hold 20% of checking account deposits as excess reserves?

7.3 The Quantity Theory of Money and Inflation
Describe the quantity theory of money and use it to explain the connection between changes in the money supply and the inflation rate.

Review Questions

3.1 What is the difference between the quantity equation and the quantity theory of money?

3.2 Explain why most economists agree that the Federal Reserve determines the inflation rate in the long run.

3.3 How accurate are the quantity theory's predictions of inflation? Briefly explain.

Problems and Applications

3.4 [Related to the Making the Connection on page 229] Would you expect that the quantity theory would do a better job of predicting inflation in high-income countries such as the United States and Germany or in less developed countries such as Kenya or Zimbabwe? Briefly explain.

3.5 In the second quarter of 2012, the money supply, M1, was $2,259 billion and nominal GDP was $15,606 billion.

MyEconLab Visit **www.myeconlab.com** to complete these exercises online and get instant feedback. Exercises that update with real-time data are marked with ⓦ.

a. What was the velocity of money measured using M1?

b. In the second quarter of 2012, M2 was $9,893 billion. What was the velocity of money measured using M2?

c. Briefly explain why these measures of velocity are different.

Source: Federal Reserve Bank of St. Louis.

3.6 A *Wall Street Journal* article on the Fed's options for reducing inflationary pressure stated, "In the old days, when the Fed wanted to tighten … the task was easy. It pulled a few billion dollars out of short-term lending markets by selling Treasury bonds." Why does the Fed's selling Treasury bonds "pull" money out of the system?

Source: Jon Hilsenrath, "As the Fed Uses Fewer Tools, Exit Plan Emerges," *Wall Street Journal*, December 15, 2009.

3.7 During the late nineteenth century, the United States experienced a period of sustained *deflation*, or a falling price level. Explain using the quantity theory of money how deflation is possible. Is it necessary for the quantity of money to decline for deflation to occur?

3.8 **[Related to** Solved Problem 7.3 **on page 230]** Assume that the growth rate of real GDP is 3%, the growth rate of velocity is 0%, the rate of growth of the money supply is 4%, and that changes in the rate of growth of the money supply do not affect real GDP.

a. What is the current rate of inflation?

b. What will happen to the inflation rate if the rate of growth of the money supply increases to 7%?

c. What will happen to the inflation rate if the rate of growth of the money supply increases to 7%, and, at the same time, the growth rate of velocity increases to 2%?

7.4 The Relationships Among the Growth Rate of Money, Inflation, and the Nominal Interest Rate

Discuss the relationships among the growth rate of money, inflation, and nominal interest rates.

Review Questions

4.1 If the inflation rate turns out to be greater than the expected inflation rate, will the expected real interest rate be higher or lower than the actual real interest rate?

4.2 Explain under what circumstances lenders gain and borrowers lose if the inflation rate differs from the expected inflation rate.

4.3 According to the Fisher effect, what must occur for the nominal interest rate to increase by 5%? To decrease by 5%?

Problems and Applications

4.4 The long-run growth rate of real GDP for the United States is about 3%, and the expected real interest rate on corporate Aaa bonds has averaged 2.8%.

a. If the growth rate of velocity is 0% and the rate of growth of the money supply is 6%, in the long run what is the nominal interest rate?

b. What will happen to the nominal interest rate in the long run if the rate of growth of the money supply falls to 3%?

c. What will happen to the nominal interest rate in the long run if the rate of growth of the money supply falls to 3% and the growth rate of real GDP falls to 2.5%?

4.5 Suppose that the inflation rate turns out to be higher than expected. Is this good news or bad news for investors who bought bonds issued when the inflation rate was expected to be lower? Briefly explain.

4.6 Suppose that inflation has been equal to 3% per year for several years and that the real interest rate that banks require on typical mortgage loans is 2%.

a. What nominal interest rate would banks currently be charging on 30-year home mortgages?

b. Suppose that the Federal Reserve unexpectedly increases the rate of growth of the money supply by 1%, and this change is expected to be permanent. How are banks likely to change the nominal interest rate they charge on mortgages?

c. What effect is the Fed's action likely to have on the real interest rate banks receive on mortgages made prior to the increase in the growth rate of the money supply?

4.7 In the summer of 2012, as worries about the possibility of the Spanish government defaulting on its sovereign debt rose, the nominal interest rate on the government's bonds increased sharply.

a. Why did the nominal interest rate increase?

b. Would you expect there to be a difference between the real interest rate and the expected real interest rates in this situation?

4.8 During the Great Depression, the price level fell during some years.

a. With a falling price level, what happens to the actual real interest rate? Does your answer depend on what happens to the nominal interest rate? Briefly explain.

b. In contrast, during the 2007–2009 financial crisis, nominal interest rates on Treasury bills were close to zero, and inflation remained positive for most of this period. What was the real interest rate on Treasury bills during this period?

c. Why would savers be willing to hold Treasury bills with the real interest rate in part (b)?

7.5 **The Costs of Inflation**
Explain the costs of a monetary policy that allows inflation to be greater than zero.

Review Questions

5.1 What is seigniorage? In what sense is it an inflation tax?

5.2 Explain how inflation can be costly to an economy, even if it is expected.

5.3 It is often said that inflation "greases the wheels of the labor market." Explain what this statement means.

Problems and Applications

5.4 [Related to the Making the Connection on page 240] Some central banks set an explicit inflation target, essentially committing themselves to keeping inflation within a certain range. How might an explicit inflation target affect the expected inflation rate?

5.5 Forty years ago, it was typical for grocery stores to post prices by labeling each individual can or box.

When prices changed, an employee would have to relabel every item in the store so that the cashier could enter them correctly into the cash register (bar code scanners had not yet been invented). Today, most prices are posted on shelf labels and scanned into cash registers using bar codes.

a. How has this change to pricing items in stores affected menu costs?

b. Are menu costs the same for all grocery store items? Briefly explain.

5.6 Suppose that consumer preferences are changing, so that more consumers want to buy chicken and fish and fewer want to buy beef and pork.

a. If inflation is low and fully anticipated, how would you expect the relative price of these goods to change, and how would that affect production of these goods?

---

b. Suppose now that inflation is volatile, so that it is difficult to tell the difference between an increase in the price of an individual good and an increase in the overall price level. How might volatile inflation lead to a misallocation of resources?

5.7 From 1939 until the early 1960s, the price of nearly all comic books was $0.10. In the late 1960s and early 1970s, as the inflation rate increased significantly, comic book publishers frequently increased their prices. Often, though, they would first sell comics at the higher price in only a few cities, selling at the old price elsewhere. Briefly explain why publishers would have expected that this strategy would increase their profits.

5.8 The idea of shoe-leather costs is that people wear out their shoes going back and forth to the bank. While people are unlikely to actually wear out their shoes in this way, what are some examples of actual costs that you might incur by trying to reduce the costs to you of inflation?

7.6 Hyperinflation and Its Causes
Explain the causes of hyperinflation.

Review Questions

6.1 What is hyperinflation, and why does it occur?

6.2 Why would a government risk experiencing hyperinflation by printing money rather than issuing bonds to finance a large budget deficit?

Problems and Applications

6.3 While hyperinflations are always caused by rapid growth in the money supply, they can be intensified by the actions of households and firms trying to protect themselves from inflation by spending money as soon as they receive it.
   a. What is likely to happen to the velocity of money during a hyperinflation?
   b. Use the quantity equation to show how the change in velocity affects the inflation rate.

6.4 Hyperinflation reduces economic growth, both through resource misallocation and by reducing saving and investment.
   a. Why does hyperinflation cause misallocation of resources?
   b. Why does hyperinflation reduce saving and investment?
   c. What effects do the misallocation of resources and reduced saving and investment have on economic growth?

6.5 Hyperinflation occurred in the South during the U.S. Civil War (1861–1865). Unable to tax effectively in a largely agricultural economy, the Confederate government was forced to print money, eventually creating a money supply of approximately 1.5 billion Confederate dollars.
   a. Explain how the rapid increase in the money supply combined with wartime scarcity of goods would cause prices to escalate.
   b. In 1864, the Confederate government attempted to reduce inflation by reducing the money supply by approximately one-third. The Confederacy forced paper currency to be converted into bonds by a specific date (or converted at a penalty after that date). What do you expect the immediate effect of this policy would have been?

6.6 [Related to the Chapter Opener on page 216] The following table shows the approximate *daily* rates of inflation from some of the worst hyperinflation episodes in history:

Country	Month with highest inflation rate	Daily inflation rate
Hungary	July 1946	195%
Zimbabwe	November 2008	98
Yugoslavia	January 1994	64.6
Germany	October 1923	20.9
Greece	October 1944	17.1
Taiwan (Republic of China)	May 1949	13.4

A simple way of calculating the approximate amount of time it will take prices to double is to divide 70 by the growth rate; this is called the Rule of 70. For each of the hyperinflations shown in the table, calculate the amount of time it would take for prices to double. [Hint: Because these are daily rates, in some cases, prices will double in a matter of hours.]

Source: Steve H. Hanke and Alex K. F. Kwok, "On the Measurement of Zimbabwe's Hyperinflation," *Cato Journal*, Vol. 29, No. 2, Spring/Summer 2009.

6.7 [Related to the Chapter Opener on page 216] By early 2009, Zimbabwe was experiencing inflation that was estimated to be 231 million percent per year. Because of the rapidly falling value of paper money, the government was forced to issue currency in larger and larger denominations, including a $50 billion note. At the time, a $50 billion note would purchase about two loaves of bread. An economist in Zimbabwe was quoted as saying, "It is a waste of resources to print Zimbabwe dollar notes now. Who accepts a currency that loses value by almost 100 percent daily?"

a. Why would printing notes be a waste of resources?

b. The government of Zimbabwe authorized many stores to make transactions in foreign currencies. What difficulties would this cause stores and consumers?

Source: "Zimbabwe Introduces $50 Billion Note," CNN. com, January 10, 2009.

Data Exercises

D7.1: Using data from the St. Louis Federal Reserve (FRED) (http://research.stlouisfed.org/fred2/), analyze the money supply.

a. Download and graph monthly data for M1 (M1SL) and M2 (M2SL) for the period from 1990 to the present. Calculate the growth rate as the percentage change from the same month in the previous year. Describe the relationship between the two measures of the money supply. Which is more volatile?

b. Download and graph the data for the "St. Louis Adjusted Monetary Base" (AMBSL) form 1990 to the present. Calculate the growth rate as the percentage change from the same month in the previous year. How does this growth rate compare to the growth rates of M1 and M2 you found in part (a)?

i. In general, what happens to M1 and M2 as the monetary base increases?

ii. Is the relationship that you found in part (i) different during the 2007–2009 period?

D7.2: [Related to the Chapter Opener on page 216] Steve Hanke at the Cato Institute (www.cato. org/zimbabwe) has calculated a hyperinflation index for Zimbabwe and other countries suffering from hyperinflations.

a. Where does Zimbabwe rank in Hanke's index? How long did it take for prices to double at the peak of the hyperinflation?

b. Search media sources to find out what the current state of Zimbabwe's economy is. How did the government get to this point?

D7.3: The World Bank (www.worldbank.org) has data on money growth rates for different countries. These data are listed under "Money and Quasi-Money" growth, which is roughly the same as M2 in the United States. Choose 10 countries to analyze.

a. Which countries have the most rapid rates of money growth? The slowest?

b. Compare the data on rate of money growth with the growth rate of consumer prices. Are the data consistent or inconsistent with the quantity theory?

D7.4: [Related to the Macro Data feature on page 239] In the chapter, we showed how to use interest rate data to calculate the expected inflation rate over 5-year and 10-year horizons. The Federal Reserve Bank of Cleveland (www.clevelandfed.org/research/data/inflation_expectations/) uses a different approach to calculate the expected inflation rate over different time periods. Go to this Web site and find the most recent data on the expected inflation rate for the next year and for the next 30 years.

D7.5: [Excel exercise] Use data from the World Bank (www.worldbank.org) to do the following:

a. Find the correlation coefficient for M2 growth and consumer price growth for each country in the group of 10 high-income countries.

b. Find the correlation coefficient for each country in the group of 10 low-income countries.

c. Now find the correlation coefficient for the entire group of 20 countries.

d. If you have had a statistics class covering regression analysis, run a regression using money growth as the independent variable and the average price growth as the dependent variable. Explain your results.

D7.6: Using data from the St. Louis Federal Reserve (FRED) (http://research.stlouisfed.org/fred2/), analyze the money supply.

a. Find the values from FRED for the M1 Money Stock (M1), the Currency Component of M1 (CURRENCY), and Total Checkable Deposits (TCD), from 1950 to the present.

b. Plot the growth rate of M1, the currency component, and total checkable deposits. What happened to each component during the 2007–2009 recession? Was this behavior typical for a recession?

c. How do the growth rates of the money supply during the 2007–2009 recession compare to the historical average growth rate?

D7.7: Using data from the St. Louis Federal Reserve (FRED) (http://research.stlouisfed.org/fred2/), analyze the relationship between the money supply and inflation.

a. Find the values for M1 (M1SL) and the personal consumption expenditure price index (PCEPI) from 1959 to the present.

b. Calculate the year-over-year growth rate for each variable.

c. In how many recessions does the inflation rate increase? In how many recessions does the inflation rate decrease?

d. What happened to the inflation rate and the growth rate of the money supply during the 2007–2009 recession? Is this consistent with the quantity theory of money? Explain.

D7.8: Using data from the St. Louis Federal Reserve (FRED) (http://research.stlouisfed.org/fred2/), analyze the money supply.

a. Find the most recent values from FRED for the M2 Money Stock (M2), the Total Savings Deposits at all Depository Institutions (SAVINGS), Retail Money Funds (WRMFSL), and Small Time Deposits - Total (WSMTIME).

b. Using the data found above, compute the most recent value of M1.

c. If consumers were to shift funds from savings accounts to checking accounts, what would happen to the values of M1 and M2?

D7.9: Using data from the St. Louis Federal Reserve (FRED) (http://research.stlouisfed.org/fred2/), analyze the money supply.

a. Find data from FRED for the M1 Money Stock (M1SL) and the M2 Money Stock (M2SL) from 1959 to the present

b. Using the data found above, calculate M1 as a proportion of M2 for each of the years.

MyEconLab   Visit **www.myeconlab.com** to complete these exercises online and get instant feedback. Exercises that update with real-time data are marked with 🔊.

c. Explain whether this proportion has increased, decreased, or remained the same over time.

D7.10: Using data from the St. Louis Federal Reserve (FRED) (http://research.stlouisfed.org/fred2/), analyze the money supply.

a. Find the most recent values from FRED for the M1 Money Stock (M1SL) and the St. Louis Adjusted Monetary Base (AMBSL).

b. Using the data found above, calculate the value of the money multiplier.

c. Assuming the multiplier is equal to the value computed in part (b), if the monetary base increases by $400 million, then by how much will the money supply increase.

D7.11: Using data from the St. Louis Federal Reserve (FRED) (http://research.stlouisfed.org/fred2/), analyze the money supply.

a. Find the most recent values from FRED for the Currency Component of M1 (CURRNS), Total Checkable Deposits (TCDSL) and Excess Reserves of Depository Institutions (EXCRESNS).

b. Using the data found above, calculate the value of the currency ratio.

c. Using the data found above, calculate the value of the excess reserve ratio.

d. Using the data found above and assuming a required reserve ratio of 11%, calculate the value of the money multiplier.

D7.12: Using data from the St. Louis Federal Reserve (FRED) (http://research.stlouisfed.org/fred2/), analyze what happened to the money multiplier.

a. Find data from FRED for Excess Reserves of Depository Institutions (EXCRESNS), the monetary base (AMBSL), M1 (M1SL) and M2 (M2SL).

b. Calculate the M1 multiplier and the M2 multiplier. Graph the value of these multipliers since 1959.

c. Graph excess reserves since 1959.

d. Why did the M1 and M2 multipliers decrease dramatically during the 2007–2009 recession?

D7.13: Using data from the St. Louis Federal Reserve (FRED) (http://research.stlouisfed.org/fred2/), analyze the velocity of money.

a. Find the most recent values and values from the same month in 1959 to the present from FRED for the Velocity of M1 Money Stock (M1V) and the Velocity of M2 Money Stock (M2V).

b. Graph the velocity of M1 and the velocity of M2.

c. The quantity theory of money assumes that velocity is constant. Is this a good assumption for either M1 or M2? Is it a good assumption during some time periods?

D7.14: Using data from the St. Louis Federal Reserve (FRED) (http://research.stlouisfed.org/fred2/), analyze the money supply and velocity of money.

a. Find the most recent values and values from the same quarter 10 years earlier from FRED for Real Gross Domestic Product (GDPC1), the GDP Price Deflator (GDPDEF), and the M2 Money Stock (M2SL).

b. Using the data found above, compute the average annual rate of change in both Real GDP and the M2 Money Stock over the given 10 year period.

c. On the assumption that velocity was constant during this period, compute the implied average annual inflation rate.

d. Using the GDP Price Deflator data found above, compute the average annual inflation rate over the given 10 year period.

e. Given the difference between the implied inflation rate and the actual inflation rate, describe what must have happened to velocity during this period.

D7.15: Using data from the St. Louis Federal Reserve (FRED) (http://research.stlouisfed.org/fred2/), analyze the money supply and velocity of money.

a. Find the most recent values and values from the same month 10 years earlier from FRED for nominal Gross Domestic Product (GDP), the M1 Money Stock (M1SL), and the M2 Money Stock (M2SL).

b. Using the data found above, compute M1 Velocity and M2 Velocity for both periods.

c. Since the velocity of money measures the volume of goods and services included in GDP that a given money stock purchases, economists sometimes casually refer to it as the "workload" performed by money. Given the values computed above, explain what has happened to this "workload" for the period under consideration.

D7.16: Using data from the St. Louis Federal Reserve (FRED) (http://research.stlouisfed.org/fred2/), analyze the money supply, velocity of money, and GDP.

a. Find, from FRED, the most recent value of Real Gross Domestic Product (GDPC1) and the value from the same quarter 8 years forward for Real Potential Gross Domestic Product (GDPPOT).

b. Using the data found above, compute the average annual rate of growth in real GDP over the given 8 year span on the assumption that the economy achieves its potential output. In other words, compute the average annual rate of growth, if real output grows from its most recent level to its potential 8 years into the future,

c. On the assumption that the quantity theory of money holds, that is, that the velocity of money will be constant during this interval, by what percentage will the money stock need to grow if price inflation is 2%?

d. Suppose this money growth target is adhered to, yet actual inflation over the period averages more than 2%. Given this average, what can you conclude about velocity during this period?

D7.17: Using data from the St. Louis Federal Reserve (FRED) (http://research.stlouisfed.org/fred2/), analyze interest rates and inflation.

a. Find the most recent values and values from the same month 5 years earlier from FRED for the the 10-Year Treasury Constant Maturity Rate (GS10), and the 10-Year Treasury Inflation-Indexed Security, Constant Maturity (FII10).

b. Using the data found above, show and explain what has happened to expected inflation between these two periods.

Appendix

The Money Multiplier

The Fed's balance sheet lists the Fed's assets and liabilities. There is a close connection between the monetary base and the Fed's balance sheet. Table 7A.1 shows a simplified version of the Fed's balance sheet that includes only the four entries that are most relevant to the Fed's actions in increasing and decreasing the monetary base. In most years, the Fed's most important assets are its holdings of U.S. Treasury securities—Treasury bills, notes, and bonds—and the discount loans it has made to banks. Recall that discount loans are loans that the Fed makes to troubled financial institutions such as commercial banks (see Chapter 3). The Fed's two most important liabilities are currency in circulation and bank reserves. Recall that the sum of currency in circulation and bank reserves equals the monetary base.

Table 7A.1 A Simplified Federal Reserve Balance Sheet

Assets	Liabilities
U.S. Treasury securities	Currency in circulation
Discount loans to banks	Reserves

Open Market Operations

The Fed can increase the money supply using open market operations, which involve buying and selling Treasury securities. Suppose that the Fed buys $1 million worth of Treasury securities from Bank of America. We can illustrate the effect of the Fed's open market purchase by using a *T-account*, which is a stripped-down version of a balance sheet. We use T-accounts to show only how a transaction *changes* a balance sheet. Although in our example, the Fed purchased securities from only one bank, in practice, the Fed typically buys securities from multiple banks at the same time. So, we use a T-account for the whole banking system to show the results of the Fed's open market purchase: The banking system's balance sheet shows a decrease in security holdings of $1 million and an increase in reserves of the same amount (note that the banking system's balance sheet simply adds together the assets and liabilities of all of the commercial banks in the United States):

Banking System

Assets	Liabilities
Securities −$1 million	
Reserves +$1 million	

255

We can use another T-account to show the changes in the Fed's balance sheet. The Fed's holdings of securities (an asset) increase by $1 million, and bank reserve deposits (a liability) also increase by $1 million:

Federal Reserve

Assets	Liabilities
Securities +$1 million	Reserves +$1 million

The Fed's open market purchase from Bank of America increases reserves by $1 million and, therefore, the monetary base increases by $1 million. A key point is that *the monetary base increases by the dollar amount of an open market purchase.* The process also works in reverse, so if the Fed sells $1 million of securities in an open market sale, the monetary base will decrease by $1 million.

The Simple Deposit Multiplier

In this section, we describe how the money supply can be increased or decreased through a process of *multiple deposit expansion.* What happens to the money supply when the Fed increases bank reserves through an open market purchase? To answer this question, we first analyze the changes that occur at a single bank and then look at changes for the whole banking system.

How a Single Bank Responds to an Increase in Reserves Suppose that the Fed purchases $100,000 in Treasury bills (or T-bills) from Bank of America, increasing the bank's reserves by $100,000. We can use a T-account to show how Bank of America's balance sheet changes to reflect these transactions:

Bank of America

Assets	Liabilities
Securities −$100,000	
Reserves +$100,000	

The Fed's purchase of T-bills from Bank of America increases the bank's excess reserves but not its required reserves. The reason is that required reserves are determined as a percentage of the bank's checking accounts. Because this transaction has no effect on Bank of America's checking account deposits, it doesn't change the amount of reserves that the bank is required to hold. Bank of America earns only a low interest rate from the Fed on the additional reserves obtained from the T-bill sale and therefore has an incentive to loan out or invest these funds.

Suppose that Bank of America loans $100,000 to Rosie's Bakery to enable it to install two new ovens. We will assume that Bank of America extends the loan by creating a checking account for Rosie's and depositing the $100,000 principal of the loan in it. Both the asset and liability sides of Bank of America's balance sheet increase by $100,000:

Bank of America

Assets	Liabilities
Securities −$100,000	Checking accounts +$100,000
Reserves +$100,000	
Loans +$100,000	

Recall that the money supply—using the M1 definition—equals currency in circulation plus checking accounts. By lending money to Rosie's, Bank of America creates checking accounts and, therefore, increases the money supply. Suppose that Rosie's then spends the loan proceeds by writing a check for $100,000 to buy the ovens from Bob's Bakery Equipment. Bob's deposits the check in its account with PNC Bank. Once the check has cleared and PNC Bank has collected the funds from Bank of America, Bank of America will have lost $100,000 of reserves and checking account deposits:

Bank of America

Assets	Liabilities
Securities −$100,000	Checking accounts $0
Loans +$100,000	
Reserves $0	

Bank of America is now satisfied because it has exchanged some of its low-interest Treasury bill holdings for a higher-interest loan. But the effect of the open market purchase on the banking system is not finished.

How the Banking System Responds to the Increase in Reserves We can trace the further effect of the open market operation by considering the situation of PNC Bank after it has received the check for $100,000 from Bob's Bakery Equipment. After PNC has cleared the check and collected the funds from Bank of America, PNC's balance sheet changes as follows:

PNC Bank

Assets	Liabilities
Reserves +$100,000	Checking accounts +$100,000

PNC's deposits and reserves have both increased by $100,000. For simplicity, let's assume that when it received Bob's deposit, PNC had no excess reserves. If the required reserve ratio is 10%, PNC must hold $10,000 (= 0.10 × $100,000) against its increase of $100,000 in checking account deposits. The other $90,000 of the reserves PNC has gained is excess reserves. PNC knows that it will lose reserves equal to the amount of any loan it grants because the amount of the loan will be spent and the funds will be deposited in another bank. So, *PNC can only safely lend out an amount equal to its excess reserves*. Suppose that PNC makes a $90,000 loan to Jerome's Printing to purchase new office equipment. Initially, PNC's assets (loans) and liabilities (checking account deposits) rise by $90,000. But this is temporary because Jerome's will spend the loan proceeds by writing a $90,000 check for equipment from Computer Universe, which has an account at SunTrust Bank. When SunTrust clears the $90,000 check against PNC, PNC's balance sheet changes as follows:

PNC Bank

Assets	Liabilities
Reserves +$10,000	Checking accounts +$100,000
Loans +$90,000	

These are the changes in SunTrust's balance sheet:

SunTrust Bank

Assets	Liabilities
Reserves +$90,000	Checking accounts +$90,000

To this point, checking account deposits in the banking system have risen by $190,000 as a result of the Fed's $100,000 open market purchase. SunTrust faces the same decisions that confronted Bank of America and PNC. SunTrust wants to use the increase in reserves to expand its loans, but it can safely lend only the increase in excess reserves. With a required reserve ratio of 10%, SunTrust must add ($90,000 × 0.10) = $9,000 to its required reserves and can lend only $81,000. Suppose that SunTrust lends the $81,000 to Howard's Barber Shop to use for remodeling. Initially, SunTrust's assets (loans) and liabilities (checking account deposits) rise by $81,000. But when Howard's spends the loan proceeds and a check for $81,000 clears against it, the changes in SunTrust's balance sheet will be as follows:

SunTrust Bank

Assets	Liabilities
Reserves +$9,000	Checking accounts +$90,000
Loans +$81,000	

If the proceeds of the loan to Howard's Barber Shop are deposited in another bank, checking account deposits in the banking system will rise by another $81,000. To this point, the $100,000 increase in reserves supplied by the Fed has increased the level of checking account deposits by $100,000 + $90,000 + $81,000 = $271,000. This process is called *multiple deposit creation*. The money supply is growing with each loan. The initial increase in bank reserves and in the monetary base results in a multiple increase in the money supply.

The process still isn't complete. The recipient of the $81,000 check from Howard's Barber Shop will deposit it, and checking account deposits at some other bank will expand. The process continues to ripple through the banking system and the economy. We illustrate the results in Table 7A.2. Note from the table that new checking account

Table 7A.2 Multiple Deposit Creation, Assuming a Fed Open Market Purchase of $100,000 and a Required Reserve Ratio of 10%

Bank	Increase in deposits	Increase in loans	Increase in reserves
PNC Bank	$100,000	$90,000	$10,000
SunTrust Bank	90,000	81,000	9,000
Third Bank	81,000	72,900	8,100
Fourth Bank	72,900	65,610	7,290
Fifth Bank	65,610	59,049	6,561
.	.	.	.
.	.	.	.
.	.	.	.
Total Increase	$1,000,000	$900,000	$100,000

deposits continue to be created each time checks are deposited and banks make new loans, but the size of the increase gets smaller each time because banks must hold part of the money at each step as required reserves.

Although the initial increase in reserves was $100,000, so the monetary base increased by $100,000, the ultimate increase in checking account deposits was $1,000,000, so the money supply increased by $1,000,000. Therefore, the *simple deposit multiplier*, the ratio of the amount of deposits created by banks to the amount of new reserves, is ($1,000,000/$100,000) = 10.

A More Realistic Money Multiplier

The simple deposit multiplier assumed that banks hold no excess reserves and that the nonbank public chooses to keep its holdings of currency constant. The equation on page 226 shows how we can derive a more realistic money multiplier by relaxing these assumptions.

CHAPTER 8

The Labor Market

Learning Objectives

After studying this chapter, you should be able to:

 Use the model of demand and supply for labor to explain how wages and employment are determined (pages 262–268)

8.2 Define unemployment and explain the three categories of unemployment (pages 269–275)

8.3 Explain the natural rate of unemployment (pages 275–284)

8.4 Explain how government policies affect the unemployment rate (pages 284–287)

If Firms Have Trouble Finding Workers, Why Is the Unemployment Rate so High?

The recession of 2007–2009 was the most severe the United States had experienced since the Great Depression of the 1930s. Real GDP declined by 5.1% during the recession, and the unemployment rate rose to over 10%. In September 2012, more than three years after the end of the recession, the unemployment rate was still high at 7.8%, and nearly half of the unemployed had been out of work for at least six months. Unemployment had been so high for so long that some economists had begun speaking of the "new normal," in which unemployment rates might be stuck at higher levels for many years.

But despite the severity of the recession and slow recovery, some firms continued to hire workers. For instance, Ernst & Young, the accounting and consulting firm, continued to hire thousands of new graduates each year. Many firms were reporting shortages of skilled workers, even while millions remained unemployed. A report by the consulting firm Deloitte found that 600,000 manufacturing jobs were going unfilled because firms could not find skilled workers. A manager at a metal-parts factory in Michigan was quoted as saying that his workers had been working 60 to 70 hours a week because he could not find additional workers with the required skills. Part of the problem was that the introduction of computers and automation into factories has raised the skill requirements for factory work. Increasingly, factory workers need to have a good understanding of mathematics to program and operate the new machines. Another metal-parts manufacturer in Michigan was quoted as saying, "Now it's: 'I need 20 guys with very specialized technical skills.' There's a mismatch."

Continued on next page

Key Issue and Question

Issue: The unemployment rate in the United States did not fall below 8% until more than three years after the end of the 2007–2009 recession.

Question: Has the natural rate of unemployment increased?

Answered on page 287

The experiences of these firms reflected two aspects of the U.S. labor market. First, economists agree that during recessions and expansions alike, the U.S. labor market creates and destroys millions of jobs every month. For example, during the worst part of the recession, from the fourth quarter of 2008 through the third quarter of 2009, more than 32 million workers lost their jobs. During the same period, though, more than 25 million workers found jobs. Net employment declined by 7 million, but even these very high job losses took place in the context of millions of workers finding jobs.

The second aspect of the labor market involves structural unemployment, which arises from a persistent mismatch between the skills of workers and the requirements of jobs. No one doubted that part of the high unemployment rates during and after the recession represented *cyclical unemployment,* or unemployment due to the severity of the recession. But was the level of structural unemployment unusually high? The experience of the manufacturing firms in Michigan suggests that it was, but some economists were skeptical that a rise in structural unemployment could account for more than a small percentage of the overall increase in unemployment. Economists and policymakers have debated the reasons why unemployment has remained persistently high since the end of the recession.

The disagreement among economists involved more than just how to categorize the unemployed. The types of economic policies Congress, the president, and the Federal Reserve might use depended at least in part on what was causing the high rates of unemployment.

Sources: U.S. Bureau of Labor Statistics, "Employment Situation Summary," June 1, 2012; U.S. Bureau of Labor Statistics, "Business Employment Dynamics—Second Quarter 2010," February 1, 2011; David Leonhardt, "Debating the Causes of Joblessness,"*New York Times*, January 21, 2011; Motoko Rich, "Factory Jobs Return, but Employers Find Skills Shortage,"*New York Times*, July 1, 2010; Neal Conan, "Job Pool for 2010 Grads Crowded with 2009 Grads," www.npr.org, May 24, 2010; and Peter Whoriskey, "Wanted: Skilled Factory Workers,"*Washington Post*, February 20, 2012.

When most people think about how well the economy is doing, they focus on the state of the labor market. How easy is it for them, members of their family, and friends to find jobs? Are they receiving pay raises or pay cuts? By the spring of their senior year, most college students are face-to-face with the state of the economy as they consider their job prospects. As we saw in Chapter 1, entering the labor force when the job market is weak can mean not only a much longer job search but also possibly having to work for years in a relatively low-paying job. Not surprisingly, the unemployment rate is probably the most closely watched macroeconomic statistic by the general public. Wall Street investors also look to labor market statistics to gauge how well the economy is performing. When the government releases new statistics on the labor market, good news usually causes stock prices to rise, and bad news causes stock prices to fall. And during the 2012 presidential election, each month after the government announced the latest data on unemployment, political commentators would adjust their predictions of President Barack Obama's chances of being reelected.

Economists devote significant time and resources to analyzing the labor market. In considering policies to address unemployment, Congress, the president, and the Federal Reserve rely on this analysis. In this chapter, we discuss what economists mean by the phrase *full employment*. As it turns out, full employment does not mean that every worker who wants a job has a job. Economists use a definition of full employment that reflects the fact that the U.S. labor market is dynamic and that workers are constantly entering and leaving employment.

8.1

Learning Objective

Use the model of demand and supply for labor to explain how wages and employment are determined.

The Labor Market

Economists rely on the basic model of demand and supply to analyze the labor market, although this market differs from the markets for final goods and services. The most obvious difference is that in the market for labor, firms are demanders, and households are suppliers. The demand for labor and other factors of production is a *derived demand* because it depends on the demand for the goods that labor produces. We briefly discuss the demand for labor before discussing the supply of labor.

Nominal and Real Wages

The price of labor is the wage, which includes "fringe benefits," such as medical insurance, retirement benefits, and bonuses. The nominal wage (W) is how much workers are paid in dollars. The real wage, w, represents the purchasing power of the nominal wage and is calculated by dividing the nominal wage by the price level, P:

$$\text{Real wage} = w = \frac{W}{P}.$$

For example, if the nominal wage in 2013 is $40 per hour and the price level is 1, then the real wage is also $40.[1] If the inflation rate is 3% while the nominal wage remains unchanged, the real wage will fall to:

$$\frac{\$40}{1.03} = \$38.83.$$

The Demand for Labor Services

Marginal product of labor (*MPL*) The extra output a firm receives from adding one more unit of labor, holding all other inputs and efficiency constant.

The labor demand curve is the same as the **marginal product of labor (*MPL*)** curve, where the marginal product of labor is the extra output a firm receives from adding one more unit of labor, holding all other inputs and efficiency constant. Due to diminishing marginal returns, the marginal product of labor will decrease as firms hire more workers. Figure 8.1 shows that diminishing marginal returns cause the demand curve for labor to slope downward.

Shifting the Demand Curve

The demand curve for labor shows the relationship between the real wage rate and the quantity of labor demanded, holding everything else constant. For labor demand, "everything else" is any variable other than the real wage that affects the willingness of firms to hire workers. Because the labor demand curve is the marginal product of labor curve, "everything else" includes factors that affect the marginal product of labor, such as the amount of capital, the skill level of workers, and technology. Changes in these variables cause the demand curve to shift.

For example, suppose that the accounting firm Ernst & Young purchases new computer software that allows its workers to audit financial statements more quickly, thereby increasing the marginal product of labor. Anything that increases the marginal product of labor will

---

[1]Note that we often express the price level in the base year as 100, rather than 1. In that case, we can think of the real wage as being calculated as $(W/P) \times 100$.

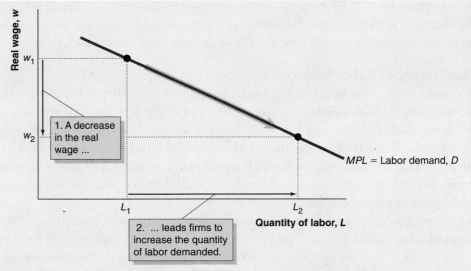

Figure 8.1

The Labor Demand Curve

The demand curve for labor is the marginal product of labor curve and slopes downward due to diminishing marginal returns. As the real wage decreases from w_1 to w_2, firms increase the quantity of labor demanded from L_1 to L_2. As firms hire more workers, the marginal product of labor decreases.

shift the labor demand curve to the right, as shown in Figure 8.2, where the labor demand curve shifts from D_1 to D_2. If the real wage remains fixed at w, the quantity of labor demanded will increase from L_1 to L_2. By similar reasoning, an increase in the capital stock would also increase the quantity of labor demanded. If Ernst & Young gives its workers more computers to work with, each worker can carry out more audits, so the marginal product of labor will increase, shifting the labor demand curve to the right.

To understand why the demand curve for labor shifts, think from the firm's point of view. Firms hire workers to produce goods and services. Anything that makes workers more productive will make the workers more valuable to the firm. The more productive workers

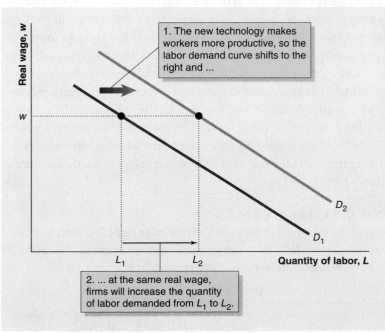

Figure 8.2

Shifting the Labor Demand Curve

If technology improves, the marginal product of labor increases, which shifts the labor demand curve to the right, from D_1 to D_2. Similar reasoning shows that an increase in the capital stock also shifts the labor demand curve to the right.

become, the more workers the firm is willing to hire at the current real wage, so the labor demand curve shifts to the right. Similarly, anything that makes workers less productive also makes them less valuable to the firm, so the labor demand curve shifts to the left.

The Supply of Labor Services

We turn now to considering how households decide the quantity of labor to supply. Of the many trade-offs each of us faces in life, one of the most important is how to divide up the 24 hours in a day between labor and leisure. Every hour spent sleeping, reading, watching television, playing sports, or in other forms of leisure is an hour less spent working. Because in devoting an hour to leisure we give up an hour's earnings from working, *the wage is the opportunity cost of leisure*. In that sense, we can consider the wage to be the price of leisure.

To understand the effect of an increase in the real wage on the quantity of labor supplied, imagine that you work for Ernst & Young and that you just received a pay increase of 10%. Would you be willing to work more hours or fewer hours? Microeconomics tells us that we consume less of a good when its price increases. Because the price of leisure increases as the wage rate increases, the wage increase should lead us to devote less time to leisure and more time to work. This response to a wage increase is called the *substitution effect* because we substitute work for leisure. However, the substitution effect is not the entire story. Microeconomics also tells us that we consume more of normal goods when our income rises. The higher wage rate increases your income, so you should consume more leisure. This response to a wage increase is called the *income effect* because you are using your higher income to purchase more leisure.

The substitution effect and the income effect are pushing the quantity of hours you supply in opposite directions: Following an increase in your real wage, the substitution effect leads you to supply more hours of labor, while the income effect leads you to supply fewer hours of labor. As an employee of Ernst & Young, whether you would increase or decrease the quantity of hours you supply in response to a 10% increase in your real wage depends on which of these tendencies is strongest *for you*.[2] If you prefer more time with your friends and family, you may decrease the quantity of labor supplied, but if you want to purchase a new car or save more to send your children to college, you may increase the quantity of labor supplied. For the aggregate labor market, which includes all the workers in the country, evidence suggests that in the short run, the substitution effect is stronger than the income effect, so an increase in the real wage leads to an increase in the quantity of labor supplied. In other words, the labor supply curve slopes upward, as shown in Figure 8.3. As the real wage increases from w_1 to w_2, the quantity of labor supplied increases from L_1 to L_2.

Factors That Shift the Labor Supply Curve

The supply curve shows the relationship between the real wage and the quantity of labor supplied, holding constant other factors that might affect the willingness of households to supply labor, such as households' wealth, preferences for leisure over labor, and

---

[2]It also depends on whether Ernst & Young allows you the flexibility to adjust the number of hours that you work.

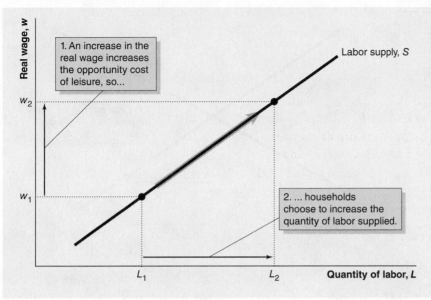

Figure 8.3

The Labor Supply Curve

Assuming the substitution effect is stronger than the income effect, an increase in the real wage from w_1 to w_2, causes the quantity of labor supplied to increase from L_1 to L_2 and the labor supply curve to slope upward.

income taxes. When these other factors change, the supply curve shifts. For example, households typically respond to an increase in wealth by "purchasing" more leisure time and supplying fewer hours of labor. The result is that when household wealth increases, the labor supply curve shifts to the left, as shown in Figure 8.4.

An increase in income tax rates will reduce after-tax income, so the opportunity cost of leisure decreases. As a result, households will purchase more leisure and decrease the quantity of labor supplied, so the labor supply curve will shift to the left. This explanation assumes, once again, that the substitution effect is larger than the income effect. Similarly, an increased preference for leisure will shift the labor supply curve to the left.

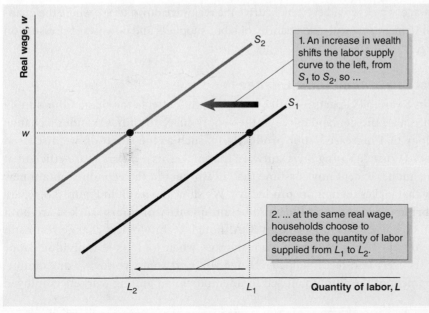

Figure 8.4

Shifting the Labor Supply Curve

The labor supply curve shifts to the left, from S_1 to S_2, if wealth increases, income taxes increase, or there is a shift in preference toward leisure. As a result, the quantity of labor that households supply decreases from L_1 to L_2 at the fixed real wage, w.

Figure 8.5

Equilibrium in the Labor Market

If the real wage equals w^*, the labor market is in equilibrium. At the real wage, w_1, the quantity of labor demanded, L_2, would exceed the quantity of labor supplied, L_1, resulting in a shortage of labor.

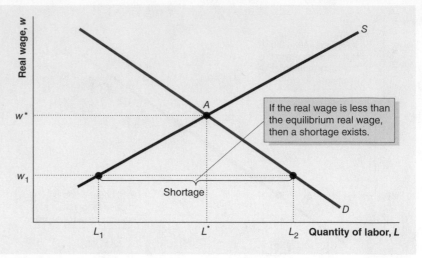

In Figure 8.4, the labor supply curve shifts to the left, from S_1 to S_2, and the quantity of labor that households supply decreases from L_1 to L_2.

Equilibrium in the Labor Market

Figure 8.5 shows equilibrium in the aggregate labor market at point A, with equilibrium wage rate w^* and equilibrium quantity of labor L^*. If the real wage is below equilibrium, as at w_1, the quantity of labor demanded, L_2, is greater than the quantity of labor supplied, L_1. Competition among firms will drive up the real wage to w^*, where the quantity of labor demanded equals the quantity of labor supplied, and upward pressure on the real wage is eliminated.

If the real wage started above the equilibrium real wage, the quantity of labor supplied would exceed the quantity of labor demanded. Some workers would offer to work for a lower real wage, which would eventually drive the real wage down to w^*, where the quantity of labor demanded equals the quantity of labor supplied, and downward pressure on the real wage is eliminated.

The Effect of Technological Change

A change in a variable, apart from the real wage, that affects the demand or supply of labor will cause the demand curve or the supply curve to shift. Consider a change in technology that increases labor productivity, such as the situation we discussed earlier, where Ernst & Young buys software that makes its workers more efficient at conducting audits. Except now, assume that all workers in the economy obtain new technology that makes them more productive. We show the result in Figure 8.6, where the equilibrium real wage and the equilibrium quantity of hours worked are both higher in the new equilibrium at point B. Although technological change results in a higher real wage in the aggregate labor market, when we look at individual labor markets, it is likely that technological change will hurt some workers. For example, the development of the automobile led to unemployment among workers employed

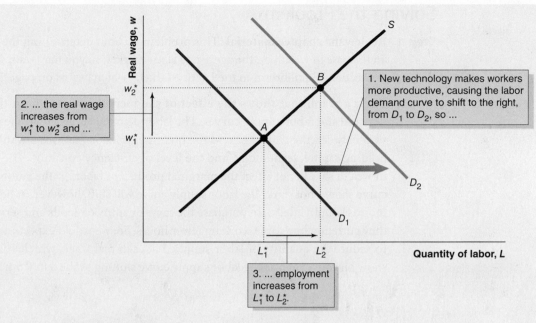

Figure 8.6 **The Effect of Technology on Labor Market Equilibrium**

When new technology makes workers more productive, the marginal product of labor increases, so the labor demand curve shifts to the right, from D_1 to D_2. As a result, the real wage increases to w_2^*, and the quantity of labor increases to L_2^*.

assembling carriages and wagons pulled by horses. Similarly, most workers employed assembling and repairing typewriters eventually lost their jobs following the introduction of personal computers. So, while the analysis in Figure 8.6 allows us to conclude that the real wage in the aggregate labor market will increase following technological change, in the markets for some jobs, the real wage may fall.

Solved Problem 8.1

Why Don't People Work as Much as They Did Decades Ago?

In the early twentieth century, it was common for someone to work 48 to 50 hour per week. Steel workers at some firms worked 12-hour days into the 1920s. Today, 40 hours is the typical workweek, and more people routinely work less than 40 hours than work more. What explains the decline? One clue comes from the work of Douglas Holtz-Eakin of the American Action Forum, David Joulfaian of the U.S. Treasury Department, and Harvey Rosen of Princeton University. They examined the effect of inheritances on labor supply decisions in the United States. They found that the larger the inheritance, the more likely the recipient was to reduce

his or her labor supply. The likely explanation is that individuals who receive large inheritances can use those funds to purchase goods and services, thereby reducing the need to work as many hours. Their result applies to individuals but also raises the issue of the effect on the aggregate labor market as a country becomes wealthier. From 1950 to 2011, total household wealth in the United States increased from $7 trillion to $52 trillion, measured in 2005 dollars. Predict the effect this increase in wealth had on the equilibrium real wage and the level of employment. Use a graph to support your answer.

↓ supply, wages ↑
     + Demand

Solving the Problem

Step 1 **Review the chapter material.** This problem is about determining the effect of an increase in wealth on the aggregate labor market, so you may want to review the section "Equilibrium in the Labor Market," which begins on page 266.

Step 2 **Draw a graph that shows the effect of the increase in wealth on the labor demand and labor supply curves.** The labor demand curve shows the relationship between the real wage and the quantity of labor that firms want to hire, holding capital, technology, and the level of efficiency constant. The increase in wealth should not affect the marginal product of labor, so the labor demand curve should not shift. The labor supply curve will shift, however. When wealth increases, individuals can purchase the same quantity of goods and services that they currently buy while working fewer hours. So, we would expect individuals to reduce the quantity of labor supplied at each real wage, which you should show on your graph as the labor supply curve shifting to the left, from S_1 to S_2.

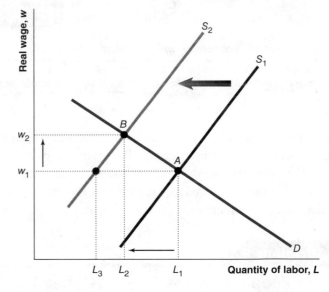

Step 3 **Use your graph to explain the effect on the real wage and quantity of labor.** The graph shows that at the original real wage of w_1, a shortage of labor exists because the quantity of labor supplied is L_3, and the quantity of labor demanded is L_1. As a result, the equilibrium real wage will rise, while the equilibrium quantity of labor will decrease, from L_1 to L_2.

Over the years, people in high-income countries such as France, Germany, and the United States have spent fewer hours working and more time in leisure. This Solved Problem helps explain why: As wealth has increased, individuals have used the increase in wealth to "purchase" more leisure time, thereby decreasing the number of hours spent working.

Source: Douglas Holtz-Eakin, David Joulfaian, and Harvey Rosen, "The Carnegie Conjecture: Some Empirical Evidence," *Quarterly Journal of Economics*, Vol. 108, No. 2, May 1993, pp. 413–435.

See related problem 1.4 at the end of the chapter.

Categories of Unemployment

Learning Objective
Define unemployment and explain the three categories of unemployment.

The demand and supply model suggests that when the labor market is in equilibrium, every worker who wants a job can find one. This observation means that any worker who does not have a job must prefer leisure to working at the prevailing real wage. If this analysis is true, then the unemployment we observe must be voluntary. It seems implausible, however, that when the unemployment rate in the United States increased from 4.6% during June 2007 to 10.1% in October 2009, it was due to a sudden increase in people's preference for leisure over work. Especially when the loss of a job can lead to bankruptcy, the loss of a home, or other severe consequences. Some of the increase in the unemployment rate was almost certainly involuntary, which means that workers who wanted jobs at the current wage could not find them.

To better understand unemployment, in this section we begin by discussing three categories of unemployment that economists have found useful in analyzing the labor market:

1. Frictional unemployment
2. Structural unemployment
3. Cyclical unemployment

Frictional Unemployment and Job Search

Workers have different skills, interests, and abilities, and jobs have different skill requirements, working conditions, and wages. As a result, most workers spend at least some time engaging in *job search*, just as most firms spend time searching for new persons to fill job openings. **Frictional unemployment** is short-term unemployment that arises from the process of matching the job skills of workers to the requirements of jobs. It takes time for workers to search for a job and for firms to search for new employees, so there will always be some workers who are frictionally unemployed because they are between jobs and in the process of searching for new ones.

Seasonal unemployment is due to factors such as weather or fluctuations in demand for certain goods or services during different times of the year. For example, stores located in beach resorts reduce their hiring during the winter, and ski resorts reduce their hiring during the summer. Department stores increase their hiring in November and December and reduce their hiring after New Year's Day. In agricultural areas, employment increases during harvest season and declines thereafter. Construction workers experience greater unemployment during the winter than during the summer. Because seasonal unemployment can make the unemployment rate seem artificially high during some months and artificially low during other months, the Bureau of Labor Statistics reports two unemployment rates each month: one that is *seasonally adjusted* and one that is not seasonally adjusted. The seasonally adjusted data eliminate the effects of seasonal unemployment. Economists and policymakers rely on the seasonally adjusted data as a more accurate measure of the current state of the labor market.

Would eliminating all frictional unemployment be good for the economy? No, because some frictional unemployment actually increases economic efficiency. Frictional unemployment occurs because workers and firms take the time necessary to ensure a good match between the skills of workers and the requirements of jobs. By

Frictional unemployment
Short-term unemployment that arises from the process of matching the job skills of workers to the requirements of jobs.

devoting time to job search, workers end up with jobs they find satisfying and in which they can be productive. Of course, having more productive and more satisfied workers is also in the best interest of firms.

Therefore, **unemployment insurance**, a government program that allows workers to receive benefits for a period of time after losing their jobs, can increase the efficiency of labor markets and the economy. Without unemployment insurance, an unemployed worker would be under severe financial pressure to accept the first job offer he or she received, regardless of whether the job suited the worker's skills and preferences. Unemployment insurance reduces this financial pressure by providing workers with some income during the job search. As a result, workers can afford to search for jobs that better suit their skills.

It is possible, though, that providing unemployment insurance for too long a period may lead unemployed workers to take too much time searching for a new job, which would reduce economic efficiency. During and after the 2007–2009 recession, the federal government extended the normal period for receiving unemployment insurance benefits several times. Economists debated the merits of these extensions. In addition to their effects on economic efficiency, unemployment insurance payments may increase the level of consumption spending by unemployed workers, thereby speeding economic recovery.

Structural Unemployment

Structural unemployment arises from a persistent mismatch between the job skills or attributes of workers and the requirements of jobs. While frictional unemployment is short term, structural unemployment can last for longer periods because workers need time to learn new skills. According to the Bureau of Economic Analysis, employment in the motor vehicle industry, which includes the major automobile producers and their suppliers, fell from 1.32 million in 1977 to 0.67 million in 2010—a nearly 50% decrease in employment. In addition, during this period, automobile production in the United States began to shift from domestic automobile firms, such as General Motors, located near Detroit and elsewhere in the Midwest to non-U.S. firms, such as Toyota, operating factories that are concentrated in the South. Some of the unemployed automobile workers near Detroit either had to move to the South or seek employment in new industries near where they lived. In either case, the workers were likely to be unemployed for a long period. For example, it might take months for a General Motors worker who installed car doors to learn the skills needed to obtain a new job in a different sector, such as health care.

Technological change is another cause of structural unemployment. Technological change in the United States has tended to eliminate unskilled jobs while increasing the demand for skilled jobs. For example, computers and information technology have eliminated many unskilled jobs, such as typist positions, and reduced the demand for clerical staff. At the same time, these innovations have increased the demand for workers who produce computers, computer software, and other related products. These latter jobs often require more skills than the jobs computers and information technology have eliminated. Low-skilled workers who are unable to acquire the skills necessary to find employment are structurally unemployed.

Unemployment insurance A government program that allows workers to receive benefits for a period of time after losing their jobs.

Structural unemployment Unemployment that arises from a persistent mismatch between the job skills or attributes of workers and the requirements of jobs.

Macro Data: Is the Decline of Industries That Produce Goods a Recent Phenomenon?

Industries that produce goods, such as cars, computers, and appliances, have become less important over time as a share of both GDP and total employment in the United States as well as other high-income countries. Correspondingly, the share of services, such as haircuts or investment advice, has become more important.

The figure shows that in the United States, the percentage of workers in goods-producing industries decreased from 37.1% of total employment in January 1939 to 13.8% in May 2012. Goods-producing industries have been in relative decline since the end of World War II in 1945, a trend that seems unlikely to be reversed. Although the *relative share* of employment in goods-producing industries has declined, the *absolute number* of workers employed in these industries has increased. Employment in goods-producing industries increased from 11.1 million workers in January 1939 to 18.3 million workers in May 2012. This increase, though, is much smaller than the increase in employment in services-producing industries from 18.8 million workers in January 1939 to 114.7 million workers in May 2012.

What explains the decline in the share of employment in goods-producing industries? Given that the decline dates back at least as far as the 1940s, recent developments, such as competition from China or other effects of globalization, cannot be the main cause. Instead, many economists believe that the decreasing importance of the goods-producing sector is

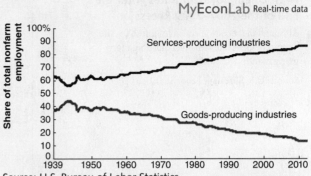

MyEconLab Real-time data

Source: U.S. Bureau of Labor Statistics.

likely due to productivity growth being much faster in goods-producing industries than in service-producing industries. For example, it still takes just as many members of an orchestra to play Beethoven's Ninth Symphony in 2012 as it did in 1939. However, each manufacturing worker is much more productive today than in 1939. As a result, the need for manufacturing workers has not grown as rapidly as the need for service workers.

The figure makes another important point: Using employment as the measure, the United States has been a service economy for a long time. In fact, services employment in 1939 was actually greater than goods employment in 2012, despite the growth in the economy and the population over the intervening 73 years.

See related problem D8.1 at the end of the chapter.

Some workers lack even basic skills, such as literacy, or have addictions to drugs or alcohol that make it difficult for them to perform adequately the duties of almost any job. These workers may remain structurally unemployed for years.

Cyclical Unemployment

When the economy enters a recession, many firms find their sales falling and cut back on production. As production falls, firms lay off workers. Workers who lose their jobs because of a recession experience *cyclical unemployment*. Economists define **cyclical unemployment** as the difference between the actual level of unemployment and the level of unemployment when the unemployment rate equals the natural rate of unemployment. The **natural rate of unemployment** is the normal rate of unemployment, consisting of frictional unemployment plus structural unemployment. It is the long-run equilibrium unemployment rate. So, when the unemployment rate equals the natural

Cyclical unemployment
Unemployment caused by a recession; measured as the difference between the actual level of unemployment and the level of unemployment when the unemployment rate equals the natural rate of unemployment.

Natural rate of unemployment
The normal rate of unemployment, consisting of frictional unemployment plus structural unemployment.

Figure 8.7

High Unemployment Rates After the End of the 2007–2009 Recession

Although the recession ended in June 2009, the unemployment rate remained quite high for many months thereafter.

Source: U.S. Bureau of Labor Statistics.

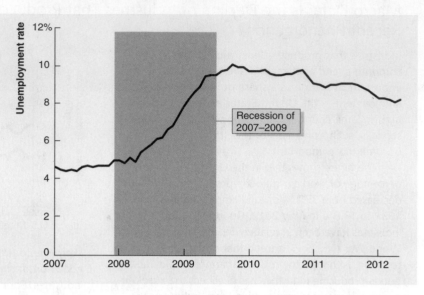

rate, cyclical unemployment is zero. Most economists believe that the natural rate of unemployment is equal to a measured unemployment rate of 5% to 6%.

Although cyclical unemployment is caused by a recession, it doesn't end when the recession ends. For example, Figure 8.7 shows that the unemployment rate in the United States continued to be well above the natural rate for many months after the recession of 2007–2009 had ended in June 2009. In 2012, the Federal Reserve was forecasting that the unemployment rate might not return to the full employment rate until after 2014. The forecasts of White House economists were even more pessimistic, with the unemployment rate projected to be at 6.5% at the end of 2016—seven and a half years after the recession ended. Some economists believed that even these gloomy forecasts might be optimistic.

Making the Connection

Did the Structural Unemployment Rate Rise During the Recession of 2007–2009?

We saw in the chapter opener that as the unemployment rate remained high long after the end of the 2007–2009 recession, some economists argued that the level of structural unemployment had increased. Cyclical unemployment rises and falls with the business cycle. It typically takes several years following the end of a recession before unemployment returns to the normal level represented by the natural rate. But the decline in unemployment following the end of the recession in June 2009 seemed particularly slow. For example, during the severe recession of 1981–1982, the unemployment rate peaked at 10.8% in November 1982. A little more than two years later, the unemployment rate was down to about 7%. In contrast, after the 2007–2009 recession, the unemployment rate continued to rise and peaked at 10.0% in October

2009. In September 2012, the unemployment rate was still high at 7.8%. Why did the unemployment rate fall so slowly during the recovery from the 2007–2009 recession?

Some economists and policymakers argued that the extent of structural unemployment had increased. Economists taking this position believed that the recession had severely affected certain industries and that the recovery of employment in these industries would be very slow. These industries might even permanently contract in size. Most notably, the residential construction industry was devastated by the recession as the housing bubble burst. From a peak in the spring of 2006, the number of jobs in residential construction declined by an extraordinary 44%. Residential and commercial construction typically decline during recessions as incomes and profits fall and families become more cautious about investing in new homes and firms reduce spending on factories and office buildings. But some economists believed that in this case, it would take years for spending on residential construction to again reach its 2006 level. As a result, many people who had worked in this sector would need to find jobs elsewhere. Doing so might require workers to learn new skills or to move to other parts of the country. The situation was similar for people who worked in industries that depend on construction, such as mortgage lending, real estate appraisals, and manufacturing of furniture, appliances, and construction equipment.

Other economists have argued that long-run changes in the economy might account for the slow growth of employment during 2009–2012 and, therefore, the slow decline in unemployment. For example, Daron Acemoglu and David H. Autor of MIT have argued that the long-run decline in jobs in manufacturing and related industries reduced earnings of workers, particularly males, who lack education beyond high school. These lower earnings resulted in more workers from these groups dropping out of the labor force. This trend, which dates back to the 1970s, was accelerated by the recession of 2007–2009, during which predominantly male jobs in manufacturing and construction were hard hit. Erica Groshen and Simon Potter of the Federal Reserve Bank of New York have argued that over time, many firms moved away from using a system of temporary layoffs to deal with a decline in demand. When firms use temporary layoffs, workers are likely to be rehired quickly once demand increases during an economic expansion. If firms use permanent layoffs following declines in demand, an "unusually high share of unemployed workers must now find new positions in different firms or industries," according to Groshen and Potter. If these arguments are correct, then the U.S. economy may face a future of "jobless recoveries" as increases in employment lag behind increases in GDP and high rates of unemployment persist for years.

Some economists, though, have been skeptical of these explanations. These economists argue that the severity of the 2007–2009 recession was caused by a particularly large decline in total spending, or *aggregate demand*. Because aggregate demand increased only slowly following the recession, GDP also grew slowly, hindering the growth in employment and keeping the unemployment rate high. In other words, the unemployment was cyclical rather than structural. For example, Christina Romer, former chair of the Council of Economic Advisers, argued that "the rise in long-term unemployment is the almost-inevitable consequence of the severe recession. We do not need to appeal to any underlying structural changes to understand it, and there is every reason to expect that long-term unemployment will come back down when aggregate demand recovers."

As we will see when we discuss short-run monetary and fiscal policies (see Chapters 12 and 13), understanding the reasons for changes in the unemployment rate is of crucial importance to policymakers.

Sources: Narayana Kocherlakota, "Back Inside the FOMC," speech delivered in Missoula, Montana, September 8, 2010; Daron Acemoglu and David H. Autor, "Skills, Tasks and Technologies: Implications for Employment and Earnings," in Orley Ashenfelter and David Card (eds.), *Handbook of Labor Economics, Vol. 4*, Amsterdam: Elsevier–North Holland, 2011; Erica L. Groshen and Simon Potter, "Has Structural Change Contributed to a Jobless Recovery?" *Current Issues in Economics and Finance*, Vol. 9, No. 8, August 2003, pp. 1–7; and Christina D. Romer, "Back to a Better Normal: Unemployment and Growth in the Wake of the Great Recession," speech delivered at the Woodrow Wilson School of Public and International Affairs, April 17, 2010.

See related problem 2.4 at the end of the chapter.

Full Employment

The term *full employment* does not mean that every worker has a job. Instead, the economy is at *full employment* when the cyclical unemployment rate is zero, or, in other words, when the unemployment rate is equal to the natural rate of unemployment. Economists sometimes call the natural rate of unemployment the *full-employment rate of unemployment*. We discuss what determines the natural rate of unemployment further in Section 8.3.

Unemployment Around the World

Figure 8.8 shows monthly unemployment rates for the United States, Japan, and the 17 countries, such as France and Germany, that use the euro for their currency. In all countries, the unemployment rate has fluctuated over time. For example, the unemployment rate for the United States varied from a low of about 4% to more than 10%. The figure also shows that the average unemployment rate has varied substantially across countries. For example, since January 1978, the unemployment rate has averaged 3.4% in Japan, 6.3% in the United States, and 9.1% for countries using the euro. The differences in average unemployment rates can change. Although not shown in the

Figure 8.8

Monthly Unemployment Rates Around the World, 1955–2011

The unemployment rate fluctuates over time for all countries, rising during recessions and falling during expansions. Note that data for the euro countries are available starting in 1990.

Source: Organisation for Economic Co-operation and Development.

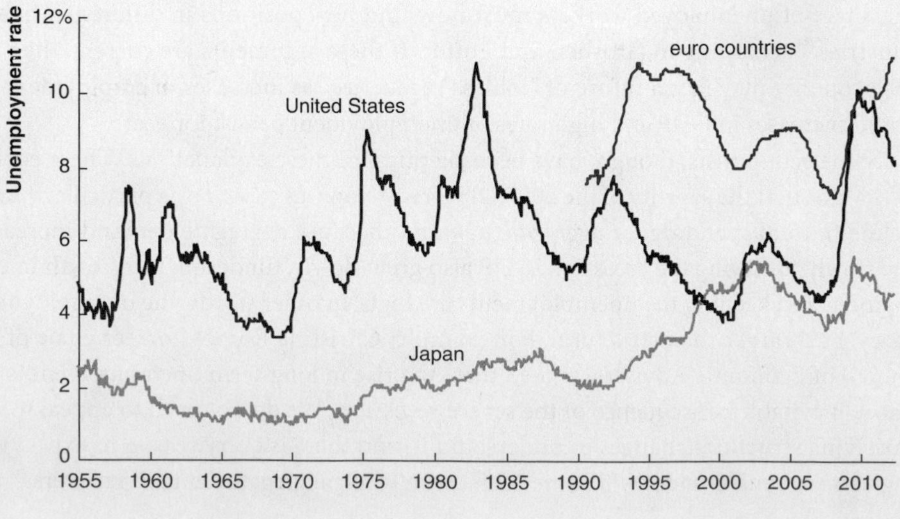

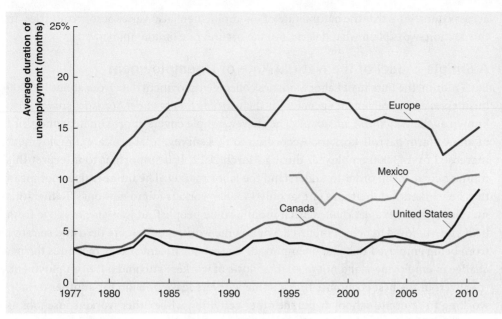

Figure 8.9

Unemployment Duration Around the World, 1977–2011

The average duration of unemployment is higher in Europe than in the United States. The difference has decreased over time but remains large. The average duration of unemployment during these years was 15.7 months in Europe but just 3.9 months in the United States. Note that data are not available for all countries for every year.

Source: Organisation for Economic Co-operation and Development.

figure, the United Kingdom and France had lower unemployment rates than the United States before the early 1980s but have had higher unemployment rates since that time. In Section 8.4, we explain why the unemployment rates in some European countries rose above the unemployment rate in the United States.

Duration of Unemployment Around the World

In addition to the variation in the average unemployment rates across countries, there is also variation in the average amount of time a worker is unemployed, or the *duration* of unemployment. Figure 8.9 shows the average duration of unemployment, measured in months, for three countries and for Europe for the years from 1977 to 2011. The average duration of unemployment was higher in Europe than in the United States even during the early 1970s. For example, in 1977, the average duration of unemployment in Europe was 9.2 months compared to only 3.3 months in the United States. The difference in the average duration of unemployment has decreased but was still large in 2011. The average duration of unemployment in Europe was 15.1 months in 2011 compared to 9.1 months in the United States.

Differences in the average duration of unemployment have important policy implications. Workers who are unemployed for long periods of time are more likely to be unemployed for structural reasons than for frictional or cyclical reasons. So, policies designed to help the long-term unemployed are more likely to be effective if they involve retraining or other programs that help workers gain new skills and move from declining industries into expanding ones.

The Natural Rate of Unemployment

As we discussed in Section 8.2, there are three categories of unemployment: cyclical, frictional, and structural. Economists call the long-run equilibrium unemployment rate the natural rate of unemployment and measure it as the sum of structural and frictional unemployment. One explanation for the differences in average unemployment rates

8.3

Learning Objective

Explain the natural rate of unemployment.

across countries is that the natural rate of unemployment also varies across countries. In this section, we explain what determines the natural rate of unemployment.

A Simple Model of the Natural Rate of Unemployment

Each month, the Bureau of Labor Statistics collects employment data from about 140,000 businesses and government agencies for the *Current Employment Statistics* survey, also known as the *establishment survey*. The survey sample covers approximately one-third of all nonfarm payroll workers. According to this survey, total nonfarm employment increased by 143,000 employees during March 2012. It is important to interpret this number correctly in order to understand the labor market. The number does not mean that no workers lost their jobs or that only 143,000 workers found new ones. Rather, this number represents a *net change*. Each month, some people find jobs and so move from being unemployed to being employed, while some workers quit or are fired and so move from being employed to being unemployed. The establishment survey measures the net change in employment and not these total flows of workers into and out of employment.

Even in the best economic times, some workers leave one job for another or stop working to return to school or pursue other activities, while other workers lose jobs as their firms close or productivity improvements make their jobs unnecessary. As a result, there is a constant flow of workers from employment to unemployment and from unemployment to employment, even when cyclical unemployment is zero.

The Bureau of Labor Statistics uses the *Job Openings and Labor Turnover Survey* (*JOLTS*) to measure job flows. The JOLTS survey consists of a sample of 16,000 business establishments made up of private businesses and government offices. According to JOLTS, during March 2012, 4.356 million workers found jobs, and 4.153 million workers left their jobs or were fired. This difference indicates that total employment increased by 203,000 during that month.[3]

Solved Problem 8.3

How Many Jobs Does the U.S. Economy Create Every Month?

The following data on total private-sector employment are from the establishment survey, as given in the June 2012 BLS Employment Situation report:

Total Private-Sector Employment (in thousands)

March	April	May
110,871	110,958	111,040

A newspaper article on the report commented, "Private companies sharply cut back on hiring last month, adding only a meager 82,000 jobs." Is the reporter accurately interpreting the data? Did the private sector create 82,000 jobs during May 2012?

---

[3]Note that the employment increase for March 2012 from the establishment survey was 143,000, while the increase from the JOLTS survey was 203,000. Because the JOLTS survey covers many fewer firms, it is less likely to give accurate estimates of month-to-month changes in employment than is the establishment survey. For more information, see John Wolford, Mary Phillips, Richard Clayton, and George Werking, "Reconciling Labor Turnover and Employment Statistics," *Proceedings of the Section on Government Statistics*, 2003. This article is available at www.bls.gov/osmr/pdf/st030080.pdf.

Solving the Problem

Step 1 **Review the chapter material.** This problem is about understanding employment flows in the U.S. labor market, so you may want to review the section "A Simple Model of the Natural Rate of Unemployment," which begins on page 276.

Step 2 **Answer the problem by explaining how to interpret the data in the BLS Employment Situation report.** The BLS Employment Situation report provides data on total employment each month, as determined by the establishment survey. The change in total employment from one month to the next tells us the *net* change in employment. The change does *not* tell us the *total* number of jobs created during a given month. So, while the reporter is correct that the change in private-sector employment during May was 82,000 (= 111,040,000 − 110,958,000), she is incorrect in saying that 82,000 private-sector jobs were created in May. As our discussion of the JOLTS data indicates, in a typical month, millions of jobs are created (and millions of jobs are lost). This reporter is making a common mistake of confusing the net change in employment with the total amount of job creation.

Sources: Bureau of Labor Statistics, "Employment Situation—May 2012," June 1, 2012; and Tami Luhby, "May Jobs Report: Hiring Slows, Unemployment Rises," CNNMoney, June 1, 2012.

See related problem 3.9 at the end of the chapter.

One way to think of the natural rate of unemployment is as the rate of unemployment that exists in the long run when the economy is in a steady state and the flow of workers into employment equals the flow of workers into unemployment. Let's explore this point further. First, assume for simplicity that the labor force is constant. The labor force is the sum of employed and unemployed workers:

$$\text{Labor force} = \text{Employed} + \text{Unemployed}.$$

Every month, some unemployed workers find jobs. We call the percentage of unemployed workers who find jobs the *rate of job finding*, or *f*. Every month, some employed workers leave, or separate from, their jobs either voluntarily or involuntarily. We call the percentage of employed workers who separate from jobs the *rate of job separation*, or *s*.

The total number of workers moving from unemployed to employed status is:

$$f \times \text{Unemployed},$$

while the total number of workers moving from employed to unemployed status is:

$$s \times \text{Employed}.$$

When the labor market is in equilibrium and unemployment is at the natural rate, the number of workers finding jobs equals the number of workers separating from jobs, so:

$$f \times \text{Unemployed} = s \times \text{Employed}.$$

We can use a bathtub analogy (see Chapter 6) to understand what determines the number of unemployed workers: The stock variable (the level of water in the bathtub) is the number of unemployed workers. The number of workers separating from their jobs (the water flowing into the bathtub) is the flow of workers into the stock of unemployed workers. The number of workers finding jobs (the water flowing out of the bathtub) is the flow of workers out of the stock of unemployed. When these two flows are equal, the number of unemployed workers is constant, the labor market is in equilibrium, and unemployment is at the natural rate.

The unemployment rate equals the number of unemployed workers divided by the labor force. Using this definition, we can derive an expression of the natural rate of unemployment, U:[4]

$$U = \frac{1}{1 + (f/s)}. \qquad = \quad \frac{s}{s + f}$$

This equation tells us that the natural rate of unemployment depends on the rate at which workers find jobs and the rate at which workers separate from jobs. As the rate of workers finding jobs increases, the unemployment rate decreases. As the rate of workers separating from jobs increases, the unemployment rate increases.

The job-finding and separation rates fluctuate with economic conditions. When these rates are constant and the flows into and out of employment are equal, the unemployment rate equals the natural rate of unemployment. So, the previous equation represents a model for the natural rate of unemployment. For example, suppose that in the long run, 1.5% of the employed lose their jobs each month while 25% of the unemployed find a job each month. Therefore, $s = 0.015$ and $f = 0.250$. The natural rate of unemployment would then be:

$$U = \frac{1}{1 + (0.250/0.015)} = 0.0566 \text{ or } 5.7\%.$$

This model of the natural rate of unemployment provides important guidance to policymakers. The model tells us that if policymakers want to lower the natural rate, they must find ways either to reduce the rate of job separation or increase the rate of job finding. We discuss government policies to reduce the natural rate of unemployment in Section 8.4.

---

[4]This is how we arrived at the equation for the natural rate of unemployment: We know that Employed = Labor force − Unemployed, so
$$f \,(\text{Unemployed}) = s \,(\text{Labor force} - \text{Unemployed}).$$

Next, we can divide each side of the above equation by the labor force to obtain:
$$f\left(\frac{\text{Unemployed}}{\text{Labor force}}\right) = s\left(1 - \frac{\text{Unemployed}}{\text{Labor force}}\right).$$

Because the unemployment rate equals: $\dfrac{\text{Unemployed}}{\text{Labor force}}$,

Which we can write as: $f(U) = s\,(1 - U)$.

If we solve for the natural rate of unemployment, U, we get: $U = \dfrac{s}{s + f}$.

Dividing the top and bottom of the fraction by s gives us our equation for the natural rate of unemployment.

MyEconLab **Real-time data**

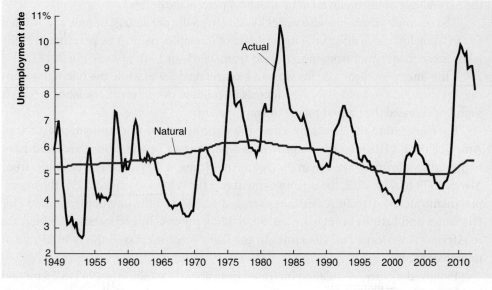

Figure 8.10

The Actual and Natural Rates of Unemployment for the United States

The natural rate of unemployment is not constant, but it fluctuates much less than the actual unemployment rate. The Congressional Budget Office estimates that the natural rate of unemployment is currently 5.4% for the United States.

Sources: U.S. Bureau of Labor Statistics; and U.S. Congressional Budget Office.

What Determines the Natural Rate of Unemployment?

Figure 8.10 plots estimates for the natural rate of unemployment by the Congressional Budget Office (CBO) against the actual rate of unemployment. The CBO is a nonpartisan agency of Congress that, among other things, gathers data to help Congress analyze economic policy. Figure 8.10 shows that while the natural rate of unemployment is not constant, it fluctuates much less than does the actual unemployment rate.

The natural rate of unemployment changes when either the amount of structural or frictional unemployment changes. Structural and frictional unemployment vary over time and across countries based on:

1. *Demographics*, including changes in the age, gender, and race of the population
2. *Public policy*, including changes in unemployment insurance, taxes, and laws governing the labor market
3. *Technological change*, including the introduction of new products that displace old products and increases in labor productivity
4. *Sectoral shifts*, including the growth and decline of different industries and changes in where industries locate

Demographics Younger workers have fewer skills and change jobs more frequently than do older workers. In addition, it often takes younger workers longer to find a job when entering the labor force. As the workforce ages, the average worker finds a job more easily, so frictional and structural unemployment decline. The unemployment rate for people aged 16 to 24 averaged 11.8% from January 1948 to May 2012. During the same time period, the unemployment rate for people aged 25 and older averaged just 4.4%. The United States experienced high birthrates from the mid-1940s to the mid-1960s—the baby boom—and lower birthrates in the years since. The average age of the U.S. labor force began to rise in the 1970s, and it has continued to increase. This aging has reduced the natural rate of unemployment by about 0.4 percentage points.[5]

The unemployment rate also varies by gender, so the percentage of men and women in the labor force also affects the natural rate of unemployment. The percentage of the labor force made up of women increased from 28.6% in 1948 to 46.6% in 2011. Since 2000, the unemployment rate for women has averaged 5.9%, while the unemployment rate for men has averaged 6.5%. The increasing number of women in the labor force has slightly decreased the natural rate of unemployment.

Race and ethnicity also may affect the natural rate of unemployment. African Americans and Hispanics have grown as a percentage of the labor force and have higher unemployment rates than do Asian Americans and Whites. For example, from March 1973 to May 2012, the unemployment rate for Whites averaged 5.7%, the unemployment rate for African Americans averaged 12.3%, and the unemployment rate for Hispanics and Latinos averaged 9.2%. So, holding other factors constant, the increase in African Americans and Hispanics in the labor force increased the natural rate of unemployment.

Finally, the prison population increased from about 0.5 million in 1980 to 2.3 million in 2011. Most of this increase came from young males with low skills. If these inmates had been in the labor force rather than in prison, many would have been unemployed. Therefore, the increase in the size of the prison population has likely reduced the natural rate of unemployment by 0.1 to 0.2 percentage points.[6]

Public Policy Public policies that affect the incentives people have to work affect the natural rate of unemployment. For example, unemployment insurance is a government program that allows unemployed workers to receive payments for a period of time after losing their jobs. In the United States, workers are usually eligible to receive a portion of their previous salary for up to 26 weeks. During recessions, the federal government often extends the duration of unemployment insurance, as it did during the recession of 2007–2009. Suppose that you lose your job as an accountant at Ernst & Young and are receiving unemployment insurance payments. You are less likely to accept a job working at Wal-Mart than you would be without unemployment insurance. If you have unemployment insurance and do not take a job at Wal-Mart, the unemployment rate will be higher than if you do take the job, so unemployment insurance has led to a higher unemployment rate.

Economists have long known that unemployment insurance may decrease the incentive to find a job and so may increase the unemployment rate. However, there is no consensus on how large this effect is, although it is unlikely that it adds more than 0.5 percentage point to the unemployment rate. Because the unemployment rate

[5]Lawrence Katz and Alan Krueger, "The High-Pressure Labor Market of the 1990s," *Brookings Papers on Economic Activity*, Vol. 1, 1999, pp. 1–65; and Robert Shimer, "Why Is the U.S. Unemployment Rate So Much Lower?" in Ben Bernanke and Julio Rotemberg (eds.), *NBER Macroeconomics Annual*, Vol. 13, Cambridge, MA: MIT Press, 1998, pp. 11–61.

[6]Lawrence Katz and Alan Krueger, "The High-Pressure Labor Market of the 1990s," *Brookings Papers on Economic Activity*, Vol. 1, 1999, pp. 1–65.

during the 2007–2009 recession increased from 5% to 10%, unemployment insurance made at most a minor contribution to the overall increase in the unemployment rate; most of the rise in the unemployment rate was caused by the large decline in GDP during the recession. In many European countries, workers receive larger unemployment insurance payments and receive them for longer periods of time than in the United States. These differences in unemployment insurance programs may explain some of the differences in long-run unemployment rates between the United States and Europe.

In 1984, the federal government passed the Social Security Disability Reform Act, which made it easier for workers to receive a portion of their wages when physically or psychologically unable to work. Partially as a result of the act, the number of workers on disability tripled between 1984 and 2012. People on disability are not in the labor force, so they do not count as unemployed. Low-skilled workers are more likely to perform physically demanding jobs, such as construction and manufacturing work, so they account for most of the increase in those receiving disability benefits. Because low-skilled workers tend to have high unemployment rates, disabled workers leaving the labor force reduced the natural rate of unemployment by about 0.5 percentage point.[7]

Marginal tax rates can affect how people decide to divide their time between work and leisure. The marginal tax rate is the fraction of each dollar earned that must be paid in taxes. The higher the marginal tax rate, the lower the after-tax wage from another hour of work. Countries in Western Europe not only have higher unemployment rates than in the United States, but workers in those countries on average work fewer hours per year. Nobel Laureate Edward Prescott of Arizona State University argues that differences in the natural rate of unemployment between the United States and Europe are mainly due to differences in marginal tax rates. For Prescott's explanation to be correct, however, changes in marginal tax rates need to have a large effect on households' labor supply decision. In other words, the *elasticity of labor supply* with respect to the after-tax wage would have to be large. Many estimates of the elasticity of labor supply indicate that it is very low. As a result, the observed increases in income tax rates in Western Europe do not appear to be large enough by themselves to explain the large increases in leisure taken by workers in those countries.

Some economists argue that the more restrictive labor market regulations in Europe provide a better explanation for higher unemployment rates and fewer hours worked. In most European countries, for example, it is difficult to fire workers, which makes firms more cautious about hiring them in the first place. Firms may also adopt more capital-intensive technology that reduces the need to hire workers, or they may be reluctant to expand operations. Both of these actions may decrease the rate of job finding and therefore increase the natural rate of unemployment.

In addition, European unions have bargained for longer vacations and more liberal leave policies than are typical in the United States.

---

[7]David Autor and Mark Duggan, "The Rise in the Disability Rolls and the Decline in Unemployment," *Quarterly Journal of Economics*, Vol. 118, No. 1, February 2003, pp. 157–205.

Making the Connection

Are Strict Labor Laws to Blame for Unemployment in France?

In July 2012, French carmaker Peugeot shocked the government of the new president of France, François Hollande, when it announced plans to close a factory outside Paris and lay off thousands of workers. Peugeot's decision followed a loss of €700 million ($860 million) in the first half of 2012. Analysts place much of the blame for Peugeot's woes on its high unit labor costs, due in part to France's strict labor laws and high payroll taxes.

Peugeot is not the only French company to suffer from high labor costs. Unless employees steal or are extremely negligent, it is difficult for any firm in France to fire workers. Economist Elie Cohen, a former board member of France Télécom, a telecommunications company that has had difficulty competing with firms from countries with less restrictive labor laws, said, "In France, you can't fire people just because your industry or technology is changing." Another cost of doing business in France and other European countries is workers' guaranteed annual vacation leave, which can run from four to six weeks. The Court of Justice of the European Union ruled in 2012 that workers in all 27 European Union countries are entitled to extended time off if they become ill on their vacations. The extra time off is equal to the number of days workers are ill while on vacation.

Not surprisingly, many firms are reluctant to hire in the first place. This reluctance can reduce the rate of job finding and increase the natural rate of unemployment. Economists have offered a number of reasons for the differences between unemployment rates in Western Europe and the United States, including different preferences among workers, differences in tax rates, and the influence of labor unions. The table below confirms that the unemployment rate in the United States was lower than the unemployment rates in France, Germany, and Italy from 2005 to 2008. In 2009 and 2010, however, the unemployment rate was higher in the United States than in any of these Western European countries. The financial crisis of 2007–2009 hit the United States very hard, and even though the recession ended in the summer of 2009, the unemployment rate remained above 8% through 2011. Could it be that the high unemployment rate in the United States reflected an increase in structural unemployment—an increase in the mismatch between available workers and job openings—and an increase in the natural rate of unemployment? As we saw in the *Making the Connection* on page 272, this remains a point of debate among economists.

Unemployment Rates for the United States and Selected European Countries

Year	United States	France	Germany	Italy
2005	5.1%	9.0%	11.2%	7.8%
2006	4.6	8.9	10.3	6.9
2007	4.6	8.1	8.7	6.2
2008	5.8	7.5	7.6	6.8
2009	9.3	9.2	7.8	7.9
2010	9.6	9.5	7.1	8.5
2011	8.9	9.4	6.0	8.5

Sources: Lelia Abboud, "At France Télécom, Battle to Cut Jobs Breeds Odd Tactics," *Wall Street Journal*, August 14, 2006; U.S. Bureau of Labor Statistics, *International Comparisons of Annual Labor Force Statistics, Adjusted to U.S. Concepts, 16 Countries, 1970–2011*, www.bls.gov/fls/flscomparelf/

tables.htm#table01_ur; Rob Valletta and Katherine Kuang, "Is Structural Unemployment on the Rise?" *Economic Letter*, Federal Reserve Bank of San Francisco, November 8, 2010; "National Lampoon's European Vacation," *Wall Street Journal*, June 27, 2012; and Carol Matlack, "Layoffs at Peugeot Signal France's Deepening Problems," *Bloomberg Businessweek*, July 12, 2012.

See related problem 3.10 at the end of the chapter.

We can conclude that a generous unemployment insurance system, high tax rates, and restrictive labor regulations tend to increase the natural rate of unemployment, while a generous system of long-term government disability payments tends to decrease it. Of course, all these policies have effects beyond the natural rate of unemployment. For example, policymakers may believe that restrictive labor regulations provide important protections to workers. So, policymakers often face a tradeoff between attempting to reduce the natural rate of unemployment while retaining policies that serve other purposes.

Technological Change Increases in productivity can reduce employment in the short run because new technology and other sources of improved productivity make some jobs obsolete. However, new technology can increase employment by creating demand for new products. For example, employment in the newspaper business has declined over the past two decades, as many people get their news online or from cable television channels. But the growth of online news and cable television has created new jobs. Workers who lose their jobs producing newspapers and who cannot make the transition to the new jobs online or on cable may become structurally unemployed, which would cause the natural rate of unemployment to increase. However, as labor and resources flow from the old to the new industries, the new technology actually leads to *higher* overall employment in the following way: In the long run, technological change and increased labor productivity lead to higher real wages. Higher real wages increase the quantity of labor that workers are willing to supply.

We can conclude that *technological change and increases in labor productivity ultimately make workers as a group better off*, even though some individual workers may be made worse off. The loss of jobs by workers at newspapers and the increase in jobs for workers in online and cable news is an example of what economists call *creative destruction*, a phrase first used by the Austrian economist Joseph Schumpeter, who taught for many years at Harvard. New technology destroys existing jobs but simultaneously creates jobs making new and better products elsewhere in the economy. Overall, technological change has a large effect on the mix of employment across industries, but it probably has at most a small effect on the natural rate of unemployment.

Sectoral Shifts Changes in the prices of key raw materials, such as oil, can cause employment to shift across sectors and increase structural unemployment. The price of a barrel of oil rose from $2.00 in December 1973 to $32.63 in July 1980. U.S. households responded to the large price increase by conserving energy, by, for example, switching from large automobiles with low gas mileage to smaller automobiles—often imported from Japan—with high gas mileage. As a result, the demand for autoworkers in the United States decreased dramatically. Autoworkers who could not develop the new skills needed for another career became structurally unemployed.

Economists refer to the process of output and employment increasing in some industries while declining in other industries as *sectoral shifts*. As sectoral shifts occur, markets work to move labor from one industry to another. During the transition, some workers will have difficulty finding new jobs and may become structurally unemployed. The figure in the *Macro Data* box on page 271 showed a long-term movement of labor from the goods-producing sector to the service-producing sector in the United States. This trend is not unique to the United States. The decrease in the relative importance of the manufacturing sectors is particularly evident in high-income countries. For countries in the Organisation of Economic Co-operation and Development (OECD) such as France, Germany, and the United States, manufacturing as a percentage of GDP decreased from 20% in 1998 to 15% in 2009. Because nonmanufacturing output—in particular, services such as accounting, business consulting, and healthcare—increased even faster, the relative importance of manufacturing declined.

In contrast, the manufacturing sector has been relatively constant in countries such as China and India. The Chinese manufacturing sector was 32% of GDP in 1998 and 2009, while the Indian manufacturing sector was 16% of GDP in 1998 and 15% of GDP in 2009. In high-income countries, labor has been flowing from the manufacturing sector to the service sector, while in many low-income countries, labor has been flowing from the agricultural sector to the manufacturing sector. As these reallocations take place, the natural rate of unemployment may temporarily increase.

The growing importance of temporary employment agencies has also affected the natural rate of unemployment. Temporary workers allow firms to increase output without committing to hiring workers who receive full benefits such as health insurance or pension contributions. Temporary employment provides a means for workers who cannot find full-time jobs to still find some employment. In addition, temporary jobs can enable young workers to make the transition to full-time employment. Since the 1980s, temporary employment has become more common, so the job-finding rate has increased. Holding other factors constant, this increase has reduced the natural rate of unemployment by 0.2 to 0.4 percentage point.[8]

8.4

Learning Objective

Explain how government policies affect the unemployment rate.

Why Does Unemployment Exist?

At equilibrium in the labor market model from Section 8.1, all workers who want jobs can find them. But then why is there unemployment? The answer is that, in reality, there are many types of *frictions* that prevent the real wage from adjusting to maintain the labor market continually at equilibrium.

Equilibrium Real Wages and Unemployment

Figure 8.11 shows a labor market with unemployment. At point A, the labor market is in equilibrium because the quantity of labor demanded and the quantity of labor supplied both equal L_1. All the workers who want jobs can find them, so there is no unemployment.

---

[8]Lawrence Katz and Alan Krueger, "The High-Pressure Labor Market of the 1990s,"*Brookings Papers on Economic Activity*, Vol. 1, 1999, pp. 1–65; and Maria Otoo, "Temporary Employment and the Natural Rate of Unemployment," *Finance and Economics Discussion Series*, Paper No. 1999-66, Washington, DC: Board of Governors of the Federal Reserve System, December 1999.

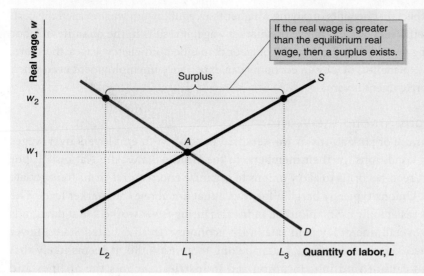

Figure 8.11

A Labor Market with Unemployment

If the real wage, w_2, is at a level above the equilibrium real wage, w_1, then the quantity of labor supplied is greater than the quantity of labor demanded. Some workers who would prefer to have a job at a real wage of w_2 cannot find one.

(In figure) If the real wage is greater than the equilibrium real wage, then a surplus exists.

However, if the real wage, w_2, is above the equilibrium real wage, w_1, the quantity of labor supplied by households, L_3, is greater than the quantity of labor demanded by firms, L_2. Because the quantity of labor employed cannot be greater than the quantity of labor demanded, L_2 also represents employment in the economy. As a result, some workers would like to have a job at the prevailing wage, w_2, but cannot find one. In other words, there is unemployment equal to $L_3 - L_2$.

Why doesn't the real wage quickly decline to restore equilibrium in the labor market and eliminate unemployment? In this section, we provide three explanations for why the real wage may remain above the equilibrium real wage for a period of time: efficiency wages, labor unions, and minimum wage laws.

Efficiency Wages

Some firms can ensure that workers work hard by supervising them. For example, a telemarketing firm can monitor workers electronically to ensure that they make the required number of phone calls per hour. Most firms, however, must rely on workers being motivated to work hard. Therefore, some firms voluntarily pay an **efficiency wage**, which is a higher-than-market wage that a firm pays to motivate workers to be more productive and to increase profits. If you receive an efficiency wage that is more than you would earn at your next best alternative job, you are less likely to take actions that will get you fired. For example, you are more likely to show up on time, take only necessary sick days, and work harder when you are at the job.

An efficiency wage also makes workers less likely to switch jobs because most alternative jobs will pay only the market wage. When a worker quits a job, the firm incurs the cost of finding and training a new worker. If that cost is high enough, the efficiency wage may actually increase profits. Firms may also pay efficiency wages to improve the quality of their workers. If wages are currently above the equilibrium real wage and a firm *reduces* its wage, some of the best workers are likely to quit and work for competitors that are paying higher wages.

Efficiency wage
A higher-than-market wage that a firm pays to motivate workers to be more productive and to increase profits.

Firms expect that benefits of paying a higher than equilibrium wage exceed the cost. Because the efficiency wage is above the market wage, it results in the quantity of labor supplied being greater than the quantity of labor demanded. Efficiency wages, therefore, provide one explanation of why an economy can experience unemployment even when cyclical unemployment is zero.

Labor Unions Around the World

Labor unions are organizations of workers that bargain with employers over wages and working conditions for their members. In the United States, the National Labor Relations Act requires firms to allow unions to organize and requires firms to negotiate with unions. Unions typically bargain for wages that are above the market level. The higher wages result in firms in unionized industries hiring fewer workers. But do unions increase the overall unemployment rate in the economy? In the United States, fewer than 7% of workers in the private sector belong to a union. So, it seems likely that workers who cannot find jobs in unionized industries, such as the airlines and telecommunications industries, can find jobs in other industries.

In the United States, unionization rates are much higher in the public sector, where more than 36% of workers are members of unions. In 2011, as state and local governments attempted to deal with budget deficits, some economists and policymakers argued that public-sector unions had succeeded in bargaining for wages and benefits—particularly pension benefits—that were far above those being paid by private firms. There remained some disagreements about the extent to which this observation was correct because some government jobs do not have direct counterparts at private firms. After many years of steady increases, employment by state and local governments declined about 650,000 between August 2008 and May 2012. These job losses contributed to the high levels of unemployment during this period.

Unionization rates vary across counties, with more than two-thirds of the labor force unionized in many European countries. More than 95% of the labor force is unionized in France and Belgium. Countries in East Asia, such as Japan and South Korea, have lower unionization rates that are comparable to the unionization rate in the United States. Because labor unions contribute to keeping real wages above their equilibrium levels, the higher unionization rates in Europe have contributed to higher unemployment rates.

The relative strength of unions has declined dramatically in recent years in many countries due to increased competition arising from globalization and the slow growth in the demand for labor in goods-producing industries, where unions tend to be concentrated.

Minimum Wage Laws

A *minimum wage* is a legal minimum hourly wage rate that employers are required to pay employees. The federal government has had a national minimum wage law since 1938. In 2012, the federal minimum wage was $7.25 per hour. Some state and local governments also impose minimum wages. For example, in 2012, the minimum wage in the state of California was $8.00 per hour, while the minimum wage in the city of San Francisco was $10.24.

If the minimum wage is set above the market wage determined by the demand and supply of labor, the quantity of labor supplied will be greater than the quantity of labor demanded. As a result, some workers will be unemployed who would have been employed if there had been no minimum wage. However, while the nominal national minimum wage increased from $0.25 per hour in 1938 to $7.25 per hour in 2012, the real minimum wage has not steadily increased. Measured in 2012 dollars, the real minimum wage rose from $3.99 per hour in 1938 to $10.35 per hour in 1968, before declining to $7.25 per hour in 2012, as the average price level rose more than did the nominal minimum wage.

How much does the federal minimum wage increase unemployment? In 2011, just 5.2% of workers received the federal minimum wage. By itself, this low percentage suggests that the federal minimum wage may not have an important effect on the overall unemployment rate. However, the minimum wage may significantly increase the unemployment rate for certain groups of low-skilled workers. For example, during 2011, 11.1% of workers without a high school degree earned the minimum wage, while just 2.2% of workers with a bachelor's degree or higher earned the minimum wage. Minimum wage workers are also primarily young workers. For workers under age 25, 13.1% earned the minimum wage, but just 3.2% of workers age 25 and older earned the minimum wage. So, minimum wage laws may have important effects on younger, less educated workers. But because teenagers and other workers receiving the minimum wage are a relatively small part of the labor force, most economists believe that, at its present level, the effect of the minimum wage on the unemployment rate in the United States is fairly small.

Answering the Key Question

Continued from page 260

At the beginning of the chapter, we asked:

"Has the natural rate of unemployment increased?"

There was a very large increase in the unemployment rate during the 2007–2009 recession. High unemployment rates persisted for several years after the official end of the recession. There are a number of explanations for these high unemployment rates. Several extensions of unemployment benefits reduced the incentive of unemployed workers to accept job offers. Being unemployed can act as a negative signal of worker quality, which makes it more difficult for unemployed workers who do want jobs to find them. In addition, the skill level of workers can deteriorate as they remain unemployed. The long duration of unemployment for many workers is certainly consistent with an increase in the natural rate of unemployment. Much of the increase in the unemployment rate was probably due to cyclical factors, however. While many firms, especially in some manufacturing industries, have trouble finding workers, the number of unemployed workers far exceeds the number of job openings. As a result, it is likely that a majority of the increase in unemployment was due to cyclical factors rather than to an increase in the natural rate of unemployment.

Key Terms and Problems

Key Terms

Cyclical unemployment, p. 271

Efficiency wage, p. 285

Frictional unemployment, p. 269

Marginal product of labor (*MPL*), p. 262

Natural rate of unemployment, p. 271

Structural unemployment, p. 270

Unemployment insurance, p. 270

8.1 The Labor Market

Use the model of demand and supply for labor to explain how wages and employment are determined.

Review Questions

1.1 Why is the demand curve for labor downward sloping?

1.2 How do the income and the substitution effects determine the slope of the labor supply curve?

1.3 What variables shift the labor demand curve? What variables shift the labor supply curve?

Problems and Applications

1.4 [**Related to** Solved Problem 8.1 **on page 267**] Draw a graph of the aggregate labor market in equilibrium and then consider each of the following situations. In each case, indicate whether the demand for labor, the supply of labor, or both will shift, and indicate what will happen to the equilibrium real wage and the equilibrium quantity of labor.

a. A technological change occurs that increases the productivity of all workers.

b. The government increases income tax rates.

c. Worker preferences change so that the workers prefer consumption of market goods to consumption of leisure.

d. The government reduces payroll taxes that firms pay when they hire workers.

1.5 According to Claudia Goldin of Harvard University, in the United States prior to 1940, most married women who worked had limited education and came from lower-income families. She argues, "Their decisions were made as secondary workers and their market work evaporated when family incomes rose sufficiently."

a. Discuss the likely relative sizes of the income and substitution effects for women during these years.

b. Given your answer to part (a), discuss the shape of the labor supply curve for women during these years.

Source: Claudia Goldin, "The Quiet Revolution That Transformed Women's Employment, Education, and Family," *American Economic Review, Papers and Proceedings*, Vol. 96, No. 2, May 2006, pp. 1–21.

1.6 Suppose that workers become concerned about the future and therefore wish to increase their hours of work relative to leisure. At the same time, there is an increase in the capital stock, which makes workers more productive.

a. Draw a graph of the labor market, showing the effect of these changes.

b. Can you predict the effect on the equilibrium quantity of labor? On the real wage?

1.7 In countries with declining populations, governments have begun to offer income subsidies for families with children. What effect is such a subsidy likely to have on the labor market, all other things being equal? Support your answer with a graph.

1.8 Discussing job openings during the recession, Cheryl Peterson, a director of the American Nurses Association, was quoted as saying: "Until the downturn, it was easy for [nurses] to find employment. . . . Now it is a little more difficult because the number of job openings has fallen and we have more retired nurses . . . coming back."

a. Why might retired nurses reenter the job market during a recession?

b. Use a graph to explain what is happening in the labor market for nurses.

Source: Louis Uchitelle, "Despite Recession, High Demand for Skilled Labor," *New York Times*, June 23, 2009.

1.9 Consider the following statement: "Increases in the capital stock are harmful to workers because the increases are the result of firms substituting capital for labor, thus reducing overall employment." Do you agree with this statement? Briefly explain.

1.10 The graph below shows the labor market. The initial equilibrium is at point A. The new equilibrium is at point B.

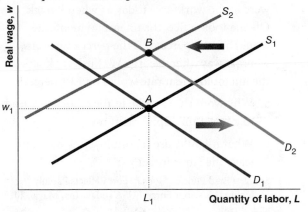

a. What factors could have caused the shifts shown on the graph?

b. Show the new equilibrium real wage and quantity of labor on the graph. Did the real wage and employment increase or decrease?

c. How would your answer to part (b) change if the size of the labor demand shift had been greater than the size of the labor supply shift?

8.2 **Categories of Unemployment**
Define unemployment and explain the three categories of unemployment.

Review Questions

2.1 When the economy is at full employment, are all workers employed? Briefly explain.

2.2 Briefly describe the three categories of unemployment.

2.3 What is seasonal unemployment? Why does the Bureau of Labor Statistics report unemployment rates each month that are both seasonally adjusted and not seasonally adjusted?

Problems and Applications

2.4 [Related to the Making the Connection on page 272] Structural unemployment can result from the development of new products that replace old products. A classic example is typewriters being replaced by personal computers.

a. How might technological change cause structural unemployment?

b. Would you expect a similar effect on unemployment when companies develop new flavors of soft drinks or new styles of clothing?

2.5 For each of the following examples, identify the category of unemployment.

a. Marty has been laid off from her job at an aircraft plant but expects to be recalled when the economy starts expanding.

b. Jada has just graduated from college and hasn't found a job yet.

c. Kishore works as a lobster man in Maine in the summer, but the industry shuts down in the winter.

d. Doug worked in an automobile plant in Michigan, but the plant was shut down permanently.

2.6 Suppose that the government wants to reduce the rate of frictional unemployment.

a. What types of measures might target frictional unemployment?

b. There is some evidence that frictional unemployment has decreased over the past two decades. What might explain this decrease?

2.7 Suppose that the government wants to reduce the rate of structural unemployment.

a. What types of measures might target structural unemployment?

b. Do measures such as the extension of unemployment insurance in industries affected by technological change tend to increase or decrease structural unemployment? Briefly explain.

2.8 Consider the following statement: "Because there will always be frictional and structural unemployment, there is no reason for government policymakers to be concerned about them. They should only be concerned about cyclical unemployment." Do you agree with this statement? Briefly explain.

2.9 [Related to the Chapter Opener on page 260] In April 2012, the unemployment rate fell from 8.2% to 8.1%, but the number of people in the labor force decreased by 342,000. Recent declines in the labor force have had a large effect on the unemployment rate. An article on USAToday.com noted that: "If the same percentage of adults were in the workforce today as when Barack Obama took office, the unemployment rate would be 11.1 percent. If the percentage was where it was when George W. Bush took office, the unemployment rate would be 13.1 percent."

a. Why would a decrease in the labor force lead to a lower unemployment rate?

b. What might cause unemployed workers to leave the labor force?

Sources: Brad Plumer, "Jobs Report Reflects Rapidly Shrinking U.S. Labor Force," USAToday.com, May 6, 2012; and Bureau of Labor Statistics.

8.3 The Natural Rate of Unemployment
Explain the natural rate of unemployment.

Review Questions

3.1 Define the natural rate of unemployment in terms of flows into and out of the labor market. Write the equation that expresses the natural rate of unemployment in terms of these flows.

3.2 What factors can cause the natural rate of unemployment to change?

Problems and Applications

3.3 Suppose that the rate of job separation is 2% and the job-finding rate is 18%.

a. What is the natural rate of unemployment?

b. If the job-finding rate doubles, what is the new natural rate of unemployment?

c. Return to the original scenario. If the rate of job separation is cut in half, what is the new natural rate of unemployment?

d. Which has a larger effect: a doubling of the job-finding rate or a halving of the job-separation rate? Does your result have any implications for government policy? Briefly explain.

3.4 Briefly explain the effect of each of the following factors on the natural rate of unemployment:

a. There is an increase in the rate of technological change.

b. The percentage of wages replaced by unemployment benefits is increased.

c. Improvements in information technology speed the matching of jobs and workers.

d. There is a recession.

3.5 The CBO estimated that the natural rate of unemployment was 6.2% in 1979 and 5.0% in 2001. If you examine Figure 8.10 on page 279 carefully, you can see that the natural rate remained relatively constant during the 1980s and then fell more rapidly during the 1990s.

a. Considering only the frictional component of the natural rate of unemployment, what might explain this change?

b. Productivity growth was slow during the 1980s. One theory about this slow growth was that innovations in computer technology were not increasing productivity in ways that were directly measurable. Productivity growth

---

increased in the 1990s, and at the same time, the natural rate fell. Does this fact suggest anything about structural unemployment in the 1980s and 1990s?

3.6 Increases in the generosity (percentage of wages replaced) and duration of unemployment benefits can be associated with increases in the natural rate of unemployment. Why do governments provide unemployment benefits if doing so might increase unemployment rates?

3.7 Demographic studies show that the Hispanic population of the United States is increasing. Traditionally, Hispanics have had higher-than-average rates of unemployment. However, it is also true that Hispanic women tend to have lower labor force participation rates (in other words, are less likely to enter the labor force) than women of other ethnic groups. How would these demographic trends be likely to affect the natural rate of unemployment?

3.8 In an article about the effect of the 2007–2009 recession on the labor market, Bloomberg.com quotes Lawrence Mishel, president of the Economic Policy Institute in Washington, as saying: "People tend to think that when you come out of a recession you get the labor market you had when you entered it. This time you may get something quite different." Why might a prolonged recession cause changes in the natural rate of unemployment?

Source: Matthew Benjamin and Rich Miller, "'Great' Recession Will Redefine Unemployment as Jobs Vanish," Bloomberg.com, May 3, 2009.

3.9 [Related to Solved Problem 8.3 on page 276] The employment–population ratio measures the percentage of the working-age population that is employed. The employment–population ratio declined by 5 percentage points during the 2007–2009 recession and increased only slightly during the following three years. By contrast, the unemployment rate declined by 2 percentage points between 2009 and 2012. Briefly discuss the pros and cons of using the employment–population ratio rather than the unemployment rate to evaluate the state of the labor market.

3.10 [Related to the Making the Connection on page 282] Some European companies have U.S. subsidiaries, and the labor practices they employ in the United States may be very different from those they employ in Europe. *Bloomberg Businessweek* reports: "With more than 5 million Americans now employed by foreign-owned companies, U.S. labor unions are starting to export their grievances." If U.S. unions are successful in getting these companies to follow European practices, what would you expect to see happen to the natural rate of employment in the United States?

Source: Carol Matlack, "U.S. Labor Takes Its Case to European Bosses," *Bloomberg Businessweek*, January 22, 2010.

8.4 | Why Does Unemployment Exist?
Explain how government policies affect the unemployment rate.

Review Questions

4.1 How does a real wage above the equilibrium wage cause unemployment?

4.2 Briefly explain the reasons the real wage may remain above the equilibrium wage for a period of time.

Problems and Applications

4.3 Suppose the equations for the demand and supply of labor are given by:

$$L_D = 100 - 2w$$
$$L_S = 10 + 3w,$$

where w is the real wage and L_D and L_S are the quantity of labor demanded and supplied, respectively.

a. Solve for the equilibrium wage and the quantity of employment and graph your results.

b. Assume that the government imposes a $20 minimum wage. Find the new quantity of labor demanded and supplied.

c. How many people lose their jobs because of the new minimum wage? How many workers are now unemployed?

4.4 In 1914, Ford Motor Company doubled its wage to $5 per day, a rate that was considerably above the average wage at that time.

a. In terms of efficiency wages, explain why Ford would have had an incentive to use this wage policy.

b. What data would you need to determine whether Ford's wage increase was successful in achieving its goals?

4.5 Some craft unions, such as electricians, restrict the number of workers who can join the union and then negotiate with employers to hire only union workers. Use a demand and supply graph to illustrate the effect of a craft union on employment and wages in an industry.

4.6 Unemployment in the labor market is increased by forces that keep wages from falling to the equilibrium level. Other than efficiency wages, unionism, and minimum wages, what other factors might cause this wage stickiness?

Data Exercises

D8.1: [Related to Macro Data feature **on page 271**]
The CIA *World Factbook* (https://www.cia.gov/library/publications/the-world-factbook/) gives for most countries the sectoral composition of GDP, that is, how production is divided up among agriculture, industry, and services.

a. Examine the sectoral compositions for France, Germany, the United Kingdom, and Japan. Are they similar to or different from those of the United States?

b. Examine the sectoral compositions for China, India, Bangladesh, and Kenya. How do these sectoral compositions compare to those you found in part (a)?

c. What implications might the different sectoral compositions have for natural rates of unemployment?

D8.2: Under the World Bank's Labor and Social Protection data bank (see data.worldbank.org/topic/labor-and-social-protection), there is information on long-term unemployment by country.

a. In which of the following countries: the United States, France, Germany, Spain, and Italy, is the percentage of long-term unemployed individuals (as a percentage of total unemployed individuals) the highest? The lowest?

b. Can you relate the differences in the duration of unemployment to differences in labor markets in these countries?

D8.3: Using data from the St. Louis Federal Reserve (FRED) (http://research.stlouisfed.org/fred2/), analyze unemployment rates.

a. Download monthly data on the unemployment rate (UNRATE) from 2002 to the present. What was the average rate of unemployment for the 2002–2006 period?

b. What has been the average rate of unemployment from 2007 to the present?

c. At this time, does it appear that the labor market has recovered from the 2007–2009 recession?

d. Twice a year the Fed releases its *Monetary Policy Report to the Congress* (http://www.federalreserve.gov/monetarypolicy/mpr_default.htm). Search the report for the Fed's forecast for the unemployment rate. How long does the Fed expect it will take for the unemployment rate to return to the average rate for the 2002–2006 period?

D8.4: Using data from the St. Louis Federal Reserve (FRED) (http://research.stlouisfed.org/fred2/), analyze the duration of unemployment.

a. For the period from 1948 to the present, download monthly data on the percent of unemployed who are unemployed for less than 5 weeks (LNS13008397), 5 to 14 weeks (LNS13025701), 15 to 26 weeks (LNS13025702) and 27 weeks or more (LNS13025703). Chart the data series on a graph.

b. The three most severe U.S. recessions since World War II occurred from November 1973 to March 1975, July 1981 to November 1982, and December 2007 to June 2009. Based on your graph, which of the three recessions was the most severe? Briefly explain.

c. Some economists argue that structural unemployment and, therefore, the natural rate of unemployment increased during the 2007–2009 recession. Are the data on the duration of unemployment consistent with this view? Briefly explain.

D8.5: [Excel exercise] Using data from the St. Louis Federal Reserve (FRED) (http://research.stlouisfed.org/fred2/), analyze the unemployment rate.

a. Download monthly data on the U-3 unemployment rate (UNRATE) and the broader U-6 unemployment rate (U6RATE) from 1994 to the present. Chart the two data series in a graph.

b. Calculate the average value and the standard deviation for each data series from 1994 to the present. Which measure of the unemployment is higher on average? Which measure is more volatile as measured by its standard deviation?

c. Calculate the correlation coefficient between the U-3 and U-6 measures of the unemployment rate.

d. Are the unemployment rate data consistent with the view that the natural rate of unemployment increased after the 2007-2009 recession? Explain.

D8.6: Using data from the St. Louis Federal Reserve (FRED) (http://research.stlouisfed.org/fred2/), analyze CPI (the consumer price index) and wages.

a. Find the most recent values and the values from one year earlier from FRED for the Consumer Price Index for All Urban Consumers: All Items (CPIAUCNS) and Average Hourly Earnings of Production and Nonsupervisory Employees: Total Private (AHETPI).

b. Using the CPI data and nominal wage data (AHETPI) from above, compute the average hourly real wage for each year.

c. Over the one-year interval under examination, calculate the percentage change in the average hourly nominal wage and the average hourly real wage.

D8.7: Using data from the St. Louis Federal Reserve (FRED) (http://research.stlouisfed.org/fred2/), analyze the natural rate of unemployment.

a. Download quarterly data on the natural rate of unemployment (NROU) from 1950 to the present. Chart the data series in a graph.

b. The U-3 unemployment rate rose from 4.8% during the fourth quarter of 2007 when then 2007-2009 recession began, to 9.5% during the second quarter of 2009, when the recession ended. How much of this increase can you attribute to increases in the natural rate of unemployment?

c. Given your answer to part (b), should the government focus on policies to reduce cyclical unemployment or the natural rate of unemployment? Briefly explain.

CHAPTER 9

Business Cycles

Learning Objectives

After studying this chapter, you should be able to:

9.1 Explain the difference between the short run and the long run in macroeconomics (pages 296–301)

9.2 Understand what happens during a business cycle (pages 301–315)

9.3 Explain how economists think about business cycles (pages 315–319)

9.4 Use the aggregate demand and aggregate supply model to explain the business cycle (pages 319–324)

9.A Appendix: Derive the formula for the expenditure multiplier (page 331)

Is the Housing Cycle the Business Cycle?

You have lived through the worst economic recession the United States is likely to experience in your lifetime: the recession of 2007–2009. It was easily the worst recession since the Great Depression of the 1930s. What caused the recession? The simple answer is that it was caused by the bursting of an epic housing bubble. During the bubble, new houses were built at a record pace in many parts of the country. The prices of new and existing houses soared. With the bursting of the bubble, spending on new housing collapsed. This collapse in spending brought on a financial crisis that affected the entire economy.

The recession of 2007–2009 was particularly bad, but it was not unusual in being caused by a decline in spending on new houses. In fact, economist Edward

Leamer of the University of California at Los Angeles argues that fluctuations in spending on new residential housing are the main reason the U.S. economy experiences a business cycle. Not all economists agree with Leamer that "Housing *Is* the Business Cycle," as he titled one of his articles, but economists do agree that spending on housing plays an important role in business cycles. Housing is also a key focus of the Federal Reserve's attempts to use monetary policy to stabilize the economy. The importance of housing may not seem surprising. Clearly, houses are expensive; the largest purchase you are ever likely to make will be a house. But even at the peak of the housing bubble, spending on new houses was only about 6% of GDP.

Continued on next page

Key Issue and Question

Issue: Economies around the world experience a business cycle.

Question: Does the business cycle impose significant costs on the economy?

Answered on page 324

There are two key facts that make housing important to the business cycle: (1) Spending on housing fluctuates a lot, and (2) the prices of houses are inflexible downward (that is, people don't like to sell their house for less than they paid for it). Total spending on food and clothing is greater than total spending on houses, but spending on food and clothing increases steadily, even during a recession. In contrast, since 1960 there have been quarters when spending on residential construction has increased by more than 85% and quarters when it has fallen more than 50% on an annual basis. The swings in consumption have been much smaller.

In the markets for most goods and services, when demand declines, so do prices. But when the demand for housing declines, prices are sticky or inflexible downward. When there is a bumper crop of oranges, the price of oranges falls. When investors reduce their demand for Apple stock, the price of that stock falls. Price changes are the way in which markets adjust to remain in equilibrium with the quantity demanded equal to the quantity supplied. Following the bursting of the housing bubble, house prices did fall, but not by nearly enough to maintain equilibrium in the housing market. When prices are sticky, a fall in demand for a product results in a big decline in the quantity of the product. In fact, many economists believe that sticky prices are a key reason—some would say the main reason—that there is a business cycle.

The causes and consequences of the business cycle were not always a significant part of the study of economics. Modern macroeconomics began during the 1930s, as economists and policymakers struggled to understand why the Great Depression was so severe. It was not just the housing market that declined during those years. Over just the first two years of the Great Depression, from 1929 to 1931, the Ford Motor Company's sales declined by almost two-thirds, General Motors's sales fell by nearly one-half, and U.S. Steel's sales declined by nearly three-quarters. From the business cycle peak in 1929 to the business cycle trough in 1933, real GDP declined by 27%, real investment spending declined by an astonishing 81%, and the S&P 500 stock price index declined by 85%—the largest decline in U.S. history. Unemployment soared from less than 3% in 1929 to more than 20% in 1933, and it remained above 11% as late as 1939.

As economists studied the events of the Great Depression, they came to understand more clearly that although real GDP experiences an upward trend in the long run, it fluctuates around this trend in the short run. The business cycle refers to these short-run fluctuations in real GDP, consisting of alternating periods of expansion and recession.

The U.S. economy has experienced business cycles dating back to at least the early nineteenth century. The business cycle is not uniform: Periods of expansion are not all the same length, nor are periods of recession, but every period of expansion in U.S. history has been followed by a period of recession, and every period of recession has been followed by a period of expansion.

Economists have developed short-run macroeconomic models to analyze the business cycle. British economist John Maynard Keynes developed a particularly influential model in 1936 in response to the Great Depression. In this chapter, we begin our discussion of the macroeconomic short run.

Sources: Bureau of Economic Analysis; Edward E. Leamer, "Housing Is the Business Cycle," in *Housing, Housing Finance, and Monetary Policy*, Federal Reserve Bank of Kansas City, August 2007; David R. Weir, "A Century of U.S. Unemployment, 1890–1990," in Roger L. Ransom, Richard Sutch, and Susan B. Carter (eds.), *Research in Economic History, Vol. 14*, Westport, CT: JAI Press, 1992, Table D3, pp. 341–343; and Robert J. Shiller, *Irrational Exuberance*, Princeton, NJ: Princeton University Press, 2005, as updated at www.econ.yale.edu/~shiller/data.htm.

As we have seen, the analysis of long-run economic growth is a key part of modern macroeconomics. In this chapter, we begin to shift our focus from the long run to the short run.

9.1

Learning Objective

Explain the difference between the short run and the long run in macroeconomics.

The Short Run and the Long Run in Macroeconomics

In microeconomic analysis, economists rely heavily on the model of demand and supply. Economists usually assume that the markets they are analyzing are in equilibrium: For example, they assume that the quantity of oranges demanded equals the quantity of oranges supplied. Put another way, economists typically assume that markets *clear* because prices rise to eliminate shortages and fall to eliminate surpluses. We know that it is not literally true that all markets for goods are in equilibrium all the time. If you can't find a popular toy during the holidays or can't get a reservation at a favorite restaurant on a Saturday night or are waiting in line to buy Apple's latest electronic gadget, you know that prices do *not* adjust continuously to keep all markets cleared all the time. Still, these examples of *nonmarket clearing*, or *disequilibrium*, are exceptions to typical market behavior, and assuming that markets are in equilibrium does not distort in any significant way our usual microeconomic analysis.

Potential GDP The level of real GDP attained when firms are producing at capacity and labor is fully employed.

We made the same assumption of market clearing in analyzing long-run economic growth when we ignored the fact that unemployment sometimes exists in labor markets and that the level of real GDP does not always equal *potential GDP*. **Potential GDP** is the level of real GDP attained when firms are producing at capacity and labor is fully employed. In the long run, nominal wages and prices are flexible, so capital and labor are fully employed. Our analysis of economic growth takes the long-run perspective, so we could safely ignore the possibility that labor might be unemployed and firms might be producing below capacity. In this chapter, we shift our focus to the short run, in which nominal wages and prices are not flexible enough to maintain full employment. We begin our discussion of the short run by considering the **business cycle**, or the alternating periods of **expansion** and **recession** that the U.S. economy has experienced for more than 200 years. Two key facts about the business cycle are:

Business cycle Alternating periods of economic expansion and recession.

Expansion The period of a business cycle during which real GDP and employment are increasing.

Recession The period of a business cycle during which real GDP and employment are decreasing.

1. Unemployment rises—and employment falls—during a recession, and unemployment falls—and employment rises—during an expansion.
2. Real GDP declines during a recession, and real GDP increases during an expansion.

The Keynesian and Classical Approaches

Keynesian economics The perspective that business cycles represent disequilibrium or nonmarket-clearing behavior.

Do the movements in employment and output during the business cycle represent equilibrium, market-clearing, behavior? Or do these movements represent disequilibrium, non-market-clearing, behavior? Economists have debated these questions for many years. An early focal point in that debate was the 1936 publication of *The General Theory of Employment, Interest, and Money* by the British economist John Maynard Keynes. In that book, Keynes argued that the high levels of unemployment and low levels of output that the world economy was experiencing during the Great Depression represented disequilibrium. He labeled the perspective that the economy was always in equilibrium as *classical economics*. Economists continue to use these labels today. **Keynesian economics** refers to the perspective that business cycles represent disequilibrium or nonmarket-clearing behavior, and **classical economics** refers to the perspective that business cycles can be explained using equilibrium analysis.

Classical economics The perspective that business cycles can be explained using equilibrium analysis.

If the Keynesian view is correct, then the increase in cyclical unemployment during a recession primarily represents *involuntary unemployment*, or workers who are unable to find jobs at the current wage rate. So, the quantity of labor supplied is greater than the quantity of labor demanded. Similarly, the decline in real GDP occurs primarily because some firms would like to sell more goods or services at prevailing prices but are unable to do so. In the markets for some goods and services, the quantity supplied is greater than the quantity demanded.

If the classical view is correct, the labor market and the markets for goods and services remain in equilibrium during the business cycle. Although employment and output decline during a recession, they do so because of the voluntary decisions of households to supply less labor and firms to supply fewer goods and services.

The majority of economists believe that the essentials of the Keynesian view of the business cycle are correct, although the details of their explanations of the business cycle are significantly different from those that Keynes offered in 1936. Some economists, however, believe that the classical view is correct. The views of these economists are sometimes called the *new classical macroeconomics*, where the word *new* is used to distinguish their views from the views of economists writing before 1936.

In this and the following chapters, although we will focus on the Keynesian view, we will also keep in mind the new classical view.

Macroeconomic Shocks and Price Flexibility

The word *cycle* in the phrase *business cycle* can be misleading because it suggests that the economy follows a regular pattern of recessions and expansions of the same length and intensity, in a self-perpetuating cycle. Although decades ago some economists thought of business cycles in more or less this way, today most do not. Instead, most economists—of both the Keynesian and classical schools—see the business cycle as resulting from the response of households and firms to *macroeconomic shocks*. A **macroeconomic shock** is an unexpected exogenous event that has a significant effect on an important sector of the economy or on the economy as a whole.[1] Examples of macroeconomic shocks are a financial crisis, the collapse of a housing bubble, a significant innovation in information technology, a significant unexpected increase in oil prices, or an unexpected change in monetary policy or fiscal policy.

> **Macroeconomic shock**
> An unexpected exogenous event that has a significant effect on an important sector of the economy or on the economy as a whole.

Macroeconomic shocks require many households and firms to change their behavior. For example, the collapse of the housing bubble in the United States during 2006 reduced the demand for housing. Firms engaged in residential construction and workers employed by those firms had to adjust to the decline in demand by moving to non-residential construction or by leaving the construction industry entirely. Similarly, as use of personal computers spread during the 1980s, firms making large mainframe computers, typewriters, and other office equipment had to adjust to a decline in demand by switching to producing personal computers or by entering other industries.

One of the benefits of the market system is its flexibility. Every month in the United States, new firms open and existing firms expand their operations, creating millions of jobs, while at the same time other firms close or contract their operations, destroying millions of jobs. Generally, a market system handles well the flow of resources—labor,

---

[1]Recall that economists refer to something that is taken as given as *exogenous* and something that will be explained by the model as *endogenous* (see Chapter 1).

capital, and raw materials—from declining industries to expanding industries. The manufacturing sector has been shrinking for decades and capital and labor have had to flow from manufacturing towards industries such as banking and insurance.

A macroeconomic shock, however, requires an economy to make these adjustments quickly, so the results can be disruptive. For example, at the height of the housing bubble in the United States from 2004 to 2006, residential construction averaged more than 6% of GDP. By the end of the recession in June 2009, residential construction was only about 2.5% of GDP. That decline may sound small, but it amounted to reduced spending on new houses of over $470 *billion*. If total output and total employment in the U.S. economy were not to decline, then substantial resources, including more than 2 million workers, would have to leave the residential construction industry and find employment elsewhere—a difficult task to accomplish in a short period of time. While the economy initially adjusted smoothly to the decline in residential construction, the economy did enter a recession in December 2007, as oil prices rose and the financial crisis developed. As a result, employment and output in the U.S. economy declined substantially.

We know from microeconomic analysis that markets adjust to changes in demand and supply through changes in prices. One reason an economy may have difficulty smoothly adjusting to a macroeconomic shock is that prices and wages may not fully adjust to the effects of the shock in the short run. In fact, many economists believe that a key difference between the short run and the long run is that *in the short run nominal prices and nominal wages are "sticky," while in the long run nominal prices and nominal wages are flexible.* By "sticky," economists mean that prices and wages do not fully adjust in the short run to changes in demand or supply, while in the long run they do fully adjust.

Recall the important distinction between nominal and real variables. A nominal price is the stated price of a product, not corrected for changes in the price level, while a real price is corrected for changes in the price level. Similarly, a nominal wage is not corrected for changes in the price level, while a real wage is corrected. When we refer to price and wage stickiness, we are referring to nominal prices and wages, not real prices and wages. Economists call the slow adjustment of nominal prices and wages to shocks *nominal price and wage rigidity* or *nominal price and wage stickiness*. Keynesian economists initially focused on nominal wage stickiness because that is what Keynes emphasized in *The General Theory*. In recent years, *new Keynesian economists* have shifted the focus to nominal price stickiness.

Why Are Prices Sticky in the Short Run?

The fact that prices are often sticky in the short run is a key reason macroeconomic shocks can result in fluctuations in total employment and total output. So, understanding why prices can be sticky is an important macroeconomic issue.

Two key factors cause price stickiness. First, most firms are in *imperfectly competitive* markets. Unlike in a *perfectly competitive* market, firms in imperfectly competitive markets have some control over prices, so prices do not instantly adjust to movements in demand and supply. Therefore, one source of price stickiness is that firms that have some control over the prices they charge may decide not to reduce them following a decline in demand.

Second, there are often costs to firms from changing prices. If changing prices is costly, firms face a trade-off when demand or supply curves shift. For example, when the demand curve for a firm's product shifts to the left, a firm will benefit from cutting prices because quantity demanded does not fall by as much as it would if the firm held price constant. We would expect that a firm will lower its price following a decline in demand if the benefit to doing so would be greater than the cost. The firm will not lower its prices if the benefit would be less than the cost. The same is true following an increase in demand: If the benefit from raising the price does not exceed the cost, the firm will hold its price constant.

Why is it costly for firms to change prices? Firms such as JCPenney and IKEA print catalogues and create Web sites that list the prices of their products. If prices change, these firms must take the time and incur the cost to reprint their catalogues, update their Web sites, and change the prices marked on their store merchandise.

Customers may also be angered if a firm raises prices, as might happen, for instance, if a hardware store raised the price of snow shovels after a winter storm. Customers and firms may also agree to long-term contracts. For instance, customers of some fuel oil companies have signed contracts to buy home heating oil at a fixed price during the coming year.

In addition, before firms adjust their prices, they must determine how much demand and supply have shifted in their individual markets and how long-lived these shifts might be. For example, the manager of a hotel may realize that the economy has moved into a recession and may expect that demand for rooms in the hotel has declined. But rather than lower prices right away—and run the risk of annoying customers if she ends up quickly raising them again—the manager may want to see how much the recession affects tourism and business travel in that city. In this case, we can think of the cost of changing prices as the cost of determining how the firm should respond to a macroeconomic shock.

These various costs to firms of changing prices are called **menu costs** because one of the original examples of the expense of changing prices was the cost of printing new restaurant menus.

> **Menu costs** The costs to firms of changing prices.

How Long are Prices Sticky? Economic research has shown that most firms in Western Europe and the United States change prices just once or twice a year, with firms in the service sector typically changing prices less frequently than manufacturing firms.[2] Economists have also found that firms are more likely to change prices as a result of shocks to the firm's sector than as a result of shocks to the aggregate economy.[3] For instance, book publishers may adjust prices fairly quickly in response to changes in the cost of paper but respond more slowly to changes in the demand for books that results from the bursting of a housing bubble.

---

[2]Alan Blinder, "On Sticky Prices: Academic Theories Meet the Real World," in N. Gregory Mankiw (ed.), *Monetary Policy*, Chicago: University of Chicago Press, 1994; and Campbell Leith and Jim Malley, "A Sectoral Analysis of Price-Setting Behavior in U.S. Manufacturing Industries," *Review of Economics and Statistics*, Vol. 89, No. 2 March 2007, pp. 335–342.

[3]Jean Boivin, Marc Giannoni, and Ilian Mihov, "Sticky Prices and Monetary Policy: Evidence from Disaggregated U.S. Data," *American Economic Review*, Vol. 99, No. 1, March 2009, pp. 350–384.

Making the Connection

The Curious Case of the 5-Cent Bottle of Coke

There is price stickiness, and then there is the case of the price of a bottle of Coke. As we have seen, there are reasons firms may not fully adjust the prices of their products to changes in demand and supply in the short run. The period involved, though, is usually a year or two. After that time has passed, firms will typically have fully adjusted their prices. Over a period of decades, most firms experience many shifts in demand and supply. Despite short-run price stickiness, these shifts ought to result in the prices of the firm's products changing many times. Not so with a bottle of Coca-Cola, however. Between 1886 and 1955, the price of a standard, 6.5-ounce glass bottle of Coke remained unchanged, at 5 cents.

During this nearly 70-year period, wars, the Great Depression, the passage and repeal of a ban on selling alcoholic beverages, a tripling of the price of sugar, and changes in the technology of producing soft drinks all occurred, but Coca-Cola held the price of its most important product constant.

Coca-Cola was introduced in 1886 by an Atlanta, Georgia, druggist named John Stith Pemberton. At first, he sold it as a "patent medicine." Patent medicines were bottled liquids that their sellers claimed would cure a variety of physical ailments. Pemberton claimed that Coca-Cola acted as a nerve tonic and stimulant and could cure headaches. Although patent medicines were typically sold in large bottles for a price of $0.75 to $1.00, Pemberton came up with the idea of selling Coca-Cola in single servings for a nickel, thereby expanding the number of consumers who could afford to buy it. At first, most Coke was sold by the glass at soda fountains, drug stores, and restaurants. Following the introduction of the distinctive 6.5-ounce "hobble skirt" bottle in 1916, bottle sales, particularly through vending machines, became increasingly important.

Daniel Levy and Andrew T. Young of Emory University have provided the most careful account of why Coca-Cola kept the price of its most important product fixed for decades. Levy and Young argue that three main factors account for this extraordinary episode of price rigidity:

1. From 1899 to 1921, the firm was obligated by long-term contracts to provide its bottlers with the syrup that Coca-Cola is made from at a fixed price of $0.92 per gallon. Although Coca-Cola manufactured the syrup, the bottlers that actually produced the soft drink and distributed it for sale were independent businesses. After 1921, the price Coca-Cola charged its bottlers for syrup varied, and this no longer became an important reason for inflexibility in the retail price.
2. Vending machines could accept only a single coin and could not make change. Coca-Cola, therefore, could not adjust the price of a bottle in penny increments.
3. Coca-Cola believed that it was important that consumers be able to buy the signature 6.5-ounce Coke bottle using a single coin. This meant that to raise the price from a nickel, the firm would have to start charging a dime, which would be a 100% increase in price. During the 1950s, Robert Woodruff, who was then president of Coca-Cola, tried to get around this problem by urging newly elected President Eisenhower, who happened to be Woodruff's friend and hunting companion, to

have the U.S. Treasury begin issuing a 7.5-cent coin. Eisenhower forwarded the proposal to the Department of the Treasury, but the Treasury did not pursue the idea further.

Ultimately, rising costs and advances in vending machine technology led Coca-Cola to abandon its fixed-price strategy. By 1955, Coke was selling for 5, 6, 7, or even 10 cents in different parts of the country. In 1959, 6.5-ounce bottles of Coke were no longer selling for 5 cents anywhere in the United States.

The saga of the nickel Coke provides an extreme example of why a firm may consider it profitable to hold the price of a product constant, despite large swings in demand and costs.

Sources: Daniel Levy and Andrew T. Young, "'The Real Thing': Nominal Price Rigidity of the Nickel Coke, 1886–1959," *Journal of Money, Credit, and Banking*, Vol. 36, No. 4, August 2004, pp. 765–799; Richard S. Tedlow, *New and Improved: The Story of Mass Marketing in America*, New York: Basic Books, 1990; and E. J. Kahn, Jr., *The Big Drink: The Story of Coca-Cola*, New York: Random House, 1960.

See related problem 1.7 at the end of the chapter.

Nominal Wage Rigidity Firms are likely to hold their prices constant if the wages they pay are constant. For most firms, wages are their largest cost. Many firms adjust the wages or salaries they pay only once per year. Long-term labor contracts explain some nominal wage stickiness. For example, when a firm negotiates a long-term labor contract with a labor union, the contract fixes the nominal wage for the duration of the contract, which is typically several years. Even if economic conditions change, it is often difficult and costly to renegotiate long-term contracts. In addition to formal contracts, firms often arrive at *implicit contracts* with workers. An implicit contract is not a written, legally binding agreement. Instead, it is an informal arrangement a firm enters into with workers in which the firm refrains from making wage cuts during recessions in return for workers being willing to accept smaller wage increases during expansions. Firms may also refrain from cutting wages during recessions for fear that their best workers will quit to find jobs at other firms once an economic expansion improves conditions in the labor market. Firms also sometimes pay higher than equilibrium real wages known as *efficiency wages* to motivate workers to be more productive. Efficiency wage considerations can also lead firms to maintain wages during a recession. All these reasons help to explain why nominal wages are typically sticky in the short run.

What Happens During a Business Cycle?

Economists think of the business cycle as resulting from macroeconomic shocks that push real GDP away from potential GDP. For example, the United States experienced three large shocks during 2007–2009: the collapse of the housing bubble, a financial crisis that increased the cost to households and firms of obtaining loans, and a large increase in the price of imported oil. As a result of these shocks, the growth rate of real GDP decreased from 1.7% during the fourth quarter of 2007 to −8.9% during the fourth quarter of 2008.

9.2

Learning Objective
Understand what happens during a business cycle.

MyEconLab Real-time data

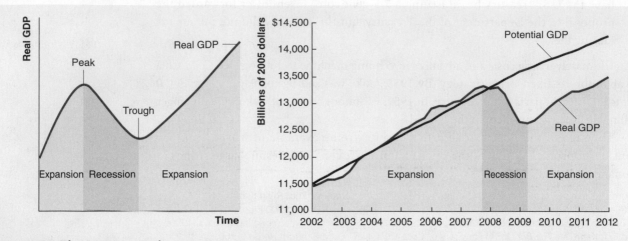

Figure 9.1 The Business Cycle

Panel (a) shows an idealized business cycle, with real GDP increasing smoothly in an expansion to a business cycle peak and then decreasing smoothly in a recession to a business cycle trough, followed by another expansion. The periods of expansion are shown in green, and the period of recession is shown in red.

Panel (b) shows the severe recession of 2007–2009, with real GDP remaining below potential GDP well into the expansion.

Sources: U.S. Bureau of Economic Analysis; Congressional Budget Office; and National Bureau of Economic Research.

The financial crisis and the increase in oil prices were global shocks that affected most countries. Among countries using the euro for their currency, the growth rate of real GDP decreased from 1.6% during the fourth quarter of 2007 to −6.8% during the fourth quarter of 2008, before falling to −10.9% during the first quarter of 2009.

Figure 9.1 illustrates the phases of the business cycle. Panel (a) shows an idealized business cycle, with real GDP increasing smoothly in an expansion to a business cycle peak and then decreasing smoothly in a recession to a business cycle trough, followed by another expansion. Panel (b) shows the period before, during, and after the recession of 2007–2009. The figure shows that a business cycle peak was reached in December 2007. The following recession was the most severe since the Great Depression of the 1930s. Panel (b) also shows the growth of potential GDP during this period. Notice that even when the economy was in a business cycle expansion after the second quarter of 2009, real GDP remained well below potential GDP.

Why do we care about the business cycle? Declining real GDP is always accompanied by declining employment. As people lose jobs, their incomes and standard of living decline. In severe recessions, the long-term unemployed can encounter severe financial hardship, even destitution. Declining GDP also increases business bankruptcies, with some entrepreneurs having a lifetime's investment in a business wiped out in a year or two. Expanding GDP, in contrast, opens up employment opportunities to millions of additional workers and makes it possible for more entrepreneurs to realize the dream of opening a business.

The Changing Severity of the U.S. Business Cycle

One way to gauge the severity of the economic fluctuations caused by a business cycle is to look at annual percentage changes, or growth rates, in real GDP. Figure 9.2 shows the annual growth rates for real GDP between 1901 and 2011. The fluctuations in real

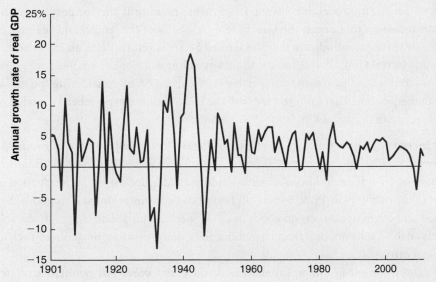

Figure 9.2

Fluctuations in Real GDP, 1901–2011

The annual growth rate of real GDP fluctuated more before 1950 than it has since 1950.

Sources: For 1901–1929: Louis D. Johnston and Samuel H. Williamson, "What Was the U.S. GDP Then?" www.measuringworth.org/usgdp, 2010; and for 1930–2011: U.S. Bureau of Economic Analysis.

GDP were clearly more severe before 1950 than after 1950. In particular, there were eight years before 1950 during which real GDP declined by 3% or more, but there were no years with such declines after 1950 until 2008 and 2009. The increased stability of real GDP after the early 1980s, as well as the mildness of the recessions of 1991–1992 and 2001, led some economists to describe the period as the *Great Moderation*. The recession that began in December 2007, though, was the most severe since the Great Depression of the 1930s, suggesting that the Great Moderation was over.

We can also see the unusual severity of the 2007–2009 recession by comparing its length to the lengths of other recent recessions. Table 9.1 shows that in the late nineteenth century, the average length of recessions was the same as the average length of expansions. During the first half of the twentieth century, the average length of expansions decreased slightly, and the average length of recessions decreased significantly. As a result, expansions were about six months longer than recessions during those years. The most striking change came after 1950, when the length of expansions greatly increased and the length of recessions decreased. In the second half of the twentieth century, expansions were more than six times as long as recessions. In other words, in the late nineteenth century, the U.S. economy spent as much time in recession as it did in expansion, but after 1950, the U.S. economy experienced long expansions interrupted by relatively short recessions.

Table 9.1 The Changing Duration of Expansions and Contractions

Period	Average length of expansions	Average length of recessions
1870–1900	26 months	26 months
1900–1950	25 months	19 months
1950–2009	62 months	11 months

Note: The World War I and World War II periods have been omitted from the computations in the table.

Source: National Bureau of Economic Research.

The recession of 2007–2009 is an exception to this experience of relatively short, mild recessions. This recession lasted 18 months, making it the longest since the 43-month recession that began the Great Depression. Does the length and severity of the 2007–2009 recession indicate that the United States is returning to an era of severe fluctuations in real GDP? A full answer to this question will not be possible for several more years. But we can gain some perspective on the question by considering the explanations that economists have offered for why the U.S. economy experienced a period of relative macroeconomic stability from 1950 to 2007:

- *The increasing importance of services and the declining importance of goods.* As services, such as medical care and investment advice, have become a much larger fraction of GDP, there has been a corresponding relative decline in the production of goods. For example, in 1929, 54% of all household consumption was on goods, but just 34% of consumption was on goods in 2011. Spending on goods, especially durable goods such as automobiles, fluctuates more than does spending on services such as medical care.

- *The establishment of unemployment insurance and other government transfer programs that provide funds to the unemployed.* Before the 1930s, programs such as unemployment insurance, which provides government payments to workers who lose their jobs, and Social Security, which provides government payments to retired and disabled workers, did not exist. These and other government programs make it possible for workers who lose their jobs during recessions to have higher incomes and, therefore, to spend more than they would otherwise spend. This additional spending may have helped to shorten recessions.

- *Active federal government policies to stabilize the economy.* Before the Great Depression of the 1930s, the federal government did not attempt to end recessions or prolong expansions. Because the Great Depression was so severe, with the unemployment rate rising to more than 20% of the labor force and real GDP declining by almost 30%, public opinion began favoring government attempts to stabilize the economy. In the years since World War II, the federal government has actively tried to use policy measures to end recessions and prolong expansions.

  Many economists believe that these government policies have played a key role in stabilizing the economy. Other economists, however, argue that activist policy has had little effect. This macroeconomic debate is an important one, so we will consider it further in later chapters when we discuss the federal government's monetary and fiscal policies.

- *The increased stability of the financial system.* The severity of the Great Depression of the 1930s was caused in part by instability in the financial system. More than 5,000 banks failed between 1929 and 1933, reducing the savings of many households and making it difficult for households and firms to obtain the credit needed to maintain their spending. In addition, a decline of more than 80% in stock prices reduced the wealth of many households and made it difficult for firms to raise funds by selling stock. Most economists believe that the return of financial instability during the 2007–2009 recession is a key reason the recession was so severe. If the United States is to return to macroeconomic stability, stability will have to return to the financial system.

How Do We Know the Economy Is in an Expansion or a Recession?

The federal government produces many statistics that make it possible to monitor the economy. But the federal government does not officially decide when a recession begins or when it ends. Instead, most economists accept the decisions of the Business Cycle Dating Committee of the National Bureau of Economic Research (NBER), a private research group located in Cambridge, Massachusetts. Nine economists on the NBER's Business Cycle Dating Committee determine the beginning and ending of recessions. Although journalists often define a recession as two consecutive quarters of declining real GDP, the NBER has a broader definition:

> A recession is a significant decline in economic activity spread across the economy, lasting more than a few months, normally visible in production, employment, real income, and other indicators. A recession begins when the economy reaches a peak of activity and ends when the economy reaches its trough. Between trough and peak, the economy is in an expansion.[4]

The Business Cycle Dating Committee declares a recession when its members conclude that there is enough evidence that a recession has started. Typically, this declaration does not occur until several months after the recession has begun. For example, in December 2008, the committee announced that a recession had begun in December 2007—a year earlier. Although the committee regards gross domestic product (GDP) and gross domestic income (GDI) as the "two most reliable comprehensive estimates of aggregate domestic production," it does not use these two data series exclusively when dating the beginning and ending of recessions. The official GDP and GDI data are available only quarterly, and the committee dates the beginning and ending of recessions to a specific month. Therefore, the committee also looks at monthly data on payroll employment, aggregate hours worked, and real personal income excluding transfer payments. The committee also considers monthly estimates of real GDP constructed by Macroeconomic Advisers, a private, nonpartisan economic research group and a second monthly real GDP series constructed by James Stock of Harvard University and Mark Watson of Princeton University, two economists on the committee.

Measuring Business Cycles

Looking at panel (b) of Figure 9.1 on page 302, you can think of actual real GDP as being composed of two parts, both of which change over time. The first part is potential GDP, and the second part is the deviation of actual real GDP from potential GDP. Economists typically use the deviation of real GDP from potential GDP as the best measure of the size of the economic fluctuations associated with a business cycle. For a particular time period, we can write:

Real GDP = Potential GDP + Deviation from potential GDP,

or:

$$Y = Y^p + (Y - Y^p),$$

where Y is real GDP, Y^p is potential GDP, and $(Y - Y^p)$ is the deviation of real GDP from its potential level.

---

[4]Business Cycle Dating Committee, National Bureau of Economic Research, September 20, 2010. www.nber.org/cycles/sept2010.html.

Solved Problem 9.2

Dating U.S. Recessions

You may have heard a recession defined as two consecutive quarters of declining real GDP. In fact, though, the NBER does not use this rule of thumb in dating recessions. According to the NBER, the U.S. economy was in a recession from March 2001 to November 2001. The following table shows the growth rate of real GDP for the United States around the time of the recession. Use the rule of thumb to date the beginning and end of the 2001 recession. Based on the rule of thumb, did the United States experience a recession in 2001? Why is there a difference between the dates using the rule of thumb and the dates from the NBER?

Quarter	Growth rate of real GDP	Quarter	Growth rate of real GDP	Quarter	Growth rate of real GDP
2000 Q1	1.1%	2001 Q1	−1.3%	2002 Q1	3.5%
2000 Q2	8.0	2001 Q2	2.6	2002 Q2	2.1
2000 Q3	0.3	2001 Q3	−1.1	2002 Q3	2.0
2000 Q4	2.4	2001 Q4	1.4	2002 Q4	0.1

Solving the Problem

Step 1 **Review the chapter material.** The problem asks you to think about dating business cycles, so you may want to review the section "How Do We Know the Economy Is in an Expansion or a Recession?" which begins on page 305.

Step 2 **Use the rule of thumb to determine if a recession occurred.** The rule of thumb states that a recession begins with two consecutive negative quarters of real GDP growth. Although economic growth slowed dramatically in 2000 from the late 1990s, the first quarter of negative real GDP growth occurs during the first quarter of 2001. However, economic growth was positive during the second quarter before becoming negative again during the third quarter. Therefore, according to the rule of thumb, there was no recession during 2001.

Step 3 **Explain why there is a difference between the rule of thumb and the NBER dates.** As noted in the text, the NBER defines a recession as "a significant decline in economic activity . . . lasting more than a few months." In determining whether a recession has occurred, the NBER looks at many data series, not just real GDP. So, it is possible, as happened during 2001, for the NBER to decide a recession has occurred even during a period when real GDP did not decline for two consecutive quarters.

See related problems 2.4 and D9.1 at the end of the chapter.

Because potential GDP grows over time, economists measure economic fluctuations as the percentage deviation of actual real GDP from potential GDP rather than the absolute dollar difference. This percentage deviation of real GDP from potential GDP is called the output gap. To obtain this measure, we divide $(Y - Y^p)$ by potential output:

Output gap The percentage deviation of actual real GDP from potential GDP.

$$\text{Output gap} = \frac{(Y - Y^p)}{Y^p}.$$

The output gap measures how fully the economy is employing its resources, such as labor, natural resources, and physical and human capital. For example, in the first quarter of 2012, real GDP was $13,491 billion, and potential GDP was $14,270 billion. Therefore, the deviation from potential GDP was $13,491 billion – $14,270 billion = –$779 billion, so the output gap was:

$$-\$779 \text{ billion} / \$14,270 \text{ billion} = -0.055 \text{ or } -5.5\%.$$

When the output gap equals zero, the economy is producing at its long-run capacity and so is producing the maximum sustainable level of goods and services. If the output gap is greater than zero, the economy is operating at a level that is greater than it can sustain in the long run. If the output gap is less than zero, the economy is operating below its capacity.

— overheating?

Figure 9.3 shows the output gap for the United States from the first quarter of 1949 to the first quarter of 2012. The shaded areas represent recessions. During a recession, real GDP declines below potential GDP, and the output gap becomes negative. Even

MyEconLab Real-time data

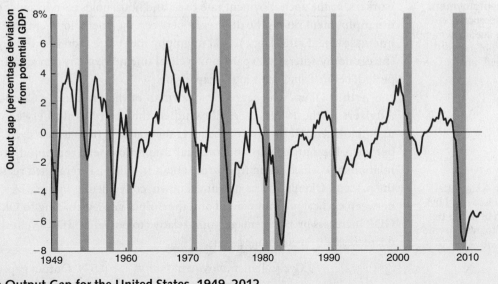
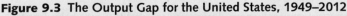

Figure 9.3 The Output Gap for the United States, 1949–2012

During a recession, real GDP declines below potential GDP, and the output gap becomes negative. Even after an expansion begins and real GDP begins to increase, real GDP typically remains below potential GDP for a considerable time, so the output gap remains negative. Eventually, as the expansion continues, real GDP will rise above

potential GDP, and the output gap will become positive. Shaded areas represent recessions.

Sources: U.S. Bureau of Economic Analysis; Congressional Budget Office; and National Bureau of Economic Research.

after an expansion begins and real GDP begins to increase, it typically remains below potential GDP for a considerable time, so the output gap remains negative. Eventually, as the expansion continues, real GDP will rise above potential GDP, and the output gap will become positive.

Costs of the Business Cycle

Should we care about the fluctuations in real GDP that occur during the business cycle? As real GDP per capita increases over time, the effects of economic growth should overwhelm the effects of the business cycle on the average person's well-being. Moreover, the business cycle results in real GDP sometimes being below potential GDP, but it also results in periods during which real GDP is above potential GDP. It might seem as if the costs of economic fluctuations will average out across the business cycle. Actually, though, economic research and simple observations of the effects of recessions on workers and firms indicate that economic fluctuations have costs—and the costs can be large. Furthermore, recent research suggests that the business cycle may affect the level of potential GDP. We discuss the costs of the business cycle in the sections that follow.

Okun's Law and Unemployment Economists and policymakers focus on two key costs of the business cycle: the lost income that occurs when real GDP is below potential GDP and the inflation that often develops when the economy is operating above potential GDP. To explain the costs of operating below potential GDP, we focus on labor markets.

When real GDP falls below potential GDP during a recession, firms lay off workers, so the unemployment rate rises, and households earn less income. The **cyclical unemployment rate** is the difference between the unemployment rate and the natural unemployment rate. The cyclical unemployment rate increases during recessions. As the economy enters an expansion, cyclical unemployment may continue to rise for a period, before falling later in the expansion.

Arthur Okun, who served as chairman of the President's Council of Economic Advisers in the 1960s, carefully studied the relationship between real GDP and unemployment. He discovered that over the course of the business cycle, the relationship between the output gap and cyclical unemployment remained fairly close. This relationship, which Okun first wrote about in 1962, has remained reasonably stable to the present. **Okun's law**, as it is now known, conveniently summarizes the relationship between cyclical unemployment and the output gap. According to Okun's law, as real GDP increases by 1 percentage point relative to potential GDP, cyclical unemployment decreases by 0.5 percentage point:

$$\text{Cyclical unemployment rate} = -0.5 \times \text{Output gap.}$$

Figure 9.4 shows the actual cyclical unemployment rate and the rate calculated using Okun's law for the period from the first quarter of 1950 to the first quarter of 2012. The figure shows that Okun's law provides a reasonable approximation of the behavior of unemployment during the business cycle.

Cyclical unemployment rate The difference between the unemployment rate and the natural unemployment rate.

Okun's law A statistical relationship discovered by Arthur Okun between the cyclical unemployment rate and the output gap.

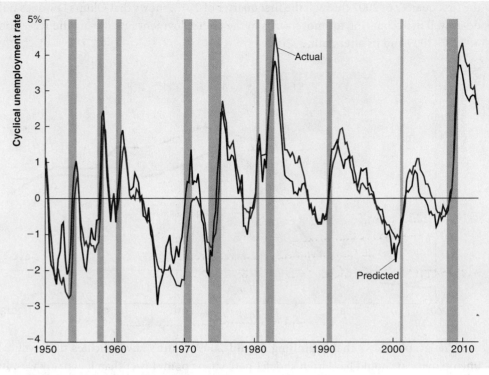

Figure 9.4

Actual and Predicted Cyclical Unemployment Rates, Based on Okun's Law

Okun's law does a good job expressing how the output gap and cyclical unemployment are related: As real GDP increases by 1 percentage point relative to potential GDP, cyclical unemployment decreases by 0.5 percentage point. Shaded areas represent recessions.

Sources: U.S. Bureau of Economic Analysis; and Congressional Budget Office.

Making the Connection

Did the 2007–2009 Recession Break Okun's Law?

During 2009 and 2010, White House economists were criticized for their inaccurate predictions of the unemployment rate. In early 2009, Christina Romer, who was then chair of the President's Council of Economic Advisers, and Jared Bernstein, economic adviser to Vice President Joe Biden, predicted that if Congress passed President Barack Obama's stimulus program of higher federal government spending and tax cuts, unemployment would peak at about 8% in the third quarter of 2009 and then decline in the following quarters. Although Congress passed the stimulus program, the unemployment rate was 9.6% in the third quarter of 2009. It rose to 9.9% in the fourth quarter of 2009 and was still at 9.6% in the fourth quarter of 2010. The unemployment rate fell below 9.0% in October 2011, but was still high at 7.8% in September 2012.

Romer and Bernstein were hardly alone in failing to forecast the severity of unemployment during and after 2009. One reason for the faulty forecasts was that until the fourth quarter of 2011 the unemployment rate was significantly higher than expected from the size of the output gap, given Okun's law. Figure 9.4 shows that for the whole period since 1950, Okun's law does a good job of accounting for movements in the unemployment rate. The graph on the next page, which covers just the period from the first quarter of 2007 through the first quarter of 2012, shows that Okun's law does not do as well in accounting for movements in the unemployment rate during the recession of 2007–2009 and its aftermath.

MyEconLab Real-time data

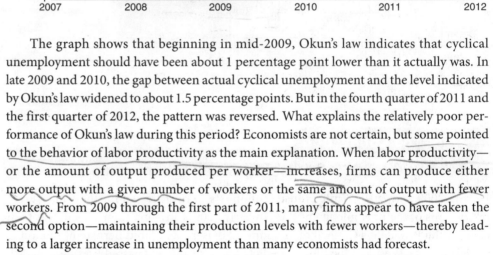

The graph shows that beginning in mid-2009, Okun's law indicates that cyclical unemployment should have been about 1 percentage point lower than it actually was. In late 2009 and 2010, the gap between actual cyclical unemployment and the level indicated by Okun's law widened to about 1.5 percentage points. But in the fourth quarter of 2011 and the first quarter of 2012, the pattern was reversed. What explains the relatively poor performance of Okun's law during this period? Economists are not certain, but some pointed to the behavior of labor productivity as the main explanation. When labor productivity—or the amount of output produced per worker—increases, firms can produce either more output with a given number of workers or the same amount of output with fewer workers. From 2009 through the first part of 2011, many firms appear to have taken the second option—maintaining their production levels with fewer workers—thereby leading to a larger increase in unemployment than many economists had forecast.

But in the fourth quarter of 2011 and the first quarter of 2012, cyclical unemployment as predicted by Okun's law was *greater* than the actual cyclical unemployment rate. Why did Okun's law shift from underpredicting the actual unemployment rate to overpredicting it? Some economists believe that because the 2007–2009 recession was so severe, many firms worried that they might be forced into bankruptcy. As a result, they took actions to cut their costs by laying off more workers than they ordinarily would have, given the extent of the decline in their sales. By late 2011, firms had become more optimistic about the economic expansion continuing and substantially increased their hiring. Okun's law also had difficulty accurately accounting for the unemployment rate following the severe recession of 1981–1982, raising the possibility that Okun's law may not be accurate during severe recessions.

Some economists argue that changes in the labor market may account for problems with Okun's law. For example, Robert Gordon of Northwestern University believes that a decline in unionization and a rise in temporary employment may have increased the willingness for firms to lay off workers in a recession. If true, these changes will make it difficult for Okun's law to accurately predict changes in unemployment during recessions.

It remains to be seen whether the strong relationship between changes in output and changes in unemployment Arthur Okun discovered 50 years ago will continue to hold.

Sources: Christina Romer and Jared Bernstein, "The Job Impact of the American Recovery and Reinvestment Plan," January 10, 2009; Mary Daly and Bart Hobjin, "Okun's Law and the Unemployment Surprise of 2009," *Federal Reserve Bank of San Francisco Economic Letter*, March 8, 2009; Robert J. Gordon, "The Demise of Okun's Law and of Procyclical Fluctuations in Conventional and Unconventional Measures of Productivity," paper presented at the NBER Summer Institute, July 21, 2010; and Jon Hilsenrath, "Piecing Together the Job-Picture Puzzle," *Wall Street Journal*, March 12, 2012.

See related problem 2.7 at the end of the chapter.

The Costs of the Business Cycle to Workers Okun's law illustrates the ebb and flow of cyclical unemployment across the business cycle. The income unemployed workers lose is one of the most important costs of the business cycle. Although cyclical unemployment falls and household incomes rise during expansions, the costs of the business cycle do not necessarily average out across the cycle for four reasons:

1. A business cycle consists of an expansion and a recession, but recessions do not necessarily have the same magnitude as expansions. As a result, real GDP may be below potential GDP more than half the time. For example, real GDP rose above potential GDP only briefly and by a small amount during the expansion that began in November 2001.

2. If workers are unemployed for long periods of time, their skills may deteriorate. In the extreme case, this deterioration can be severe enough to make some workers structurally unemployed and increase the natural rate of unemployment. Some economists believe that a prolonged period of unemployment can result in *hysteresis*, in which the natural rate of unemployment may increase for a number of years. Hysteresis may have occurred in the United States during the 1930s and in some Western European countries during the 1980s. In the case of Western Europe, an increase in unemployment initially due to recessions brought on by sharp increases in oil prices persisted for years. For example, while the unemployment rate in France averaged 3.8% during the 1970s, it averaged 9.0% during the 1990s. Similarly, while the unemployment rate in the United Kingdom averaged 4.4% during the 1970s, it averaged 10.1% during the 1980s.

3. The unemployment and lost income resulting from a recession is concentrated among low-income workers. The wages of workers with a lower level of education are affected more by high unemployment than are the wages of workers with a higher level of education. Low-income workers and workers who lack skills do particularly well during periods of low unemployment, such as the late 1990s, but much more poorly during periods of high unemployment.

4. The negative effects of recessions on workers can last many years. Economist Lisa Kahn of Yale University has studied the effects on workers of graduating from

college during a recession. Not surprisingly, Kahn found that graduating during a recession reduced a worker's wage and job prospects. However, what is surprising is that these effects lasted for up to 15 years.[5] Losing a job is not just painful for new workers. Experienced workers who lose their jobs during a recession have significantly lower incomes over their lifetimes than do workers who lose their jobs during expansions.

The Effect of the Business Cycle on Inflation Business cycles typically affect the inflation rate. As actual GDP increases relative to potential GDP, resources become fully employed, so it becomes difficult for firms to find idle labor, capital, and natural resources to produce goods and services. As a result, the prices of these inputs begin to rise, and firms try to pass along the cost increases to consumers in the form of higher prices, thereby increasing inflation. Inflation, especially high and variable inflation, makes the economy less efficient and can discourage capital accumulation due to distortions in the tax system. As a result, fluctuations in the inflation rate represent another important cost of the business cycle.

Links Between Business Cycles and Growth It is possible that business cycles affect potential GDP and have long-lasting effects on the economy as a whole. The uncertainty associated with business cycles can reduce investment spending, providing one possible link between business cycles and potential GDP. The greater the uncertainty about the future demand for a firm's product, the more difficult it is for the firm to determine whether investment in machinery or a new factory will be profitable. This uncertainty also makes it difficult for the firm to determine the size of the factory to build and the most appropriate technology to use in the factory. Because of uncertainty, the firm may choose not to pursue the investment at all. Business cycles, particularly when they are severe, can cause uncertainty about future demand. An economy with more severe business cycles experiences greater uncertainty about future demand, so it may invest less than an economy with milder business cycles.

Garey Ramey and Valerie Ramey of the University of California, San Diego, have found that average growth rates of real GDP are lower for countries with more severe business cycles, such as the Democratic Republic of the Congo, Guyana, and Zambia.[6] Gadi Barlevy of the Federal Reserve Bank of Chicago shows that eliminating business cycles would raise the growth rate of per capita consumption by 0.4% per year.[7] While this percentage may seem small, small changes in growth rates become large differences in the standard of living over time due to the power of compounding. So, an increase in the growth rate of this magnitude would have a very large effect on households' well-being in the long run.

[5]Lisa Kahn, "The Long-Term Labor Market Consequences of Graduating from College in a Bad Economy," *Labour Economics*, Vol. 17, No. 2, April 2010, pp. 303–316.

[6]Garey Ramey and Valerie Ramey, "Cross-Country Evidence on the Link Between Volatility and Growth," *American Economic Review*, Vol. 85, No. 5, December 1995, pp. 1138–1151.

[7]Gadi Barlevy, "The Cost of Business Cycles Under Endogenous Growth," *American Economic Review*, Vol. 94, No. 4, September 1994, pp. 964–990.

Movements of Economic Variables During the Business Cycle

In studying business cycles, economists are interested in movements of economic variables relative to the cycle. An economic variable is a **procyclical variable** if it moves in the same direction as real GDP and other measures of aggregate economic activity: increasing during business cycle expansions and decreasing during recessions. For example, employment, investment spending, and spending on durable goods tend to increase during expansions and decrease during recessions, so these variables are procyclical. An economic variable is a **countercyclical variable** if it moves in the opposite direction from real GDP and other measures of aggregate economic activity: decreasing during expansions and increasing during recessions. For example, the unemployment rate tends to decrease during expansions and increase during recessions, so the unemployment rate is countercyclical.

Economists also study the timing of fluctuations in economic variables relative to the timing of fluctuations in real GDP. The Conference Board, a private nonprofit economic research firm, classifies economic variables by whether the fluctuations in the variables lead, lag, or occur at the same time as fluctuations in real GDP. Table 9.2 shows the Conference Board's classification of economic variables. **Leading indicators**

Procyclical variable An economic variable that moves in the same direction as real GDP—increasing during expansions and decreasing during recessions.

Countercyclical variable An economic variable that moves in the opposite direction as real GDP—decreasing during expansions and increasing during recessions.

Leading indicators Economic variables that tend to rise and fall in advance of real GDP.

Table 9.2 Movements of Economic Variables Relative to Real GDP

Leading economic indicators

1. Average weekly hours in the manufacturing sector
2. Average weekly initial claims for unemployment insurance
3. Building permits for new private housing units
4. Interest rate spread, which is the interest rate on 10-year Treasury bonds minus the federal funds rate
5. Index of consumer expectations
6. Index of supplier deliveries
7. Manufacturers' new orders received for consumer goods and materials
8. Manufacturers' new orders received for nondefense capital goods
9. Money supply, M2
10. Stock prices of 500 common stocks

Coincident economic indicators

1. Employees on nonagricultural payrolls
2. Industrial production
3. Manufacturing and trade sales
4. Personal income minus transfer payments

Lagging economic indicators

1. Average duration of unemployment
2. Average prime interest rate charged by banks
3. Commercial and industrial loans
4. Consumer price index for services
5. Inventories-to-sales ratio in manufacturing and trade
6. Labor cost per unit of output in the manufacturing sector
7. Ratio of consumer installment credit—such as credit card balances—to personal income

Source: The Conference Board, www.conference-board.org/data/bci/index.cfm?id=2160.

are economic variables that tend to rise and fall in advance of real GDP and other measures of aggregate economic activity. For example, stock prices, such as the S&P 500, tend to peak and then decrease prior to the start of a recession. The S&P 500 peaked on March 24, 2000, a full year before the 2001 recession began, and it bottomed on September 21, 2001, two months before the recession ended. **Coincident indicators** are economic variables that tend to rise and fall at the same time as real GDP and other measures of aggregate economic activity. The coincident indicators that the Conference Board follows include most of the data series that the Business Cycle Dating Committee of the NBER relies on when determining the official beginning and ending dates of recessions. **Lagging indicators** are economic variables that tend to rise and fall after real GDP and other measures of aggregate economic activity have already risen or fallen. For example, the median duration of unemployment was 6.6 weeks at the beginning of the 2001 recession in March 2001, but it fell to 6.0 weeks in June 2001, during the middle of the recession. Therefore, unemployment duration was falling during the first months of the 2001 recession. By the end of the recession, in November 2001, the median duration of unemployment was 7.7 weeks. The duration of unemployment kept rising after the expansion began, and it peaked at 11.5 weeks in June 2003—a full 19 months after the end of the recession.

Coincident indicators
Economic variables that tend to rise and fall at the same time as real GDP.

Lagging indicators
Economic variables that tend to rise and fall after real GDP.

The Global Business Cycle

The U.S. economy is not alone in experiencing business cycles. Figure 9.5 shows the deviation of real GDP from potential GDP from 1965 to 2011 for the United States, Japan, and the European countries using the euro.

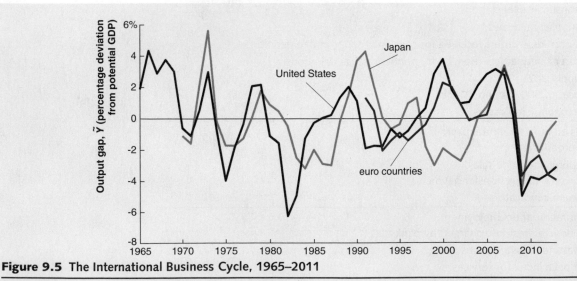

Figure 9.5 The International Business Cycle, 1965–2011

Business cycles in Japan and the United States appear synchronized from the 1970s to the mid-1980s, but during the 1990s, the relationship was not as strong. Business cycles in the euro countries and the United States appear synchronized between 1991 and 2002,

but the relationship was weaker between 2002 and 2008. Note that data for the euro countries became available starting in 1990.

Source: Organisation for Economic Co-operation and Development.

Business cycles across countries are related but not perfectly synchronized. For example, business cycles in Japan and the United States appear synchronized from the 1970s to the mid-1980s, but during the 1990s, the relationship was not as strong. Business cycles in the countries using the euro and the United States appear synchronized between 1991 and 2002, but the relationship was weaker between 2002 and 2008. From 2008 to 2011, all three areas—Japan, the United States, and countries using the euro—experienced a large decrease in real GDP relative to potential GDP due to the financial crisis.

Two key factors explain why business cycles are related across countries. First, countries trade with one another, so a downturn in one country can spread to other countries. If the United States enters a recession, then U.S. imports from Canada, Japan, and European countries decline. For example, falling incomes in the United States will reduce purchases of LED televisions from Japan and South Korea and expensive wine from France, among many other products. As a result, real GDP in those countries will decrease as well. Second, shocks, such as the oil price shocks of 1973 and 1990 and the financial market shock of 2007–2009, are often global in nature. In such cases, all countries experience a similar shock at the same time, so it is not surprising that business cycles appear to be synchronized across countries.

Shocks and Business Cycles

9.3

Learning Objective
Explain how economists think about business cycles.

The many markets that make up the economy are constantly buffeted by shocks that affect the consumption and investment decisions of households and firms. Some shocks affect many markets in the economy at once. For example, when oil prices spiked in the early 1970s, households faced higher gasoline prices, and firms faced higher fuel costs and higher costs for goods, such as plastics, that are made from oil. Households responded to this shock by reducing consumption spending on products other than gasoline, and firms reduced production as their costs rose. These reductions in spending and increases in production costs contributed to the 1973–1975 recession. Iraq's invasion of Kuwait in August 1990 caused a spike in oil prices and a drop in consumer confidence that some economists believe contributed to the 1990–1991 recession. The terrorist attacks of September 11, 2001, in the United States led to a dramatic decline in consumption for that month, which worsened the 2001 recession. Some shocks arise in financial markets. The collapse of stock prices that began in March 2000 following the end of the "dot-com bubble" contributed to the 2001 recession in the United States. Natural disasters can also act as shocks. When Hurricane Katrina struck the Gulf Coast region in 2005, it reduced consumer confidence and disrupted the availability of refined oil products in the United States, although this shock was not large enough to cause a recession.

Shocks also have effects beyond the sector that is first affected. Although the collapse in stock market prices starting in March 2000 was a financial market event, stocks are a component of household wealth, so when stock prices decline, household wealth also declines. When their wealth declines, households have fewer resources to finance consumption either today or in the future. As a result, households cut back on consumption.

When nominal wages and prices are flexible, markets absorb shocks, so the shocks do not have a large effect on real GDP. However, when nominal wages and prices are sticky, quantities in individual markets respond to these shocks. Changes in quantities reverberate through the economy because, as output changes, so does income. Changes in income can lead to changes in spending and further changes in output and employment.

Multiplier Effects

Multiplier effect A series of induced increases (or decreases) in consumption spending that results from an initial increase (or decrease) in autonomous expenditure; this effect amplifies the effect of economic shocks on real GDP.

The effects of shocks are amplified through **multiplier effects**, which refers to a series of induced increases (or decreases) in consumption spending that results from an initial increase (or decrease) in *autonomous expenditure*, which refers to spending that does not depend on income. Examples of changes in autonomous expenditure include a change in government purchases or taxes, a decline in consumer spending as a result of a decline in consumer confidence, or a decline in investment spending resulting from firms becoming more pessimistic about the future profitability of capital.

The basic idea behind the multiplier effect comes from the circular-flow diagram shown in Figure 2.1 on page 30. That diagram shows that every $1 that households spend on consumption goods generates $1 of revenues for some firm (for simplicity, we ignore spending on imports). The firm then uses that $1 to hire labor, capital, and other inputs to produce goods and services. Because households own all inputs, the $1 ultimately goes to households as income. Those households spend part of the increase in income, while using the rest of the increase to pay taxes or to save. This extra spending initiates a second round of spending and income changes in the circular flow, and so on.

Consider an example of the multiplier effect. To keep the example simple, we will ignore taxes and spending on imports. We will assume that households spend $0.90 of each additional dollar of income and save the remaining $0.10.

Suppose a shock, such as an increase in consumer confidence, causes households to increase spending on goods and services by $1 billion. This additional $1 billion in spending generates an additional $1 billion in revenues for firms. Firms hire labor, capital, and natural resources to produce goods and services, so the $1 billion in revenues generates $1 billion in income for households, who own these inputs. Households use this increase in income to purchase additional goods and services, such as appliances, furniture, and vacations, so the initial increase in expenditure generates a second round of spending. The new spending during the second round is $1 billion × 0.90 = $900 million, which, in turn, provides $900 million in additional revenues to firms and $900 million in additional income for households. These households spend 90% of this extra $900 million in income on goods and services. Therefore, there is a third round through the circular flow in which spending increases by $900 million × 0.90 = $810 million. Each time through the circular flow, the increase in income and spending gets smaller because households spend only 90% of an increase in income, saving the other 10%. So, the new income generated eventually becomes zero as the number of rounds increases. The total change in income is large, however, because additional income is generated during each round through the circular flow:

$$\text{Total income generated} = \$1 \text{ billion} + \$900 \text{ million} + \$810 \text{ million}$$
$$+ \ \$729 \text{ million} + \$656 \text{ million} + \ldots = \$10 \text{ billion}.$$

Because the change in total income equals the change in GDP, in this example, a $1 billion increase in consumption spending results in a $10 billion increase in GDP. In the appendix to this chapter, we demonstrate why the total increase in GDP in this example is $10 billion. The fact that the total income generated is greater than the initial change in household spending is the result of the multiplier effect. The **multiplier** is the change in equilibrium GDP divided by the change in autonomous expenditure. In this case the multiplier equals $10 billion/$1 billion = 10.

The multiplier is the same whether government purchases increase by $1 billion, the government cuts taxes so investment or consumption increase by $1 billion, or consumers become optimistic about the future and decide to increase spending by $1 billion.

Our example shows a multiplier of 10, but in the real world the multiplier is much smaller, partly because of the effects of taxes and expenditures on imports. Economists measure the magnitude of the business cycle relative to potential GDP, so they often measure the multiplier effect relative to potential GDP as well. In that case, we would have:

$$\left(\frac{\text{Change in autonomous expenditure}}{\text{Potential GDP}} \right) \times \text{Multiplier effect} = \left(\frac{\text{Change in real GDP}}{\text{Potential GDP}} \right).$$

Table 9.3 shows estimates of the multiplier measured in this way for the U.S. economy. The estimates, which come from an economic model that economists at the Organisation for Economic Co-operation and Development (OECD) use, allow for the possibility of income taxes and household purchases of imported goods, as well as other factors that can reduce the size of the multiplier effect.

The estimate for the multiplier in the first year is 1.1, which means a 1-percentage-point increase in expenditure as a percentage of potential GDP increases real GDP by 1.1 percentage points relative to potential GDP. Notice that the effect gets smaller over time because nominal wages and prices adjust to the shock as the economy moves from the short run to the long run. The estimates in the table show the multiplier effect resulting from an increase in government purchases, but these estimates would also apply to changes in consumption, investment, and net exports.

Multiplier The change in equilibrium GDP divided by the change in autonomous expenditure.

Table 9.3 Multiplier Estimate for the United States

Year after the expenditure increase	Increase in real GDP relative to potential GDP (as a percentage of potential GDP)
Year 1	1.1%
Year 2	1.0
Year 3	0.5
Year 4	0.2
Year 5	0.1

Source: Thomas Dalsgaard, Christophe Andre, and Peter Richardson, "Standard Shocks in the OECD Interlink Model," Organisation for Economic Co-operation and Development Working Paper 306, September 6, 2001.

The values for the multiplier in Table 9.3 are estimates based on historical data. The actual value of the multiplier may be larger or smaller, depending on the circumstances. For the multiplier effect to operate, there must be some idle resources so that firms can hire more labor, capital, and other inputs when demand increases. The further real GDP is below potential GDP, the greater the amount of idle resources and the larger the multiplier effect may be. Put another way, the worse the economy is performing, the larger the multiplier effect may be.

We can summarize our account of economic fluctuations during a business cycle with the following simple schematic:

Shock → Spending response by households and firms → Multiplier effect → Change in real GDP.

An Example of a Shock with Multiplier Effects: The Bursting of the Housing Bubble

We can illustrate the multiplier effect by looking at the effects of the bursting of the housing bubble. The Federal Reserve Board estimates that measured in 2005 dollars, the value of real estate owned by households declined by $2,330 billion from the first quarter of 2007 to the first quarter of 2008.[8] According to the Congressional Budget Office, for every $1 change in real estate wealth, consumption changes by $0.07.[9] So, the change in total consumption was:

$$- \$2,330 \text{ billion} \times 0.07 = - \$163.1 \text{ billion}.$$

This amount represents an initial reduction in expenditure in the circular flow, which then had multiplier effects. Potential GDP was $13,423 billion in 2008, so the initial change in consumption represents:

$$- \$163.1 \text{ billion} / \$13,423 \text{ billion} = - 1.2\% \text{ of potential GDP}.$$

Using the estimate of the multiplier for the first year after an expenditure shock from Table 9.3, we have:

Total change in real GDP relative to potential GDP

= Initial change in expenditure relative to potential GDP × Multiplier
= −1.2% × 1.1
= −1.3%.

Real GDP was 0.7% above its potential level in 2007, so holding everything else constant, we would have expected real GDP to fall below potential in 2008. The multipliers in Table 9.3 decrease as we move from year 1 to year 5, so the effect of the decrease in housing prices on output becomes smaller over time, as nominal wages and prices

---

[8]Calculated using the Flow of Funds Account from June 5, 2008. The data for the value of real estate owned by households come from Table B.100, line 4. Nominal values were converted to real values using the chain-type price index for real GDP.

[9]Congressional Budget Office, "Housing Wealth and Consumer Spending," January 2001. The CBO considers two estimates: a high estimate of 0.07, which we use here, and a low estimate of 0.03.

adjust to the shock and help move real GDP back to potential GDP. The estimates of the multiplier effect suggest that the collapse in housing prices would reduce real GDP relative to its potential level by the following:

$$-1.2\% \times 1.0 = -1.2\% \text{ in } 2009$$
$$-1.2\% \times 0.5 = -0.6\% \text{ in } 2010$$
$$-1.2\% \times 0.2 = -0.2\% \text{ in } 2011$$
$$-1.2\% \times 0.1 = -0.1\% \text{ in } 2012$$

Because of the multiplier effect, a reduction in housing prices may reduce real GDP for years into the future.

A Simple Model of the Business Cycle: Aggregate Demand and Aggregate Supply

To this point in the chapter, we have concentrated on what happens during business cycles and the way in which the effects of shocks are multiplied. In this section, we take a step further by introducing a simple model of how the economy adjusts to shocks. Although we present more detailed models in the following chapters, the basic *aggregate demand–aggregate supply model*, or *AD–AS model*, provides us with the tools for understanding some of the key facts about the business cycle. As we saw at the beginning of the chapter, some economists follow the Keynesian approach, which emphasizes the consequences of short-run wage and price stickiness. Other economists follow the classical approach, which holds that wage and price stickiness is unimportant, and that there are other reasons why output and employment fluctuate in response to shocks. One advantage of the *AD–AS* model is that it can be used to illustrate both approaches.

9.4

Learning Objective

Use the aggregate demand and aggregate supply model to explain the business cycle.

Aggregate Demand and Aggregate Supply: An Introduction

Figure 9.6 shows the three components of the *AD–AS* model:

1. The aggregate demand (*AD*) curve
2. The short-run aggregate supply (*SRAS*) curve
3. The long-run aggregate supply (*LRAS*) curve

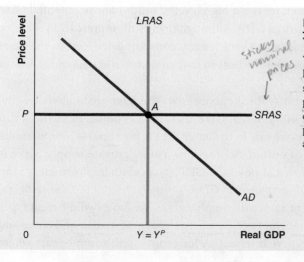

Figure 9.6

The Aggregate Demand–Aggregate Supply Model

The aggregate demand (*AD*) curve slopes downward because as the price level decreases, aggregate expenditures increase. The short-run aggregate supply (*SRAS*) curve is horizontal to reflect the view that nominal wages and prices are sticky in the short run. The long-run aggregate supply (*LRAS*) curve is vertical at potential GDP to reflect the view that nominal wages and prices are flexible in the long run. Long-run equilibrium is at point *A* where all three curves intersect.

The aggregate demand (*AD*) curve shows the relationship between the aggregate price level and the total amount of expenditure on domestically produced goods and services. As the aggregate price level falls, expenditure on domestic goods and services increases, so real GDP increases. Because the aggregate demand curve looks like the demand curve for an individual good, such as oranges, it is tempting to say that as the price level increases, the quantity demanded of real GDP decreases because goods and services are more expensive. However, this explanation for a downward-sloping demand curve works only for individual markets where we assume that total income is held constant. For the economy as a whole, as the price level rises, so do the incomes of households and firms. So, we need a macroeconomic explanation of why the aggregate demand curve is downward sloping. We provide a more complete discussion in later chapters, but at this point, we can briefly provide three reasons for the shape of the aggregate demand curve:

1. *The wealth effect.* As the price level increases, the *real value* of household wealth declines, reducing consumption.

2. *The interest rate effect.* A higher price level increases the demand for money, causing an increase in the interest rate (see Chapter 3). A higher interest rate will reduce firms' spending on investment goods and households' spending on consumer durables, such as cars and appliances, and on new houses.

3. *The international trade effect.* If the price level in the United States rises relative to the price levels in other countries, U.S. exports will become relatively more expensive and foreign imports will become relatively less expensive. So, net exports will decrease. In addition, the higher interest rate may increase demand for the U.S. dollar, increasing its exchange value. A higher value of the dollar will also cause a decline in net exports.

The short-run aggregate supply (*SRAS*) curve shows the relationship between the aggregate price level and the quantity of real GDP that firms would like to produce when the aggregate price level is constant. Earlier in the chapter, we saw that nominal wages and prices are often sticky in the short run. If we assume for simplicity that the price level is constant in the short run, then the short-run aggregate supply curve is a horizontal line. With a horizontal short-run aggregate supply curve, firms are supplying the level of output demanded, whether it is a high level of output above potential GDP or a low level of output below potential GDP. Although firms will respond to an increase in demand by supplying more goods and services at a constant price level in the short run, in the long run wages and prices will adjust so that an increase in demand results in a higher price level.

The long-run aggregate supply (*LRAS*) curve shows the relationship between the aggregate price level and the quantity of real GDP that firms produce in the long run when the price level is flexible. As we saw in earlier chapters, potential GDP represents the long-run equilibrium level of output. So, the long-run aggregate supply curve is vertical at potential GDP. Recall that at potential GDP, cyclical unemployment is zero, so potential GDP is also called *full-employment GDP*.

Because we have two different aggregate supply curves, we have two different types of equilibrium. A short-run equilibrium occurs where the aggregate demand curve and the short-run aggregate supply curve intersect. A long-run equilibrium occurs where the aggregate demand curve, the short-run aggregate supply curve, and the long-run aggregate supply curve intersect. Figure 9.6 shows the long-run equilibrium is at point A because all three curves intersect at that point. Next, we discuss factors that might cause the economy to temporarily move away from its long-run equilibrium.

Aggregate Supply Shocks and the Business Cycle

We have seen that macroeconomic shocks cause households and firms to change their behavior, which changes their expenditures, which in turn causes real GDP to change.

An *aggregate supply shock* results in a change to firms' costs of production. If a shock causes the costs of production to decrease, then the short-run aggregate supply curve shifts down. If the costs of production increase, then the short-run aggregate supply curve shifts up. For example, if oil prices increase, the cost of producing many goods and services increases. As costs rise, firms will increase their prices and the short-run aggregate supply curve will shift up. A shock that increases the costs of production is a *negative aggregate supply shock* because it results in lower real GDP and employment. A shock that decreases the costs of production is a *positive aggregate supply shock* because it results in higher real GDP and employment.

Figure 9.7 shows the effect on the economy of an increase in oil prices. The short-run aggregate supply curve shifts up from $SRAS_1$ to $SRAS_2$, and the new short-run equilibrium is at point B. The increase in oil prices has caused real GDP, Y_2, to fall below potential GDP, Y^P, so the economy is in a recession.

The decrease in real GDP from Y^P to Y_2 causes the cyclical unemployment rate to rise. Eventually, higher unemployment puts downward pressure on nominal wages, which reduces the costs of production for firms. The price level will fall, and the $SRAS$ curve will shift down. As the price level falls, real GDP increases toward potential GDP. The recession ends when the price level has fallen from P_2 back to P_1 and the economy is back in long-run equilibrium at point A. The recession ends without any intervention by the government. Therefore, economists believe that the economy has an *automatic mechanism* that causes real GDP to return to potential GDP in the long run.

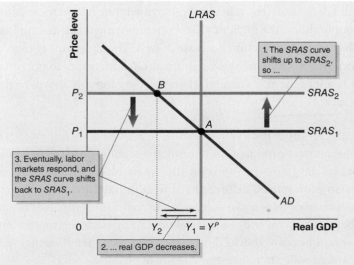

Figure 9.7

Negative Aggregate Supply Shock

Shocks that initially increase the costs of production, such as an increase in oil prices, cause the short-run aggregate supply curve to shift up, and short-run equilibrium moves from point A to point B. In the short run, real GDP decreases, and the cyclical unemployment rate increases, so these shocks are called *negative aggregate supply shocks*. Eventually, falling wages causes the short-run aggregate supply curve to shift back from $SRAS_2$ to $SRAS_1$ and the economy returns to long-run equilibrium at point A.

Figure 9.8

Negative Aggregate Demand Shock

A negative aggregate demand shock causes the aggregate demand curve to shift from AD_1 to AD_2. The new short-run equilibrium is at point B. Eventually, wages fall and the short-run aggregate supply curve shifts down from $SRAS_1$ to $SRAS_2$, bringing the economy back to long-run equilibrium at point C.

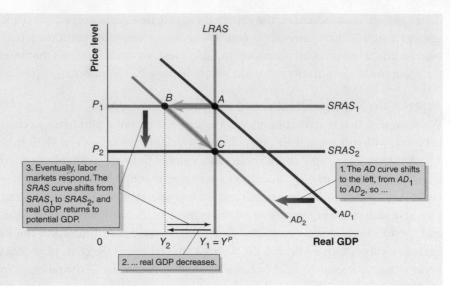

Aggregate Demand Shocks and the Business Cycle

An *aggregate demand shock* causes the aggregate demand curve to shift. For example, suppose that firms become more uncertain about the future state of the economy. Fearing that their profits may be lower than they had previously believed, firms become less willing to purchase new capital goods and build new factories, so investment spending decreases and the aggregate demand curve shifts to the left. A shock that reduces expenditure is called a *negative aggregate demand shock*, and a shock that increases expenditure is called a *positive aggregate demand shock*.

Figure 9.8 uses the *AD–AS* model to analyze the effect of a decline in investment spending. The aggregate demand curve shifts to the left, from AD_1 to AD_2. The new short-run equilibrium occurs at point B, where the new aggregate demand curve intersects the initial short-run aggregate supply curve. At point B, real GDP, Y_2, is below potential GDP, Y^P, so the increase in uncertainty has caused a recession.

Because real GDP has decreased, the cyclical unemployment rate has increased. Just as with an aggregate supply shock, the higher cyclical unemployment causes nominal wages to decrease, so the costs of production decrease as well. The short-run aggregate supply curve shifts down, from $SRAS_1$ to $SRAS_2$, and real GDP increases to potential GDP. Once again, as a result of the automatic mechanism, the economy moves to the new long-run equilibrium at point C.

Should Policy Try to Offset Shocks?

How long does it take the automatic mechanism to bring the economy back to potential GDP following a shock? Economists are split on this question. Most economists, including new Keynesian economists, believe that the automatic mechanism acts relatively slowly because nominal wages and prices are sticky in the short run. As a result, real GDP can remain below potential and the cyclical unemployment rate can remain positive for years following a negative shock. If this view is correct, then it strengthens the argument for government policy to reduce the severity of business cycles.

However, classical economists believe that nominal wages and prices respond quickly to shocks, so the automatic mechanism will keep real GDP close to potential GDP most of the time. Classical economists believe that fluctuations in real GDP are actually movements in potential GDP rather than movements in real GDP relative to potential GDP. In other words, classical economists believe that most shocks, such as changes in labor productivity, represent movements in the long-run aggregate supply curve. These shocks cause fluctuations in potential GDP to occur while nominal wages and prices quickly adjust to keep real GDP equal to potential GDP. In the classical view, attempts by the government to reduce the severity of business cycles are unnecessary because households and firms are responding optimally to the shock. Under these circumstances, policy is likely to make households and firms worse off rather than better off.

Making the Connection

How Important Is Housing in the Business Cycle?

We have seen that a demand shock can arise from an unexpected decline in any type of spending. In practice, though, most recessions in the United States since World War II have begun with a decline in residential construction. As we noted in the chapter opener, Edward Leamer of the University of California at Los Angeles has gone so far as to argue that "housing is the business cycle," meaning that declines in residential construction are the most important reason for the declines in aggregate demand that lead to recessions. The shaded periods in the graph below represent recessions. The graph shows that spending on residential construction has declined prior to every recession since 1955.

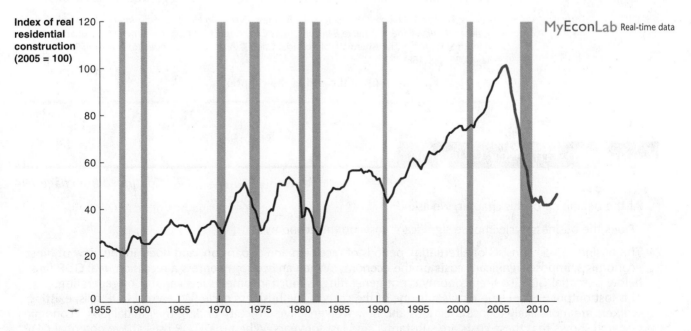

The figure shows again a fact that we noted earlier in the chapter: The decline in residential construction during the 2007–2009 recession was particularly severe.

Spending on residential construction declined by almost 60% from the fourth quarter of 2005 to the second quarter of 2010. Largely because of these problems in the housing sector, the decline in real GDP during the recession of 2007–2009 was larger than during any other recession since the Great Depression of the 1930s.

Notice that residential construction begins to decline *before* a recession begins, so the decline in construction is not primarily due to falling incomes resulting from the recession. The one exception since 1955 is the recession of 2001, which was caused by the collapse of the dot-com stock bubble. In Leamer's words: "Housing provides an extremely accurate alarm of oncoming recessions."

What causes declines in spending on residential construction, and why was the decline that preceded the 2007–2009 recession so severe? Late in a business cycle expansion, the inflation rate and interest rates start to increase. Higher interest rates often result from monetary policy actions as the Federal Reserve tries to slow down the economy and reduce the rate of inflation (see Chapter 12). Higher interest rates reduce consumer demand for new houses by increasing the cost of loans.

But the collapse in residential construction prior to and during the recession of 2007–2009 was due more to the deflating of the housing bubble of 2002–2005 and to the financial crisis that began in 2007 than to higher interest rates. Research by Carmen M. Reinhart and Kenneth S. Rogoff of Harvard University shows that declines in aggregate demand that result from financial crises tend to be larger and more long lasting than declines due to other factors. This analysis is borne out by the fact that only in mid-2012 did the U.S. housing market show signs of a significant recovery. Many economists argued that the slow recovery of the housing market helped account for the slow growth in the overall economy. For instance, in the second quarter of 2012, real GDP grew by only 1.3% on an annual basis, far below its long-run annual growth rate of about 3%.

Sources: Edward E. Leamer, "Housing Is the Business Cycle," in *Housing, Housing Finance, and Monetary Policy*, Federal Reserve Bank of Kansas City, August 2007; and Carmen M. Reinhart and Kenneth S. Rogoff, "The Aftermath of Financial Crises," *American Economic Review*, Vol. 99, No. 2, May 2009, pp. 466–472.

See related problem 4.8 at the end of the chapter.

Answering the Key Question

Continued from page 294

At the beginning of this chapter, we asked:

"Does the business cycle impose significant costs on the economy?"

The business cycle consists of alternating periods of recession and expansion, and does, in the view of most economists, impose significant costs on the economy. When an economy enters a recession, real GDP falls below potential GDP, so the economy is not generating as much income as it is capable of generating. This lost output and income represents one of the costs of the business cycle. When real GDP falls, existing workers are more likely to lose their jobs and new workers have difficulty finding their initial jobs. Economic research shows that these costs are substantial and last for years. When real GDP rises above potential GDP, inflation may rise, which can also impose significant costs on the economy. There is also some evidence that countries with severe business cycles grow more slowly over long periods of time than countries with mild business cycles. Taken together, these costs can be significant.

Key Terms and Problems

Key Terms

Business cycle, p. 296

Classical economics, p. 296

Coincident indicators, p. 314

Countercyclical variable, p. 313

Cyclical unemployment rate, p. 308

Expansion, p. 296

Keynesian economics, p. 296

Lagging indicators, p. 314

Leading indicators, p. 313

Macroeconomic shock, p. 297

Menu costs, p. 299

Multiplier, p. 317

Multiplier effect, p. 316

Okun's law, p. 308

Output gap, p. 307

Potential GDP, p. 296

Procyclical variable, p. 313

Recession, p. 296

9.1 The Short Run and the Long Run in Macroeconomics
Explain the difference between the short run and the long run in macroeconomics.

Review Questions

1.1 What is an expansion? What is a recession?

1.2 What is a macroeconomic shock? How do macroeconomic shocks relate to the business cycle?

1.3 What are sticky prices? What are two key factors that cause price stickiness? What effect might sticky prices have on an economy that has experienced a macroeconomic shock?

Problems and Applications

1.4 One possible explanation for higher natural rates of unemployment in Western Europe than the United States is stronger labor unions (see Chapter 8). Strong labor unions may also increase the severity of a business cycle by increasing wage stickiness. Draw a graph of the aggregate labor market in equilibrium. Then assume that the demand for labor decreases due to an economic downturn and that nominal wages and prices are sticky in the short run. Show the effect on the quantity of labor employed and the quantity unemployed.

1.5 Consider the following statement: "If all nominal wages and prices adjusted instantly, there would be no business cycle." Do you agree with this statement? Briefly explain.

1.6 What effect would each of the following factors have on the stickiness of nominal wages and

prices? Briefly explain whether these factors increase or decrease the severity of the business cycle.

a. Grocery stores change from stamping individual prices on products to using bar codes to scan prices into a cash register.

b. The size of the unionized manufacturing sector increases relative to the size of the nonunionized service sector.

c. More firms move to selling via the Internet rather than using printed catalogues.

1.7 [Related to the Making the Connection on page 300] An *Associated Press* article about sticky prices states: "That's what analysts call it when companies slap higher prices on products and keep them there even though the rationale for the price hikes . . . is gone."

a. Prices for goods such as cereal and toothpaste did not fall during the 2007–2009 recession. Why might these prices be sticky?

b. Prices for goods such as oil and wheat did fall during the 2007–2009 recession. Why are these prices different from the prices for goods such as cereal and toothpaste?

Source: Christopher Leonard, "Despite Threat of Recession, 'Sticky Prices' Keep Bills High," Associated Press, October 19, 2008.

MyEconLab Visit **www.myeconlab.com** to complete these exercises online and get instant feedback. Exercises that update with real-time data are marked with (W).

1.8 Economist P. Nicholas Rowe of Carleton College notes that one source of sticky prices is what he calls "sticky coordination":

> Each individual firm can adjust its price easily, but one firm's equilibrium price depends on the prices it expects other firms to set. And it is difficult for all firms to coordinate a change in all their prices. Each firm does not know whether the other firms

will change their prices, and each waits for the others to go first.

Why would one firm's equilibrium price depend on other firms' prices? How might this dependence lead to price stickiness following a negative demand shock?

Source: P. Nicholas Rowe, "Sticky Prices vs. Sticky Coordination; Inflation vs. NGDP Targeting," Worthwhile Canadian Initiative blog, March 3, 2012.

9.2 What Happens During a Business Cycle?
Understand what happens during a business cycle.

Review Questions

2.1 How is the output gap measured?

2.2 Briefly discuss the reasons for macroeconomic stability in the United States from 1950 until the start of the recession of 2007–2009.

2.3 Explain why the costs of the business cycle do not always average out over the cycle.

Problems and Applications

2.4 [Related to the Solved Problem 9.2 on page 306]

The following table shows data on the quarterly growth rate of real GDP for the U.S. economy:

Quarter	Growth rate (percentage)
1973 Q1	10.6%
1973 Q2	4.7
1973 Q3	−2.1
1973 Q4	3.9
1974 Q1	−3.5
1974 Q2	1.0
1974 Q3	−3.9
1974 Q4	−1.6
1975 Q1	−4.8
1975 Q2	3.1
1975 Q3	6.9
1975 Q4	5.3

a. Using the rule-of-thumb definition of a recession, did this economy experience any recessions during this period? Briefly explain.

b. The NBER says that a recession began during the fourth quarter of 1973 and ended during the first quarter of 1975. How does your answer in part (a) compare to the official NBER dates?

2.5 Suppose that potential GDP in a small country is $10,000 in year 1, and real GDP is also $10,000. Potential GDP grows at a rate of 3% per year.

a. Calculate potential GDP for the next six years.

b. If real GDP in year 4 is $10,500, what is the output gap?

c. If real GDP in year 6 is $11,700, what is the output gap?

2.6 Refer to problem 2.5. Use Okun's law to answer the following questions:

a. What is the cyclical rate of unemployment in year 1?

b. What is the cyclical rate of unemployment in year 4?

c. What is the cyclical rate of unemployment in year 6?

2.7 [Related to the Making the Connection on page 309] An article in the *Wall Street Journal* in 2012 noted: "Under [Okun's law], it would take growth between 4% and 5% to explain the improvements in unemployment in the past year—much more than the recovery has actually delivered." In the situation the reporter was describing, was Okun's law predicting that there would be more or less unemployment than there actually was? What factors can account for the inaccurate prediction of the unemployment rate by Okun's law during this period?

Source: Jon Hilsenrath," Piecing Together the Job-Picture Puzzle," *Wall Street Journal*, March 12, 2012.

2.8 What would each of the following tend to indicate about the state of the economy? That is, in each of these situations, is the economy likely to be headed for a recession, in a recession, headed for an expansion, or in an expansion?

    a. A sharp decline in real GDP

    b. A decrease in international trade

    c. A decrease in the unemployment rate below the natural rate

2.9 Briefly explain whether you agree with the following statement: "Large countries such as the United States, in which a relatively small portion of GDP comes from international trade, are not likely to be affected by business cycles in other countries."

2.10 In September 2012, the U.S. unemployment rate was 7.8%. If the natural rate of unemployment is assumed to be 5.5%, what is the output gap?

2.11 Discussing business cycles, an article from the Federal Reserve Bank of Dallas stated: "Volatility can also spill over into real and financial asset markets, where severe price movements can produce seemingly arbitrary redistributions of wealth."

    a. What does the article mean when it says that price movements can produce arbitrary wealth redistributions?

    b. This article was written before the 2007–2009 recession. Do you think that this recession caused arbitrary redistributions of wealth? What evidence would support your answer?

Source: Evan Koenig and Nicole Ball, "The 'Great Moderation' in Output and Unemployment Volatility: An Update," *Economic Letter*, Vol. 2, No. 9, September 2007.

9.3   Shocks and Business Cycles

Explain how economists think about business cycles.

Review Questions

3.1 What is a multiplier effect? Give an example.

3.2 Explain why macroeconomic shocks have a larger effect on real GDP when prices and wages are sticky than when prices and wages are flexible.

Problems and Applications

3.3 [Related to the Chapter Opener **on page 294**] One cause of the 2007–2009 recession was the decline in housing prices due to the bursting of the housing bubble. The housing industry is closely linked to many other markets and to the spending and saving decisions of households. Carefully explain some of the ways in which a decline in housing prices may affect the rest of the economy.

3.4 A decline in stock prices reduces household wealth and consumption spending. Estimates of U.S. stock market losses in 2008 are around $7,000 billion.

    a. It is estimated that the propensity to spend out of stock market wealth is relatively small. Assume that consumers spend $0.03 out of every additional $1 of stock market wealth. Estimate the decline in expenditure due to the fall in the stock market during 2008.

    b. Assuming that potential GDP was $13,423 billion in 2008, what effect did the loss of wealth from the stock market have on the output gap? Assume a multiplier of 1.1.

3.5 The costs of the Japanese earthquake and tsunami of March 2011 include the direct cost of cleanup and additional costs, such as the loss of revenues from seafood harvests, tourism, and related industries. Using the concept of multipliers, explain how this disaster may affect the Japanese economy as a whole.

3.6 Suppose that the following unlikely event had occurred: Because of the severity of the 2007–2009 recession, all U.S.-based automobile firms had closed.

  a. What would be the direct effect of the failure of the automobile industry?

  b. What other industries are closely connected to the automobile industry? How would these industries have been affected by the failure of the U.S. automobile firms?

  c. Would there have been other multiplier effects? If so, briefly describe them.

9.4 **A Simple Model of the Business Cycle: Aggregate Demand and Aggregate Supply**

Use the aggregate demand and aggregate supply model to explain the business cycle.

Review Questions

4.1 Explain why the short-run aggregate supply curve is horizontal but the long-run aggregate supply curve is vertical.

4.2 Explain the differences between aggregate demand shocks and aggregate supply shocks.

Problems and Applications

4.3 Draw an aggregate demand–aggregate supply graph to illustrate each of the following scenarios. Make sure to identify the short-run and long-run equilibrium points. Assume that the economy is initially in long-run equilibrium.

  a. The economy experiences a positive aggregate supply shock.

  b. The economy experiences a negative aggregate supply shock.

  c. The economy experiences a positive aggregate demand shock.

  d. The economy experiences a negative aggregate demand shock.

4.4 Suppose that the economy is initially in long-run equilibrium and unexpectedly experiences a large decrease in oil prices. In each part of the problem, draw a graph to illustrate your answer.

  a. What will initially happen to short-run aggregate supply, long-run aggregate supply, and aggregate demand?

  b. What will happen to the price level and real GDP in the short run?

  c. What will happen in the long run to short-run aggregate supply, long-run aggregate supply, and aggregate demand?

  d. What will happen in the long run to the price level and real GDP?

4.5 Suppose that the economy is initially in long-run equilibrium and unexpectedly experiences a large increase in housing prices. In each part of the problem, draw a graph to illustrate your answer.

  a. What will initially happen to short-run aggregate supply, long-run aggregate supply, and aggregate demand?

  b. What will initially happen to the price level and real GDP?

  c. What will happen in the long run to short-run aggregate supply, long-run aggregate supply, and aggregate demand?

  d. What will happen in the long run to the price level and real GDP?

4.6 Explain whether each of the following best represents an aggregate demand shock or an aggregate supply shock and whether the shock is positive or negative.

  a. The government unexpectedly doubles military spending due to a war.

b. Households become concerned about whether they will lose their jobs, so they reduce consumption and increase savings.

c. Major technological progress occurs in the market for alternative energy sources.

d. A tsunami wipes out 50% of the manufacturing capacity of an economy.

e. Stock prices unexpectedly increase by 50%.

4.7 In a blog on the *Economist* web site, correspondent Matt Yglesias makes the following statement: "[We] need to note that rising oil prices represent both demand shocks and supply shocks to the American economy." Explain how increases in oil prices could be considered both a demand shock and a supply shock to an economy. Draw a graph illustrating your answer.

Source: Matt Yglesias, "Oil: When the Supply Shocks Are Demand Shocks and the Demand Shocks Are Supply Shocks," *Economist*, February 26, 2012.

4.8 [Related to the Making the Connection **on page 323**] Edward Leamer has made the following argument:

> Don't forget that the P in GDP refers to production. . . . Thus volumes matter for real GDP accounting, not prices. . . . But what is crystal clear is that the stickiness of home prices is a big problem for home volumes.

a. Why might home prices be particularly sticky?

b. What does Leamer mean by "the stickiness of home prices is a big problem for home volumes"?

c. Is the stickiness of home prices also a problem for the economy as a whole? Briefly explain.

Source: Edward E. Leamer, "Housing Is the Business Cycle," in *Housing, Housing Finance, and Monetary Policy*, Federal Reserve Bank of Kansas City, August 2007.

Data Exercises

D9.1: [Related to the Solved Problem 9.2 **on page 306**] The National Bureau of Economic Research's (NBER's) Web site is located at www.nber.org.

a. Find the NBER listing of all business cycle peaks and troughs since 1854. Do these data support the claim that the length of recessions has declined over time?

b. Find the most recent NBER announcement of the beginning or end of a recession. Which data series does the NBER mention as being relevant to its decision?

D9.2: The Leading Economic Index (LEI) is published by the Conference Board (www.conference-board.org).

a. Go to the Conference Board's Web site and find the LEI. What does the most recent value for the index indicate about the state of the economy?

b. Are all components of the index moving in the same direction?

D9.3: The Conference Board (www.conference-board.org) publishes a Leading Economic Indicators (LEI) index for the euro zone.

a. How is this index calculated compared to the LEI for the United States?

b. What does the most recent value indicate? What effect is this value likely to have on the United States?

D9.4: Using data from the St. Louis Federal Reserve (http://research.stlouisfed.org/fred2/), analyze the relationship between the output gap and cyclical unemployment.

a. Download quarterly data on nominal GDP (GDP), nominal potential GDP (NGDPPOT), the unemployment rate (UNRATE), and the natural rate of unemployment (NROU) for the most recent quarter. Use the data to calculate the output gap.

b. Based on the GDP gap that you found in (a), what does Okun's law indicate that the value of cyclical unemployment was in the most recent quarter?

c. Calculate the cyclical unemployment rate. How well did Okun's law do at estimating this value?

D9.5: [Excel exercise] While it is preferable to use quarterly data to follow business cycles, it is often difficult to find consistent data for a broad range of countries. The International Monetary Fund's *World Economic Outlook* (http://www.imf.org/external/pubs/ft/weo/2012/01/weodata/index.aspx) has annual data on the output gap as a percentage of potential GDP for most countries from 1980 to the present.

a. Choose two countries that you think have interrelated economies (for example, the United States and Canada). Graph the data and calculate the correlation coefficient. How closely correlated are the output gaps for these countries? Do business cycles appear to be related in the two countries?

b. Repeat the steps above for two countries that you think are less likely to be closely related, such as the United States and Chile. Briefly explain how your answers here are different from your answers in part (a).

D9.6: Using data from the St. Louis Federal Reserve (http://research.stlouisfed.org/fred2/), examine the relationship between the slope of the yield curve and recessions. Many people believe that if the slope of the yield curve becomes negative then a recession is likely to start within the next twelve months. Using monthly data, we can measure the slope of the yield curve as the difference between the constant maturity 10-year Treasury rate (GS10) and the federal funds rate (FEDFUNDS).

You can find the dates of U.S. recessions from the National Bureau of Economic Research's website at: http://www.nber.org/cycles/cyclesmain.html.

a. Calculate and graph the slope of the yield curve from January 1955 to the present. How many times does the slope of the yield curve become negative.

b. How many times does a negative slope correctly predict a recession within the next twelve months?

c. How many times does a negative slope incorrectly predict a recession within the next twelve months?

d. How many times does a recession occur without the slope of the yield curve becoming negative?

e. Do you think that the slope of the yield curve is a useful predictor of a recession? Briefly explain.

D9.7: Using data from the St. Louis Federal Reserve (http://research.stlouisfed.org/fred2/), examine the relationship between financial market risk and recessions. One way to measure the degree of risk in financial markets is to look at the TED spread which is the difference between the 3-month London Interbank Offer Rate (LIBOR) (USD3MTD156N) and the 3-month U.S. Treasury bill (DGS3MO). The higher the value of the TED spread the more expensive it is for banks to borrow relative to what it costs the U.S. government to borrow which means financial markets have become riskier.

You can find the dates of U.S. recessions from the National Bureau of Economic Research's website at: http://www.nber.org/cycles/cyclesmain.html.

a. Calculate and graph the TED spread from 1986 to the present.

b. The United States experienced a severe recession from December 2007 to June 2009. What happened to the TED spread during the 2007–2009 recession? Did the TED spread begin to rise before or after the recession began?

c. How does the behavior of the TED spread during the 2007–2009 recession compare to its behavior during earlier recessions? What does this suggest about financial markets during the 2007–2009 recession?

Appendix

The Formula for the Expenditure Multiplier

We can find the total increase in real GDP resulting from an increase in autonomous expenditure by using the formula for an infinite series. Suppose that there is an initial increase of $1,000 in government purchases and that households spend $0.90 of each additional dollar of income. In each subsequent round through the circular flow, new spending is 90% of the spending from the previous round. Therefore:

Learning Objective

Derive the Formula for the Expenditure Multiplier.

$$\text{Total increase in spending} = \$1,000 + 0.9 \times \$1,000 + 0.9 \times (0.9 \times \$1,000) + \ldots$$
$$= \$1,000 + 0.9 \times \$1,000 + 0.9^2 \times \$1,000 + 0.9^3 \times \$1,000 + \ldots$$
$$= (1 + 0.9 + 0.9^2 + 0.9^3 + \ldots) \times \$1,000.$$

The expression in parentheses is an infinite series, and it equals:

$$(1 + 0.9 + 0.9^2 + 0.9^3 + \ldots) = 1/(1 - 0.9) = 10.$$

Therefore, the total change in real GDP is:

$$\text{Total increase in spending} = \text{Total increase in real GDP} = 10 \times \$1,000 = \$10,000,$$

where 10 is the value of the multiplier.

To derive a general formula for the multiplier, let f represent the fraction of income spent during each round through the circular flow (0.9 in the above example). The infinite sum m in parentheses represents the multiplier:

$$m = (1 + f + f^2 + f^3 + \ldots).$$

To solve for the value of the multiplier, multiply both sides of the equation by f to get:

$$fm = (f + f^2 + f^3 + \ldots).$$

Now, subtract fm from m to get:

$$m - fm = (1 + f + f^2 + f^3 + \ldots) - (f + f^2 + f^3 + \ldots).$$

Now, solve for m to get:

$$m = 1/(1 - f).$$

So, if $f = 0.9$, then $m = 10$. We could introduce the effects of income taxes and spending on imports into the f term, but the procedure for arriving at a value for the multiplier would not change.

CHAPTER 10

Explaining Aggregate Demand: The *IS–MP* Model

Learning Objectives

After studying this chapter, you should be able to:

10.1 Explain how the *IS* curve represents the relationship between the real interest rate and aggregate expenditure (pages 334–346)

10.2 Use the monetary policy, *MP*, curve to show how the interest rate set by the central bank helps to determine the output gap (pages 346–353)

10.3 Use the *IS–MP* model to understand why real GDP fluctuates (pages 353–363)

10.A Appendix: Use the *IS–LM* model to illustrate macroeconomic equilibrium (pages 370–379)

Fear of Falling (into a Recession)

By late 2012, the U.S. economy was three years into a recovery from the severe recession of 2007–2009. But the recovery was relatively weak, with real GDP still more than 5% below potential GDP and the unemployment rate just below 8%. Even with U.S. GDP still far from potential GDP, some economists and policymakers feared that a new recession might soon begin. Here are three headlines from articles that appeared in the *Wall Street Journal* during this time:

> "CBO Sees 2013 Recession Risk"
> "Recession, Recession, Everywhere"
> "Will World Doom Drag U.S. Back into Recession?"

Policymakers and economists feared that the U.S. economy might fall into recession for two reasons: First,

it seemed possible that the federal government would sharply raise taxes and cut spending in 2013. Second, economic problems in Europe could affect the U.S. economy. Why, though, would higher taxes, reduced government spending, or problems in Europe lead to a recession in the United States? Based on our discussion of long-run growth, we can conclude that changes in taxes or government spending will affect the mix of goods and services produced, but will leave the level of *total* production or potential GDP unaffected. Similarly, if economic problems cause Europeans to buy fewer U.S. goods and services, then *in the long run* households in the United States will buy more U.S.-produced goods and services, once again leaving total production and potential GDP unaffected.

Continued on next page

Key Issue and Question

Issue: The U.S. economy has experienced 11 recessions since the end of World War II.

Question: What explains the business cycle?

Answered on page 364

Most economists believe, though, that there is an important difference between the *short run* and the *long run* in macroeconomics. The existence of the business cycle shows that in the short run, real GDP can fall below or rise above potential GDP. As we noted in the previous chapter, British economist John Maynard Keynes began the modern analysis of the short run in macroeconomics. In a famous passage from his 1923 book *A Tract on Monetary Reform*, Keynes argued against focusing on the long run during periods of high unemployment or inflation:

> But this *long run* is a misleading guide to current affairs. *In the long run,* we are all dead. Economists set themselves too easy, too useless a task if in tempestuous seasons they can only tell us that when the storm is long past the ocean is flat again.

Keynes's macroeconomic analysis was not universally accepted when he first developed it, and it remains controversial among economists and policymakers today.

In particular, some economists argue that the economy typically adjusts smoothly to changes in taxes, declines in exports, or other short-run shocks to the economy. These economists, contrary to Keynes, argue that policymakers would be better off taking measures to promote long-run growth rather than attempting to offset short-run shocks to the economy. In fact, these economists argue that government policies contribute to fluctuations in unemployment and inflation rather than reducing them.

The severity of the recession of 2007–2009 led the federal government to take unprecedented fiscal and monetary actions. The debate over these actions highlights the differences among economists over how best to understand the business cycle. Would a sharp increase in taxes or a decline in exports to Europe, in fact, push the U.S. economy into recession? These questions are important not just to economists and policymakers but also to the owners and managers of firms and to the millions of workers whose incomes depend on the answers.

Sources: Alen Mattich, "Recession, Recession, Everywhere," *Wall Street Journal*, May 24, 2012; Damian Paletta, "CBO Sees 2013 Recession Risk," *Wall Street Journal*, May 23, 2012; John Hilsenrath, "Will World Doom Drag the U.S. Back Into Recession?" *Wall Street Journal*, May 25, 2012; Jack Ewing, "Ford's Challenges Mount in Europe," *New York Times*, April 26, 2012; and John Maynard Keynes, *A Tract on Monetary Reform*, London: Macmillan, 1923, p. 80.

We have already considered the basic facts of the business cycle. We saw that the unemployment rate and the inflation rate rise and fall during recessions and expansions. During the Great Depression of the 1930s, the most severe economic downturn in U.S. history, the unemployment rate rose above 20% and the economy experienced significant *deflation*, or declines in the price level. While the unemployment rate in the United States has never again been as high as 20%, the unemployment rate did rise above 10% during the 1981–1982 and 2007–2009 recessions. High rates of unemployment and large declines in GDP can result in severe hardships for many households and can drive firms into bankruptcy. In 2009, the U.S. economy also experienced its first deflation since the 1950s, although it was a mild decline of less than −0.5%.

In the previous chapter, we saw that the simple *AD–AS model* can help us understand the causes of the business cycle. Although aggregate supply shocks are capable of causing recessions, most economists believe that aggregate demand shocks typically cause recessions. In this chapter, we look more closely at aggregate demand. Our aim is to develop a model that can help to explain changes in the unemployment rate, real GDP, interest rates, and the inflation rate. The *IS–MP model* we develop in this chapter is a short-run model that assumes that the price level is fixed, or, equivalently, that the short-run aggregate supply curve is horizontal. In the next chapter, we complete the model by considering a longer period over which the price level adjusts to changes in aggregate demand.

Learning Objective

Explain how the *IS* curve represents the relationship between the real interest rate and aggregate expenditure.

IS–MP **model** A macroeconomic model consisting of an *IS* curve, which represents equilibrium in the goods market; an *MP* curve, which represents monetary policy; and a Phillips curve, which represents the short-run relationship between the output gap (which is the percentage difference between actual and potential real GDP) and the inflation rate.

IS curve A curve in the *IS–MP* model that shows the combination of the real interest rate and aggregate output that represents equilibrium in the market for goods and services.

MP curve A curve in the *IS–MP* model that represents Federal Reserve monetary policy.

Phillips curve A curve that represents the short-run relationship between the output gap (or the unemployment rate) and the inflation rate.

The *IS* Curve: The Relationship Between Real Interest Rates and Aggregate Expenditure

Economists' ideas about short-run macroeconomics have evolved over the years since Keynes first studied these issues in the 1930s. The most important of these ideas are captured in the **IS–MP model**, which is a macroeconomic model that economists use to analyze the determinants of real GDP, the inflation rate, the unemployment rate, and the real interest rate.[1] We can also use the *IS–MP* model to analyze the effects of *monetary policy* and *fiscal policy*. Economic forecasters who work for manufacturing firms, financial firms, and the government typically use macroeconomic models similar to the *IS–MP* model.

The *IS–MP* model consists of three parts:

1. The **IS curve**, which represents equilibrium in the market for goods and services
2. The **MP curve**, which represents Federal Reserve monetary policy
3. The **Phillips curve**, which represents the short-run relationship between the output gap (the percentage difference between real GDP and potential GDP) or the unemployment rate and the inflation rate

In this chapter, we focus on the *IS* and *MP* curves, leaving the Phillips curve for the next chapter. The interaction of the *IS* curve and the *MP* curve allows us to analyze the effect of monetary policy on equilibrium in the goods market. The *IS* and *MP* curves ultimately determine the position and shape of the aggregate demand curve. As we have seen, the aggregate demand curve and the short-run aggregate supply curve determine equilibrium real GDP and the price level in the short run.

We begin our discussion by analyzing the *IS* curve.

Equilibrium in the Goods Market

A key idea behind the *IS–MP* model is that *changes in aggregate expenditure cause changes in real GDP*. Economists define *aggregate expenditure* (*AE*), or total spending on real GDP, as the sum of:

C = consumption expenditure

I = investment expenditure on capital goods, such as factories, houses, and machinery, and changes in business inventories

G = government purchases of goods and services

NX = net exports of goods and services

or:

$$AE = C + I + G + NX.$$

The *goods market* includes trade in all final goods and services that the economy produces during a particular period of time—in other words, all goods that are included in real GDP. Equilibrium occurs in the goods market when the value of goods and services demanded—aggregate expenditure, *AE*—equals the value of goods and services produced—real GDP, *Y*. So, at equilibrium:

$$AE = Y.$$

---

[1]Economists love acronyms, even if they can sometimes be mysterious. In this case, *IS* stands for *investment and saving*, and *MP* stands for *monetary policy*.

Suppose the economy starts in equilibrium but then aggregate expenditure declines so that it is less than real GDP. In that case, total spending, or aggregate expenditure, will be less than total production, or GDP, so some goods that were produced will not be sold, and inventories of unsold goods will unexpectedly increase. For example, if in a particular month, General Motors (GM) produces and ships 250,000 cars to dealers but sells only 225,000 cars, inventories of cars on the lots of GM's dealers will rise by 25,000 cars. (Notice that because inventories are counted as part of investment, in this situation, *actual investment spending* will be greater than *planned investment spending*.) If the decline in spending is affecting not just automobiles but other goods and services as well, firms are likely to reduce production and lay off workers: Real GDP and employment will decline, and the economy will be in a recession.

If aggregate expenditure is greater than GDP, however, total spending will be greater than total production, and firms will sell more goods and services than they had expected to sell. If GM produces 250,000 cars but sells 300,000, then inventories of cars on dealers' lots will decline by 50,000 cars. (In this case, because dealers are unexpectedly drawing down inventories, actual investment spending will be less than planned investment spending.) The dealers will be likely to increase their orders from GM's factories. If sales exceed production not just for automobiles but for other goods and services as well, firms will increase production and hire more workers: Real GDP and employment will increase, and the economy will be in an expansion.

Only when aggregate expenditure equals GDP will firms sell what they expected to sell. In that case, firms will not experience unexpected changes in their inventories, and they will not have an incentive to increase or decrease production. The goods market will be in equilibrium. Table 10.1 summarizes the relationship between aggregate expenditure and GDP.

To analyze the effect of changes in aggregate expenditure on GDP, we make the simplifying assumption that of the four components of aggregate expenditure—C, I, G, and NX—changes in real GDP affect only C, consumption. To see why consumption depends on GDP, remember that when we measure the value of total production, we are at the same time measuring the value of total income. (Sales taxes and some other relatively minor items cause a difference between the value for GDP and the value for *national income*, as shown in the federal government's statistics. But this difference is not important for our analysis.)

Recall that disposable income, Y^D, equals total income (Y) plus transfer payments (TR) minus taxes (T), or:

$$Y^D = Y + TR - T.$$

Table 10.1 The Relationship Between Aggregate Expenditure and GDP

If aggregate expenditure is ...	then ...	and ...
equal to GDP	there are no unexpected changes in inventories	the goods market is in equilibrium.
less than GDP	inventories rise	GDP and employment decrease.
greater than GDP	inventories fall	GDP and employment increase.

used to buy the necessities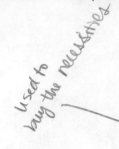

Studies have shown that households spend more when their current disposable income increases and spend less when their current disposable income decreases.[2] The relationship between current consumption spending and disposable income is called the *consumption function*. Economists often assume that only part of consumption depends on disposable income:

$$C = \overline{C} + (MPC \times Y^D),$$

where $\overline{C}$ represents consumption that does not depend on disposable income. (We use the "bar" designation over the C to indicate that this expenditure is *autonomous*, or independent of changes in income.) The amount by which consumption spending changes as disposable income changes is called the **marginal propensity to consume (*MPC*)**, which we can write as:

Marginal propensity to consume (*MPC*)
The amount by which consumption spending changes when disposable income changes.

$$MPC = \frac{\Delta C}{\Delta Y^D}.$$

measured out of a new dollar / how much will be consumed

The *MPC* has a value between 0 and 1. For instance, if the *MPC* is 0.90, then households spend \$0.90 of every additional dollar they earn. If taxes and transfer payments are constant, then a change in disposable income is the same as a change in total income, and we can also write:

$$MPC = \frac{\Delta C}{\Delta Y}.$$

Relying on the assumption that I, G, and NX don't depend on GDP, we have the following expression for aggregate expenditure, substituting in the expression above for C:

$$AE = \overline{C} + (MPC \times Y) + \overline{I} + \overline{G} + \overline{NX}.$$

Panel (a) of Figure 10.1 shows equilibrium in the goods market using a *45°-line diagram*. On the vertical axis, we measure planned aggregate expenditure. On the horizontal axis, we measure real GDP, or real total income, Y. The 45° line represents all points that are equal distances from the two axes—that is, all the points where $AE = Y$. Therefore, any point along the 45° line is potentially a point of equilibrium in the goods market. At any particular time, though, equilibrium is the point where the aggregate expenditure line crosses the 45° line. We draw the aggregate expenditure line as upward sloping because as GDP increases, consumption increases, while the other components of aggregate expenditure remain constant.

Review!!

Panel (a) of Figure 10.1 shows that equilibrium in the goods market occurs at Y_1, where the AE line crosses the 45° line. Panel (b) shows why the goods market is not in equilibrium at other levels of real GDP. For example, if real GDP is initially Y_2, aggregate expenditure is only AE_2. With spending less than production, there is an unexpected increase in inventories. Rising inventories cause firms to cut production until the goods market reaches equilibrium at Y_1. If real GDP is initially Y_3, aggregate expenditure is AE_3. With spending greater than

---

[2]Many economists believe that consumption is better explained by a household's *permanent income* than by its current income. A household's permanent income is the level of income that it expects to receive over time. A household's current income might differ from its permanent income due to a temporary job loss, an illness, winning a lottery, having a year of particularly high or low investment income, and so forth. For our analysis, we ignore this complication here. (We provide a more detailed discussion of the determinants of consumption in Chapter 16.)

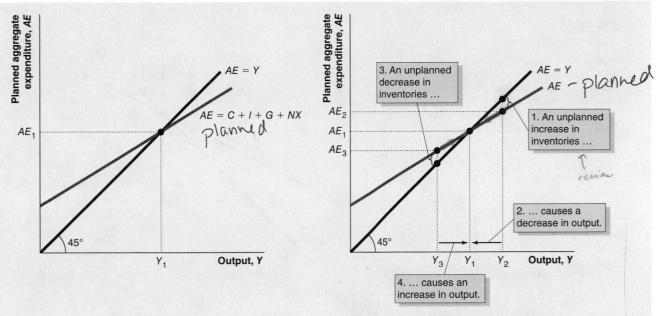

Figure 10.1 Illustrating Equilibrium in the Goods Market

Panel (a) shows that equilibrium in the goods market occurs at Y_1, where the AE line crosses the 45° line. In panel (b), if the level of real GDP is initially Y_2, aggregate expenditure is AE_2. Rising inventories cause firms to cut production, and the economy will move down the

AE line until it reaches equilibrium at Y_1. If real GDP is initially Y_3, aggregate expenditure is AE_3. Falling inventories cause firms to increase production, and the economy will move up the AE line until it reaches equilibrium at Y_1.

production, there is an unexpected decrease in inventories. Falling inventories cause firms to increase production until the goods market reaches equilibrium at Y_1.

The Multiplier Effect

How does a change in aggregate expenditure affect equilibrium real GDP? In Figure 10.2, initially equilibrium occurs at point *A*. Assume that spending on residential construction, a component of *I*, declines. As a result, the aggregate expenditure line shifts down from AE_1 to AE_2, and equilibrium is now at point *B*. Notice that the initial decrease in investment spending results in a larger decrease in equilibrium real GDP. The decrease in investment spending has had a *multiplied effect* on equilibrium real GDP. It is not only investment spending that will have this multiplied effect; any decrease in *autonomous expenditure* will shift down the aggregate expenditure function and lead to a multiplied decrease in equilibrium GDP. Autonomous expenditure does not depend on the level of GDP. In the aggregate expenditure model, investment spending, government spending, and net exports are all autonomous expenditures.

As we have seen, consumption has both an autonomous component, which does not depend on the level of GDP, and a nonautonomous—or induced—component that does depend on the level of GDP. For example, if households decide to save more of their incomes—and spend less—at every level of income, there will be an autonomous decrease in consumption spending, and the aggregate expenditure function will

Figure 10.2

The Multiplier Effect

Point *A* shows the economy initially at equilibrium with real GDP, Y_1, equal to potential GDP, Y^P. Then investment, *I*, declines. As a result, the aggregate expenditure line shifts from AE_1 to AE_2. Short-run equilibrium is now at point *B*, with a new level of real GDP, Y_2. The decline in equilibrium GDP is greater than the initial decline in investment spending that caused it.

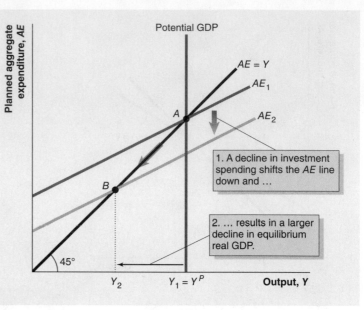

1. A decline in investment spending shifts the *AE* line down and …

2. …, results in a larger decline in equilibrium real GDP.

shift down. If, however, real GDP decreases and households decrease their consumption spending, as indicated by the consumption function, the decrease in consumption spending will be induced rather than autonomous.

Suppose, for instance, that spending on residential construction declines by $10 billion. Income will also decline by $10 billion, which leads to an *induced* decline in consumption. As spending on residential construction declines, homebuilders cut production, lay off workers, and reduce their demand for construction materials. Falling incomes in the construction industry lead households to reduce their spending on cars, furniture, appliances, and other goods and services. If the *MPC* is 0.75, then an initial $10 billion decline in income results in an induced decline in consumption of $7.5 billion. This $7.5 billion decline in consumption results in a $7.5 billion decline in income and another 0.75 × $7.5 billion = $5.625 billion induced decline in consumption, and so on through multiple rounds of decreased income and decreased consumption. Note, though, that because the *MPC* is less than 1, each round of spending decreases will be smaller than the previous round until the rounds of spending eventually stop.

Multiplier The change in equilibrium GDP divided by the change in autonomous expenditure.

Economists calculate the result of the process just described by using the **multiplier**, which equals the change in equilibrium GDP divided by the initial change in autonomous expenditure. The series of induced changes in consumption that results from an initial change in autonomous expenditure is called the **multiplier effect**. We can write the multiplier for a change in investment spending as:

Multiplier effect A series of induced increases (or decreases) in consumption spending that results from an increase (or decrease) in autonomous expenditure; this effect amplifies the effect of economic shocks on real GDP.

$$\text{Multiplier} = \frac{\Delta Y}{\Delta \bar{I}}.$$

We could use a similar expression for the multiplier resulting from a change in $\bar{C}$, $\bar{G}$, or $\overline{NX}$. How large is the multiplier? We can calculate it by using the expression for aggregate expenditure:

$$AE = \bar{C} + (MPC \times Y) + \bar{I} + \bar{G} + \overline{NX},$$

and the expression for equilibrium in the goods market:

$$AE = Y.$$

Substituting, we have:

$$Y = \overline{C} + (MPC \times Y) + \overline{I} + \overline{G} + \overline{NX}.$$

We are focusing on the effect on equilibrium GDP of a change in *I*, holding the other components of aggregate expenditure constant. If these other components are constant, then changes in them are zero, so we have:

$$\Delta Y = (MPC \times \Delta Y) + \Delta\overline{I}.$$

Rearranging terms, we have the expression for the multiplier:

$$\frac{\Delta Y}{\Delta \overline{I}} = \frac{1}{(1 - MPC)}.$$

In general, the expression for the *expenditure multiplier* is:

$$\frac{\Delta Y}{\Delta \text{Autonomous expenditure}} = \frac{1}{(1 - MPC)}.$$

If, as we assumed earlier, the *MPC* is 0.75, then the value of the multiplier for investment expenditure is:

$$\frac{\Delta Y}{\Delta \overline{I}} = \frac{1}{(1 - 0.75)} = \frac{1}{0.25} = 4.$$

So, a decline in investment spending of $1 billion would lead to a decline in equilibrium real GDP of $4 billion. When Keynes and his colleagues developed multiplier analysis in the 1930s, they believed that the multiplier might be as large as 10.[3] With a large multiplier, a relatively small decline in investment spending could have led to the large declines in GDP experienced in the United States and Europe during the Great Depression. For reasons we will discuss later in this chapter, economists today believe that the size of the multiplier is closer to 2 (or less) than to 10.

The multiplier effect works in both directions: An increase in investment spending causes a multiplied increase in equilibrium real GDP, just as a decrease in investment spending causes a multiplied decrease in equilibrium real GDP.

The Government Purchases and Tax Multipliers

During a recession, the federal government can take action to increase real GDP by increasing government purchases or by cutting taxes. For example, an increase in government spending on bridges and highways will have a multiplied effect on

---

[3]John Maynard Keynes, *The Theory of Employment, Interest, and Money*, London: Macmillan, 1936, p. 51. Because macroeconomic statistics were not yet available in the 1930s, Keynes was unable to provide more than a rough estimate of the multiplier. He did note (p. 56) that Simon Kuznets's early estimates of investment and national income for the United States implied a multiplier of about 2.5. But he thought the value of the marginal propensity to consume used in the calculation was "implausibly low" given the economic conditions in the United States during the 1930s.

equilibrium GDP in the same way that an increase in investment spending would. So, the *government purchases multiplier* is:

$$\text{Government purchases multiplier} = \frac{\Delta Y}{\Delta \overline{G}} = \frac{1}{(1 - MPC)}.$$

Similarly, if the government cuts the personal income tax, disposable income will increase, leading to an increase in consumption. The amount of spending that is subject to the multiplier equals $MPC \times \Delta T$ because households will save part of an increase in disposable income. So, the *tax multiplier* is:

$$\text{Tax multiplier} = \frac{\Delta Y}{\Delta \overline{T}} = \frac{-MPC}{(1 - MPC)}.$$

Notice that because a *decrease* in taxes *increases* disposable income and real GDP, the tax multiplier is negative. With an *MPC* of 0.75, the tax multiplier is $-0.75/(1-0.75) = -3$. So, while a $1 billion increase in government purchases will increase equilibrium GDP by $4 billion, a $1 billion decrease in taxes will increase equilibrium GDP by $3 billion.[4]

----

[4]What happens to the value of the government purchases multiplier if we take into account the *tax rate* that households pay on their income? It turns out that changing the tax rate changes the value of the multiplier.

To see this, suppose that the tax rate is 20%, or 0.2. In that case, an increase in household income of $10 billion will increase disposable income by only $8 billion [or $10 billion $\times (1-0.2)$]. In general, an increase in income can be multiplied by $(1-t)$ to find the increase in disposable income, where t is the tax rate. So, we can rewrite the consumption function as:

$$C = \overline{C} + MPC(1 - t)Y.$$

We can use this expression for the consumption function to find an expression for the government purchases multiplier, using the same method we used previously:

$$\text{Government purchases multiplier} = \frac{\Delta Y}{\Delta \overline{G}} = \frac{1}{1 - MPC(1 - t)}.$$

We can see the effect of changing the tax rate on the size of the multiplier by trying some values. First, assume that $MPC = 0.75$ and $t = 0.2$. Then:

$$\text{Government purchases multiplier} = \frac{\Delta Y}{\Delta \overline{G}} = \frac{1}{1 - 0.75(1 - 0.2)} = 2.5.$$

This value is smaller than the multiplier of 4 that we calculated earlier by assuming that there was only a fixed amount of taxes (which is the same as assuming that the tax rate was zero). This multiplier is smaller because spending in each period is now reduced by the amount of taxes households must pay on any additional income they earn.

We can calculate the multiplier for an *MPC* of 0.75 and a lower tax rate of 0.1:

$$\text{Government purchases multiplier} = \frac{\Delta Y}{\Delta \overline{G}} = \frac{1}{1 - 0.75(1 - 0.1)} = 3.1.$$

So, cuttitng the tax rate from 20% to 10%, increased the value of the government purchases multiplier from 2.5 to 3.1.

Solved Problem 10.1

Calculating Equilibrium Real GDP

The 45°-line approach is too simplified to address all of the key macroeconomics issues, but it can

help us understand the role of aggregate expenditure in determining equilibrium real GDP.

a. Use the following information to calculate equilibrium real GDP (all values are in trillions of 2005 dollars):

Consumption:	$C = \$1.0 + 0.75Y^D$
Investment:	$\bar{I} = \$1.9$
Government purchases:	$\bar{G} = \$2.0$
Net exports:	$\overline{NX} = -\$0.5$
Taxes:	$\bar{T} = 0$
Government transfer payments:	$\overline{TR} = 0$

b. Now suppose that all of the information given in part (a) remains the same except that taxes equal $2.5 trillion and transfers equal $2.0 trillion. Calculate equilibrium real GDP.

c. Now suppose that potential GDP equals $17.0 trillion. If equilibrium real GDP equals the amount you calculated in part (b), use the value for the government purchases multiplier to calculate how much government purchases would have to change for equilibrium GDP to equal potential GDP (assuming that taxes remain unchanged). Use the value for the tax multiplier to calculate how much the government has to change taxes for equilibrium GDP to equal potential GDP (assuming that government purchases remain changed). Use a graph to illustrate your answer.

Solving the Problem

Step 1 **Review the chapter material.** This problem is about determining equilibrium in the 45°-line diagram and the government purchases and tax multipliers, so you may want to review the sections "Equilibrium in the Goods Market," which begins on page 334, and "The Government Purchases and Tax Multipliers," which begins on page 339.

Step 2 **Answer part (a) by solving for equilibrium in the 45°-line model.** We can calculate equilibrium by keeping in mind that $AE = C + I + G + NX$, and that at equilibrium, $Y = AE$. Also note that because $\bar{T} = 0$ and $\overline{TR} = 0$, $Y = Y^D$:

$$AE = C + I + G + NX$$
$$= \$1.0 + 0.75Y + \$1.9 + \$2.0 - \$0.5$$
$$= \$4.4 + 0.75Y.$$

At equilibrium, $Y = AE$, so:

$$Y = \$4.4 + 0.75Y$$
$$Y - 0.75Y = \$4.4$$
$$Y = \$4.4/(1 - 0.75)$$
$$Y = \$17.6 \text{ trillion.}$$

Step 3 **Answer part (b) by substituting the values for taxes and transfers into the consumption function and solving again for equilibrium.** Including taxes and transfers, the consumption function becomes:

$$C = \$1.0 + 0.75(Y + \$2.0 - \$2.5).$$

So, at equilibrium:

$$Y = \$4.4 + 0.75Y + (0.75 \times \$2.0) - (0.75 \times \$2.5)$$
$$Y - 0.75Y = 4.025$$
$$Y = \$4.025/(1 - 0.75)$$
$$Y = \$16.1 \text{ trillion.}$$

Step 4 **Begin answering part (c) by using the values for the government purchases and tax multipliers to calculate the changes necessary in government purchases and taxes.** The value of the government purchases multiplier is:

$$\frac{\Delta Y}{\Delta \overline{G}} = \frac{1}{(1 - MPC)} = \frac{1}{(1 - 0.75)} = 4.$$

The necessary change in equilibrium real GDP is $17.0 trillion − $16.1 trillion = $0.9 trillion. Therefore, government purchases need to increase by:

$$\Delta G = \frac{\Delta Y}{\text{Multiplier}} = \frac{\$0.9 \text{ trillion}}{4} = \$0.225 \text{ trillion, or } \$225 \text{ billion.}$$

The value of the tax multiplier is:

$$\frac{\Delta Y}{\Delta \overline{T}} = \frac{-MPC}{(1 - MPC)} = \frac{-0.75}{(1 - 0.75)} = -3.$$

So, taxes need to be cut by:

$$\Delta T = \frac{\Delta Y}{\text{Multiplier}} = \frac{\$0.9 \text{ trillion}}{-3} = -\$0.3 \text{ trillion, or } \$300 \text{ billion.}$$

Notice that because the tax multiplier is smaller (in absolute value) than the government purchases multiplier, the cut in taxes needs to be larger than the increase in government purchases to result in the same increase in equilibrium real GDP. Bear in mind, though, that the 45°-line approach is simplified.

Step 5 **Finish answering part (c) by drawing a graph that shows the changes in government purchases or taxes necessary for short-run equilibrium to occur at real GDP of $17.0 trillion.**

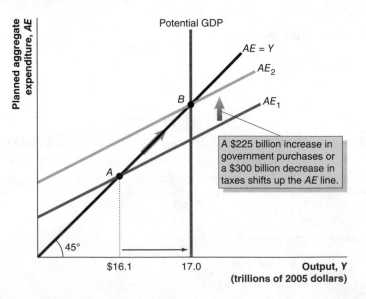

See related problem 1.10 at the end of the chapter.

Constructing the *IS* Curve

The 45°-line diagram illustrates the important insight that changes in aggregate expenditure cause changes in real GDP. This analysis is incomplete, though, because it doesn't include the effects of changes in interest rates on spending. To understand how monetary policy and financial markets affect GDP, we need to bring interest rates into the analysis.

Changes in the real interest rate affect consumption, investment, and net exports:

- A decrease in the real interest rate increases consumption because it gives consumers an incentive to spend rather than save and reduces their cost of borrowing.
- A decrease in the real interest rate increases investment spending because it makes firms more willing to invest in plant and equipment and makes households more likely to purchase new houses.
- A decrease in the domestic real interest rate makes returns on domestic financial assets less attractive to investors relative to the returns on foreign assets, decreasing the exchange rate. The decrease in the exchange rate increases exports and decreases imports, thereby increasing net exports.

— remember

An increase in the real interest rate will have the opposite effect—decreasing consumption, investment, and net exports.

Panel (a) of Figure 10.3 uses the 45°-line diagram to show the effect of changes in the real interest rate on equilibrium in the goods market. With the real interest rate initially at r_1, the aggregate expenditure line is $AE(r_1)$, and the equilibrium level of real

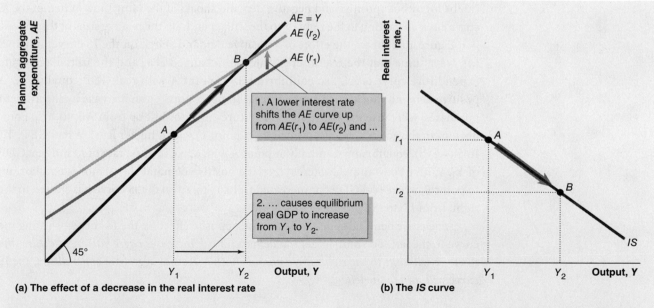

(a) The effect of a decrease in the real interest rate

(b) The *IS* curve

Figure 10.3 Deriving the *IS* Curve

Panel (a) uses the 45°-line diagram to show the effect of changes in the real interest rate on equilibrium in the goods market. With the real interest rate initially at r_1, the aggregate expenditure line is $AE(r_1)$ and the equilibrium level of real GDP is Y_1 (point A). If the interest rate falls from r_1 to r_2, the aggregate expenditure line shifts up from $AE(r_1)$ to

$AE(r_2)$, and the equilibrium level of real GDP increases from Y_1 to Y_2 (point B). In panel (b), we plot the points from panel (a) to form the *IS* curve. The points A and B in panel (b) correspond to the points A and B in panel (a).

GDP is Y_1 (point A). If the interest falls from r_1 to r_2, the aggregate expenditure line shifts up from $AE(r_1)$ to $AE(r_2)$, and the equilibrium level of real GDP increases from Y_1 to Y_2 (point B).

In panel (b), we use the results from panel (a) to construct the *IS* curve, which shows the combinations of the real interest rate and real GDP for which the goods market is in equilibrium. We know that at every equilibrium point in the 45°-line diagram in panel (a), planned aggregate expenditure equals real GDP. In panel (b), we plot these points on a graph with the real interest rate on the vertical axis and the level of real GDP on the horizontal axis. Points A and B in panel (b) correspond to points A and B in panel (a). The *IS* curve is downward sloping because a lower real interest rate causes an increase in planned aggregate expenditure and a higher equilibrium level of real GDP.

Shifts of the *IS* Curve

The *IS* curve shows the effect of changes in the real interest rate on aggregate expenditure, holding constant all other factors that might affect the willingness of households, firms, and governments to spend. Therefore, an increase or a decrease in the real interest rate results in *a movement along the IS curve*. Changing other factors that affect aggregate expenditure will cause a *shift of the IS curve*. These other factors that lead to changes in aggregate expenditure are called *demand shocks*. For example, spending on new residential construction in the United States declined by about 60% between 2005 and 2010. This decline in a component of I was a *negative demand shock* that shifted the *IS* curve to the left. Between 2006 and 2011, net exports increased by almost 60%. This increase in *NX* was a *positive demand shock* that shifted the *IS* curve to the right. Note that the economy can be hit by both positive and negative demand shocks at the same time. Whether the *IS* curve ends up shifting to the right or to the left depends on the relative sizes of the shocks.

Figure 10.4 shows the effect of a positive demand shock on the *IS* curve. In panel (a), we assume that the real interest rate is unchanged at r_1 and the initial aggregate expenditure curve is AE_1, so equilibrium is at point A with real GDP equal to Y_1. A positive demand shock, such as an increase in net exports or an increase in government purchases, will cause the aggregate expenditure curve to shift up from AE_1 to AE_2. Equilibrium in the goods market now occurs at point B, with a higher level of real GDP, Y_2. In panel (b), equilibrium is initially at point A with a real interest rate of r_1 and real GDP of Y_1. With a constant real interest rate, the positive demand shock moves equilibrium to point B, where real GDP has increased from Y_1 to Y_2, so the *IS* curve has shifted to the right, from IS_1 to IS_2.

A negative demand shock will have the opposite effect on the *IS* curve—shifting the curve to the left. To summarize: *If a demand shock increases aggregate expenditure, the* IS *curve will shift to the right. If a demand shock decreases aggregate expenditure, the* IS *curve will shift to the left.*

The *IS* Curve and the Output Gap

Economists measure economic fluctuations using the *output gap*, which is the percentage difference between real GDP and potential GDP. The Federal Reserve focuses on the output gap rather than on the level of real GDP when conducting

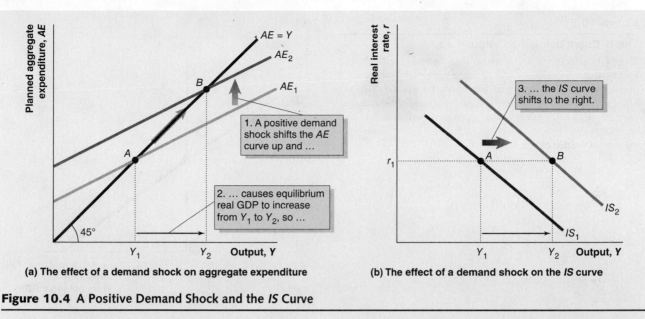

Figure 10.4 A Positive Demand Shock and the *IS* Curve

In panel (a), the positive demand shock shifts up the *AE* curve, and equilibrium moves from point *A* to point *B*.

In panel (b), the *IS* curve shifts to the right, from IS_1 to IS_2. Points *A* and *B* represent the same combination of the real interest rate and level of real GDP in both panels.

monetary policy. So, it is helpful to use the output gap rather than the level of real GDP in the *IS* curve graph. During a recession, the output gap becomes negative when real GDP is below potential GDP. When output increases during an expansion, the output gap eventually becomes positive, as real GDP rises above potential GDP.

We can replace the level of real GDP with the output gap in the *IS* curve graph, with the following qualification: We should think of changes in the real interest rate as affecting the level of investment spending, consumption spending, and net exports *relative to potential GDP*. For instance, when the real interest rate falls and *C*, *I*, and *NX* increase, the increase in aggregate expenditure will cause real GDP, *Y*, to increase relative to potential GDP, Y^P. In that case, when we graph the *IS* curve with the real interest rate on the vertical axis and the output gap on the horizontal axis, the *IS* curve is still downward sloping.

Figure 10.5 shows the *IS* curve graph with the output gap on the horizontal axis. We use the symbol $\tilde{Y}$ to distinguish the output gap from real GDP, *Y*. As a reference, we have included a vertical line where $Y = Y^P$, which is also the point where the output gap is zero. Normally, we draw graphs with the vertical axis beginning at 0 on the horizontal axis. In this case, though, our graphs are easier to understand if we move the vertical axis to the left, leaving zero in the middle of the horizontal axis. It's important to note that values to the left of zero on the horizontal axis represent negative values for the output gap, and values to the right of zero on the horizontal axis represent positive values for the output gap.

Figure 10.5

The *IS* Curve Using the Output Gap

The graph shows the output gap, rather than the level of real GDP, on the horizontal axis. Values to the left of 0 on the horizontal axis represent negative values for the output gap—periods during which real GDP is below potential GDP—and values to the right of zero on the horizontal axis represent positive values for the output gap—periods during which real GDP is above potential GDP. The vertical line, $Y = Y^P$, is drawn from the point at which the output gap is zero.

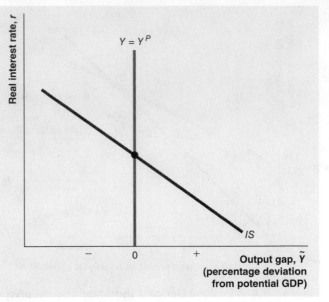

Learning Objective

Use the monetary policy, *MP*, curve to show how the interest rate set by the central bank helps to determine the output gap.

The Monetary Policy Curve: The Relationship Between the Central Bank's Target Interest Rate and Output

The *IS* curve represents equilibrium in the goods market because it shows every combination of the real interest rate and real GDP for which aggregate expenditure equals production. The second component of the *IS–MP* model is the monetary policy, or *MP*, curve. The Federal Reserve conducts monetary policy by managing the money supply and interest rates to pursue macroeconomic policy objectives such as price stability, high employment, and economic growth. During the past several decades, the Fed, like most other central banks, has generally focused its monetary policy actions on interest rates. Therefore, we call the curve showing the effect of the real interest rate on the output gap the monetary policy, or *MP*, curve.

One problem the Fed faces in carrying out monetary policy is that it controls a key short-term nominal interest rate, the *federal funds rate*, but not long-term real interest rates. It is the long-term real interest rates on mortgage loans or on corporate bonds that households and firms consider when they make decisions about buying houses and investing in new factories, equipment, and office buildings. The federal funds rate is the interest rate that banks charge each other on short-term loans.

In this section, we explore the link between the federal funds rate that the Fed controls and long-term real interest rates that affect aggregate expenditure. After this discussion, we will see that while the Fed *influences* long-term real interest rates, it does not have complete *control* over them.

Term structure of interest rates The relationship among the interest rates on bonds that are otherwise similar but that have different maturities.

The Link Between the Short-Term Nominal Interest Rate and the Long-Term Real Interest Rate

Recall that the **term structure of interest rates** is the relationship among the interest rates on bonds that are otherwise similar but that have different maturities. The interest rate on a long-term bond equals the average of the expected interest rates on short-term bonds plus a *term premium* to compensate lenders for the possibility that interest rates will change while they own the long-term bond. Recall also that when interest rates fluctuate, so do the prices of bonds, thereby potentially causing losses to investors in bonds. The **term premium** is the additional interest that investors require in order to buy a long-term bond rather than a comparable sequence of short-term bonds. Therefore, if there is a difference between the short-term nominal interest rate (such as the interest rate on a three-month Treasury bill) and the long-term nominal interest rate (such as the interest rate on a 10-year Treasury note), the difference is due to two factors:

Term premium The additional interest that investors require in order to be willing to buy a long-term bond rather than a comparable sequence of short-term bonds.

1. Investors' expectations of future short-term interest rates, as given by the term structure
2. The term premium

Combined, these two factors are called the *term structure effect*, or *TSE*. The difference between the short-term nominal interest rate, i, and the long-term nominal interest rate, i_{LT}, is:

$$i_{LT} = i + TSE.[5]$$

This equation shows that if the Fed increases the short-term nominal interest rate today and the term structure effect stays constant, the long-term nominal interest rate will also increase. The equation also shows that lower expected short-term interest rates in the *future* will reduce long-term interest rates *today* because *TSE* will become smaller. That is, expectations about the future can have an important effect on interest rates today and, therefore, on current spending. (If you are having trouble understanding how expectations of future short-term rates affect long-term rates today, you may want to review the discussion of the term structure in Chapter 3 on pages 96–99.) Similarly, if the term premium that investors require to invest in long-term bonds increases, then *TSE* will increase, which increases the long-term nominal interest rate, i_{LT}.

---

[5]An expression for *TSE* can be derived as follows for the simple case where the long-term bond is a two-year bond; i_t is the interest rate on the one-year (short-term) bond today; i_{2t} is the interest rate on the two-year (long-term) bond today; i^e_{t+1} is the interest rate expected on the one-year bond one year from now; and i^{TP} is the term premium on the two-year bond:

$$i_{2t} = \frac{i_t + i^e_{t+1}}{2} + i^{TP}.$$

Replacing i_{2t} with i_{LT}, i_t with i, and keeping in mind that $\dfrac{i}{2} = i - \dfrac{i}{2}$,

we have:

$$i_{LT} = i + \frac{i^e_{t+1}}{2} - \frac{i}{2} + i^{TP}.$$

Therefore, the expression for *TSE* is: $TSE = \dfrac{i^e_{t+1}}{2} - \dfrac{i}{2} + i^{TP}$. This expression shows that an increase in the short-term nominal interest rate *reduces* the *TSE* term. However, a one-percentage-point increase in the short-term nominal interest rate will decrease the *TSE* term by just 0.5 percentage point. So, an increase in the short-term nominal interest rate will still increase the long-term nominal interest rate, and the basic message of the equation in the text is correct: Increases in the short-term nominal interest rate will increase the long-term nominal interest rate, and decreases in the short-term nominal interest rate will decrease the long-term nominal interest rate.

Risk structure of interest rates The relationship among interest rates on bonds that have different characteristics but the same maturity.

Default risk The risk that a borrower will fail to make payments of interest or principal.

— higher default risk w/ more time

The **risk structure of interest rates** shows the relationship among interest rates on bonds that have different characteristics but the same maturity. A key way in which bonds differ is with respect to **default risk**, which is the risk that a borrower will fail to make payments of interest or principal. The bonds of private corporations have higher interest rates than do comparable bonds issued by the U.S. Treasury to compensate investors for the possibility that the corporations might default on the bonds. This higher interest rate is called a *default-risk premium*. Households must also pay a default-risk premium when they borrow money because they may not be able to make all the interest and principal payments on loans they receive. If we let *DP* stand for the default-risk premium, then we have the following relationship between the long-term nominal interest rate and the short-term nominal interest rate:

$$i_{LT} = i + TSE + DP.$$

Finally, we need to consider the link between the long-term *nominal* interest rate and the long-term *real* interest rate. To calculate the expected real interest rate, we subtract the expected inflation rate from the nominal interest rate:

$$r = i - \pi^e.$$

This relationship holds for both short-term and long-term interest rates. So, we can say that the long-term real interest rate equals the long-term nominal interest rate minus the expected inflation rate, or:

$$r_{LT} = i_{LT} - \pi^e.$$

Using this last relationship, we have our final equation for the real interest rate:

$$r_{LT} = i + TSE + DP - \pi^e.$$

Because the Fed has good control over the short-term nominal interest rate, it controls the long-term real interest rate as well, *provided that term structure effects, the default-risk premium, and the expected inflation rate all remain unchanged*. In practice, the Fed's job can be difficult because these other three factors may move in ways that offset the Fed's policy action. For example, the Fed might want to stimulate the economy by lowering the real interest rate. To achieve this goal, the Fed lowers the short-term nominal interest rate. However, the long-term real interest rate may not decline if (1) lenders, including investors in the bond market, believe that future short-term nominal rates will be higher; or (2) lenders require a higher default-risk premium; or (3) lenders lower their expectations of the future inflation rate. These factors may make the Fed's attempts to stimulate the economy ineffective.

The Fed does have *some* influence over these three factors. For instance, if the Fed is able to convince lenders that it will keep short-term nominal rates low for an extended period of time, then the term structure effect will likely be unchanged. The Fed may actually bring about a reduction in the default-risk premium if lenders believe that the Fed's expansionary policy will bring the economy out of a recession, thereby reducing the probability that borrowers will default on loans. Still, events beyond the Fed's control can drive movements in the long-term real interest rate.

Macro Data Box: Real Interest Rates and the Global Savings Glut

Our explanation of the *MP* curve suggests that the Fed can increase long-term real interest rates just by increasing the federal funds rate. However, in practice, it is not quite that easy for the Fed to increase real interest rates. The figure below shows the nominal target federal funds rate from 2003 to 2008 along with the real interest rate on a 10-year U.S. Treasury security (Treasury Inflation-Protected Security).

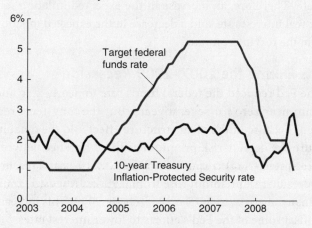

The United States experienced a recession in 2001, and the recovery from that recession was initially extremely slow. In 2003, the Fed was worried that the economy might slow down further so it took two steps considered dramatic at the time: (1) lowering the target federal funds rate to just 1% and (2) keeping the federal funds rate at this low level for a full year. In June 2004, after the recovery began to strengthen, the Fed started to increase its target federal funds rate.

According to our discussion, what should have happened to long-term real interest rates? Our explanation of the *MP* curve indicates that holding everything else constant, an increase in the target federal funds rate should lead to higher long-term real interest rates. However, the figure above shows that the real interest rate on a 10-year U.S. Treasury security did not rise. In fact, real interest rates initially fell from 2.2% in June 2004 to 1.6% in February 2005. Long-term real rates didn't rise during the 2004 to 2007 period nearly as much as the increase in the target federal funds rate would suggest. We can therefore conclude that monetary policy had very little effect on long-term real interest rates and the *MP* curve from 2004 to 2007.

In a speech he gave in 2005, prior to becoming Governor of the Federal Reserve Board, Ben Bernanke argued that there was a "global savings glut" that kept long-term real interest rates low despite the changes in the target federal funds rate. Bernanke argued that the aging population in developed economies, such as Japan, led them to increase savings. Savings also increased in developing nations for two additional reasons. First, many developing nations, such as South Korea and Thailand, experienced financial crises in the 1990s and responded with policies that led to lower government deficits and higher savings rates. Second, many developing nations were oil exporters and as the price of oil rose, national income and national savings also rose. The combined effect of these changes was a large increase in saving in global financial markets. When the Fed increased the target federal funds rate, it put upward pressure on long-term real interest rates *holding everything else constant*. However, everything else was not constant. The increase in global saving put downward pressure on long-term real interest rates in the market for loanable funds. As a result, there was little change in long-term real interest rates during this period.

Source: Ben Bernanke, "The Global Savings Glut and the U.S. Current Account Deficit," March 10, 2005; and Board of Governors of the Federal Reserve System.

See related problems 2.8 and D10.1 at the end of the chapter.

The effect of Fed actions on the expected inflation rate can be complex. If the Fed lowers the short-term nominal interest rate to stimulate the economy, lenders, households, and firms may believe that increased economic activity will lead to a higher inflation rate. An increase in the expected inflation rate would reinforce the Fed's action by further decreasing the real interest rate. Similarly, if the Fed increases the short-term nominal interest rate to slow down the economy, the expected inflation rate may fall. A decrease in the expected inflation rate would reinforce the Fed's action by further increasing the real interest rate. However, the *Fisher effect* indicates that increases in expected inflation typically result in increases in long-term nominal interest rates (see Chapter 7). In the long run, a one-percentage-point increase in the expected inflation rate will result in a one-percentage-point increase in the long-term nominal interest rate, leaving the real interest rate unchanged. For example, assume that the long-term nominal interest rate is 5% and the expected inflation rate is 2%, so the long-term real interest rate is 3%. If as a result of Fed policy, the expected inflation rate increases from 2% to 4%, the long-term nominal interest rate will increase from 5% to 7%, leaving the long-term real interest rate unchanged, at 3%. In the short run, though, the long-term nominal interest rate usually does not rise and fall percentage point for percentage point with the expected inflation rate. Therefore, an increase in the expected inflation rate may result in a decrease in the real interest rate, and a decrease in the expected inflation rate may result in an increase in the real interest rate.

Interest Rate Movements During the 2007–2009 Recession

During the financial crisis, the Fed reduced the federal funds rate to nearly zero and indicated that it would remain near zero for several years. But the long-term real interest rate did not fall to zero because of the term structure effect and the default-risk premium. We can measure the default-risk premium as the difference between the interest rate on the highest-rated (Aaa) corporate bond and a 10-year Treasury note. Measured this way, the default-risk premium rose from 0.9% on August 1, 2007, before the beginning of the financial crisis, to 3.0% on March 18, 2009. This increase in the default-risk premium offset some of the Fed's efforts to lower interest rates.

The default-risk premium did not increase steadily through the entire financial crisis. Instead, there were episodes of sudden large increases in the default-risk premium. For example, in September 2008, investment bank Lehman Brothers defaulted on its bonds, loans, and other debts and filed for bankruptcy. The default-risk premium increased from 1.8% on September 2, 2008, to 2.6% on October 17, 2008, to compensate investors for the increased likelihood that borrowers would default, thereby offsetting some of the effects of the Fed's lowering of short-term interest rates.

Deriving the *MP* Curve Using the Money Market Model

The Federal Reserve and other central banks have interest rate targets and adjust the money supply to keep interest rates at those targets. The Fed explicitly targets the federal funds rate, but other short-term interest rates usually move closely with the federal funds rate. Figure 10.6 plots three short-term nominal interest rates—the federal funds rate, the three-month Treasury bill rate, and the three-month commercial paper rate for the years between 1997 and 2012. (Corporations use *commercial paper* to borrow funds for a short period, generally three months or less.) Notice how the rates move very closely together. This movement shows that the Fed can be confident that when it takes actions to increase or decrease one short-term rate, other short-term rates will move in the same direction. So which short-term nominal interest rate we focus on is not important.

We can derive the *MP* curve using the money market model (see Chapter 3). For convenience, we make the following assumptions:

1. The *TSE* and *DP* terms are constant.
2. The expected inflation rate, π^e, is constant.

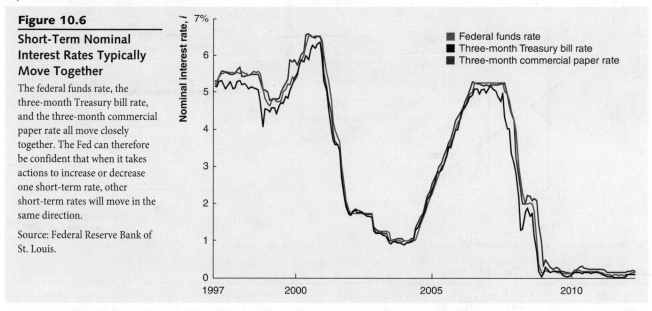

Figure 10.6

Short-Term Nominal Interest Rates Typically Move Together

The federal funds rate, the three-month Treasury bill rate, and the three-month commercial paper rate all move closely together. The Fed can therefore be confident that when it takes actions to increase or decrease one short-term rate, other short-term rates will move in the same direction.

Source: Federal Reserve Bank of St. Louis.

Given these assumptions, by changing the short-term nominal interest rate, the Fed can change the long-term real interest rate.

In Figure 10.7, equilibrium is initially at point A in panel (b), with the output gap equal to $\tilde{Y}_1$ and the real interest rate equal to r. Suppose that real GDP increases so that the output gap changes from $\tilde{Y}_1$ to $\tilde{Y}_2$. The increase in real GDP leads households and firms to purchase more goods and services, so the demand for money in panel (a) shifts to the right, from MD_1 to MD_2. If the Fed keeps the money supply constant, the increase in the demand for money will cause the interest rate to increase. But if the Fed has a target nominal interest rate, it will increase the money supply to keep the interest rate at the target. As a result, the short-term nominal interest rate remains constant, and with the term structure effect, the default-risk premium, and the expected inflation rate all remaining constant, the long-term real interest rate will also remain constant. With the real interest rate constant and the output gap at $\tilde{Y}_2$ we move to point B in panel (b). The result is that the MP curve will be horizontal at r.

Shifts of the MP Curve

The MP curve is determined by the Fed's target short-term nominal interest rate along with the term structure effect, TSE, the default-risk premium, DP, and the expected inflation rate, π^e. If any of these four variables change, the MP curve will shift. In Figure 10.8, we begin at point A with the Fed's initial federal funds rate target consistent with a real interest rate of r_1, so the MP curve is MP_1.[6]

---

[6]In this chapter, we have used r_{LT} for the long-term real interest rate. For simplicity, we are dropping the LT subscript from r. For the remainder of this chapter and in the following chapters, r will be the long-term real interest rate.

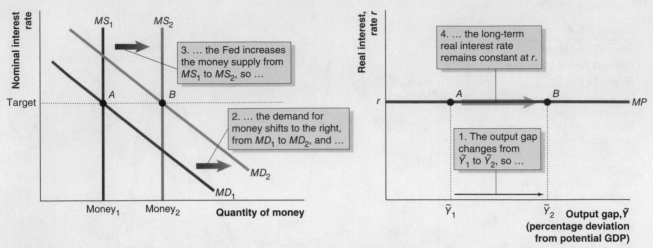

(a) The central bank adjusts the money supply

(b) The *MP* curve

Figure 10.7 Deriving the *MP* Curve

As the output gap changes from $\tilde{Y}_1$ to $\tilde{Y}_2$ in panel (b), the money demand curve shifts to the right in panel (a). The central bank increases the money supply in panel (a) to keep the short-term nominal interest rate at the target interest rate. If the short-term nominal interest rate is constant, then so is the long-term nominal interest rate. If expected inflation is also constant, then the long-term real interest rate also remains constant, and equilibrium moves from point *A* to point *B* in both panels.

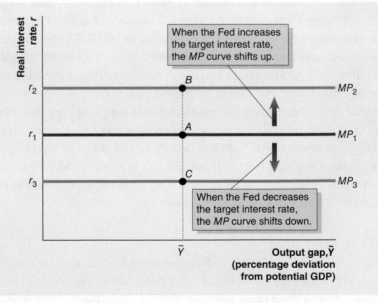

Figure 10.8

Changes in the Interest Rate Target and the *MP* Curve

When the Fed increases its target for the short-term nominal interest rate, the long-term nominal interest rate increases. Assuming that expected inflation, the term structure effect, and the default-risk premium are constant, the long-term real interest rate increases, so the *MP* curve shifts up, from MP_1 to MP_2. When the Fed decreases its target for the short-term nominal interest rate, the long-term nominal interest rate decreases, and the *MP* curve shifts down, from MP_1 to MP_3.

Suppose that the Fed then decides to increase its interest rate target. If expected inflation, the term structure effect, and the default-risk premium are constant, the increase in the target for the short-term nominal interest rate will increase the long-term real interest rate from r_1 to r_2. As a result, the *MP* curve will shift up from MP_1 to

MP_2. Assuming that the output gap is unchanged, we move from point A to point B. Similarly, if the Fed decides to decrease its target for the short-term nominal interest rate, the long-term real interest rate will decrease from r_1 to r_3. As a result, the MP curve will shift down, from MP_1 to MP_3, and we move from point A to point C.

Fed policy is not the only factor that affects the real interest rate. For instance, increases in the default-risk premium increase the real interest rate in much the same way as does an increase in the target interest rate. As we have seen, the default-risk premium increased after the bankruptcy of Lehman Brothers in September 2008, so real interest rates in financial markets increased, shifting up the MP curve. Table 10.2 summarizes the factors that cause the MP curve to shift. (Note that the table shows the shift in the MP curve that results from an *increase* in each of the factors. A *decrease* in these factors would cause the MP curve to shift in the opposite direction.)

Central banks usually increase their interest rate target during expansions to help reduce inflation and decrease their target during recessions to help increase output and reduce unemployment. For example, as the U.S. housing market began to overheat in the mid-2000s, the Fed increased its target interest rate from 1.0% in June 2004 to 5.25% on June 29, 2006. As the financial crisis began, the Fed reduced its target in a series of steps until, by December 2008, it had been lowered to between 0% and 0.25%.

Equilibrium in the *IS–MP* Model

We constructed the *IS* curve to describe how changes in the real interest rate affect equilibrium real GDP. And we constructed the *MP* curve to describe how Federal Reserve policy, acting through financial markets, determines the real interest rate. Combining the *IS* and *MP* curves allows us to determine short-run macroeconomic equilibrium, under the assumption that the price level remains constant. In this section, we combine the *IS* and *MP* curves to understand how macroeconomic shocks can affect the output gap and how government policy can respond to the effects of shocks.

Figure 10.9 on page 355 shows equilibrium in the *IS–MP* model. For a given *IS* curve, the Fed's choice of the real interest rate determines the equilibrium output gap. If the Fed sets the real interest rate at r_1, then real GDP equals potential GDP and the output gap, $\widetilde{Y}_1$, equals zero. So, firms are producing at their normal capacity and there is no cyclical unemployment, leaving the economy at the natural rate of unemployment.

Through its control of the short-term nominal interest rate, the Fed has an important effect on the long-term real interest rate, but the Fed's policy is not the only factor that affects the long-term real interest rate. As these other factors change, the *MP* curve will shift, which will cause the level of real GDP and the output gap to change. Similarly, demand shocks will shift the *IS* curve, which will also cause the output gap to change.

Demand Shocks and Fluctuations in Output

In Section 10.1, we saw how demand shocks affect the *IS* curve. We now explain how these shocks will cause real GDP to fluctuate if the Fed keeps the real interest rate constant. For example, suppose that a collapse in consumer confidence leads households to reduce

10.3
Learning Objective
Use the *IS–MP* model to understand why real GDP fluctuates.

Table 10.2 Factors That Shift the *MP* Curve

If …	the long-term real interest rate will …	and the *MP* curve will shift
the Fed increases its target for the short-term nominal interest rate (*i* increases),	increase	
investors increase the short-term interest rate they expect in the future (*TSE* increases),	increase	
investors increase the term premium they require on long-term bonds (*TSE* increases),	increase	
the default-risk premium increases (*DP* increases),	increase	
the expected inflation rate increases (π^e increases),	decrease	

see p. 359 for some graphs but w/ IS curve as well

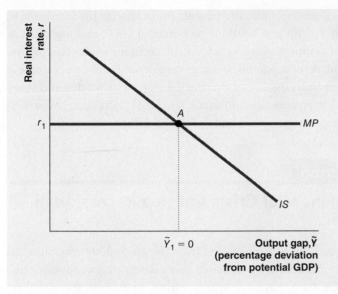

Figure 10.9

Equilibrium in the *IS–MP* Model

The economy is in equilibrium where the *MP* and *IS* curves intersect at point *A*, with real GDP equal to potential GDP, so the output gap equals 0.

consumption. Many economists believe that declining consumer confidence contributed to the 1990–1991 recession. Iraq invaded Kuwait on August 1990. Fears that the invasion would lead to sharply higher gasoline prices helped push the University of Michigan's Index of Consumer Sentiment down from 88.2 during July 1990 to 63.9 during October 1990. The decrease in consumer sentiment contributed to the 3.1% decrease in consumption spending during the fourth quarter of 1990, which helped cause the recession.

Figure 10.10 shows the effect of the decrease in consumer confidence using the *IS–MP* model. Initially, equilibrium is at point *A*, with real GDP equal to potential GDP, so $\tilde{Y}_1 = 0$. As households reduce consumption, the *IS* curve shifts to the left, from IS_1

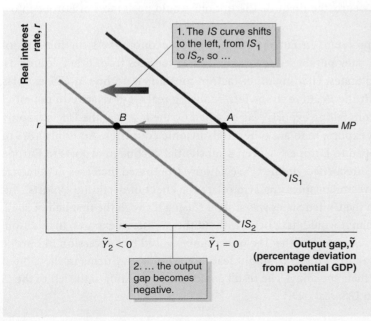

Figure 10.10

A Negative Demand Shock and Equilibrium Real GDP

A negative demand shock shifts the *IS* curve to the left, from IS_1 to IS_2. If the Fed keeps the real interest rate constant, the output gap becomes negative and equilibrium moves from point *A* to point *B*.

to IS_2. Assuming that the Fed does not initially take action to change the interest rate, equilibrium is now at point *B*, with real GDP below potential GDP, making $\widetilde{Y}_2 < 0$. In other words, the economy has moved into a recession, with declining levels of output and rising levels of unemployment. A reduction in consumer confidence is just one example of a negative demand shock that shifts the *IS* curve to the left. Any negative demand shock would have a similar effect. Any positive demand shock, such as an increase in investment by firms, would increase aggregate expenditure and shift the *IS* curve to the right.

Making the Connection

Will the European Financial Crisis Cause a Recession in the United States?

In 2012, the U.S. economy had not fully recovered from the 2007–2009 recession. Yet many economists and policymakers were concerned that a developing economic crisis in Europe might push the United States back into recession. In Europe, the global recession caused large increases in government spending on unemployment benefits and other transfer payments and reductions in tax revenues as incomes and profits declined. Budget deficits soared, particularly in Greece, Ireland, Spain, Portugal, and Italy. Governments financed the resulting budget deficits by selling bonds. By the spring of 2010, many investors had come to doubt the ability of Greece, in particular, to make the interest payments on the bonds. The International Monetary Fund and the European Central Bank made loans to these countries but insisted on *austerity policies* of lower government spending and higher taxes. By 2012, voters in several of these countries had begun to reject continuing austerity. Investors began to believe that Greece might abandon using the euro and resume using its earlier currency, the drachma. Investors had similar concerns about Spain. Many economists and policymakers believed that if several countries were to stop using the euro, the financial disruptions would push most of Europe into a recession.

How did these problems in Europe affect the U.S. economy? As the incomes of Europeans declined, they purchased fewer goods and services from other countries, including the United States. Holding other factors constant, a decline in U.S. exports to Europe would shift the *IS* curve to the left, reducing real GDP relative to potential GDP. The damage from falling exports was lessened by the fact that the U.S. economy is less dependent on exports than are other high-income countries. And only 18% of U.S. exports are shipped to Europe. So, even a substantial decline in exports to Europe has a relatively small direct effect on the U.S. economy. Continued increases in domestic consumption and investment spending also offset the effect of declining exports. But although real GDP in the United States was still increasing through the first half of 2012, growth was slower than it would have been without the decline in exports. In addition, some economists were concerned that the uncertainty caused by a recession in Europe and the possible breakup of the euro might lead households and firms in the United States to cut back on their spending. The result could be a larger shift to the left of the *IS* curve and a decline in U.S. real GDP.

Problems in Europe could also affect the U.S. economy through the financial system. Financial flows among countries have greatly increased in recent years. As a result, many U.S. banks and other financial firms have invested in European sovereign debt or have financial dealings with European banks. Many European banks have suffered losses, and some appeared to be in danger of failing. Some policymakers worried that problems at European banks might spill over and cause significant losses or even failures at U.S. banks. Most economists were less concerned about failures of U.S. banks, however, because the sovereign debt crisis unfolded fairly slowly, and U.S. banks had had time to sell European sovereign debt as well as some of their holdings with European banks. In addition, the financial position of most U.S. banks had improved significantly since the 2007–2009 financial crisis, and the banks were in a position to withstand losses they might suffer on European securities. However, indirect effects of European problems might be more important than the direct effects. If a financial crisis developed in Europe, Europeans might sharply curtail their lending, including lending to U.S. firms, and both European and U.S. investors might also switch to only the safest assets—so-called safe-haven investments. In fact, by mid-2012, investors were bidding up the prices of U.S. Treasury bonds to very high levels. As funds flowed into safe-haven investments, they were less available to firms hoping to borrow to finance expansions in production and employment.

As this book went to press, the ultimate outcome of the European economic crisis was uncertain. Clearly, though, in an increasingly global economic and financial system, the Federal Reserve and other U.S. policymakers had to be prepared to deal with economic developments outside the United States.

Sources: Vanessa Fuhrmans and Dana Cimilluca, "Business Braces for Europe's Worst," *Wall Street Journal*, May 31, 2012; Alex Brittain and Brian Blackstone, "Euro-Zone Reports Deepen Gloom," *Wall Street Journal*, June 1, 2012; Kathleen Madigan, "Forecasters Flying Blind When Predicting Repercussions of Greek Exit," *Wall Street Journal*, May 25, 2012; Jack Ewing, "Euro Zone Economy Skirts Recession," *New York Times*, May 15, 2012; and "A Central-Bank Failure of Epic Proportions," *Economist*, June 1, 2012.

See related problems 3.4 and D10.2 at the end of the chapter.

Monetary Policy and Fluctuations in Real GDP

In the previous section, we saw that a negative demand shock can push the economy into recession when the Fed keeps the real interest rate unchanged. In practice, though, if the Fed recognizes that a negative demand shock has occurred, it will try to offset the effects of the shock by lowering its target for the federal funds rate. (We will discuss monetary policy more completely in Chapter 12.) For now, we can look at the effects of the Fed's lowering its target for the federal funds rate on macroeconomic equilibrium.

Figure 10.11 shows the effect of a decrease in the Fed's target interest rate on the output gap. We assume that the economy has been hit by a negative demand shock, therefore we begin in short-run equilibrium at point A, with real GDP less than potential GDP, so $\widetilde{Y}_1 < 0$. A decrease in the Fed's target for the federal funds rate decreases the real interest rate from r_1 to r_2. The *MP* curve shifts down, from MP_1 to MP_2, causing planned

Figure 10.11

The Fed Ends a Recession

A decrease in the Fed's target for the federal funds rate causes the long-term real interest rate to decrease from r_1 to r_2. As a result, aggregate expenditure increases, causing real GDP to rise back to potential GDP and the output gap to return to zero at $\widetilde{Y}_2$. Equilibrium moves from point *A* to point *B*, and the Fed has ended the recession.

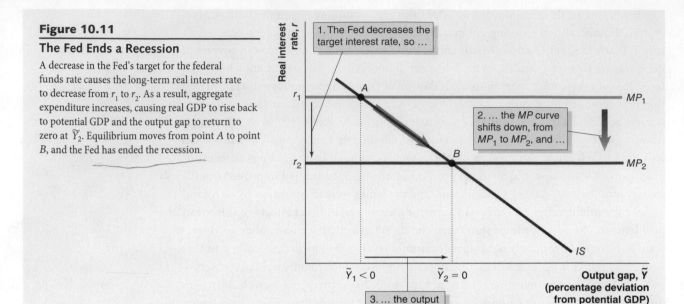

aggregate expenditure to increase, so real GDP increases back to potential GDP. In the new equilibrium at point *B*, the output gap is again zero at $\widetilde{Y}_2$, and the Fed has ended the recession.

Although the *IS–MP* model used in Figure 10.11 is simplified, it captures how the Fed responds to a recession—by lowering its target for the federal funds rate. The Fed's target for the federal funds rate was 6.5% just before the 2001 recession. To stimulate the economy, the Fed reduced this target interest rate to 2.0% by the end of the recession in November 2001, and it further reduced the target rate to 1.0% by June 2003 to help speed the following economic expansion. (As we will see in the next chapter, the downside to reducing interest rates is that low interest rates might cause the inflation rate to increase.)

Other central banks also use reductions in short-term nominal interest rates to fight recessions. During the early 1990s, Japan experienced the collapse of both real estate and stock prices, and the Japanese economy grew very slowly during the 1990s. In an attempt to increase real GDP, the Bank of Japan lowered its target short-term nominal interest rate in a series of steps to essentially 0% by 1999. Unfortunately, there are situations—particularly when short-term rates hit 0%—when lowering the target interest rate is not enough to eliminate an output gap (see Chapter 12). In this case, the Japanese economy did not fully recover, and it has experienced sluggish economic growth for nearly 20 years.

Table 10.3 summarizes the effects of different shocks and changes in policy on real GDP and the real interest rate in the *IS–MP* model.

Table 10.3 Summary of the *IS–MP* Model

The following change ...	causes ...	Graph of the effect ...
a positive demand shock	aggregate expenditure to increase at every interest rate.	
an increase in the target federal funds rate (*i* increases)	the long-term real interest rate to increase and aggregate expenditure to decrease.	
an increase in the short-term interest rate investors expect in the future (*TSE* increases)	the long-term real interest rate to increase and aggregate expenditure to decrease.	
an increase in the term premium investors require on long-term bonds (*TSE* increases)	the long-term real interest rate to increase and aggregate expenditure to decrease.	
an increase in the default-risk premium (*DP* increases)	the long-term real interest rate to increase and aggregate expenditure to decrease.	
an increase in the expected inflation rate (π^e increases)	the long-term real interest rate to decrease and aggregate expenditure to increase.	

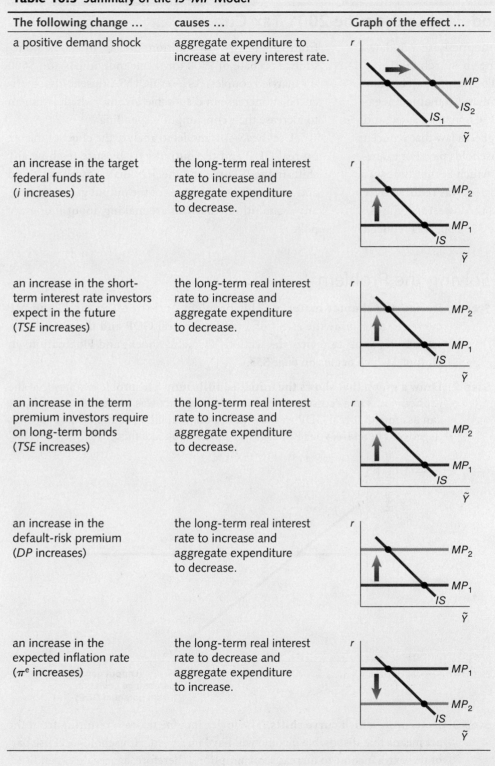

Solved Problem 10.3

Using the *IS–MP* Model to Analyze the 2001 Tax Cut

The National Bureau of Economic Research dates the 2001 recession as starting in March 2001 and ending in November 2001. The output gap became negative during the recession and remained negative until 2005. In June 2001, Congress passed and President George W. Bush signed a law that reduced the income tax rates that households pay. For example, the top income tax rate, which at that time was levied on income above $288,350, was reduced over time from 39.6% to 35%, and the lowest income tax rate, levied on income below $26,250, was reduced from 15% to 10%. In addition, the law included a one-time tax rebate of $300 for single individuals and $600 for married couples. As a result, U.S. households experienced an increase in disposable income, which led them to increase their consumption spending.

Use the *IS–MP* model to analyze the effect of the tax on real GDP and the output gap. Be sure to show any shifts in the *IS* curve and the *MP* curve, as well as the old and new equilibrium values of the output gap. Also state any assumptions that you are making about monetary policy.

Solving the Problem

Step 1 **Review the chapter material.** This problem is about using the *IS* and *MP* curves to determine the effect of a tax cut on real GDP and the output gap, so you may want to review the section "Demand Shocks and Fluctuations in Output," which begins on page 353.

Step 2 **Draw a graph that shows the initial equilibrium.** The problem states that the economy was in a recession at the time that the act was passed. As a result, we can assume that real GDP was less than potential GDP, so the output gap was negative. Therefore, your initial graph should look like this:

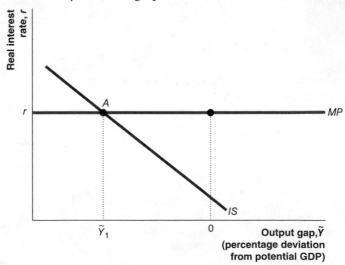

Step 3 **Determine which curve shifts.** The lower income tax rate resulting from the act means that disposable income will have increased. Households will use part of this extra income to increase consumption. Therefore, aggregate expenditure should now be higher for any given real interest rate. Table 10.3 on page 359

tells us that a shock that increases aggregate expenditure will shift the *IS* curve to the right, from IS_1 to IS_2.

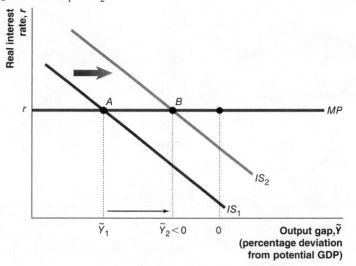

Step 4 **State your assumption about monetary policy and explain the effect of the act on real GDP and on the output gap.** The simplest assumption is that the Fed keeps the real interest rate constant. In that case, if the *IS* curve shifts to the right, short-run equilibrium will move from point *A* to point *B* in the graph in Step 3. The higher level of consumption causes real GDP to increase relative to potential GDP, so the equilibrium output gap changes from $\tilde{Y}_1$ to $\tilde{Y}_2 < 0$. The problem states that the output gap in the United States remained negative until 2005, so your graph in Step 3 should show that the output gap is still negative after the effect of the tax cut.

This analysis indicates that the 2001 tax cut increased consumption and real GDP. As a result, the tax cut made the 2001 recession less severe.

EXTRA CREDIT: Although the 2001 tax cuts served in the short run to increase disposable income and aggregate expenditure, they had another purpose—increasing economic growth. Some macroeconomic policies also have effects in the long run (see Chapter 15). In this case, President Bush and the members of Congress who voted for the act hoped that cutting tax rates would increase the incentive to work, save, and invest, which would in the long run increase potential GDP.

See related problem 3.5 at the end of the chapter.

IS–MP and Aggregate Demand

We mentioned at the beginning of the chapter that *IS–MP* is a model of the aggregate demand curve. In the previous chapter, we defined the aggregate demand curve as representing all the equilibrium combinations of real GDP and the price level. We can adjust that definition slightly to say that the aggregate demand curve (*AD*) is all of the equilibrium combinations of the *output gap* and the price level.

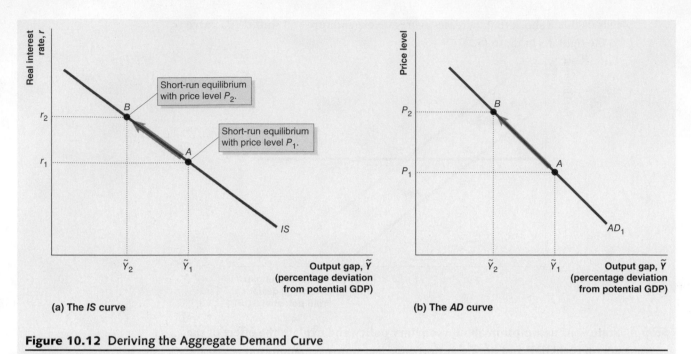

Figure 10.12 Deriving the Aggregate Demand Curve

Panel (a) shows that an increase in the price level from P_1 to P_2 causes a movement along the *IS* curve from point *A* to point *B*. Plotting the equilibrium combinations of the price level and the output gap from panel (a) gives us the aggregate demand curve in panel (b).

Figure 10.12 illustrates how we can derive the aggregate demand curve from the *IS–MP* model. Consider the effect of an increase in the price level on the *IS* curve. In the money market, an increase in the price level causes the demand for money curve to shift to the right, increasing the equilibrium interest rate. A higher interest rate leads to a decline in aggregate expenditure, which causes a movement up along the *IS* curve, resulting in a lower level of real GDP relative to potential GDP. In panel (a), we start in equilibrium at point *A*, with the price level equal to P_1, the interest rate equal to r_1, and the output gap equal to $\widetilde{Y}_1$. The increase in the price level from P_1 to P_2 causes a movement along the *IS* curve from point *A* to point *B*. At point *B*, the interest rate is r_2 and the output gap is $\widetilde{Y}_2$. So panel (a) shows two pairs of values for the price level and the output gap that represent short-run equilibrium. In panel (b), we plot these two points in a graph with the price level on the vertical axis and the output gap on the horizontal axis. Points *A* and *B* in panel (b) correspond to points *A* and *B* in panel (a). If we kept varying the price level and plotting the effects on the *IS* curve in panel (a), we would have plotted all the points on the aggregate demand curve (*AD*) in panel (b).

We have shown that an increase in the price level will cause an increase in the interest rate, *provided that the Fed allows the interest rate to rise.* The Fed could offset the effects of an increase in the price level on the interest rate by keeping the interest rate constant. The Fed could keep the interest rate constant by increasing the supply of money in the money market. In practice, though, the Fed will typically allow the interest rate to increase following persistent increases in the price level. So the analysis illustrated in Figure 10.12 is accurate. We discuss the Fed's actions when the price level is increasing in more detail in the next chapter.

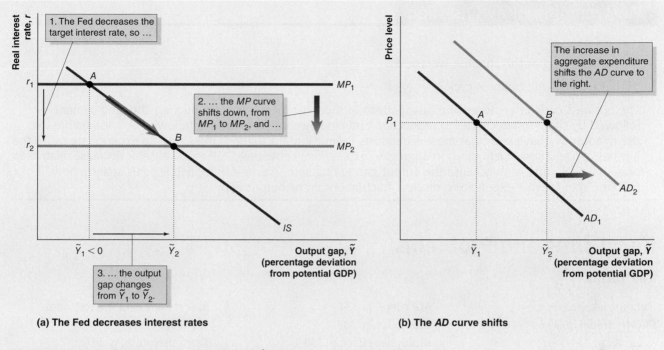

Figure 10.13 An Expansionary Monetary Policy

Panel (a) shows the effect of an expansionary monetary policy in the *IS–MP* model. The *MP* curve shifts down from MP_1 to MP_2. Equilibrium moves from point *A* to point *B*, with the interest rate declining from r_1 to r_2, and the output gap changing from $\widetilde{Y}_1$ to $\widetilde{Y}_2$. In panel (b), the increase in aggregate expenditure causes the *AD* curve to shift from AD_1 to AD_2. Equilibrium moves from point *A* to point *B*.

We know that demand shocks will cause the *IS* curve to shift. A shift of the *IS* curve represents a larger or smaller level of spending at each interest rate, so a shift of the *IS* curve will cause the *AD* curve to shift in the same direction. For example, a decline in spending on residential construction causes the *IS* curve to shift to the left and, therefore, will also cause the *AD* curve to shift to the left. Similarly, expansionary fiscal policy shifts the *IS* curve to the right, thereby also shifting the *AD* curve to the right. If the Fed engages in an expansionary monetary policy by lowering its target interest rate, the *MP* curve will shift down. The lower interest rate results in a movement down the *IS* curve. Because aggregate expenditure has increased at a given price level, the *AD* curve will shift to the right.

Figure 10.13 illustrates the effects of an expansionary monetary policy. In panel (a), an expansionary monetary policy results in the *MP* curve shifting down from MP_1 to MP_2. Equilibrium moves from point *A* to point *B*, with the real interest rate falling from r_1 to r_2 and the output gap changing from $\widetilde{Y}_1$ to $\widetilde{Y}_2$. In panel (b), equilibrium is initially at point *A*, with a price level of P_1 and an output gap of $\widetilde{Y}_1$. The expansionary monetary policy increases aggregate expenditure, which shifts the *AD* curve from AD_1 to AD_2. At point *B*, equilibrium occurs at price level P_1 and output gap $\widetilde{Y}_2$.

In the next chapter, we will complete the *IS–MP* model by incorporating the Phillips curve into the model. The complete *IS–MP* model allows us to determine the equilibrium inflation rate as well as the output gap.

Answering the Key Question

Continued from page 332

At the beginning of this chapter, we asked:

"What explains the business cycle?"

The business cycle refers to the irregular pattern of short-run increases in production and employment followed by short-run decreases in production and employment—expansions followed by contractions. In this chapter, we have seen that most economists believe that fluctuations in aggregate expenditure cause the business cycle. These fluctuations in aggregate expenditure cause real GDP to increase or decrease relative to potential GDP; that is, they cause the output gap to fluctuate. The *IS–MP* model helps us analyze how fluctuations in aggregate expenditure result in fluctuations in the output gap.

Key Terms and Problems

Key Terms

Default risk, p. 348

IS–MP model, p. 334

IS curve, p. 334

Marginal propensity to consume (*MPC*), p. 336

MP curve, p. 334

Multiplier, p. 338

Multiplier effect, p. 338

Phillips curve, p. 334

Risk structure of interest rates, p. 348

Term premium, p. 347

Term structure of interest rates, p. 346

10.1 The *IS* Curve: The Relationship Between Real Interest Rates and Aggregate Expenditure

Explain how the *IS* curve represents the relationship between the real interest rate and aggregate expenditure.

Review Questions

1.1 What are the components of aggregate expenditure? Explain how equilibrium output is determined in the goods market.

1.2 What is the multiplier effect? What are the formulas for the government purchases and tax multipliers?

1.3 Explain how the *IS* curve represents equilibrium in the goods market. Why is the *IS* curve downward sloping?

1.4 Give an example of a shock that could shift the *IS* curve to the left. Give an example of a shock that could shift the *IS* curve to the right.

Problems and Applications

1.5 Draw a 45°-line diagram and identify the equilibrium level of real GDP. Use your graph to show the effect on equilibrium real GDP of each of the following:

a. Households become more pessimistic about their future incomes and decide to buy fewer new homes.

b. The federal government increases transfer payments without changing taxes.

c. The federal government launches a major program to rebuild the interstate highway system without increasing taxes.

d. Europe enters a severe recession.

1.6 The graph below shows the goods market initially in equilibrium at output Y_1. Then the aggregate expenditure function shifts from AE_1 to AE_2.

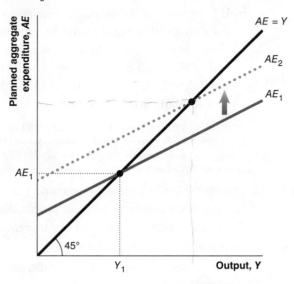

a. Give three examples of events that might have caused this shift in aggregate expenditure.

b. Carefully explain the process by which the economy will adjust to the new equilibrium.

1.7 A newspaper article quotes Gary Painter, a professor at the University of Southern California as arguing: "Increased housing demand definitely has multiplier effects throughout the economy." What does he mean by "multiplier effects"? Why would increased housing demand have multiplier effects?

Source: Catherine Rampell, "As New Graduates Return to Nest, Economy Also Feels the Pain," *New York Times*, November 16, 2011.

1.8 For each of the following values of the marginal propensity to consume (*MPC*), find the value of the government purchases multiplier and the tax multiplier.

a. $MPC = 0.80$

b. $MPC = 0.75$

c. $MPC = 0.60$

1.9 Suppose that the marginal propensity to consume is 0.80.

a. If the government increases spending by $10 billion, what is the change in equilibrium real GDP?

b. If the government increases taxes by $10 billion, what is the change in equilibrium real GDP?

c. If the government increases taxes by $10 billion *at the same time* that it increases spending by $10 billion, what is the change in equilibrium real GDP?

1.10 [**Related to** Solved Problem 10.1 **on page 340**] Consider the following information on an economy (all values are in trillions of 2005 dollars):

Consumption:	$C = \$1.2 + 0.6Y^D$
Investment:	$\overline{I} = \$2.0$
Government purchases:	$\overline{G} = \$2.1$
Net exports:	$\overline{NX} = -\$0.5$
Taxes:	$\overline{T} = 0$
Government transfer payments:	$\overline{TR} = 0$

a. Calculate equilibrium real GDP.

b. Now suppose that all the information given in part (a) remains the same except that taxes equal $2.0 trillion and transfers equal $1.5 trillion. Calculate equilibrium real GDP.

c. Now suppose that potential GDP equals $15.0 trillion. If equilibrium real GDP equals the amount you calculated in part (b), use the value for the government purchases multiplier to calculate how much government purchases would have to change for equilibrium GDP to equal potential GDP (assuming that taxes remain unchanged). Use the value for the tax multiplier to calculate how much the government has to change taxes for equilibrium GDP to equal potential GDP (assuming that government purchases remain unchanged). Use a graph to illustrate your answer.

1.11 For each of the following changes, (1) identify whether there is a shift in the *IS* curve or a movement along the curve, and (2) if the curve shifts, state the direction in which it shifts.

a. The real interest rate increases.

b. Firms become more pessimistic about the future profitability of investment.

c. Government spending increases.

d. Real GDP falls.

1.12 Briefly explain whether you agree with the following statement: "The *IS* curve slopes downward because a fall in the short-term nominal interest rate increases the money supply and decreases investment spending."

1.13 A study by the Congressional Budget Office notes that the size of the multiplier effect is difficult to determine exactly. The study notes that few economists believe that the value for the government purchases multiplier is greater than 2.5 or that the value for the tax multiplier is greater than 1.5 in absolute value.

a. Why do most economists believe that the value for the government purchases multiplier is greater than the value for the tax multiplier?

b. If Congress and the president were considering a policy of increasing government purchases or cutting taxes in order to increase real GDP, would the relative sizes of the two multipliers be the only factor they should take into account? Briefly explain.

Source: Congressional Budget Office, *Estimated Impact of the American Recovery and Reinvestment Act on Employment and Economic Output from July 2011 Through September 2011*, November 2011, Table 2, p. 6.

1.14 During the 1960s, a major restructuring of the tax code decreased taxes for most people. Also during these years, the war in Vietnam required increased government purchases.

a. Which components of real GDP did these events affect?

b. How did these events affect the goods market?

c. Would these events affect the *IS* curve? Briefly explain.

10.2 **The Monetary Policy Curve: The Relationship Between the Central Bank's Target Interest Rate and Output**

Use the monetary policy, *MP*, curve to show how the interest rate set by the central bank helps to determine the output gap.

Review Questions

2.1 Over which interest rates does a central bank have the most control? Briefly explain.

2.2 Briefly explain the effect of each of the following on the long-term real interest rate, assuming everything else is constant:

a. The default-risk premium declines.

b. Investors expect future short-term interest rates to rise.

c. The expected inflation rate increases.

2.3 Briefly explain how we can derive the *MP* curve from the money market model.

2.4 List two factors that would cause the *MP* curve to shift up and two factors that would cause the *MP* curve to shift down.

Problems and Applications

2.5 An article in the *Economist* magazine argues that the expected inflation rate in the United States followed "a steady downward trend" between December 2007 and May 2012.

a. Holding other factors constant, what would be the effect of this trend on the long-term real interest rate?

b. If the Fed had wanted to offset the effect you describe in part (a), what action could it have taken? Briefly explain.

Source: "What's Inflation Telling Us About the Output Gap?" *Economist*, May 20, 2012.

2.6 Suppose the Fed increases the target for the federal funds rate.

a. Show the effect using a graph for the money market.

b. Show the effect using a graph of the *MP* curve.

2.7 For each of the following changes, (1) identify whether there is a shift in the *MP* curve or a movement along the curve, and (2) if the curve shifts, state the direction in which it shifts.

a. The Fed decreases the target federal funds rate.

b. Real GDP increases.

c. Government purchases increase.

2.8 **[Related to** Macro Data feature **on page 349]** Briefly explain whether you agree with the following statement: "Central banks control only short-term interest rates, but long-term interest rates are most important for economic activity. Therefore, monetary policy is not important in determining output."

10.3 **Equilibrium in the *IS–MP* Model**
Use the *IS–MP* model to understand why real GDP fluctuates.

Review Questions

3.1 How does a shift to the right of the *IS* curve affect the output gap and the real interest rate?

3.2 How does a shift up of the *MP* curve affect the output gap and the real interest rate?

3.3 Briefly explain how the *AD* curve can be derived from the *IS–MP* model.

Problems and Applications

3.4 **[Related to the** Making the Connection **on page 356]** An article in the *Wall Street Journal* was titled "Forecasters Flying Blind When Predicting Repercussions of Greek Exit."

a. How would countries abandoning the euro be likely to affect the U.S. economy?

b. Why might forecasters have trouble estimating the size of these effects on the U.S. economy?

Source: Kathleen Madigan, "Forecasters Flying Blind When Predicting Repercussions of Greek Exit," *Wall Street Journal*, May 25, 2012.

3.5 **[Related to** Solved Problem 10.3 **on page 360]** In the early 1990s, the Japanese economy experienced a number of shocks due to the bursting of bubbles in real estate and the stock market.

a. Use an *IS–MP* graph to show how the shocks affected the economy. Briefly explain what happened to the real interest rate, real GDP, and the output gap.

b. The Bank of Japan responded to the shocks by reducing its target interest rate. Use an *IS-MP* graph to show how this action would affect the output gap.

3.6 **[Related to the** Chapter Opener **on page 332]** In a column in the *New York Times*, economist Robert Shiller of Yale University wrote that the ideas of John Maynard Keynes "enabled us to think of the economy as something that can spontaneously fail, that the government can stimulate to get going again and make everyone better off."

a. What did Shiller mean in saying that the economy can "spontaneously fail"?

b. How can the government stimulate the economy and make everyone better off?

c. Would you expect that the government policies you described in part (b) would make people better off in just the short run or in both the short run and the long run?

Source: Robert J. Shiller, "Making the Most of Our Financial Winter," *New York Times*, October 15, 2011.

3.7 The effectiveness of monetary policy in changing output depends on the slope of the *IS* curve, which in turn depends on the responsiveness of investment and consumption to the real interest rate. The graph on the right side shows two *IS* curves. *IS*$_1$ shows the case where households and firms do not increase consumption and investment much in response to lower interest rates; for *IS*$_2$, households and firms are more responsive to lower interest rates.

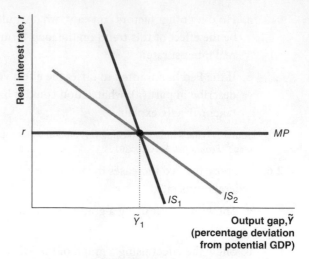

a. Show the effect on the output gap of a decrease in the target federal funds rate, given each of the *IS* curves.

b. Along which *IS* curve is the ability of monetary policy to change real GDP greater? Briefly explain.

Data Exercises

D10.1: [Related to the Macro Data feature **on page 349**] Using data from the St. Louis Federal Reserve (FRED) (http://research.stlouisfed.org/fred2/), analyze the relationship between the federal funds rate and the long-term interest rate. The Fed and other central banks usually target short-term nominal interest rates. Figure 10.6 showed that there is a close relationship between the federal funds rate and other short-term nominal interest rates in the economy. However, what matters for spending decisions are long-term real interest rates.

a. For 1984 to the present, download monthly data on the nominal effective federal funds rate (FEDFUNDS) and the nominal 10-year constant maturity U.S. Treasury security (GS10). Chart the two data series on a graph.

b. Is the relationship between the federal funds rate and long-term nominal interest rates as strong as the relationship between the federal funds rate and other short-term nominal interest rates? Briefly explain. Hint: Think of the term-structure of interest rates.

c. Now add the monthly interest rate of the 30-year fixed rate mortgage (MORTG) to your graph. Is the relationship between the federal funds rate and the mortgage rate stronger or weaker than the relationship between the federal funds rate and the interest rate on 10-year U.S. Treasury notes? Briefly explain. In particular, comment on the behavior of mortgage interest rates during the first part of the 2007–2009 recession. Hint: Think of the risk-structure of interest rates.

D10.2: [Excel Exercise] [**Related to** Making the Connection **on page 356**] The Bureau of Economic Analysis (BEA) provides data on U.S. exports of goods and services to euro zone countries and data on nominal GDP for the United States. The annual data is available at the website www.bea.gov.

a. Go to the BEA website and get data for both the nominal value of exports and nominal GDP.

b. What was the percentage decrease in exports to the euro zone between 2008 and 2009?

c. Suppose that a similar percentage decrease in 2012 occurred due to the financial crisis in Europe and that the expenditure multiplier is 1.1. What will be the decrease in GDP for the United States in 2012?

D10.3: Using data from the St. Louis Federal Reserve (FRED) (http://research.stlouisfed.org/fred2/), analyze the default-risk premium. One way to calculate the default-risk premium is took look at the difference between the interest rate on Aaa rated corporate bonds and the interest rate on U.S. Treasury securities.

a. For 1953 to the present, download monthly data on the interest rate on AAA rated corporate bonds (AAA) and the interest rate on constant maturity 10-year U.S. Treasury securities (GS10). Calculate the default-risk premium and plot the data series on a graph.

b. You can find the dates of U.S. recessions at the website of the National Bureau of Economic Research (http://www.nber.org/cycles/cyclesmain.html). What happens to the default-risk premium during recessions? Holding everything else constant,

what should happen to the *MP* curve during recessions?

c. What would the Fed have to do to offset the effect of the increase in the default-risk premium on the *MP* curve?

D10.4: Using data from the St. Louis Federal Reserve (FRED) (http://research.stlouisfed.org/fred2/), analyze the long-term real interest rate.

a. For 2003 to the present, download monthly data for the 10-year constant maturity U.S. Treasury security (GS10) as a measure of the nominal interest rate and the 10-year U.S. Treasury inflation protected security (FII10) as a measure of the real interest rate. The Fisher relationship tells us that the expected inflation rate is the nominal interest rate minus the real interest rate. Calculate the expected inflation rate over the next ten years using this data.

b. For 2003 to the present, download monthly data on Aaa corporate bonds (AAA). The Fisher relationship also tells us that the real interest rate equals the nominal interest rate minus the expected inflation rate. Calculate the real interest rate for Aaa corporate bonds. Chart the series on a graph.

c. What happened to the real interest rate from the beginning of the recession in December 2007 to August 2008? Does this suggest that shifts in the *IS* curve or *MP* curve were responsible for the start of the recession? Explain.

d. What happens to the real interest rate from September 2008 to November 2008? Does this suggest that shifts in the *IS* curve or *MP* curve were responsible for the deepening of the recession during the fall of 2008? Explain.

Appendix

IS–LM: An Alternative Short-Run Macroeconomic Model

10.A

Learning Objective
Use the *IS–LM* model to illustrate macroeconomic equilibrium.

***IS–LM* model** A macroeconomic model which assumes that the central bank targets the money supply.

The *IS–MP* model we developed in this chapter assumes that the Fed adjusts the money supply in order to hit its target for the short-term nominal interest rate. We presented the *IS–MP* model in the chapter because many central banks today target short-term nominal interest rates. However, central banks may target economic variables other than the short-term nominal interest rate. For example, the Federal Reserve did not have an official short-term nominal interest rate target until 1990. In this appendix, we examine the ***IS–LM* model**, which assumes that the central bank targets the money supply.[7] Whether the Fed targets interest rates or the money supply, it affects the economy by first intervening in the money market. Therefore, the *IS–MP* model and *IS–LM* model are similar. In fact, we can derive the *MP* curve by using the *IS–LM* model. As a result, *you should think of the models as being complementary models rather than competing models.*

As the names suggest, both the *IS–MP* model and *IS–LM* model use the *IS* curve to show the negative relationship between the real interest rate and aggregate expenditure: Households and firms purchase fewer goods and services when interest rates are high, and they purchase more goods and services when interest rates are low. The two models differ in the way they include financial markets. While the *IS–MP* model analyzes the money market using the *MP* curve, which assumes that the Fed has a short-term nominal interest rate target, the *IS–LM* model analyzes the money market by using the *LM* curve, which assumes that the Fed has a target level of the money stock. The ***LM* curve** shows the combinations of the interest rate and output that result in equilibrium in the money market. We start the discussion by deriving the *LM* curve.

***LM* curve** A curve that shows the combinations of the real interest rate and output that result in equilibrium in the money market.

Asset Market Equilibrium

Savers have a variety of ways to allocate their wealth. To simplify, we can think of savers as choosing between two broad categories of assets: money assets, such as checking accounts and cash, and non-money assets, such as stocks and bonds. The markets for money and non-money assets are in equilibrium when the total quantities demanded equal the total quantities supplied. Therefore, for the economy as a whole, the total demand for money balances, M_d, and non-money assets, N_d, equals total wealth, W, or:

$$M_d + N_d = W.$$

On the supply side, total wealth, W, equals the sum of the total quantity of money supplied, M_s, and the total quantity of non-money assets supplied, N_s, or:

$$M_s + N_s = W.$$

---

[7]*LM* refers to the combinations of r and Y for which the demand for money (L, for demand for liquidity) equals the supply of money (M, for money). *LM* is shorthand for $L = M$.

In equilibrium, the quantity of an asset demanded equals the quantity of the asset supplied. Combining the equations for the demand and supply for assets, we get:

$$M_d + N_d = M_s + N_s.$$

We can combine terms to show the *excess demand* for each type of asset:

$$(M_d - M_s) + (N_d - N_s) = 0,$$

so the excess demand for the different types of assets must sum to zero. Alternatively, we can write this equation as:

$$M_d - M_s = N_s - N_d.$$

When the total quantity of money demanded exceeds the quantity supplied, or $M_d > M_s$, there is an excess demand for money. When the total quantity of non-money assets supplied exceeds the quantity demanded, or $N_s > N_d$, there is an excess supply of non-money assets. So, an *excess demand* for one of the two assets (money or non-money) equals the *excess supply* of the other. In equilibrium, asset prices adjust so that there is no excess demand or supply in either market. In other words, the left side and the right side of the equation above must both equal zero. So, the money market is in equilibrium only if the market for non-money assets is in equilibrium. Knowing that the equilibrium in one of the two asset markets is related to the equilibrium in the other, we can make an important simplification: Any combination of real GDP and the real interest rate that results in an equilibrium in the money market also results in an equilibrium in the market for non-money assets. We use this simplification to focus on the variables that determine equilibrium in the money market.

Deriving the *LM* Curve

To derive the *LM* curve, we use a modified version of our money market model from Chapter 3. In that chapter, we used a nominal money demand curve and a nominal money supply curve to determine the short-term nominal interest rate. Because equilibrium in the goods market, as shown by the *IS* curve, depends on the real interest rate, we will make the simplifying assumption that the expected inflation rate is constant, so that a change in the nominal interest rate is equivalent to a change in the real interest rate. In addition, we will assume that a change in short-term nominal interest rates results in a change in long-term nominal interest rates in the same direction. If these two conditions hold, the equilibrium real interest rate is determined in the money market.

We will use the real money supply curve and the real money demand curve to determine the short-term real interest rate. The real money supply is the nominal money supply divided by the aggregate price level, and real money demand is the nominal money demand divided by the aggregate price level. In constructing the *LM* curve, we assume that the central bank keeps the nominal money supply constant. In both panel (a) and panel (b) of Figure 10A.1, the economy begins in equilibrium at point A. If real GDP increases relative to potential GDP, the output gap changes from $\widetilde{Y}_1$ to $\widetilde{Y}_2$, and households and firms make more purchases, which shifts the demand for money in panel (a) from MD_1 to MD_2. The Fed keeps the real money supply constant, so the equilibrium real interest rate increases from r_1 to r_2. Equilibrium is now at point B in both panel (a) and panel (b). Therefore, as real GDP increases, the interest rate necessary

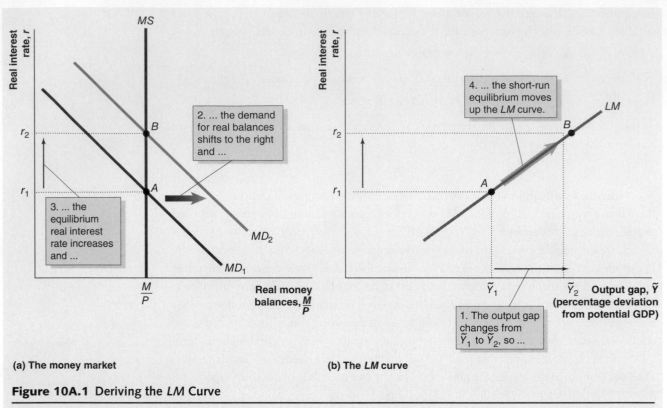

(a) The money market

(b) The *LM* curve

Figure 10A.1 Deriving the *LM* Curve

As real GDP increases relative to potential GDP, the output gap changes from $\widetilde{Y}_1$ to $\widetilde{Y}_2$ in panel (b), and households purchase more goods and services, so the real money demand curve shifts to the right and the equilibrium real interest rate increases in panel (a). As a result, the real

interest rate also increases in panel (b) and the *LM* curve shows a positive relationship between the equilibrium combinations of the output gap and the real interest rate.

to keep the money market in equilibrium also increases, and the *LM* curve is upward sloping, as shown in panel (b).

Shifting the *LM* Curve

The *LM* curve shows the combinations of the output gap and the real interest rate that result in equilibrium in the money market. If factors that affect the money market (other than the output gap) change, the *LM* curve will shift. For example, Figure 10A.2 shows the effect of an increase in the money supply on the *LM* curve. The economy begins in equilibrium at point *A*, with the output gap equal to $\widetilde{Y}_1$ and the real interest rate equal to r_1. In panel (a), suppose that the Fed decides to increase the nominal money supply. If the price level remains constant, the real money supply increases, so the money supply curve shifts to the right, from MS_1 to MS_2. The equilibrium real interest rate decreases from r_1 to r_2, and equilibrium in the money market is at point *B*. The increase in the real money supply reduces the equilibrium real interest rate from r_1 to r_2. In panel (b), if output remains at $\widetilde{Y}_1$ and the equilibrium real interest rate is now r_2, equilibrium is at point *B*. Point *B* is not on the original *LM* curve, so the *LM* curve shifts to the right, from LM_1 to LM_2.

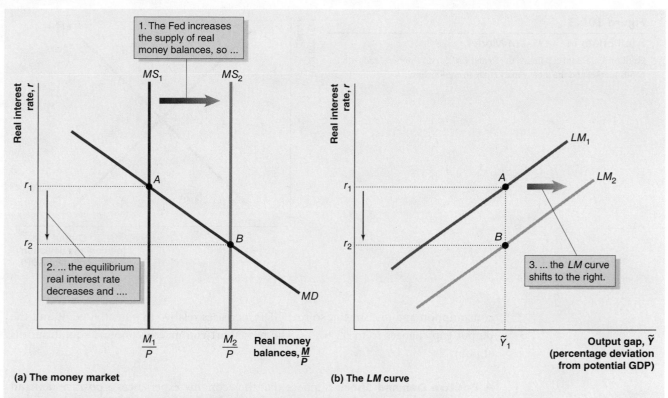

Figure 10A.2 The Effect of an Increase in the Money Supply on the *LM* Curve

In panel (a), the price level is constant. An increase in the nominal money supply shifts the real money supply curve to the right, from MS_1 to MS_2, and lowers the real interest rate. The real interest rate is now lower for any given level of the output gap, so the *LM* curve shifts to the right in panel (b).

Equilibrium in the *IS–LM* Model

In the *IS–LM* model, the *IS* curve shows the relationship between changes in the real interest rate and the output gap, and the *LM* curve shows the effect of changes in the output gap on the real interest rate. The market for goods and services and the money market are both in equilibrium at the point where the *IS* curve intersects the *LM* curve in Figure 10A.3. At point *A*, the real interest rate equals the equilibrium real interest rate r_1, and real GDP equals potential GDP, so $\widetilde{Y} = 0$.

Using Monetary Policy to Increase Output We derived the *LM* curve by assuming that the Fed kept the nominal money supply constant. Of course, the Fed can always change the nominal money supply, and we have already seen that when the nominal money supply increases, the *LM* curve shifts to the right. Figure 10A.4 shows the effect of an increase in the nominal money supply on the equilibrium output gap and the real interest rate. The economy is initially in short-run macroeconomic equilibrium at point *A*. The Fed increases the nominal money supply, so the *LM* curve shifts to the right, from LM_1 to LM_2. At the initial equilibrium real interest rate, there is now an excess supply of money, so the real interest rate falls. The lower real interest rate leads to higher

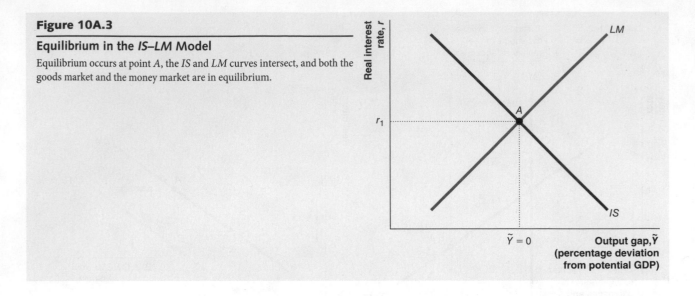

Figure 10A.3

Equilibrium in the *IS–LM* Model

Equilibrium occurs at point *A*, the *IS* and *LM* curves intersect, and both the goods market and the money market are in equilibrium.

consumption and investment, so real GDP increases relative to potential GDP, and the output gap changes from $\tilde{Y}_1$ to $\tilde{Y}_2$. The new short-run macroeconomic equilibrium is at point *B*.

A Positive Demand Shock Suppose that the economy experiences a positive demand shock due to the increased optimism of households and firms. Figure 10A.5 shows the economy initially in short-run macroeconomic equilibrium at point *A*. A positive demand shock leads to higher consumption and investment, so the *IS* curve shifts to the

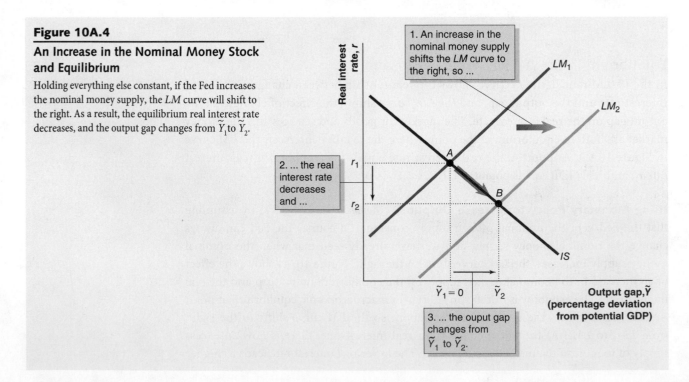

Figure 10A.4

An Increase in the Nominal Money Stock and Equilibrium

Holding everything else constant, if the Fed increases the nominal money supply, the *LM* curve will shift to the right. As a result, the equilibrium real interest rate decreases, and the output gap changes from $\tilde{Y}_1$ to $\tilde{Y}_2$.

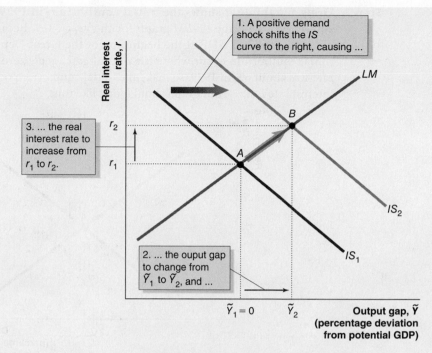

Figure 10A.5 The Effect of a Positive Demand Shock on Equilibrium

Holding everything else constant, a positive demand shock will shift the *IS* curve to the right, so the equilibrium real interest rate increases from r_1 to r_2, and the equilibrium output gap changes from $\tilde{Y}_1$ to $\tilde{Y}_2$.

right, from IS_1 to IS_2. As a result, real GDP increases relative to potential GDP and the real interest rate also increases. The new short-run macroeconomic equilibrium is at point *B*.

Solved Problem 10A.1

Monetary Policy During the Great Depression

Nobel Laureate Milton Friedman criticized the Federal Reserve for allowing the money supply to decrease during the Great Depression. The nominal money supply decreased from $26.2 billion during the third quarter of 1929 to $18.9 billion during the first quarter of 1933—a 27% decrease in just four years. Real interest rates on corporate bonds rose from 6% to about 17%, and real GDP fell by more than 25%. Real GDP equaled potential GDP at the beginning of the Great Depression, but real GDP may have been as much as 35% below potential GDP during the first quarter of 1933! In Friedman's view, the decrease in the money supply played an important role in the decrease in real GDP during the Great Depression. Is Friedman's view consistent with the *IS–LM* model?

Solving the Problem

Step 1 **Review the chapter material.** This problem is about applying the *IS-LM* model, so you may want to review the section "Equilibrium in the *IS–LM* Model," which begins on page 373.

Step 2 **Draw a graph that shows the initial equilibrium in 1929.** Draw the initial equilibrium with the *IS–LM* graph for the year 1929. Because real GDP was equal to potential GDP at the beginning of the Great Depression, make the initial equilibrium occur where the output gap equals zero. The real interest rate was about 6% in 1929, so make the initial equilibrium occur where the real interest rate is 6%. Your graph should look like this:

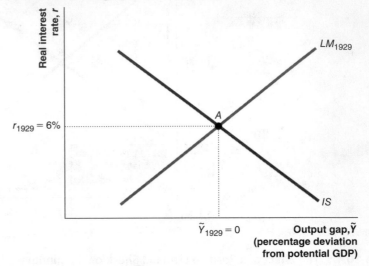

Step 3 **Determine the effect of the decrease in the nominal money supply.** The nominal money supply decreased by about 27% between 1929 and 1933. The nominal money supply is one of the factors that we hold constant when we draw the *LM* curve. Therefore, you should show the effect of the decrease in the money supply by shifting the *LM* curve to the left, from LM_{1929} to LM_{1933}. Label the new equilibrium interest rate r_{1933} and the new equilibrium output gap, $\widetilde{Y}_{1933}$. Your graph should look like this:

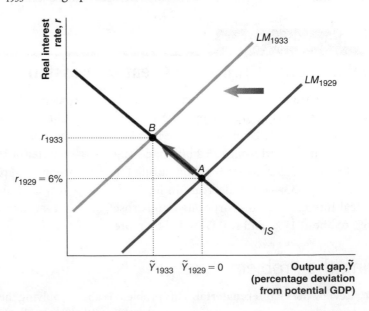

Step 4 Compare your graph to the actual experience. Your graph should show that a decrease in the nominal money supply will lead to higher real interest rates and lower real GDP. This is in fact what happened. The real interest rate rose from 6% to about 17%, while the output gap fell from 0% to about −35%. Therefore, the *IS–LM* model is consistent with Milton Friedman's view that the decrease in the nominal money supply contributed to the severity of the Great Depression.

See related problem 10A.8 at the end of the appendix.

An Alternative Derivation of the MP Curve

When the Fed targets interest rates, it makes sense to use the *MP* curve to represent monetary policy, but when the Fed targets the money supply, it makes sense to use the *LM* curve to represent monetary policy. Because both the *LM* and *MP* curves are derived from the money market model, the *IS–LM* model is similar to the *IS–MP* model. Holding the expected inflation rate, term structure effects, and the default-risk premium constant, the real interest rate is set by the Fed. If the Fed adjusts the money supply to keep the market interest rate at the target interest rate, then the *IS–LM* and *IS–MP* models are essentially the same model.

Consider the effect of a positive demand shock, as shown in Figure 10A.6. Before the positive demand shock, the economy is in short-run macroeconomic equilibrium

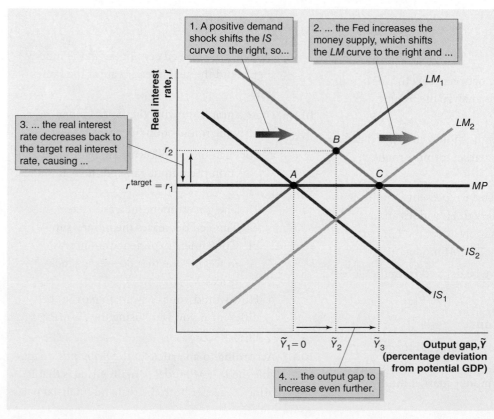

1. A positive demand shock shifts the *IS* curve to the right, so...

2. ... the Fed increases the money supply, which shifts the *LM* curve to the right and ...

3. ... the real interest rate decreases back to the target real interest rate, causing ...

4. ... the output gap to increase even further.

Figure 10A.6

An Alternative Derivation of the MP Curve

If the Fed targets the real interest rate, the money supply and the *LM* curve must adjust to keep the real interest rate equal to the target real interest rate. Therefore, in response to a positive demand shock, the Fed must increase the money supply, which shifts the *LM* curve to the right and reduces the real interest rate back to the target real interest rate.

at point A, where the real interest rate equals the Fed's target real interest rate, r^{target}, and real GDP equals potential GDP. If the Fed keeps the money supply constant, then the positive demand shock will cause the real interest rate to rise to r_2, which is above the target real interest rate, and the economy will be in short-run macroeconomic equilibrium at point B. If, on the other hand, the Fed targets the real interest rate, the money supply and the LM curve must adjust to keep the real interest rate at r^{target}. To maintain the target real interest rate, the Fed must increase the money supply, shifting the LM curve to the right, from LM_1 to LM_2. This shift causes the real interest rate to decrease from r_2 to r^{target}. If the Fed acts quickly enough, the real interest rate never increases at all, and the economy moves directly from point A to point C. If we connect those two points, we have a horizontal line at the target real interest rate, which we have previously called the MP curve.

We can see that the LM and MP curves are really not very different. Using the LM curve is a convenient way to represent monetary policy when the Fed targets the money supply. Using the MP curve is a convenient way to represent monetary policy when the Fed targets the interest rate, as it generally does.

Key Terms and Problems

Key Terms

IS–LM model, p. 370
LM curve, p. 370

Review Questions

10A.1 What is the difference between how the *IS–LM* and the *IS–MP* models analyze the money market?

10A.2 How is equilibrium in the money market related to equilibrium in the market for non-money assets?

10A.3 Explain how the *LM* curve represents equilibrium in the money market. How does an increase in the money supply affect the *LM* curve and equilibrium in the *IS–LM* model?

10A.4 How can the *MP* curve be derived from the *IS–LM* model?

Problems and Applications

10A.5 In earlier periods, the Fed targeted the money supply. More recently, the Fed has targeted the interest rate. Use the money market model to explain why the Fed cannot target the money supply and the real interest rate at the same time.

10A.6 Draw a graph showing the *IS–LM* model and identify the initial equilibrium.

 a. For each of the following changes, show the effect on the output gap and the real interest rate.
   i. The government increases taxes.
   ii. The Fed decreases the money supply.
   iii. Consumers experience an increase in wealth due to increases in stock prices.
 b. How would your answers to part (a) be different if you were using the *IS–MP* model?

10A.7 According to an article in the *Economist* magazine the *IS-LM* model's "main virtue is that it brings together both the real and financial parts of the economy." Briefly explain how the *IS-LM* model brings together the real and financial parts of the economy. Why would doing so be a virtue in a macroeconomic model?

Source: "A Working Model," *Economist*, August 11, 2005.

10A.8 **[Related to** Solved Problem 10A.1 **on page 375]** This appendix demonstrates why the *IS–LM* model accurately represents movements in the real interest rate and the output gap during the Great Depression.

a. Review the discussion of the 2007–2009 financial crisis in the chapter. Use the *IS–LM* model to show the approximate movements of the real interest rate and the output gap during that period.

b. Recommend a change in monetary policy that would have prevented the change in the output gap.

CHAPTER 11

The *IS–MP* Model: Adding Inflation and the Open Economy

Learning Objectives

After studying this chapter, you should be able to:

11.1 Understand the role of the Phillips curve in the *IS–MP* model (pages 381–395)

11.2 Use the *IS–MP* model to understand the performance of the U.S. economy during the recession of 2007–2009 (pages 396–398)

11.3 Understand the *IS–MP* model in an open economy (pages 398–406)

Where's the Inflation?

What if the United States began to experience significant inflation—not the 2% average inflation rate of 2000–2012, but 5% or 6%? How would this higher inflation rate affect you? We have seen that the effects of *anticipated* inflation are fairly small (see Chapter 7). If you and your employer both expect 6% inflation, that rate is likely to be reflected in your salary increases. It will also be reflected in the interest rates on your car loan and your student loans. But what if people expect 2% inflation but the inflation rate turns out to actually be 6%? Then the nominal salary your employer agreed to pay you for the year won't keep up with the increase in prices—a loss for you. But you will probably be paying a lower real interest rate on your loans—a gain for you. Unexpected changes in the inflation rate can arbitrarily create winners and losers,

which is a key reason that economists, businesses, and policymakers spend considerable time and effort trying to forecast inflation.

But inflation is not easy to forecast. In mid-2009, just as the severe recession of 2007–2009 was ending, several economists worried that the United States would soon enter a period of high inflation. Arthur Laffer, formerly of the University of Southern California, argued, "We can expect rapidly rising prices and much, much higher interest rates over the next four or five years . . ." Simon Johnson, a former chief economist at the International Monetary Fund, maintained, "The large increase in credit from the Federal Reserve can potentially push up prices. . . . The real danger . . . is that the Fed will lose control over expectations, pushing inflation above 5 percent." Allan Meltzer, an economist at Carnegie Mellon University,

Continued on next page

Key Issue and Question

Issue: The recession of 2007–2009 was the worst since the Great Depression of the 1930s.

Question: What explains the severity of the 2007–2009 recession?

Answered on page 407

worried, "If President Obama and the Fed continue down their current path, we could see a repeat of those dreadful inflationary years [of the 1970s]." These forecasts turned out to be incorrect.

What worried these and other economists was that in responding to the financial crisis and recession, the Federal Reserve had greatly increased the monetary base. Between 1960 and 2007, the monthly growth rate of the monetary base had never been above 20% at an annual rate. But during each of the seven months beginning in November 2008, the monetary base increased by at least 70% at an annual rate, and in three of those months it increased by a staggering 100%. The increases in the money supply were smaller but still substantial.

Recall that the quantity equation indicates that increases in the money supply should result in increases in the inflation rate. While the correlation between the rate of growth of the money supply and the inflation rate is strong in the long run, it can be weak in the short run. During the years from the beginning of the

recession through 2012, the link was quite weak. The following table shows values for the average annual growth rate of the M2 definition of the money supply and the Federal Reserve's preferred measure of the inflation rate for 2007 to 2011. Although in most of these years the growth rate of the money supply was relatively high, the inflation rate was very low.

Year	Annual growth rate of M2	Inflation
2007	6.2%	2.3%
2008	6.8	2.3
2009	8.0	1.6
2010	2.5	1.4
2011	7.3	1.4
2012	10.0	1.9

In this chapter, we discuss why, contrary to the forecasts of some economists, the inflation rate was so low during these years. To do so, we need to complete the *IS–MP* model by incorporating the Phillips curve.

Sources: Arthur B. Laffer, "Get Ready for Inflation and Higher Interest Rates," *Wall Street Journal*, June 11, 2009; Allan H. Meltzer, "Inflation Nation," *New York Times*, May 4, 2009; Simon Johnson, "Inflation Fears," *New York Times*, May 28, 2009; and Federal Reserve Bank of St. Louis.

In the previous chapter, we introduced the *IS–MP* model, which allowed us to determine the short-run equilibrium of the real interest rate and the output gap. We saw how movements in aggregate expenditure are the key reason real GDP fluctuates relative to potential GDP during the business cycle. In developing the *IS–MP* model, we made the assumption that we were dealing with a short enough period of time that we could consider the price level to be constant. We also did not explicitly take into account the effects of the United States being an open economy. In this chapter, we extend the *IS–MP* model by looking at how changes in the output gap affect the inflation rate and by applying the model to an open economy.

The *IS–MP* Model and the Phillips Curve

11.1

Learning Objective

Understand the role of the Phillips curve in the *IS–MP* model.

Typically, when real GDP and employment are increasing, the inflation rate increases, and when real GDP and employment are decreasing, the inflation rate decreases. In 1958, the New Zealand economist A. W. H. Phillips published the first systematic study of the relationship between the state of the economy and the inflation rate.[1] Phillips plotted data on the growth rate of nominal wages and the unemployment rate in the United Kingdom and drew a curve showing their average relationship. Generally, when wages increase, so do prices. So most economists interpreted Phillips's results as showing a

[1] A. W. H. Phillips, "The Relationship Between Unemployment and the Rate of Change of Money Wages in the United Kingdom 1861–1957," *Economica*, Vol. 25, No. 100, November 1958, pp. 283–299.

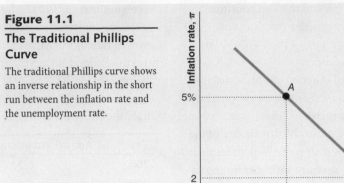

Figure 11.1

The Traditional Phillips Curve

The traditional Phillips curve shows an inverse relationship in the short run between the inflation rate and the unemployment rate.

Structural Relationship

tendency for the inflation rate to increase as the unemployment rate decreases. Since that time, a graph showing the short-run relationship between the unemployment rate and the inflation rate has been called a *Phillips curve*. Figure 11.1 is a graph similar to the one Phillips prepared. Each point on the Phillips curve represents a combination of the inflation rate and the unemployment rate that might be observed in a particular year. For example, point *A* represents the combination of a 3% unemployment rate and a 5% inflation rate in one year, and point *B* represents the combination of a 6% unemployment rate and a 2% inflation rate in another year.

Economists and policymakers initially viewed the Phillips curve as a *structural relationship* in the economy. A structural relationship depends on the basic behavior of households and firms and remains unchanged over long periods. An example of a structural relationship is that the demand curve for apples is downward sloping. If the Phillips curve is a structural relationship, policymakers face a trade-off between inflation and unemployment that will not change over time. The Fed could *permanently* reduce the unemployment rate from, say, 6% to 3%, if it were willing to accept an increase in the inflation rate from, say, 2% to 5%. Similarly, the Fed could *permanently* reduce the inflation rate if it were willing to accept a higher unemployment rate. Two events changed the view that the Phillips curve represented a permanent, stable trade-off for policymakers. First, in 1968, Nobel Laureates Milton Friedman and Edmund Phelps argued that, while in constructing the Phillips curve, economists assumed that expected inflation was constant, it was more likely that expected inflation adjusts if current inflation rates are different from past inflation rates.[2] In other words, Friedman and Phelps believed that if inflation is higher in 2014 than it has been in the past, households and firms will expect

[2]Milton Friedman, "The Role of Monetary Policy," *American Economic Review*, Vol. 58, No. 1, March 1968, pp. 1–17; and Edmund Phelps, "Money–Wage Dynamics and Labor Market Equilibrium," *Journal of Political Economy*, Vol. 76, No. 4, Part 2, July/August 1968, pp. 678–711.

the higher inflation to persist in 2015. Because expected inflation should affect the prices that firms charge and the wages that workers seek, higher expected inflation in 2015 may also increase the actual inflation rate in 2015. Friedman and Phelps believed that as the inflation rate in the United States increased during the 1960s, it was only a matter of time before the stable inverse relationship between unemployment and inflation embodied in the Phillips curve broke down.

The second event that undermined the view that the Phillips curve represented a stable trade-off between inflation and unemployment was the increase in *both* the inflation rate and the unemployment rate during the 1970s. The annual inflation rate as measured by changes in the consumer price index (CPI) was just 1.9% during January 1966, but it eventually rose to 14.6% during April 1980. Instead of decreasing during this period, the unemployment rate actually rose. The unemployment rate was 4.0% in January 1966, but rose to 6.9% in April 1980. So, over this period, the unemployment rate rose by 2.9 percentage points, and in contrast to the prediction of a stable Phillips curve, rather than falling, the inflation rate rose by 12.7 percentage points! It seemed impossible to reconcile actual macroeconomic data with a stable Phillips curve.

Friedman's and Phelps's criticism of the theory behind the Phillips curve and the actual experience of the U.S. economy during the 1970s convinced economists that the Phillips curve did not represent a stable relationship. Economists have concluded that the position of the Phillips curve can shift over time in response to *supply shocks*, such as an increase in the price of oil, and to changes in the expected inflation rate. Once we account for these two factors, the Phillips curve remains a useful tool for explaining the *short-run* trade-off between the unemployment rate and the inflation rate.

To see why changes in households' and firms' expectations about the inflation rate will shift the position of the Phillips curve, consider the following example: If workers and firms expect that the inflation rate will be 2% per year, but they experience an extended period of 4% inflation, they are likely to adjust their expectations of future inflation from 2% to 4%. Expectations of inflation can become embedded in the economy. So, if workers believe that the future inflation rate will be 4%, rather than 2%, they know that unless their nominal wage increases by at least 4%, their real wage—their nominal wage divided by the price level—will decline. Similarly, the Fisher effect indicates that an increase in the expected inflation rate will cause an increase in nominal interest rates. We can conclude that as workers, firms, and investors adjust from expecting an inflation rate of 2% to expecting an inflation rate of 4%, the inflation rate will be 2% higher at any given unemployment rate. In other words, the Phillips curve shown in Figure 11.1 will have shifted up by 2%.

Most economists believe that the best way to analyze the effect of changes in the unemployment rate on the inflation rate is by looking at the gap between the current unemployment rate and the unemployment rate when the economy is at full employment, which is called the *natural rate of unemployment*. The gap between the current rate of unemployment and the natural rate equals *cyclical unemployment* because it represents unemployment caused by a business cycle recession. When the current unemployment rate equals the natural rate, the inflation rate typically does not change, holding constant expectations of inflation and the effects of supply shocks. When the current unemployment rate is greater than the natural rate, some workers have trouble finding jobs, so wage increases will be limited, as will increases in firms' costs of production. As a result, the inflation rate will decrease. When the current unemployment rate is less than the natural rate of unemployment, labor market conditions will be tight, and wages are likely to increase, which pushes up firms' costs of production. So, the inflation rate will increase.

Taking all these factors into account gives us the following equation for the Phillips curve:

$$\pi_t = \pi_t^e - a(U_t - U^N) - s_t,$$

where:

π_t = current inflation rate
π_t^e = expected inflation rate
U_t = current unemployment rate
U^N = natural rate of unemployment
s_t = variable that represents the effects of a supply shock (s will have a negative value for a negative supply shock and a positive value for a positive supply shock.)
a = constant that represents how much the gap between the current rate of unemployment and the natural rate affects the inflation rate

The equation tells us that an increase in expected inflation or a negative supply shock, such as an increase in oil prices, will shift the Phillips curve up, while a decrease in expected inflation or a positive supply shock, such as an increase in the growth rate of productivity, will shift the Phillips curve down.

What might cause the expected rate of inflation to change? Typically, households and firms adjust their expectations of inflation as they experience persistent rates of actual inflation that are above the rates they had expected. The experience of the U.S. economy during the 1960s and 1970s provides an example of this point. Inflation during the 1960s averaged about 2% per year but accelerated to 5% per year from 1970 to 1973 and to 8.5% per year from 1974 to 1979. These persistently high rates of inflation led households and firms to revise upward their expectations of inflation, and the Phillips curve shifted up. Notice that once the Phillips curve has shifted up, the economy is worse off because, every unemployment rate becomes associated with a higher inflation rate. The decline in the inflation rate during the 1980s provides an example of how a decrease in expected inflation can lead to lower inflation. Paul Volcker became Federal Reserve chairman in August 1979, with a mandate from President Jimmy Carter to bring down the inflation rate. When the economy experienced the severe recession of 1981–1982, the inflation rate declined sharply as the unemployment rate soared and firms experienced excess capacity. From 1983 to 1986, the inflation rate averaged 3.3% per year, which was less than half its previous level. Accordingly, households and firms lowered their expectations of future inflation, and the Phillips curve shifted down.

Figure 11.2 shows the shifts of the Phillips curve associated with supply shocks and changes in expected inflation. An increase in the expected inflation rate such as the one that occurred during the 1960s and 1970s will shift the Phillips curve up, from PC_1 to PC_2.

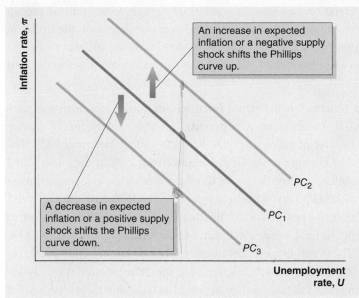

Figure 11.2

Shifts of the Phillips Curve

An increase in expected inflation or a negative supply shock shifts the Phillips curve up, so the inflation rate is now higher for any given unemployment rate. A decrease in expected inflation or a positive supply shock shifts the Phillips curve down, so the inflation rate is now lower for any given unemployment rate.

A decrease in the expected inflation rate such as the one that occurred after the 1981–1982 recession will shift the Phillips curve down, from PC_1 to PC_3.

Okun's Law, the Output Gap, and the Phillips Curve

The Phillips curve shows the short-run relationship between the inflation rate and the unemployment rate. In the last chapter, we used the *IS* curve and the *MP* curve to explain the short-run equilibrium output gap and real interest rate. If we could show the relationship between the output gap and the inflation rate, we could integrate the Phillips curve into our *IS–MP* model. Including the Phillips curve would allow us to illustrate the effects of changes in the inflation rate on Fed policy and the effects of changes in Fed policy on the inflation rate. Fortunately, there is a straightforward way of modifying the Phillips curve to change it from a relationship between the inflation rate and the unemployment rate to a relationship between the inflation rate and the output gap. This approach relies on Okun's law (see Chapter 9).

Okun's law is a relationship between the output gap, $\widetilde{Y}_t$, and the gap between the current and natural rates of unemployment, or cyclical unemployment:

$$(U_t - U^N) = -0.5\widetilde{Y}_t,$$

which we can rewrite as:

$$\widetilde{Y}_t = -2(U_t - U^N).$$

We can substitute the Okun's law relationship into the equation for the Phillips curve to obtain:

$$\pi_t = \pi_t^e + b\widetilde{Y}_t - s_t.^3$$

---

[3]To arrive at this equation, we first substitute the expression for Okun's law into the equation for the Phillips curve to get $\pi_t = \pi_t^e - a\left(\dfrac{\widetilde{Y}_t}{-2}\right) - s_t$. If we let $b = a/2$, we have the equation given in the text.

The coefficient b in the equation represents the effect of changes in the output gap on the inflation rate. The term $b\widetilde{Y}_t$ represents the effect of demand shocks on the inflation rate, and the term s_t represents the effects of supply shocks on the inflation rate. As before, the term π_t^e shows the effect of the expected inflation rate on the current inflation rate.

The Effect of Demand Shocks on Inflation Inflation often increases during expansions. For example, real GDP was about equal to potential GDP during the fourth quarter of 1963, but by the first quarter of 1966, real GDP was 5.9% above potential GDP. The inflation rate as measured by changes in the CPI increased from 1.7% at the end of 1963 to 3.8% by October 1966. Inflation often decreases during recessions, as happened during the 1981–1982 recession. Real GDP was 0.6% below potential GDP during the first quarter of 1981, but it was 7.5% below potential GDP by the end of the recession in the fourth quarter of 1982. As a result, the inflation rate fell from 11.8% during January 1981 to 3.8% during December 1982. These two experiences illustrate that when real GDP increases relative to potential GDP during economic expansions, the inflation rate typically increases as well. And when real GDP falls relative to potential GDP during recessions, the inflation rate typically decreases.

The Effect of Supply Shocks on Inflation Inflation does not always decrease during recessions, however. Inflation actually increased during the 1973–1975, 1980, and 1990–1991 recessions. What makes these recessions different? Each of these recessions was accompanied by a negative supply shock. Negative supply shocks raise firms' costs of production, which the firms typically pass along as increases in the prices of the goods they sell. Through this mechanism, a negative supply shock can increase the inflation rate.

Increases in productivity represent positive supply shocks that can reduce firms' costs and decrease the inflation rate. Productivity growth reduces costs per unit of output, so firms can produce more goods and services with the same number of workers. For example, improvements in information technology help firms produce more goods and services without incurring higher costs. Competition among firms ensures that these cost reductions are passed along to consumers in the form of lower prices.

Stagflation A combination of inflation and recession, usually resulting from a supply shock.

Two examples illustrate the effects of supply shocks. First, as oil prices rose from $3.56 per barrel to $11.16 per barrel during the 1973–1975 recession, the inflation rate increased from 8.3% at the beginning of the recession in November 1973 to 10.5% at the end of the recession in March 1975. The U.S. economy was experiencing **stagflation**, which is a combination of inflation and recession, usually resulting from a negative supply shock. The tripling of the price of oil during the 1973–1975 recession significantly increased firms' costs of production and caused the inflation rate to increase, even though real GDP fell relative to potential GDP.

The United States experienced a positive supply shock beginning in the late 1990s, when the growth rate of labor productivity increased. From 1973 to 1995, labor productivity growth averaged just 1.4% per year. But from 1996 to 2011, the growth rate of labor productivity increased, averaging 2.5% per year. Many economists believe that labor productivity growth increased during the 1990s because of the spread of information technology. The increase in Internet use during the 1990s changed how firms sell to consumers and to each other. Cell phones, laptop computers, and wireless Internet

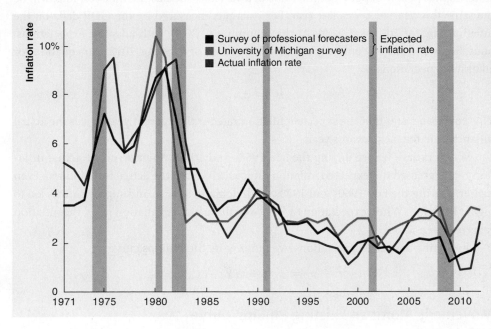

Figure 11.3

Measures of Expected Inflation for the United States, 1971–2011

Two measures of the expected inflation rate—one from the University of Michigan survey and one from a survey of professional forecasters—track the actual inflation rate fairly closely. Shaded areas represent recessions, as determined by the National Bureau of Economic Research.

Note: The University of Michigan survey begins in 1978.
Sources: Data from the U.S. Bureau of Labor Statistics, the Federal Reserve Bank of Philadelphia, and the University of Michigan.

access allow people to work away from the office, both at home and while traveling. These developments significantly increased labor productivity.

The near doubling of the growth rate of labor productivity helped keep the growth rate of firms' costs low. From 1973 to 1995, labor costs per unit of output grew at a rate of 4.7% per year, but labor costs per unit of output grew at a rate of just 1.3% per year from 1996 to 2011. The low growth rate of costs helped keep the inflation rate low during these years.

Expectations of Inflation Because they cannot observe the expected inflation rate directly, economists often rely on surveys. The Federal Reserve Bank of Philadelphia conducts the *Survey of Professional Forecasters*, which provides a consensus estimate by professional economic forecasters of the expected inflation rate over the next year. The University of Michigan conducts a monthly survey of households that includes a question about their expectations of the inflation rate for the upcoming year. Figure 11.3 shows the actual inflation rate and the expected inflation rate as measured by these two surveys. The figure shows that the two measures of the expected inflation rate track the actual inflation rate fairly closely.

The expected inflation rate rose rapidly during the late 1960s and early 1970s, but then it fell dramatically during the early 1980s, and it has been low and fairly stable since 1990. The decrease in the expected inflation rate was part of the period of sustained macroeconomic stability known as the Great Moderation.

Adaptive Expectations How do households and firms form their expectations of future inflation rates? Some economists believe that households and firms have **adaptive expectations**, which is the assumption that people make forecasts of future values of a variable using only past values of the variable. The simplest form of adaptive expectations

Adaptive expectations
The assumption that people make forecasts of future values of a variable using only past values of the variable.

assumes that people expect that the value of a variable, such as the inflation rate, will be the same this year as it was last year. For example, measured by the GDP deflator, the inflation rate for 2011 was 2.1%. At the beginning of 2012, with adaptive expectations, households and firms would expect an inflation rate of 2.1% for 2012. An equation for adaptive expectations is:

$$\pi_t^e = \pi_{t-1}.$$

This equation states that the expected inflation rate for the current year equals the actual inflation rate for the previous year.

When inflation rose during the late 1960s and 1970s, the rise in the actual inflation rate increased the expected inflation rate, which drove the actual inflation rate even higher. During the late 1960s and 1970s, both demand shocks and supply shocks led to higher inflation. When expectations adjusted to these higher inflation rates, the inflation rate rose even more.

Assuming adaptive expectations, we can rewrite the Phillips curve as:

$$\pi_t = \pi_{t-1} + b\widetilde{Y}_t - s_t.$$

Movement Along an Existing Phillips Curve

With the Phillips curve shown in Figure 11.4, we assume initially that there are no supply shocks, so $s_t = 0$. At point A, real GDP equals potential GDP, so $\widetilde{Y}_1 = 0$, and the inflation rate during the current year equals the inflation rate from the previous year, so $\pi_1 = \pi_0$. Because the inflation rate is unchanged, there are no supply shocks, and the output gap equals 0, the expected inflation rate equals the actual inflation rate, $\pi_1 = \pi^e$. Therefore, point A represents short-run equilibrium. Now suppose a positive demand shock, such as an increase in spending on residential construction, causes real GDP to increase above potential GDP, and, therefore, the output gap changes from $\widetilde{Y}_1$

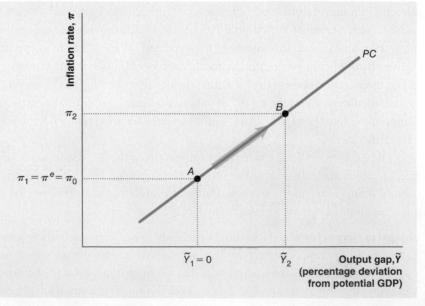

Figure 11.4

An Increase in the Output Gap Increases the Inflation Rate

As real GDP increases relative to potential GDP, firms start to run into capacity constraints and wages and other input prices increase. Firms pass along the higher costs to consumers in the form of higher prices, so the inflation rate increases and short-run equilibrium moves from point A to point B.

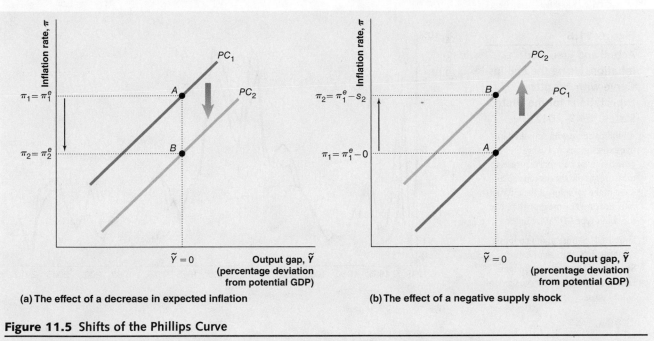

(a) The effect of a decrease in expected inflation

(b) The effect of a negative supply shock

Figure 11.5 Shifts of the Phillips Curve

In panel (a), a decrease in expected inflation shifts the Phillips curve down.

In panel (b), a negative supply shock, such as an increase in the price of oil, shifts the Phillips curve up.

to $\widetilde{Y}_2$. As firms produce beyond their normal capacity, wages and other input prices rise, which firms pass on to consumers by increasing the prices of goods and services. In the equation for the Phillips curve, $b\widetilde{Y}_t$ is greater than zero, so the inflation rate rises from π_1 to π_2, and short-run equilibrium moves from point A to point B.

The experience of the United States during the 1960s illustrates a movement along an existing Phillips curve. During the third quarter of 1963, real GDP equaled potential GDP, so the economy was at point A, with an inflation rate of 0.9%. However, by the first quarter of 1969, real GDP was 3.2% above potential GDP, and the inflation rate had increased to 4.6%. The economy was now at point B.

Shifts of the Phillips Curve

Changes in the expected inflation rate and supply shocks cause the Phillips curve to shift, as illustrated in Figure 11.5.

We first show the effect of a change in expected inflation on the Phillips curve. In panel (a), the economy is initially at point A, where real GDP equals potential GDP, so $\widetilde{Y} = 0$, and for simplicity, we assume that there are no supply shocks, so $s = 0$. As a result, $\pi_1 = \pi_1^e$. Now suppose that the expected inflation rate decreases so that $\pi_1^e > \pi_2^e$, while the output gap remains equal to 0. In this case, the new inflation rate equals $\pi_2 = \pi_2^e$, and the economy is at point B. Point B is clearly not on the original Phillips curve, so the Phillips curve must have shifted down, from PC_1 to PC_2.

Panel (b) shows the effect of an increase in oil prices that increases the cost per unit of output. The economy starts at point A, where the output gap equals 0. The initial

Figure 11.6

Actual and Predicted Inflation, Using the Phillips Curve with Adaptive Expectations for the United States, 1949–2012

A Phillips curve with simple adaptive expectations and using the growth rate of nominal oil prices to measure supply shocks can explain most of the variation in the inflation rate measured by the growth rate of the chain-type GDP price index.

Sources: U.S. Bureau of Economic Analysis; U.S. Bureau of Labor Statistics; Congressional Budget Office; and Federal Reserve Bank of Saint Louis.

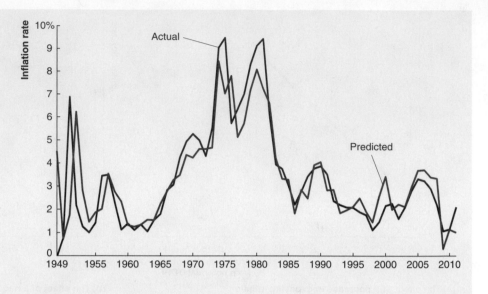

supply shock is zero, so $s_1 = 0$ and $\pi_1 = \pi_1^e - 0$. As a result of the negative supply shock, $s_2 < 0$, and the inflation rate rises to $\pi_2 = \pi_1^e - s_2$. (Recall that because s is preceded by a negative sign in the equation for the Phillips curve, when s takes on a *negative* value, the Phillips curve shifts up.) The economy is now at point B, which is not on the original Phillips curve. The Phillips curve has shifted up, from PC_1 to PC_2.

How Well Does the Phillips Curve Fit the Inflation Data?

One of the Fed's responsibilities is to keep the inflation rate low and stable, so it is important for the Fed to have a good model for how inflation is determined. Chairman Ben Bernanke and other members of the Fed use a version of the Phillips curve when conducting monetary policy. How well does the Phillips curve explain the inflation rate?

Figure 11.6 shows the actual inflation rate and the inflation rate that the Phillips curve predicts, assuming that households and firms have adaptive expectations and using changes in oil prices to measure supply shocks, s_t. Notice that the predicted inflation rate closely tracks the actual inflation rate. Therefore, the Phillips curve provides a good, though not perfect, explanation of movements in the inflation rate.

Making the Connection

Lots of Money but Not Much Inflation Following the Recession of 2007–2009

We saw in the chapter opener that in 2009, as the recession ended, a number of economists predicted that the inflation rate would increase substantially. A few economists even predicted that the United States might experience one of its worst peacetime inflations. For instance, in assessing the effects of the Fed's policies, Arthur Laffer argued: "To date what's happened is potentially far more inflationary than were the monetary policies of the 1970s, when the prime interest rate peaked at 21.5% and inflation peaked in the low double digits." In fact, though, from 2009 to 2012, the inflation rate averaged less than 2%, which was even below the Fed's inflation target.

Given that the monetary base had soared, why didn't the inflation rate take off as these economists had predicted? The answer is partly that the increases in the monetary base resulted in much smaller-than-expected increases in the money supply. More importantly, though, the recovery from the recession was slow, and the U.S. economy suffered from a large output gap and high rates of unemployment through 2012.

When the Fed purchases financial securities, such as Treasury bonds, the funds end up either in banks as bank reserves or as currency in circulation. The monetary base is the sum of bank reserves plus currency. So if, for example, the Fed purchases $100 billion in Treasury bonds, the monetary base will also increase by $100 billion. We can determine the value of the money supply by multiplying the value for the monetary base by the money multiplier (see Chapter 7). Prior to the recession of 2007–2009, the multiplier typically had a value of around 1.5. Once the Fed embarked on heavy purchases of Treasury securities and mortgage-backed securities in the fall of 2008, the money multiplier fell below 1 and remained there. In effect, the money multiplier had become a money *divisor*, and increases in the monetary base resulted in smaller increases in the money supply. The explanation for the decline in the value of the money multiplier is that banks, worried about the creditworthiness of borrowers and deterred by the low interest rates on loans, piled up huge reserves while cutting back on their loans.

Still, despite the low value of the money multiplier, if the economy had been in a strong expansion, the increases in the money supply would have been large enough to have eventually resulted in large increases in the inflation rate. Through 2012, however, the U.S. economy was a long way from experiencing a strong expansion. The figure below shows the output gap for the period from the beginning of 1990 through

MyEconLab Real-time data

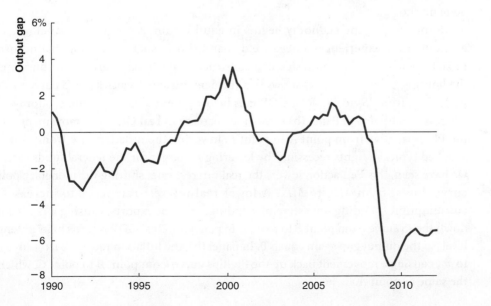

mid-2012. Even though the recession had ended three years earlier, real GDP was still more than 5% below potential GDP. Although this value was smaller than it had been during the worst of the recession, it was still much larger than the output gap had been at any time during the 1990–1991 or 2001 recessions. With real GDP so far below potential GDP, there was little pressure for wages and other costs to increase, which helped to keep the inflation rate low. As an article in the *Economist* magazine put it, "On at least some measurements, both inflation and inflation expectations are behaving *exactly* as one would expect given a persistent, large output gap."

The question remained, however, about what would happen to inflation once the economy entered a stronger expansion. The large reserves held by banks had the potential to result in large increases in the money supply once banks resumed lending at more normal levels. Federal Reserve Chair Ben Bernanke stated that once the economy resumed growing more rapidly, the Fed had an "exit strategy" that would allow it to unwind the large increases in the monetary base before inflation could accelerate. Economists disagreed over whether the Fed would be able to successfully implement this strategy or whether the predictions that inflation would accelerate would eventually prove correct.

Sources: Arthur B. Laffer, "Get Ready for Inflation and Higher Interest Rates," *Wall Street Journal*, June 11, 2009; and "What's Inflation Telling Us About the Output Gap?" *Economist*, March 20, 2012.

See related problem 1.10 at the end of the chapter.

Using Monetary Policy to Fight a Recession

In this section, we combine the *IS* and *MP* curves and the Phillips curve to explain how monetary policy responds to demand shocks. Figure 11.7 shows how the Fed can try to use monetary policy to move the economy back to potential GDP following a negative demand shock.

Suppose that the economy begins in equilibrium at point *A* in panel (a). The economy then experiences a negative demand shock, such as the one that occurred in 2007, when spending on residential construction declined following the bursting of the housing bubble. Panel (a) shows that the demand shock causes the *IS* curve to shift to the left, from IS_1 to IS_2. Real GDP falls below potential GDP, so the economy is in a recession at point *B*. Panel (b) shows the decrease in real GDP as a movement down the Phillips curve from point *A* to point *B*, lowering the inflation rate from π_1 to π_2. The Fed typically fights recessions by lowering its target for the federal funds rate. As we have seen, this Fed action lowers the real interest rate, shifting the monetary policy curve down, from MP_1 to MP_2. A lower real interest rate leads to increases in consumption spending, investment spending, and net exports, causing a movement down the *IS* curve from point *B* to point *C* in panel (a). Real GDP returns to its potential level, so the output gap again equals 0. In panel (b), the inflation rate rises from π_2 back to π_1, causing a movement back up the Phillips curve from point *B* to point *C*, which is the same as point *A*.

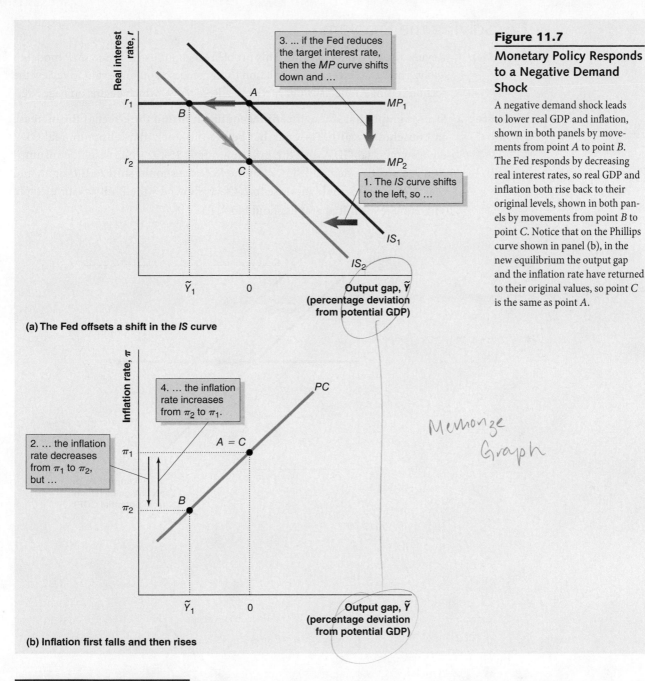

Figure 11.7

Monetary Policy Responds to a Negative Demand Shock

A negative demand shock leads to lower real GDP and inflation, shown in both panels by movements from point *A* to point *B*. The Fed responds by decreasing real interest rates, so real GDP and inflation both rise back to their original levels, shown in both panels by movements from point *B* to point *C*. Notice that on the Phillips curve shown in panel (b), in the new equilibrium the output gap and the inflation rate have returned to their original values, so point *C* is the same as point *A*.

(a) The Fed offsets a shift in the *IS* curve

(b) Inflation first falls and then rises

Solved Problem 11.1

Fed Policy to Keep Inflation from Increasing

During the expansion of the 1990s, the stock market boomed, increasing household wealth and the willingness of households to spend. As a result, aggregate expenditure increased, and the inflation rate accelerated from 1.0% during the fourth quarter of 1998 to 2.4% during the fourth quarter of 2000. What policy could the Fed have pursued to keep the inflation rate from rising? Use the *IS–MP* model to answer this question. Be sure to show any shifts in or movements along the *IS* curve, the *MP* curve, and the Phillips curve.

Solving the Problem

Step 1 **Review the chapter material.** This problem is about using the *IS–MP* model to analyze how the Fed can keep inflation from rising, so you may want to review the section "Using Monetary Policy to Fight a Recession," which begins on page 392.

Step 2 **Draw a graph that shows the initial equilibrium and the effect of the increase in household wealth.** Assume that before the stock market boom, real GDP equals potential GDP, and the inflation rate is 1%. An increase in consumption is a positive demand shock, so the *IS* curve should shift to the right, and the inflation rate should increase to 2.4%, as shown by the Phillips curve graph. Therefore, your initial graphs should look like this:

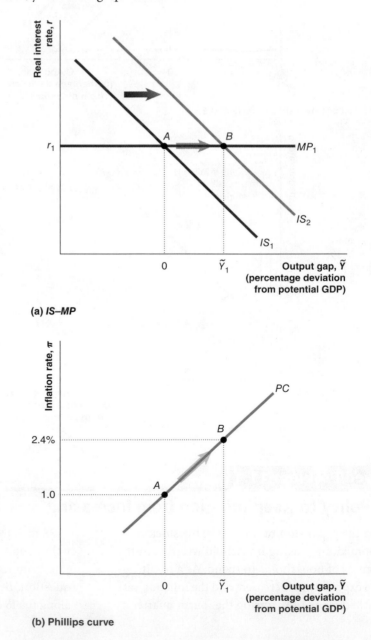

(a) *IS–MP*

(b) Phillips curve

Step 3   Determine the Fed's response. How can the Fed keep the inflation rate from increasing? The Phillips curve shows that the output gap would have to remain equal to 0 to keep the inflation rate at 1.0%. The Fed affects the output gap by changing the real interest rate and the position of the *MP* curve. To keep the output gap at 0, the real interest rate would have to increase, so the *MP* curve must shift up. Your graphs should now look like this:

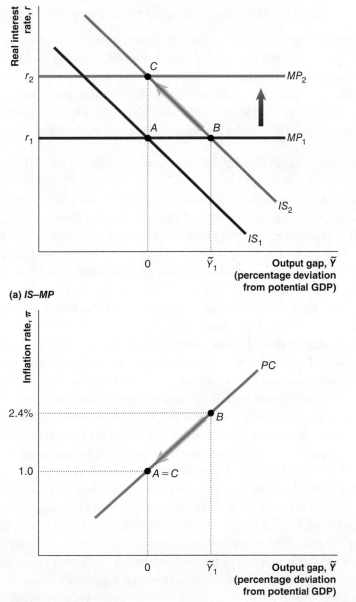

(a) *IS–MP*

(b) **Phillips curve**

In principle, the Fed could have prevented the increase in the inflation rate. The Fed did increase short-term nominal interest rates from 4.75% in June 1999 to 6.5% in May 2000. But, the Fed did not increase interest rates quickly enough to prevent the inflation rate from increasing.

See related problem 1.11 at the end of the chapter.

11.2

Learning Objective

Use the *IS–MP* model to understand the performance of the U.S. economy during the recession of 2007–2009.

The Performance of the U.S. Economy During 2007–2009

The U.S. economy experienced three shocks during the 2007–2009 period:

- A financial crisis that affected the *MP* curve by increasing the risk premium investors required before making loans and affected the *IS* curve by reducing the ability of households and firms to finance their spending
- The collapse of the housing bubble, which affected the *IS* curve
- A surge in oil prices, which affected the Phillips curve

As a result of these shocks, real GDP fell from 0.2% above potential GDP during the second quarter of 2007 to 7.4% below potential GDP during the third quarter of 2009. The inflation rate rose from 1.8% during the fourth quarter of 2006 to 3.2% during the third quarter of 2008, before decreasing to −0.4% during the second quarter of 2009. In this section, we use the *IS–MP* model to explain how the three shocks caused both the decrease in real GDP and the temporary increase in the inflation rate.

Using the *IS–MP* Model to Analyze the Financial Crisis and the Housing Crash

The default-risk premium is measured as the difference between the interest rate on Aaa corporate bonds and the interest rate on a 10-year Treasury note. The default-risk premium typically rises during recessions because investors believe that corporations are more likely to default on their loans. Typically, though, the increase in the default-risk premium does not completely offset the Fed's efforts to lower the long-term real interest rate by reducing its target for the federal funds rate.

In June 2007, the default-risk premium was 0.65%, which was just below the average of 0.77% over the 1953–2008 period. In August, the default-risk premium rose to 1.25% because investors became increasingly concerned that problems in the housing market would spill over into the wider economy. The default-risk premium continued to rise until it reached 2.13% on March 17, 2008, the day JPMorgan Chase offered to purchase the investment bank Bear Stearns, thereby saving it from bankruptcy. Because investors had become very concerned that firms might default on their bonds, they were unwilling to purchase corporate bonds except at higher interest rates. So, the default-risk premium rose, and many firms were unable to obtain financing for investment projects. Problems in financial markets also affected households as banks began to increase interest rates and to demand more collateral for loans. These changes restricted the ability of households to borrow and caused consumption and housing sales to decline. So, the financial market shock reduced both consumption and investment. If financial market turbulence had lasted a brief period, it would probably not have significantly affected investment—because it can take months or longer for firms to plan investment projects or for individuals to purchase a home. However, the default-risk premium continued to rise to 2.73% in November 2008, and it remained elevated at 1.56% as late as May 2010.

Housing prices began to decline in 2006, as the housing bubble burst. The value of a home is a major component of a household's wealth, and when wealth decreases, so does household consumption. In addition, as housing sales declined, builders cut back on construction of new homes. The growth rate of residential construction went from 6.2% during 2006 to −22.9% during 2008, and it was still −3.0% in 2010. The rapid decrease in housing prices reduced both consumption and investment.

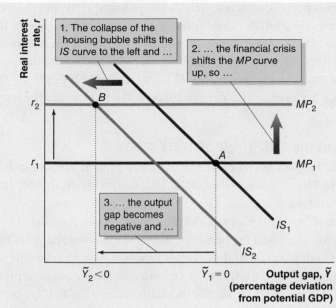

1. The collapse of the housing bubble shifts the *IS* curve to the left and …

2. … the financial crisis shifts the *MP* curve up, so …

3. … the output gap becomes negative and …

(a) *IS–MP*

Figure 11.8

The Financial and Real Estate Market Shocks and the U.S. Economy, 2007–2009

The financial crisis shifts the *MP* curve upward, and the collapse in housing prices shifts the *IS* curve to the left in panel (a). As a result, the real interest rate increases and the output gap becomes negative in panel (a), and the inflation rate decreases in panel (b). In both panels, short-run equilibrium moves from point *A* to point *B*.

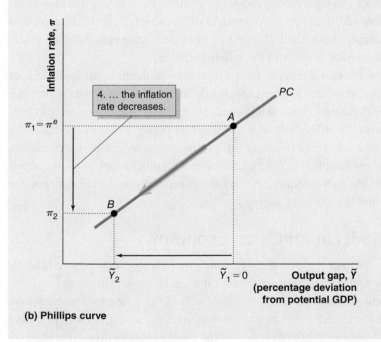

4. … the inflation rate decreases.

(b) Phillips curve

Figure 11.8 uses the *IS–MP* model to show the effects of the housing and financial market shocks. Panel (a) shows the effect of these shocks on the *IS* and *MP* curves. In mid-2007, the economy was in equilibrium at point *A*, where $\widetilde{Y}_1 = 0$. The financial crisis increased the default-risk premium, so the *MP* curve shifted up, from MP_1 to MP_2. The collapse of the housing bubble reduced wealth and residential construction, causing the *IS* curve to shift to the left. In addition, the financial crisis made it more difficult for households and firms to borrow the funds they needed to finance consumption and investment. These effects combined to shift the *IS* curve from IS_1 to IS_2. By 2009, short-run equilibrium was at point *B*, with real GDP below potential GDP and the output gap at $\widetilde{Y}_2$. Panel (b) uses the Phillips curve to show the effect of the change in the output gap on the inflation rate. As short-run equilibrium moves from point *A* to point *B*, the inflation rate falls from π_1 to π_2. The *IS–MP* model predicts that the financial crisis and the bursting of the housing bubble should have reduced real GDP *and* the inflation rate. However, we have yet to consider the effect on the economy of the surge in oil prices during 2008.

The *IS–MP* Model and the Oil Shock of 2007–2008

The price of oil rose from $56.60 a barrel in March 2007 to a high of $145.66 in July 2008, before decreasing to $30.81 in December 2008. This supply shock should have caused the inflation rate to increase.

Figure 11.9 shows the effect of the oil price shock, using the *IS–MP* model. As we just saw, the financial market shock and the housing market crash moved the short-run equilibrium to point *B* in both panel (a) and panel (b). Panel (a) reproduces panel (a) from Figure 11.8. In understanding the effect of the oil price shock, we begin at point *B*. The increase in oil prices was a negative supply shock that caused the Phillips curve in panel (b) to shift up from PC_1 to PC_2. The inflation rate increased to π_3, output remained at $\widetilde{Y}_2$, and short-run equilibrium moved to point *C*. Because the increase in inflation did not cause an additional decline in real GDP, in panel (a) point *C* is also point *B*. As a result of the supply shock, the inflation rate increased. After mid-2008, oil prices fell, the *PC* curve shifted back down, and the inflation rate fell.

The *IS–MP* model is a useful tool for analyzing short-run fluctuations in the output gap and in the inflation rate. The *IS* curve captures the effect of demand shocks that can temporarily push short-run macroeconomic equilibrium away from a zero output gap. The *MP* curve captures the effects not only of monetary policy, but also the effects of fluctuations in the real interest rate resulting from changes in the default-risk premium, changes in investors' expectations of future interest rates, and changes in the expected inflation rate. Finally, the Phillips curve captures the effect of changes in the output gap on the inflation rate and the effects of supply shocks.

Learning Objective

Understand the *IS–MP* model in an open economy.

The *IS–MP* Model in an Open Economy

To this point in our discussion of the *IS–MP* model, we have not incorporated the effect of changes in the real interest rate on the nominal exchange rate or on net exports. Doing so is important, however, because the flow of trade and financial investments between the United States and other countries is greater today than at any previous time. The details of the open economy version of the *IS–MP* model differ depending on whether the economy has a fixed or floating exchange rate system. We first consider the case of a floating exchange rate.

The *IS* Curve with a Floating Exchange Rate

The *IS* curve shows the negative relationship between the real interest rate and aggregate expenditure in the goods market. As the real interest rate increases, the cost of borrowing increases, so households and firms borrow less to finance consumption and investment. In an open economy, changes in the nominal exchange rate will affect net exports.

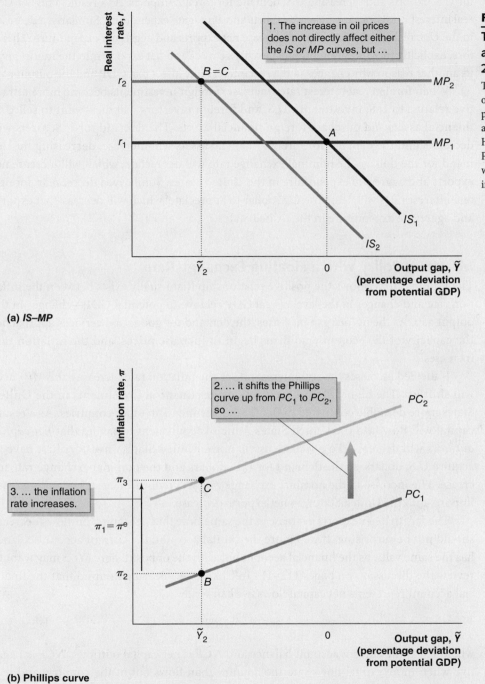

1. The increase in oil prices does not directly affect either the *IS or MP* curves, but …

2. … it shifts the Phillips curve up from PC_1 to PC_2, so …

3. … the inflation rate increases.

(a) IS–MP

(b) Phillips curve

Figure 11.9

The Oil Price Shock and the U.S. Economy, 2007–2009

The increase in the price of oil does not shift the curves in panel (a), which is the same as panel (a) in Figure 11.8. However, the increase shifts the Phillips curve up in panel (b), which puts upward pressure on inflation.

In this section, we modify the *IS* curve to take into account the effect of changes in the real interest rate on the exchange rate and net exports.

If the real interest in the United States increases, foreign investors will increase their demand for U.S. dollars in order to buy U.S. financial assets. The increased demand for U.S. dollars will increase the nominal exchange rate, thereby decreasing foreign demand for U.S. exports and increasing U.S. demand for foreign imports. As a result, a higher U.S. real interest rate should reduce net exports and aggregate expenditure. Similarly, a decrease in the U.S. real interest rate should increase net exports and aggregate expenditure. Therefore, explicitly incorporating nominal exchange rates and net exports into the model gives us another reason why changes in the real interest rate affect real GDP and the output gap.

When foreign real interest rates increase, foreign investments become more attractive relative to U.S. investments. U.S. and foreign investors will then want to sell U.S. financial assets and purchase foreign financial assets. The demand for U.S. assets will decrease, and the demand for foreign financial assets will increase, decreasing the demand for the dollar. The nominal exchange rate will depreciate, which will increase net exports and aggregate expenditure in the United States. Similarly, a decrease in foreign real interest rates will cause the U.S. dollar to appreciate, which will decrease net exports and aggregate expenditure in the United States.

Monetary Policy with a Floating Exchange Rate

The Phillips curve shows the positive relationship that usually exists between the inflation rate and changes in the level of real GDP relative to potential GDP—changes in the output gap. As the output gap increases, the demand for goods and services approaches the capacity of the economy, so firms begin to increase prices, and the inflation rate increases.

If the Fed increases the real interest rate as the inflation rate increases, the *MP* curve will shift up. The higher real interest rate makes financial investments in the United States more desirable compared to financial investments in other countries. As a result, capital will flow into the United States, which is equivalent to saying that *net capital outflows* will decrease. To purchase assets in the United States, investors first have to acquire U.S. dollars, so the demand for U.S. dollars and the nominal exchange rate increase. The increase in the nominal exchange rate will reduce U.S. exports and increase imports into the United States, so net exports decrease.

The fact that net exports decrease at the same time that net capital outflows decrease should not be surprising. If we ignore the capital account, the current account balance has the same value as the financial account but with the opposite sign. (You may want to review the discussion on pages 112–114 in Chapter 4.) Bearing in mind that the financial account represents net capital flows, we can write:

$$CA = NCF,$$

where *CA* is the current account balance and *NCF* is net capital outflows. *NCF* is negative when more capital flows into the country than flows out of the country, and it is positive when more capital flows out of the country than into the country. If a country has a current account deficit, net capital outflow is also negative. For example, because the United States ran a current account deficit in 2012, net capital outflows were also negative, so capital was flowing into the United States during 2012.

We can conclude that because changes in real interest rates have important effects on both net exports and net capital outflows, when a country has a floating exchange rate, monetary policy causes changes in net exports and net capital outflows.

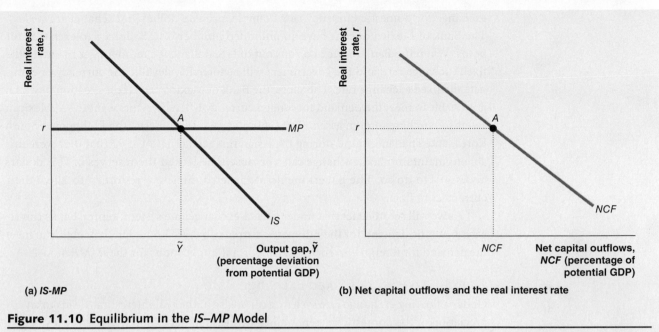

Figure 11.10 Equilibrium in the *IS–MP* Model

Equilibrium occurs in panel (a) where the *IS* and *MP* curves intersect. Panel (b) shows that net capital outflows decrease as the real interest rate increases. Because net exports equal net capital outflows, the level of net capital outflows in panel (b) is also the level of net exports.

Equilibrium in an Open Economy with a Floating Exchange Rate

Figure 11.10 shows equilibrium in the *IS–MP* model when we take into account the effect of changes in the real interest rate on net capital flows (*NCF*). Equilibrium occurs at point *A*, where the *IS* and *MP* curves intersect. The *IS–MP* graph in panel (a) determines the equilibrium real interest rate. The equilibrium real interest rate then determines net capital outflows in panel (b).

The *IS–MP* Model with a Fixed Exchange Rate

Under a fixed exchange rate system, the central bank agrees to buy and sell the domestic currency at a fixed nominal exchange rate. This policy affects the *IS–MP* model in several important ways.

If Mexico decided to fix the exchange rate of the peso at $1 = 14 pesos, the Bank of Mexico would have to be willing to buy and sell pesos at that exchange rate. A fixed exchange rate means that (1) no banks or other currency traders would sell U.S. dollars for less than 14 pesos because the Bank of Mexico is willing to pay 14 pesos for each dollar; and (2) no currency traders would pay more than 14 pesos for a dollar because the Bank of Mexico will sell dollars for 14 pesos each. In this way, the central bank can fix the nominal exchange rate.

Fixed exchange rate systems pose an interesting challenge for governments. Central banks have an unlimited ability to create their own currency, so they have no difficulty maintaining a fixed exchange rate system by providing the domestic currency in exchange for a foreign currency (for example, providing pesos in exchange for dollars). Things are a bit trickier when a central bank is asked to provide foreign currency in exchange for domestic currency (for example, provide dollars in exchange for pesos). The Bank of Mexico doesn't have an unlimited number of U.S. dollars to exchange for pesos. When the Bank of Mexico runs out of U.S. dollars, it can no longer maintain the fixed exchange rate, and the government will be forced to devalue the currency or eliminate the fixed exchange rate. Therefore, the Bank of Mexico can face a situation in which it is unable to meet the demand for foreign currency when investors want to sell Mexican assets to purchase foreign assets. The central banks of Indonesia, the Philippines, South Korea, and Thailand found during the Asian financial crisis of 1997 that they were unable to maintain fixed exchange rates because they lacked the reserves of U.S. dollars necessary to do so. The governments of those countries were forced to allow their currencies to float.

As we will see, the fact that under a fixed-exchange rate system, central banks can always meet the demand for their domestic currency but are limited in their ability to meet the demand for foreign currencies has important implications for the *IS-MP* model.

The *IS* Curve with a Fixed Exchange Rate

Under a floating exchange rate system, an increase in the real interest rate leads to an appreciation of the domestic currency and a decrease in net exports. Therefore, exchange rates and net exports provide a country with an additional mechanism through which an increase in the real interest rate will lead to lower aggregate expenditure and output. Under a fixed exchange rate system, this mechanism does not exist because the nominal exchange rate is fixed. Therefore, changes in the real interest rate do not affect the nominal exchange rate, so net exports do not change as the real interest rate changes. But the *IS* curve still slopes downward because a higher real interest rate still reduces consumption and investment. In this respect, the *IS* curve under a fixed exchange rate system is very similar to the *IS* curve for a closed economy.

With a fixed exchange rate, if the government decides to change the exchange rate, the *IS* curve will shift. For example, suppose that the government decides to reduce the fixed exchange rate, or *devalue the currency*. In that case, exports would become cheaper and imports would become more expensive, so net exports would increase, and the current account deficit would decrease. The increase in net exports would shift the *IS* curve to the right. Similarly, if the government decides to increase the fixed exchange rate or *revalue the currency*, exports would become more expensive, and imports would become cheaper. Net exports would decrease, and the *IS* curve would shift to the left.

The *MP* Curve with a Fixed Exchange Rate

Under a fixed exchange rate system, there is a limit to how low the central bank can set the domestic real interest rate. As the real interest rate decreases, the demand for domestic financial assets decreases, which causes currency traders to exchange the domestic currency for foreign currency. To meet this demand for foreign currency, the central bank needs sufficient foreign-exchange reserves. But as the real interest rate decreases, domestic financial assets become less and less attractive, so investors exchange more and more of the domestic currency for foreign currency. Eventually, the central bank will run out of foreign-exchange reserves, and the fixed exchange rate system will collapse.

The lowest real interest rate that the central bank can set while still maintaining the fixed exchange rate system is $\bar{r}$. When the real interest rate falls to this level, the central bank cannot lower it any further and still maintain the fixed exchange rate system because it does not have enough foreign exchange reserves. So, the *MP* curve cannot fall below MP_{Min} which is horizontal at $\bar{r}$. We can conclude that there is a limit to how much monetary policy can reduce the real interest rate while maintaining a fixed exchange rate.

Macro Data: Did the Gold Standard Make the Great Depression Worse?

Currently, many countries, including the United States, allow their currencies to float but occasionally intervene to buy and sell their currency or other currencies to affect exchange rates. In other words, many countries use a managed float exchange rate system. When the Great Depression started in 1929, the United States, Japan, and much of Europe used the gold standard, which is a fixed exchange rate system. Under the gold standard, a country's currency consisted of gold coins and paper currency that the government was committed to redeem for gold. Exchange rates were determined by the relative amounts of gold in each country's currency, and the size of a country's money supply was determined by the amount of gold available. The gold standard required central banks to buy and sell gold at a fixed price and to maintain a sufficient reserve of gold. Gold flowed freely across international borders. If a central bank believed that too much gold was flowing out of the country, the central bank would often increase interest rates. The higher interest rates would provide an incentive for gold to flow back into the country. Fixing the price of the currency in terms of gold eliminates exchange rate uncertainty and so makes international transactions easier. It also makes it easier for households and firms to plan for the future. However, the greatest drawback to the gold standard was that the central bank lacked control of the money supply.

Economists believe that the gold standard worsened the Great Depression. Maintaining a fixed exchange rate like the gold standard restricts how much central banks can lower interest rates during a recession. As interest rates fall, gold flows out of the country to countries with higher interest rates. Losing too much gold will force the country off of the gold standard. In fact, a central bank could be forced to increase interest rates to reduce a gold outflow, even if doing so made a recession worse. In the 1930s, the gold standard prevented central banks from aggressively responding to the Great Depression. For example, in 1930 and 1931, the Federal Reserve was faced with gold outflows and raised interest rates in response. Even though the interest rate increases allowed the United States to remain on the gold standard, many economists believe the increases worsened the Great Depression.

The figure below shows industrial production in four countries from 1929 to 1936. In 1931, Japan and the United Kingdom were the first countries to leave the gold standard.

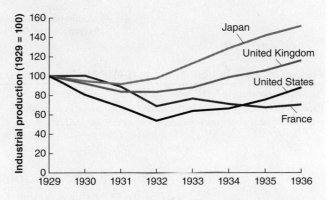

Notice that industrial production fell by less than 10% in Japan and about 17% in the United Kingdom, and both economies started to recover from the Great Depression in 1932. In contrast, the United States did not leave the gold standard until 1933 and France until 1936, and the downturn was much more severe in these two countries. Industrial production fell by over 30% in France and by nearly 50% in the United States. In the United States, the recovery from the Great Depression did not begin until March 1933 when President Franklin Roosevelt took the United States off the gold standard.

The poor economic performance of France, the United States, and other countries that were late to abandon the gold standard is the primary reason that countries did not return to the gold standard in later years.

Source: Barry Eichengreen, "The Origins and Nature of the Great Slump Revisited," *Economic History Review*, vol. 45, no. 2 (May 1992), pp. 213–239; Barry Eichengreen, *Golden Fetters: The Gold Standard and the Great Depression 1919–1939*, 1992, New York: Oxford University Press; *Statistical Year-Book of the League of Nations, 1936–37*, Geneva: League of Nations, 1937, Table 105, p. 163.

See related problem 3.6 at the end of the chapter.

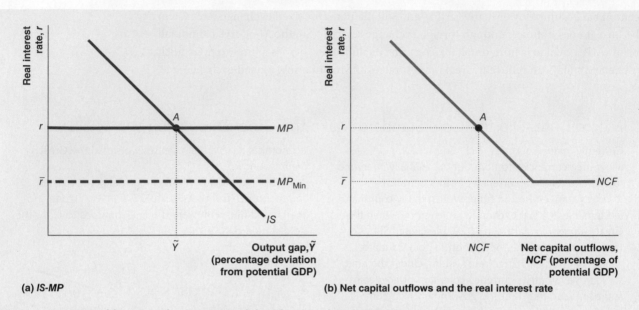

(a) IS-MP

(b) Net capital outflows and the real interest rate

Figure 11.11 Equilibrium in the *IS–MP* Model with a Fixed Exchange Rate

Equilibrium occurs in panel (a), where the *IS* and *MP* curves intersect. Panel (b) shows that net capital outflows decrease as the real interest rate increases. If the central bank is acquiring foreign-exchange reserves, it can maintain the fixed exchange rate system. However, the domestic interest rate cannot fall below $\bar{r}$, and the *MP* curve cannot shift below MP_{Min}, while maintaining the fixed exchange rate system.

Equilibrium in an Open Economy with a Fixed Exchange Rate

Figure 11.11 shows equilibrium in the *IS–MP* model under a fixed exchange rate system. Equilibrium occurs at point *A*, where the *IS* and *MP* curves intersect. The *IS–MP* graph in panel (a) determines the equilibrium real interest rate, just as it does under a floating exchange rate system. The real interest rate $\bar{r}$ indicates the lowest real interest rate compatible with the central bank being able to maintain fixed exchange rates. The equilibrium real interest rate then determines net capital outflows, *NCF*, in panel (b). At a high domestic real interest rate, investors want to purchase domestic financial assets. These purchases increase the demand for the domestic currency, so the central bank acquires foreign-exchange reserves as currency traders exchange foreign currency for the domestic currency. At a low domestic real interest rate, investors want to sell domestic financial assets. These sales decrease the demand for the domestic currency, so the central bank loses foreign-exchange reserves as currency traders exchange domestic currency for foreign currency. In panel (b), the *NCF* curve becomes horizontal at $\bar{r}$ because that is the lowest real interest rate that will occur as long as the central bank maintains a fixed exchange rate.

Making the Connection

Can the Euro Survive?

There are advantages to having a fixed exchange rate. Firms that export find it easier to plan if they know what the foreign currency price of their products will be. In addition, if the exchange rate is fixed, firms can borrow in foreign currencies with less

Model in an Open Economy **405**

risk. The appeal of fixed exchange rates eventually led the European Union (EU) in 1999 to decide to move to a common currency. In 2002, the euro replaced individual currencies in participating countries. By 2012, 17 members of the EU, including all of the largest economies with the exception of the United Kingdom, had adopted the euro. The European Central Bank assumed responsibility for monetary policy and for issuing currency.

   The period from 2001 until the beginning of the global economic downturn at the end of 2007 was one of relative economic stability in most of Europe. With low interest rates, low inflation rates, and expanding employment and production, the advantages of the euro seemed obvious. With the beginning of the financial crisis of 2007, the disadvantages of the euro also began to become obvious. Although the European Union had been taking steps to integrate the economies of the member countries, many aspects of these economies, including rates of taxation, extent of unionization, government spending and transfer policies, and so on, remained quite different. One result of these differences among economies was differences in inflation rates. The figure below shows increases in the consumer price level between 2002 and 2011 for France, Germany, Greece, and Spain. Prices in Greece and Spain increased much more than in France or Germany.

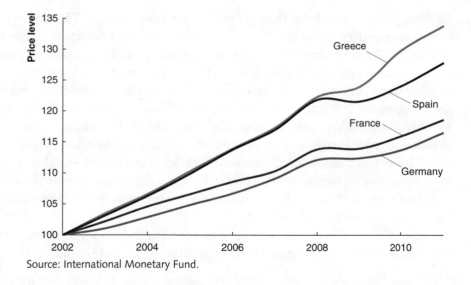

Source: International Monetary Fund.

MyEconLab Real-time data

   Recall the formula for the real exchange rate:

$$e = E \times \left(\frac{P^{\text{Domestic}}}{P^{\text{Foreign}}} \right),$$

where:
e = real exchange rate
E = nominal exchange rate
P^{Domestic} = domestic price level
P^{Foreign} = foreign price level

Once the euro was introduced, the nominal exchange rate among these countries was fixed, but the real exchange could still change as the price levels in the countries changed. As the figure shows, the price levels in Greece and Spain rose much more than the price levels in France and Germany. As a result, Greece and Spain experienced sharply higher real exchange rates than did France and Germany. The higher exchange rates reduced Greece's and Spain's net exports and slowed their recovery from the recession of 2007–2009. While France and Germany were running current account surpluses, Greece and Spain were running large current account deficits. In fact, these economies were worse off in 2011 than they had been during the worldwide financial crisis a few years earlier. In 2011, the unemployment rate in Spain was 21.6% and in Greece it was 17.3%, while in France it was 9.7% and in Germany it was 6.0%.

If Spain and Greece still had their own currencies, their nominal exchange rates could have declined, thereby increasing their exports and reducing their imports. Iceland, which does not use the euro, experienced a substantial decline in its nominal exchange rate. Partly as a result, the unemployment rate in Iceland in 2011 was only 7.4%.

There were two ways that Spain and Greece could restore competitiveness—that is, reduce the prices of their exports and of their domestic goods in competition with foreign imports:

1. *Lower inflation rates to below those of their major trading partners.* This way of restoring competitiveness was difficult because in 2010 and 2011 the inflation rates in France and Germany were lower than in Greece and Spain. Some economists and policymakers suggested that price levels in Greece and Spain would have to fall—in other words, deflation would have to occur—to restore the competitiveness of their economies. This internal devaluation was difficult to achieve because, as we have seen, wages and prices tend to exhibit downward rigidity, which means that, in practice, cutting wages and prices is difficult. Attempting to reduce wages and prices led to significant political unrest in both Spain and Greece. An alternative to deflation was for Germany, in particular, to have a significantly higher inflation rate than Spain or Greece. There was little political support for this approach in Germany, however.

2. *Abandon the euro.* If Spain and Greece reverted to using their own currencies, these currencies could depreciate against the euro, helping to restore competitiveness.

Most economists and policymakers believed that a breakup of the euro—or even the exit of a few countries—would be likely to cause extensive economic disruptions, probably pushing the euro area countries into a serious recession. In late 2012, it appeared that both Greece and Spain would continue using the euro.

Sources: David Román, Santiago Perez, and Jonathan House, "Rajoy Upbeat on Aid Plan," *Wall Street Journal*, June 10, 2012; Charles Forelle and Marcus Walker, "Dithering at the Top Turned EU Crisis to Global Threat," *Wall Street Journal*, December 29, 2011; Kathleen Madigan, "Forecasters Flying Blind When Predicting Repercussions of Greek Exit," *Wall Street Journal*, May 25, 2012; and "A Central-Bank Failure of Epic Proportions," *Economist*, June 1, 2012.

See related problem 3.7 at the end of the chapter.

Answering the Key Question

Continued from page 380

At the beginning of this chapter, we asked:

"What explains the severity of the 2007–2009 recession?"

Most economists were surprised by the severity of the 2007–2009 recession. During the previous 25 years of the Great Moderation, the U.S. economy had experienced only the mild recessions of 1990–1991 and 2001. It appeared that the Fed had learned to tame the business cycle. Even in early 2007, after it had become clear that significant problems had developed in the subprime mortgage market, many economists and policymakers, including Fed Chairman Ben Bernanke, were uncertain that a recession would occur at all, much less a recession more severe than any since the Great Depression of the 1930s. As we have seen in this chapter, the key reason the recession was so severe is that it was accompanied by a financial crisis. It is not a coincidence that both the Great Depression and the recession of 2007–2009 were accompanied by financial crises.

This chapter has discussed how a financial crisis reduces the effectiveness of the Fed's key policy tool: reducing short-term nominal interest rates. Although the Fed reduced short-term rates to historic lows, a sharp increase in the default-risk premium led to increases in the long-term real interest rates that households and firms pay when borrowing. These high real interest rates, combined with the reluctance of many banks and other financial firms to make loans at any rate of interest, led to sharp declines in consumption and investment spending and a severe recession.

Key Terms and Problems

Key Terms

Adaptive expectations, p. 387   Stagflation, p. 386

11.1 **The *IS–MP* Model and the Phillips Curve**
Understand the role of the Phillips curve in the *IS–MP* model.

Review Questions

1.1 What is the Phillips curve? Why did economists and policymakers initially believe that the Phillips curve represented a structural relationship in the economy?

1.2 What is the equation for the Phillips curve with the output gap on the horizontal axis? How does a supply shock affect the Phillips curve with the output gap on the horizontal axis?

1.3 What causes a movement along the Phillips curve with the output gap on the horizontal axis? What causes the Phillips curve to shift?

Problems and Applications

1.4 "Supply-side" government policies aim to stimulate productivity through tax cuts and work incentives. Proponents of these policies argue that changes in the individual and corporate tax codes and cuts in capital gains taxes set the stage for productivity gains during the 1990s.

a. What effect would an increase in productivity have on the Phillips curve? Illustrate your answer with a graph.

b. What effect would the productivity increase have on the inflation rate, holding other factors constant?

MyEconLab   Visit **www.myeconlab.com** to complete these exercises online and get instant feedback. Exercises that update with real-time data are marked with Ⓦ.

1.5 Suppose that the output gap is zero.

    a. Graph the economy's initial equilibrium using the *IS–MP* model including the Phillips curve.

    b. Now suppose that the government increases spending due to a war. Show the effect on output and inflation, using both the *IS–MP* and Phillips curve graphs.

1.6 Consider the following statement: "Because wages and prices are sticky, the Phillips curve relationship between inflation and the output gap is valid only when the output gap is positive." Do you agree with this statement? Briefly explain.

1.7 Recent evidence suggests that over time the Phillips curve has flattened. An article in the *Economist* states: "A flatter Phillips curve is good news when unemployment is falling. But it also implies bad news if inflation rises significantly."

    a. If firms find it difficult to raise prices, why might the result be a flatter Phillips curve?

    b. How would the effect of a demand shock be different if the Phillips curve is relatively flat than if it is relatively steep?

    c. Why does the article argue that a flatter Phillips curve may be bad news if there is high inflation?

Source: "Curve Ball," *Economist*, September 28, 2006.

1.8 In April 2012, Federal Reserve Chair Ben Bernanke stated in a press conference that inflation expectations of households and firms were "well anchored."

    a. What does it mean to refer to expectations of inflation as "well anchored"?

    b. If expectations are adaptive, are they likely to be well anchored? Briefly explain.

Source: Board of Governors of the Federal Reserve System, "Transcript of Chairman Bernanke's Press Conference April 25, 2012," April 25, 2012.

1.9 [**Related to the** Chapter Opener **on page 380**] In 2009, Simon Johnson, former chief economist at the International Monetary Fund, believed that Fed policies might lead to a sharp increase in inflation. He argued:

> The large increase in credit from the Federal Reserve can potentially push up prices, even though unemployment remains relatively high. . . . If this seems far-fetched, remember the importance of self-fulfilling expectations as far as inflation is concerned.

Use the equation for the Phillips curve to explain how it is possible to have a high inflation rate even if the unemployment rate is high.

Source: Simon Johnson, "Inflation Fears," *New York Times*, May 28, 2009.

1.10 [**Related to the** Making the Connection **on page 390**] The output gap can be difficult to measure because potential GDP must be estimated, and economists' estimates differ. In 2012, the Congressional Budget Office (CBO) estimated that potential GDP was about $1 trillion lower than the CBO's 2007 forecast had predicted.

    a. Was the output gap larger or smaller (in absolute value) in 2012 than it would have been if the CBO's 2007 forecast had been correct? Briefly explain.

    b. If the CBO's 2007 forecast had been correct, is it likely that the inflation rate in 2012 would have been higher or lower than it actually was? Briefly explain.

1.11 [**Related to** Solved Problem 11.1 **on page 393**] In the aftermath of the 2007–2009 financial crisis, the Fed became concerned about deflation.

    a. Use the *IS–MP* model including the Phillips curve to show how a decrease in aggregate expenditure could cause deflation.

    b. What policies should the Fed pursue to attempt to prevent deflation? Use the *IS–MP* model including the Phillips curve in your answer.

11.2 The Performance of the U.S. Economy During 2007–2009

Use the *IS–MP* model to understand the performance of the U.S. economy during the recession of 2007–2009.

Review Questions

2.1 Briefly explain what happened to real GDP and the inflation rate during the recession of 2007–2009.

2.2 What were the three shocks that the U.S. economy experienced during the period of 2007–2009? Explain how each of these three shocks can be shown in the *IS–MP* model including the Phillips curve.

Problems and Applications

2.3 China experienced many of the negative effects of the 2007–2009 recession. Like the United States, China was faced with higher oil prices. Unlike in the United States, however, housing prices in China did not fall. China's exports did decline sharply as the recession lowered incomes in the United States and other trading partners. Assume that China was producing at potential GDP prior to the recession. Use the *IS–MP* model including the Phillips curve to show the effects of the recession in China.

2.4 Prior to the 2007–2009 recession, China's inflation rate appeared to be increasing.

    a. What would a high and increasing rate of inflation imply about China's output gap?

    b. What would you expect to happen to China's inflation rate as a result of the U.S. recession?

2.5 Some economists were concerned that the financial crisis of 2007–2009 would lead to problems with deflation. The Federal Reserve Bank of San Francisco's *Economic Letter* stated: "A popular version of the well-known Phillips curve model of inflation predicts that we are on the cusp of a deflationary spiral in which prices will fall at ever-increasing rates over the next several years."

    a. How might a deflationary spiral occur in the Phillips curve model?

    b. Why do you think that a deflationary spiral did not occur?

Source: "The Risk of Deflation," *FRBSF Economic Letter*, March 27, 2009.

2.6 Consider the following statement: "The event that caused the recession of 2007–2009 was the failure of Lehman Brothers. If Lehman Brothers had not been allowed to fail, there would have been no effect on the default-risk premium and thus no demand shock." Do you agree with this statement? Briefly explain.

11.3 The *IS–MP* Model in an Open Economy

Understand the *IS–MP* model in an open economy.

Review Questions

3.1 How does the open-economy *IS–MP* model incorporate net exports assuming a floating exchange rate system? Assuming a fixed exchange rate system?

3.2 What is different about the *MP* curve in a fixed exchange rate system as compared to a floating exchange rate system?

3.3 Explain how the equilibrium real interest rate, net capital outflows, and the level of net exports are determined in an open economy.

Problems and Applications

3.4 For each of the following cases, use the *IS–MP* model and the *NCF* curve to explain the effect on the output gap, the real interest rate, and net capital flows, assuming that exchange rates are flexible.

a. Consumers decide to spend more and save less.

b. There is an increase in incomes in Europe, so U.S. net exports increase.

c. The Federal Reserve reduces the money supply.

d. Expected profits from newly built factories in the United States increase.

3.5 In April 2011, the European Central Bank (ECB) increased its target interest rate, while other major central banks held their target interest rates constant.

a. What effect would a rise in European interest rates be expected to have on output in Europe? What effect would it have on net capital flows?

b. How would this rise in European interest rates affect the value of the euro relative to the value of the dollar?

3.6 [**Related to the** Macro Data Box **on page 403**] The Greek unemployment rate rose from 7.5% during the first quarter of 2008 to 21.7% during the second quarter of 2012. Because Greece uses the euro rather than its own currency, the country is not able to devalue its currency in an attempt to stimulate the economy.

a. Suppose Greece abandoned the euro as its currency and reintroduced its former currency, the drachma, with an exchange rate of 1 euro = 1 drachma. Draw a graph using the open economy version of the *IS-MP* model to show the effect on Greece's output gap and inflation rate if the country then devalued the drachma to 1 euro = 2 drachma.

b. Withdrawing from the euro would create a significant amount of uncertainty. Draw a graph using the open economy version of the *IS-MP* model to show how the uncertainty caused by the withdrawal would affect Greece's output gap and inflation rate.

c. Based on the experience of countries leaving the gold standard and devaluing their currencies during the Great Depression, discuss what you think would be the ultimate effect on the Greek economy of abandoning the euro.

3.7 [**Related to the** Making the Connection **on page 404**] A column published in the *New York Times* in 2012 observes that "Greece suffers from a crippling competitiveness gap and is locked into the euro."

a. What is a "competitiveness gap"?

b. Was Greece's competitiveness gap connected to its use of the euro? Briefly explain.

Source: Katrin Bennhold, "What History Can Explain About Greek Crisis," *New York Times*, May 21, 2012.

Data Exercises

D11.1: [Excel exercise] Using data from the St. Louis Federal Reserve (http://research.stlouisfed.org/fred2/) FRED database, examine the experience of the US. economy during the 1990s. The U.S. economy experienced a positive technology shock with the spread of information communication technology and the internet after 1995.

a. Download monthly data on the Personal Consumption Expenditure price index (PCEPI) from 1981 to the present.

Calculate the inflation rate from 1982 to 2007 as the percentage change in the Personal Consumption Expenditure price index from the same month in the previous year.

b. Calculate the average inflation rate from 1982 to 1995 and the average inflation rate from 1995 to 2007.

c. Are your calculations consistent with a positive technology shock? Explain.

MyEconLab Visit **www.myeconlab.com** to complete these exercises online and get instant feedback. Exercises that update with real-time data are marked with ⓦ.

D11.2: During the 2007–2009 period, shocks affected the United Kingdom in ways similar to the United States. As in the United States, oil prices were high, and housing prices had sharply escalated after 2000. The financial crisis in the United States also affected investment in the United Kingdom, both by limiting credit and increasing risk premiums.

Using data from the St. Louis Federal Reserve (http://research.stlouisfed.org/fred2/) FRED database, examine the behavior of the U.K. economy since 2007.

a. Download quarterly data for real GDP (GBRRGDPQDSNAQ) and the GDP deflator (GBRGDPDEFQISMEI) from 2006 to the present. Calculate the growth rate of real GDP as the percentage change from the same quarter in the previous year and calculate the inflation rate as the percentage change in the GDP deflator from the same quarter in the previous year. Download data on the unemployment rate (GBRURHARMMDSMEI) for the same time period.

b. Chart the three data series from 2007 to the present in a graph.

c. How similar is the experience of the United Kingdom to the experience of the United States?

D11.3: [Excel exercise] Another way of viewing the Phillips curve relationship is to relate the inflation rate to the unemployment rate. Using data from the St. Louis Federal Reserve (http://research.stlouisfed.org/fred2/) FRED database, examine the relationship between unemployment and the annual inflation rate.

a. Download quarterly data for the unemployment rate (UNRATE) and the Personal Consumption Expenditure price index (PCEPI) from 1959 to the present. Calculate the inflation rate as the percentage change in Personal Consumption Expenditure price index from the same quarter in the previous year.

b. Chart the two data series on a graph. For what periods does there appear to be a clear inverse relationship between the inflation rate and the unemployment rate?

c. Calculate the correlation coefficient for the inflation and unemployment rates for this entire period. Now calculate the correlation coefficient for the periods for which you can identify a distinct inverse relationship.

CHAPTER **12**

Monetary Policy in the Short Run

Learning Objectives

After studying this chapter, you should be able to:

12.1 Understand the structure of the Federal Reserve (pages 414–416)

12.2 Describe the goals of monetary policy (pages 416–418)

12.3 Explain the Federal Reserve's monetary policy tools (pages 418–423)

12.4 Use the *IS–MP* model to understand how monetary policy affects the economy in the short run (pages 424–435)

 12.5 Explain the challenges in using monetary policy effectively (pages 435–444)

 12.6 Evaluate the arguments for and against central bank independence (pages 444–447)

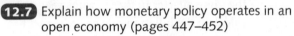 **12.7** Explain how monetary policy operates in an open economy (pages 447–452)

Why Didn't the Fed Avoid the Recession of 2007–2009?

During the 2007–2009 recession, as unemployment soared and the financial system seemed to teeter on the verge of collapse, many people asked the same question: Why hadn't government policymakers avoided this disaster? Many economists had given the Federal Reserve substantial credit for the good performance of the economy between the early 1980s and 2007. Why, then, had the Fed not been able to keep the unemployment rate from rising above 10% and real GDP from falling by more than it had since the 1930s?

As a professor of economics at Princeton, Ben Bernanke had studied the causes of the Great Depression of the 1930s. When he became Fed chairman in 2004, he vowed that the Fed would never allow such a disaster to occur again. Yet the 2007–2009 recession was the worst since the Great Depression. In the early 1960s, Milton Friedman of the University of Chicago and Anna Schwartz of the National Bureau of Economic Research published an influential discussion of the importance of bank panics in their book *A*

Continued on next page

Key Issue and Question

Issue: The Federal Reserve undertook unprecedented policy actions in response to the recession of 2007–2009.

Question: Why were traditional Federal Reserve policies ineffective during the 2007–2009 recession?

Answered on page 453

Monetary History of the United States, 1867–1960. In
A Monetary History and later writings, Friedman and
Schwartz singled out the failure in December 1930 of
the Bank of United States, a large private bank located
in New York City, as being particularly important in
explaining the severity of the Great Depression.

For Friedman and Schwartz, the failure of the Federal Reserve to stop the bank panics of the early 1930s
was the key reason the Great Depression was so severe.
In 2002, when Ben Bernanke was a member of the Fed's
Board of Governors, but not yet the chairman, he told
Friedman, "Regarding the Great Depression, you're
right, we did it. We're very sorry. But thanks to you, we
won't do it again." When the financial crisis started in
August 2007, Bernanke's words were put to the test.
At that point, Bernanke faced a dilemma similar to the
one Fed officials faced in the 1930s: If the Fed moved to
save failing financial firms, it could reduce the severity of
the financial crisis, but it might also increase the extent
of *moral hazard* in the financial system by changing the
behavior of the managers of the financial firms. The Fed
was worried that the managers of financial firms might
be more likely to make risky investments if they believed
that the Fed would bail out the firms.

In an attempt to avoid the errors the Fed committed in the 1930s, the Fed saved the Bear Stearns
investment bank from bankruptcy in March 2008 by
arranging for the bank JPMorgan Chase to purchase it.
Fear of increasing moral hazard, though, contributed
to the Fed's decision *not* to save the investment bank
Lehman Brothers, which failed on September 15, 2008.
The failure of Lehman Brothers led many lenders to
sharply cut back on their lending, thereby contributing
to the growing financial crisis. At that point, the Fed
decided to put aside concerns about moral hazard
and act aggressively to stabilize the financial system.
Among other actions, the Fed made loans to financial
institutions beyond just commercial banks, saved the

insurance giant American International Group (AIG),
and provided short-term financing for corporations by
buying the firms' commercial paper.

Although the Fed eventually took aggressive
policy actions during the financial crisis, it was initially slow to recognize the threat the crisis posed. For
example, in May 2007, Ben Bernanke gave a speech
indicating that the housing market problems developing
at that time would have little effect on financial markets and the broader economy. Bernanke was wrong,
as were many other economists. The collapse in housing prices in 2006 and 2007 helped trigger a massive
financial crisis. Then, in August 2007, just days before
the start of the crisis, the Fed indicated that it was
more concerned about inflation than about a potential
recession.

Some economists and policymakers criticized the
Fed for being slow to recognize the problems in financial markets and for having potentially increased the
extent of moral hazard in the financial system by "bail-
ing out Wall Street" in saving Bear Stearns and AIG.
As a result of the financial crisis and the criticisms of
the Fed's actions during the crisis, Bernanke's confirmation by Congress to a second term as Fed chairman
in early 2010 was contentious, with strong opposition
from some Democrats and Republicans. Senator
Richard Shelby of Alabama accused Bernanke of
sitting idly by while financial problems developed
that "greatly exacerbated the crisis." In some ways,
these criticisms were like those made by Friedman and
Schwartz of Fed policy during the Great Depression.
Ultimately, 70 senators voted to confirm Bernanke,
but the 30 votes against his confirmation represented
the most "no" votes that any nominee for Fed
chairman had ever received.

As we will see in this chapter, the monetary policy
actions the Fed took during the financial crisis remain
controversial.

Sources: Milton Friedman and Anna Schwartz, *A Monetary History of the United States, 1867–1960*, Princeton, NJ: Princeton University Press, 1963, pp. 308–313; Friedman quote from Milton Friedman, "Anti-Semitism and the Great Depression," *Newsweek*, Vol. 84, November 16, 1974; "The Very Model of a Modern Central Banker," *Economist*, August 29, 2009; Tom Braithwaite and James Politi, "Bernanke Wins New Term as Fed Chief," *Financial Times*, January 29, 2010; David Wessel, "Financial Crisis: Inside Dr. Bernanke's E.R.," *Wall Street Journal*, July 18, 2009; and Ben Bernanke, "The Subprime Mortgage Market," speech at the Federal Reserve Bank of Chicago's 43rd Annual Conference on Bank Structure and Competition, Chicago, May 17, 2007.

Monetary policy The actions the Federal Reserve takes to manage interest rates and the money supply to pursue macroeconomic goals.

Monetary policy refers to the actions the Federal Reserve takes to manage interest rates and the money supply to pursue macroeconomic goals. In this chapter, we use the *IS-MP* model to explain how the Fed can employ monetary policy to help stabilize the economy and the financial system and reduce the severity of economic fluctuations. We will also discuss how in practice it can be difficult for the Fed and other central banks to implement effective policies.

The Federal Reserve System

12.1

Learning Objective

Understand the structure of the Federal Reserve.

The organization of the Federal Reserve plays a significant role in how it conducts monetary policy. To understand why the Fed is organized as it is, we need to look briefly at earlier attempts to create a central bank in the United States.

Creation of the Federal Reserve System

Not long after the United States won its independence, Treasury Secretary Alexander Hamilton organized the Bank of the United States, which was meant to perform functions similar to those of a modern central bank.[1] The Bank of the United States was not entirely a government agency in that it had both government and private shareholders. The Bank attempted to stabilize the financial system by ensuring that local banks did not extend excessive amounts of loans. Congress granted the Bank a 20-year charter in 1791, making it the only federally chartered bank. Local banks resented the Bank's supervision of their operations. Many advocates of a limited federal government distrusted the Bank's power, and important leaders such as Thomas Jefferson believed that the Bank of the United States was unconstitutional. Farmers and owners of small businesses, particularly in the West and South, resented the Bank's interfering with their ability to obtain loans from their local banks. There was not enough congressional support to renew the charter, so the Bank ceased operations in 1811.

Partly because of the federal government's problems in financing the War of 1812, political opinion in Congress shifted back toward the need for a central bank. In 1816, Congress established the Second Bank of the United States, also under a 20-year charter. The Second Bank of the United States encountered many of the same controversies as the First Bank of the United States. Although Congress passed a bill to recharter the Bank, President Andrew Jackson vetoed the bill, and the Bank's charter expired in 1836.

The disappearance of the Second Bank of the United States left the nation without a central bank and, therefore, without an official lender of last resort to make loans to banks during **bank runs**, when large numbers of depositors would lose confidence in banks and withdraw their funds. Without a lender of last resort, banks suffering temporary problems with deposit withdrawals could be forced to close. Severe nationwide financial panics in 1873, 1884, 1893, and 1907—and accompanying economic downturns—raised fears in Congress that the U.S. financial system was unstable. The severity of the panic of 1907 convinced many that the United States needed a central bank to make loans to banks experiencing runs. In 1913, President Woodrow Wilson signed the Federal Reserve Act

Bank run The process by which large numbers of depositors who have lost confidence in a bank simultaneously withdraw enough funds to force the bank to close.

---

[1]Note that this bank is unrelated to the bank with a similar name, Bank of United States, that failed during the 1930s.

into law. The act established the **Federal Reserve System** (the Fed) as the central bank of the United States.

The Structure of the Federal Reserve System

Many in Congress believed that a unified central bank based in Washington, DC would concentrate too much economic power in the hands of the officials running the bank. Congress also wanted to avoid having a single central bank with branches, which had been the structure of the First and Second Banks of the United States. So, the Federal Reserve Act divided the United States into 12 Federal Reserve districts, each of which has a *Federal Reserve Bank*. Among other responsibilities, the Federal Reserve Bank in each district makes short-term loans called *discount loans* to banks within the district. These loans were intended to provide liquidity to banks, thereby fulfilling, in a decentralized way, the system's role as lender of last resort and making bank panics less likely. Figure 12.1 shows the Federal Reserve districts and the locations of the Federal Reserve Banks. Although the federal government created them, technically Federal Reserve Banks have a certain degree of independence from the government. Federal Reserve Banks are owned by commercial banks within their districts. In addition, each Federal Reserve Bank selects its own president to oversee operations and take part in monetary policy decisions. We discuss central bank independence in more detail in Section 12.6.

Federal Reserve System
The central bank of the United States; commonly referred to as "the Fed."

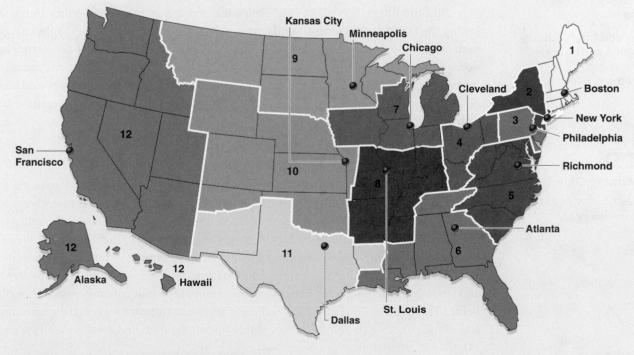

Figure 12.1 Federal Reserve Districts and Banks

The Federal Reserve System is divided into 12 districts, each of which has a district bank identified by a purple dot in the figure. The federal government created the Federal Reserve System, but each regional Federal Reserve Bank is owned by the commercial banks within its district. Note that Hawaii and Alaska are included in the Twelfth Federal Reserve District.

Board of Governors
The governing board of the Federal Reserve System, consisting of seven members appointed by the president of the United States.

In addition to the 12 regional Federal Reserve Banks, the Fed has a **Board of Governors** headquartered in Washington, DC. The board's seven members are appointed by the president of the United States and confirmed by the U.S. Senate. Governors serve nonrenewable terms of 14 years that are staggered so that one term expires every other January.[2] The intent was to limit the number of members that one president can appoint. The president appoints one member of the board to serve as the chairman for a renewable four-year term. For instance, Ben Bernanke was appointed chairman in January 2006 by President George W. Bush and reappointed in January 2010 by President Barack Obama. The chairman acts as the public face of the Federal Reserve and often testifies before Congress on monetary policy and the state of the U.S. economy.

Federal Open Market Committee (FOMC)
The 12-member Federal Reserve committee that directs open market operations.

Open market operations
The Federal Reserve's purchases and sales of securities, usually U.S. Treasury securities, in financial markets.

The Board of Governors oversees the entire Federal Reserve System. In recent decades, however, the 12-member **Federal Open Market Committee (FOMC)** has been at the center of Fed policymaking. The FOMC conducts **open market operations**, the purchases and sales of U.S. Treasury securities. Voting members of the FOMC are the chairman of the Board of Governors, the other 6 Fed governors, the president of the Federal Reserve Bank of New York, and the presidents of 4 of the other 11 Federal Reserve Banks (who serve on a rotating basis). Although only 5 Federal Reserve Bank presidents are voting members of the FOMC, all 12 attend meetings and participate in discussions. The committee is scheduled to meet eight times a year, but it may meet more frequently, as economic conditions warrant.

Federal funds rate The interest rate that banks charge each other on short-term loans.

Until the financial crisis of 2007–2009, the Fed's most important policy tool was setting the target for the **federal funds rate**, which is the interest rate that banks charge each other on short-term loans. During the financial crisis, Fed Chairman Ben Bernanke needed to make decisions rapidly and to use new policy tools. As a result, the focus of monetary policy moved away from the federal funds rate. As more normal conditions return to the economy and financial system, the federal funds rate will resume its previous importance.

12.2

Learning Objective
Describe the goals of monetary policy.

The Goals of Monetary Policy

Most economists and policymakers agree that the overall aim of monetary policy is to advance the economic well-being of the population. Although there are many ways to assess economic well-being, it is typically determined by the quantity and quality of goods and services that individuals can enjoy. Economic well-being arises from the efficient employment of labor and capital and the steady growth in output. In addition, stable economic conditions—minimal fluctuations in production and employment, and smoothly functioning financial markets—are qualities that enhance economic well-being. The Federal Reserve has several goals intended to promote a well-functioning economy: (1) price stability, (2) high employment, (3) financial market stability, and (4) interest rate stability.

---

[2]Technically, a governor could be appointed to fill out the term of a governor who had resigned and then be later nominated to a new 14-year term. In this way, Alan Greenspan was able to serve as chairman of the Board of Governors from 1987 to 2006.

Price Stability

Inflation, or persistently rising prices, erodes the value of money. Especially since inflation rose dramatically and unexpectedly during the 1970s, policymakers in most high-income countries have set price stability as a policy goal. In a market economy, in which prices communicate information about costs and demand for goods and services to households and firms, inflation makes prices less useful as signals for resource allocation. When the overall price level changes, among other problems, families have trouble deciding how much to save for their children's education or for retirement, and firms facing uncertain future prices hesitate to enter into long-term contracts with suppliers or customers. Fluctuations in inflation can also arbitrarily redistribute income, as when lenders suffer losses when inflation is higher than expected.

In practice, the Fed's goal of price stability means that it attempts to achieve low and stable inflation rather than zero inflation. With low and stable inflation, market prices efficiently allocate resources in the economy, so the economy is more productive and living standards are higher in the long run. In 2012, the Fed announced that it considers an inflation rate of 2% consistent with the goal of price stability.

High Employment

The second goal of the Federal Reserve is high employment, or a low rate of unemployment. Unemployed workers and underused factories and machines lower output. Unemployment causes financial distress and decreases the self-esteem of workers who lack jobs. Congress and the president share responsibility with the Fed for the goal of high employment.

The Fed does not aim for zero unemployment. Indeed, if the unemployment rate were zero, then cyclical unemployment would be negative, and real GDP would be far above potential GDP. The Phillips curve tells us that the result would be an increase in the inflation rate. So, zero unemployment is not compatible with the Fed's goal of price stability. Instead, the Fed attempts to keep cyclical unemployment as close to zero as possible, or, looked at another way, the Fed attempts to keep the actual unemployment rate equal to the natural rate of unemployment. In 2012, the Fed announced that the members of the FOMC believe the natural rate of unemployment is between 5.2% and 6%, which is also consistent with estimates from the Congressional Budget Office.

Financial Market Stability

When financial markets and institutions are not efficient in matching savers and borrowers, the economy loses resources. Firms with the potential to produce high-quality products and services cannot obtain the financing they need to design, develop, and market these products and services. Savers waste resources looking for satisfactory investments. The stability of financial markets and institutions makes possible the efficient matching of savers and borrowers.

Congress and the president created the Federal Reserve in response to the financial market turmoil of 1907, so it is not surprising that financial market stability is a goal of monetary policy. Banks and financial institutions are prone to *liquidity problems* because they borrow short-term—sometimes overnight—and use the funds to make long-term investments. Therefore, if a large number of depositors want to withdraw funds, a bank may have trouble providing the funds because they have been invested in long-term loans and securities. In a system without deposit insurance, depositors may worry that unless they are among the first to withdraw their money when their bank encounters trouble, they may not be able to retrieve all of it. If many depositors try to withdraw their funds at the same time, the result is a bank run that may cause the bank to fail. The failure of one bank may lead depositors at other banks to withdraw their money in a process called *contagion*. Many banks may be forced to close in a *bank panic*. A central bank can aim to head off such a panic by acting as a *lender of last resort* to help troubled banks get through temporary liquidity problems. As the 2007–2009 financial crisis showed, any financial firm that borrows short term and uses the funds to lend long term can be subject to a run.

Interest Rate Stability

Like fluctuations in price levels, fluctuations in interest rates make planning difficult for households and firms. Increases and decreases in interest rates make it hard for firms to plan investments in plant and equipment and make households more hesitant about long-term investments in houses. Because people often blame the Fed for increases in interest rates, the Fed's goal of interest rate stability is motivated by political pressure as well as by a desire for a stable saving and investment environment. In addition, sharp interest rate fluctuations cause problems for banks and other financial firms that borrow in short-term markets and lend in long-term markets. So, stabilizing interest rates can help to stabilize the financial system.

The Fed's Dual Mandate

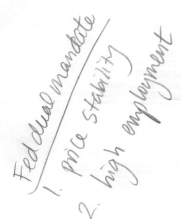

Congress has authorized the Fed to pursue the goals of price stability, maximum employment, and moderate long-term interest rates. How can the Fed pursue all these goals at once? As it turns out, these goals are really just two goals: price stability and maximum employment. If inflation is low and stable, then long-term interest rates will also be moderate. Therefore, many economists and commentators refer to the Fed's *dual mandate* as price stability and high employment. An open question is whether the Fed's dual mandate is necessarily consistent with financial market stability, as we discuss next.

Monetary Policy Tools

To achieve its goals, the Fed has a variety of policy tools. The three traditional monetary policy tools are (1) open market operations, (2) discount loans, and (3) reserve requirements. In this section, we discuss the Fed's three traditional policy tools and two new policy tools that the Fed introduced starting in the fall of 2008.

Open Market Operations

The FOMC conducts open market operations—the purchase and sale of government securities in financial markets—with the goal of affecting the federal funds rate. The FOMC sets a target for the federal funds rate, but the actual rate is determined by the interaction between the demand and supply for bank reserves in the *federal funds market*. Banks demand reserves both to meet their legal obligation to hold required reserves and because they might want to hold excess reserves to meet their short-term liquidity needs. When interest rates are very low, as they were during and after the financial crisis of 2007–2009, banks may also decide to hold reserves if they cannot find sufficiently profitable lending opportunities. If a bank finds that it has insufficient reserves, it can borrow reserves from other banks. Similarly, if a bank has more reserves than it needs, it can loan reserves to other banks. The Fed supplies bank reserves through open market operations. So, although the Fed controls the supply of reserves, banks control the demand for reserves. The result is that the Fed can usually come close to hitting its target for the federal funds rate, but is not always able to hit the target exactly.

The Fed can decrease the federal funds rate by increasing the supply of bank reserves, and it can increase the federal funds rate by decreasing the supply of bank reserves. To decrease bank reserves, the Fed engages in an *open market sale*. To increase bank reserves, the Fed engages in an *open market purchase*. For example, suppose the Fed wants to buy $1 billion of Treasury bills from banks. Banks have reserve accounts with the Fed, so the Fed pays for the securities by increasing the banks' reserves by $1 billion. This increase in the supply of reserves reduces the federal funds rate. If the Fed wanted to increase the federal funds rate, it could sell $1 billion in Treasury bills to banks. In paying for the Treasury bills, banks will reduce their reserves by $1 billion. This decrease in the supply of reserves increases the federal funds rate.

At the end of each of its meetings, the FOMC issues a statement that includes its target for the federal funds rate and its assessment of the economy, particularly with respect to its policy goals of price stability and economic growth. In addition, the FOMC issues a *policy directive* to the Federal Reserve System's account manager, who is a vice president of the Federal Reserve Bank of New York and who is responsible for implementing open market operations and hitting the FOMC's target for the federal funds rate. The Open Market Trading Desk at the Federal Reserve Bank of New York carries out open market operations. The trading desk is linked electronically through a system called the Trading Room Automated Processing System (TRAPS) to about 20 primary dealers, who are private securities firms that the Fed has selected to participate in open market operations. Each morning, the trading desk notifies the primary dealers of the size of the open market purchase or sale being conducted and asks them to submit offers to buy or sell Treasury securities. The dealers have just a few minutes to respond. Once the Fed's account manager receives the dealers' offers, the manager goes over the list, accepts the best offers, and has the trading desk buy or sell the securities until the volume of reserves reaches the Fed's desired goal.

How does the account manager know what to do? The manager interprets the FOMC's most recent policy directive, holds daily conferences with two members of the FOMC, and personally analyzes financial market conditions. Then the manager compares the level of reserves in the banking system with the level of reserves the trading desk staff estimates will be necessary to hit (or maintain) the target federal funds rate. If the level of reserves needs to be increased over the current level, the account manager orders the trading desk to purchase securities. If the level of reserves needs to be decreased, the account manager orders the trading desk to sell securities.

Discount Loans and the Lender of Last Resort

To fulfill the system's role as a lender of last resort, the 12 Federal Reserve Banks lend to commercial banks in their districts through the *discount window*. The loans the Fed makes to banks are discount loans, and they are typically for very short periods, usually overnight, although they can be for as long as 90 days. The interest rate the Fed charges on

Macro Data: Does the Federal Reserve Hit Its Federal Funds Rate Target?

The FOMC conducts monetary policy by setting a target for the federal funds rate. The Open Market Trading Desk at the New York Federal Reserve Bank then carries out open market operations each morning to keep the federal funds rate close to the target rate. Although the Federal Reserve controls the supply of bank reserves, the federal funds rate is a market interest rate that is determined by both demand and supply. Fluctuations in the demand for bank reserves may cause the federal funds rate in the market to deviate from the target federal funds rate. The figure in the next column shows the relationship between the target federal funds rate set by the Federal Reserve and the federal funds rate in the market, using daily data from 1986 to 2012. The figure shows that the Federal Reserve has generally been successful at keeping the market rate close to the target rate. The Fed can offset fluctuations in the demand for reserves by changing the supply of reserves.

Beginning in September 2008, as the financial crisis deepened, the federal funds rate persistently fell below the target rate as the Federal Reserve injected reserves into the banking system. For example, the target federal funds rate was 2.0% on October 2, but the effective

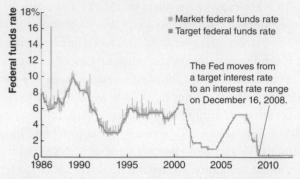

Source: Board of Governors of the Federal Reserve System.

federal funds rate in the market was just 0.7%. This unusual situation reflected the Fed's desire to increase reserves as much as required to help deal with the financial crisis, even if the result was to miss its federal funds rate target. In December 2008, the Fed temporarily abandoned having a single target for the federal funds rate in favor of a target *range* between 0.00% and 0.25%. The actual federal funds rate has remained in the target range every week through September 2012.

See related problem D12.1 at the end of the chapter

Discount rate The interest rate that the Federal Reserve charges on discount loans.

discount loans is called the **discount rate**. Because the Federal Reserve provides discount loans to banks in the form of increases in the banks' reserves, an increase in the quantity of discount loans from the Fed to banks will increase the monetary base (currency plus bank reserves), unless the Fed offsets the effect through another policy action. All else held constant, an increase in the monetary base will cause an increase in the money supply.

Discount loans can provide liquidity to troubled financial institutions. However, because the discount rate is set above the federal funds rate, only banks that are unable to borrow from other banks use them. As a result, in normal times, the volume of discount loans is very low. For example, between January 2000 and July 2007—the month before the financial crisis began—the volume of discount loans averaged just $219 million per month, while total bank reserves averaged $42.8 billion.

Reserve Requirements

The Federal Reserve requires that banks hold a certain percentage of their checking account deposits as either vault cash—currency held in the bank—or as deposits with the Fed. Banks that have reserves above the required levels are free to loan them to households and firms or invest them in Treasury bills or other securities.[3] Because these

---

[3]U.S. law prohibits commercial banks from owning stock of non-financial firms.

reserves exceed reserve requirements, economists call them *excess reserves*. **Reserve requirements** provide the Fed with a monetary policy tool because raising the *required reserve ratio*, or the percentage of checking account deposits that banks must hold as reserves, reduces the ability of banks to make loans and other investments. Lowering the required reserve ratio increases the ability of banks to make loans and other investments.

Banks must hold reserves, but reserve requirements are the least-used policy tool in part because banks find it disruptive to adjust to frequent changes in the required reserve ratio. While the Fed can easily reverse an open market purchase by carrying out an open market sale, quickly reversing an increase or a decrease in the required reserve ratio would cause significant problems for banks. As a result, the Fed has not changed the required reserve ratio since 1992. Other central banks, though, still use this policy tool frequently. For example, the People's Bank of China reduced required reserves several times in late 2011 and early 2012, in an effort to stimulate lending and economic activity.

New Monetary Policy Tools in Response to the 2007–2009 Financial Crisis

The traditional monetary policy tools allow the Fed to respond to most economic problems. However, the financial crisis that started in August 2007 forced the Fed to develop new policy tools to achieve its goals. The Fed used some of the policy tools for just a short period of time, but it is still using two new tools that involve paying interest to banks:

1. Interest on bank reserves
2. Interest on funds deposited at the Fed for more than one day

Interest on Bank Reserves Banks had long complained that the Fed's failure to pay interest on the banks' required reserve deposits amounted to a tax because banks do not have the opportunity to loan out and earn interest income from required reserves. To respond to banks' complaints and to give the Fed greater control over movements in bank reserves, Congress, in 2006, authorized the Fed to begin paying interest on bank reserve deposits beginning in October 2011. In response to the financial market crisis, Congress moved this date ahead to October 2008, and the Fed immediately began to pay interest on reserves. Paying interest on reserves gives the Fed another monetary policy tool. By increasing the interest rate on reserves, the Fed can increase the level of reserves banks are willing to hold, thereby restraining bank lending and the increases in the money supply that would result. Lowering the interest rate would have the opposite effect.[4]

Interest on Funds Deposited at the Fed for more than One Day To provide greater control over bank reserve accounts, the Fed created a second policy tool, the Term Deposit Facility (TDF). Term deposits are similar to the certificates of deposit that banks offer to households and firms. The Fed offers term deposits to banks in periodic auctions. The interest rates are determined by the auctions and have been slightly above the interest rate the Fed offers on reserve balances. For example, in July 2012, the interest rate on the Fed's auction of $3 billion in 28-day term deposits was 0.26%, which was higher than the interest rate of 0.25% the Fed was paying on reserve deposits. The TDF

Reserve requirements
Regulations that require banks to hold a fraction of checking account deposits as vault cash or deposits with the Fed.

---

[4]Technically, the Fed can set separate interest rates on required reserve balances and on excess reserve balances. As of September 2012, the interest rate on both types of balances was the same: 0.25%.

gives the Fed another tool in managing bank reserve holdings because the funds that banks place in term deposits are removed from their reserve accounts. So, the more funds banks place in term deposits, the less they will have available to expand loans and the money supply.

Other Nontraditional Policy Actions From its founding in 1913 until 1980, with a few brief exceptions, the Fed made loans only to commercial banks that were members of the Federal Reserve System. In 1980, Congress authorized the Fed to make loans to all depository institutions. By the beginning of the financial crisis in 2007, however, a *shadow banking system* of investment banks, money market mutual funds, hedge funds, and other nonbank financial firms had grown to be as large as the commercial banking system. The initial stages of the financial crisis involved these shadow banks rather than commercial banks. When the crisis began, the Fed was handicapped in its role as a lender of last resort because it had no recent tradition of lending to anyone but banks.

The Fed did, however, have the authority to lend more broadly. Section 13(3) of the Federal Reserve Act authorizes the Fed in "unusual and exigent circumstances" to lend to any "individual, partnership, or corporation" that could provide acceptable collateral and could demonstrate an inability to borrow from commercial banks. The Fed used this authority to set up several temporary lending programs that provided credit to primary dealers, issuers of commercial paper, and buyers of certain securitized loans. The Fed ended these innovative loan programs in 2010, with the financial system having recovered from the worst of the crisis.

Figure 12.2 shows that there was an explosion in all types of lending by the Fed during the financial crisis. Borrowing from the Fed amounted to just $2.1 billion as late as

MyEconLab Real-time data

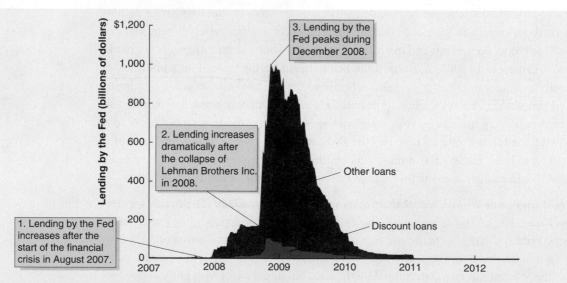

Figure 12.2 Lending by the Fed During the Financial Market Shock

During the financial crisis, lending by the Federal Reserve increased from just a few hundred million dollars to $993.5 billion during December 2008. Since that time, lending by the Fed has steadily decreased.

Source: Board of Governors of the Federal Reserve System.

December 5, 2007. However, as the financial crisis worsened during the first months of 2008, financial institutions borrowed more and more from the Fed. After the collapse of Bear Stearns on March 19, 2008, total borrowing from the Fed had increased to $108.9 billion. On September 17, 2008, just days after Lehman Brothers filed for bankruptcy, total borrowing had reached $271.3 billion, skyrocketing from there to $993.5 billion on December 10, 2008, during the worst part of the financial crisis. Since that time, borrowing from the Fed has decreased steadily; it had fallen to $2.6 billion by August 2012.

Making the Connection

On the Board of Governors, Four Can Be a Crowd

Because the Fed's most important monetary policy tool is setting the target for the federal funds rate, by the 1980s, the key monetary policy debates within the Fed took place during meetings of the FOMC. Economists and Wall Street analysts closely watched the outcome of each meeting for clues about the direction of Fed policy. During the financial crisis of 2007–2009, however, it became clear that the Fed could not confine its actions to changes in the target for the federal funds rate. As in other recessions, the FOMC moved to cut the target beginning in September 2007. But by December 2008, the FOMC had effectively cut the target to zero, yet the economy continued to contract, and the financial system was in crisis.

As discussed earlier, during the financial crisis, Fed Chairman Ben Bernanke instituted a series of policy actions, some of which were unprecedented. Because the crisis was spreading quickly, it was not feasible to wait for the next FOMC meeting to discuss potential policy moves. In addition, because the FOMC consists of all the members of the Board of Governors and 5 of the 12 district bank presidents, its size was a barrier to quick decision making. The alternative of relying on the Board of Governors was also problematic. In 1976, Congress passed the Government in the Sunshine Act, which requires most federal government agencies to give public notice before a meeting. If four or more members of the Board of Governors meet to consider a policy action, it is considered an official meeting under the act and cannot be held without prior public notice. Given that Bernanke needed to make decisions rapidly as events unfolded hour by hour, the requirement of prior public notice made it infeasible for him to meet with more than two other members of the Board of Governors.

As a result, Bernanke relied on an informal group of advisers consisting of Board of Governors members Donald Kohn and Kevin Warsh and Federal Reserve Bank of New York president Timothy Geithner. Geithner was a member of the FOMC but not of the Board of Governors, so his presence at meetings did not trigger the Sunshine Act requirement. The "four musketeers," as they came to be called, were the key policymaking body at the Fed during the crisis. The unintended consequence of the Sunshine Act requirements was to drastically limit the input of the other members of the Board of Governors into monetary policymaking.

Source: David Wessel, *In Fed We Trust: Ben Bernanke's War on the Great Panic*, New York: Crown Business, 2009.

See related problem 3.6 at the end of the chapter.

12.4

Learning Objective

Use the *IS–MP* model to understand how monetary policy affects the economy in the short run.

Monetary Policy and the *IS–MP* Model

In this section, we use the *IS–MP* model to analyze the Fed's monetary policy actions.

Monetary Policy and Aggregate Expenditure

Recall that the nominal interest rate is the stated interest rate on a bond or loan. The real interest rate is adjusted for inflation. Usually, we calculate the real interest rate by subtracting the expected inflation rate from the nominal interest rate. As we have seen, the Fed is able to keep the nominal federal funds rate close to its target. But long-term real interest rates, such as those a homebuyer would pay on a 30-year mortgage or a firm would pay on a 30-year bond, are more relevant in determining consumption and investment. Long-term nominal interest rates are linked to short-term nominal interest rates through the *term structure of interest rates* and the default risk premium. The long-term nominal interest rate, i_{LT}, equals the short-term nominal interest rate, i, plus the term structure effect, *TSE*, and the default-risk premium, *DP*:

$$i_{LT} = i + TSE + DP.$$

We will typically assume that if the Fed increases its target for the short-term nominal interest rate, the term structure effect and the default-risk premium will remain unchanged. Therefore, an increase or decrease in the Fed's target for the federal funds rate will result in an increase or decrease in the long-term nominal interest rate.

The long-term real interest rate is important in determining consumption and investment. The long-term real interest rate, r, equals the long-term nominal interest rate minus the expected inflation rate, π^e:

$$r = i_{LT} - \pi^e.$$

For simplicity, we will assume that households and firms expect the inflation rate next year to be the same as the inflation rate this year. In other words, we will assume that households and firms have *adaptive expectations*. Adaptive expectations imply that, because the expected inflation rate is constant, any increase in nominal interest rates will also increase real interest rates. If at the beginning of 2012, a bank is offering car loans with a nominal interest rate of 5% when the expected inflation rate is 2%, then the real interest rate is 5% − 2% = 3%. If at the beginning of 2013, the bank increases the nominal interest rate to 6%, then, because the expected inflation rate is unchanged, the real interest rate increases to 6% − 2% = 4%. Therefore, if the nominal interest rate increases by a given number of percentage points, the real interest rate will increase by that same number of percentage points. Similarly, any decrease in the nominal interest rate will result in a decrease in the real interest rate.

Although households and firms cannot borrow or lend at the federal funds rate, as Figure 12.3 shows, the federal funds rate, the mortgage interest rate, and the interest rates on corporate bonds generally move together. Note, though, that the federal funds rate often increases and decreases more than these long-term rates. For example, for several years after 2000, all interest rates fell, but the interest rates on mortgages and corporate bonds did not fall by as much or as rapidly as the federal funds rate. In this case, investors did not believe that these low short-term rates would persist for very long. In other words, investors expected that future short-term rates would increase,

MyEconLab Real-time data

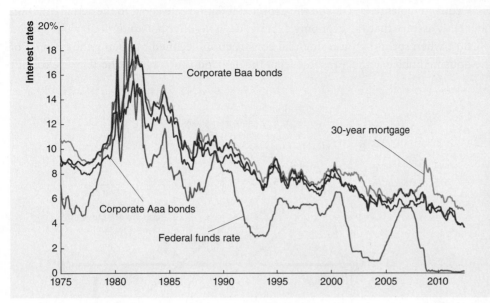

Figure 12.3

The Federal Funds Rate and the Interest Rates on Corporate Bonds and Mortgages

The Fed controls the federal funds rate. The long-term interest rates that households pay to purchase a house or that corporations pay to finance investment generally rise and fall with the federal funds rate.

Source: Board of Governors of the Federal Reserve System.

increasing the *TSE* term. Generally, though, if the Fed increases or decreases its target for the federal funds rate, long-term nominal interest rates—for example, the interest rate on a 30-year mortgage—will also increase or decrease. If the expected inflation rate is constant, then the long-term real interest rate will also increase or decrease.

When the Fed lowers its target for the federal funds rate, it is conducting an *expansionary monetary policy*. If interest rates decline, it will become less expensive for households and firms to borrow, so consumption and investment will increase, which will increase aggregate expenditure. An increase in aggregate expenditure will cause real GDP and employment to also increase. When the Fed raises its target for the federal funds rate—typically in response to a rising inflation rate—in an attempt to decrease real GDP and employment, it is conducting a *contractionary monetary policy*. Table 12.1 summarizes how the Fed conducts monetary policy by using open market operations to affect real GDP.

Using Monetary Policy to Fight a Recession

One of the Fed's goals is high employment. To achieve this goal, during recessions, the Fed carries out expansionary monetary policy to try to reduce the cyclical unemployment rate.

Table 12.1 Open Market Operations and Real GDP

When the Fed ...	bank reserves and the money supply ...	causing the federal funds rate and long-term real interest rates to ...	and causing consumption and investment to ...	so, real GDP ...
sells government bonds	decrease	increase	decrease	decreases.
buys government bonds	increase	decrease	increase	increases.

In Figure 12.4, equilibrium is initially at point *A* in panels (a) and (b), with real GDP equal to potential GDP and the expected inflation rate equal to the actual inflation rate. Now assume that the economy experiences a *negative demand shock*, as happened in 2007, when spending on residential construction declined following the collapse of the housing bubble. Panel (a) shows that the demand shock causes the *IS* curve to shift

Figure 12.4

Expansionary Monetary Policy

In panel (a), a demand shock causes the *IS* curve to shift to the left, from IS_1 to IS_2. Real GDP falls below potential GDP, so the economy has a negative output gap at $\tilde{Y}_2$ and enters a recession. Panel (b) shows that a negative output gap results in a movement down the Phillips curve, lowering the inflation rate from π_1 to π_2. The Fed lowers the real interest rate, shifting the monetary policy curve down from MP_1 to MP_2—down the *IS* curve. Real GDP returns to its potential level, so the output gap is again zero. In panel (b), the inflation rate rises from π_2 back to π_1.

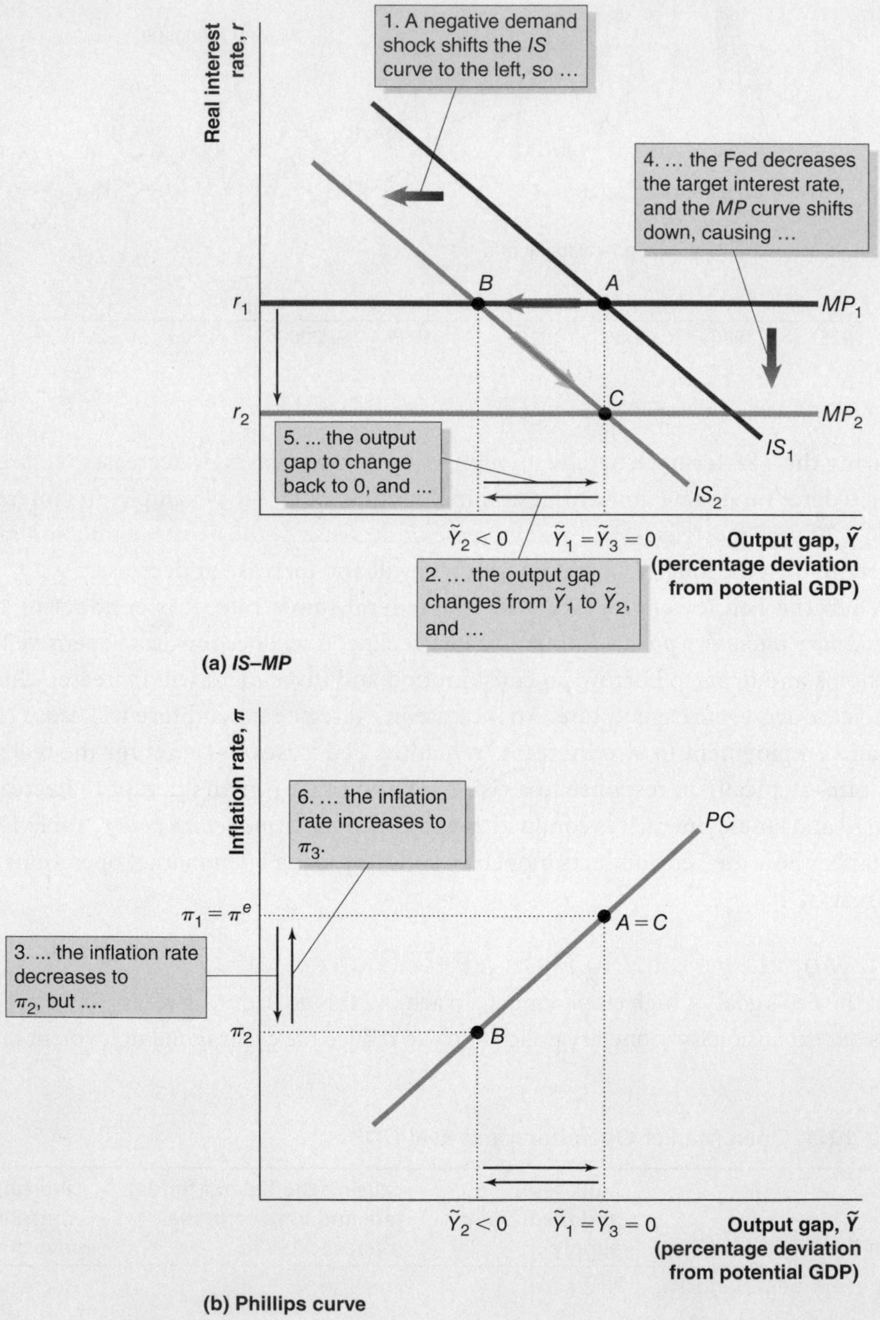

1. A negative demand shock shifts the *IS* curve to the left, so …

4. … the Fed decreases the target interest rate, and the *MP* curve shifts down, causing …

5. … the output gap to change back to 0, and …

2. … the output gap changes from $\tilde{Y}_1$ to $\tilde{Y}_2$, and …

$\tilde{Y}_2 < 0$ $\tilde{Y}_1 = \tilde{Y}_3 = 0$ **Output gap, $\tilde{Y}$ (percentage deviation from potential GDP)**

(a) IS–MP

6. … the inflation rate increases to π_3.

3. … the inflation rate decreases to π_2, but ….

$\tilde{Y}_2 < 0$ $\tilde{Y}_1 = \tilde{Y}_3 = 0$ **Output gap, $\tilde{Y}$ (percentage deviation from potential GDP)**

(b) Phillips curve

to the left, from IS_1 to IS_2. Real GDP falls below potential GDP, so the output gap becomes negative and the economy enters a recession. Panel (b) shows that a negative output gap pushes short-run equilibrium down the Phillips curve, from point A to point B, reducing the inflation rate from π_1 to π_2. The Fed typically fights recessions by lowering its target for the federal funds rate. This action lowers the real interest rate, shifting the monetary policy curve down from MP_1 to MP_2. A lower real interest rate leads to increases in consumption, investment, and net exports, moving short-run equilibrium from point B to point C on the IS curve. Real GDP returns to its potential level, so the output gap is again zero. In panel (b), the inflation rate rises from π_2 back to π_1.

Using Monetary Policy to Fight Inflation

During the economic expansion of the 1990s, real GDP in the United States increased from 0.4% above potential GDP in the second quarter of 1998 to 3.2% above potential GDP in the second quarter of 2000. During the same period, the inflation rate as measured using the CPI rose from 1.6% to 3.8%. Figure 12.5 on page 428 shows how the Fed can use monetary policy to reduce the inflation rate and achieve its goal of price stability.

Suppose a positive demand shock has pushed real GDP above potential GDP, so that short-run equilibrium is at point A in panels (a) and (b) (for simplicity, we do not show the initial shift of the IS curve). At point A, the output gap is positive and the inflation rate is greater than expected, $\pi_1 > \pi^e$. To reduce the inflation rate, the Fed increases the interest rate from r_1 to r_2, causing the MP curve to shift up from MP_1 to MP_2. Short-run equilibrium is now at point B, and real GDP equals potential GDP, so $\widetilde{Y}_2 = 0$. Along the Phillips curve, the output gap changes from $\widetilde{Y}_1$ to $\widetilde{Y}_2$, so the inflation rate decreases to π_2. At point B in panels (a) and (b), both the inflation rate and the output gap have been reduced.

Using Monetary Policy to Deal with a Supply Shock

In the two previous examples, the Fed used changes in its target interest rate to offset the effects on the economy of demand shocks. In theory, when demand shocks cause the output gap and the inflation rate to fluctuate, it is clear which policy the Fed should use to achieve its goals. But what should the Fed do when dealing with a supply shock, such as a significant increase in oil prices? The correct policy for the Fed to pursue following a supply shock is less clear.

The U.S. economy suffered from a large supply shock in the 1970s, when the price of a barrel of oil nearly tripled from $3.56 per barrel in July 1973 to $11.16 per barrel in October 1974. This increase in oil prices significantly raised the costs of production for many firms. As firms raised prices in response to these higher costs, the inflation rate rose. Figure 12.6 on page 429 illustrates the effects of a supply shock. The short-run equilibrium before the supply shock is shown by point A in both panels. As panel (b) shows, the supply shock causes the Phillips curve to shift up, from PC_1 to PC_2, as the inflation rate increases for every value of the output gap.

Panel (b) of Figure 12.6 on page 429 illustrates the dilemma that supply shocks pose for the Fed. If the Fed keeps the real interest rate unchanged, then the inflation rate will rise, undermining the Fed's goal of price stability. The Fed could attempt to maintain the inflation rate at its initial level by raising the real interest rate from r_1 to r_2. But, as shown in panel (a), the higher interest rate would result in a movement along the IS

Figure 12.5

Contractionary Monetary Policy

After a positive demand shock, the economy is at point A in panels (a) and (b), in which the output gap is positive and inflation is greater than expected. To reduce inflation, the Fed increases the real interest rate, which shifts up the MP curve in panel (a). As a result, the output gap changes from $\widetilde{Y}_1$ to $\widetilde{Y}_2$. The Phillips curve in panel (b) shows us that the inflation rate will also decrease.

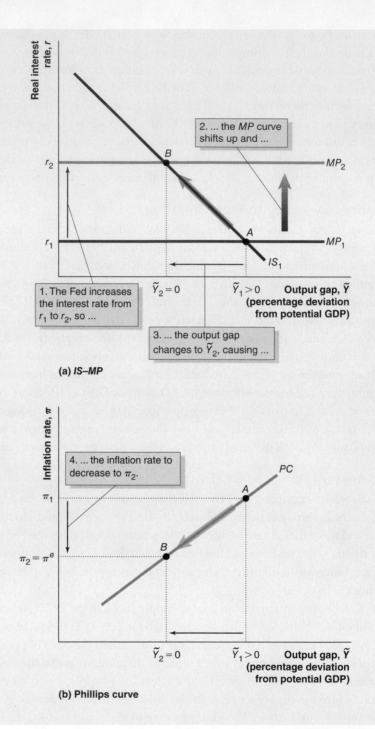

1. The Fed increases the interest rate from r_1 to r_2, so ...

2. ... the MP curve shifts up and ...

3. ... the output gap changes to $\widetilde{Y}_2$, causing ...

4. ... the inflation rate to decrease to π_2.

(a) *IS–MP*

(b) Phillips curve

curve from point A to point C, as consumption, investment, and net exports all decline. At point C, real GDP falls below potential GDP, so the output gap is negative. The Fed has succeeded in keeping the inflation rate constant at point C in panel (b) but only by failing to meet its goal of high employment. Unfortunately for the Fed, supply shocks require it to choose between its goals of price stability and high employment.

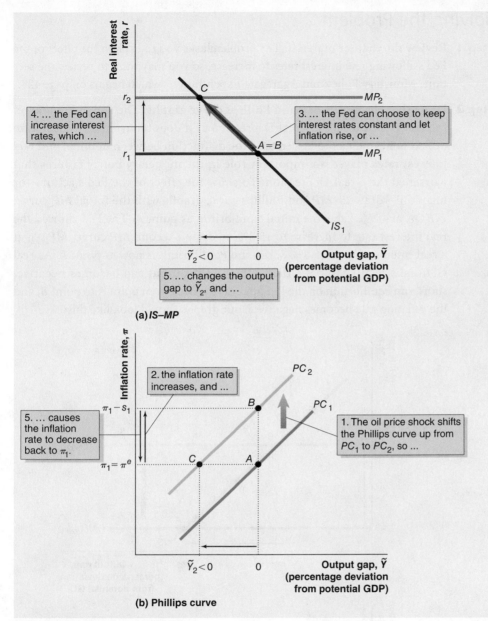

(a) *IS–MP*

4. ... the Fed can increase interest rates, which ...

3. ... the Fed can choose to keep interest rates constant and let inflation rise, or ...

5. ... changes the output gap to $\tilde{Y}_2$, and ...

2. the inflation rate increases, and ...

5. ... causes the inflation rate to decrease back to π_1.

1. The oil price shock shifts the Phillips curve up from PC_1 to PC_2, so ...

(b) Phillips curve

Figure 12.6

Monetary Policy and an Increase in Oil Prices

After an increase in oil prices, the economy's equilibrium is at point *B* in panels (a) and (b), in which the actual inflation rate is greater than the expected inflation rate. In this situation, the Fed faces a choice. The Fed can increase the real interest rate to decrease the inflation rate, which would shift the economy's short-run equilibrium to point *C* in panels (a) and (b), but this measure comes at the cost of lower real GDP. Alternatively, the Fed can keep interest rates constant, so the economy's equilibrium remains at point *B* in panels (a) and (b), but this action leaves the economy with a higher inflation rate.

Solved Problem 12.4

Did the Federal Reserve Make the Great Depression Worse?

The Great Depression was the most severe economic contraction that the United States has ever experienced. During the first years of the Great Depression in the early 1930s, the Fed thought that its monetary policy was expansionary because interest rates were low and stable. For example, the *nominal* interest rate on the safest corporate bonds varied from 4.4% to 5.4%. The Fed thought that these low interest rates

represented an expansionary policy, so that there was no need to change policy. Because the United States experienced deflation during these years, however, the *real* interest rate on the safest corporate bonds increased from 4.8% in October 1929 when the stock market crashed to 15.8% in May 1932! Use the *IS–MP* model to show the effect of a monetary policy that allowed the real interest rate to increase from 4.8% to 15.8%.

Solving the Problem

Step 1 **Review the chapter material.** The problem asks you to explain the effect of the Fed's allowing real interest rates to increase, so you may want to review the section "Monetary Policy and Aggregate Expenditure," which begins on page 424.

Step 2 **Draw the relevant *IS–MP* and Phillips curve graphs.** The Fed did not target interest rates during the Great Depression as it does today. In fact, the failure of Fed policymakers to understand the distinction between nominal and real interest rates played an important role in the monetary policy failures that worsened the Great Depression. To show the effect of the Fed's action—or inaction!—draw *IS–MP* and Phillips curve graphs with the initial *MP* curve, MP_{1929}, at 4.8%. Label the initial equilibrium as point *A*. The Fed allowed the real interest rate to increase to 15.8%, so draw a second *MP* curve, MP_{1932}, at a real interest rate of 15.8%. Short-run equilibrium is now at point *B*. As real GDP falls relative to potential GDP and the output gap becomes negative, short-run equilibrium on the Phillips curve moves from point *A* to point *B*, and the inflation rate becomes negative. Your graphs should look like this:

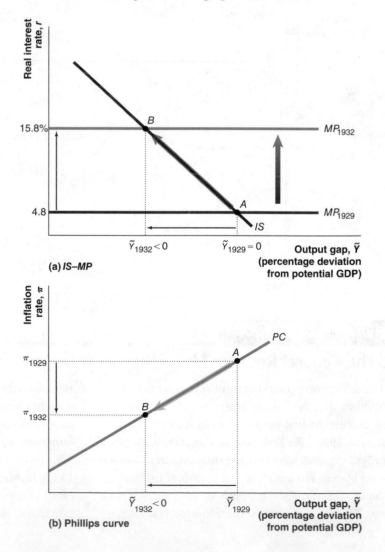

(a) *IS–MP*

(b) Phillips curve

Step 3 Discuss the effects of a rising real interest rate on the economy. If the Fed's policy made the Great Depression worse, the increase in the real interest rate would have led to lower real GDP. In fact, real GDP did fall. The increase in the real interest rate made it more expensive for households and firms to borrow to finance consumption and investment, so aggregate expenditure decreased and real GDP fell between 1929 and 1932. The Phillips curve in panel (b) in Step 2 shows that as real GDP declined far below potential GDP, the economy experienced deflation, or a falling price level.

As Milton Friedman argued, the Fed's policies were at least partly responsible for the severity of the Great Depression. Friedman emphasized the Fed's failure to stop the bank panics and the decline in the money supply, but the Fed's failure to distinguish real interest rates from nominal interest rates was also a serious policy mistake. The Fed did learn from the experience of the Great Depression, which is why Ben Bernanke is quoted as saying at the start of the chapter, "we won't do it again."

See related problems 4.4 and 4.5 at the end of the chapter.

The Liquidity Trap, the Zero Lower Bound, and Alternative Channels of Monetary Policy

Economists refer to the ways in which monetary policy can affect real GDP and prices as the *channels of monetary policy*. In the *IS–MP* model, monetary policy works through the effects that changes in the federal funds rate ultimately have on the output gap and the inflation rate. Economists call this monetary policy channel the *interest rate channel*.

There are two important instances in which monetary policy may not be able to stimulate the economy through the interest rate channel. The first step in stimulating the economy is for the central bank to purchase short-term bonds, which leads to lower short-term nominal interest rates. The short-term nominal interest rate is the opportunity cost of holding your wealth as money. John Maynard Keynes argued that when short-term nominal interest rates get low enough, the opportunity cost is so low that households will always prefer to hold money rather than short-term bonds. In that case, the Fed cannot push short-term nominal interest rates below some low positive interest rate, the interest channel stops functioning, and monetary policy may become powerless to stimulate the economy. Because the interest rate is "trapped" at a low level, Keynes called this phenomenon the *liquidity trap*.

Economists have debated whether the liquidity trap is just a theoretical curiosity or a real phenomenon. Clearly, though, the Fed cannot push the federal funds rate below 0%. A negative interest rate means that the *lender* is paying the *borrower* to borrow the lender's money. A negative federal funds rate means that one bank would be willing to *pay* another bank to borrow its reserves—an event that is about as likely as Wells Fargo paying you to take out a car loan or a student loan. As a consequence, when short-term nominal interest rates are already at 0%, the Fed cannot decrease them further. The inability of the Fed to lower interest rates to negative values is referred to as the *zero bound constraint*. At the zero bound constraint, the Fed cannot decrease real interest rates by decreasing nominal interest rates.

In the liquidity trap or at the zero bound constraint, short-term nominal interest rates cannot fall any further. In this situation, is monetary policy unable to increase aggregate expenditure and real GDP? Not necessarily. The effect of open market operations on interest rates is important, but there are two additional channels through which monetary policy can affect real GDP and inflation:

1. Credit channels
2. Quantitative easing

Credit Channels Monetary policy may affect credit markets in ways that are independent of the interest rate. These channels exist due to *asymmetric information* in the financial system. **Asymmetric information** occurs when one party in an economic transaction has better information than the other party. The *bank lending channel* of monetary policy emphasizes the behavior of borrowers who depend on bank loans. Firms have much better information about their true financial condition than do potential investors who might be willing to buy their stocks or bonds. Some firms, such as Starbucks and Google, are so large and well known that most of the information investors need is publicly available, and the firms can borrow directly from financial markets by selling corporate bonds. However, some firms are not well known, and investors are not willing to buy their bonds. These firms are forced to rely on banks and other financial intermediaries for loans. Banks develop specialized knowledge about firms. For example, a local bank may have made loans to a neighborhood bakery or beauty salon over a period of years, so the bank knows the owner's history of repaying loans and the owner's general creditworthiness. Many households also rely on banks to finance consumption and investment, by borrowing money to buy cars and homes.

Now consider how the open market purchase of government securities affects the bank lending channel. The Fed purchases government securities, so bank reserves increase. Banks can use the increased reserves to make new loans. Borrowing from banks increases, so consumption and investment increase. The increase in spending leads firms to increase output. An open market sale of government securities would have the opposite effect: The sale of government securities to banks reduces reserves and leads banks to decrease lending. As a result, some households and firms will not be able to obtain loans, so consumption and investment will decrease. The decrease in spending leads firms to decrease output. Notice, though, that the bank lending channel operates regardless of the short-term nominal interest rate. The bank lending channel provides one way in which monetary policy may still be effective even when short-term nominal interest rates equal zero.

The *balance sheet channel* provides an alternative way for monetary policy to affect households and firms that are dependent on banks for loans. Banks often require firms and households to post collateral for a loan. The more collateral that a firm has, the easier it is for the firm to get a loan because the loan becomes less risky for the bank. The same is also true of households that borrow to finance consumption or the purchase of a house. Expansionary monetary policy will often increase stock prices and the value of other assets. An increase in asset values can increase the net worth of firms and the wealth of households, providing them with more collateral to use for loans. As a

Asymmetric information
The situation in which one party to an economic transaction has better information than the other party.

result, expansionary monetary policy may increase the amount of lending and, therefore, consumption and investment—even if interest rates do not change.

Quantitative Easing Even if the federal funds rate is zero, the Fed can still add reserves to the banking system through open market purchases of long-term securities. By December 2008, the Fed had driven the target for the federal funds rate nearly to zero, while the financial crisis and the economic recession had deepened. These continuing problems led the Fed to take the unusual step of buying more than $1.7 trillion in mortgage-backed securities and longer-term Treasury securities during 2009 and early 2010. This policy of a central bank attempting to stimulate the economy by buying long-term securities is called **quantitative easing**. The Fed's objective was to reduce the interest rates on mortgages and on 10-year Treasury notes. By buying large amounts of Treasury securities and mortgage-backed securities, the Fed would increase the demand for them, forcing up their prices. The price and the interest rate on a financial asset, such as a 10-year Treasury note, move in opposite directions: When the price of a Treasury note increases, its interest rate decreases. Lower interest rates on mortgage-backed securities would translate into lower interest rates on mortgages, helping to increase sales of new homes. The Fed's purchases of mortgage-backed securities also helped to reduce the default-risk premium on mortgages. Because the Fed was buying mortgage-backed securities, banks could pass the risk of default to the Fed, so mortgages became less risky for banks.

Quantitative easing A central bank policy that attempts to stimulate the economy by buying long-term securities.

The interest rate on the 10-year Treasury note plays a particularly important role in the financial system because it is a benchmark default-free interest rate. A lower interest rate on 10-year Treasury notes can help to lower interest rates on corporate bonds, thereby increasing investment spending. In November 2010, the Fed announced a second round of quantitative easing (dubbed QE2). With QE2, the Fed bought an additional $600 billion in long-term Treasury securities through June 2011. In September 2012, the Fed announced a third round of quantitative easing (QE3), focused on purchases of mortgage-backed securities. The Fed pledged to continue QE3 until growth in real GDP and employment returned to more normal levels.

We can use our discussion of the *MP* curve to analyze the effects of quantitative easing. Recall that the expression for the long-run real interest rate, r, is:

$$r = i + TSE + DP - \pi^e.$$

With conventional monetary policy, the Fed reduces r by lowering its target for the federal funds rate, i, thereby shifting down the *MP* curve. This strategy will be successful if the expected inflation rate, the term structure effect, and the default risk premium remain unchanged. During the 2007–2009 financial crisis and its aftermath, however, the Fed had already pushed the federal funds rate as low as it could. Therefore, to increase real GDP and employment, the Fed needed another way of shifting down the *MP* curve. Quantitative easing gave the Fed the means to do so. Using quantitative easing to reduce the interest rate on 10-year Treasury notes allowed the Fed to directly reduce the real interest rate, causing the *MP* curve to shift down. The policy was intended to reduce the term premium in the term structure effect by reducing long-term interest rates relative to short-term interest rates. In practice, the market for U.S. Treasury securities is very large, so the Fed's purchases had only a small effect on the interest rate on 10-year Treasury notes. Therefore, it is unclear whether quantitative easing had a significant effect on real GDP and employment.

The Bank of Japan tried using quantitative easing as the Japanese economy struggled through a decade of extremely slow economic growth throughout the 1990s. During 2001–2006, the Bank of Japan set targets for the volume of bank reserves and purchased long-term government securities until reserves hit the target level. At one point, the Bank of Japan set a target of 30–35 trillion yen for bank reserves when the required level of bank reserves was just 6 trillion yen. The target created a huge supply of excess reserves that Japanese banks could lend to households and firms if they so chose. During this experiment with quantitative easing, the Bank of Japan purchased not only government securities but also stocks and commercial paper. Economists still debate whether the Bank of Japan's quantitative easing helped the economy, but the Japanese economy has yet to return to the growth rates it experienced prior to the 1990s.

Figure 12.7 shows the effects of the Fed's policies during the financial crisis of 2007–2009 and the period immediately following on the value of assets on the *Fed's balance sheet*. The turmoil following the collapse of Lehman Brothers on September 15, 2008, led to a dramatic change in Fed policy. The Fed's assets exploded from $927 billion before the Lehman Brothers bankruptcy to $2.2 trillion on November 12, 2008. The increase came primarily from new loans to financial institutions and attempts to increase

MyEconLab Real-time data

Figure 12.7

Federal Reserve Assets, 2007–2012

After the collapse of Lehman Brothers, the Fed dramatically increased the assets it owned from $927 billion to $2.2 trillion. Some of the increase came from loans to financial institutions and the rest came from purchases of assets such as commercial paper and mortgage-backed securities.

Source: Board of Governors of the Federal Reserve System.

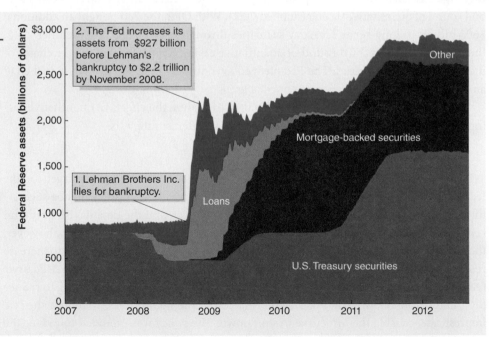

the liquidity of key markets such as commercial paper. Access to the commercial paper market is critical to the day-to-day operations of many large firms.

Quantitative easing has a drawback: By increasing bank reserves and the monetary base, it has the potential to significantly increase inflation. Although critics of the Fed were concerned that inflation would increase as early as 2009, in fact, inflation remained at low levels through the end of 2012. When inflation did not increase, many economists saw it as an indication of the severity of the 2007–2009 recession and the weakness of the subsequent recovery.

Operation Twist In September 2011, the Fed announced that it would purchase $400 billion of long-term securities while also selling $400 billion of short-term securities. The financial press referred to this policy as *Operation Twist*. The policy's name reflects its goal of twisting the yield curve by increasing short-term interest rates and lowering long-term interest rates. In effect, Operation Twist would reduce the term premium in the term structure effect. Because Operation Twist attempted to directly reduce long-term interest rates through bond purchases, it was similar in its effects to quantitative easing. By selling $400 billion of short-term bonds at the same time that it bought $400 billion of long-term securities, the Fed did not increase the monetary base or the threat of future inflation. Most economists believe that Operation Twist had only modest success in increasing real GDP and employment, although in mid-2012, Fed Chairman Bernanke argued that the effect of the policy was "still working its way through the system."

The Limitations of Monetary Policy

Our discussion thus far may make it seem easy for central banks to eliminate economic fluctuations and achieve price stability, high employment, and stable interest rates following a demand shock. In fact, though, central banks face several important challenges to implementing policy successfully.

The Fed's ability to quickly recognize the need for a change in monetary policy is a key to its success. If the Fed is late in recognizing that a recession has begun or that the inflation rate is increasing, it may not be able to implement a new policy soon enough to avoid a significant recession or a significant increase in inflation. In fact, particularly when dealing with small demand shocks, if the Fed implements a policy too late, it may actually destabilize the economy.

Policy Lags

In practice, the Fed is not instantly aware that a significant demand shock or supply shock has occurred. Even after the Fed becomes aware that a shock has occurred, it takes time to decide on an appropriate policy. Then, it takes time for the new policy to actually affect real GDP, employment, and inflation. Due to *lags* between the time a shock occurs and the time the effects of the policy change occur, monetary policy cannot immediately offset the effects of shocks. In this section, we discuss *policy lags* further.

Learning Objective
Explain the challenges in using monetary policy effectively.

Recognition lag The period of time between when a shock occurs and when policymakers recognize that the shock has affected the economy.

A **recognition lag** is the period of time between when a shock occurs and when policymakers recognize that the shock has affected the economy. Economic data become available to policymakers with a delay of up to several months. For example, the first estimate for the growth rate of the U.S. economy for 2012 was not available until the end of January 2013. In addition, initial estimates of economic variables, such as employment and real GDP, are often inaccurate, so it is difficult to know if a shock has had a large effect on the economy. This uncertainty makes it difficult for policymakers to know if a shock requires a policy response. For example, NASDAQ (a stock index based largely on high-tech companies) peaked on March 10, 2000, and then rapidly declined as the dot-com bubble burst. The destruction in stock market wealth contributed to the 2001 recession. However, it was not initially clear that the economy would enter a recession after the dot-com bubble burst. In fact, on May 16, 2000, at which point the NASDAQ had decreased by 26.4%, the Fed actually increased interest rates from 6.0% to 6.5% because it was still worried that inflation was accelerating.

Implementation lag The period of time between when policymakers recognize that a shock has occurred and when they adjust policy to the shock.

An **implementation lag** is the period of time between when policymakers recognize that a shock has occurred and when they adjust policy to the shock. Implementation lags exist because once the Fed recognizes that a shock has occurred, it still takes time to determine whether and how to respond. Implementation lags by themselves are short for monetary policy. The FOMC meets eight times a year and, if necessary, can authorize changes in policy between regularly scheduled meetings. For example, in response to the financial crisis, the FOMC cut the target federal funds rate by 0.50% on October 8, 2008, even though the FOMC was not scheduled to meet until October 28, 2008.

Impact lag The period of time between a policy change and the effect of that policy change.

An **impact lag** is the period of time between a policy change and the effect of that policy change on real GDP, employment, inflation, and other economic variables. Nobel Laureate Milton Friedman famously described the lags for monetary policy as "long and variable," which means that it can take months or years for changes in monetary policy to affect real GDP and inflation and that the lags vary based on historical circumstances. Figure 12.3 on page 425 illustrates part of the reason these lags exist. Once the Fed reduces the target federal funds rate, it takes time for the interest rates that affect corporate and household behavior to also decline. Then it takes time for corporations to identify newly profitable investment projects, obtain loans from banks or arrange to sell corporate bonds, and start spending the borrowed funds. Similarly, it takes time for families to respond to lower mortgage interest rates by buying houses. As a result, the full effect of a change in monetary policy is typically spread out over several years.

Economic Forecasts

Because it can take a long time for the effect of a change in monetary policy to affect real GDP, central banks do not respond to the current state of the economy. Instead, they respond to the state of the economy they think will exist in the future, when the policy change actually affects the economy. For example, the Fed cut its federal funds rate target by 0.5% on October 8, 2008. Given the impact lags associated with monetary policy, the full effect of that rate cut on real GDP was likely to be spread out over several years. In making that cut, the Fed was thinking about the economy's future performance.

Table 12.2 Federal Reserve Forecasts for Real GDP Growth During 2007 and 2008

Forecast date	Forecast growth rate	
	2007	2008
February 2006	3% to 4%	—
July 2006	2.5% to 3.25%	—
February 2007	2.25% to 3.25%	2.5% to 3.25%
July 2007	2% to 2.75%	2.5% to 3.0%
February 2008	—	1.0% to 2.2%
July 2008	—	1.0% to 1.6%

Source: Board of Governors of the Federal Reserve System, *Monetary Report to the Congress*, various dates.

For a central bank to succeed in reducing the severity of business cycles, it must often act *before* the size of a shock is apparent in the economic data. So, good policy requires good economic forecasts based on models that describe accurately how the economy functions. Unfortunately, economic forecasts and models can be unreliable because the factors determining real GDP can change quickly. Shocks by their nature are unpredictable. For example, the forecasts of most economists at the end of 2006 and the beginning of 2007 did not anticipate the severity of the economic slowdown that began in December 2007. Only after financial market conditions began to deteriorate rapidly did economists significantly reduce their forecasts of GDP growth in 2008 and 2009.

Table 12.2 shows the Fed's estimates for the growth rate of real GDP for 2007 and 2008 in its *Monetary Policy Report to Congress*. To avert the economic slowdown in 2007, the Fed would have had to change policy before 2007. However, in February 2006, the Fed expected the economy to grow by 3% to 4% in 2007, so it had little reason to change policy. Similarly, the Fed could have changed policy in an attempt to keep the economy growing in 2008, but it would have had to change policy before 2008, and as late as July 2007, the Fed still expected the economy to grow by 2.5% to 3.0% in 2008. In fact, real GDP increased by only 1.9% in 2007 and declined by 0.3% in 2008. In principle, the Fed could have taken actions to avert or at least greatly reduce the severity of the 2007–2009 recession. In practice, the Fed could not prevent the recession because it did not see the recession coming.

Model Uncertainty

An issue related to poor economic forecasts is model uncertainty. Even if the Fed is convinced that the economy will enter a recession or that inflation will accelerate next year, it still faces problems in implementing monetary policy. Why? Economic models are just approximations of how the world works. As a result, economists do not know precisely how any given event will change real GDP and inflation, how any change in the target short-term nominal interest rate will change the long-term real interest rate, how much consumption and investment will respond to changes in the long-term real interest rate, how much real GDP will respond to the changes in consumption and investment, or how much inflation will respond to changes in real GDP.

Economic models are not sophisticated enough to tell us precisely how much an event will change aggregate expenditure. For example, we know that consumption responds to changes in wealth, so a reduction in real estate values should reduce consumption. The key question for central bankers is: By how much? According to the Congressional Budget Office, recent estimates of the responsiveness of consumption to a $100 increase in real estate wealth range from $1.70 to $21. The high estimate is more than 10 times larger than the low estimate, so it is difficult for the Fed to know exactly the effects of a change in housing wealth. In addition, there is only a *tendency* for long-term interest rates to decrease as the Fed reduces its target short-term nominal interest rate. Figure 12.3 on page 425 shows that the interest rates are related but that the relationship is not perfect. As a result, the Fed does not know for certain how much it must reduce its target short-term nominal interest rate to get the long-term real interest rate to be at the desired level. Economic models have not advanced to the point where economists know exactly how responsive consumption and investment are to interest rates, so the Fed does not know exactly by how much to reduce interest rates to prevent a recession. Finally, economic models also cannot tell us exactly how much inflation will respond to changes in real GDP, or the output gap.

Consequences of Policy Limitations

Policy lags and the inherent uncertainty of economic forecasts mean that policymakers may make mistakes. Figure 12.8 provides an example of a poorly timed monetary policy. Suppose that stock market wealth falls by 10% on a single day. Based on its models and economic forecasts, assume the Fed believes the result will be reduced consumption, leading to a recession. Therefore, the Fed believes that short-run equilibrium will occur at point A in panels (a) and (b).

At point A, real GDP is below potential GDP, so $\widetilde{Y}_1 < 0$, and cyclical unemployment is positive. In response, the Fed decreases the target interest rate to increase consumption, investment, and net exports—and shift short-run equilibrium to point B. If the IS curve remains at IS_1, then when the Fed reduces interest rates, real GDP increases relative to potential GDP and the output gap moves to $\widetilde{Y}_2$. The change in the output gap causes the inflation rate to increase to π_2. Short-run equilibrium is now at point B, and the recession has ended. The lags for monetary policy are long and variable, so it takes time for the change in monetary policy to increase output. In the time it takes monetary policy to have its effect, the stock market may have recovered or other events may have increased aggregate expenditure. Short-run equilibrium could be at point C when real GDP begins responding to policy. The recession will be over *before* the change in policy affects real GDP. Therefore, the change in policy will move the short-run equilibrium to point D in panel (a), where $\widetilde{Y}_4 > 0$. With the output gap equal to $\widetilde{Y}_4$, the inflation rate increases to π_4, and short-run equilibrium is now at point D in panel (b). In this case, monetary policy has pushed real GDP beyond potential GDP, causing the inflation rate to increase.

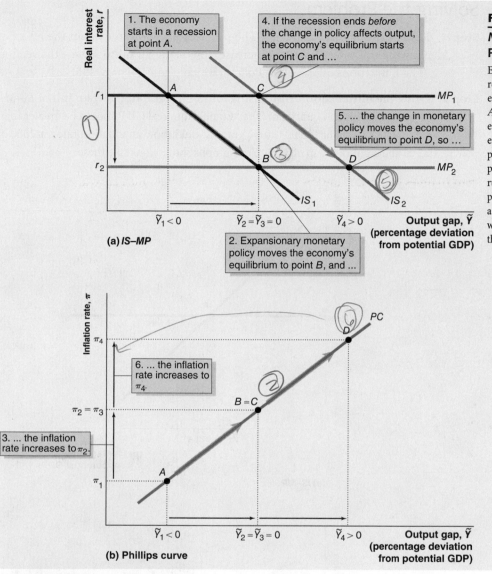

1. The economy starts in a recession at point *A*.

4. If the recession ends *before* the change in policy affects output, the economy's equilibrium starts at point *C* and ...

5. ... the change in monetary policy moves the economy's equilibrium to point *D*, so ...

2. Expansionary monetary policy moves the economy's equilibrium to point *B*, and ...

(a) *IS–MP*

6. ... the inflation rate increases to π_4.

3. ... the inflation rate increases to π_2.

(b) Phillips curve

Figure 12.8

Monetary Policy That Is Poorly Timed

Expansionary monetary policy results in the economy's short-equilibrium moving from point *A* to point *B* in panels (a) and (b), ending a recession. If a recession ends before the change in monetary policy affects the economy, the policy change will move the short-run equilibrium from point *C* to point *D* in panels (a) and (b). As a result of poor timing, the policy will increase the inflation rate after the recession has already ended.

Solved Problem 12.5

Did the Fed Help Cause the 2001 Recession?

Real GDP was 1.1% greater than potential GDP during the third quarter of 1998, but it rose to 3.5% above potential GDP by the second quarter of 2000. With real GDP above potential GDP, the inflation rate began to increase. The inflation rate as measured by the CPI increased from 1.4% during September 1998 to 3.7% during June 2000. The Fed responded by increasing the target federal funds rate from 5.0% in September 1998 to 6.5% in May 2000. The last increase in the target rate came after the dot-com bubble burst and all

major stock indexes started to decline. By March 2001, the U.S. economy had entered a recession that worsened after the terrorist attacks on September 11, 2001, led households and firms to reduce consumption and investment. The recession was short, ending in November 2001, but the economy recovered slowly, and real GDP was 1.9% below potential GDP as late as the first quarter of 2003. Did the Fed's decision to increase the federal funds rate contribute to the recession and the slow recovery? Use the *IS–MP* model to show the effect of the Fed's policy.

Solving the Problem

Step 1 **Review the chapter material.** The problem asks you to explain the effect of allowing real interest rates to increase, so you may want to review the section "The Limitations of Monetary Policy," which begins on page 435.

Step 2 **Draw the initial equilibrium using an *IS–MP* graph.** Draw an initial *IS–MP* graph for the second quarter of 2000. Equilibrium real GDP should be greater than potential GDP. Your Phillips curve graph should show an inflation rate for 2000 of 3.7% and an output gap of 3.5%. Your graphs should look like these:

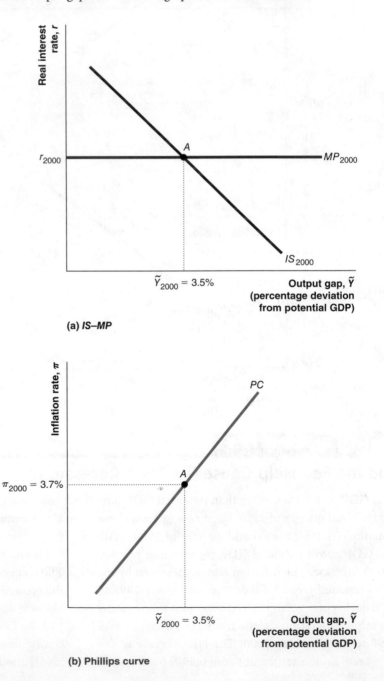

(a) *IS–MP*

(b) Phillips curve

Step 3 **Show the effect of the increase in interest rates.** The Fed increased the federal funds rate, which should increase long-term real interest rates. Assume that the Fed knows exactly how much to increase interest rates to move real GDP to potential GDP. Therefore, you should shift the *MP* curve up on the *IS–MP* graph and you should show the short-run equilibrium moving down the Phillips curve. Your graphs should now look like these:

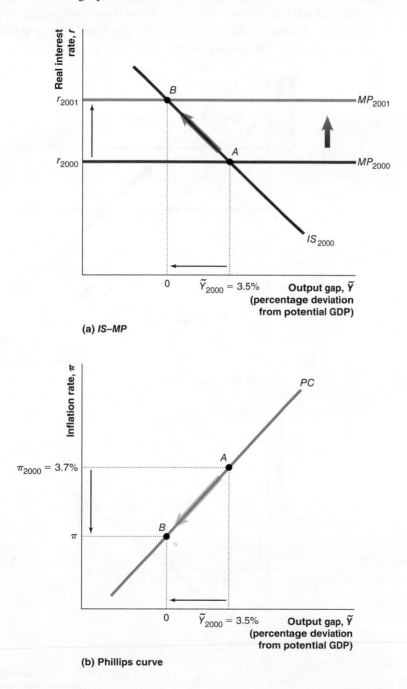

(a) *IS–MP*

(b) **Phillips curve**

Step 4 **Show the effect of the collapse in stock prices and the terrorist attacks.** A stock market collapse such as the one that occurred in 2000 reduces household wealth, which reduces consumption. The stock market collapse also increases uncertainty about the future, leading firms to reduce investment spending and leading households to further reduce consumption. The terrorist attacks also increased uncertainty, leading firms and households to reduce expenditures on goods and services. Show the effect of the decrease in aggregate expenditure by shifting the *IS* curve to the left in the *IS–MP* graph and by moving the short-run equilibrium further down the Phillips curve. Your graphs should look like these:

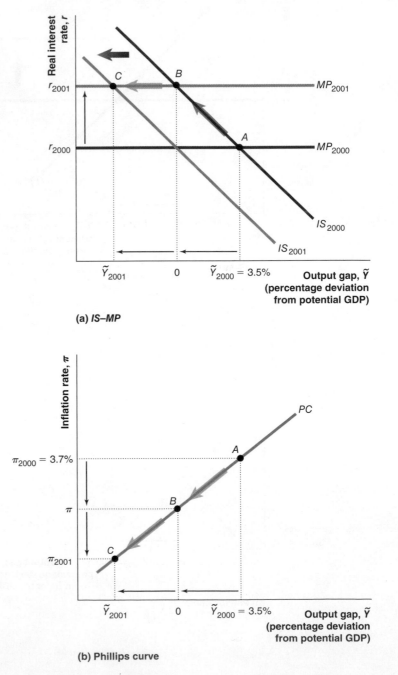

(a) *IS–MP*

(b) **Phillips curve**

The Fed could not be certain where the *IS* curve would be for the year 2001. Therefore, it based its policy decisions in 2000 on where it *thought* the *IS* curve would be. The Fed may have underestimated the effect of the stock market collapse on consumption and investment, and it could not have anticipated the terrorist attacks or their effect on the U.S. economy. The Fed may have anticipated that the *IS* curve would remain at IS_{2000}, but the actual *IS* curve was IS_{2001}. As a result, the Fed's decision to increase the federal funds rate during 2000 may have contributed to the 2001 recession and to the slow recovery.

See related problem 5.4 at the end of the chapter

Moral Hazard

Financial investments are inherently risky, and it is possible for financial institutions to earn huge profits. It is often the case, however, that the larger the potential profits, the larger the potential losses. Ordinarily, managers of financial institutions have a strong financial incentive to carefully balance potential reward against risk. Sometimes, however, a financial institution becomes so large that its failure would damage the financial system and, potentially, the broader economy. If the federal government adopts a **too-big-to-fail policy**, it does not allow large financial firms to fail for fear of damaging the financial system. A goal of monetary policy is financial market stability, so the Fed and central banks in other countries often make loans to troubled financial institutions during a crisis. By saving troubled financial institutions, central banks may achieve financial stability in the short run, but they also may increase *moral hazard*, which could destabilize the financial system in the long run if financial institutions take larger risks.

Too-big-to-fail policy A policy in which the federal government does not allow large financial firms to fail for fear of damaging the financial system.

Making the Connection

"Too Big to Fail"—The Legacy of Continental Illinois

The Federal Reserve responded to the financial crisis very aggressively in 2008, providing loans not only to commercial banks but also to investment banks and private companies. While many analysts credit the Fed's actions with preventing the crisis from worsening, these actions also reinforced the belief that there were institutions that were "too big to fail." Therefore, it came as a great shock in the fall of 2008 when the Fed allowed the investment bank Lehman Brothers to declare bankruptcy.

According to Neil McLeish, an analyst at Morgan Stanley, "Prior to Lehman, there was an almost unshakable faith that the senior creditors and [trading partners] of large, systemically important financial institutions would not face the risk of outright default." This "almost unshakable faith" was partly the result of the failure of another financial institution. Continental Illinois Bank, one of the largest banks in the United States, had suffered heavy losses on its loans, and many of its customers withdrew their deposits in 1984, after the bank's weakened financial condition became known. Many other smaller banks held deposits in Continental Illinois, and there was concern among regulators that these banks might fail if Continental Illinois failed. To avoid these losses to the banking system and potential harm to the wider economy, the Federal Deposit

Insurance Corporation (FDIC) seized the assets of Continental Illinois. When a bank fails, the FDIC pays back depositors and helps to settle the bank's other debts. Investors who have bought the bank's bonds or made loans to the bank are typically paid back less than the face value of the debts. The possibility of such losses discourages investors from buying the bonds of or making loans to banks that are poorly managed. But in the case of Continental Illinois, bondholders were fully paid back. In effect, the bank's creditors did not pay a penalty for the failure of Continental Illinois.

Although neither the federal government nor the Federal Reserve had an official too-big-to-fail policy, the government's response to Continental Illinois encouraged executives at other large financial firms and their creditors to assume that policymakers would rescue them in the event of another crisis. This approach, which some refer to as "constructive ambiguity"—saving large banks without a formal policy of doing so—proved to be unworkable in 2008 as the Fed became concerned with increasing moral hazard. Congress, the Federal Reserve, and other bank regulators were challenged to find alternatives to constructive ambiguity.

There clearly remain many financial firms that are "too big to fail." In 2012, the following five banks held about $8.5 trillion in assets: JPMorgan Chase, Bank of America, Citigroup, Wells Fargo, and Goldman Sachs. Relative to the size of the U.S. economy, these five banks were about twice as large as they were in 2001. Gary Stern, former president of the Federal Reserve Bank of Minneapolis, commented: "Market participants believe that nothing has changed, that too-big-to-fail is fully intact." Some analysts have suggested that these institutions should be reduced in size in order to improve the credibility of a government pledge to allow them to fail. In 2012, Sanford Weill, former head of Citigroup, surprised many analysts by endorsing this position. Another suggestion is to more heavily regulate institutions to reduce the risk of failure.

Sources: Michael J. De La Merced, "Weill Calls for Splitting Up Big Banks," *New York Times*, July 25, 2012; Gerald P. Dwyer, "Too Big to Fail," *Notes from the Vault*, Federal Reserve Bank of Atlanta, February 2010; "The Hazard in Moral Hazard," *Economist*, October 13, 2008; and David J. Lynch, "Big Banks: Now Even Too Bigger to Fail," *BloombergBusinessWeek*, April 19, 2012.

See related problem 5.6 at the end of the chapter.

In pursuing the goals of monetary policy, central banks may inadvertently create moral hazard and make the financial system and the economy less stable. In July 2010, Congress passed the Wall Street Reform and Consumer Protection Act, often referred to as the *Dodd-Frank Act*. The act contains provisions intended to eliminate the too big-to-fail policy. Some economists were skeptical, though, that when faced with the failure of a large financial firm the federal government would not still feel obliged to rescue it.

12.6

Learning Objective
Evaluate the arguments for and against central bank independence.

Central Bank Independence

Governments create central banks, and governments also appoint the heads of central banks. This process does not necessarily mean, however, that governments control the decisions of central bankers. The Federal Reserve System of the United States provides a good example of how a central bank that is created by the government can nevertheless maintain substantial independence in how it conducts monetary policy.

The Independence of the U.S. Federal Reserve

Congress created the Federal Reserve System in 1913 and set out its policy goals. The president nominates and the Senate confirms members of the Federal Reserve's Board of Governors. The chairman of the Federal Reserve is required to testify before Congress twice each year to explain monetary policy decisions. So, the Federal Reserve acts within boundaries established by Congress and the president. The Fed, though, has a great deal of flexibility in meeting the goals of monetary policy. The Federal Open Market Committee decides the target federal funds rate without direct input from either the president or Congress. During the financial crisis of 2007–2009, the Fed developed a number of new policy tools without direct approval from either the president or Congress. Chairman Ben Bernanke had to explain the Fed's actions to Congress, but the Fed was able to pursue major new policies without approval from the government.

Congress intended that the structure of the Fed would insulate it from political pressure. The members of the Federal Reserve Board are appointed to 14-year nonrenewable terms, so once confirmed, they are relatively free of political pressure. In addition, the Fed is not dependent on the federal government for funding. The Fed owns a large amount of U.S. Treasury securities and pays for its operations with the interest income from these securities. Unlike federal agencies such as the Department of Defense or the Department of the Treasury, the Fed does not have to go to Congress each year to request funding. In fact, the Fed typically spends less than it earns and returns these profits to the Treasury. Because the Fed greatly increased its holdings of securities during the financial crisis, it was able to return $78 billion to the U.S. Treasury in 2010 and $77 billion in 2011.

If Congress and the president become dissatisfied with the Fed's performance, they are free to change how the Fed operates by amending the Federal Reserve Act. As we saw in the chapter opener, the reappointment of Ben Bernanke in 2010 was politically contentious. During the debate over the Dodd-Frank Act in 2010, there were several proposals to substantially reduce the Fed's independence, although none of the proposals was included in the final bill. The debate over the Fed's independence is likely to continue. In the next two sections, we briefly review some arguments for and against Fed independence.

The Case for Fed Independence The main argument for Fed independence is that monetary policy—which affects inflation, interest rates, exchange rates, and economic growth—is too important and technical for politicians to determine. Because of the frequency of elections, politicians may be concerned with the short-term benefits of policies, without regard for the policies' potential long-term costs. In particular, the short-term desire of politicians to be reelected may clash with the country's long-term interest in low inflation. The public may well prefer that the experts at the Fed, rather than politicians, make monetary policy decisions.

Another argument for Fed independence is that complete control of the Fed by elected officials increases the likelihood of fluctuations in the money supply caused by political pressure. For example, particularly just before an election, those officials might pressure the Fed to assist the Treasury's borrowing efforts by buying government bonds, which would increase the money supply and temporarily increase real GDP and employment, but at the risk of increasing inflation in the long run.

The Case Against Fed Independence The importance of monetary policy for the economy is also the main argument against central bank independence. Supporters of reducing the Fed's independence argue that in a democracy, elected officials should make public policy. Because the public holds elected officials responsible for monetary policy problems, some analysts advocate giving those officials more control over it. While some economists argue that monetary policy is too technical for elected officials to understand, other economists argue that elected officials have experience dealing with equally complex tasks, such as fiscal policy, national security, and foreign policy. In addition, critics of central bank independence argue that placing the central bank under the control of elected officials could confer benefits by coordinating monetary policy with government taxing and spending policies.

Those in favor of greater government control argue that the Fed has not always used its independence well. For example, critics note that the Fed's concern about inflation contributed to its failure to assist the banking system during the Great Depression. Critics also note that Fed policies were too inflationary in the 1960s and 1970s. Some analysts believe that the Fed acted too slowly in addressing credit problems during the recession of the early 1990s. Finally, some economists argue that the Fed kept interest rates too low for too long after the 2001 recession, which helped fuel the housing market bubble.

These examples illustrate that central bank independence is by no means a guarantee of sound monetary policy. However, research on central bank independence indicates that the more independent the central bank, the better the economy's performance. Alberto Alesina and Lawrence Summers, economists at Harvard University, examined the relationship between central bank independence and macroeconomic performance for 16 high-income countries from 1955 to 1988. Figure 12.9 shows their findings on

Figure 12.9

Central Bank Independence and the Average Inflation Rate

For 16 high-income countries, the greater the degree of central bank independence from the rest of the government, the lower the inflation rate.

Source: Alberto Alesina and Lawrence Summers, "Central Bank Independence and Macroeconomic Performance: Some Comparative Evidence," *Journal of Money, Credit, and Banking*, May 1993, Vol. 25, No. 2, pp. 151–162. Copyright © 1993. Reproduced with permission of Blackwell Publishing Ltd.

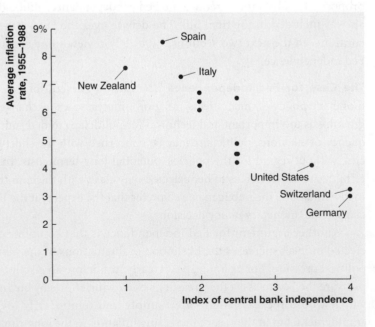

the relationship between central bank independence and average inflation rates. Alesina and Summers measured central bank independence using an index ranging from 1 (minimum independence) to 4 (maximum independence). Their results show that the more independent the central bank, the lower the average inflation rate. During this time period, New Zealand's central bank was least independent, and the inflation rate averaged 7.6%. In contrast, the central banks for Germany and Switzerland were most independent and experienced average inflation rates of about 3%. This result is consistent with the view that independent central banks resist political pressure to stimulate the economy in the short run at the cost of higher inflation in the long run. Alesina and Summers also found that central bank independence reduces the volatility of both the inflation rate and the real interest rate. More stable prices and real interest rates makes it easier for households and firms to make long-term plans such as saving for retirement or deciding to build a new factory. Therefore, central bank independence improves the performance of the economy. The benefits of improved economic performance, however, must be weighed against the cost of having a central bank that is not directly responsible to the voters conduct monetary policy.

Monetary Policy in an Open Economy

Learning Objective
Explain how monetary policy operates in an open economy.

The United States is an open economy and experiences extensive trade and flows of financial investment with other countries. To this point, we have not considered in detail international trade and international monetary flows when discussing monetary policy. We have also not taken into account the exchange rate policies that governments pursue. A country can either allow the exchange rate for its currency to float, so the exchange rate changes from day to day, or a country can try to fix the exchange rate at some level. As it turns out, the decision to either fix the exchange rate or let it float can help determine the effectiveness of expansionary monetary policy.

Monetary Policy with Floating Exchange Rates

Panel (a) of Figure 12.10 shows the effect of an expansionary monetary policy. The Fed reduces the real interest rate, shifting down the MP curve from MP_1 to MP_2. This shift decreases the real interest rate, from r_1 to r_2, so short-run equilibrium moves from point A to point B, and the output gap changes from $\widetilde{Y}_1$ to $\widetilde{Y}_2$. The lower real interest rate makes investment in the United States less attractive, so investors purchase fewer U.S. assets and net capital outflows increase from NCF_1 to NCF_2, as shown in panel (b). Because investors purchase fewer U.S. assets, they need fewer U.S. dollars, so the demand for U.S. dollars decreases, causing the dollar to depreciate in value. Because net exports equal net capital outflows, net exports also increase from NCF_1 to NCF_2.

In a closed-economy version of the IS–MP model, an expansionary monetary policy would reduce interest rates, leading to higher consumption and investment. Lower interest rates still lead to higher consumption and investment and an increase in real GDP relative to potential GDP in an open-economy version of the model. However, now lower real interest rates also lead to higher net exports, so expansionary monetary policy increases real GDP for a third reason: The lower real interest rates cause the domestic currency to depreciate, so net exports increase.

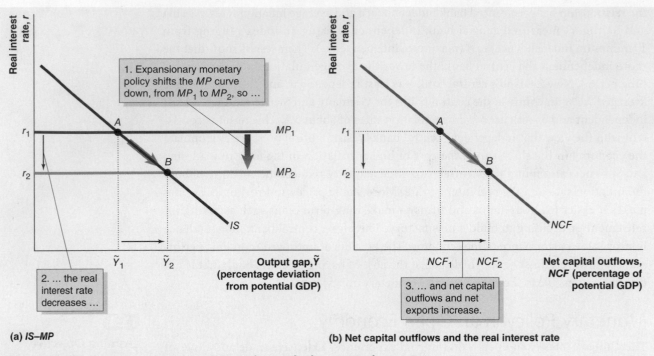

Figure 12.10 An Expansionary Monetary Policy with Floating Exchange Rates

An expansionary monetary policy decreases the real interest rate in panel (a). The decrease in the real interest rate causes the exchange rate to depreciate, so net capital outflows increase in panel (b) and net exports also increase. In both panels, equilibrium moves from point A to point B.

Monetary Policy with a Fixed Exchange Rate

With a fixed exchange rate, a country needs enough reserves of foreign currency to maintain the fixed exchange rate. However, if real interest rates fall below some critical level, $\bar{r}$, then investors will pull their funds out of a country, and the country will exhaust its reserves of foreign currency. When the country no longer has enough foreign reserves, it will be forced to abandon the fixed exchange rate. As a result, $\bar{r}$ represents a lower bound for the real interest rate.

Expansionary Monetary Policy Figure 12.11 shows the effect of an expansionary monetary policy. As long as the initial real interest rate is greater than $\bar{r}$, the central bank can increase real GDP with an expansionary monetary policy that shifts the MP curve down, from MP_1 to MP_2. The expansionary monetary policy has the usual effect: The output gap changes from $\widetilde{Y}_1$ to $\widetilde{Y}_2$ in panel (a) and net capital outflows increase from NCF_1 to NCF_2 in panel (b). However, once the IS curve intersects MP_2 where the real interest rate is $\bar{r}$, the central bank cannot increase real GDP and maintain the fixed exchange rate. Once the central bank exhausts its foreign-exchange reserves, the government will be forced to abandon the fixed exchange rate or devalue the currency. A fixed exchange rate clearly puts severe limits on the ability of conventional monetary policy to stimulate the economy. An alternative policy available to a country with a fixed exchange rate is a *currency devaluation*.

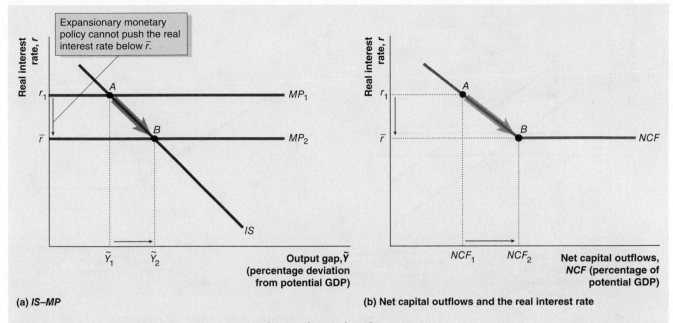

(a) *IS–MP*

(b) Net capital outflows and the real interest rate

Figure 12.11 An Expansionary Monetary Policy with Fixed Exchange Rates

With fixed exchange rates, an expansionary monetary policy cannot shift the *MP* curve below the lower bound of $\bar{r}$ in panel (a). As a result, the central bank cannot push the output gap beyond $\widetilde{Y}_2$ while maintaining the fixed exchange rate. In panel (b), net capital outflows can increase from NCF_1 to NCF_2, but not beyond. In both panels, monetary policy results in short-run equilibrium moving from point *A* to point *B*.

Devaluing the Currency If a country operates under a fixed exchange rate system, policymakers have an additional way to affect economic activity. The government can decide to maintain a fixed exchange rate system but with a devalued currency. If the government devalues the currency, then there is a one-time decrease in the nominal exchange rate. The decrease in the nominal exchange rate will make exports cheaper and imports more expensive, so net exports will increase. Figure 12.12 shows that the increase in net exports will shift the *IS* curve to the right from IS_1 to IS_2, in panel (a). It is possible for the central bank to lower the real interest rate further while still maintaining the new lower nominal exchange rate so $\bar{r}$ decreases from $\bar{r}_1$ to $\bar{r}_2$. As a result of these changes, real GDP increases relative to potential GDP in panel (a). According to the Phillips curve, the change in the output gap leads to higher inflation, so the central bank increases the real interest rate and the *MP* curve shifts up from MP_1 to MP_2. The real interest rate increases, so net capital outflows decrease in panel (b).

The Policy Trilemma for Economic Policy

Our discussion of macroeconomic theory and the real-world experience of many countries shows that a country cannot achieve all three of the following policy goals:

1. Exchange rate stability
2. Monetary policy independence
3. Free capital flows

We consider why each of these goals is desirable and then explore why they cannot be simultaneously attained.

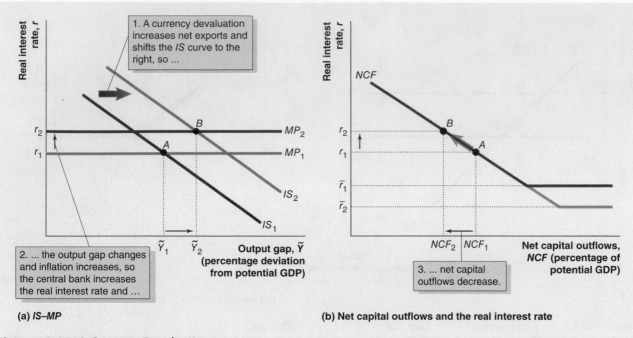

Figure 12.12 A Currency Devaluation

A currency devaluation increases net exports, so the *IS* curve shifts to the right from IS_1 to IS_2 in panel (a). In addition, $\bar{r}$ decreases from $\bar{r}_1$ to $\bar{r}_2$, so monetary policy can now reduce real interest rates further than before.

As the central bank increases the real interest rate, net capital outflows decreases, as panel (b) shows. In both panels, equilibrium moves from point *A* to point *B*.

Exchange Rate Stability Exchange rate stability is desirable because it reduces the uncertainty of buying, selling, and investing across borders. For example, if a Mexican firm knows that the exchange rate between the U.S. dollar and the Mexican peso will always be 12.8 pesos per dollar, then it is easier for the firm to know whether it will be profitable to build a factory to export goods to the United States. Uncertainty about the exchange rate makes the firm less likely to invest. Uncertainty about exchange rates also means that U.S. investors will be less willing to purchase Mexican assets, such as stocks and bonds, due to the risk that the exchange rate will change and reduce the rate of return on the investment. Remember that the nominal exchange rate is a price, so the benefits of nominal exchange rate stability are similar to the benefits of general price stability (see Chapter 7). As with stability in other prices, stable nominal exchange rates make it easier for households and firms to plan.

Monetary Policy Independence *Monetary policy independence* means the ability of the central bank to use monetary policy to achieve macroeconomic objectives such as stable prices and high employment, without regard to movements in exchange rates. If monetary policy can respond to demand and supply shocks, then it is possible for monetary policy to reduce the severity of business cycles. Recall that one of the reasons that economists think that business cycles in the United States were so mild from the early 1980s to 2007 was that the Fed effectively responded to shocks.

In the United States, the Fed is free to adjust monetary policy to pursue macroeconomic objectives because the United States has a floating exchange rate, so the Fed does not have to adjust nominal interest rates to maintain the value of the dollar. In contrast, countries with fixed exchange rates and free capital flows must adjust the interest rate to maintain their fixed exchange rate, so they cannot also adjust interest rates to achieve price stability and high employment.

Free Capital Flows The free flow of capital across borders is the third desirable policy goal. One way for a country to finance gross private investment is through capital flows from abroad. These flows can also finance government budget deficits so that the deficits do not crowd out domestic private investment.

While access to capital flows seems desirable, some countries believe that large capital flows make economic activity more volatile. For example, a large increase in capital out-flows will reduce the demand for the domestic currency and lead to a rapid depreciation of the currency. The rapid depreciation of the currency can make critical imports, such as food and fuel, more expensive for households and firms. As a result, some countries impose *capital controls*, which are legal limits or restrictions on the flow of financial capital into and out of a country. Capital controls can limit the excessive swings in the nominal exchange rate by limiting the ability of capital to flow into and out of a country. In the extreme, capital controls may prohibit international transactions in assets such as stocks and bonds, or the controls may require official government permission to engage in these international transactions. Alternatively, governments may impose taxes on international transactions that make these transactions more costly and, therefore, discourage or limit their volume. In recent years, developing countries such as Brazil (1993–1997), Chile (1991–1998), Colombia (1993–1998), Malaysia (1998–1999), and Thailand (1995–1997) have all used capital controls to restrict short-term capital flows into and out of their countries. Capital controls have an important drawback, however. If foreign firms believe that they will have difficulty exchanging local currency for foreign currency, they may be reluctant to invest in the country. Particularly for developing countries, foreign direct investment and foreign portfolio investment may be indispensible for economic growth.

The Policy Trilemma for Economic Policy The hypothesis that it is impossible for a country to have exchange rate stability, monetary policy independence, and free capital flows at the same time is called the **policy trilemma**. This hypothesis is based on the work of Nobel Laureate Robert Mundell of Columbia University and Marcus Fleming of the International Monetary Fund. If the hypothesis is correct, it is possible to achieve at most two of the policy goals at the same time. Therefore, policymakers must choose which goal they do not wish to pursue. Figure 12.13 shows the policy trilemma. Each side of the triangle indicates one of the desirable policy goals, and each point of the triangle indicates which policy goal is unattainable.

The lower left of the triangle indicates that if policymakers choose to allow free capital flows and have an independent monetary policy, they must let the exchange rate float. The United States currently allows free flow of capital, and the Federal Reserve is free to use monetary policy to pursue macroeconomic objectives such as low inflation and high employment. As a consequence, the United States must let the U.S. dollar float in foreign-exchange markets. Why? Changes in the nominal exchange rate depend not only on domestic monetary policy but also on monetary policy in other countries. If the Federal Reserve uses monetary policy to keep inflation low, then the U.S. dollar will appreciate or depreciate depending on monetary policy in other countries. These fluctuations create exchange rate risk for U.S. firms and households seeking to invest abroad and for foreign firms and households seeking to invest in the United States.

Policy trilemma The hypothesis that it is impossible for a country to have exchange rate stability, monetary policy independence, and free capital flows at the same time.

Figure 12.13

The Policy Trilemma

It is impossible for a country to achieve the goals of exchange rate stability, monetary policy independence, and free capital flows at the same time. At most, a country can achieve two of the three goals, and there is no clear consensus on which two are the best to pursue.

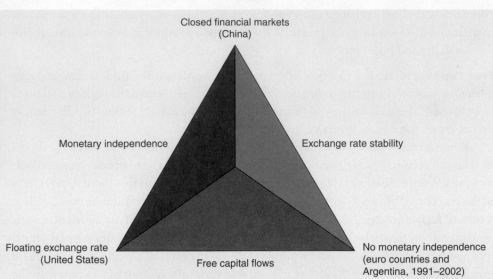

The lower-right point of the triangle indicates that if policymakers choose to allow free capital flows and have exchange rate stability, they must give up monetary policy independence. Argentina from 1991 to 2002 maintained a currency board that exchanged Argentine pesos for U.S. dollars at the rate of 1 peso per dollar. Argentina also allowed free capital flows across its borders, so it could not use monetary policy to respond to macroeconomic shocks. Why? Consider what would happen if the Federal Reserve increased interest rates in the United States. The increase would make U.S. assets more attractive relative to Argentine assets, so investors would sell Argentine assets to purchase U.S. assets. This shift would decrease the demand for Argentine pesos, so the peso would depreciate below the official exchange rate. To maintain the official exchange rate of $1 per peso, the Argentine currency board would have to use dollars to purchase pesos. Consequently, the supply of pesos in the foreign-exchange market would fall, so the peso would appreciate back to $1 per peso. Alternatively, Argentina could increase interest rates along with the United States to prevent Argentinian assets from becoming unattractive. Either way, if a country such as Argentina wants to keep a fixed exchange rate in addition to free capital flows, the country must use monetary policy to maintain the official exchange rate rather than to stabilize the domestic economy.

The top of the triangle indicates that, if policymakers choose monetary policy independence and a stable exchange rate, they must restrict the flow of capital. China maintains an independent monetary policy and has essentially fixed the value of the yuan, also known as the renminbi, against a market basket of foreign currencies, so it has had to restrict capital flows. Why? If China allowed free capital flows, it would be vulnerable to a large drop in the demand for Chinese assets, which would reduce the demand for its currency. This reduction in the demand for yuan would cause a large depreciation in the yuan. By restricting capital flows into and out of the country, China keeps the value of the assets that foreigners own in China relatively stable, so the demand for yuan in foreign-exchange markets is also relatively stable. For example, during 1997, many Asian countries, such as Indonesia, South Korea, and Thailand, experienced dramatic devaluations of their currencies as foreign capital fled those countries. However, China was able to maintain the stability of the yuan partly because the country restricted the outflow of foreign capital.

Answering the Key Question

Continued from page 412

At the beginning of this chapter, we asked:

"Why were traditional Federal Reserve policies ineffective during the 2007–2009 recession?"

The traditional Fed policy response to a recession is to reduce the short-term nominal interest rate. Normally, this policy will decrease the long-term real interest rate, provided that term structure effects, the default-risk premium, and the expected inflation rate remain constant. This traditional interest rate channel could not operate through much of the 2007–2009 recession because by December 2008, the Fed had pushed its target for the federal funds rate nearly to zero. As a result, the Fed was forced to craft new policies in an attempt to increase real GDP and employment.

Key Terms and Problems

Key Terms

Asymmetric information, p. 432

Bank run, p. 414

Board of Governors, p. 416

Discount rate, p. 420

Federal funds rate, p. 416

Federal Open Market Committee (FOMC), p. 416

Federal Reserve System, p. 415

Impact lag, p. 436

Implementation lag, p. 436

Monetary policy, p. 414

Open market operations, p. 416

Policy trilemma, p. 451

Quantitative easing, p. 433

Recognition lag, p. 436

Reserve requirements, p. 421

Too-big-to-fail policy, p. 443

12.1 ## The Federal Reserve System
Understand the structure of the Federal Reserve.

Review Questions

1.1 What is the Federal Open Market Committee (FOMC), and why is it important?

1.2 Briefly discuss the reasons for the disappearance of the First and Second Banks of the United States. Given the failures of those banks, why did Congress create the Federal Reserve System in 1913?

Problems and Applications

1.3 Why are the terms of members of the Board of Governors both very long and staggered?

1.4 In 1913, Congress created 12 Federal Reserve districts spread over the country. Why did Congress divide the country into districts?

1.5 Consider the following statement: "Because the Chairman of the Fed is appointed by the president of the United States and serves a four-year term, the president controls the Fed." Briefly explain whether you agree with this statement.

12.2 The Goals of Monetary Policy
Describe the goals of monetary policy.

Review Questions

2.1 What are the primary goals of a central bank?

2.2 Explain what is meant by the Fed's *dual mandate*.

Problems and Applications

2.3 The Fed views price stability as keeping the inflation rate at 2%. Why doesn't the Fed target a 0% rate of inflation?

2.4 Consider the following statement: "On average, rates of unemployment in Europe are higher than rates of unemployment in the United States. Thus, the Fed must be doing a good job of maintaining high employment." Briefly explain whether you agree with this statement.

2.5 Most economists estimate that the natural rate of unemployment is between 5% and 6%. However, some evidence suggests that the natural rate of unemployment may have increased after the recession of 2007–2009. If the Fed believed that the natural rate of unemployment was lower than it actually is, what would be the consequences for the economy?

2.6 When financial markets do not function well, savers and investors waste resources, and the economy is less efficient.

   a. How might problems in financial markets affect employment and economic growth?

   b. Some people argue that the Fed should not interfere in financial markets. Why is maintaining the stability of financial markets important to the Fed's other goals?

12.3 Monetary Policy Tools
Explain the Federal Reserve's monetary policy tools.

Review Questions

3.1 Explain how the Fed uses open market operations to target the federal funds rate. Why does the value of the federal funds rate matter?

3.2 Why is it important to have a central bank to act as a lender of last resort?

3.3 Describe the Fed's three traditional monetary policy tools. How can the Fed use each of these tools to either increase or decrease bank reserves?

Problems and Applications

3.4 Briefly explain how the Fed can reduce the federal funds rate. Why is the federal funds rate considered important if no households or firms (other than banks) can borrow or lend at this rate?

3.5 Explain how each of the following tools allows the Fed to increase its control of bank reserves:

   a. The ability to pay interest on reserves

   b. The Term Deposit Facility (TDF)

3.6 [Related to the Making the Connection on page 423] At an August 2011 meeting of the FOMC, three Federal Reserve Bank presidents publicly dissented from a decision to maintain the federal funds rate at a near-zero level through 2013. (At a later meeting the date was extended through mid-2015.) The dissents were notable because FOMC members have typically voted unanimously on interest rate decisions. One of the dissenting votes came from Narayana Kocherlakota, the president of the Federal Reserve Bank of Minneapolis, who explained that he favored low interest rates but objected to the Fed making a commitment to maintain low rates over a specific period of time. He stated that the decision would make it more difficult to maintain the Fed's commitment to keep the rate of inflation from exceeding its target of 2%. Explain what Kocherlakota's reasoning may have been.

Source: Brad Allen, "Kocherlakota's Priority: Federal Reserve Transparency," *Minnpost.com*, February 15, 2012.

MyEconLab Visit **www.myeconlab.com** to complete these exercises online and get instant feedback. Exercises that update with real-time data are marked with ⓜ.

12.4 Monetary Policy and the *IS–MP* Model

Use the *IS–MP* model to understand how monetary policy affects the economy in the short run.

Review Questions

4.1 How can monetary policy affect aggregate expenditure? How can the Fed use monetary policy to fight a recession? How can the Fed use monetary policy to fight inflation?

4.2 What is quantitative easing, and under what circumstances would a central bank use it to stimulate the economy?

4.3 What is Operation Twist? Why did the Fed pursue this policy beginning in 2011?

Problems and Applications

4.4 [Related to Solved Problem 12.4 **on page 429**] In 1999 and early 2000, the Fed increased the target federal funds rate repeatedly, partly because it believed that the economy was overheating and that inflation would increase. The following graph shows the position of the economy prior to the Fed's actions:

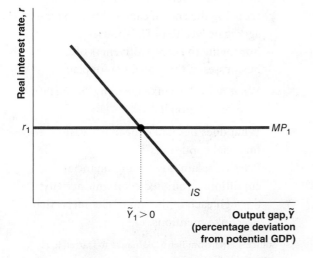

a. Carefully explain in words how the Fed's actions would be expected to affect the economy.

b. Show the effect of the Fed's actions on the *IS–MP* graph including the Phillips curve.

4.5 [Related to Solved Problem 12.4 on page 429] Economic activity in the United States peaked in March 2001 and then began to decline with the NASDAQ crash resulting from the collapse of the dot-com bubble. The terrorist attacks on the United States on September 11, 2001, worsened the recession.

a. Draw an *IS–MP* graph to show the position of the economy in late 2001.

b. What actions would you expect the Fed to have taken in this situation?

c. Use your *IS–MP* graph from part (a) to show the effect of the Fed's actions.

4.6 During the 1990s, changes in technology lowered costs. Use the *IS–MP* model, including the Phillips curve, to analyze the situations described below.

a. Suppose the Fed does not change the real interest rate following this positive supply shock. What will happen to the inflation rate?

b. Draw a graph to show what actions the Fed can take if it decides to keep the inflation rate constant.

4.7 Suppose that rather than expectations being strictly adaptive, increases in the money supply cause the expected inflation rate to increase immediately.

a. In this case, when the Fed increases the money supply, what happens to long-term real interest rates?

b. How does the link between money supply increases and expected inflation change the Fed's ability to affect the economy through the interest rate channel?

4.8 During the 2007–2009 financial crisis, banks faced liquidity problems, in part due to the illiquidity of some of their assets. These problems made some banks reluctant to lend, making it difficult for households and firms to borrow funds, which in turn caused economic activity to decline.

   a. Explain how the Fed can use the bank lending channel and the balance sheet channel to solve this problem.

   b. Was the Fed effective in using these channels during this period? Briefly explain.

4.9 Consider the following statement: "If the short-term nominal interest rate is zero, monetary policy can have no further expansionary effect on the economy." Briefly explain whether you agree with this statement.

4.10 In early 2011, unrest in the Middle East caused a sharp increase in the price of oil. Suppose that the economy was below potential GDP at $\widetilde{Y}_1$ prior to the oil shock, as shown at point A on the following Phillips curve graph:

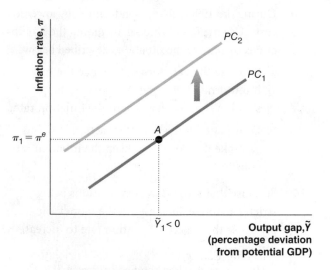

   a. If the Fed keeps the real interest rate constant, show on the graph a possible short-run equilibrium inflation rate and output gap.

   b. If the Fed acts to keep the inflation rate constant, use Phillips curve to show the new short-run equilibrium.

4.11 An article in the *Economist* magazine observed that when the Fed's "policy rate is effectively zero and long-term rates are close to all-time record lows. . . . [doesn't] additional easing amount to little more than pushing on a string?"

   a. What is the Fed's "policy rate"?

   b. What does the author mean by "additional easing"?

   c. What does the author mean when he compares additional easing to "pushing on a string"?

   d. With short-term and long-term interest rates at or near zero, do you think that additional quantitative easing by the Fed would amount to little more than pushing on a string? Briefly explain.

Source: "Is the Fed Pushing on a String?" *Economist*, July 3, 2012.

4.12 In a letter to a member of Congress, Fed Chairman Ben Bernanke made the following statement:

> The monetary accommodation provided by the Federal Reserve has substantially helped the U.S. economy by easing financial conditions. . . . The easing in financial conditions has promoted economic activity through a variety of channels, including reducing the cost of capital, boosting the aggregate wealth of U.S. households, and improving the competitiveness of U.S. businesses in the global marketplace.

   a. What does Bernanke mean by "monetary accommodation"?

   b. What does Bernanke mean by "easing financial conditions"?

   c. Briefly explain how easing financial conditions promoted economic activity through each of the three "channels" that Bernanke mentions.

Source: Letter from Ben S. Bernanke to Darrell E. Issa, August 22, 2012.

12.5 The Limitations of Monetary Policy
Explain the challenges in using monetary policy effectively.

Review Questions

5.1 What are the lags associated with monetary policy? How long are these lags?

5.2 Briefly discuss why timing is important when conducting monetary policy and how poorly timed monetary policy can negatively affect the economy.

Problems and Applications

5.3 In a letter to a member of Congress, Fed Chairman Ben Bernanke made the following statement, "the stance of policy must necessarily be set in light of a forecast of the future performance of the economy."

   a. What did Bernanke mean by "the stance of policy"?

   b. Why must the stance of policy be set by a forecast of the future performance of the economy rather than by the present state of the economy?

   Source: Letter from Ben S. Bernanke to Darrell E. Issa, August 22, 2012.

5.4 [Related to Solved Problem 12.5 on page 439] The initial recovery from the 2001 recession was very slow. As a result, the Fed reduced the federal funds rate to just 1% in 2003 and kept it there for a full year. Some economists argue that the low federal funds rate kept mortgage rates too low for too long and helped cause housing prices to rise. The rise in housing prices in 2001–2006 was a key factor in setting the stage for the financial crisis of 2007–2009.

   a. Why might the Fed have kept interest rates too low for too long? Frame your answer in terms of policy lags and the uncertainty of modeling.

   b. Illustrate your answer by drawing an *IS–MP* graph, including the Phillips curve.

5.5 Consider the following statement. "Because economic models cannot precisely predict the effect of policy changes, policymakers should not use them to make predictions about the economy." Briefly explain whether you agree with this statement.

5.6 [Related to the Making the Connection on page 443] Some analysts claim that many wealthy depositors prefer maintaining accounts with large "too-big-to-fail" banks, even if they could earn higher interest rates from smaller banks.

   a. Briefly explain why these depositors use this strategy.

   b. Are there any negative consequences for the efficiency of the economy from depositors following this strategy? Briefly explain.

5.7 [Related to the Chapter Opener on page 412] The chapter opener notes that Senator Richard Shelby of Alabama accused Chairman Bernanke of sitting idly by while financial problems developed, which "greatly exacerbated the crisis." In the early 1960s, Milton Friedman made the same criticism of the Fed's monetary policy during the Great Depression. In light of the problems of lags, forecasting, and economic uncertainty presented in Section 12.5, to what extent do you think it is reasonable to hold the Fed accountable for the policy failures that led to the financial crisis of 2007–2009 and the Great Depression?

5.8 The slow pace of economic recovery had Fed officials considering additional stimulus measures in mid-2012, but as a *Wall Street Journal* article reported, "The Fed is once again finding itself in a difficult spot. Officials aren't yet sure if the recent slowdown in growth is transitory or permanent." Explain why it is important for the Fed to understand if an economic slowdown is transitory or permanent when considering stimulus measures and how misreading the situation could create additional problems for the economy.

   Source: Jon Hilsenrath and Kristina Peterson, "Fed Weighs More Stimulus," *Wall Street Journal*, July 11, 2012.

MyEconLab Visit **www.myeconlab.com** to complete these exercises online and get instant feedback. Exercises that update with real-time data are marked with 🅜 .

12.6 Central Bank Independence

Evaluate the arguments for and against central bank independence.

Review Questions

6.1 What does it mean to describe a central bank as independent? Why might independence be desirable?

6.2 Describe the relationship between central bank independence and inflation rates. What are the reasons for this relationship?

6.3 Explain how the importance of monetary policy can be the main argument both for *and* against central bank independence.

Problems and Applications

6.4 In 2010, the European Central Bank (ECB) purchased bonds issued by Greece and other euro-zone economies with excessive government debt. This bailout raised a number of concerns, as discussed in the *Economist*: "Even as the bank's dealers were pushing cash into the bond markets of selected euro-zone countries, its president . . . was trying to reassure Germans that the ECB had not lost . . . its independence."

 a. What risks would be created by a loss of ECB independence?

 b. Does it matter what people in Germany think of ECB independence?

 Source: "After the Fall, "*Economist*, May 10, 2010.

6.5 It is frequently said that people "vote with their pocketbooks."

 a. What monetary policies would a president who was solely interested in reelection wish to pursue?

 b. What risks for the economy would such monetary policies present?

6.6 In July 2012, legislation was introduced in Congress that would require audits of monetary policy by the nonpartisan Government Accountability Office. Fed Chairman Ben Bernanke argued that if passed, the law would reduce the Fed's independence because it would result in "political meddling in monetary policy decisions." Briefly discuss the pros and cons of subjecting the Fed's monetary policy actions to government-controlled audits.

 Source: David Lawder, "US House Passes Fed Audit Bill; Measure Seen Dying in Senate," *Reuters*, July 25, 2012.

12.7 Monetary Policy in an Open Economy

Explain how monetary policy operates in an open economy.

Review Questions

7.1 How do imports and exports relate to the *IS* curve under a floating exchange rate system? Under a fixed exchange rate system?

7.2 What are the effects on interest rates and real GDP of expansionary monetary policy in an open economy with floating exchange rates? With fixed exchange rates?

7.3 What is the policy trilemma?

Problems and Applications

7.4 The International Monetary Fund (IMF) makes loans to countries that are running out of reserves of foreign currency.

 a. How would a loan of foreign currency help a country maintain a fixed exchange rate?

 b. The IMF makes loans only when it believes that currency problems are temporary. Why would a country have temporary currency problems?

What must happen to the exchange rate if these problems persist rather than being temporary?

7.5 A currency devaluation can stimulate economic activity in the short run.

    a. Draw an *IS–MP* graph to show the effect of a currency devaluation.

    b. Why don't countries with fixed exchange rates use devaluation more often as a policy tool?

7.6 China has used a fixed exchange rate to keep the value of its currency below its market level.

    a. Why is it easier for a country to undervalue a currency than to overvalue it?

    b. How does China's exchange rate policy affect its purchase of U.S. Treasury securities?

    c. What is likely to happen to China's imports, exports, and purchases of U.S. securities if the exchange rate is allowed to float?

7.7 Because the Fed is not constrained by a fixed exchange rate, it is free to set monetary policy without concerns about the effect on the value of the dollar.

    a. How would the Fed's actions during the 2007–2009 financial crisis have been constrained if the exchange rate had been fixed?

    b. The value of the dollar actually increased at some points during the 2007–2009 recession. Is this increase the result you would have expected? If not, how can you explain this increase?

7.8 Suppose that a country has a fixed exchange rate and no capital controls. Due to a political crisis, projections for economic growth in coming years are revised sharply downward. As a result of the new projections, savers wish to purchase financial assets in other countries.

    a. What is the likely effect of having savers purchase foreign assets on the ability of the country to maintain its exchange rate?

    b. How would the situation be different if there were a flexible exchange rate?

7.9 Capital flows can cause problems for exchange rate stability. So, why do most countries allow the free movement of capital?

Data Exercises

D12.1: [Related to the Macro Data feature on page 420]

The *Macro Data* box shows the relationship between the effective federal funds rate and the target rate. Using data from the St. Louis Federal Reserve (FRED) (http://research.stlouisfed.org/fred2/), analyze the relationship between the effective federal funds rate and the target range.

    a. Obtain daily data since December 16, 2008 for the effective federal funds rate (DFF), the upper limit of the target range for the federal funds rate (DFEDTARU), and the lower limit for the target range (DFEDTARL). Plot all three data series on a graph.

    b. Has the Fed been able to keep the effective federal funds rate within the target range? Explain.

D12.2: Go to the Web site of the Bank of England, www.bankofengland.co.uk. The interactive database for the Bank of England has a section entitled *Monetary financial institutions' balance sheets, income and expenditure.* That section has data on the Bank of England's balance sheet. What happened to the bank's balance sheet after 2007? How does these changes compare to the changes in the Fed's balance sheet?

D12.3: [Excel exercise] The text discussion of discount loans states that average monthly borrowing of banks from the Fed from 2000 to 2007 was $219 million. Using data from the St. Louis Federal Reserve (FRED) (http://research.stlouisfed.org/fred2/), examine the amount of discount loans.

MyEconLab   Visit **www.myeconlab.com** to complete these exercises online and get instant feedback. Exercises that update with real-time data are marked with ⬤.

a. Obtain monthly data on discount loans (DISCBORR) since 2000. Based on the discount loan data, briefly explain when you think the financial crisis began. Briefly explain when you think the financial crisis ended.

b. Using your answers to part (b), calculate the mean and standard deviation for discount loans for the pre-crisis, crisis, and post-crisis periods.

c. How unusual was the crisis period?

D12.4: Using data from the St. Louis Federal Reserve (FRED) (http://research.stlouisfed.org/fred2/), analyze the federal funds rate and the discount rate.

a. Find the most recent values and values from two years earlier from FRED for the Effective Fed Funds Rate (FEDFUNDS) and the Primary Credit Rate (MPCREDIT). The Primary Credit Rate is typically referred to as the Federal Reserve Discount Rate.

b. Using the data you found in part (a), describe what has happened to short-term interest rates over the past two years.

CHAPTER 13

Fiscal Policy in the Short Run

Learning Objectives

After studying this chapter, you should be able to:

13.1 Explain the goals and tools of fiscal policy (pages 463–467)

13.2 Distinguish between automatic stabilizers and discretionary fiscal policy and understand how the budget deficit is measured (pages 468–476)

13.3 Use the *IS–MP* model to understand how fiscal policy affects the economy in the short run (pages 476–487)

13.4 Use the *IS–MP* model to explain the challenges of using fiscal policy effectively (pages 488–494)

13.5 Explain how fiscal policy operates in an open economy (pages 494–496)

Driving Toward a "Fiscal Cliff"

It was a lot harder to find a job in mid-2012 than it should have been. More than three years after the end of the recession of 2007–2009, employment was still nearly 10 million jobs below its normal level.[1] The persistence of high unemployment meant that by 2012, the unemployed were out of work for an average of nearly 40 weeks, which was twice as long as during the deep recession of 1981–1982.

Clearly, part of the reason for the poor employment picture was the severity of the 2007–2009 recession. The global financial crisis that began in August 2007 ended nearly 25 years of economic stability in the United States and other developed countries. The recession was worldwide, affecting Asian countries, including Japan, Singapore, and Hong Kong; European countries, including Germany, Ireland, Greece, and the United Kingdom; and countries in the Americas, including Canada, Mexico,

Continued on next page

Key Issue and Question

Issue: During the 2007–2009 recession, Congress and the president undertook unprecedented fiscal policy actions.

Question: Was the American Recovery and Reinvestment Act of 2009 successful at increasing real GDP and employment?

Answered on page 496

[1]In July 2012, the employment–population ratio was 58.4%. The same number of months after the end of the 2001 recession, the ratio was 62.4%. With a working-age population of 243,354,000, the difference in the employment–population ratios indicates a gap of 9.7 million jobs.

and the United States. Many economists referred to the 2007–2009 downturn as the "Great Recession."

But the severity of the recession was not the only thing holding back job creation in the United States in 2012. The U.S. economy appeared to be headed toward what Fed Chairman Ben Bernanke called a "fiscal cliff." He was referring to a combination of significant increases in federal taxes and reductions in federal government spending scheduled to take effect in January 2013. Some tax cuts first enacted under President George W. Bush in 2001 were scheduled to expire at the end of 2012. In addition, Congress had enacted legislation that beginning in 2013 would significantly cut federal spending. Bernanke argued that the combination of lower federal spending and higher taxes would reduce aggregate expenditure by as much as $600 billion and push the economy into a recession in 2013. The recession could result in 1.25 million lost jobs. The Congressional Budget Office forecasts were similar.

By the summer and fall of 2012, the effects of the potential tax increases and spending cuts were already being felt. When a firm considers expanding by building a new factory, store, or office and by hiring new employees, it looks not just at the present but also at the future. Expanding a business during a recession can turn into a financial disaster for a firm. In 2012, many firms were anticipating the fiscal cliff and decided it was not a good time to expand. For example, the CEO of Hubbell Incorporated, a manufacturer of electronic and electrical products, was quoted as saying: "The fiscal cliff is the primary driver of uncertainty, and a person in my position is going to make a decision to postpone hiring and investments. . . . We don't have to get to the edge of the cliff before the damage is done." The CEO of Kindred Healthcare Inc., which operates nursing homes and rehabilitation centers, asserted: "If you can't plan, you don't spend. And if you don't spend you don't hire."

President Barack Obama and leaders in Congress acknowledged the dangers of driving the economy over the fiscal cliff, but they had difficulty coming to an agreement to do anything about it. Because the federal government was spending far more than the taxes it was taking in, the government was running a large budget deficit. Bernanke recommended that the president and Congress avoid large tax increases or spending cuts in 2013, when the economy was still weak, while committing to future spending cuts and tax increases that would balance the budget in later years. Many economists and policymakers supported this approach.

Congress and the president had difficulty coming to an agreement partly because 2012 was a presidential election year, when political maneuvering can make agreement on legislation difficult. Also involved, though, was a disagreement over *fiscal policy*. In February 2009, President Obama proposed, and Congress passed, the American Recovery and Reinvestment Act (often referred to as "the stimulus package"). This act involved increases in government spending and tax cuts that totaled $840 billion. The debate over whether these spending increases and tax cuts had been effective in reducing the severity of the recession formed the background for the debate during 2012 over avoiding the fiscal cliff.

As this chapter was being written, it was not yet clear whether the president and Congress would agree on a proposal to avoid the fiscal cliff. In any event, debate over the effectiveness of fiscal policy had intensified.

Sources: Nelson D. Schwartz, "Partisan Impasse Drives Industry to Cut Spending," *New York Times*, August 6, 2012; Dennis K. Berman, "A Business Message to D.C.: Stop Fighting, We'll Spend," *Wall Street Journal*, August 9, 2012; Ben S. Bernanke, *Semiannual Monetary Policy Report to the Congress*, July 17, 2012; Congressional Budget Office, "Economic Effects of Reducing the Fiscal Restraint That Is Scheduled to Occur in 2013," May 22, 2012; Congressional Budget Office, *The Budget and Economic Outlook: Fiscal Years 2012 to 2022*, Washington, DC: Government Printing Office, January 2012; and U.S. Bureau of Labor Statistics.

Fiscal policy Changes in federal government taxes, purchases of goods and services, and transfer payments that are intended to achieve macroeconomic policy objectives.

In this chapter, we use the *IS-MP* model to explain how *fiscal policy* affects the economy in the short run. **Fiscal policy** refers to changes the federal government makes in taxes, purchases of goods and services, and transfer payments that are intended to achieve macroeconomic policy objectives. As we will see, fiscal policy can encounter problems in achieving its goals.

The Goals and Tools of Fiscal Policy

Long before the Great Recession of 2007–2009, there was the Great Depression of the 1930s. The Great Depression was the worst economic downturn in U.S. history. Real GDP decreased by more than 25% between 1929 and 1933, which was about six times the decrease in real GDP from 2007 to 2009. The unemployment rate, which had been 3% in 1929, soared to over 20% in 1933. And the Great Depression was prolonged, with the unemployment rate not returning to 3% until 1942, after the United States had entered World War II. The dramatic increase in government spending on goods and services to fight World War II caused real GDP to increase by nearly 50% between 1941 and 1944, while the unemployment rate fell to about 1%.

Some economists and policymakers were concerned that the end of the war and the demobilization of the military might cause a return to the high unemployment rates of the 1930s. In response to these concerns, Congress and President Harry Truman enacted the Employment Act of 1946. This act stated:

> The Congress hereby declares that it is the continuing policy and responsibility of the Federal Government to use all practicable means . . . to promote maximum employment, production, and purchasing power.

What "all practicable means" might be is unclear, but this act was important because for the first time, the federal government explicitly took responsibility for achieving macroeconomic policy goals. This responsibility continues today. As we saw at the start of the chapter, the U.S. government took several macroeconomic policy actions, including passing the American Recovery and Reinvestment Act, to reduce the severity of the 2007–2009 recession.

Who Conducts Fiscal Policy?

In most countries, the central government conducts fiscal policy, although the specific structure and mechanisms vary from country to country. In the United States, fiscal policy requires agreement between the Congress and the president. Members of the House of Representatives and the Senate introduce bills to change government spending and taxes, debate their differences over the bills, and revise the bills. For a bill passed by Congress to become law, either the president must sign it, or, if the president vetoes the bill, Congress must override the president's veto with two-thirds majorities in the House and Senate. This process normally takes considerable time and can slow the response of fiscal policy to changes in economic conditions. For instance, during 2012, President Obama proposed ways to avoid some of the increases in taxes and spending cuts scheduled for 2013. The leaders of the House of Representatives passed a bill containing a competing plan. The leaders of the Senate had yet a third plan. By the fall of 2012, though, the president and Congress had not reached consensus on a bill, despite warnings by Fed Chairman Ben Bernanke and the Congressional Budget Office that failure to address the issue might tip the economy into a recession.

In the United States, the federal, state, and local governments all have responsibility for taxing and spending. Economists typically use the term *fiscal policy* to refer only to

13.1

Learning Objective
Explain the goals and tools of fiscal policy.

fiscal actions of federal government

the actions of the federal government. State and local governments sometimes change their taxing and spending policies to aid their local economies, but these are not fiscal policy actions because they are not intended to affect the national economy. The federal government makes many decisions about taxes and spending, but not all of these decisions are fiscal policy actions because they are not intended to achieve macroeconomic policy goals. For example, a decision to cut the taxes of people who buy hybrid cars is an environmental policy action, not a fiscal policy action. Similarly, the spending increases to fund the wars in Iraq and Afghanistan were part of defense and homeland security policy, not fiscal policy. While changes in tax policy to help the environment and military spending on a war may affect the national economy, they are not fiscal policy in the strict sense of the term.

Just as with monetary policy, the goal of fiscal policy is to reduce the severity of economic fluctuations. Typically, though, in the United States and most other countries, fiscal policy focuses on employment and production and leaves price stability to the central bank.

Traditional Tools of Fiscal Policy

Fiscal policy can affect the economy in the short run by causing changes in aggregate expenditure. In the sections that follow, we discuss three fiscal policy tools that affect real GDP:

1. Government purchases
2. Taxes
3. Transfer payments

Government Purchases The federal government purchases goods, such as computers for government offices and aircraft carriers, and purchases services, such as those provided by soldiers and FBI agents. Holding everything else constant, an increase in government purchases, G, will increase aggregate expenditure, AE. The increase in aggregate expenditure means that firms sell more goods and services, which leads them to expand production, increasing real GDP. Governments have traditionally used spending on infrastructure projects to try to stimulate the economy during a recession. For example, the Japanese government during the 1990s, the U.S. government during 2007–2009, and the Chinese government during 2008 and 2009, spent billions of dollars on building and repairing domestic infrastructure, including roads and bridges. While building and repairing infrastructure may be valuable in its own right, the specific reason the Chinese, Japanese, and U.S. governments increased infrastructure spending was to provide a stimulus to the economy in the short run. Holding all else constant, we would expect:

An increase in government purchases → An increase in aggregate expenditure → An increase in real GDP and employment.

Taxes Governments obtain tax revenue from many different sources. The U.S. government levies a *personal income tax*, *a payroll tax*, and a *corporate income tax*. Some governments also tax consumption. For example, most of the states in the United

States have a sales tax that applies to most consumer purchases. Most European countries have a *value-added tax* (VAT), which is collected from firms, rather than from consumers, and is paid on the difference between the price consumers pay and the cost firms incur to produce the good or service. The federal government does not have a national sales tax or a VAT, but it does levy excise taxes on specific goods, such as gasoline and alcohol.

Changes in taxes affect the consumption and investment components of aggregate expenditure, as we discuss next.

Consumption Changes in taxes on personal income increase or decrease **disposable income**, which equals national income plus transfer payments minus personal tax payments. Households either spend their disposable income or save it. If income taxes increase, then, holding everything else constant, disposable income decreases, so household spending and saving both decrease. As a result, consumption, *C*, and aggregate expenditure, *AE*, decrease, which reduces spending on goods and services, leading firms to decrease production and employment. Similarly, a decrease in taxes will increase consumption and aggregate expenditure, leading firms to increase production and employment. Governments sometimes use cuts in personal income taxes to fight recessions. For example, in 2001, President George W. Bush and Congress reduced taxes to increase spending during a recession. (Changing tax rates can also have important effects on the willingness of households to work and invest. We discuss these long-run effects later in this chapter.) To summarize, holding all else constant, we would expect:

> A decrease in the tax rate on personal income → An increase in disposable income → An increase in consumption → An increase in aggregate expenditure → An increase in real GDP and employment.

Sales taxes or a VAT also affect consumption. An increase in these taxes makes goods and services more expensive by raising prices, so households reduce their consumption. As a result, consumption and aggregate expenditure decrease, which leads firms to decrease production and employment. Holding all else constant, we would expect:

> An increase in consumption taxes → An increase in prices of consumption goods → A decrease in consumption → A decrease in aggregate expenditure → A decrease in real GDP and employment.

Investment An increase in corporate income taxes reduces the *after-tax* profitability of investment projects. So, an increase in corporate income tax rates will cause firms to abandon their least profitable investment projects, reducing spending on new plant and equipment. As a result, investment and aggregate expenditure decrease. This decrease in aggregate expenditure reduces firms' sales, leading them to reduce production and employment. Holding all else constant, we would expect:

> An increase in corporate income taxes → A decrease in the after-tax profitability of investment projects → A decrease in investment → A decrease in aggregate expenditure → A decrease in real GDP and employment.

Disposable income
National income plus transfer payments minus personal tax payments.

$IN + TR - T$

Transfer Payments *Transfer payments*, such as unemployment insurance, are payments by the government to individuals for which the individuals do not provide a good or service in return. An increase in transfer payments will increase disposable income and lead to more spending on goods and services. As a result, consumption and aggregate expenditure increase, leading firms to increase production and employment. During the 2007–2009 recession, both President Bush and President Obama signed laws that extended the duration of unemployment insurance payments for unemployed workers whose benefits had expired. Holding all else constant, we would expect:

> An increase in transfer payments → An increase in disposable income →
> An increase in consumption → An increase in aggregate expenditure →
> An increase in real GDP and employment.

Expansionary Policy and Contractionary Policy Economists distinguish between *expansionary fiscal policy* and *contractionary fiscal policy*. Expansionary fiscal policy is intended to increase real GDP and employment by increasing aggregate expenditure. Expansionary fiscal policy actions include increases in government purchases, reductions in taxes, and increases in transfer payments. Contractionary fiscal policy is intended to reduce aggregate expenditure to fight inflation. Contractionary fiscal policy actions include decreases in government purchases, increases in taxes, and reductions in transfer payments.

Making the Connection

Why Was the Severity of the 2007–2009 Recession So Difficult to Predict?

At the time the Obama administration prepared the stimulus bill in early 2009, the administration's economists presented forecasts of real GDP and unemployment that turned out to be much too optimistic. Other policymakers, economists, and corporate CEOs also were surprised by the severity of the 2007–2009 recession in the United States. A key reason for the surprise was that the United States had not experienced a financial crisis since the 1930s, and so economists had no recent experience with the effects of a financial crisis on the economy.

The recession of 2007–2009 was the first since the 1930s to be accompanied by a bank panic, although it was primarily in the "shadow banking system" of investment banks, mutual funds, and insurance companies rather than in the commercial banking system. Both the Great Depression and the recession of 2007–2009 were severe. Was their severity the result of the accompanying bank panics? More generally, do recessions accompanied by bank panics tend to be more severe than recessions that do not involve bank panics?

Carmen Reinhart and Kenneth Rogoff of Harvard University have gathered data on recessions and bank panics, or bank crises, in a number of countries in an attempt to answer this question. The table on the following page shows the average change in key economic variables during the period following a bank crisis for the United States during the Great Depression and a variety of other countries in the post–World War II era, including Japan, Norway, Korea, and Sweden. The table shows that for these countries, on average, the recessions following bank crises were quite severe. Unemployment rates increased by 7 percentage points—for example, from 5% to 12%—and continued increasing for nearly five years after a crisis had begun. Real GDP per capita also declined sharply, and the average length of a recession following a bank crisis has been nearly two years. Adjusted for inflation, stock prices dropped by more than half, and housing prices dropped by more than one-third. Government debt soared by 86%. The increased public debt was partly the result of increased government spending, including spending to bail out failed financial institutions. But most of the increased debt was the result of government budget deficits resulting from sharp declines in tax revenues as incomes and profits fell as a result of the recession.

Economic variable	Average change	Average duration of change	Number of countries involved
Unemployment rate	+7 percentage points	4.8 years	14
Real GDP per capita	−9.3%	1.9 years	14
Real stock prices	−55.9%	3.4 years	22
Real house prices	−35.5%	6 years	21
Real government debt	+86%	3 years	13

The table below shows some key indicators for the 2007–2009 U.S. recession compared with other U.S. recessions of the post–World War II period:

	Duration	Decline in real GDP	Peak unemployment rate
Average for postwar U.S. recessions	10.4 months	−1.7%	7.6%
U.S. recession of 2007–2009	18.0 months	−4.1%	10.0%

Note: In this table, the duration of recessions is based on National Bureau of Economic Research (NBER) business cycle dates; the decline in real GDP is measured as the simple percentage change from the quarter of the cyclical peak to the quarter of the cyclical trough; and the peak unemployment rate is the highest unemployment rate in any month following the cyclical peak.

Consistent with Reinhart's and Rogoff's findings that recessions that follow bank panics tend to be unusually severe, the 2007–2009 recession was the worst in the United States since the Great Depression of the 1930s. The recession lasted nearly twice as long as the average of earlier postwar recessions, GDP declined by more than twice the average, and the peak unemployment rate was about one-third higher than the average.

A key reason that most people did not anticipate the severity of the 2007–2009 recession is that they failed to see the financial crisis coming.

Sources: The first table is adapted from data in Carmen M. Reinhart and Kenneth S. Rogoff, *This Time Is Different: Eight Centuries of Financial Folly*, Princeton, NJ: Princeton University Press, 2009, Figures 14.1–14.5; the second table uses data from the U.S. Bureau of Economic Analysis and National Bureau of Economic Research.

See related problem 1.8 at the end of the chapter.

13.2

Learning Objective

Distinguish between automatic stabilizers and discretionary fiscal policy and understand how the budget deficit is measured.

Discretionary fiscal policy Government policy that involves deliberate changes in taxes, transfer payments, or government purchases to achieve macroeconomic policy objectives.

Automatic stabilizers Taxes, transfer payments, or government expenditures that automatically increase or decrease along with the business cycle.

Budget Deficits, Discretionary Fiscal Policy, and Automatic Stabilizers

Some changes in government spending and taxes occur due to the effects of existing laws, and some changes occur because the government decides to change current laws to achieve its macroeconomic policy objectives. In this section, we distinguish between these two types of fiscal policies.

Discretionary Fiscal Policy and Automatic Stabilizers

Discretionary fiscal policy involves deliberate changes in taxes, transfer payments, or government purchases to achieve macroeconomic policy objectives. The American Recovery and Reinvestment Act of 2009 is an example of discretionary fiscal policy that both increased government purchases and decreased taxes in an attempt to increase real GDP and employment. On rare occasions, governments have used fiscal policy to try to contain inflation. For example, in 1968, the federal government levied a temporary 10% surcharge on personal and corporate income in an attempt to reduce aggregate expenditure and prevent inflation from accelerating. For the most part, however, Congress and the president have let the Federal Reserve take the lead in controlling inflation.

Some types of government spending and taxes automatically respond to changes in output and employment. **Automatic stabilizers** refer to taxes, transfer payments, or government expenditure that automatically increase or decrease along with the business cycle. Unexpected events—"shocks"—accentuated by the multiplier effect lead to fluctuations in real GDP. Automatic stabilizers help reduce the severity of these fluctuations by reducing the size of the multiplier. Consider the case of unemployment insurance, a government program that replaces a portion of the lost wages of recently unemployed workers. Without this insurance, the disposable income of a worker who loses her job may drop to zero. She would have to pay for food, clothing, and rent by drawing down savings or by borrowing. As a result, she would likely significantly decrease consumption. With unemployment insurance, the unemployed worker's disposable income would decline, but not all the way to zero. Because consumption would not fall by as much as it would without unemployment insurance, the size of the multiplier effect is reduced, as is the total effect on real GDP of any initial decrease in aggregate expenditure.

The income tax system in the United States also acts as an automatic stabilizer. During a recession, as unemployment rises, household income falls, but personal income taxes will also automatically fall. The effect is similar to a tax cut, so disposable income and consumption will decrease less than they otherwise would have. Similarly, during an economic expansion, as households' incomes rise, so will personal income taxes, restraining the growth of disposable income and consumption.

The Budget Deficit and the Budget Surplus

During the debate over federal spending and taxes in 2012, a key issue was the size of the federal government's budget deficit. The budget shows the relationship between

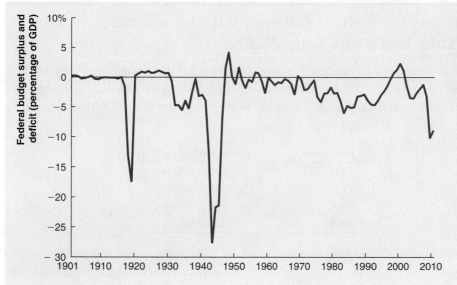

Figure 13.1

The Federal Budget Surplus and Deficit, 1901–2011

During wars, government spending increases far more than tax revenues, increasing the budget deficit. The budget deficit also increases during recessions, as government spending increases and tax revenues fall. The federal government has run a budget deficit most years since 1970.

Sources: *Budget of the United States Government, Fiscal Year 2009, Historical Tables*, Washington, DC: U.S. Government Printing Office, 2008; and U.S. Bureau of Economic Analysis.

the federal government's expenditure—including both federal government purchases of goods and services and transfer payments—and its tax revenue. If the federal government's expenditure is greater than its tax revenue, a **budget deficit** results. If the federal government's expenditure is less than its tax revenue, a **budget surplus** results.

As with other macroeconomic variables, it is useful to consider the size of the surplus or deficit relative to the size of the overall economy. Figure 13.1 shows that, as a percentage of GDP, the largest deficits of the twentieth century came during World Wars I and II. During major wars, higher taxes only partially offset massive increases in government expenditure, leaving large budget deficits. The figure also shows large deficits during recessions. During recessions, government expenditure on transfer payments increases and tax revenues fall, automatically increasing the budget deficit. In addition, fiscal policy actions during recessions tend to increase deficits further. In 1970, the federal government entered into a long period of continuous budget deficits. From 1970 through 1997, the federal government's budget was in deficit every year. From 1998 through 2001, there were four years of budget surpluses. The recessions of 2001 and 2007–2009, tax cuts, and increased government spending on the wars in Iraq and Afghanistan contributed to keeping the budget in deficit in the years after 2001. The effects on the federal budget deficit of the Obama administration's American Recovery and Reinvestment Act can also be seen in Figure 13.1. In 2009, the federal budget deficit reached 8% of GDP for the first time since World War II. During 2012, President Obama, Republican presidential nominee Mitt Romney, and Republican and Democratic leaders in Congress all proposed plans to reduce the federal budget deficit in the long run.

Budget deficit The situation in which the government's expenditure is greater than its tax revenue.

Budget surplus The situation in which the government's expenditure is less than its tax revenue.

> ### Making the Connection
>
> ## How Did the Federal Government Run a Budget Surplus in the Late 1990s and Early 2000s?
>
> When the federal government is running annual budget deficits of over $1 trillion, as it has been doing since 2009, it is difficult to believe that the government had a budget surplus as recently as fiscal year 2001.[2] In fact, as the table below shows, 2001 was the fourth consecutive year of budget surpluses:
>
> | Fiscal year | Federal budget surplus |
> |---|---|
> | 1998 | $69.3 billion |
> | 1999 | 125.6 billion |
> | 2000 | 236.2 billion |
> | 2001 | 128.2 billion |

Before 1998, the federal government had not had a budget surplus since 1969, so this four-year period was unusual. There are several explanations for the surplus years. The U.S. economy emerged from a brief recession in 1991, when the budget deficit was $269.2 billion. The 1990–1991 recession was followed by a 10-year expansion that added 24 million jobs. As a result, federal tax receipts in fiscal year 2001 were $1,991.1 billion, about 89% higher than in 1991. But the increase in revenue was not the only reason for the budget surpluses. In 1990, Congress passed the Budget Enforcement Act (BEA). The law had two significant parts: It placed a limit on annual federal expenditure, and it required that any increases in spending or tax cuts that would increase the deficit (or decrease the surplus) be offset by a reduction in spending or an increase in taxes elsewhere in the budget. Although the federal government did not always meet the "pay-as-you-go" rules, the rules did check increases in federal spending somewhat, and the presence of large deficits when the act was passed made it politically difficult for legislators to recommend new spending programs. Congress extended the BEA several times, but it expired in 2002.

Several other factors made it easier to control the growth of federal expenditure during the 1990s. The sudden collapse of the Soviet Union in the late 1980s and early 1990s allowed the United States to reduce defense spending. Adjusted for inflation, defense outlays in 1998 were about $100 billion less than they were in 1989. During President Clinton's administration, the federal government's main transfer program to low-income households, Aid to Families with Dependent Children (AFDC), was revised. There were 6.5 million fewer recipients of federal funding under the new program, Temporary Assistance for Needy Families (TANF), in 1996 than there had been under AFDC in 1993. In addition to these developments on the expenditure side of the budget, the federal government increased taxes during the administrations of President George H. W. Bush in 1990 and President Bill Clinton in 1993.

Federal budget surpluses came to an end in 2001, in part because the recession that began that year reduced revenue and increased expenditures on transfer programs.

---

[2]The federal government's *fiscal year* does not correspond to the calendar year. The federal government's fiscal year begins on October 1 and extends to the following September 30. For example, fiscal 2012 began October 1, 2011, and ended September 30, 2012.

Congress also approved income tax reductions and increases in defense and national security spending after the terrorist attacks on September 11, 2001. The recession of 2007–2009 and the expenditure programs enacted to pull the economy out of the recession sent the federal budget deficit to record levels. The budget deficit for fiscal year 2012 was $1.1 trillion. The total debt of the federal government in 2012 exceeded the value of U.S. GDP.

Economists Carmen and Vincent Reinhart and Kenneth Rogoff examined the effect that high levels of government debt have had on economic growth in 22 countries since 1800. They found that when debt equaled 90% or more of GDP, on average, economic growth declined by 1.2 percentage points per year, even though some of the countries experienced relatively low real interest rates, despite the high debt levels. The authors explained that the lower growth rates were a product of higher taxes and lower spending that governments used to reduce the debt burdens.

As we saw in the chapter opener, during 2012, the president and Congress struggled to find a way to ensure that in the long run, the budget deficit would be greatly reduced without taking steps that might push the economy into a recession.

Sources: Allen Schick, "A Surplus, if We Can Keep It: How the Federal Budget Surplus Happened," www.brookings.edu, Winter 2000; *Economic Report of the President*, Washington, DC: U.S. Government Printing Office, 2011, Table B-80, p. 285; "The Budget Surplus," *Economist*, February 10, 2000; "Budget Deficit Running Slightly Lower Than Last Year: CBO," *Reuters*, August 7, 2012; and Carmen M. Reinhart, Vincent R. Reinhart, and Kenneth S. Rogoff, "Debt Overhangs: Past and Present," National Bureau of Economic Research Working Paper 18015, April 2012.

See related problem 2.9 at the end of the chapter.

Looking at the budget deficit in isolation can provide a misleading picture of discretionary fiscal policy because the deficit automatically rises and falls with the business cycle. When the economy enters an expansion, output, employment, and income increase. The higher level of income means that the government will receive more tax revenue, and the higher level of employment means that payments for unemployment insurance and other transfer payments, such as Temporary Assistance for Needy Families and Medicaid, decrease. Therefore, an economic expansion automatically reduces a budget deficit (or increases a budget surplus). By the same token, when the economy moves into recession, the budget deficit automatically increases (or the surplus decreases) as tax revenues fall and expenditures on unemployment insurance and other programs rise. Notice that these changes in the budget deficit happen automatically without Congress or the president undertaking discretionary fiscal policy.

The tax systems, the unemployment insurance systems, and the programs to provide income to low-income households vary from country to country, so the size of automatic stabilizers also varies from country to country. In general, policies in Europe provide more of an automatic fiscal stimulus than do those in the United States. As the global economy experienced a recession during 2008 and 2009, the spending increases and tax reductions due to automatic stabilizers increased by 1.6% of potential GDP in the United States and 1.8% in Japan, while they increased by 2.7% in France and Germany and by 2.9% in the United Kingdom.

Cyclically adjusted budget deficit or surplus
The deficit or surplus in the federal government's budget if real GDP equaled potential GDP; also called the full-employment budget deficit or surplus.

We can think of the government's actual budget deficit in any particular year as resulting from two factors: discretionary fiscal policy and the response of automatic stabilizers to the state of the economy. To focus on that part of the budget deficit that is due to discretionary fiscal policy, economists often use the **cyclically adjusted budget deficit or surplus**, which measures what the deficit or surplus in the federal government's budget would be if real GDP equaled potential GDP. (Economists sometimes call the cyclically adjusted budget deficit the *full-employment budget deficit* because it is the budget deficit that would exist if workers were fully employed.) In other words:

Budget deficit = Cyclically adjusted budget deficit + Effect of automatic stablizers.

Because the cyclically adjusted budget deficit removes the effects of economic fluctuations—and therefore automatic stabilizers—on the budget deficit, the cyclically adjusted budget deficit tells us whether discretionary fiscal policy is expansionary or contractionary. If the government is running a cyclically adjusted budget deficit, discretionary fiscal policy is expansionary because it increases aggregate expenditure. If the government is running a cyclically adjusted budget surplus, discretionary fiscal policy is contractionary because it decreases aggregate expenditure.

Figure 13.2 shows the cyclically adjusted budget deficits for Japan, the United Kingdom, the United States, and countries using the euro, such as France and Germany, from 1994 to 2011. A positive number indicates a cyclically adjusted budget surplus, so discretionary fiscal policy is contractionary. A negative number indicates a cyclically adjusted budget deficit, so discretionary fiscal policy is expansionary. Each country experienced an increase in its cyclically adjusted budget deficit during the 2007–2009 period, but the size of the deficits differed across countries. From 2007 to 2009, the cyclically adjusted budget deficit increased by 6.4% of potential GDP in the United Kingdom and 6.1% in the United States but by just 2.8% in Japan and 2.3% for countries using the euro. Figure 13.2 shows that the United Kingdom and the United States had particularly large cyclically adjusted budget deficits during the 2007–2009 recession, which means

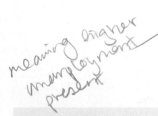

(handwritten margin notes: "this means that gov't is using expansionary policy to REDUCE the deficit" and "meaning higher unemployment present")

Figure 13.2

Cyclically Adjusted Budget Deficit or Surplus for Japan, the United Kingdom, the United States, and countries using the euro, 1994–2011

The United States and the United Kingdom used discretionary fiscal policy to a greater extent during the 2007–2009 financial crisis than did Japan or the euro countries as a group. As a result, the United States and the United Kingdom experienced a much larger increase in their cyclically adjusted budget deficits.

Source: Organisation for Economic Co-operation and Development.

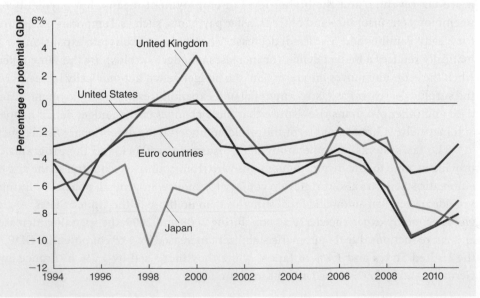

Macro Data: Did Fiscal Policy Fail During the Great Depression?

Modern macroeconomic analysis began during the 1930s, with the publication of *The General Theory of Employment, Interest, and Money* by John Maynard Keynes. One conclusion that many economists drew from Keynes's book was that an expansionary fiscal policy would be necessary to pull the United States out of the Great Depression. When Franklin D. Roosevelt became president in 1933, federal government expenditure increased as part of his New Deal program. The United States experienced a federal budget deficit each remaining year of the decade, except for 1937. The U.S. economy recovered very slowly, however, and did not reach potential GDP again until the United States entered World War II in 1941.

Some economists and policymakers at the time argued that because the economy recovered slowly, despite increases in government spending, fiscal policy had been ineffective. During the debate over President Obama's 2009 stimulus package, some economists again raised the argument that fiscal policy failed during the Great Depression. Economic historians have argued, however, that despite the increases in government spending, Congress and the president had not, in fact, implemented an expansionary fiscal policy during the 1930s. In separate studies, economists E. Cary Brown of the Massachusetts Institute of Technology and Larry Peppers of Washington and Lee University argued that there

was a cyclically adjusted budget deficit during only one year of the 1930s—and that this one deficit was small. The table below provides data supporting their arguments. (Dollar values in the table are presented in nominal rather than real terms.) The second column shows that federal government expenditure increased from 1933 to 1936, fell in 1937, and then increased in 1938 and 1939. The third column shows a similar pattern, with the federal budget being in deficit each year after 1933, except for 1937. The fourth column, however, shows that in each year after 1933, the federal government ran a cyclically adjusted budget *surplus*. Because the level of income was so low and the unemployment rate was so high during these years, tax collections were far below what they would have been if the economy had been at potential GDP. As the fifth column shows, in 1933 and again in the years 1937 to 1939, the cyclically adjusted surpluses were quite large relative to GDP.

Although President Roosevelt proposed many new government spending programs, he had also promised during the 1932 presidential election campaign to balance the federal budget. He achieved a balanced budget only in 1937, but his reluctance to allow the actual budget deficit to grow too large helps explain why the cyclically adjusted budget remained in surplus. Therefore, rather than reduce the severity of the Great Depression, fiscal policy may actually have slowed the recovery.

(1) Year	(2) Federal government expenditure (billions of dollars)	(3) Actual federal government budget deficit or surplus (billions of dollars)	(4) Cyclically adjusted budget deficit or surplus (billions of dollars)	(5) Cyclically adjusted budget deficit or surplus as a percentage of GDP
1929	$2.6	$1.0	$1.24	1.20%
1930	2.7	0.2	0.81	0.89
1931	4.0	−2.1	−0.41	−0.54
1932	3.0	−1.3	0.50	0.85
1933	3.4	−0.9	1.06	1.88
1934	5.5	−2.2	0.09	0.14
1935	5.6	−1.9	0.54	0.74
1936	7.8	−3.2	0.47	0.56
1937	6.4	0.2	2.55	2.77
1938	7.3	−1.3	2.47	2.87
1939	8.4	−2.1	2.00	2.17

Sources: E. Cary Brown, "Fiscal Policy in the 'Thirties: A Reappraisal," *American Economic Review*, Vol. 46, No. 5, December 1956, pp. 857–879; Larry Peppers, "Full Employment Surplus Analysis and Structural Changes: The 1930s," *Explorations in Economic History*, Vol. 10, No, 2, Winter 1973, pp. 197–210; and U.S. Bureau of Economic Analysis.

See related problem 2.10 at the end of the chapter.

that they relied much more on fiscal policy than did the other countries. Figure 13.2 also shows that in the United States, discretionary fiscal policy may have contributed to the recession of 2001. The cyclically adjusted budget went from a deficit equal to –0.9% of potential GDP in 1997 to a surplus equal to 0.2% of potential GDP in 2000; so, discretionary fiscal policy moved from expansionary to slightly contractionary just before the start of the 2001 recession.

The Deficit and the Debt

Every time the federal government runs a budget deficit, the U.S. Treasury must borrow funds from investors by selling Treasury securities. For simplicity, we will refer to all Treasury securities as "bonds." When the federal government runs a budget surplus, the Treasury pays off some existing bonds. Figure 13.1 on page 469 shows that there are many more years of federal budget deficits than years of federal budget surpluses. As a result, the total number of Treasury bonds has grown over the years. The total value of U.S. Treasury bonds outstanding is referred to as the *federal government debt* or, sometimes, as the *national debt*. Formally, **gross federal debt held by the public** includes U.S. Treasury bonds and a small amount of securities issued by other federal agencies.[3] Each year the federal budget is in deficit, the federal government debt grows. Each year the federal budget is in surplus, the debt shrinks.

Figure 13.3 shows the gross federal debt held by the public as a percentage of GDP since 1790. Over the long run, the federal debt has increased during wars and decreased during peace. The debt increased during the 1930s and early 1940s as a result of the large federal budget deficits during the Great Depression and World War II. After the end of World War II, GDP grew faster than the debt until the early 1970s, which caused the ratio of debt to GDP to fall. The large budget deficits of the 1980s and early 1990s sent the debt-to-GDP ratio climbing. The budget surpluses of 1998 to 2001 caused the debt-to-GDP ratio to fall, but it rose again with the return of deficits beginning in 2002. There were major tax cuts in 2001 and 2003, and further tax cuts in 2008, 2009, and 2011, in response to the recession of 2007–2009 and its aftermath. There were also several major increases in government spending during these years. In 2003, President George W. Bush and Congress enacted a new prescription drug benefit for Medicare patients. Both President Bush and President Obama extended unemployment benefits, and President Obama increased spending on infrastructure projects and other programs during the 2007–2009 recession. Finally, the wars in Afghanistan and Iraq increased defense spending during this period.

The dollar value of federal debt held by the public in 1945 was $252 billion versus $10,128 billion in 2011. This comparison makes the debt in 2011 look much larger than the debt in 1945. However, a comparison of the dollar value of the debt across time can

Gross federal debt held by the public Debt that includes the bonds and other securities issued by the U.S. Treasury (and a small amount of securities issued by federal agencies) not held by the federal government; also called the national debt.

---

[3]Some federal government debt is owned by the Federal Reserve System, and some is held by the Social Security trust fund (formally called the Old-Age and Survivors Insurance [OASI] Trust Fund) or other federal trust funds. The Federal Reserve has accumulated Treasury bonds in the course of conducting monetary policy, while the Social Security Administration has accumulated bonds in anticipation of the effect on the Social Security system of the retirements of millions of baby boomers. When the baby boomers retire, the trust fund will sell Treasury bonds to make payments to retirees. Ultimately, however, taxpayers in the future will have to provide the tax revenue to repay the Treasury bonds.

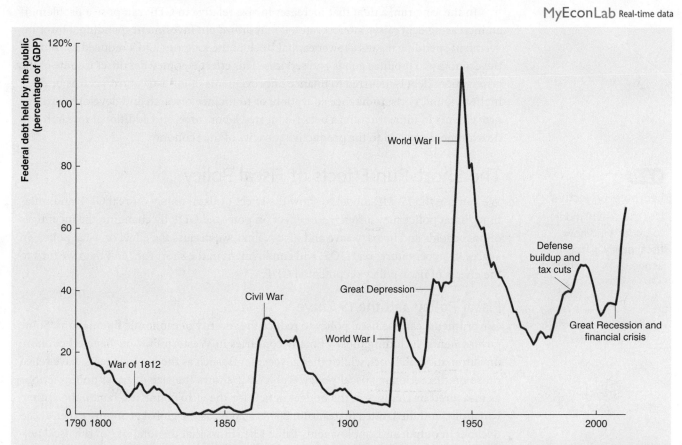

Figure 13.3 Federal Debt Held by the Public as a Percentage of GDP for the United States, 1790–2011

The federal debt increased during the Great Depression and also during the recession of 2007–2009 due to declining tax revenue and increased federal spending. The federal debt also rose in the 1980s due to tax cuts and increased military spending.

Source: Congressional Budget Office.

be misleading. If we look at the debt relative to GDP, we can see that it was 67% of GDP in 2011, but 113% of GDP in 1945.

also not taking Δ in price level into account

Is the Federal Debt a Problem?

Debt can be a problem for a government for the same reasons it can be a problem for a household or a business. If members of a family have difficulty making the monthly mortgage payment, they will have to cut back spending on other things. If they are unable to make the payments, they will have to default on the loan and will probably lose their house. The federal government is in no danger of defaulting on its debt. Ultimately, the government can raise the funds it needs through taxes to make the interest payments on the debt. If the debt becomes very large relative to the economy, however, the government may have to raise taxes to high levels or cut back on other types of spending to make interest payments. Interest payments were about 6% of total federal expenditure in 2011. At this level, large tax increases or significant cutbacks in other types of federal spending are not required.

In the long run, a debt that increases in size relative to GDP can pose a problem. If an increasing debt raises interest rates, it may *crowd out* investment spending. Lower investment spending means a lower capital stock in the long run and a reduced capacity of the economy to produce goods and services. This effect is somewhat offset if some of the government debt is incurred to finance improvements in infrastructure, such as bridges, highways, and ports; to finance education; or to finance research and development. Improvements in infrastructure, a better-educated labor force, and additional research and development can add to the productive capacity of the economy.

13.3

Learning Objective

Use the *IS–MP* model to understand how fiscal policy affects the economy in the short run.

The Short-Run Effects of Fiscal Policy

We can use the *IS–MP* model to show the effect of fiscal policy on real GDP and inflation. Fiscal policy may also have an effect on potential GDP by changing the incentives of households and firms to save and invest. First, we discuss the effect of fiscal policy on aggregate expenditure, real GDP, and employment in the short run, and then we turn to the effects of fiscal policy on potential GDP.

Fiscal Policy and the *IS* Curve

Governments can use fiscal policy to reduce the severity of economic fluctuations. Some governments, including those of many countries in Western Europe, have relied more on automatic stabilizers, while other governments, such as the United States, have relied more on discretionary fiscal policy. Table 13.1 shows the size of fiscal policy actions as measured by changes in the budget deficit for the euro countries, Japan, the United Kingdom, and the United States from 2008 to 2009, as the global economy experienced declines in output and employment. Table 13.1 shows that the total size of the fiscal policy action was somewhat smaller in the euro countries than in other countries because the euro countries chose to rely much more on automatic stabilizers than did other countries. We turn now to analyzing how both automatic stabilizers and discretionary fiscal policy can help reduce the severity of economic downturns.

Fiscal policy affects aggregate expenditure, which causes the *IS* curve to shift. All else being equal, an increase in government purchases causes aggregate expenditure

Table 13.1 Fiscal Policy in Advanced Economies, 2008–2009

	Change in the cyclically adjusted budget deficit (as a percentage of potential GDP)	Change in automatic stabilizers (as a percentage of potential GDP)	Change in the budget deficit (as a percentage of potential GDP)
Euro countries	−1.5%	−2.7%	−4.1%
Japan	−2.8	−1.8	−4.6
United Kingdom	−4.5	−2.9	−7.4
United States	−3.1	−1.6	−4.7

Note: Negative numbers indicate that the budget deficit became larger, and so fiscal stimulus increased.

Sources: Organisation for Economic Co-operation and Development and authors' calculations.

Table 13.2 Fiscal Policy Tools and Real GDP

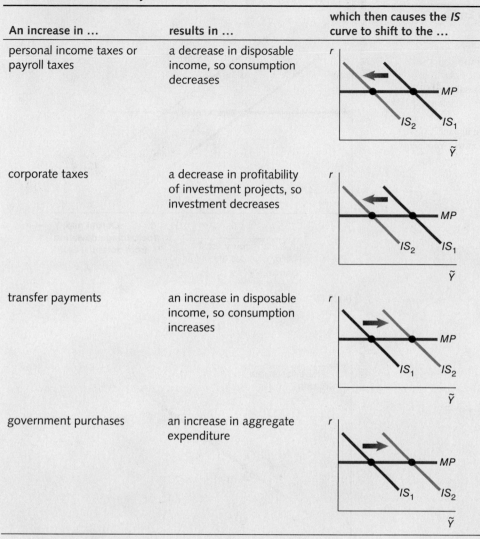

An increase in ...	results in ...	which then causes the *IS* curve to shift to the ...
personal income taxes or payroll taxes	a decrease in disposable income, so consumption decreases	
corporate taxes	a decrease in profitability of investment projects, so investment decreases	
transfer payments	an increase in disposable income, so consumption increases	
government purchases	an increase in aggregate expenditure	

to increase, and firms respond by increasing output and employment. Graphically, we can show an increase in government purchases as a shift of the *IS* curve to the right. An increase in taxes will shift the *IS* curve to the left, while an increase in transfer payments will shift the *IS* curve to the right. Table 13.2 above summarizes the relationship between fiscal policy and real GDP.

Using Discretionary Fiscal Policy to Fight a Recession

As mentioned at the start of the chapter, President Obama signed the American Recovery and Reinvestment Act into law on February 17, 2009. The act consisted of increases in transfer payments, increases in government spending on goods and services, tax cuts to households and firms, and aid to state and local governments. China

Figure 13.4

Discretionary Fiscal Policy to End a Recession

Increases in government purchases and transfer payments or decreases in taxes all increase aggregate expenditure and shift the *IS* curve to the right, from IS_1 to IS_2, as shown in panel (a). As a result, real GDP again equals potential GDP, ending the recession and increasing the inflation rate from π_1 to π_2, which was its value before the recession, as shown in panel (b). In both panels, short-run equilibrium moves from point *A* to point *B*.

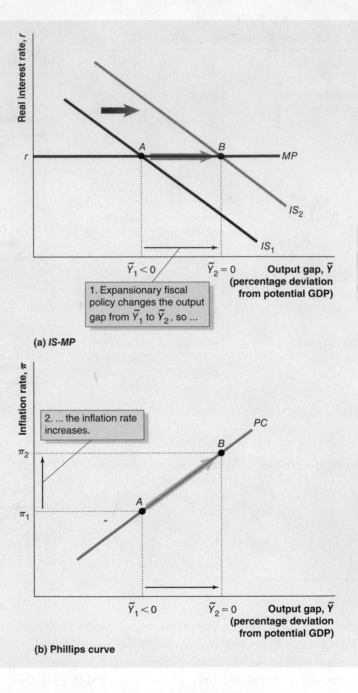

1. Expansionary fiscal policy changes the output gap from $\tilde{Y}_1$ to $\tilde{Y}_2$, so ...

(a) *IS-MP*

2. ... the inflation rate increases.

(b) Phillips curve

passed a similar $586 billion stimulus package in 2009. We can use the *IS–MP* model to analyze the effects of these policies.

The U.S. and Chinese fiscal stimulus packages increased aggregate expenditure, shifting the *IS* curve to the right. Figure 13.4 shows how discretionary fiscal policy can help end a recession. For simplicity, we show the effect of an increase in government purchases, but a decrease in taxes or an increase in transfer payments would have similar effects.

We assume that the economy is already in a recession, so in panel (a) short-run equilibrium is at point A, where $\widetilde{Y}_1 < 0$. Real GDP is less than its potential level, so cyclical unemployment is greater than zero. Because the economy is in a recession and real GDP is less than potential GDP, in panel (b) the inflation rate, π_1, is less than it would be at potential GDP. Congress and the president increase government purchases, so the IS curve shifts to the right, from IS_1 to IS_2. Real GDP increases back to potential GDP, so the output gap changes from $\widetilde{Y}_1$ to $\widetilde{Y}_2$, and in panel (b) the inflation rate increases to π_2. Short-run equilibrium is now at point B and the recession has ended. The government has achieved the goal of higher real GDP and employment, with the inflation rate returning to its value before the recession.

Automatic Stabilizers

The expansionary effect of automatic stabilizers varies from recession to recession. During the severe recessions of 1973–1975, 1981–1982, and 2007–2009, automatic stabilizers in the United States were −2.1%, −1.6%, and −2.1% of potential GDP, respectively, but during the milder recessions of 1990–1991 and 2001, automatic stabilizers were just −0.8% and −1.1% of potential GDP. We can also use the IS–MP model to analyze the effects of automatic stabilizers on the economy.

Because of automatic stabilizers, there is an immediate fiscal policy response to a decline in aggregate expenditure, even without Congress and the president taking action. This automatic fiscal response reduces the adverse consequences of the demand shock, so any given decrease in aggregate expenditure has a smaller effect on real GDP and employment. Figure 13.5 shows the automatic stabilizers at work in response to an increase in uncertainty that leads to reduced investment.

In panel (a), short-run equilibrium is at point A, with real GDP equal to potential GDP. Suppose that uncertainty about the future state of the economy increases, causing investment to decrease. If there are no automatic stabilizers, the IS curve shifts to the left, from IS_1 to $IS_{2(\text{no stabilizers})}$, which equals the decline in investment spending times the expenditure multiplier. Real GDP decreases, so the output gap changes to $\widetilde{Y}_{2(\text{no stabilizers})}$, cyclical unemployment is greater than zero, and the economy is in a recession. In panel (b), as the output gap changes from $\widetilde{Y}_1$ to $\widetilde{Y}_{2(\text{no stabilizers})}$, there is a movement down the Phillips curve from point A to point B, so the inflation rate declines to $\pi_{2(\text{no stabilizers})}$, which is less than the initial inflation rate, π_1. Short-run equilibrium is now at point B in both panel (a) and panel (b).

If there are automatic stabilizers, such as unemployment insurance, then the initial decrease in investment is the same, but the multiplier is smaller, so the effect of the shock on the economy is smaller. To see why, recall the expression for disposable income: $Y^D = Y + TR - T$. Disposable income will not fall as much when automatic stabilizers are triggered because some decreases in income from higher unemployment are offset by higher transfers and lower taxes. So, the automatic stabilizers result in a smaller shift in the IS curve, to $IS_{2(\text{stabilizers})}$. Real GDP falls, but not by as much, so the recession is less severe. Automatic stabilizers reduce the magnitude of the multiplier and so reduce the size of the decline in real GDP. In panel (b), the smaller decline in real GDP means that the inflation rate only decreases to $\pi_{2(\text{stabilizers})}$. Short-run equilibrium is now at point C in panel (a) and panel (b).

Figure 13.5

Automatic Stabilizers and a Decrease in Aggregate Expenditure

Automatic stabilizers reduce the size of the multiplier. As a result, a shock such as an increase in uncertainty has a smaller effect on real GDP and the output gap. Without automatic stabilizers, the *IS* curve shifts to $IS_{2(\text{no stabilizers})}$ and the output gap moves to $\tilde{Y}_{2(\text{no stabilizers})}$. With automatic stabilizers, though, the *IS* curve shifts only to $IS_{2(\text{stabilizers})}$, so real GDP declines by less and the output gap moves only to $\tilde{Y}_{2(\text{stabilizers})}$ in panel (a), and the inflation rate only decreases to $\pi_{2(\text{stabilizers})}$ in panel (b).

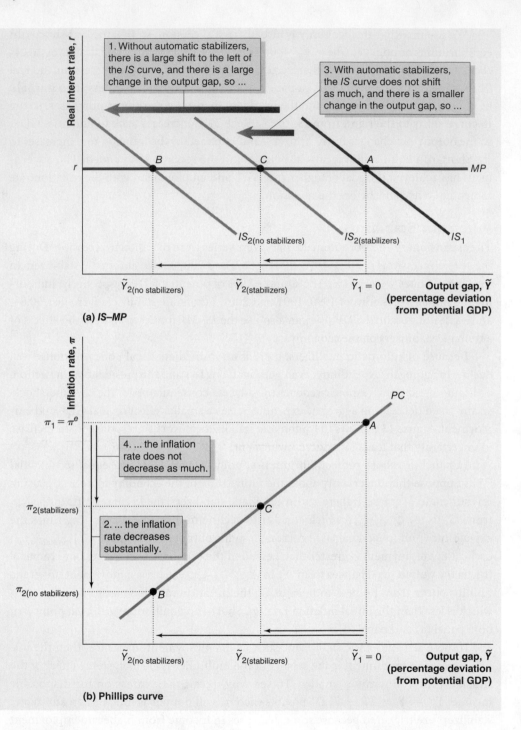

How effective are automatic stabilizers? Economists Darrel Cohen and Glenn Follette of the Federal Reserve Board estimate that automatic stabilizers in the United States reduce the multiplier associated with shocks to aggregate expenditure by 10%.[4]

[4]Darrel Cohen and Glenn Follette, "The Automatic Fiscal Stabilizers: Quietly Doing Their Thing," *FRBNY Economic Policy Review*, Vol. 6, No. 1, April 2000, pp. 35–68.

The findings of Cohen and Follette suggest that automatic stabilizers have a modest effect on reducing the severity of business cycles but that such stabilizers are nonetheless important because they represent an immediate policy response that does not require direct government action. In addition, even if the effect of automatic stabilizers on the output gap is relatively small, these policies still help reduce the negative effect of economic fluctuations on lower-income groups and those who lose their jobs.

Solved Problem 13.3A

Should the Federal Government Eliminate the Budget Deficit?

The United States ran a $1.4 trillion budget deficit in 2009 and $1.3 trillion deficits in 2010 and 2011. As a result, the amount of federal government debt held by the public increased from $5.8 trillion at the end of 2008 to $10.1 trillion at the end of 2011. The projected increases in the debt in future years are so large that some people argue that the government should immediately reduce the budget deficit to zero. As we saw in the chapter opener, during 2012 there was heated debate over the federal government's budget. Use the *IS-MP* model to analyze the effect on the output gap and employment if the government eliminated a budget deficit when real GDP was below potential GDP.

Solving the Problem

Step 1 **Review the chapter material.** The problem asks you to determine how eliminating a budget deficit when real GDP is below potential GDP will affect the economy, so you may want to review the section "The Short-Run Effects of Fiscal Policy," which begins on page 476.

Step 2 **Draw an *IS–MP* graph showing the economy experiencing a negative output gap.** Make sure that you label each curve and indicate that the initial equilibrium occurs where real GDP is less than potential GDP. Your graph should look like this:

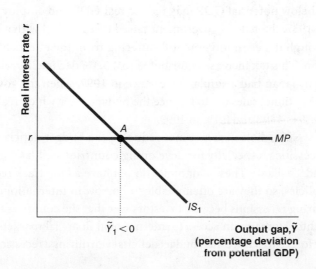

Step 3 **Determine the effect on the *IS* curve of eliminating the budget deficit.** To eliminate the budget deficit, the government must decrease government purchases, decrease transfer payments, increase taxes, or some combination of the three. Decreasing government purchases reduces aggregate expenditure, all else being equal. Decreasing transfer payments reduces disposable income, which leads households to consume less, so aggregate expenditure decreases. If the government increases taxes on households, then disposable income decreases, so consumption and aggregate expenditure will decrease. If the government increases taxes on firms, then investment is less profitable and investment and aggregate expenditure decrease. This reasoning suggests that regardless of how the government decides to eliminate the budget deficit, aggregate expenditure decreases. So, eliminating the budget deficit will cause the *IS* curve to shift to the left.

Step 4 **Add the new *IS* curve to your *IS–MP*.** The size of the output gap has increased, so real GDP is now further away from potential GDP:

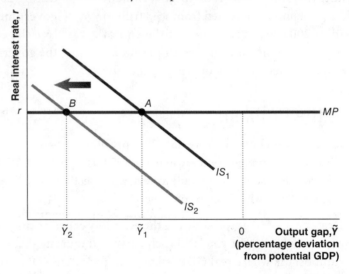

This analysis shows that eliminating a budget deficit when the economy is below potential GDP may reduce real GDP and employment. For example, in 1937, the federal government raised taxes to deal with a budget deficit, even though the economy was still suffering from the effects of the Great Depression. This tax increase contributed to a 3.4% decline in real GDP the following year. Japan had a similar experience in 1997, when the government increased the national sales tax to balance the budget, after which real GDP decreased by 2.0% in 1998 and 0.1% in 1999.

Nevertheless, sometimes reducing the budget deficit is necessary during recessions, especially for developing countries such as Mexico, South Korea, and Thailand. These economies do not have a long track record of sound fiscal policies, so they are often unable to borrow in international financial markets during recessions because investors fear that the countries may default on their debts. To maintain access to international financial markets, the countries may be forced to reduce their budget deficits even during a recession. Some economists believe that in the future even high-income countries such as Germany, Japan, and the United States may face limits on their ability to borrow. The willingness of investors to lend depends on investors' confidence that a country will repay the loans as promised. Once that confidence disappears, it can become very difficult for a country to borrow.

See related problem 3.5 at the end of the chapter.

Conceptually, using fiscal policy to reduce the severity of economic fluctuations is straightforward: The government uses fiscal policy to offset the effect of an increase or a decrease in aggregate expenditure by adjusting government purchases of goods and services, transfer payments, and taxes. In practice, implementing a successful fiscal policy may be difficult for many of the same reasons that monetary policy is difficult to implement. We discuss these difficulties in the next section.

Making the Connection

State and Local Government Spending During the 2007–2009 Recession

The recession that began in late 2007 severely reduced the tax revenues of state and local governments and increased the demand for their services. The decline in state and local tax receipts was the most severe since World War II. Although the recession ended in 2009, the combined budget deficit for all states at the beginning of fiscal 2012 was still about $107 billion. Most state governments in the United States have balanced-budget requirements that prevent planned spending from exceeding expected revenues. The details of the restrictions vary, but they limit the ability of states to run budget deficits during recessions. Recessions reduce state revenues for the same reason that recessions reduce federal revenues: As people lose their jobs and firms' profits decline, tax revenues decrease.

The budget crisis forced lawmakers to make difficult spending decisions. California was one of several states that instituted involuntary furloughs for state employees. The furloughs forced nearly 200,000 state employees to take Fridays off without pay in 2008. While furloughs help to reduce state expenditure, they also reduce the incomes of state employees. These employees and their families are forced to cut back on expenditures, which hurts local businesses.

Brian Lucking and Dan Wilson, economists with the Federal Reserve Bank of San Francisco, estimated the effect of total government spending—local, state, and federal—on the U.S. economy during and after the recession of 2007–2009. Although federal spending was highly expansionary during this period, Lucking and Wilson noted that state and local spending rose less than would be expected, given the severity of the recession and spending increases in past recessions. As state governments tried to reduce their deficits and balance their budgets, state and local spending fell significantly from 2009 to 2011. Lucking and Wilson also noted that state and local government spending declined during 2011 and 2012 more rapidly than would be expected based on spending in past business cycles and the slow rate of economic growth since the end of the recession. Lucking and Wilson predicted that fiscal policies in place in 2012 would be contractionary over the next few years. State and local government officials did not want to hear this prediction because they were anxiously awaiting an improvement in the national economy that would increase their tax receipts and decrease their spending on transfer payments.

Sources: Phil Oliff, Chris Mai, and Vincent Palacios, "States Continue to Feel Recession's Impact," *Center on Budget and Policy Priorities*, June 27, 2012; Brian Lucking and Daniel Wilson, "U.S. Fiscal Policy: Headwind or Tailwind?" *FRBSF Economic Letter*, July 2, 2012; Jeremy Gerst and Daniel Wilson, "Fiscal Crises of the States: Causes and Consequences," *FRBSF Economic Letter*, June 28, 2010; Jon Ortiz and Jim Wasserman, "State Furloughs: Unpaid Fridays May Not Be Over," *Sacramento (California) Bee*, June 19, 2010; and U.S. Bureau of Economic Analysis.

See related problem 3.6 at the end of the chapter.

Personal Income Tax Rates and the Multiplier

A change in personal income tax rates has a more complicated effect on real GDP than does a tax cut of a fixed dollar amount, such as the targeted tax cuts that were part of President Obama's 2009 stimulus plan. The *marginal income tax rate*, which is the fraction of each additional dollar of income that must be paid in taxes, is one of the automatic stabilizers in the economy. Recall that automatic stabilizers reduce the size of the expenditure multiplier. Why do taxes have this effect?

Assume that the Fed is keeping the real interest rate constant, so we can focus on shifts in the *IS* curve. If the income tax rate is 20%, the government takes 20% of a household's income in taxes. The household can spend or save the remaining 80%. Therefore, if total income is Y, then disposable income is given by:

$$Y^D = (1 - t)Y,$$

where t is the marginal income tax rate and a 20% tax rate means that t equals 0.20. Consumption is based on disposable income, so:

$$C = \overline{C} + MPC(Y^D) = \overline{C} + MPC(1 - t)Y.$$

Therefore, aggregate expenditure is given by:

$$AE = \overline{C} + MPC(1 - t)Y + \overline{I} + \overline{G} + \overline{NX}.$$

In equilibrium:

$$Y = AE.$$

So, substituting, we have:

$$Y = \overline{C} + MPC(1 - t)Y + \overline{I} + \overline{G} + \overline{NX},$$

or, rearranging terms:

$$Y = \frac{\overline{C} + \overline{I} + \overline{G} + \overline{NX}}{[1 - (1 - t)MPC]}.$$

If investment changes, while autonomous consumption, government purchases, and net exports remain unchanged, we have:

$$\Delta Y = \frac{\Delta \bar{I}}{[1 - (1 - t)MPC]},$$

or, rearranging terms:

$$\frac{\Delta Y}{\Delta \bar{I}} = \frac{1}{[1 - (1 - t)MPC]}.$$

In an earlier example (see Chapter 10, page 339), we set the tax rate equal to 0, and the *MPC* was 0.75, so the multiplier equaled:

$$\frac{\Delta Y}{\Delta \bar{I}} = \frac{1}{[1 - (1 - 0)0.75]} = \frac{1}{[1 - 0.75]} = \frac{1}{0.25} = 4.$$

If the tax rate were to increase from 0 to 0.20, then the multiplier would equal:

$$\frac{\Delta Y}{\Delta \bar{I}} = \frac{1}{[1 - (1 - 0.20)0.75]} = \frac{1}{[1 - (0.80)0.75]} = \frac{1}{[1 - 0.60]} = \frac{1}{0.40} = 2.5.$$

Taking account of the income tax significantly reduces the value of the multiplier. Other automatic stabilizers, such as unemployment insurance, similarly reduce the value of the multiplier. With unemployment insurance, rising real GDP and employment will cause a less-than-proportional increase in disposable income because rising employment means a lower level of unemployment insurance payments.

Our example was for a change in autonomous investment, but the formulas are equally valid for autonomous changes in government purchases, consumption, and net exports.

Solved Problem 13.3B

Calculating Equilibrium Real GDP and the Expenditure Multiplier with Income Taxes

Assume that the Fed is keeping the real interest rate constant. Use the following data to calculate the equilibrium level of real GDP and the value of the investment expenditure multiplier:

$C = \overline{C} + MPC(1 - t)Y = \$1.0 \text{ trillion} + 0.8(1 - 0.20)Y$
$I = \$1.6 \text{ trillion}$
$G = \$1.3 \text{ trillion}$
$NX = -\$0.4 \text{ trillion}$

Solving the Problem

Step 1 Review the chapter material. The problem asks you to calculate equilibrium real GDP and the value of the expenditure multiplier, so you may want to review the section "Personal Income Tax Rates and the Multiplier," which begins on page 484.

Step 2 **Use the data to calculate equilibrium real GDP.** We know that in equilibrium, aggregate expenditure equals real GDP. The expression for aggregate expenditure is:

$$AE = \overline{C} + MPC(1 - t)Y + \overline{I} + \overline{G} + \overline{NX}.$$

So, at equilibrium:

$$Y = AE = \overline{C} + MPC(1 - t)Y + \overline{I} + \overline{G} + \overline{NX}.$$

Substituting the values above gives us:

$$Y = \$1.0 \text{ trillion} + 0.80(1 - 0.20)Y + \$1.6 \text{ trillion} + \$1.3 \text{ trillion} - \$0.40 \text{ trillion}$$

$$Y = 0.64Y + \$3.5 \text{ trillion}$$

$$0.36\,Y = \$3.5 \text{ trillion}$$

$$Y = \frac{\$3.5 \text{ trillion}}{0.36} = \$9.7 \text{ trillion}.$$

Step 3 **Calculate the value of the multiplier from the data given.** The expression for the investment expenditure multiplier is:

$$\frac{\Delta Y}{\Delta \overline{I}} = \frac{1}{[1 - (1 - t)MPC]}.$$

With $MPC = 0.80$ and $t = 0.20$, the value of the multiplier is:

$$\frac{\Delta Y}{\Delta \overline{I}} = \frac{1}{[1 - (1 - 0.20)0.80]} = \frac{1}{[1 - (0.80)0.80]} = \frac{1}{[1 - 0.64]} = \frac{1}{0.36} = 2.8.$$

See related problem 3.9 at the end of the chapter.

The Effects of Changes in Tax Rates on Potential GDP

So far, we have concentrated on the effect of fiscal policy on aggregate expenditure, but changes in marginal tax rates may also have important effects on potential GDP. Potential GDP is determined by the quantity of labor, the quantity of capital goods, and the overall level of efficiency in the economy. To the extent that marginal tax rates affect these three factors, changes in marginal tax rates will cause changes in potential GDP.

Tax wedge The difference between the before-tax and after-tax return to an economic activity.

The difference between the before-tax and after-tax return to an economic activity is known as the **tax wedge**. For example, the U.S. federal income tax has several tax brackets, which are the income ranges within which a tax rate applies. In 2012, for a single taxpayer, the tax rate was 10% on the first $8,700 earned during the year. The tax rate rises for higher income brackets. In 2012, the highest tax rate was 35% on income above $388,350. Suppose you are paid a wage of $20 per hour. If your marginal income tax rate is 25%, then for every additional hour you work, your after-tax wage is $15, and the tax wedge is $5. Cutting the marginal tax rate on income results in a larger quantity of labor supplied because the after-tax wage would be higher (see Chapter 8). Similarly, a reduction in the tax rate increases the after-tax return to saving, causing an increase in the supply of loanable funds, a lower equilibrium real interest rate, and an increase in investment. In general, economists believe that the smaller the tax wedge for any economic activity—working, saving, investing, or starting a business—the more of that economic activity that will occur.

We can look briefly at the effects on potential GDP of cutting each of the following taxes:

- *Individual income tax.* Reducing the marginal tax rates on individual income will reduce the tax wedge workers face, thereby increasing the quantity of labor supplied. The increase in the labor supplied will increase potential GDP. Many small businesses are *sole proprietorships*, whose profits are taxed at the individual income tax rates. So cutting the individual income tax rates also raises the return to entrepreneurship, encouraging the opening of new businesses. Most household saving is also taxed at the individual income tax rates. Reducing marginal income tax rates increases the return to saving resulting in more funds available for investment. As the economy accumulates more capital goods, potential GDP will increase.

- *Corporate income tax.* The federal government taxes the profits earned by corporations under the corporate income tax. In 2012, most large corporations faced a marginal corporate tax rate of 35% at the federal level. Cutting this tax rate would encourage investment by increasing the return corporations receive from new investments in equipment, factories, and office buildings. Because innovations are often embodied in new investment goods, cutting the corporate income tax rate can potentially increase the pace of technological change and the overall level of efficiency in the economy. Increased capital and increased efficiency will increase potential GDP.

- *Taxes on dividends and capital gains.* Corporations distribute some of their profits to shareholders in the form of payments known as *dividends*. A *capital gain* is the change in the price of an asset, such as a share of stock. Rising profits usually result in rising stock prices and capital gains to shareholders. Individuals pay taxes on both dividends and capital gains (although the tax on capital gains can be postponed if the stock is not sold). Lowering the tax rates on dividends and capital gains increases the return to saving, thereby increasing investment. So, all else being equal, decreasing taxes on capital gains and dividends leads to a larger capital stock and increases potential GDP.

The increases in potential GDP due to the increases in capital, labor, and the overall level of efficiency are sometimes called the *supply-side effects* of fiscal policy. Most economists would agree that there is a supply-side effect from reducing taxes, but the magnitude of the effect is the subject of considerable debate. For example, some economists argue that the increase in the quantity of labor supplied following a tax cut will be limited because many people work a number of hours set by their employers and lack the opportunity to work additional hours. Similarly, some economists believe that tax changes have only a small effect on saving and investment. In this view, saving and investment are affected much more by changes in income or changes in expectations of the future profitability of new investment due to technological change or improving macroeconomic conditions than they are by tax changes.

Ultimately, the size of the supply-side effects of tax policy can be resolved only through careful study of the effects of differences in tax rates on labor supply and on saving and investment decisions.

13.4

Learning Objective

Use the *IS–MP* model to explain the challenges of using fiscal policy effectively.

The Limitations of Fiscal Policy

Fiscal policy, like monetary policy, faces many challenges in attempting to reduce the severity of business cycles. For a fiscal policy to be implemented successfully, Congress and the president must quickly recognize that a recession has started. If Congress and the president are late to respond, the policy may not be of much help. In fact, if Congress and the president respond slowly enough, policy may actually destabilize the economy by increasing aggregate expenditure when a recovery is well underway.

Policy Lags

We have seen that three policy lags make it difficult for monetary policy to reduce the severity of economic fluctuations: recognition, implementation, and impact lags. Congress and the president have access to the same information as do monetary policymakers at the Fed, so the recognition lag for both monetary and fiscal policy is typically several months.

The response lag is different for automatic stabilizers than for discretionary fiscal policy. As we noted earlier, in the United States, discretionary fiscal policy requires coordination between Congress and the president, so the lag for discretionary fiscal policy can be several months or longer. By contrast, automatic stabilizers respond immediately, without the need for political coordination.

The impact lag for fiscal policy can last from several months to several years. The government can often immediately adjust taxes and transfer payments, and these changes result in immediate changes in disposable income. However, there is no guarantee that households will immediately use their extra disposable income to consume more goods and services; indeed, households may instead choose to save the additional disposable income. If the government cuts tax rates on corporate profits, it takes time for firms to evaluate and pursue new investment projects. Therefore, the impact lags for discretionary changes to taxes and transfer programs can be long. The impact lag for government purchases can also be long because even after the federal government authorizes new expenditures on, say, roads and bridges, it takes time to plan the new projects.

The American Recovery and Reinvestment Act of 2009 provides an example of the lags associated with discretionary fiscal policy. The act was intended to stimulate the economy and to help reduce the severity of the 2007–2009 recession. Ideally, the act should have had its greatest effect during 2009, but much of the effect appears to have occurred *after* 2009. Table 13.3 shows that just 20.9% of the spending and 30.6% of the tax cuts authorized by the act occurred in 2009. The act provided tax cuts to households and firms, including incentives for first-time homebuyers to purchase new homes. However, it takes time for households to find a home that they want and can afford, and it takes time for firms to find new investment projects. In addition, the act provided funds for increased spending on infrastructure projects, but the projects needed to be planned and coordinated with state and local governments before they could begin. Much of the debate over the act centered on whether there were enough "shovel-ready projects" in 2009—that is, infrastructure projects that had received all the necessary approvals so they could start at any time but were waiting for government funding—to have a

Table 13.3 Initial Estimates of the Timing of Government Expenditure and Tax Changes from the American Recovery and Reinvestment Act

Year	Billions of dollars per year			Percentage		
	Expenditure	Taxes	Total	Expenditure	Taxes	Total
2009	$120.1	−64.8	$184.9	20.9%	30.6%	23.5%
2010	219.3	−180.1	399.4	38.1	85.0	50.7
2011	126.2	−8.2	134.4	21.9	3.9	17.1
2012	46.1	10.0	36.1	8.0	−4.7	4.6
2013	30.3	2.7	27.6	5.3	−1.3	3.5
2014	27.9	5.5	22.4	4.8	−2.6	2.8
2015	11.7	7.0	4.7	2.0	−3.3	0.6

Note: The CBO estimated the cost of the American Recovery and Reinvestment Act over the 2009 to 2019 period. We show only the cost over the years from 2009 to 2015, so the percentages in the last three columns do not necessarily add to 100. The values in the Taxes column are positive after 2011 because some of the changes to the tax code resulted in higher taxes in those years.

Source: U.S. Congressional Budget Office.

sufficiently large effect on the economy. Not many shovel-ready projects were available in 2009, so most of the spending from the 2009 act occurred in 2010 and 2011, after the recession had ended. In this case, though, the impact lag was not as significant because the recession had been so severe that real GDP was still well below potential GDP in 2010 and 2011.

Economic Forecasts

Because of lags, Congress and the president must make changes to discretionary fiscal policy based on their forecasts of how the economy will be performing several months or years in the future. In this respect, Congress and the president face the same problem the Federal Reserve faces in conducting monetary policy: They must rely on economic forecasts that are not always accurate. Mistakes in economic forecasts may limit the effectiveness of fiscal policy in reducing the severity of economic fluctuations. For example, in November 2008, the professional forecasters surveyed by the Federal Reserve Bank of Philadelphia expected real GDP to decrease by 0.2% in 2009 and the unemployment rate to increase to 7.4%. As it turns out, these forecasts were overly optimistic. Real GDP actually decreased by 2.6% during 2009, and the unemployment rate rose to 10.0% in October and averaged 9.3% for the entire year. Even after the severe financial distress following the bankruptcy of Lehman Brothers in September 2008, most forecasters failed to predict the severity of the economic downturn.

The Uncertainty of Economic Models

We have seen that economic models do not provide exact estimates of how real GDP, employment, or inflation will respond to changes in policy. Such uncertainty makes fiscal policy challenging because Congress and the president do not know exactly how much a change in government purchases or taxes will affect output or inflation.

Recent debates about fiscal policy have centered on the magnitude of the multipliers for changes in government purchases and taxes.

As Table 13.4 shows, estimates of the size of the multiplier vary. It is not even clear whether tax cuts or spending increases have a larger effect on GDP. The uncertainty over the magnitude of the multipliers made it difficult for economists to provide policymakers with clear advice on whether the American Recovery and Reinvestment Act should contain more increases in government spending or more tax cuts. However, as Table 13.3 on page 489 shows, the final act relied more heavily on spending increases than it did on tax cuts.

Table 13.4 Estimates of the Multiplier from Various Academic and Government Sources

Economist or organization	Type of multiplier	Estimated size of multiplier
Christina Romer (prior to serving as chair of the Council of Economic Advisers from 2009–2010) and David Romer, University of California, Berkeley	Tax	2–3
Robert J. Barro, Harvard University, and Charles J. Redlick, Bain Capital, LLC	Tax	1.1
Congressional Budget Office	Tax	0.6–1.5 (2-year tax cut for lower- and middle-income people) and 0.2–0.6 (1-year tax cut for higher-income people)
Tommaso Monacelli, Roberto Perotti, and Antonella Trigari, Universita Bocconi	Government purchases	1.2 (after 1 year) and 1.5 (after 2 years)
Ethan Ilzetzki, London School of Economics, and Enrique G. Mendoza and Carlos A. Vegh, University of Maryland	Government purchases	0.8
Congressional Budget Office	Government purchases	1.0–2.5
John Cogan and John Taylor, Stanford University, and Tobias Cwik and Volker Wieland, Gothe University	A permanent increase in government purchases	0.4
Christina Romer, University of California, Berkeley, and Jared Bernstein, Chief Economist and Economic Policy Adviser to Vice President Joseph Biden	A permanent increase in government purchases	1.6
Valerie Ramey, University of California, San Diego	Military expenditure	0.6–1.1
Robert J. Barro, Harvard University, and Charles J. Redlick, Bain Capital, LLC	Military expenditure	0.4–0.5 (after 1 year) and 0.6–0.7 (after 2 years)

Sources: Tommaso Monacelli, Roberto Perotti, and Antonella Trigari, "Unemployment Fiscal Multipliers," *Journal of Monetary Economics*, Vol. 57, No. 5, July 2010, pp. 531–553; Ethan Ilzetzki, Enrique G. Mendoza, and Carlos A. Vegh, "How Big (Small?) Are Fiscal Multipliers?" National Bureau of Economic Research, Working Paper 16479, October 2010; Robert J. Barro and Charles J. Redlick, "Macroeconomic Effects from Government Purchases and Taxes," National Bureau of Economic Research Working Paper 15369, September 2009; Congressional Budget Office, *Estimated Impact of the American Recovery and Reinvestment Act on Employment and Economic Output from April 2010 Through June 2010*, August 2010; Jared Bernstein and Christina Romer, "The Job Impact of the American Reinvestment and Recovery Plan," January 9, 2009; John Cogan, Tobias Cwik, John Taylor, and Volker Wieland, "New Keynesian Versus Old Keynesian Government Spending Multipliers," *Journal of Economic Dynamics and Control*, Vol. 34, No. 3, March 2010, pp. 281–295; Valerie Ramey, "Identifying Government Spending Shocks: It's All in the Timing," *Quarterly Journal of Economics*, Vol. 126, No. 1, February 2011, pp. 1–50; Christina Romer and David Romer, "The Macroeconomic Effects of Tax Changes: Estimates Based on a New Measure of Fiscal Shocks," *American Economic Review*, Vol. 100, No. 3, June 2010, pp. 763–801; and U.S. Congressional Budget Office, "Estimated Impact of the American Recovery and Reinvestment Act on Employment and Economic Output from October 2009 Through December 2009," February 2010.

Crowding Out and Forward-Looking Households

Two phenomena help explain why the multiplier may not be large (and possibly even less than one): crowding out and the forward-looking behavior of households and firms. **Crowding out** is a reduction in private investment caused by government budget deficits. The government running a deficit affects the ability of households and firms to borrow. For example, suppose the government borrows $100 billion to spend on infrastructure projects. A $100 billion increase in government purchases will reduce national saving by $100 billion, and, according to the loanable funds model, this reduction should lead to higher real interest rates. When real interest rates increase, firms find it more expensive to borrow to finance investment, so investment decreases. As a result of crowding out, aggregate expenditure increases by less than $100 billion. If the budget deficit crowds out, say, $30 billion of private investment, aggregate expenditure increases by $70 billion (the $100 billion increase in government purchases minus the $30 billion decrease in private investment). The exact degree of crowding out depends on how much of the deficit is financed by households, firms, and governments outside the United State; how much real interest rates increase; and the sensitivity of investment to the real interest rate. Higher real interest rates may also encourage households to save rather than consume, so consumption may also decrease. Crowding out is likely to be greater the closer the economy is to potential GDP.

Most economists believe that households and firms are forward looking in the sense that they care about the future when they make decisions about how much to consume and invest. Households need to save for future spending on things such as cars, homes, college educations, and retirement. So households care not only about taxes this year but also about taxes in the future. Similarly, the profits earned from investing in factories and other capital goods are earned for many years into the future, so firms care about taxes in the future.

When the government borrows to run a budget deficit, it must pay back the loans at some point in the future, which may require higher taxes. As households and firms anticipate paying higher taxes in the future, they may reduce consumption and investment today. Robert Barro of Harvard University calls the idea that households reduce consumption when the government cuts taxes *Ricardian equivalence* because it was first discussed in the early nineteenth century by British economist David Ricardo. In principle, Ricardian equivalence might reduce to zero the multiplier effect of increases in government spending or cuts in taxes. The multiplier would be zero if a decrease in taxes led households and firms to reduce current spending by exactly the amount of the tax cut. Most economists doubt that Ricardian equivalence reduces multipliers to zero, but opinions differ over how important Ricardian equivalence is.

When Will Fiscal Multipliers Be Large?

Economists have identified two situations in which expenditure and tax multipliers are likely to be large. First, multipliers are likely to be large during severe recessions when there are substantial unemployed resources in the economy. The multiplier story depends on the ability of firms to use additional revenue to hire resources, such as labor, to produce more goods and services. For example, if the government spends an additional $10 billion on building roads, firms hire $10 billion of labor, materials, and

Crowding out A reductio[n] in private investment caused by government budget deficits.

equipment to build the roads. Imagine what would happen if all workers were already employed at the time the government increases expenditures by $10 billion. To produce the $10 billion in roads, firms would have to hire workers away from other firms that produce other goods and services. The result would be an additional $10 billion of roads but $10 billion less of private goods and services, so real GDP would not increase. If the economy is already at full employment, the likely effect of an expansionary fiscal policy would be to increase nominal wages and prices but leave output unchanged. So, the further away from full employment the economy is, the larger the multiplier is likely to be.

Second, if the central bank keeps real interest rates constant, then the multipliers for fiscal policy are more likely to be large. Crowding out occurs when government borrowing increases the real interest rate that firms must pay when borrowing to finance investment. So, if monetary policy keeps real interest rates from rising, the multiplier will be larger.

Moral Hazard

Fiscal policy, like monetary policy, creates moral hazard because it can insulate households and firms from the consequences of poor decisions, making these decisions more likely. Poor decisions by households and firms can make economic fluctuations more severe.

For example, the Emergency Economic Stabilization Act of 2008 created the $700 billion Troubled Asset Relief Program (TARP) to help stabilize financial markets. Because the failure of some large firms could cause severe disruption to the financial system or the broader economy, the government used TARP funds to purchase stock in banks such as Citigroup and Bank of America, the insurance company AIG, and the automobile companies Chrysler and General Motors. To the extent that TARP funds prevented those firms from going bankrupt, TARP reduced the severity of the 2007–2009 recession. However, TARP may also have sent a signal to U.S. firms that if they are large enough, the federal government will not let them go bankrupt. As a result, large firms have less incentive to avoid risky investments. If their investments work out well, the firms get to keep the profits, but if the investments fail, taxpayers may protect them from bankruptcy.

The federal government has recognized the risks inherent in programs such as TARP, and it has taken steps to reduce moral hazard. First, the government restricted the ability of firms receiving TARP funds to pay dividends to shareholders until the funds were repaid. Not receiving expected dividend payments hurts the firms' shareholders. Second, the government placed limits on executive compensation for firms that accepted TARP funds. Because executives do not want limits on their compensation, these limits represent a cost to executives of seeking government funds. It is not yet clear how much moral hazard TARP has created or how much limits on dividends and executive compensation reduced moral hazard.

Consequences of Policy Limitations

During 2009, real GDP in the United States was 7.2%, or about $1 trillion, below potential GDP. How much would the U.S. government have had to increase spending to eliminate the gap between actual and potential real GDP? The answer depends on the size of the multiplier. Refer again to Table 13.4 on page 490. If the government purchases multiplier is at the high end of the CBO's estimates, the government would have had to increase spending by $1 trillion divided by 2.5, or $400 billion. In contrast, if the multiplier is on the low end of the CBO's estimates, the government would have had to increase spending by $1 trillion ($1 trillion divided by 1). If the lowest estimate shown in the table is correct, the government would have had to spend nearly $1 trillion divided by 0.4, or $2.5 trillion to eliminate the gap. Therefore, the estimates of the magnitude of government spending increase necessary to have ended the 2007–2009 recession in the United States range from $400 billion to $2.5 trillion! This simple example tells us that the size of the government spending increase or tax cut required to increase output to potential and end a recession is far from certain. This uncertainty makes it difficult to design a fiscal policy to reduce the severity of economic fluctuations.

Evaluating the American Recovery and Reinvestment Act

When President Obama first proposed the American Recovery and Reinvestment Act, his economic team forecast that the act would keep the unemployment rate from rising over 8%, but the unemployment rate eventually rose to 10%. Economists, policymakers, and political commentators have advanced two opposing interpretations of why unemployment rose more than had been expected:

1. The act did not succeed in increasing real GDP and employment.
2. The act worked as intended, but the recession turned out to be much more severe than policymakers realized at the start of 2009.

It remains unclear which of these two interpretations is correct.

Appraising exactly the effect of the act is difficult. First, we cannot go back in time and see what would have happened to real GDP and the unemployment rate if there had been no stimulus package. Second, as we saw earlier, estimates of the size of fiscal policy multipliers vary widely.

Studies examining the effect of the act have used different approaches. First, separate studies by the CBO and by Alan Blinder of Princeton University and Mark Zandi of Moody's Analytics have found that the act had a large positive effect on real GDP and employment.[5] The CBO found that during 2010, the act increased real GDP by between 1.5% and 4.2%, increased employment by between 1.9 million and 4.8 million workers, and reduced the unemployment rate by between 0.7 percentage points and 1.8 percentage points. Blinder and Zandi found similar results. However, both these studies are based on economic models that assume large multiplier effects. The studies tell us the effect of the act if the multipliers are as large as the authors assumed them to be. If the multipliers are smaller than assumed in these studies, the effect of the act will be correspondingly smaller.

---

[5]Congressional Budget Office, "Estimated Impact of the American Recovery and Reinvestment Act on Employment and Economic Output from January 2010 through March 2010," May 2010; and Alan Blinder and Mark Zandi, "How the Great Recession was Brought to an End," Economy.com, July 27, 2010.

A second approach to determining the effect of the act is to compare the historical paths for real GDP and employment with a forecast of GDP and employment, assuming that the act had not been passed. This approach has the advantage of not assuming that multipliers are large or small. Instead, it calculates the magnitude of the multiplier by looking at the difference between the historical path and the forecast path. President Obama's Council of Economic Advisers used this approach to estimate the effect of the act on GDP and employment.[6] The council's estimates show that by the second quarter of 2010 the act had increased GDP by 3.2% and employment by 3.6 million. However, as the council itself points out, its approach cannot distinguish between the effects of the act and other policy changes, such as changes in monetary policy and other government policies, such as TARP. At best, the council's report shows that the total effect of all fiscal policy and monetary policy actions to fight the 2007–2009 recession was to increase real GDP and employment significantly.

Moreover, the analysis of Cogan, Taylor, Cwik, and Wieland mentioned in Table 13.4 suggests that the multipliers for the act were as small as 0.4. If their estimate is correct, the effect of the act is likely to have been even smaller than the CBO's lower estimates. The varying estimates of the effect of the act indicate that there is no consensus among economists on the effectiveness of fiscal policy or even which fiscal policy tools are likely to have the largest effect. Economists will likely be analyzing the effect of the American Recovery and Reinvestment Act for many years to come.

13.5

Learning Objective

Explain how fiscal policy operates in an open economy.

Fiscal Policy in an Open Economy

Taking into account the effect of international trade, international financial flows, and exchange rate policies changes our analysis of monetary policy (see Chapter 12). The same is true of fiscal policy.

Fiscal Policy with Floating Exchange Rates

The United States allows its exchange rate to float. As we will see, a floating exchange rate reduces the effectiveness of fiscal policy. Panel (a) of Figure 13.6 shows the effect of an increase in government purchases that shifts the IS curve to the right, from IS_1 to IS_2. The increase puts upward pressure on inflation. Typically, the Fed responds to an increase in the inflation rate by shifting up the MP curve from MP_1 to MP_2, which increases the real interest rate from r_1 to r_2. Short-run equilibrium moves from point A to point B. The higher real interest rate makes investment in the United States more attractive, so investors purchase more U.S. assets and net capital outflows decrease from NCF_1 to NCF_2, as shown in panel (b). To purchase U.S. assets, investors need U.S. dollars, so the demand for U.S. dollars increases, causing the dollar to appreciate in value. Because net exports equal net capital outflows, net exports also decrease.

In the closed-economy version of the IS–MP model, a higher real interest rate reduces private consumption and investment. The open-economy version of

---

[6]Council of Economic Advisers, "The Economic Impact of the American Recovery and Reinvestment Act of 2009: Fourth Quarterly Report," July 14, 2010.

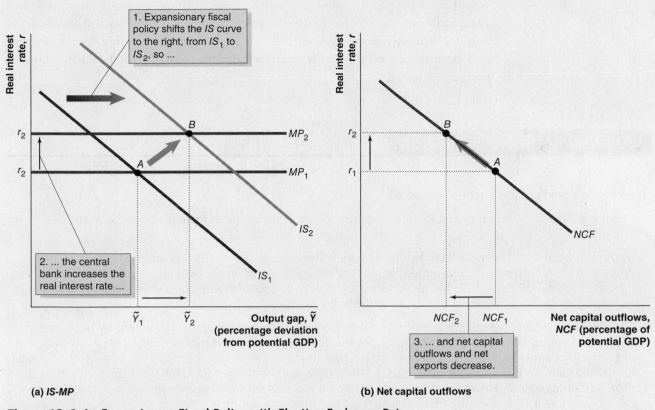

Figure 13.6 An Expansionary Fiscal Policy with Floating Exchange Rates

Panel (a) shows that under a floating exchange rate system, an increase in government purchases typically leads the Federal Reserve to shift up the MP curve from MP_1 to MP_2. Short-run equilibrium moves from point A to point B.

In panel (b), the increase in the real interest rate causes the exchange rate to appreciate, so net capital outflows and net exports decrease. Short-run equilibrium moves from point A to point B.

the IS–MP model shows that expansionary fiscal policy will also reduce net exports due to the appreciation of the domestic currency. Therefore, fiscal policy is less effective at increasing real GDP in an open economy with a floating exchange rate than in a closed economy. In the eyes of U.S. policymakers, this potential drawback to a floating exchange rate is not enough to offset the advantages (see Chapter 4).

Fiscal Policy with a Fixed Exchange Rate

Some countries pursue a fixed exchange rate policy. As it turns out, with a fixed exchange rate, an expansionary fiscal policy is more effective than in a closed economy.

Suppose that Mexico has a fixed exchange rate. If the Mexican government decides to pursue an expansionary fiscal policy, the result will be both an increase in real GDP and a higher inflation rate. If the Bank of Mexico was not concerned about the exchange rate, then it would respond to the higher inflation rate by increasing the real interest rate, as the Fed did in our earlier example. However, increasing the real interest rate would cause the peso to appreciate, which would violate the Bank's commitment to a fixed exchange rate. To prevent the peso from appreciating, the Bank will have to act to keep the real interest rate constant. As a result, investment spending does not decline and expansionary fiscal policy is even more effective than it would be under a floating exchange rate.

Answering the Key Question

Continued from page 461

At the beginning of this chapter, we asked:

"Was the American Recovery and Reinvestment Act of 2009 successful at increasing real GDP and employment?"

In the short run, fiscal policy affects aggregate expenditure, which then causes changes in real GDP and employment. An increase in government purchases will increase aggregate expenditure, which will cause an increase in real GDP and employment. A decrease in personal taxes increases disposable income, which will increase aggregate expenditure, real GDP, and employment.

The American Recovery and Reinvestment Act tried to increase real GDP and employment by both increasing government purchases and cutting taxes. As the discussion in the text makes clear, economists have not yet come to a consensus on how effective the act was. If the expenditure multiplier is as large as the Obama administration and the Congressional Budget Office believe, then the act substantially increased both real GDP and employment. However, if the expenditure multiplier is smaller, as other studies indicate, then the act increased real GDP and employment by a relatively modest amount.

Key Terms and Problems

Key Terms

Automatic stabilizers, p. 468

Budget deficit, p. 469

Budget surplus, p. 469

Crowding out, p. 491

Cyclically adjusted budget deficit or surplus, p. 472

Discretionary fiscal policy, p. 468

Disposable income, p. 465

Fiscal policy, p. 462

Gross federal debt held by the public, p. 474

Tax wedge, p. 486

13.1 The Goals and Tools of Fiscal Policy
Explain the goals and tools of fiscal policy.

Review Questions

1.1 What is fiscal policy? Who is responsible for conducting fiscal policy?

1.2 What are the goals of fiscal policy? What tools have policymakers traditionally used to achieve these goals?

1.3 Describe how changes in personal income taxes, corporate income taxes, and transfer payments affect real GDP and employment.

MyEconLab Visit **www.myeconlab.com** to complete these exercises online and get instant feedback. Exercises that update with real-time data are marked with (🌀).

Problems and Applications

1.4 For each of the following situations, choose a fiscal policy and explain how it could be used to correct the economic problem.

    a. Real GDP is above potential GDP after a stock market boom.

    b. The economy is in a recession due to a decline in spending on residential construction.

1.5 In the United States, consumption taxes (such as sales taxes) are typically state or local rather than federal taxes. In Europe, consumption taxes are imposed nationally rather than regionally, and are typically far higher than U.S. consumption taxes.

    a. If the United States were to reduce income taxes and impose a national sales tax, briefly explain what the effects would be on consumption and investment.

    b. Would you expect a consumption tax to have a different effect on consumer savings than would an income tax? Briefly explain.

1.6 In the United Kingdom, national debt as a percentage of GDP rose from 37% in 2007 to over 66% in mid-2012. A primary reason for the large increase in the national debt was the recession of 2007–2009 and the subsequent slow recovery.

The government of the U.K. follows a rule that the national debt as a percentage of GDP should not exceed 40%.

    a. What fiscal policies could the government of the U.K. use to reduce the national debt and keep the economy in line with its debt rule?

    b. What effect would these policies have on the economy of the U.K.?

1.7 Consider the following statement: "Monetary policy and fiscal policy are really the same thing because they both can involve the buying and selling of U.S. Treasury securities." Briefly explain whether you agree with this statement.

1.8 [Related to the *Making the Connection* on page 466] The chapter suggests that one reason it was difficult to predict the severity of the 2007–2009 recession is that most economists did not anticipate the financial crisis.

    a. What might the failure to anticipate the recession imply about the effectiveness of fiscal policy in preventing or reducing the severity of the recession?

    b. What fiscal policies might have been implemented earlier if economists had more accurately predicted the severity of the recession?

13.2 Budget Deficits, Discretionary Fiscal Policy, and Automatic Stabilizers
Distinguish between automatic stabilizers and discretionary fiscal policy and understand how the budget deficit is measured.

Review Questions

2.1 How is discretionary fiscal policy different from automatic stabilizers? List examples of both discretionary fiscal policy and automatic stabilizers during the 2007–2009 recession.

2.2 What is a cyclically adjusted budget deficit or surplus? How is it used to determine whether fiscal policy is expansionary or contractionary?

2.3 Describe the difference between a federal budget surplus, a federal budget deficit, and the national

debt. Briefly describe trends in the U.S. federal budget surplus and deficit, and the national debt since the start of the Great Depression.

Problems and Applications

2.4 Briefly explain whether each of the following is an example of (1) a discretionary fiscal policy, (2) an automatic stabilizer, or (3) not a fiscal policy.

    a. The federal government increases spending on rebuilding highways

b. The Federal Reserve sells Treasury securities

c. The total the federal government pays out for unemployment insurance increases during a recession

d. Personal income revenues decline during a recession

e. The federal government changes the required gasoline mileage for new cars

f. Congress and the president enact a 5% increase in all income tax rates

2.5 According to the chapter, contractionary fiscal policy is rarely used. But during the late 1990s, the U.S. government ran a budget surplus. Does this surplus imply that fiscal policy in this period was contractionary? Briefly explain.

2.6 As mentioned in the chapter, in 1968, the U.S. government placed a temporary 10% surcharge on personal and corporate income in an attempt to prevent the economy from overheating and causing inflation to accelerate. This surtax remained in effect through 1970.

a. What type of policy was this surtax?

b. Economic research has shown that consumers are more likely to make changes in consumption spending when there is a permanent change in their income. Given this finding, would you expect that the surcharge had the desired result?

c. Why might Congress and the president chose a temporary tax change over a permanent tax change?

2.7 Most of the programs that we think of as automatic stabilizers did not exist in 1929. Suppose that the automatic stabilizers existed in 1929. Briefly explain the effect these stabilizer would have had on the severity of the Great Depression.

2.8 [Related to the Chapter Opener on page 461] While addressing Congress in July 2012, Fed Chairman Ben Bernanke offered the following opinion:

"The most effective way that Congress could help to support the economy right now, would be to work to address the nation's fiscal challenges in a way that takes into account both the need for long-run sustainability and the fragility of the recovery."

a. What "fiscal challenges" was the United States facing in 2012?

b. Why was Bernanke worried that Congress might take actions that would not be advisable given the "fragility of the recovery"?

Source: Ben S. Bernanke, *Semiannual Monetary Policy Report to the Congress*, July 17, 2012.

2.9 [Related to the Making the Connection on page 470] One reason given for the Bush tax cuts in 2001 was to reduce the size of the government budget surplus.

a. How might tax cuts reduce the size of the budget surplus?

b. Why might the government want to reduce the size of the budget surplus?

c. Shortly after the tax cuts were passed, various events occurred that policymakers could not have predicted, such as the terrorist attacks on September 11, 2001. What happened to the government's budget surplus?

2.10 [Related to the Macro Data feature on page 473] In January 2012, the Congressional Budget Office (CBO) predicted that the U.S. federal government would have a budget deficit equal to 2.0% of GDP and a cyclically adjusted budget surplus equal to 0.7% of GDP in 2014.

a. Was the CBO forecasting that discretionary fiscal policy would be expansionary or contractionary? Briefly explain.

b. What effect did the CBO forecast that automatic stabilizers would have on the economy? Briefly explain.

Source: Congressional Budget Office, "The Budget and Economic Outlook: Fiscal Years 2012 to 2022," January 31, 2012. Available at: http://www.cbo.gov/publication/42905

13.3 **The Short-Run Effects of Fiscal Policy**
Use the *IS–MP* model to understand how fiscal policy affects the economy in the short run.

Review Questions

3.1 How are changes in discretionary fiscal policy shown in the *IS–MP* model? Include the Phillips curve in your discussion.

3.2 How are automatic stabilizers shown in the *IS–MP* model? Include the Phillips curve in your discussion.

3.3 How does a change in the personal income tax rate affect the multiplier? How does a change in the size of the multiplier affect the economy?

3.4 Explain how cuts in individual income taxes, corporate income taxes, and taxes on dividends and capital gains affect potential GDP.

Problems and Applications

3.5 [Related to Solved Problem 13.3A **on page 481**] In 1968, the U.S. government placed a temporary 10% surcharge on personal and corporate income in an attempt to prevent the economy from overheating and inflation from accelerating. The graph below shows short-run equilibrium prior to the surcharge. Assume that the economy was already experiencing inflation at that time. Use the graph to illustrate the effect of the surcharge on the economy. Explain the likely effect of the surcharge on the Phillips curve and the output gap.

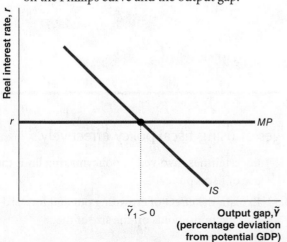

3.6 [Related to the Making the Connection **on page 483**] From 1991 to 2000, the Japanese economy grew so slowly that those years have become known as the "Lost Decade." Nevertheless, the Japanese government increased the national sales tax in 1997 because it had become concerned about its budget deficit. As a result, real GDP decreased by 2.0% in 1998 and 0.1% in 1999. The graph below shows short-run equilibrium in the Japanese economy in 1997 prior to the sales tax increase. The graph assumes that growth had been slow but not negative, so the economy was at or near full employment.

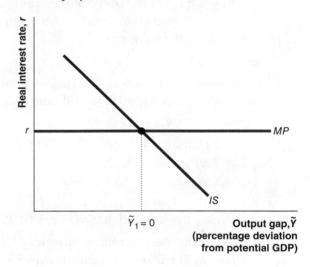

a. Show the effect of the sales tax on the *IS–MP* graph and describe any change that would take place on the Phillips curve.

b. If the primary goal of the government is full employment, was increasing the national sales tax in 1997 a wise policy? Briefly explain.

3.7 Consider the following statement: "Because automatic stabilizers are built into the economy, there is no need for discretionary fiscal policy." Do you agree with this statement? Briefly explain.

3.8 Unemployment insurance usually expires after approximately 26 weeks. During the 2007–2009 crisis, unemployment benefits were extended for some workers. Congress has subsequently passed additional extensions, the latest of which was set to expire at the end of 2012. Discussing one of these extensions, an article in the *Economist* states, "Congress had never before failed to extend benefits when unemployment remained above 7.2%, and this week's action marked the seventh extension in this recession."

a. Use the *IS–MP* graph to show how an automatic stabilizer such as unemployment benefits works.

b. What would have been the consequences of having let unemployment insurance benefits expire after 26 weeks?

c. Can you think of any reason why extensions of unemployment insurance benefits might be harmful to the economy?

Source: "Read This Shirt," *Economist*, July 22, 2010.

3.9 **[Related to Solved Problem 13.3B on page 485]** An economy can be described by the following data:

$$C = \overline{C} + MPC(1 - t)Y$$
$$\quad = \$1.0 \text{ trillion} + 0.758(1 - 0.25)Y$$
$$I = \$2.0 \text{ trillion}$$
$$G = \$3.0 \text{ trillion}$$
$$NX = \$0.5 \text{ trillion}$$

a. Calculate the equilibrium level of real GDP.

b. Suppose that the government increases purchases by $1 trillion. Calculate the change in real GDP.

c. What is the value of the multiplier?

3.10 An economy has a marginal propensity to consume of 0.90. The tax rate is 0.10.

a. What is the value of the multiplier?

b. What would the value of the multiplier be if the tax rate increased to 0.15?

c. Suppose that the government increases purchases by $2 billion in (a) and (b). What is the change in real GDP in each case?

d. How do changes in the tax rate affect the amount by which equilibrium real GDP changes as government purchases change?

3.11 For each of the following, describe the change in consumption, investment, and aggregate expenditure and explain what happens to the *IS* curve and the Phillips curve.

a. The government increases infrastructure spending on roads and bridges by 25%.

b. The government cuts the corporate tax rate in half.

c. Payroll taxes are increased on workers who earn over $100,000.

d. Personal income tax rates are reduced for anyone earning less than $40,000.

e. The length of time an individual can collect unemployment insurance is reduced from 99 weeks back to 26 weeks.

13.4 The Limitations of Fiscal Policy
Use the *IS–MP* model to explain the challenges of using fiscal policy effectively.

Review Questions

4.1 How are lags different for fiscal policy than for monetary policy? How are they the same?

4.2 How does the accuracy of economic forecasts present a problem for fiscal policy? How do the uncertainties involved in policymaking limit the use of fiscal policy?

4.3 Explain the effect of crowding out and forward-looking households on the size of the multiplier.

4.4 Why is the multiplier likely to be large during a severe recession or when the Fed keeps real interest rates constant?

Problems and Applications

4.5 During the 2007–2009 financial crisis, among policymakers, the Fed was the first to respond with a reduction in short-term nominal interest rates in September 2007. Fiscal policy actions came later. Comment on the length of fiscal and monetary policy lags and why a monetary policy action occurred first.

4.6 The table in the next column shows U.S. budget deficits from 2007 to 2012. Compared to the data for 2007, the size of the federal budget deficit was significantly higher each year beginning in 2009 due to (1) the stimulus package of 2009, (2) reduced tax collections, and (3) increased government spending on transfer payments.

a. If households are forward looking, what effect will increased budget deficits have on their spending and saving choices?

b. Discuss the relevance of these spending and saving choices for the effectiveness of fiscal policy.

Year	Surplus or deficit (−), (millions of dollars)
2007	−$160,701
2008	−458,553
2009	−1,412,688
2010	−1,293,489
2011	−1,299,595
2012 (estimate)	−1,326,948

Source: www.whitehouse.gov.

4.7 The size of the expenditure multiplier varies depending on economic conditions and the conduct of monetary policy. Suppose that the government decides to spend an extra $100 billion on infrastructure projects and that the central bank targets an inflation rate of 2%. In addition, assume that the central bank always adjusts policy to hit this target. Use the *IS-MP* diagram and the Phillips curve to explain the effect of the increase in government spending on the economy.

13.5 Fiscal Policy in an Open Economy
Explain how fiscal policy operates in an open economy.

Review Questions

5.1. Briefly explain whether fiscal policy is more or less effective in an open economy with a floating exchange rate than in a closed economy.

5.2. Briefly explain whether fiscal policy is more or less effective in an open economy with a fixed exchange rate than in a closed economy.

Problems and Applications

5.3. Consider the difference between the effectiveness of fiscal policy in a small economy, such as Sweden, when the economy is closed and when it is open. Is the difference in the effectiveness of fiscal policy likely to be larger or smaller than for the United States? Briefly explain.

5.4. In July 2012, the government of newly elected French president François Hollande announced that it would sharply increase taxes to try to close a government budget deficit. Use the *IS–MP* model to analyze the effect of this tax increase on the output gap and the inflation rate, assuming that the real interest rate remains unchanged. Is the effect of the tax increase greater if you assume that France is a closed economy or an open economy? Briefly explain.

Source: "François Hollande's Fiscal Puzzle," *Economist*, July 7, 2012.

Data Exercises

D13.1: [Excel exercise] The International Monetary Fund publishes the World Economic Outlook. Go to www.imf.org and look at the most recent version available. Look at the data for the cyclically adjusted budget deficit (which the World Economic Outlook calls "General Government Structural Balance") for Brazil, China, France, and Germany from 2000 to 2017. Use the series for the cyclically adjusted budget deficit that is measured as a percentage of potential GDP.

  a. Download the data and plot the data in a graph. Which country relied the most on discretionary fiscal policy in response to the financial crisis of 2008 and 2009?

  b. How do these countries' discretionary fiscal policies compare to the countries in Table 13.1 on p. 476?

  c. From 2012 to 2017, which of these four countries is expected to have the most expansionary discretionary fiscal policy? Briefly explain.

D13.2: Go to www.recovery.gov, where you will find information about the American Recovery and Reinvestment Act. According to this site, how were the dollars authorized by the act spent? According to the site, how many jobs has the economy gained as a result of the act?

D13.3: Using data from the St. Louis Federal Reserve (FRED) (http://research.stlouisfed.org/fred2/), analyze the relationship between government spending, tax revenue, and the business cycle.

  a. Download quarterly data from 1947 to the present for federal government consumption expenditures and gross investment (FGCE), federal government current receipts (FGRECPT), nominal GDP (GDP), and the chain-type GDP price index (GDPCTPI).

  b. Calculate real GDP, real federal consumption expenditures and investment, and real federal current receipts. Calculate the annual growth rate for each of these series as the percentage change from the same quarter in the previous year.

  c. Calculate the correlation between the growth rate of real GDP and the growth rate of real federal consumption expenditures and investment. Calculate the correlation between the growth rate of real GDP and real federal current receipts.

  d. One way to measure the business cycle is to look at the growth rate of real GDP. Based on the correlations you previously calculated, has U.S. fiscal policy made the business cycle more severe or less severe? Briefly explain.

D13.4: [Excel exercise] The Congressional Budget Office provides data on the actual and cyclically adjusted budget deficits. Find data from 1959 to 2011 in this Excel file: www.cbo.gov/doc.cfm?index=10544&type=2.

  a. Graph the budget deficit or surplus and the cyclically adjusted deficit or surplus for this period. (Note that the deficit or surplus is called "Government Saving" in this file.)

  b. What was the average surplus or deficit? What was the average cyclically adjusted surplus or deficit? What is the correlation coefficient between the actual deficit and the cyclically adjusted deficit?

  c. Calculate the standard deviation for each series and comment on your results.

D13.5: The International Monetary Fund publishes the World Economic Outlook. Go to www.imf.org and look at the most recent version available. Look at the data on the forecasted output gap for Japan, the United Kingdom, and the United States for 2012 to 2017.

a. Based on these data, design a fiscal policy for each year that would make the output gap equal to zero.

b. Describe at least two problems that these countries would have in implementing your suggested policies.

D13.6: [Excel exercise] The International Monetary Fund publishes the World Economic Outlook. Go to www.imf.org and look at the most recent version available. Look at the data for cyclically adjusted budget deficit (which the World Economic Outlook calls "General Government Structural Balance") and output gap from 1980 to 2011 for France and the United Kingdom. Use the series for the cyclically adjusted budget deficit that is measured as a percentage of potential GDP.

a. If these countries used discretionary fiscal policy to try to stabilize the economy (that is, to keep the output gap close to 0), then what should be the correlation between the cyclically adjust budget deficit and the output gap?

b. Plot the output gap and the cyclically adjusted budget deficit for France on the same graph. Does the correlation between the two series look as if it is positive or negative? Repeat your analysis for the United Kingdom.

c. Calculate the correlation between the output gap and the cyclically adjusted budget deficit for France. Is the correlation consistent with a discretionary fiscal policy that stabilizes the economy? Repeat your analysis for the United Kingdom.

CHAPTER 14

Aggregate Demand, Aggregate Supply, and Monetary Policy

Learning Objectives

After studying this chapter, you should be able to:

14.1 Understand how aggregate demand is determined (pages 506–512)

14.2 Explain the relationship between aggregate supply and the Phillips curve (pages 512–515)

14.3 Use the aggregate demand and aggregate supply model to analyze macroeconomic conditions (pages 515–526)

14.4 Discuss the implications of rational expectations for macroeconomic policymaking (pages 526–530)

14.5 Discuss the pros and cons of the central bank's operating under policy rules rather than using discretionary policy (pages 530–536)

Did the Fed Create and Then Kill the Great Moderation?

The key short-run macroeconomic problem is the business cycle. Most economists believe that business cycles make households and firms worse off. If macroeconomic policy can reduce the severity of business cycles, people will find jobs more easily, entrepreneurs will have an easier time starting new businesses, and households will not have to worry about high inflation rates eroding the value of their savings.

Unfortunately, macroeconomic policy has often failed to reach its objectives. Sometimes monetary and fiscal policy have actually made macroeconomic conditions worse rather than better. A number of

policy mistakes contributed to the Great Depression. Most economists believe that mistakes by the Federal Reserve made the Great Depression longer and deeper than it would otherwise have been. In addition, some economists believe fiscal policy mistakes during this period also made the Depression worse.

Many economists have also criticized macroeconomic policy during the 1970s. Until the 1970s, the United States had experienced high inflation rates only during wartime, but by 1974, the inflation rate soared to more than 10%. The inflation rate declined during the next few years, only to rise again sharply beginning

Continued on next page

Key Issue and Question

Issue: Between the early 1980s and 2007, the U.S. economy experienced a period of macroeconomic stability known as the Great Moderation.

Question: Did discretionary monetary policy kill the Great Moderation?

Answered on page 536

in 1978. In early 1980, the inflation rate was above 14% for five months. These high inflation rates imposed serious costs on many households and firms. Workers whose nominal wages did not keep pace with these high inflation rates suffered large declines in real wages. Bondholders, people receiving fixed-dollar pensions, and banks that had made fixed-interest-rate loans all suffered losses. Most economists believe that monetary policy could have been used more skillfully to keep inflation from reaching such high levels. To add to the problems of the 1970s and early 1980s, the economy suffered severe recessions in 1973–1975 and 1981–1982. In late 1982, the unemployment rate hit a peak of 10.8%, which remains the highest unemployment rate since the 1930s. This combination of high inflation and high unemployment, dubbed *stagflation*, left much of the general public wondering whether Fed policymakers knew what they were doing.

After the early 1980s, however, the performance of the economy improved, and so did the reputation of Fed policymakers. Following the end of the 1981–1982 recession, the United States experienced 92 straight months of economic expansion, ending with the brief and mild recession of 1990–1991. The following expansion was 120 months long—the longest in U.S. history—and was followed by another short and mild recession during 2001. The inflation rate was also well under control, averaging just 2.6% between December 1982 and December 2007. This 25-year run of long expansions, short and mild recessions, and low inflation

was arguably the longest period of macroeconomic stability in the history of the United States. The period was a sufficiently sharp break with the past that economists James Stock of Harvard University and Mark Watson of Princeton University named it the "Great Moderation." Having received a good share of the blame for previous periods of macroeconomic instability, should the Fed receive credit for the Great Moderation? Certainly many economists, Wall Street analysts, and members of Congress seemed convinced that Alan Greenspan, who served as Fed chair from 1987 to 2006, had somehow managed to tame the business cycle. As we will see in this chapter, however, some economists were skeptical that better Fed policy was the key to the Great Moderation.

The Great Moderation ended abruptly in 2007. As we discussed in earlier chapters, the 2007–2009 recession was the worst since the Great Depression of the 1930s. Did Fed policies play a role in ending the Great Moderation? In hindsight, a number of economists and policymakers argued that Fed policies during the early 2000s, although widely seen as successful at the time, actually led to the recession of 2007–2009. To some economists, Alan Greenspan's reputation was turned on its head—from hero to villain—in just a few years.

As we have already seen, explaining business cycles is not an easy task. In this chapter, we will look more closely at monetary policy, with the aim of being better able to evaluate the Fed's role in the Great Moderation and in the severe recession of 2007–2009.

Sources: U.S. Bureau of Economic Analysis; U.S. Bureau of Labor Statistics; and James Stock and Mark Watson, "Has the Business Cycle Changed and Why?" *NBER Macroeconomics Annual*, 2002, pp. 159–218.

We used the aggregate demand and aggregate supply model to illustrate changes in real GDP and the price level during the business cycle (see Chapter 9). We also saw how *IS–MP* is a model of aggregate demand. Our initial discussion illustrated the aggregate demand and aggregate supply model using a graph with real GDP on the horizontal axis and the price level on the vertical axis. Now that we have explored the *IS–MP* model, including the Phillips curve, we can present a more complete version of the aggregate demand and aggregate supply (*AD-AS*) model using graphs with the output gap on the horizontal axis and the inflation rate on the vertical axis. This approach makes it easier to use the model to analyze the business cycle and macroeconomic policies. The *AD-AS* model completes our discussion of business cycles.

14.1

Learning Objective

Understand how aggregate demand is determined.

Aggregate Demand Revisited

We can begin constructing the aggregate demand and aggregate supply model by noting that one of the main goals of central banks is price stability. To achieve this goal, central banks set either an implicit or explicit inflation target, π_{Target}. Some central banks, such as the Federal Reserve in the United States, have announced inflation targets that they are not legally obliged to meet. Other central banks, such as the Reserve Bank of New Zealand, have an explicit inflation target specified by law. When inflation is greater than the target rate, central banks increase interest rates to reduce aggregate expenditure and real GDP, which in turn will reduce the inflation rate. When inflation is less than the target rate, central banks decrease interest rates to increase aggregate expenditure and real GDP, which in turn will raise the inflation rate.

We can think of the central bank's response to changes in inflation as a **central bank reaction function**, which is a rule or formula that a central bank uses to set interest rates in response to changing economic conditions. The line in Figure 14.1 illustrates the central bank's reaction function. When the real interest rate equals r_1, the level of aggregate expenditure is consistent with the central bank's target inflation rate, π_{Target}. The reaction function slopes upward because the central bank increases the real interest rate as the inflation rate increases and decreases the real interest rate as the inflation rate decreases. There are two key components of the reaction function. First, the target inflation rate is the inflation rate that the central bank wants to achieve in the long run. Second, the slope of the reaction function indicates how much the central bank responds to short-run differences between the actual inflation rate and the target inflation rate: The steeper the reaction function, the more the central bank increases the interest rate in response to the current inflation rate being above the target inflation rate and the more the central bank decreases the real interest rate in response to the actual inflation rate being below the target inflation rate. The flatter the reaction function, the smaller the changes the central bank makes in the real interest rate in response to differences between the actual inflation rate and the target inflation rate. In other words, if the reaction function is steep, the central bank responds more aggressively to differences between the actual inflation rate and the target inflation rate than if the reaction function is flat.

Central bank reaction function A rule or formula that a central bank uses to set interest rates in response to changing economic conditions.

Figure 14.1

The Central Bank Reaction Function

The reaction function slopes upward, indicating that the central bank increases the real interest rate as the inflation rate increases and decreases the real interest rate as the inflation rate decreases.

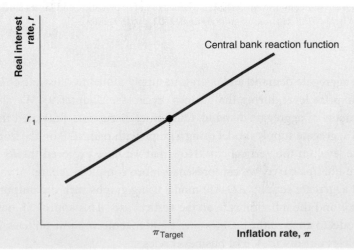

The reaction function in Figure 14.1 somewhat simplifies the actual policy situation that central banks face. For one thing, central banks typically have goals beyond just price stability. The Federal Reserve, for example, is charged by Congress with achieving high employment and financial market stability, as well as price stability. So, in some circumstances, a reaction function focusing on just inflation may not be consistent with the Fed's other goals. We consider more complicated reaction functions later in this chapter. The reaction function illustrated in Figure 14.1 also assumes that the central bank controls the *long-term real interest rate*, but the Fed, like other central banks, actually controls the *short-term nominal interest rate*. Recall that the long-term real interest rate depends on the short-term nominal interest rate, the term structure effect, the default risk premium, and the expected inflation rate. At this point, we are assuming that these factors are unchanged, so a change in the short-term nominal interest rate will change the long-term real interest rate.

The Aggregate Demand Curve

The reaction function shows how the Fed adjusts its target for the real interest rate in response to changes in the inflation rate. Raising the target for the real interest rate makes it more costly for households and firms to borrow to finance consumption and investment. A higher real interest rate also increases the exchange rate between the U.S. dollar and foreign currencies, which reduces net exports. Because aggregate expenditure and real GDP decrease as the real interest rate increases, there is a negative relationship between the real interest rate and the quantity of real GDP demanded by households and firms. As we saw in earlier chapters, we express this negative relationship with the *IS* curve.

We can use the *IS–MP* model to derive the **aggregate demand (AD) curve**, which is a curve that shows the relationship between the inflation rate and aggregate expenditure on goods and services by households and firms. Figure 14.2 shows how we can derive the aggregate demand curve by using the *IS–MP* model and the central bank reaction function.

In the figure, short-run equilibrium is initially at point A in both panel (a) and panel (b), with real GDP equal to potential GDP, so the output gap equals zero at $\widetilde{Y}_1$. The inflation rate, π_1, is equal to the Fed's target rate, π_{Target}. Given the Fed's reaction function, it sets the real interest rate at r_1, so the *MP* curve is MP_1. Now suppose that in panel (b) the inflation rate increases from π_1 to π_2, which is above the Fed's target rate. The reaction function indicates that the Fed will increase the real interest rate as the inflation rate increases. Accordingly, we show the real interest rate increasing from r_1 to r_2 in panel (a). As a result, aggregate expenditure will fall below potential GDP and the output gap changes from $\widetilde{Y}_1$ to $\widetilde{Y}_2$. The new equilibrium combination of inflation and real GDP demanded is π_2 and $\widetilde{Y}_2$, so short-run equilibrium is now at point B in both panel (a) and panel (b). Drawing a line connecting points A and B gives us the aggregate demand curve. Because an increase in the inflation rate leads the Fed to increase the real interest rate, there is an inverse relationship between the inflation rate and the output gap. This relationship is represented by the aggregate demand curve. Changes in the inflation rate cause movements along the aggregate demand curve.

The reaction function tells us how much the real interest rate changes as the inflation rate increases, so it is important in deriving the aggregate demand curve. If the Fed focuses

Aggregate demand (*AD*) curve A curve that shows the relationship between aggregate expenditure on goods and services by households and firms and the inflation rate.

Figure 14.2

Deriving the Aggregate Demand Curve

The aggregate demand curve shows the relationship between aggregate expenditure and the inflation rate. An increase in the inflation rate from π_1 to π_2 in panel (b) causes the Fed to increase the real interest rate, so the MP curve shifts from MP_1 to MP_2, causing a movement along the IS curve from point A to point B in panel (a). Consumption, investment, and net exports all decline, which reduces real GDP. As a result, the output gap changes from $\widetilde{Y}_1$ to $\widetilde{Y}_2$, and in panel (b), short-run equilibrium moves from point A to point B on the AD curve.

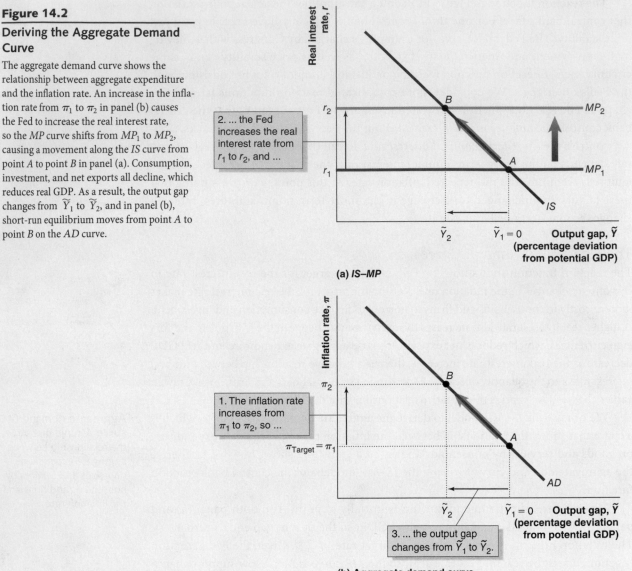

2. ... the Fed increases the real interest rate from r_1 to r_2, and ...

(a) IS–MP

1. The inflation rate increases from π_1 to π_2, so ...

3. ... the output gap changes from $\widetilde{Y}_1$ to $\widetilde{Y}_2$.

(b) Aggregate demand curve

on price stability, it will increase interest rates substantially when inflation rises, so aggregate expenditure will decrease substantially. The result is a relatively flat aggregate demand curve, which shows that aggregate expenditure is very sensitive to changes in the inflation rate. If, however, the Fed is less sensitive to changes in the inflation rate, it will not increase the real interest rate as much when the inflation rate increases, so aggregate expenditure will not decrease as much. The result in this case is a steep aggregate demand curve, which shows that aggregate expenditure is not very sensitive to changes in the inflation rate.

Shifts of the Aggregate Demand Curve

The AD curve tells us what happens to the quantity of real GDP demanded relative to potential GDP if the inflation rate increases, *holding everything else constant*. There-fore, a change in the inflation rate causes a *movement along* a particular AD curve. If a

factor that would affect the demand for goods and services other than the inflation r
changes, the *AD* curve will *shift* either to the right or to the left.

In deriving the *AD* curve, we assumed that variables that shift the *IS* curve rema
constant. Anything that causes the *IS* curve to shift will cause the *AD* curve to shi
Several factors cause the *IS* curve to shift: changes in autonomous consumption, inves
ment, and government purchases of goods and services, changes in taxes and transfe
payments, and changes in net exports. For example, if the government increases spend
ing on infrastructure projects, such as highways and bridges, both the *IS* curve and the
AD curve will shift to the right.

Figure 14.3 shows the effect of an increase in government purchases on the *AD*
curve. In panel (b), the inflation rate equals π and the output gap initially equals $\widetilde{Y}_1$, so

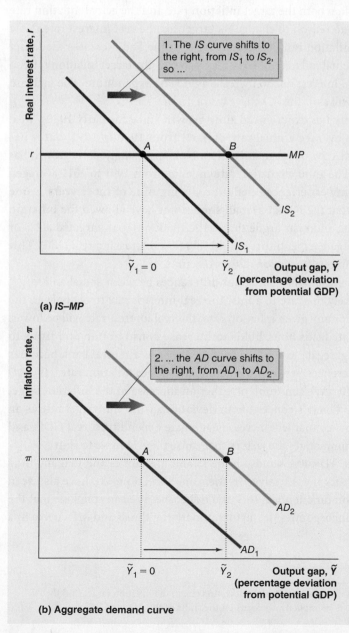

(a) *IS–MP*

(b) Aggregate demand curve

Figure 14.3

An Increase in Government Purchases Shifts the Aggregate Demand Curve

An increase in government purchases increases aggregate expenditure, so the *IS* curve shifts to the right from IS_1 to IS_2, which causes the *AD* curve to shift to the right from AD_1 to AD_2. Any increase in autonomous spending that causes the *IS* curve to shift to the right in panel (a) will also cause the *AD* curve to shift to the right in panel (b). Similarly, any decrease in autonomous spending that causes the *IS* curve to shift to the left will also cause the *AD* curve to shift to the left.

short-run equilibrium is initially at point A on AD_1. As government purchases increase, the IS curve in panel (a) shifts to the right, from IS_1 to IS_2. At the original real interest rate, short-run equilibrium is now at point B, and the output gap equals $\widetilde{Y}_2$. If the inflation rate remains constant, the new equilibrium combination of the inflation rate and the output gap is π and $\widetilde{Y}_2$. Short-run equilibrium is at point B in panel (b), which is to the right of the original AD curve. Therefore, the AD curve has shifted to the right, from AD_1 to AD_2.

A change in the central bank reaction function will also cause the AD curve to shift. There are two key components of the reaction function: (1) the central bank's inflation target and (2) how responsive the central bank is to differences between the actual and target inflation rates. When either of these two components changes, the AD curve will shift. Consider the case when both the target inflation rate and the actual inflation rate equal 2%, so the Fed has no reason to change its target for the real interest rate. Now suppose that the actual inflation rate remains at 2%, but the Fed increases the target inflation rate to 3%. The actual inflation rate is now 1% below the target inflation rate, so the Fed will reduce the real interest rate to increase aggregate expenditure. The increase in aggregate expenditure will shift the AD curve to the right.

The Japanese economy has experienced slow growth since the early 1990s. Real GDP in Japan grew at an average annual rate of 4.5% from 1970 to 1991, but it has grown at a rate of less than 1.5% per year since then. Not surprisingly, slow growth has led to low inflation rates. The annual inflation rate in Japan from 1991 to 2011 averaged just 0.2%, and the economy experienced deflation during nine of those years. Some economists have argued that the Bank of Japan should not have allowed the inflation rate to fall so low. These economists argue that if the Bank of Japan targeted a 2% or 3% rate of inflation, aggregate expenditure would increase, increasing real GDP. This argument is consistent with our discussion of the AD curve.

The less concerned central banks are about differences between actual and target inflation rates, the less likely they are to adjust the real interest rate to changes in the inflation rate. Therefore, for any given inflation rate, the real interest rate will be lower. The lower real interest rate leads households to increase consumption and firms to increase investment, so aggregate expenditure is higher. So if a central bank becomes less concerned about differences between the actual and target inflation rates, the AD curve will shift to the right.[1] We can think of either an increase in the inflation target or a decrease in the central bank's concern with deviations from this target rate as an expansionary monetary policy that will increase aggregate expenditure, real GDP, and employment. Table 14.1 summarizes the factors that cause the AD curve to shift.

We have seen that the AD curve builds on the IS and MP curves and that anything that shifts the IS curve shifts the AD curve in the same direction. We have also seen that changes in the reaction function will shift the AD curve. We can conclude that the aggregate demand curve incorporates the factors underlying the IS and MP curves in a single curve.

---

[1]Changes in the responsiveness of the central bank to deviations from the inflation target shift the AD curve and also change its slope. For simplicity, we focus on the shifts of the AD curve.

Table 14.1 Factors That Shift the Aggregate Demand Curve

An increase in ...	will ...	so the *AD* curve shifts ...
aggregate expenditure that is independent of the real interest rate	increase real GDP and the output gap at every inflation rate	
the target inflation rate	increase the inflation rate at every level of the output gap	
the central bank's concern about deviations of inflation from the target inflation rate	decrease the inflation rate at every level of the output gap	

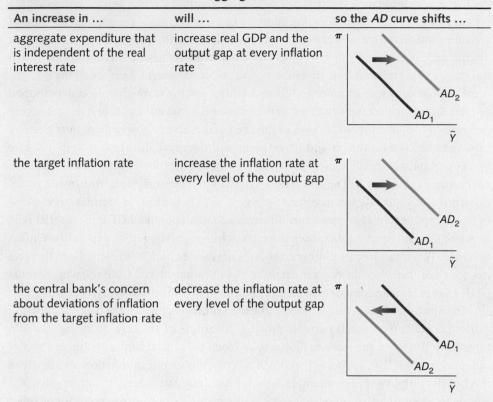

When Are Shifts to the Aggregate Demand Curve Permanent?

In Figure 14.3 on page 509, we used the example of an increase in government purchases to demonstrate a shift to the right of the *AD* curve. This shift is not permanent, and the *AD* curve will eventually shift to the left, from AD_2 to AD_1. Why? We know that in long-run equilibrium, aggregate expenditure, real GDP, and potential GDP are all equal. Therefore, aggregate expenditure cannot exceed potential GDP in long-run equilibrium. If point *A* in Figure 14.3 is the long-run equilibrium, then aggregate expenditure equals potential GDP at point *A*, and aggregate expenditure is 100% of potential GDP. Suppose that government purchases are initially 20% of potential GDP, so consumption, investment, and net exports are 80% (= 100% − 20%) of potential GDP. If government purchases increase from 20% to 25% of potential GDP, and all other expenditures are initially constant, then aggregate expenditure is now 105% (= 25% + 80%) of potential GDP. Both the *IS* curve and the *AD* curve shift to the right, and real GDP increases, but this higher real GDP is not a long-run equilibrium because aggregate expenditure cannot remain 105% of potential GDP indefinitely.

There are two ways in which real GDP can return to potential GDP. First, if the increase in government purchases is temporary, government purchases decline back to 20% of potential GDP. The temporary surge in government purchases during wars is an example of a temporary shift in the *AD* curve. In such cases, aggregate expenditure declines to 100% of potential GDP when government purchases decrease. Second, if the increase in government purchases to 25% of potential GDP is permanent, as with a permanent increase in spending on education or highways and bridges, then the sum of consumption, investment, and net exports must decrease to 75% of potential GDP. Our discussion of the loanable funds model (see Chapter 4) suggests a mechanism by which this decrease in consumption, investment, and net exports can take place. If the government permanently spends more and finances this spending through budget deficits, real interest rates will increase, which will cause investment, consumption, and net exports to decrease. If the government chooses to finance the increase in government purchases by raising taxes, consumption and investment will decrease. Either way, expenditure by the private sector will decrease in the long run to offset the effect of the increase in government purchases. We reach the same conclusion if consumption, investment, or net exports initially increase to cause the *AD* curve to shift to the right. A permanent increase in one component of aggregate expenditure as a share of potential GDP means that one, or some combination, of the other three components of aggregate expenditure must decrease. When this decrease occurs, the *AD* curve shifts back to the left. Therefore, we can conclude that when the economy starts at equilibrium with real GDP equal to potential GDP, changes in autonomous expenditure cause temporary shifts to the *AD* curve.

In contrast to changes in autonomous expenditure, changes in the reaction function cause the *AD* curve to shift permanently. Our example of an increase in the inflation target from 2% to 3% provides an illustration. When the central bank announces a higher inflation target, it is announcing that it will accept a higher rate of inflation for any given level of the output gap. For example, when the output gap is zero, the central bank is willing to accept an inflation rate of 3% rather than 2%. This result also holds for all other values of the output gap, so the shift in the *AD* curve is permanent.

When we discuss the complete aggregate demand and aggregate supply model in Section 14.3, it will be important to keep these two results in mind: *Shifts in the* IS *curve temporarily shift the* AD *curve, but changes to the reaction function permanently shift the* AD *curve.* Knowing the difference between permanent and temporary shifts in the *AD* curve helps in understanding how the economy adjusts toward long-run equilibrium. It is also important to note that while the *AD* curve may shift permanently, in the long run, real GDP will always return to its potential level. We will explore why in the next section.

Aggregate Supply and the Phillips Curve

14.2

Learning Objective

Explain the relationship between aggregate supply and the Phillips curve.

Aggregate supply (*AS*) curve A curve that shows the total quantity of output, or real GDP, that firms are willing and able to supply at a given inflation rate.

We now consider the **aggregate supply (*AS*) curve**, which shows the total quantity of output, or real GDP, that firms are willing and able to supply at a given inflation rate. This definition of the *AS* curve is similar to the definition of the Phillips curve because, in fact, the two curves are the same.[2] As we saw when we first discussed the Phillips curve (see Chapter 11), there are three sources of inflationary pressure in the short run: changes in the expected inflation rate, demand shocks, and supply shocks.

---

[2]Why two names for the same curve? The traditional name for a curve that relates the inflation rate to the output gap (or to the unemployment rate) is the Phillips curve, which was first derived in the 1950s by the New Zealand economist A. W. H. Phillips. We could have continued to use that name in this chapter, but in the context of a model that includes aggregate demand, it is less confusing to call the curve an aggregate supply curve.

The expected inflation rate is important because firms set their prices based on the prices they expect their competitors to charge and the prices they expect to pay their suppliers and employees. If firms expect inflation to increase, they will increase the prices they charge. In this section, we assume that expectations are adaptive in the sense that households and firms expect that the inflation rate from the previous period will persist into the future. For example, if the inflation rate in 2013 is 2%, the expected inflation rate for 2014 will also be 2%. But if the inflation rate rises to 4% in 2014, the expected inflation rate for 2015 will also rise to 4%.

Inflation can occur as a result of a supply shock when, for instance, the price of a key input, such as oil, unexpectedly rises, and firms pass along some of the price increase to the consumers of final goods and services. An increase in the inflation rate as a result of a supply shock tends to be temporary. For example, a 10% increase in oil prices will increase the inflation rate for a time. But once the economy adjusts to the higher price of oil, the inflation rate will return to its previous level unless oil prices increase again.

Inflation can increase following a demand shock that causes real GDP to increase relative to potential GDP because firms experience capacity constraints as raw materials and labor become harder to find at existing prices. For this reason, we would expect a positive relationship between the inflation rate and the output gap. So, just as we draw the Phillips curve as an upward-sloping line, we also draw the aggregate supply curve as an upward-sloping line.

Figure 14.4 shows the aggregate supply curve for an economy. Short-run equilibrium is initially at point A, with the inflation rate, π_1, equal to the expected inflation rate, π^e, and real GDP equal to potential GDP. If short-run equilibrium moves from point A to point B, real GDP increases relative to potential GDP, so the output gap changes from $\widetilde{Y}_1$ to $\widetilde{Y}_2$, and the inflation rate rises from π_1 to π_2. Notice that a change in the output gap causes a *movement along* an aggregate supply curve from point A to point B.

Because the aggregate supply curve is the same as the Phillips curve, we can use the equation for the Phillips curve to represent the aggregate supply curve:

$$\pi_t = \pi^e_t + b\,\widetilde{Y}_t - s_t,$$

where:

π_t = current inflation rate
π^e_t = expected inflation rate
$\widetilde{Y}_t$ = output gap
b = sensitivity of the inflation rate to changes in the output gap
s_t = effect of supply shocks

A negative sign appears in front of the supply shock term because an increase in oil prices or other negative supply shock increases the inflation rate, and a positive supply shock, such as an increase in productivity, decreases the inflation rate. We have assumed adaptive expectations, so the expected inflation rate in the current year equals the actual inflation rate in the previous year:

$$\pi^e_t = \pi_{t-1}.$$

We have also assumed that b is positive because the inflation rate increases as real GDP and the output gap increase.

Figure 14.4

The Aggregate Supply Curve

The aggregate supply curve is drawn assuming that the expected inflation rate is constant. As aggregate expenditure increases and the output gap changes from $\widetilde{Y}_1$ to $\widetilde{Y}_2$, real GDP pushes up against the capacity constraints of firms. In response, some firms increase prices, the inflation rate increases from π_1 to π_2, and short-run equilibrium moves from point A to point B on the AS curve.

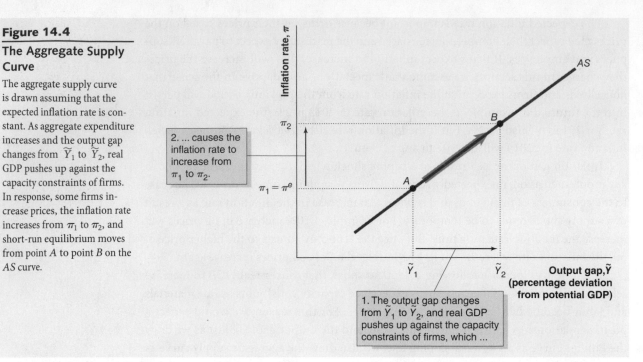

2. ... causes the inflation rate to increase from π_1 to π_2.

1. The output gap changes from $\widetilde{Y}_1$ to $\widetilde{Y}_2$, and real GDP pushes up against the capacity constraints of firms, which ...

Shifts in the Aggregate Supply Curve

When we drew the aggregate supply curve in Figure 14.4, we held supply shocks and expected inflation constant. If either of these factors changes, the aggregate supply curve will shift. The experience of the U.S. economy during the 1981–1982 recession provides an example of a shift in the aggregate supply curve. The unemployment rate during the recession of 1981–1982 rose to 10.8%, which is the highest it has been since the Great Depression. There was one positive result from the recession, however: The inflation rate fell dramatically. The inflation rate, calculated using the consumer price index, fell from 10.8% at the beginning of the 1981–1982 recession to 3.8% by its end. Figure 14.5 illustrates how the severe 1981–1982 recession helped usher in a period of low and

Figure 14.5

A Decrease in Inflationary Expectations and the Aggregate Supply Curve

The expected inflation rate decreases from π_1^e to π_2^e. So, when real GDP equals potential GDP, $\widetilde{Y}_1 = 0$, and the value of supply shocks is zero, the inflation rate will decrease from π_1 to π_2. Inflation is now lower for any given level of real GDP, and the AS curve shifts down, from AS_1 to AS_2.

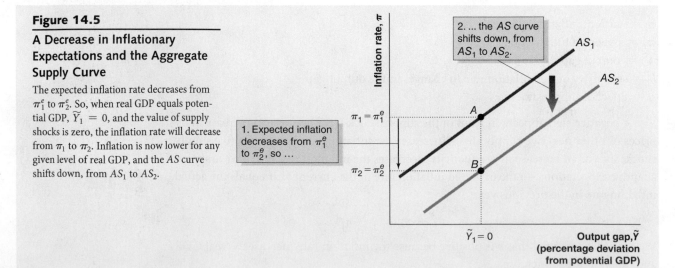

2. ... the AS curve shifts down, from AS_1 to AS_2.

1. Expected inflation decreases from π_1^e to π_2^e, so ...

Table 14.2 Factors That Shift the Aggregate Supply Curve

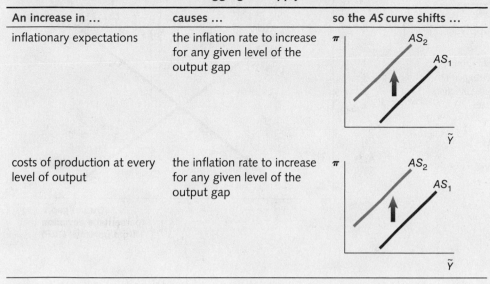

An increase in ...	causes ...	so the *AS* curve shifts ...
inflationary expectations	the inflation rate to increase for any given level of the output gap	
costs of production at every level of output	the inflation rate to increase for any given level of the output gap	

stable inflation by reducing the expected inflation rate. The figure shows the effect of a decrease in expected inflation on the aggregate supply curve.

For simplicity, in Figure 14.5 we assume that the effect of supply shocks is zero. Short-run equilibrium is initially at point *A* on AS_1. Real GDP equals potential GDP, so the output gap is zero, and inflation, π_1, equals expected inflation, π_1^e. Expected inflation decreases to π_2^e, so when real GDP equals potential GDP, $\widetilde{Y}_1 = 0$, inflation equals π_2. Short-run equilibrium is at point *B*, which is not on the original *AS* curve. Therefore, the *AS* curve has shifted down, from AS_1 to AS_2. Notice that on AS_2, inflation is now lower for any given level of the output gap, so the economy faces a more favorable trade-off between changes in inflation and changes in the output gap. A positive supply shock caused by a decrease in oil prices or an increase in productivity growth would have the same effect on the aggregate supply curve. Table 14.2 summarizes the factors that cause the aggregate supply curve to shift.

The Aggregate Demand and Aggregate Supply Model

The **aggregate demand and aggregate supply (*AD–AS*) model** explains short-run fluctuations in the output gap and in the inflation rate. To explore the model, we first discuss how long-run equilibrium is determined and then analyze what factors cause the equilibrium to change.

Equilibrium in the *AD–AS* Model

The long-run equilibrium in the *AD–AS* model is characterized by two conditions—one for real GDP and one for the inflation rate. The economy is in long-run equilibrium when:

1. Real GDP equals potential GDP: $\widetilde{Y} = 0$, and
2. The inflation rate equals both the central bank's target inflation rate and the expected inflation rate: $\pi = \pi^e = \pi_{\text{Target}}$.

14.3

Learning Objective
Use the aggregate demand and aggregate supply model to analyze macroeconomic conditions.

Aggregate demand and aggregate supply (*AD–AS*) model A model that explains short-run fluctuations in the output gap and the inflation rate.

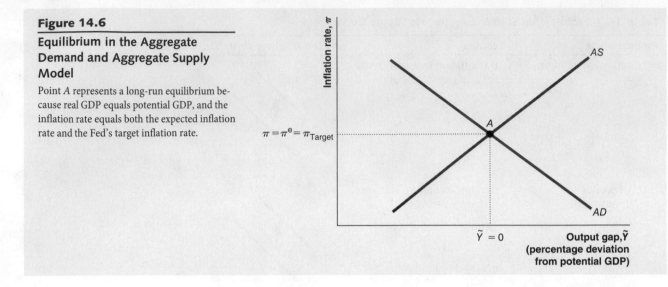

Figure 14.6

Equilibrium in the Aggregate Demand and Aggregate Supply Model

Point A represents a long-run equilibrium because real GDP equals potential GDP, and the inflation rate equals both the expected inflation rate and the Fed's target inflation rate.

In Figure 14.6 long-run equilibrium in the AD–AS model occurs at point A, where the aggregate demand and aggregate supply curves intersect. Point A is a long-run equilibrium because real GDP equals potential GDP, so the output gap is zero, and the inflation rate equals both the expected inflation rate and the Fed's target inflation rate.

We are most interested in using the AD–AS model to explain how the output gap and the inflation rate respond to shocks such as an increase in oil prices, a change in the central bank reaction function, or a collapse in stock prices. To accomplish this goal, we discuss how the economy responds to shifts in the aggregate supply curve and the aggregate demand curve.

The Effects of a Supply Shock

In 1983, James Hamilton of the University of California, San Diego, showed that seven of the eight post–World War II recessions up to that time had been preceded by large and unexpected increases in the price of oil.[3] Since the publication of Hamilton's article, the U.S. economy has experienced three more recessions: 1990–1991, 2001, and 2007–2009. All three recessions were associated with large increases in the price of oil. For example, the price of oil doubled after Iraq's invasion of Kuwait in August 1990. Many economists believe that this increase in oil prices was a critical factor in causing that recession.

Stagflation A combination of high inflation and recession, usually resulting from a supply shock such as an increase in the price of oil.

Oil price increases can play an important role in causing **stagflation**, which is a period of both high inflation and recession, usually resulting from a supply shock. The classic case of stagflation is the severe 1973–1975 global recession. The world economy experienced an oil shock in late 1973, after the Organization of the Petroleum Exporting Countries (OPEC) imposed an oil embargo in response to U.S. and European support of Israel in the 1973 Arab–Israeli War. The price of a barrel of oil rose from $4.31 during December 1973 to $10.11 during January 1974—a 135% increase in just one month! Such a large increase in the price of a key input generates inflation as firms pass their

---

[3]James Hamilton, "Oil and the Macroeconomy Since World War II," *Journal of Political Economy*, Vol. 91, No. 2, April 1983, pp. 228–248.

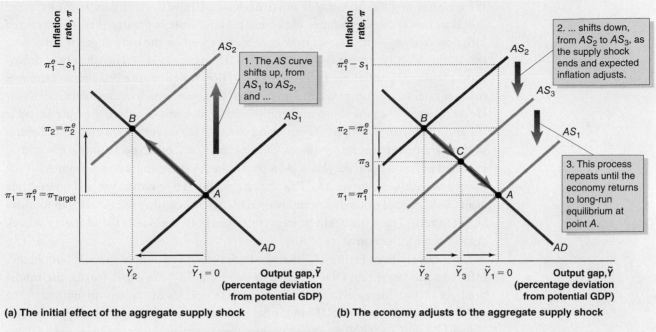

Figure 14.7 The Long-Run and Short-Run Effects of a Supply Shock

In panel (a), a supply shock causes the AS curve to shift up, from AS_1 to AS_2. Short-run equilibrium moves from point A to point B. Eventually, the expected inflation rate adjusts to the actual inflation rate.

In panel (b), the decline in the expected inflation rate causes the AS curve to shift first from AS_2 to AS_3, moving short-run equilibrium from point B to point C. As expected inflation decreases further, the AS curve shifts from AS_3 to AS_1, moving short-run equilibrium from point C back to point A. Therefore, in response to a supply shock, there is no trade-off between inflation and unemployment even in the short run.

increased costs to consumers in the form of higher prices for final goods and services. In the United States, real GDP fell from 4.5% *above* potential GDP during the second quarter of 1973 to 4.7% *below* potential GDP during the first quarter of 1975. Inflation rose from 6.6% during the second quarter of 1973 to 12.2% during the fourth quarter of 1974. In contrast to most prior recessions, inflation actually rose substantially during the 1973–1975 recession, so the U.S. economy experienced stagflation.

Figure 14.7 shows how an economy adjusts to a supply shock. For simplicity, we assume that oil prices increase during the first year and then remain constant. In panel (a), the economy starts off at long-run equilibrium at point A, where real GDP equals potential GDP, and the inflation rate, the expected inflation rate, and the target inflation rate are equal. The increase in the price of oil is a negative supply shock, so the inflation rate increases. If the output gap remained at $\widetilde{Y}_1 = 0$, the inflation rate would increase to $\pi_1^e - s_1$. However, following its reaction function, the Fed increases the real interest rate, which reduces consumption and investment. As a result of this decline in aggregate expenditure, real GDP falls and the output gap changes to $\widetilde{Y}_2$, so the inflation rate increases only to π_2 in panel (a). The AS curve shifts up, from AS_1 to AS_2, and short-run equilibrium moves from point A to point B.

Oil prices stop rising after the first year, so the supply shock is now zero, but the AS curve does not immediately shift back to AS_1 because expected inflation has increased.

We are assuming that households and firms have adaptive expectations, so the expected inflation rate increases because the actual inflation rate is greater than the expected inflation rate: $\pi_2 > \pi_1^e$. So, we now have $\pi_2 = \pi_2^e$ when the output gap is zero. As a result, the *AS* curve in panel (b) shifts down, from AS_2 to AS_3. This shift puts downward pressure on inflation. Following its reaction function, the Fed reduces the real interest rate, so consumption and investment increase, which causes real GDP to increase as well. The new short-run equilibrium is at point *C*, where the output gap is $\widetilde{Y}_3$ and the inflation rate has fallen to π_3. Point *C* is not yet a long-run equilibrium, so the adjustment process continues. Because $\pi_3 < \pi_2^e$ and expectations are adaptive, expected inflation again decreases. As a result, the *AS* curve shifts down, from AS_3 back toward the initial *AS* curve, AS_1. This shift allows the Fed to reduce the real interest rate again, so aggregate expenditure and real GDP increase causing the output gap to move closer to zero. This adjustment process continues until eventually the economy is back at long-run equilibrium at point *A*.

We can see from Figure 14.7 that the initial effect of a supply shock is both higher inflation and lower real GDP relative to potential GDP. In other words, the model predicts that an increase in oil prices can cause periods of stagflation similar to the 1973–1975 recession. The *AD–AS* model also makes another important point: With higher inflation, real GDP decreases, so the unemployment rate increases as the inflation rate increases. Therefore, there is no trade-off between inflation and unemployment—even in the short run—in response to a supply shock.

Permanent Demand Shocks: Changes in the Central Bank Reaction Function

We have seen that the Fed may have difficulty carrying out an expansionary monetary policy when the short-term nominal interest rate reaches zero. The inability of the Fed to lower interest rates to negative values is called the *zero bound constraint*. In that case, other channels of monetary policy may still operate, such as quantitative easing and credit channels. Changing the target inflation rate provides another possible channel through which the central bank can affect real GDP and employment when facing a zero bound constraint. In their discussion of monetary policy in Japan during the 1990s, some economists suggested that the Bank of Japan should increase expected inflation by increasing the target inflation rate. We can use the *AD–AS* model to explain how changing the target inflation rate can provide the central bank with another way to affect the economy when facing a zero bound constraint.

Nominal interest rates cannot fall below zero, but real interest rates can. Recall that the expression for the expected real interest rate is $r = i - \pi^e$. So, the real interest rate can become negative if the expected inflation rate is greater than the nominal interest rate. For example, suppose that the nominal interest rate is 0%, and expected inflation and target inflation equal 2%. In this case, the expected real interest rate is −2% (= 0% − 2%). If the Fed announces that it has increased the target inflation rate to 5% and households and firms believe the Fed will meet its target, the expected real interest rate will decrease to −5% (= 0% − 5%). Therefore, the announcement of a higher inflation target decreases the expected real interest rate. The lower real interest rate will increase consumption, investment, and net exports, resulting in an increase in real GDP and employment.

Macro Data: Are Oil Supply Shocks Really That Important?

Research by Lutz Kilian of the University of Michigan challenges the view that the OPEC oil embargo and other cost shocks caused the stagflation of the 1970s. Kilian believes that once you measure oil supply shocks correctly, they account for very little of the quarter-to-quarter fluctuation in nominal oil prices. Kilian points out that the prices of many industrial commodities were rising during the early 1970s due to increases in worldwide demand driven by increases in global real GDP prior to the oil embargo. So, Kilian argues that most of the nominal oil price increase during the period was due to *demand* factors rather than supply factors.

Kilian's research also shows that a 10% reduction in oil supply has little effect on either the growth rate of U.S. real GDP or the inflation rate, calculated using the CPI. For example, an oil supply shock increases CPI inflation by only about 1 percentage point six to nine months after the shock. The effect that Kilian estimated is much smaller than macroeconomists had previously believed, and is too small to have caused the stagflation of the 1970s.

Kilian and Robert Barsky of the University of Michigan argue that "stop-and-go" monetary policy rather than oil price increases caused the stagflation of the 1970s. According to their view, in 1972, the Fed stimulated the economy, thereby causing both real GDP and the inflation rate to increase. When the Fed became concerned about the rising inflation rate, it increased interest rates in 1973 and inadvertently caused a recession. They argue that inflation adjusts slowly to monetary policy, so the inflation rate continued to increase even as the economy entered a recession. The result was that the economy experienced stagflation. In effect, Kilian and Barsky argue that the Fed followed a discretionary monetary policy rather than a rules-based monetary policy. We discuss the differences between these two approaches to monetary policy further later in the chapter.

Athanasios Orphanides, an economist and the current governor of the Central Bank of Cyprus, argues that poor policy decisions due to measurement problems caused the inflation rate to increase. Policymakers receive economic data with a lag, and the initial estimates for key variables such as inflation and the output gap are often incorrect. Orphanides looked at the data available to policymakers *at the time they made their decisions* and found that they underestimated how much inflation was increasing and overestimated the level of potential GDP, which caused them to believe that real GDP was further from potential GDP than it actually was. As a result, monetary policy turned out to be more expansionary than it would have been had the Fed had more accurate data. We discuss the possibility that monetary policy caused the poor economic performance during the 1970s in greater detail in the next section.

While most economists continue to believe that an oil price shock was the main reason for the stagflation of the mid-1970s, the effect of oil price shocks on the economy remains an active area of macroeconomic research.

Sources: Lutz Kilian, "Exogenous Oil Supply Shocks: How Big Are They and How Much Do They Matter for the U.S. Economy?" *Review of Economics and Statistics*, Vol. 90, No. 2, May 2008, pp. 216–240; Lutz Kilian and Robert Barsky, "Do We Really Know That Oil Caused the Great Stagflation? A Monetary Alternative," in Ben Bernanke and Kenneth Rogoff, eds., *NBER Macroeconomics Annual*, Cambridge, MA: MIT Press, 2001, pp. 137–183; and Athanasios Orphanides, "The Quest for Prosperity Without Inflation," *Journal of Monetary Economics*, Vol. 50, No. 3, April 2003, pp. 633–663.

See related problem 3.8 at the end of the chapter.

Figure 14.8 shows how we can use the *AD–AS* model to explain the effect of a change in the monetary policy rule. Initially, long-run equilibrium is at point *A*, with real GDP equal to potential GDP and with the actual inflation rate, the expected inflation rate, and the initial target inflation rate all equal. Now suppose that the Fed increases the target inflation rate from π_{Target} to π'_{Target}. To hit the new higher target inflation rate, the Fed will have to decrease the real interest rate. The lower real interest rate causes consumption, investment, and net exports to rise, so the *AD* curve shifts to the right, from AD_1 to AD_2, and real GDP increases, causing the output gap to move to $\widetilde{Y}_2$. Short-run equilibrium is now at point *B*. Note that at point *B*, with a higher level of real GDP, the

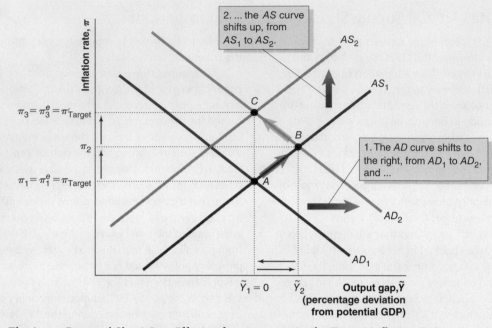

Figure 14.8 The Long-Run and Short-Run Effects of an Increase in the Target Inflation Rate

From an initial long-run equilibrium at point A, the Fed decides to increase the target inflation rate by lowering the real interest rate, which shifts the AD curve to the right, from AD_1 to AD_2. As a result, the economy moves to a new short-run equilibrium at point B. Eventually, the expected inflation rate increases, which causes the AS curve to shift up,

from AS_1 to AS_2. The economy returns to long-run equilibrium at point C, with real GDP equal to potential GDP. At point C, the inflation rate equals the new higher target inflation rate. The result is a higher inflation rate and no change in the unemployment rate.

unemployment rate will be lower than it was at point A. Point B is not a long-run equilibrium, however, because real GDP is above potential GDP and the actual inflation rate, π_2, is greater than the expected inflation rate, π_1^e. Because expectations are adaptive, the expected inflation rate will increase, and the AS curve will shift up, from AS_1 to AS_2. As the AS curve shifts up, the output gap moves back to zero, and the inflation rate increases to the new target inflation rate, π'_{Target}. The new long-run equilibrium is at point C, where the output gap is zero and the inflation rate equals both the expected inflation rate and the target inflation rate.

Figure 14.8 shows that a central bank can temporarily increase real GDP and decrease the unemployment rate by announcing a higher inflation target. The model makes another important point: In the short run, the central bank can achieve a higher level of real GDP and a lower unemployment rate by tolerating a higher inflation rate. However, once the expected inflation rate adjusts, real GDP will return to potential GDP, and the unemployment rate will increase back to its initial level. *As a result, there is no trade-off between the inflation rate and the unemployment rate in the long run. In fact, even to achieve a temporarily higher level of real GDP and a lower unemployment rate, a central bank has to accept a permanently higher inflation rate.*

Many central banks have either a formal or informal inflation target of about 2% because the costs of inflation are thought to be relatively small when the inflation rate is low and stable. However, Japan's experience of slow growth and low inflation since the 1990s and the slow growth in many countries during and after the 2007–2009 recession led some economists to advocate an increase in the target inflation rate above 2%. We have already seen that a higher inflation target can increase real GDP and employment when the short-term nominal interest rate reaches zero.

More recently, Olivier Blanchard, Giovanni Dell'Ariccia, and Paolo Mauro, economists at the International Monetary Fund (IMF), have argued that central banks around the world should permanently increase the target inflation rate from 2% to 4%.[4] Blanchard, Dell'Ariccia, and Mauro believe that the costs of inflation are still low when the inflation rate is 4%, but with a higher expected inflation rate, central banks can cut interest rates more before the interest rate reaches zero and the central banks are forced to resort to nontraditional monetary policy tools such as quantitative easing. Most central bankers disagree with Blanchard, Dell'Ariccia, and Mauro's argument for permanently higher inflation rates. For example, Fed Chairman Ben Bernanke and former European Central Bank President Jean-Claude Trichet have suggested that a higher inflation target would be counterproductive because higher inflation rates tend to be more volatile. When the volatility of the inflation rate increases, it becomes harder to predict, so it is more likely that fluctuations in the inflation rate will cause arbitrary redistributions in wealth. Central bankers may never adopt higher inflation targets, but the fact that economists raised the possibility indicates how the 2007–2009 recession has forced economists to rethink their policy advice.

Making the Connection

The End of Stagflation and the Volcker Recession

Paul Volcker was chairman of the Federal Reserve from August 1979 to August 1987. During his tenure, the United States experienced two recessions. One of these, the severe 1981–1982 recession, became known as the "Volcker Recession" because many commentators have argued that the Federal Reserve deliberately caused the recession. Volcker denies the charge. "We didn't deliberately go out to create a recession. You recognize that there are risks to things happening, but you don't deliberately do it." There is no doubt that Volcker and the Fed took strong action to bring down the actual and expected inflation rates by allowing the nominal federal funds rate to increase to 22% by the end of 1980. The Fed may have taken this unprecedented action to convince the public that it was serious about bringing down the inflation rate. Normally, the inflation rate falls during a recession, but the inflation rate rose during the 1973–1975 and 1980 recessions, remaining above 12% at the end of 1980. As a result, many people thought the Fed was not serious about keeping inflation low, so the expected inflation rate was also high.

There did not appear to be a short-run trade-off between inflation and unemployment during the 1970s. Such a trade-off, though, assumes that the aggregate supply

---

[4]Olivier Blanchard, Giovanni Dell'Ariccia, and Paolo Mauro, "Rethinking Macroeconomic Policy," *Journal of Money, Credit, and Banking,* Vol. 42, No. S1, September 2010, pp. 199–215.

curve is constant, while the aggregate demand curve shifts. Figure 14.7 on page 517 shows that if the aggregate supply curve shifts up, as it did during the 1970s due to an increase in oil prices, the inflation rate increases and real GDP decreases. The decrease in real GDP leads to an increase in unemployment. So, the apparent lack of a short-run trade-off between inflation and unemployment during the 1970s is most likely the result of negative supply shocks during that decade.

Volcker believed that increasing interest rates to fight inflation was necessary: "I . . . felt that in the long run, there wasn't any question that the economy was going to operate more efficiently; productivity would be greater; you would have less instability in the future if you could manage to stabilize prices. . . . I think the evidence is at least consistent with that view."

We can think of Volcker's determination to bring the inflation rate down as a decrease in the inflation target, which will shift the *AD* curve to the left and cause both the inflation rate and real GDP to decrease. The decrease in real GDP will cause the unemployment rate to increase, which is what happened. The inflation rate fell from 10.8% during the first month of the recession in July 1981 to 3.8% during the month after the recession ended in December 1982. In contrast, the unemployment rate rose dramatically during the same period, from 7.2% in July 1981 to 10.8% in December 1982. The inflation rate fell as the unemployment rate rose, so the short-run trade-off between inflation and unemployment had reappeared.

Because the Fed was willing to tolerate such a severe recession, many economists believe that the 1981–1982 recession provided an effective signal of the Fed's determination to bring down the inflation rate. Current Federal Reserve Chairman Ben Bernanke praised Volcker's ability to withstand the intense political pressure he faced as interest rates and the unemployment rate rose. Bernanke explained that it was common practice for pieces of wood to be sent to Volcker's office with "stop killing construction" and "save the farmer" scrawled on them. Bernanke keeps some of these on his desk "to remind me that . . . we always have to pay attention to price stability."

Sources: U.S. Bureau of Economic Analysis; U.S. Bureau of Labor Statistics; Board of Governors of the Federal Reserve System; Leonard Silk, "Volcker on the Crash," *New York Times*, November 8, 1987; "Paul Volcker Interview," *The First Measured Century*, PBS, 2000, www.pbs.org/fmc/interviews/volcker.htm; and "Bernanke Pays Homage to Predecessors," centralbanking.com, March 23, 2012.

See related problems 3.6 and 3.7 at the end of the chapter.

Temporary Demand Shocks: Changes in Aggregate Expenditure

In the mid-1990s, innovations in information and communications technology, such as development of the World Wide Web and the rapid decline in the prices of personal computers, encouraged optimism about the future profits of Internet-based firms. Investors rushed to purchase the stocks of firms such as Amazon, Yahoo, and American Online (AOL). The stocks of many technology companies trade on the NASDAQ stock market, where the average stock price soared by more than 500% between January 1995 and March 2000. This period became known as the *dot-com bubble*. Unfortunately for investors, the expected profits from many Internet firms, such as eToys and Pets.com, failed to materialize, and beginning in the spring of 2000, investors fled Internet stocks,

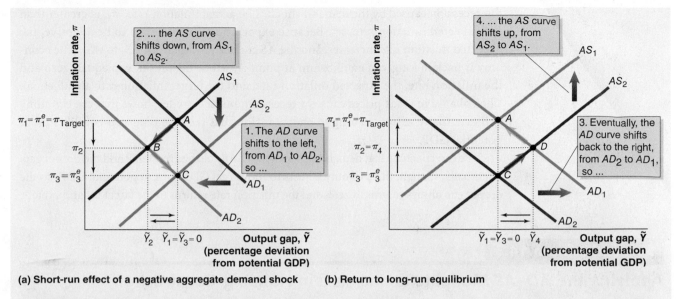

Figure 14.9 Short-Run and Long-Run Effects of a Negative Demand Shock

Panel (a) shows the effect of a negative demand shock, which temporarily shifts the AD curve to the left, from AD_1 to AD_2. As expected inflation decreases, the AS curve shifts down, from AS_1 to AS_2, and equilibrium moves from point B to point C. Eventually the AD curve shifts back to the right, from AD_2 to AD_1 in panel (b), so equilibrium moves to point D. Expected inflation adjusts, causing the AS curve to shift up, from AS_2 to AS_1. Equilibrium is now at point A, which is the long-run equilibrium. A negative demand shock causes a pattern of recession and expansion.

causing their prices to collapse. The fall in stock prices had two important effects on the economy: It reduced household wealth, which led households to reduce consumption, and it increased uncertainty about the future, which decreased firms' willingness to invest and further decreased the willingness of households to consume. The decrease in investment and the slowdown in consumption growth contributed to the recession that began in March 2001.

In Figure 14.9, we use the AD–AS model to show the effect of a negative demand shock such as a stock market crash. The initial long-run equilibrium occurs at point A, where the output gap equals zero and the inflation rate, the expected inflation rate, and the target inflation rate are all equal. The collapse in stock prices shifts the AD curve to the left, from AD_1 to AD_2. So, in panel (a), equilibrium moves from point A to point B. The economy enters a recession, with real GDP declining, as the output gap moves from $\widetilde{Y}_1$ to $\widetilde{Y}_2$. At point B, the actual inflation rate, π_2, is less than the expected inflation rate, π_1^e. Because we assume that expectations are adaptive, the expected inflation rate will decrease, and the AS curve will shift down, from AS_1 to AS_2. The decrease in the inflation rate allows the Fed to decrease the real interest rate, so consumption and investment increase, increasing real GDP. The new short-run equilibrium is at point C.

Point C is not a long-run equilibrium because the inflation rate is now less than the Fed's target inflation rate. In the long run, the AD curve will shift to the right, from AD_2 back to AD_1 as stock prices recover and uncertainty declines. Short-run equilibrium moves to point D in panel (b). Real GDP increases, moving the output gap from $\widetilde{Y}_3$ to $\widetilde{Y}_4$. In other words, the economy experiences an expansion as it recovers from the recession caused by the demand shock. The actual inflation rate, π_4, is greater than the expected inflation rate, π_3^e. Because expectations are assumed to be adaptive, the expected inflation rate increases, and the AS curve shifts up, from AS_2 to AS_1. The economy is back in long-run equilibrium at point A, where the output gap equals zero and the inflation rate, the expected inflation rate, and the target inflation rate are all equal. The collapse in stock prices causes a recession, but the model shows that the economy will eventually adjust, leading to an expansion that restores long-run equilibrium at potential GDP.

We can conclude that demand shocks *temporarily* change real GDP and the output gap. Eventually, though, the economy adjusts to move real GDP back to potential GDP, so the output gap always returns to zero, and the inflation rate returns to the target inflation rate.

Solved Problem 14.3

Applying the *AD–AS* Model to an Increase in Housing Construction

In the mid-2000s, the U.S. economy underwent a housing boom. Use the *AD–AS* model to analyze the short-run and long-run effects on real GDP and inflation of the surge in residential construction.

Solving the Problem

Step 1 **Review the chapter material.** The problem asks you to use the *AD–AS* model to determine the effect of an increase in residential construction on real GDP and inflation, so you may want to review the section "Temporary Demand Shocks: Changes in Aggregate Expenditure," which begins on page 522.

Step 2 **Draw an *AD–AS* graph that shows the initial equilibrium and discuss which curve will shift as a result of the positive demand shock.** Your graph should show the initial equilibrium as point A, where the aggregate demand and aggregate supply curves intersect:

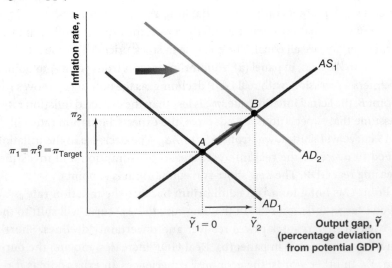

At point *A*, real GDP equals potential GDP, and the inflation rate equals the target inflation rate and the expected inflation rate. So, point *A* is a long-run equilibrium. New residential construction is one of the components of investment, so the housing boom causes aggregate expenditure to increase, and the *AD* curve shifts to the right from AD_1 to AD_2. Your graph should show the new short-run equilibrium is at point *B*.

Step 3 **Explain how the economy moves back to potential GDP.** Point *B* is not a long-run equilibrium because the output gap is greater than zero, and the inflation rate is greater than the expected inflation rate. In our earlier examples, we saw that when the actual inflation rate is greater than the expected inflation rate, the expected inflation rate will adjust, shifting the aggregate supply curve, which will return the output gap to zero. Assume expectations are adaptive. Your graph should show $\pi_2 > \pi_1^e$, so the expected inflation rate will increase, shifting up the *AS* curve from AS_1 to AS_2. Following its reaction function, the Fed increases the real interest rate as the inflation rate increases, so the output gap moves back to zero. Your graph should show that the new equilibrium is at point *C*.

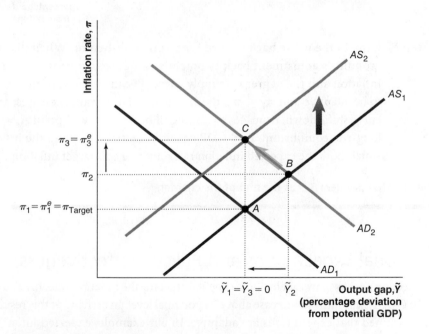

Step 4 **Explain how the aggregate demand curve shifts as the economy adjusts back to long-run equilibrium.** Even though the output gap is zero, point *C* is not a long-run equilibrium because $\pi_3 > \pi_{\text{Target}}$. At first, firms wanted to build more residential housing at every given level of the real interest rate. Eventually, the profitability of new residential housing decreases, so the demand shock ends, and the *AD* curve shifts to the left, from AD_2 to AD_1. Therefore, you should draw a new graph and show a new equilibrium at the

intersection of AD_1 and AS_2. Now the short-run equilibrium is at point D, so real GDP is less than its potential level.

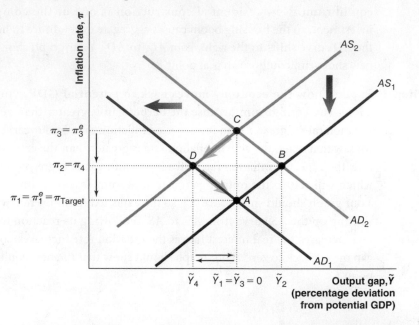

Step 5 **Explain the move back toward long-run equilibrium.** When discussing the economy's adjustment back to potential GDP, we have focused on expected inflation and the aggregate supply curve. Because expectations are assumed to be adaptive and $\pi_4 < \pi_3^e$, the expected inflation rate decreases, and the AS curve shifts down, from AS_2 to AS_1. Equilibrium is now at point A, which is the long-run equilibrium: Real GDP equals potential GDP, and the inflation rate equals both the expected inflation rate and the Fed's target inflation rate.

See related problem 3.9 at the end of the chapter.

14.4

Learning Objective

Discuss the implications of rational expectations for macroeconomic policymaking.

Rational Expectations and Policy Ineffectiveness

In Section 14.3, we saw that by increasing its target for the inflation rate, the Fed can cause real GDP temporarily to increase above its potential level. In arriving at this result, though, we assumed that expectations are adaptive. In our example, expected inflation always lagged behind actual inflation, and expectations only caught up with actual inflation when real GDP equaled potential GDP. But is the assumption of adaptive expectations correct? When inflation is increasing, firms and households will continually predict an inflation rate that is too low if they rely on adaptive expectations.

Consider a simple example to show the costs a firm may incur from using adaptive expectations. Suppose that the Fed has a target inflation rate of 2%, the Fed always hits its target for inflation, and inflation has been 2% for several years. Furthermore, assume that Apple Inc. sets the price of a basic model for the iPad at $500 and wants to keep the real price of the iPad constant in order to maximize profits. That is, the firm wants to increase the price of its product at the same rate as the inflation rate. In 2013, the nominal and real prices of the iPad equal $500, and inflation in 2013 is 2%—so the firm expects that inflation will be 2% in 2014.

Based on expected inflation of 2%, Apple should set the price in 2014 at $510. Now suppose that the Fed announces on January 1, 2014, that it will decrease its target for inflation to 0%. If the Fed successfully reduces the inflation rate to 0%, Apple's actual profit-maximizing price turns out to be $500. If Apple has adaptive expectations, it will set its price too high—at $510—and it will lose customers to its competitors. Apple would make a costly pricing mistake by ignoring the Fed's announcement that it intended to reduce the target inflation rate.

It makes sense that households and firms will use all information available to them in order to avoid making inaccurate predictions of inflation. **Rational expectations** is the assumption that people make forecasts of future values of a variable using all available information. In our previous example, if Apple has rational expectations, it would take into account the Fed's announcement of a new lower target for the inflation rate and following the Fed's announcement, Apple would set the price of the iPad at $500. Rational expectations are consistent with profit maximization, while adaptive expectations may not be. As a result, many economists believe that rational expectations may better describe the way households and firms form expectations than do adaptive expectations.

Rational expectations
The assumption that people make forecasts of future values of a variable using all available information; formally, the assumption that expectations equal optimal forecasts, using all available information.

The rational expectations assumption is closely associated with new classical theories of the business cycle (see Chapter 9). As we discuss next, the assumption of rational expectations led many new classical economists to a surprising conclusion about the effectiveness of monetary policy.

Rational Expectations and Anticipated Policy Changes

Suppose that the Fed announces that it will permanently increase its target inflation rate and that households and firms believe the announcement. That is, there is strong **central bank credibility**, which is the degree to which households and firms believe the central bank's announcements about future policy. Because the policy is announced and credible, we can say that the change represents an *anticipated policy* change. With adaptive expectations, expectations of inflation adjust slowly because the actual inflation rate has to change before the expected inflation rate changes. But with rational expectations, expectations of inflation adjust immediately.

Central bank credibility
The degree to which households and firms believe the central bank's announcements about future policy.

Refer to Figure 14.8 on page 520 to see why this difference is important when discussing monetary policy. Assuming rational expectations, the increase in the inflation target still shifts the AD curve to the right. But because rational individuals take into account all available information, the expected inflation rate increases the moment the central bank announces a higher inflation target. The aggregate supply curve *immediately* shifts from AS_1 to AS_2, and equilibrium immediately moves from point A to point C. As a result, the inflation rate immediately increases from π_1 to π_3. In contrast to the result when expectations are adaptive, there is no movement to point B. That is, the economy never experiences a temporary expansion. Therefore, a central bank cannot achieve a temporary increase in real GDP, even if it is willing to tolerate permanently higher inflation. *We can conclude that there is no trade-off between inflation and unemployment, even in the short run, when expectations are rational and policy changes are anticipated.*

This surprising result is called the *policy ineffectiveness proposition* and was developed by Robert Lucas of the University of Chicago, Thomas Sargent of New York University, and Neil Wallace of Pennsylvania State University.[5] According to this proposition, households and firms use all available information, including information about monetary policy rules, to form expectations of the inflation rate. When expected inflation increases, households and firms immediately adjust nominal prices. For example, if the Fed announces a 4% inflation target, Apple will increase the nominal price of the iPad by 4%, to $520. As a result, the real price of the iPad will remain unchanged, so monetary policy has no effect on the real price of the iPad. Therefore, the Fed's announced change in the inflation target will not have any effect on the quantity of iPads sold. What is true of Apple's iPad is also true of all other goods and services, so an announced change in the inflation target will not affect real GDP, *assuming that there is no cost to adjusting wages and prices.*

The policy ineffectiveness proposition led many new classical economists to conclude that because households and firms take into account changes in central bank policy when forming their expectations of inflation, announced and credible monetary policy do not affect real GDP and employment.

Rational Expectations and Unanticipated Policy Changes

Rational expectations do not imply that all changes in monetary policy are ineffective. For the policy ineffectiveness result to hold, policy changes must be anticipated and credible. If a policy change is a surprise or if households and firms do not believe that the Fed will actually follow through and change the policy, they will not respond to the announcement of the policy change. In these cases, the aggregate supply curve in Figure 14.8 on page 520 will not shift immediately, the short-run equilibrium will move to point *B*, and the economy will experience an expansion. If the policy change is unannounced or not credible, then the change in the policy has the same result on the economy as it does when we assume that households and firms have adaptive expectations.

Rational Expectations and Demand Shocks

If expectations are rational, then any anticipated demand shock should affect only the inflation rate. However, to the extent that households and firms do not anticipate the shock or understand how the shock will affect the economy, demand shocks can still affect real GDP. For example, if the decrease in stock prices we discussed in Figure 14.9 on page 523 had been expected, firms would have expected a lower inflation rate and changed their pricing decisions accordingly. The aggregate supply curve would have immediately adjusted, real GDP would never have decreased, the output gap would have remained zero, and the unemployment rate would never have increased. If households and firms have rational expectations, there is no trade-off between inflation and unemployment in either the short run or the long run when events such as a change in

---

[5]Robert Lucas, "Some International Evidence on Real GDP-Inflation Tradeoffs," *American Economic Review*, Vol. 63, No. 3, June 1973, pp. 326–324; and Thomas Sargent and Neil Wallace, "Rational Expectations and the Theory of Economic Policy," *Journal of Monetary Economics*, Vol. 2, No. 2, April 1976, pp. 169–183.

policy or a decrease in asset prices are anticipated. If a demand shock is unanticipated, however, then there is a trade-off between inflation and unemployment in the short run, although not in the long run.

Are Anticipated and Credible Policy Changes Actually Ineffective?

The assumption of rational expectations is compelling to many economists because it is consistent with the view that households and firms act systematically to achieve goals— maximizing utility in the case of households, and maximizing profit in the case of firms. But not all economists accept rational expectations or the policy ineffectiveness proposition. Some economists argue that even if expectations are rational, changes in policy can affect real GDP even if the changes are both anticipated and credible. For the policy ineffectiveness proposition to hold, firms must change prices in response to a change in expected inflation. But we know that it can be costly for firms to change prices. If the cost of changing prices is high enough, Apple, for instance, may not adjust the price of its iPads even when its expectations of the inflation rate change. In this case, real GDP and employment may increase even when households and firms have rational expectations.

Some economists also question whether the assumption of rational expectations is realistic. Rational expectations imply that households and firms know the actual model of how the economy operates, that they have all the relevant information, and that they know how to use that information to make predictions about inflation and other economic variables. Critics of the rational expectations assumption argue that households and firms typically lack the technical sophistication and time to completely analyze all relevant information. Given these constraints, households and firms may disregard information and make decisions according to simple rules of thumb that require less time and effort. For instance, firms may use adaptive expectations and expect the following year's inflation rate to be the same as the current year's inflation rate. Moreover, as we saw when discussing the limitations of monetary and fiscal policy, there is a great deal of uncertainty over the values for key economic parameters, such as the marginal propensity to consume or the multiplier, so it is unlikely that households and firms are using a macroeconomic model capable of yielding optimal forecasts.

The evidence on whether anticipated changes in monetary policy can affect real GDP is mixed. Thomas Sargent of New York University argued that the hyperinflation in Germany at the end of World War I ended when the government announced a credible commitment to a lower inflation rate. If expectations of inflation were adaptive, then ending the hyperinflation would have required a severe recession. Germany did not experience a severe recession as the hyperinflation ended, which Sargent interprets as evidence in favor of the rational expectations assumption.

Sargent's research provides some evidence in favor of the policy ineffectiveness proposition. Other studies, however, find that anticipated monetary policy does affect real GDP.[6] As a result, many economists take the view that anticipated changes in

---

[6]Two classic studies that find that anticipated changes in policy can affect output are Frederic S. Mishkin, "Does Anticipated Monetary Policy Matter? An Econometric Investigation," *Journal of Political Economy*, Vol. 90, No. 1, February 1982, pp. 22–51; and Robert J. Gordon, "Price Inertia and Policy Effectiveness in the United States, 1890–1980," *Journal of Political Economy*, Vol. 90, No. 6, December 1982, pp. 1087–1117.

monetary policy do affect real GDP, although by less than do unanticipated changes in policy. These economists argue that households and firms take actions to offset the effects of changes in monetary policy, but because they are not able to calculate exactly what the effects of the changes will be on monetary policy and because it is costly to change prices, real GDP and employment respond to changes in policy. Clearly, in conducting monetary policy, the Fed assumes that changes in policy affect real GDP and employment. Partly in response to the research of Lucas, Sargent, and others, the Fed goes to great lengths to ensure that households and firms view its policies as credible.

Economists continue to research how households and firms form their expectations of inflation and the extent to which the assumption of rational expectations matches actual behavior.

14.5

Learning Objective

Discuss the pros and cons of the central bank's operating under policy rules rather than using discretionary policy.

Monetary Policy: Rules Versus Discretion

Central banks are responsible for keeping inflation low and stable, but they are not always successful. The annual inflation rate in the United States measured by the CPI rose steadily from the early 1960s through 1980. To reduce inflation, the Federal Reserve allowed the federal funds rate to rise to over 20% in mid-1981, which helped cause the severe recession of 1981–1982. Our discussion of rational expectations and the evidence cited by Thomas Sargent and other economists suggests that reducing inflation rates does not have to be so costly.

Reducing inflation was costly during the 1970s in part because the Fed pursued a *discretionary policy*, which means that it conducted monetary policy in whatever way it believed would achieve its goals of price stability and high employment. As the Fed switched its focus during those years back and forth from containing inflation to stimulating real GDP and employment, the federal funds rate fluctuated widely, as did the unemployment and inflation rates. By the time Paul Volcker became Fed chair in 1979, the Fed had lost credibility because it had allowed the inflation rate to rise. An alternative to using discretionary policy is a **monetary rule**, which is a commitment by the central bank to follow specific and publicly announced guidelines for monetary policy.

Monetary rule A commitment by the central bank to follow specific and publicly announced guidelines for monetary policy.

The Taylor Rule

Monetary policy rules can take many forms. Some rules place severe restrictions on the central bank's ability to conduct monetary policy, while other rules are more guidelines for good policy than they are formal rules. Nobel Laureate Milton Friedman proposed that the central bank follow a policy rule such that the nominal money supply would grow at a constant rate, regardless of economic conditions.[7] Friedman's proposal, which was based on his belief in the importance of the quantity theory of money as a guide to policy, was a central idea in *monetarism*. Friedman and other monetarists argued that because the effects of monetary policy were powerful, but the lags with which it affected the economy were "long and variable," the Fed would be likely to destabilize the economy if it did not follow a *money growth rule*. If in the quantity equation, velocity was stable, setting the growth rate of the money supply equal to the long-run growth rate of real GDP would result in a stable price level. Although a significant minority of economists found the monetarist arguments

[7]Milton Friedman, *A Program for Monetary Stability*, New York: Fordham University Press, 1960.

persuasive in the 1960s and 1970s, support waned when financial innovation beginning in 1980 caused M1 and M2 velocity to move erratically (see Chapter 7).

Currency boards are monetary policy rules where the central bank maintains a specific value for the exchange rate of the domestic currency against another country's currency or a broad basket of currencies from various countries. The gold standard is a special type of currency board where the central bank commits to maintaining a specific price of gold. The gold standard was widely adopted during the nineteenth and early twentieth centuries. Hong Kong, Bulgaria, and Lithuania all operate currency boards, and Argentina operated a currency board from 1991 to 2002. The policy rules discussed to this point strictly limit the central bank's ability to pursue other policy goals because the central bank is mandated by law to take specific actions. Not all policy rules are this restrictive.

The Fed does not follow an official policy rule. Actual Fed deliberations are complex and incorporate many factors about the economy. John Taylor of Stanford University has summarized these factors in the **Taylor rule** for federal funds rate targeting.[8] The general equation representing the Taylor rule is:

$$i_{\text{Target}} = r^{*} + \pi_t + g(\pi_t - \pi_{\text{Target}}) + h\,\widetilde{Y}_t,$$

where:

i_{Target} = target for the nominal federal funds rate
r^{*} = long-run equilibrium real federal funds rate
π_t = current inflation rate
π_{Target} = target inflation rate
g = how much the nominal target federal funds rate responds to a deviation of inflation from its target
h = how much the nominal target federal funds rate responds to the output gap

Taylor rule A monetary policy guideline developed by economist John Taylor for determining the target for the federal funds rate.

Notice that the Taylor rule differs from our earlier central bank reaction function because the Taylor rule explicitly takes into account how the Fed responds to both the inflation rate and the output gap. As a result, the Taylor rule is consistent with the Fed's *dual mandate* of price stability and maximum sustainable employment.

The Fed has announced that it has a target inflation rate of 2%, and many economists believe that the equilibrium real federal funds rate is also 2%. Taylor found that assuming these values the rule does a good job of predicting the Fed's behavior when $g = 0.5$ and $h = 0.5$. In other words, the Taylor rule does a good job when it assumes that the Fed weights inflation and the output gap as equally important. Figure 14.10 shows the actual federal funds rate and the level of the federal funds rate that would have occurred if the Fed had strictly followed the Taylor rule. Because the two lines are close together during most years, the Taylor rule does a reasonable job of explaining Federal Reserve policy.

There are, however, some periods when the lines diverge significantly. During the late 1960s and early to mid-1970s, the federal funds rate predicted from the Taylor rule was consistently above the actual federal funds rate. This gap is consistent with the view of most economists that in the face of a worsening inflation rate during those years, the Fed should have raised the target for the federal funds rate more than it did. Figure 14.10

---

[8]Taylor's original discussion of the rule appeared in John Taylor, "Discretion Versus Policy Rules in Practice," *Carnegie-Rochester Conference Series on Public Policy*, Vol. 39, No. 1, December 1993, pp. 195–214.

MyEconLab Real-time data

Figure 14.10

The Taylor Rule and Federal Reserve Behavior, 1955–2012

The Taylor rule does a good job of predicting the nominal federal funds rate from the mid-1980s to the end of the 2001 recession. Shaded areas represent recessions, as determined by the National Bureau of Economic Research.

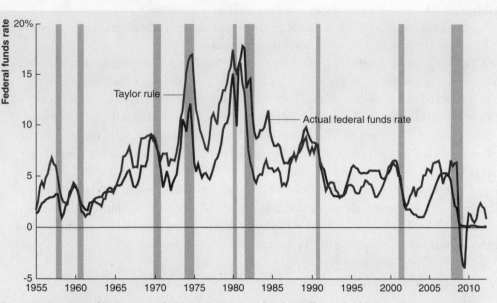

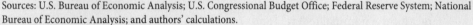

Sources: U.S. Bureau of Economic Analysis; U.S. Congressional Budget Office; Federal Reserve System; National Bureau of Economic Analysis; and authors' calculations.

also indicates that the Fed lowered the federal funds rate following the severe 1981–1982 recession more slowly than is consistent with the Taylor rule. The Fed also kept the target federal funds rate at levels well below those indicated by the Taylor rule during the recovery from the 2001 recession. Some economists and policymakers have argued that by keeping the target federal funds at a very low level for an extended period, the Fed helped fuel the housing boom of the mid-2000s. The argument is that a low federal funds rate contributed to low mortgage interest rates, thereby encouraging the housing boom. At the time, Fed Chairman Alan Greenspan argued that low interest rates were needed to guard against the possibility that the economy might lapse into a period of deflation. Current Fed Chairman Ben Bernanke has argued that a *global savings glut,* rather than Fed policy, was the main reason long-term interest rates were low in the United States during the early 2000s. Finally, notice that the Taylor rule indicates that the federal funds rate should have been negative throughout 2009. This result is another indication of the severity of the 2007–2009 recession and helps to explain why the Fed resorted to nontraditional monetary policy tools such as quantitative easing.

The United States was not the only country to allow interest rates to persist at low levels during the early 2000s, with consequences for the housing market. Economists Rudiger Ahrend, Boris Cournede, and Robert Pierce of the Organisation for Economic Co-operation and Development (OECD) examined the deviations of short-term nominal interest rates from those suggested by the Taylor rule for countries such as Ireland and Spain.[9] Ahrend, Cournede, and Pierce found that the more the central bank deviated

[9]Rudiger Ahrend, Boris Cournede, and Robert Pierce, "Monetary Policy, Market Excesses and Financial Turmoil," Organisation for Economic Co-operation and Development Economics Department working paper 597, March 2008.

from the nominal interest rate suggested by the Taylor rule, the more the countries' resources flowed into residential and nonresidential construction. These economists believe their research indicates that low nominal interest rates helped contribute to the rapid rise in residential housing during this period. So, to the extent that the collapse in housing markets contributed to the 2007–2009 recession, overly expansionary monetary policy may bear part of the blame.

The Taylor Rule and the Real Interest Rate

The Taylor rule applies to the nominal federal funds rate, but real interest rates are far more important for determining the level of economic activity. To see the relationship between the target federal funds rate and the real federal funds rate, consider the Taylor rule under the assumption that the Fed has an inflation rate target of 2%, the equilibrium real federal funds rate is 2%, and the values of g and h are both 0.5:

$$i_{\text{Target}} = 2 + \pi_t + 0.5(\pi_t - 2) + 0.5\widetilde{Y}_t = 1 + 1.5\pi_t + 0.5\widetilde{Y}_t.$$

According to the Taylor rule, the Fed should increase the target nominal federal funds rate by 1.5 percentage points for each 1-percentage-point increase in inflation. This observation is important because the Fisher relationship tells us that the real interest rate equals the nominal interest rate minus the inflation rate. If inflation increases by 1 percentage point, then the target nominal federal funds rate will increase by 1.5 percentage points, so the real interest rate will increase by 0.5 percentage point. The result is that a higher inflation rate results in a higher real interest rate. The higher real interest rate reduces consumption and investment, which slows the growth of real GDP and lowers the inflation rate. By following this rule, monetary policy helps keep the inflation rate stable.

The Case for Discretion

Economists who believe that policymakers should be allowed discretion argue that simple rules such as the Taylor rule or Friedman's constant money growth rate rule cannot accommodate new and unexpected events. So, policymakers must be free to use all available information in setting monetary policy and not just the information incorporated in a simple rule. For example, the Fed cut the target federal funds rate in response to the stock market crash of October 1987, even though the inflation rate and the output gap had not changed. The interest rate cut sent a signal to households and firms that the Fed was determined to prevent the stock market crash from harming the economy. Advocates of discretion argue that the stock market crash was a unique event that no rule could have accounted for, so the proper policy response required the Fed to use discretion.

In addition, rules often assume that key economic values are constant, when they often are not. For example, financial innovation and financial crises change the value of velocity in the quantity equation and the value of the money multiplier. Therefore, if policymakers at the Fed were to follow Friedman's constant money growth rate rule, policy might destabilize the economy. With respect to the Taylor rule, it is possible that the equilibrium real interest rate changes over time in response to technological change and other factors that affect the economy's long-run equilibrium. In those circumstances, strict adherence to the Taylor rule could potentially increase fluctuations in unemployment and inflation.

The Case for Rules

Economists who believe that policymakers should follow a monetary policy rule argue that the period between the mid-1960s and early 1980s, when inflation rose steadily, shows the problems associated with discretionary policy. As we discussed earlier, during this period, the Fed repeatedly switched back and forth between fighting inflation and keeping real GDP close to potential GDP. The Fed lost credibility with the general public, and both the actual and expected inflation rates increased. Some economists also argue that a policy rule avoids the **time-inconsistency problem**, which is the tendency of policymakers to announce one policy in order to change the expectations of households and firms and then to follow another policy after households and firms have made economic decisions based on the announced policy. For example, a central bank may announce a target inflation rate of 2% for the next year to get households and firms to make decisions about nominal prices, nominal wages, and nominal interest rates based on an expectation of 2% inflation. Then the central bank could actually increase the target inflation rate to 5%, which would lower the real wage and real interest rate, resulting in increased aggregate expenditure and real GDP.

Nobel Laureates Finn Kydland of the University of California, Santa Barbara, and Edward Prescott of Arizona State University have analyzed the time-inconsistency problem that central banks face.[10] Policymakers have an incentive to promise to achieve low inflation to reduce the expected inflation rate. A lower expected inflation rate results in a lower actual inflation rate as households and firms build the lower expected inflation rate into their pricing decisions. Once households and firms have made their pricing decisions, the central bank has achieved a favorable trade-off between real GDP and inflation. Now the central bank has an incentive to exploit that trade-off by lowering interest rates to increase real GDP and employment. It appears that the central bank can fool households and firms to stimulate the economy. Unfortunately, households and firms are not so easily fooled because they understand that the central bank has an incentive to break a promise to achieve low inflation. As a result, households and firms will expect the central bank to break its promise, so the expected inflation rate and, therefore, the actual inflation rate will remain high. Many economists believe that the time-inconsistency problem explains the poor economic performance of the mid-1960s to the early 1980s.

Advocates of rules argue that following a monetary policy rule provides the central bank with credibility because it is easier for individuals and firms to verify whether it is behaving as promised. Once the central bank achieves credibility, the expected inflation rate will fall, households and firms will build the lower expected inflation rate into their pricing decisions, and inflation will decrease.

Following a rule can also reduce uncertainty about monetary policy and improve economic performance in two other ways. First, when households and firms know how the central bank will respond to changes in the economy, they can more easily plan for the future. Second, rules provide discipline for the central bank, so that it does not constantly switch from trying to fight inflation to trying to keep the output gap close to zero.

Time-inconsistency problem The tendency of policymakers to announce one policy in advance in order to change the expectations of households and firms and then to follow another policy after households and firms have made economic decisions based on the announced policy.

---

[10]Finn Kydland and Edward Prescott, "Rules Rather Than Discretion: The Inconsistency of Optimal Plans," *Journal of Political Economy*, Vol. 85, No. 3, June 1977, pp. 473–491.

Uncertainty will still exist with rules because no one can predict shocks, but following a policy rule does eliminate the uncertainty that discretionary monetary policy might create.

Making the Connection

Central Banks Around the World Try Inflation Targeting

In January 2012, the Federal Reserve announced that it would join the ranks of central banks that had adopted an explicit inflation target. The Fed stated that its target inflation rate is 2%, as measured as the growth rate of the personal consumption expenditure price index. Previously, the Fed had set what was considered an informal target inflation range—most recently about 1.7 to 2%. Since 1989, when the Reserve Bank of New Zealand became the first central bank to adopt an explicit inflation target, the number of central banks doing so has grown to around 40, including high-income economies such as Canada and the United Kingdom and emerging markets such as Colombia, Hungary, and South Africa. Inflation targeting usually involves an explicit statement that the central bank will pursue price stability as its sole or primary objective, along with an explicit target inflation rate, usually between 1% and 3%. Sometimes penalties for missing the target rate are also involved. For example, the head of New Zealand's central bank can be fired for not meeting the inflation target.

An explicit inflation target acts as a rule to constrain the discretion of the central bank and provide it with credibility as an inflation fighter. Therefore, having an explicit inflation target may be a way to reduce the time-inconsistency problem. The central bank does retain some discretion in pursuing goals other than price stability because most countries allow the central bank to keep inflation within a specified range. For example, the central bank can increase inflation to the higher end of the range to stimulate the economy, if necessary.

The reason that countries adopt inflation targets is to bring down the inflation rate, but has it worked? The evidence is mixed. Laurence Ball of Johns Hopkins University and Niamh Sheridan of the International Monetary Fund (IMF) found that inflation did decrease after central banks adopted explicit inflation targets but that the decrease was about the same size as decreases in countries without explicit inflation targets. However, a recent study by economists at the IMF found that the surge in oil prices during 2007 caused a smaller increase in the inflation rate in countries that had explicit inflation targets. This connection provides some evidence that explicit inflation targets may help keep actual and expected inflation rates low and stable.

Inflation targeting is still a relatively new strategy, and it is too soon to tell if it will become standard practice for more central banks in the future. But some economists and banking officials have expressed doubts. Virabongsa Ramangkura, chairman of the Bank of Thailand, stated that globalization has rendered inflation targeting ineffective. Thailand has used inflation targets since 2000, but Chairman Ramangkura claims that now "commodity prices are driven by global supply and demand, not policy of a particular country . . . monetary policy shouldn't be used to deal with inflation because we can't do anything." Jeffrey Frankel, an economist at Harvard University's Kennedy School of Government, questioned the usefulness of inflation targeting because countries that had adopted targeting were not immune to the collapse of asset prices in 2008. Some economists have argued that by fixing the central bank's focus on inflation, an inflation target may cause the central bank to be less concerned with rising unemployment. Some critics argued that the European Central Bank failed to take actions to reduce unemployment during and after the 2007-2009 recession because it was focused too closely on inflation. Christina Romer of the University of California, Berkeley, and former chair of President Obama's Council of Economic Advisers, Bennett McCallum of Carnegie Mellon University, and Scott Sumner of Bentley University have called for the Fed to target either the level of nominal GDP or its growth rate. These economists believe adopting a nominal GDP target would communicate to consumers and businesses that the Fed would do whatever is necessary to push the economy toward full employment.

Sources: Karl Habermeier, et al., "Inflation Pressures and Monetary Policy Options in Emerging and Developing Countries: A Cross Regional Perspective," International Monetary Fund working paper 09/1, January 2009; Scott Roger, "Inflation Targeting Turns 20," *Finance and Development*, March 2010, pp. 46–49; Jonathan Spicer, "In Historic Shift, Fed Sets Inflation Target," *Reuters*, January 25, 2012; Suttinee Yuvejwattana, "Bank of Thailand's Virabongsa Says Inflation Target Ineffective," *Bloomberg Businessweek*, August 7, 2012; Jeffrey Frankel, "The Death of Inflation Targeting," *Project Syndicate*, May 16, 2012; and Christina Romer, "Dear Ben: It's Time for Your Volcker Moment," *New York Times*, October 29, 2011.

See related problem 5.4 at the end of the chapter.

Answering the Key Question

Continued from page 504

At the beginning of this chapter, we asked:

"Did discretionary monetary policy kill the Great Moderation?"

The Great Moderation ended when the collapse of the housing bubble led to the financial crisis and the Great Recession of 2007–2009. In this chapter, we have seen that discretionary monetary policy can lead to poor decisions by the central bank. We have also seen that the federal funds rate was far below the rate suggested by the Taylor rule during the time that the housing market bubble was developing in the United States. Furthermore, many countries experienced a housing bubble at the same time, and the extent of those bubbles is related to how far their central banks deviated from well-established monetary policy rules. While this evidence is not conclusive, it does suggest that discretionary monetary policy during the 2001–2006 period contributed to a housing bubble and to the resulting financial crisis that ended the Great Moderation.

Key Terms and Problems

Key Terms

Aggregate demand (*AD*) curve, p. 507

Aggregate demand and aggregate supply (*AD–AS*) model, p. 515

Aggregate supply (*AS*) curve, p. 512

Central bank credibility, p. 527

Central bank reaction function, p. 506

Monetary rule, p. 530

Rational expectations, p. 527

Stagflation, p. 516

Taylor rule, p. 531

Time-inconsistency problem, p. 534

14.1 Aggregate Demand Revisited
Understand how aggregate demand is determined.

Review Questions

1.1 What is a central bank reaction function? What are its key components? What does the slope of the reaction function indicate?

1.2 What is the aggregate demand curve? Explain how the aggregate demand curve is derived using the *IS–MP* model and the central bank reaction function.

1.3 What factors shift the aggregate demand curve?

Problems and Applications

1.4 In January 2012, the Federal Reserve changed its policy of implicitly targeting inflation to setting an explicit inflation target of 2%. According to a *Reuters* article, "Skeptics, particularly among congressional Democrats, have in the past worried that an explicit inflation target would relegate the full employment goal to the back burner." Why might setting an explicit inflation target conflict with a goal of full employment?
Source: Jonathan Spicer, "In Historic Shift, Fed Sets Inflation Target," *Reuters*, January 25, 2012.

1.5 Briefly explain whether you agree with the following statement: "Until the Fed set an explicit inflation target, it did not have a reaction function."

1.6 For each of the following scenarios, state the short-run effect on the *AD* curve.

a. There is an increase in government purchases.

b. Costs of production increase.

c. Investors become more pessimistic.

d. The central bank becomes less tolerant of deviations in inflation from the target rate.

e. The price level increases.

f. The target inflation rate increases.

14.2 Aggregate Supply and the Phillips Curve
Explain the relationship between aggregate supply and the Phillips curve.

Review Questions

2.1 What is the aggregate supply curve? Explain how the aggregate supply curve is related to the Phillips curve.

2.2 What demand factors contribute to inflation? What cost factors contribute to inflation? How do these factors relate to the aggregate supply curve?

2.3 Explain what factors cause the aggregate supply curve to shift.

Problems and Applications

2.4 For each of the following scenarios, state the short-run effect on the *AS* curve.

a. An increase in government spending causes aggregate expenditure and real GDP to increase.

b. Nominal wages increase rapidly.

c. Lower inflation is expected in the future.

d. A change in technology lowers the costs of production.

2.5 Write two equations for the *AS* curve. In both cases, assume that expectations are adaptive and that the effect of supply shocks is zero. For the first equation, assume that the inflation rate is very sensitive to changes in the output gap. For the second equation, assume that it is not. Graph your two curves.

MyEconLab   Visit **www.myeconlab.com** to complete these exercises online and get instant feedback. Exercises that update with real-time data are marked with ⓦ.

2.6 Briefly explain whether you agree with the following statement: "The supply shock inflation parameter, s, must always be positive because supply shocks always increase production costs."

2.7 In a March 2012 interview on Bloomberg Television's "In The Loop," former Federal Reserve Governor Randall Kroszner described inflation expectations in the United States as "well anchored." Expected inflation is well anchored when it is stable and households and firms expect the Fed will keep the actual inflation rate close to the expected inflation rate. What would happen to the AS curve if inflation expectations were not well anchored?

Source: "Kroszner Says Inflation Expectations Are 'Well Anchored,'" Bloomberg Television interview, March 23, 2012.

14.3 The Aggregate Demand and Aggregate Supply Model
Use the aggregate demand and aggregate supply model to analyze macroeconomic conditions.

Review Questions

3.1 What are the long-run equilibrium conditions in the AD–AS model? What is the relationship between the AD–AS model and the IS–MP model?

3.2 What is stagflation, and how does it occur? How does the economy readjust to long-run equilibrium after a period of stagflation, assuming that the Fed does not change its reaction function?

3.3 Using the AD–AS model, briefly explain how the economy responds differently to demand shocks and changes in the central bank reaction function.

Problems and Applications

3.4 Draw a graph of the AD–AS model. Label the curves and axes carefully. Then show the effects of the following:
  a. a positive demand shock
  b. a positive supply shock

  How are the effects of these changes on the output gap different from the effects on inflation? If you observed an increase in real GDP so the output gap moved to a value greater than zero, how could you tell whether AD or AS had shifted?

3.5 The slope of the aggregate supply curve will vary based on the sensitivity of inflation to the output gap. The following graph shows a curve that is sensitive to inflation changes (AS_1) and a curve that is less sensitive (AS_2):

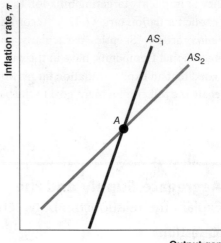

a. Draw an AD curve and assume that the equilibrium point represents the long-run equilibrium point. For simplicity, have the AD curve intersect the AS curves at point A.

b. Suppose that a housing boom takes place. Show the effect on AD and explain how the short-run changes in inflation and the output gap are different in the two cases.

3.6 [Related to the Making the Connection on page 521] Problem 2.7 states that, according to former Federal Reserve Governor Randall Kroszner, inflation expectations in 2012 were well anchored. The *Making the Connection* "The End of Stagflation and the Volcker Recession" discusses how the Fed may have induced a recession to reduce both current and expected inflation.

a. Suppose that inflation expectations lose their anchor; in other words, assume that households and firms now expect that inflation will be considerably higher next period. Use the *AD–AS* model to show the short-run effect of this change.

b. What will the Fed have to do to reduce inflation? Carefully analyze using the *AD–AS* model.

3.7 **[Related to the** Making the Connection **on page 521]** During Paul Volcker's tenure as chairman of the Federal Reserve Board, contractionary monetary policy was successfully used to reduce the rate of inflation in the United States. More recently, expansionary policy has been less successful in helping the economy to recover quickly from the recession of 2007–2009. Unemployment was still 7.8% in September 2012, more than three years after the end of the 2007–2009 recession. Why was monetary policy more effective in reducing the rate of inflation in the early 1980s than it was in stimulating the economy after 2007?

3.8 **[Related to the** Macro Data feature **on page 519]** Real oil prices decreased significantly during the 1990s. The following graph shows the initial equilibrium at point *A* and the shift in aggregate supply due to lower oil prices:

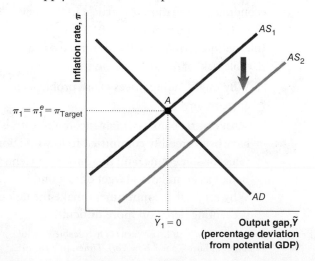

a. Identify the new equilibrium output gap and inflation rate.

b. Assuming that monetary policy does not change, show on the graph how the economy will adjust to the new long-run equilibrium.

3.9 **[Related to** Solved Problem 14.3 **on page 524]** Suppose that a severe recession in Europe causes a sharp decline in U.S. exports. Use the *AD–AS* model to show the short- and long-run effects of the European recession on the U.S. economy.

3.10 Assume that the central bank has an inflation target of 2% and always adjusts monetary policy to keep the inflation rate at 2%. Now assume that the government announces an expansionary fiscal policy of more spending on infrastructure projects and lower taxes. Given the central bank's monetary policy, will this fiscal policy have any effect on the output gap and inflation? Briefly explain.

3.11 In early 2010, consumer prices in the United Kingdom rose above 3%, even though the economy was growing slowly. An article in the *Economist* commented: "This may not be stagflation, 1970s-style; rather it is slumpflation, given that the economy is bumping along the bottom of the biggest hole dug in GDP since the Second World War."

a. What does the article mean by "slumpflation"?

b. Why would we not expect to see rising inflation during a time of slow economic growth?

c. The article also stated that the inflation rate was expected to decline. Explain this expectation using the *AD–AS* model.

Source: "Storm Before the Calm," *Economist*, February 11, 2010.

3.12 During the financial crisis, the Federal Reserve developed a number of new policy tools and allowed the monetary base to triple. However, the Fed never indicated that it was willing to allow the inflation rate to rise above its inflation target of 2%.

a. What would be the effect on the output gap and the inflation rate of the Fed's indicating it is willing to increase its target inflation rate?

MyEconLab Visit **www.myeconlab.com** to complete these exercises online and get instant feedback. Exercises that update with real-time data are marked with ⓜ.

b. Charles Evans, president of the Federal Reserve Bank of Chicago, gave a speech in January 2012 in which he argued that the Fed should pursue an expansionary monetary policy until the unemployment rate fell below 7% or the inflation rate rose above 3%. Do you think that

this policy would be more effective than actual Fed policy in stimulating the economy? Explain.

Source: "Managing Monetary Policy Risks," Charles Evans, delivered at the Indiana Bankers Association, Economic Outlook Forum, January 13, 2012. Available at: http://www.chicagofed.org/webpages/publications/speeches/2012/01_13_12_indy_outlook.cfm

14.4 Rational Expectations and Policy Ineffectiveness
Discuss the implications of rational expectations for macroeconomic policymaking.

Review Questions

4.1 What are rational expectations? What is the difference between adaptive expectations and rational expectations?

4.2 How might rational expectations make monetary policy ineffective?

4.3 Explain why monetary policy might be effective if expectations are rational but a change in policy is a surprise.

4.4 If expectations are rational, explain how anticipated and unanticipated demand shocks will affect real GDP.

4.5 Are there reasons to doubt the policy ineffectiveness proposition? Briefly explain.

Problems and Applications

4.6 Suppose that inflation has increased at an annual rate of 2% for several years. Also assume that the central bank's target inflation rate is 2%.

a. If sellers all charge $100 for their products and expectations are adaptive, what price will they charge next year, assuming that the relative demand for their products is unchanged?

b. Suppose that the central bank now announces that its target inflation rate has increased to 5%, and the actual inflation rate also becomes 5%. What price should sellers charge to keep real prices constant? What price will they actually charge if expectations are adaptive?

c. If expectations are adaptive, what will be the consequences for the economy as a result of the situation described in part (b)?

4.7 In problem 4.6, answer parts (b) and (c) again assuming that expectations are rational rather than adaptive.

4.8 Brazil experienced high inflation in the late 1980s and early 1990s. To bring prices under control, the country changed its currency to a new currency unit, the real. Explain why Brazil might use a strategy of introducing a new currency in order to lower the inflation rate.

4.9 Briefly explain whether you agree with the following statement: "Rational expectations assumes that all people are completely rational, and because this probably is not true, this theory doesn't help us to evaluate the effectiveness of monetary policy."

4.10 Briefly explain whether you agree with the following statement: "Currently, interest rates are very low. Because everyone knows that the Fed will raise rates at some point, raising rates will have no effect on real GDP or employment when it happens."

4.11 Deflation can be as great a problem for economies as inflation. An article in the *New York Times* reported in July 2012 that the International Monetary Fund warned of "'a sizeable risk' of deflation in the euro zone."

a. Why might falling prices cause problems for an economy?

b. Most central banks in high-income countries have been credibly committed to low inflation rates for some time, and the European Central Bank has an inflation target of just under 2%. Why might this commitment make the task of preventing deflation more difficult?

Source: Jack Ewing, "IMF Warns of a 'Sizeable Risk' of Deflation in Euro Zone," *New York Times*, July 18, 2012.

14.5 Monetary Policy: Rules Versus Discretion

Discuss the pros and cons of the central bank's operating under policy rules rather than using discretionary policy.

Review Questions

5.1 Explain the difference between a rules strategy and discretionary policy. What are the primary arguments in favor of a rules approach and of a discretionary approach when conducting monetary policy?

5.2 What is the Taylor rule? How might deviations from the Taylor rule have contributed to the 2007–2009 recession?

Problems and Applications

5.3 If central banks follow the Taylor rule, how does the real interest rate change during the business cycle?

5.4 [Related to the Making the Connection on page 535] Some central banks have explicit inflation targets, while others have implicit targets.

    a. In the context of topics discussed in this section, what is the advantage of having an explicit target?

    b. What is the advantage of having an implicit target or no target at all?

5.5 [Related to the Chapter Opener on page 504] Explain how the Fed may have created the Great Moderation. In what way may the Fed have contributed to the end of the Great Moderation?

5.6 A very simple monetary rule might be: "Increase the money supply at the rate of growth of real GDP."

    a. What would be the advantages of this monetary rule? What would be the problems?

    b. What if the rule said: "Increase the money supply at the rate of growth of real GDP plus 2%." Now what would be the advantages and problems?

    c. What if the rule said: "Increase the money supply at the rate of growth of real GDP plus 2% plus one-half of the output gap." Now what would be the advantages and problems?

5.7 Briefly explain whether you agree with the following statement: "Because the business cycle is unpredictable and real-time data are usually unobtainable, monetary policy rules probably won't be successful."

5.8 Both Alan Greenspan and Ben Bernanke have claimed that monetary policy was not responsible for the housing bubble. Instead, they blame a change in the relationship between short-term interest rates and long-term mortgage rates. An article in the *Economist* that summarizes their positions states part of the Greenspan explanation as follows: "The rise in desired global saving relative to desired investment caused a global decline in long-term rates, which became delinked from the short-term rates that central bankers control." How would the delinking of short- and long-term rates create a problem for monetary policy and policy rules?

Source: "It Wasn't Us," *Economist*, March 18, 2010.

5.9 A column in the *Economist* magazine argues that:

    Central banks should focus their efforts on measures of demand—nominal GDP, nominal income, nominal spending—rather than measures of inflation. If nominal GDP is at a level that's inconsistent with full employment, demand is too low and the central bank should do more.

    a. In what ways is a central bank targeting nominal GDP different from a central bank targeting the inflation rate?

    b. If a central bank is targeting nominal GDP, what actions would it take to "do more" if the economy was not at full employment?

Source: "Rethinking Macro," *Economist*, July 26, 2012.

Data Exercises

D14.1: [Excel exercise] Using data from the St. Louis Federal Reserve (FRED) (http://research. stlouisfed.org/fred2/), examine the effect on the Brazilian inflation rate of the introduction of the real on July 1, 1994.

   a. Download quarterly data on the consumer price index (BRACPIALLQINMEI) from January 1980 to the present. Calculate the inflation rate as the percentage change from the same quarter in the previous year. Plot the data on a graph.

   b. Describe the differences in the inflation rate before and after July 1, 1994.

   c. Calculate the mean and standard deviation of the inflation rate before and after July 1, 1994.

   d. Are your results in parts (b) and (c) consistent with the view that the introduction of the real reduced the inflation rate and made the inflation rate less volatile? Briefly explain.

D14.2: Using data from the St. Louis Fed's database (FRED) (research.stlouisfed.org/fred2/) analyze the source of business cycles in the United States. Recall that an aggregate demand shock causes inflation and the output gap to move in the same direction while an aggregate supply shock causes inflation and the output gap to move in opposite directions. Dates for U.S. business cycles can be found on the National Bureau of Economic Research's website at: http://www.nber.org/cycles/cyclesmain.html.

   a. Download quarterly data on nominal GDP (GDP), nominal potential GDP (NGDPPOT) and the chain-type price index for GDP (GDPCTPI) from 1949 to the present.

   b. Calculate the output gap and the inflation rate as the compound annual growth rate. Plot both series on a graph.

   c. Based on these data, which recessions do you think were caused primarily by aggregate demand shocks and which recessions were caused primarily by aggregate supply shocks? Briefly explain.

D14.3: The growth rate of real GDP is an alternative to the output gap as a measure of the business cycle. Using data from the St. Louis Fed's database (FRED) (research.stlouisfed.org/fred2/) analyze the sources of business cycles in the United Kingdom.

   a. Download quarterly data from 1955 to the present for the growth rate of real GDP (GBRGDPRQPSMEI) and the level of the GDP implicit price deflator (GBRGDPDEFQISMEI). FRED also has a monthly indicator variable for recessions (GBRRECM) for the United Kingdom.

   b. Calculate the inflation rate as the growth rate of the GDP implicit price deflator from the same quarter the previous year.

   c. Plot the growth rate of real GDP and the inflation rate on the same graph.

   d. Based on these data, which recessions do you think were caused primarily by aggregate demand shocks and which recessions were caused primarily by aggregate supply shocks? Briefly explain.

D14.4: [Excel exercise] It is possible that the relationship between short- and long-term interest rates may have weakened during the 1980–2011 period. Using data from the St. Louis Fed's database (FRED) (research.stlouisfed.org/fred2/) analyze this relationship.

   a. Download monthly data on the 3-month constant maturity U.S. Treasury bill (GS3M) and the 30-year conventional mortgage (MORTG) from January 1985 to the present.

   b. What is the correlation coefficient between the two rates over the entire period?

   c. If you split the data into 5-year periods beginning with 1985, is the correlation coefficient the same for each period?

   d. Are your results consistent with the view that the relationship between short- and long-term interest rates has weakened? Briefly explain.

CHAPTER 15

Fiscal Policy and the Government Budget in the Long Run

Learning Objectives

After studying this chapter, you should be able to:

15.1 Discuss basic facts about the U.S. government's fiscal situation (pages 544–551)

15.2 Explain when fiscal policy is sustainable and when it is not sustainable (pages 551–555)

15.3 Understand how fiscal policy affects the economy in the long run (pages 556–559)

15.4 Explain the fiscal challenges facing the United States (pages 559–565)

15.A Appendix: Derive the conditions for a sustainable fiscal policy (pages 571–572)

15.B Appendix: Derive the equation showing the relationship between budget deficits and private expenditure (page 572)

Drowning in a Sea of Debt?

Most people have debt: They owe money on student loans, car loans, or mortgage loans. What about the debt that the government has, in effect, taken out in their name? In June 2012, the national debt of the United States stood at $15.9 trillion, or $50,000 for every person in the United States. At some point, will the government raise your taxes to help pay off the national debt? If so, should you change your spending and saving behavior now to prepare for the possibility of paying higher taxes in the future?

Most high-income countries, including the United States, Germany, and Japan, suffer from rising national debts. National debts are increasing because these countries are currently running large deficits and are likely to

continue to do so for years into the future. The current deficits are largely the result of the lower tax revenues and higher government spending associated with the slow recovery from the 2007–2009 recession. The future deficits are primarily due to aging populations and expected increases in healthcare costs and government-funded pensions, such as the Social Security system in the United States.

Economists often measure budget deficits as a fraction of GDP. For reasons we will discuss in this chapter, when the deficit rises above about 3% of GDP, it reaches levels that governments find difficult to sustain in the long run. The federal government's budget

Continued on next page

Key Issue and Question

Issue: In 2012, the federal government's budget deficit and the national debt were on course to rise to unsustainable levels.

Question: How can the United States solve its long-run fiscal problem?

Answered on page 566

deficit averaged 2.5% of GDP from 1969 to 2007, which was sustainable. In 2009, however, the deficit soared to above 10%, and it remained above 7% in 2012, levels previously seen only during major wars such as World War I and World War II, and it was not projected to fall back to 3% until 2014 at the earliest. The United States is not alone in running large budget deficits. Economists at the Organisation for Economic Co-operation and Development (OECD) estimated that several member countries of the OECD were facing similarly large government budget deficits.

These high deficits have contributed to long-term fiscal problems for many countries. Japan's national debt was more than 200% of GDP in 2012. As of mid-2012, the national debts of Portugal, Ireland, Italy, and Greece were above 100% of GDP. At these levels of debt, the interest payments the government must make to bondholders rises to levels that squeeze out other spending. The U.S. public debt rose to "only" about 75% of GDP in 2012, but if current taxing and spending policies remain in place, the debt will exceed 100% of GDP in the decades ahead.

With aging populations and rising health care and pension costs, countries face hard choices: Governments must choose among (1) reducing health care and pension benefits for the elderly, (2) reducing other spending, and (3) raising taxes to levels that might significantly reduce economic efficiency.

In the United States, the challenge of dealing with future deficits and rising national debt is so great that a recent survey of economists by the National Association for Business Economics ranked the federal deficit as the country's biggest long-term problem. How governments choose to deal with these looming fiscal problems will have important consequences for the future of their economies.

Sources: Congressional Budget Office, *Budget and Economic Outlook: Fiscal Years 2012 to 2022*, January 2012; Chris Isidore, "Economists' Biggest Worry: Federal Budget Deficit," CNNMoney.com, February 28, 2011, money.cnn.com/2011/02/28/news/economy/economists_federal_deficit_worries/index.htm; Organisation for Economic Co-operation and Development (OECD); and World Bank, *World Development Indicators*.

The Federal Reserve uses monetary policy to pursue macroeconomic policy goals (see Chapter 12). In the long run, monetary policy affects only nominal variables such as the inflation rate and leaves real variables such as output and employment unchanged. By the *long run*, we mean a period of time sufficiently long so that nominal wages and prices are flexible and real GDP always equals potential GDP. The government also uses fiscal policy, such as changes in taxes and government purchases, to achieve macroeconomic goals in the short run (see Chapter 13). In this chapter, we explain how fiscal policy affects real variables in the long run.

15.1

Learning Objective

Discuss basic facts about the U.S. government's fiscal situation.

Gross federal debt held by the public Debt that includes the bonds and other securities issued by the U.S. Treasury (and a small amount of securities issued by federal agencies) not held by the federal government.

Debt and Deficits in Historical Perspective

To provide context for understanding how fiscal policy affects an economy in the long run, it is important to first review some historical facts and key definitions. **Gross federal debt held by the public** includes the bonds and similar securities issued by the U.S. Treasury (and a small amount of securities issued by federal agencies) not held by the federal government. Federal debt has tended to increase during wars and decrease during times of peace. The notable exceptions include the Great Depression, the 1980s, and the 2000–2012 period when the national debt rose substantially even though the United States was not involved in a major war. Before we can analyze the key issues connected with the federal debt, though, we need to understand the government's budget constraint, which spells out how governments finance their spending.

The Government Budget Constraint

Households face a budget constraint because the total amount that a household spends cannot exceed its income plus the amount it can borrow. The government faces a similar budget constraint. The government purchases goods and services (G) and makes transfer payments (TR) to households. The government must also make interest payments on existing debt. If i is the nominal interest rate on existing government bonds (B), then interest payments today are:

$$i_t B_{t-1},$$

where:

t = the current year
$t - 1$ = the previous year.

The government can finance its purchases of goods and services, transfer payments, and interest payments through tax revenue (T), issuing new government bonds (ΔB), or increasing the monetary base (ΔMB). In other words, the government must pay for its spending through taxes, borrowing, or creating money by increasing the monetary base. Increasing the monetary base is called **seigniorage** because it represents a transfer of wealth from individuals holding currency to the government (see Chapter 7). The government's budget constraint is then:

$$G_t + TR_t + i_t B_{t-1} = T_t + \Delta B_t + \Delta MB_t.$$

The terms on the left of the equation represent the *uses* of government funds, and the terms on the right side represent the *sources* of government funds. If we move taxes to the left side, we have:

$$G_t + TR_t - T_t + i_t B_{t-1} = \Delta B_t + \Delta MB_t.$$

The left side of the equation is the **budget deficit**, which is the difference between government expenditure and tax revenue.[1] The right side of the equation tells us that the budget deficit is financed by issuing new government securities and seigniorage. To focus on the government's operations, we define the **primary budget deficit (*PD*)** as:

$$PD_t = G_t + TR_t - T_t.$$

The primary budget deficit is the difference between government purchases of goods and services plus transfer payments minus tax revenue, but does not include the interest payments that the government makes. We can rewrite the equation for the budget deficit as:

$$PD_t + i_t B_{t-1} = \Delta B_t + \Delta MB_t.$$

For example, during 2011, federal government expenditure on goods and services plus transfer payments was $3,371 billion, and revenue was $2,302 billion, so the primary budget deficit was $1,069 billion. The government also made interest payments of

Seigniorage The government's profit from issuing fiat money; also called the inflation tax.

Budget deficit The difference between government expenditure and tax revenue.

Primary budget deficit (*PD*) The difference between government purchases of goods and services plus transfer payments minus tax revenue.

---

[1]In this chapter, we will use the convention that a positive number represents a budget deficit and a negative number represents a budget surplus. This convention is different from the one we used in earlier chapters, where a negative number was a budget deficit and a positive number was a surplus. We make this change in order to make the algebra easier to follow.

Figure 15.1

The Total Budget Deficit and Primary Budget Deficit for the United States, 1962–2011

Because interest payments are always positive, the primary budget deficit is always less than the total budget deficit. The primary budget deficit was negative, and therefore in surplus, most recently in 2007.

Source: U.S. Bureau of Economic Analysis.

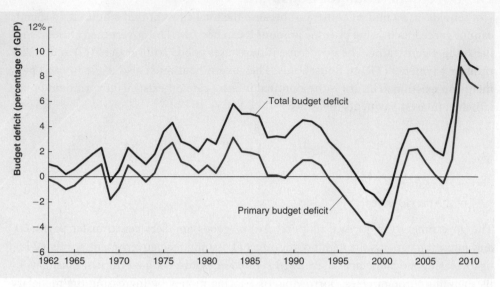

$227 billion, however, so the total deficit for the year was $1,296 billion. As you can see, the difference between the total and the primary deficits can be hundreds of billions of dollars per year. Figure 15.1 shows the total and the primary budget deficits as a percentage of GDP for the United States from 1962 to 2011. The total budget deficit and primary budget deficit track each other closely over time. The primary deficit was last negative—meaning that the primary budget was in surplus—in 2007, while the total budget deficit was last negative (the total budget was in surplus) in 2001.

The Relationship Between the Deficit and the National Debt

The debt is the total value of government bonds outstanding, B. Putting aside changes in the monetary base, we can think of the budget deficit as the yearly flow of new government bonds, ΔB. The value of bonds outstanding increases when the government runs a budget deficit and decreases when the government runs a budget surplus.

We can think in terms of the bathtub analogy (see Chapter 6). The level of water in a bathtub (the dollar value of the debt) is a stock variable, while the water flowing into the tub (the dollar value of government expenditure) and flowing out of the tub (the dollar value of tax revenue) are flow variables. During years that expenditures are greater than tax revenue, the government runs a budget deficit, more water flows into the bathtub than flows out, and the stock of government bonds and the federal debt increases. During years that expenditures are less than tax revenue, the government runs a budget surplus, more water flows out of the bathtub than flows in, and the stock of government bonds and the federal debt decreases.

Whether we focus on the deficit, the debt, or both depends on the question we are asking. If we want to know the effect of fiscal policy on the ability of households and firms to borrow to finance consumption and investment when the economy is at potential GDP, we should look to the yearly budget deficit. Remember that if the government increases its budget deficit, it reduces the pool of national saving available to households and firms to finance consumption and investment. If we want to know whether the government's fiscal policy is sustainable, we need to focus on both the debt and the deficit. There is a limit to how much financial markets will lend to governments, so the debt-to-GDP ratio cannot increase forever. We call a fiscal policy *sustainable* when the debt-to-GDP ratio is constant or decreasing, and we call a fiscal policy *unsustainable* when the debt-to-GDP ratio is increasing. A fiscal policy that results in an increasing debt-to-GDP ratio must eventually change so that the ratio either remains constant or begins to decrease.

Gross Federal Debt Versus Debt Held by the Public

Figure 15.2 shows gross federal debt and gross federal debt held by the public. **Gross federal debt** is the total dollar value of Treasury bonds plus the dollar value of the small amount of bonds and other securities issued by other federal agencies. Gross federal debt held by the public includes just those bonds held outside the federal government. The federal government owes some of its debt to itself because some government programs have trust funds that have purchased Treasury bonds. Some government programs, such as Social Security, have specific taxes and fees associated with the program. If the revenues from these taxes and fees exceed what the program pays out that year, the program runs a surplus. Legally, the program must use the surplus to purchase Treasury bonds. Because the Social Security Administration is part of the federal government, one branch of the federal government (the Treasury) owes a debt to another branch of the federal government (the Social Security Administration).

Gross federal debt at the end of June 2012 was $15,880 billion. Of that amount, $11,073 billion was owned by the public, and $4,807 billion was owned by various federal government agencies. The Federal Reserve has also accumulated large holdings of Treasury bonds in the course of conducting monetary policy. Because of the Fed's special status as a public–private agency that is technically independent of the rest of the

Gross federal debt
The total dollar value of Treasury bonds plus the dollar value of the small amount of bonds and other securities issued by other federal agencies.

MyEconLab Real-time data

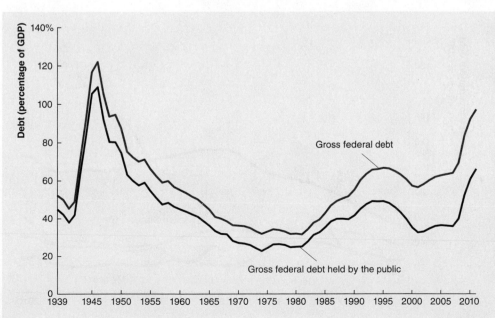

Figure 15.2

Gross Federal Debt and Gross Federal Debt Held by the Public for the United States, 1939–2011

Gross federal debt is greater than debt held by the public, but the two measures of federal debt track each other closely over time. Debt is calculated as the ratio of fiscal year debt to calendar year GDP.

Sources: U.S. Bureau of Economic Analysis; and White House Council of Economic Advisers.

federal government, the Fed's holdings of Treasury bonds are included with the holdings of the public rather than with the holdings of federal agencies. At the end of June 2012, the Fed held $1,660 billion in Treasury debt. If we subtract the debt held by the Fed from the debt held by the public, we have the *debt held by private investors*, which was $9,413 billion at the end of June 2012.

When economists evaluate the size of the government's debt, they tend to focus on the gross federal debt held by the public. If the Treasury borrows $20 billion from the Social Security Administration, that borrowing does not affect the funds available to the private sector to finance consumption and investment. However, the $20 billion affects the economy because it represents a future liability of the federal government to pay retirement benefits to the workers who pay Social Security taxes.

The Debt-to-GDP Ratio

In this chapter, we emphasize the debt-to-GDP ratio rather than focus on the dollar value of the debt because the debt-to-GDP ratio does a better job of measuring whether fiscal policy is sustainable. The federal government obtains most of its revenues through taxes, and GDP represents the income potentially available to be taxed. Thinking about the debt of an individual helps us understand why it makes sense to measure debt relative to a nation's income. Is $1 million a high level of debt? It depends. If your income is $50,000 per year, then $1 million in debt is extremely high. However, if you are a rich entrepreneur who earns $50 million per year, then $1 million is a low level of debt. It makes sense to measure debt relative to income because income represents your ability to pay the debt.

Figure 15.3 shows the debt of the U.S. federal government and of the central governments of several other countries in the Organisation for Economic Co-operation and Development (OECD). Measuring debt as a percentage of GDP, the debt levels for

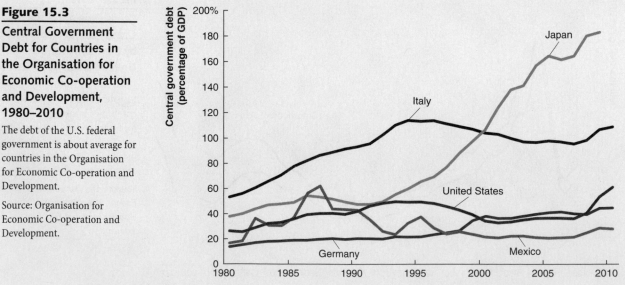

Figure 15.3

Central Government Debt for Countries in the Organisation for Economic Co-operation and Development, 1980–2010

The debt of the U.S. federal government is about average for countries in the Organisation for Economic Co-operation and Development.

Source: Organisation for Economic Co-operation and Development.

the United States are about average for OECD countries. Several countries had debt of about 100% of GDP, while Japan's debt was nearly 200% of its GDP. Figure 15.3 shows that the debt-to-GDP ratio is relatively stable for OECD countries, apart from Japan. Because the population is aging in most OECD countries, government expenditures on programs for the elderly will likely cause the debt-to-GDP ratio to increase in the future. Figures 15.1 through 15.3 together suggest that the current level of debt for the U.S. federal government is not high by U.S. historical standards or by the standards of other advanced countries. This situation will change, though, if the federal government continues to run large deficits, causing the debt-to-GDP ratio to increase.

Composition of Federal Government Revenue and Expenditure

To understand the fiscal challenges the United States faces, it is helpful to first understand the composition of federal government expenditure and revenue and how the composition has changed since the 1960s.

Federal Government Revenue As mentioned earlier, the federal government obtains most of its revenue through taxes:

- *Individual income taxes* are the taxes that households pay on their wage and non-wage income.
- *Social insurance taxes* are the *payroll taxes* that households and firms pay to support Social Security and Medicare. *Medicare* is the federal government's program to provide health care for the elderly.
- *Corporate income taxes* are taxes that corporations pay on their profits.

Figure 15.4 shows that since 1962, total federal revenue has averaged about 18% of GDP. The relative importance of the three categories of taxes has changed somewhat over the years. There are year-to-year fluctuations in individual income tax revenue as a

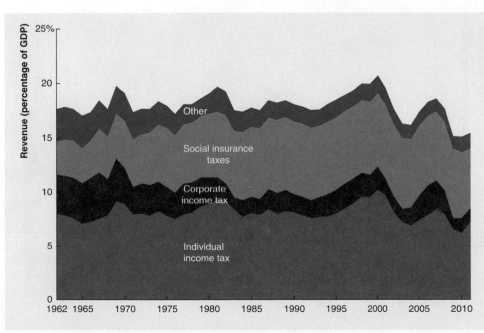

Figure 15.4

Composition of Federal Government Revenue, 1962–2011

Since 1962, corporate income taxes have become relatively less important, while social insurance taxes for Social Security and Medicare have become more important. Data used for this figure are based on the fiscal year rather than the calendar year. The category "other" includes revenue from tariffs on imports, estate taxes, and excise taxes such as federal gasoline taxes.

Source: U.S. Congressional Budget Office.

percentage of GDP, reflecting the effects of the business cycle and changes in tax law. But there is no long-term trend over the entire period: Individual income tax revenue was 7.8% of GDP in 1962 and 7.3% in 2011. In contrast, corporate income tax revenue was on a downward trend from 3.6% of GDP in 1962 to 1.2% of GDP in 2011. Revenue from social insurance taxes, on the other hand, increased from 3.0% to 5.5% of GDP during the same time period.

Seigniorage Tax revenue is by far the most important source of revenue for the federal government, but the government also obtains revenue from seigniorage. When the Federal Reserve increases the monetary base, the purchasing power of previously existing currency eventually decreases, so increasing the monetary base essentially transfers wealth from those who own existing currency to the government. For governments in high-income countries, seigniorage is usually not an important source of revenue; it averaged just 0.2% of GDP from 1990 to 2008 for the United States, while personal income taxes, social insurance taxes, and corporate income taxes combined averaged 17.8% of GDP.

Federal Government Expenditure

The changing composition of federal government expenditure helps us understand the fiscal challenges the government faces. Figure 15.5 shows federal government expenditure as a percentage of GDP for the United States from 1962 to 2011. Over this period, federal government expenditure has averaged 20.6% of GDP. Federal expenditure rose to 25.2% of GDP in 2009, as the government undertook policies to fight the 2007–2009 recession, and expenditure remained at 24.1% in 2011. The composition of federal expenditure has changed dramatically. In 1962, defense expenditure was 9.3% of GDP, but it decreased to 4.7% in 2011. In contrast, Medicare and Medicaid spending rose from nothing in 1962 (the programs were introduced a few years later) to 5.5% of

Figure 15.5

Composition of Federal Government Expenditure, 1962–2011

Transfer payments such as Medicare, Medicaid, and Social Security were a much larger percentage of GDP in 2011 than in the 1960s, while defense spending was a much smaller percentage.

Source: U.S. Congressional Budget Office.

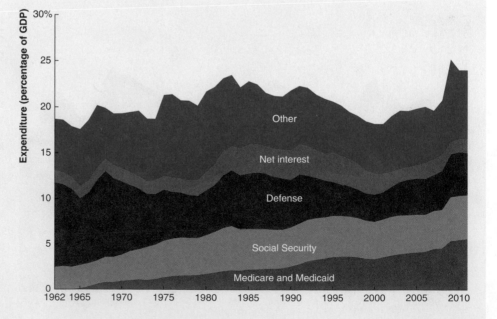

GDP in 2011, and spending on Social Security rose from 2.5% to 4.8% of GDP during the same time period. In other words, military expenditure has become much less important over time, while spending on transfer payments such as Medicare, Medicaid, and Social Security has become much more important.

The Sustainability of Fiscal Policy

Learning Objective

Explain when fiscal policy is sustainable and when it is not sustainable.

The federal government ran very large budget deficits beginning in 2009. As the economy returns to full employment, the size of the deficit will shrink. Longer term, though, as the population of the United States gets older and if medical costs continue to rise faster than the inflation rate, the federal government is likely to spend increasing amounts on Medicare, Medicaid, and Social Security. In this section, we examine whether the federal government's fiscal policy is sustainable.

Expressing the Deficit as a Percentage of GDP

We begin by taking our earlier equation for the government's budget constraint and expressing it as values relative to nominal GDP, which equals P_tY_t:

$$\frac{PD_t}{P_tY_t} + i_t\frac{B_{t-1}}{P_tY_t} = \frac{\Delta B_t}{P_tY_t} + \frac{\Delta MB_t}{P_tY_t}.$$

This equation is equivalent to:[2]

$$\Delta\left(\frac{B_t}{P_tY_t}\right) = \frac{PD_t}{P_tY_t} + [\,i_t - (\pi_t + g_y)\,]\frac{B_{t-1}}{P_{t-1}Y_{t-1}} - \frac{\Delta MB_t}{P_tY_t},$$

where:

π_t = inflation rate
g_y = growth rate of real GDP.

Nominal GDP growth equals the inflation rate plus the growth rate of real GDP, or $\pi_t + g_y$. The debt-to-GDP ratio is stable when the change in the debt-to-GDP ratio, which is the expression on the left side of this equation, equals zero.

Notice that the debt-to-GDP ratio increases when the primary deficit-to-GDP ratio is greater than zero or when seigniorage decreases. The middle term in the equation shows the effects on the debt-to-GDP ratio of past debt and the growth rate of nominal GDP. The higher the nominal interest rate, the larger the interest payments the government must make during the year. Holding everything else constant, these interest payments will increase the debt-to-GDP ratio. And, holding everything else constant, nominal GDP growth will reduce the debt-to-GDP ratio.

The Solow growth model (see Chapter 6) tells us that, in the long run, the growth rate of real GDP equals the growth rate of the labor force plus the rate of technological change. So, if either the growth rate of the labor force or the rate of technological change increases, the debt-to-GDP ratio will decrease.

---

[2]We show the full derivation of this equation in Appendix 15A at the end of the chapter.

The effect of an increase in the growth rate of the money supply is more difficult to analyze because the inflation rate also affects the nominal interest rate. When the nominal interest rate is constant, an increase in the growth rate of the money supply increases the inflation rate and reduces the debt-to-GDP ratio. However, the Fisher effect tells us that the increase in the inflation rate will lead to a higher nominal interest rate, and that increase will, in turn, raise the debt-to-GDP ratio. Therefore, the net effect of an increase in the growth rate of the money supply is ambiguous and may be zero. This observation raises an important point: *It is difficult to finance budget deficits simply by printing more money because nominal interest rates adjust upward, causing interest payments to also increase.* This effect is one explanation for the unsustainable hyperinflation in Germany from 1922 to 1923 (see Chapter 7).

Making the Connection

The European Debt Crisis

The United States was not the only country to experience an increase in debt during and after the financial crisis of 2007–2009. During the spring of 2010, many investors became reluctant to buy Greek government bonds because they were afraid that the government might default on the bonds. If the Greek government could not sell new bonds, the ΔB term in the government budget constraint equation would become zero. Because Greece uses the euro as its currency, the European Central Bank, rather than the central bank of Greece, controls the Greek monetary base. Greece does not have the option of expanding the monetary base to finance a budget deficit, and ΔMB is constant. Accordingly, the Greek government faced the hard choice of either defaulting on the interest payments due on its debt or dramatically reducing its primary budget deficit by raising taxes and cutting spending. To help prevent a default, the other countries using the euro and the International Monetary Fund (IMF) put together a bailout package of €110 billion. To receive these funds, the Greek government had to agree to increase taxes and cut spending. European countries and the IMF also created a €750 billion fund to help other European governments that might have difficulty financing their debts. The goal of the fund was to reassure investors that no country using the euro would default on its debt.

Unfortunately, the sovereign debt crisis that started with Greece during the spring of 2010 spread to Ireland during the fall. Ireland had kept government spending under control, but the collapse of its real estate market greatly weakened Irish banks. In an attempt to calm financial markets and assure the public that Irish banks were safe, the Irish government guaranteed the debt of Irish banks. As a result, the Irish government's budget deficit reached 32% of GDP during 2010. Ireland eventually had to accept a bailout of €85 billion from other European nations and the IMF in November 2010. Despite the bailout, investors were concerned that even with these funds, the Irish government would not be able to make the changes to its budget necessary to stabilize its economy. To make matters worse, the same concerns that forced a bailout of the Irish government led to problems in Spain.

Although Spain's sovereign debt burden was much less than that of Greece, by 2012, the Spanish economy was saddled with over €600 billion of private loans, which the Spanish government could not finance by itself. The real estate industry's collapse led to massive unemployment in Spain's construction industry. Total unemployment in Spain reached 25% in 2012. Although euro-zone countries created a €780 billion bailout fund, critics worried that this would not be enough to ensure that Spain would be able to continue making payments on its debt. But committing more money to the fund met resistance among many in Europe, especially in Germany, who would like countries in Southern Europe to do more to address their own economic problems. Europe's financial woes even led Moody's Investors Service to consider lowering its triple-A ratings on the debt of Germany, the Netherlands, and Luxembourg—Europe's strongest economies—due to the rising uncertainty about Europe's debt crisis.

The debt crisis has forced many countries to reevaluate the benefits of government programs relative to the long-term costs of maintaining those programs.

Sources: Jack Ewing, "The Euro Zone Crisis: A Primer," *New York Times*, May 22, 2012; "Saving the Euro: Ireland's Woes Are Largely of Its Own Making but German Bungling Has Made Matters Worse," *Economist*, November 18, 2010; "No Easy Exit," *Economist*, December 4, 2010; and Stephen Castle, "Economic Divisions in Euro Zone Are Seen as Threat," *New York Times*, November 30, 2010.

See related problem 2.4 at the end of the chapter.

When Is Fiscal Policy Sustainable?

Recall that the real interest rate, r, equals the nominal interest rate minus the inflation rate. We can use this relationship to eliminate the nominal interest rate and the inflation rate from the government budget constraint and rewrite the equation as:

$$\Delta\left(\frac{B_t}{P_t Y_t}\right) = \frac{PD_t}{P_t Y_t} + (r_t - g_y)\frac{B_{t-1}}{P_{t-1} Y_{t-1}} - \frac{\Delta MB_t}{P_t Y_t}.$$

This equation allows us to discuss whether a country's fiscal policy is sustainable. Fiscal policy is sustainable when the debt-to-GDP ratio is either constant or declining. Because seigniorage is normally very small, we can simplify our discussion by assuming that it is zero. We will also assume that the government's primary deficit is zero, so the above equation becomes:

$$\Delta\left(\frac{B_t}{P_t Y_t}\right) = (r_t - g_y)\frac{B_{t-1}}{P_{t-1} Y_{t-1}}.$$

This equation shows that the change in the debt-to-GDP ratio depends only on the real interest rate and the growth rate of real GDP. If the real interest rate is greater than the growth rate of real GDP:

$$r_t > g_y,$$

then:

$$\Delta\left(\frac{B_t}{P_t Y_t}\right) > 0,$$

so the debt-to-GDP ratio will increase even if the government has a primary deficit of zero. In this case, the government is forced to run a primary surplus just to prevent the debt-to-GDP ratio from rising to higher and higher levels. However, if:

$$r_t < g_y,$$

then:

$$\Delta\left(\frac{B_t}{P_tY_t}\right) < 0,$$

so the debt-to-GDP ratio will decrease. In this case, it is possible to have a primary deficit greater than zero and still have a sustainable fiscal policy.

Consider the United States during 2011. According to the Congressional Budget Office (CBO), the debt-to-GDP ratio for the United States was 62.8% during 2010. During 2011, the average real interest rate that the United States paid on long-term bonds was 1.2%, and the growth rate of real GDP was 1.8%. Assuming that the primary deficit and seigniorage are both zero, we have:

$$\Delta\left(\frac{B_t}{P_tY_t}\right) = (0.012 - 0.018)0.628 = -0.004, \text{ or } -0.4\%.$$

That is, if the U.S. government had a primary budget deficit of zero, the debt-to-GDP ratio for the United States would have decreased by 0.4%. However, the U.S. government actually ran a primary deficit during 2011, so the debt-to-GDP ratio rose to 67.7% by the end of 2011. The 1.8% growth rate of real GDP was well below the U.S. long-run average, so this calculation suggests that the U.S. government could reduce the debt-to-GDP ratio through economic growth if it found a way to reduce the primary budget deficit to zero.

Solved Problem 15.2

Can Japan Grow Its Way Out of Debt?

In Japan, the government debt reached 215% of GDP during 2010. Since 1990, economic growth in Japan has averaged just 0.7% per year, and the inflation rate (calculated as the growth rate of the GDP deflator) has averaged −0.7%. The Ministry of Finance reported that the average nominal interest rate that the government paid to borrow for 10 years was 1.2%. Given this information, was Japanese fiscal policy sustainable? If not, what would the primary budget deficit have to be to make fiscal policy sustainable?

Solving the Problem

Step 1 **Review the chapter material.** The problem asks you to determine whether fiscal policy is sustainable, so you may want to review the section "When Is Fiscal Policy Sustainable?" which begins on page 553.

Step 2 **Determine whether Japanese fiscal policy is sustainable.** To determine whether the debt is sustainable, you have to compare the real interest rate with the growth rate of real GDP. You know that the growth rate of real GDP was just 0.7%. You also know that the nominal interest rate was 1.2% and that the inflation rate was −0.7%. Using the definition of the real interest rate, you can calculate the real interest rate as:

$$r = 1.2 - (-0.7) = 1.9\%.$$

Because:

$$r > g_y,$$

Japan's debt was not sustainable, so even if the Japanese government had a primary deficit of zero, the debt-to-GDP ratio would continue to increase.

Step 3 **Determine the primary deficit necessary to make the debt stable.** You can use the equation for the government budget constraint from page 553:

$$\Delta\left(\frac{B_t}{P_tY_t}\right) = \frac{PD_t}{P_tY_t} + (r_t - g_y)\frac{B_{t-1}}{P_{t-1}Y_{t-1}} - \frac{\Delta MB_t}{P_tY_t}.$$

Seigniorage is usually small, so you can rewrite the preceding equation without seigniorage:

$$\Delta\left(\frac{B_t}{P_tY_t}\right) = \frac{PD_t}{P_tY_t} + (r_t - g_y)\frac{B_{t-1}}{P_{t-1}Y_{t-1}}.$$

The real interest rate was 1.9%, or 0.019, and the growth rate of real GDP has averaged 0.7%, or 0.007, so plugging these values into the preceding equation, you get:

$$\Delta\left(\frac{B_t}{P_tY_t}\right) = \frac{PD_t}{P_tY_t} + (0.019 - 0.007)\frac{B_{t-1}}{P_{t-1}Y_{t-1}}.$$

In 2010, the debt-to-GDP ratio was 215%, or 2.15, so you should plug this value in for the lagged debt-to-GDP ratio. Because the debt-to-GDP ratio is sustainable when the ratio is constant, you should plug in a value of 0 for the change in the debt-to-GDP ratio on the left side:

$$0 = \frac{PD_t}{P_tY_t} + (0.019 - 0.007)2.15.$$

Now, you can solve for the primary deficit:

$$\frac{PD_t}{P_tY_t} = -0.026, \text{ or } -2.6\%.$$

A negative number means that the Japanese government would have to run a primary *surplus* of 2.6% of GDP to make the debt sustainable. However, Japan actually had a primary *deficit* of 8.8% in 2010, so the debt is not sustainable. Unless Japan significantly increases its growth rate in the near future, it will not be able to grow its way out of the debt. Due to the slow growth of real GDP, moving to a sustainable fiscal policy will require Japan to run a primary surplus by increasing taxes and cutting spending.

See related problem 2.7 at the end of the chapter.

15.3

Learning Objective

Understand how fiscal policy affects the economy in the long run.

The Effects of Budget Deficits in the Long Run

In earlier chapters, we discussed the short-run effects of fiscal policy. In this section, we shift the focus to the long-run effects of fiscal policy.

The Budget Deficit and Crowding Out

The national income identities are useful because they must hold, given the definition of the variables (see Chapter 2). So, the identities act as constraints. Recall the following identity:

$$Y = C + I + G + NX.$$

As we show in Appendix 15B, we can modify the preceding equation to become:

$$[(G + TR) - T] = S_{\text{Household}} - I - NX,$$

where:

$$S_{\text{Household}} = Y + TR - T - C$$
$$[(G + TR) - T] = \text{the budget deficit}$$

This equation tells us that the government's budget deficit is financed by some combination of private savings, reduced private investment, and net exports. It might sound strange to say that net exports finance government deficits, but a trade deficit means that financial capital from abroad flows into the country. In effect, the country is borrowing from abroad to finance its budget deficit.

Suppose the government decides to decrease income taxes by $100 billion. To keep the deficit from increasing, the government could (1) reduce purchases by $100 billion; or (2) reduce transfer payments by $100 billion; or (3) increase other taxes by $100 billion.

If the government does not change policy, the budget deficit will increase by $100 billion. The government will have to issue $100 billion in new Treasury bonds, which requires the private sector to adjust. One possibility is that households may increase savings by $100 billion to purchase the new bonds. In this case, domestic households could reduce consumption by $100 billion. In effect, domestic households finance the higher deficit by cutting their own consumption. Alternatively, firms and households could decrease investment by $100 billion. This decline is called **crowding out**, which is a reduction in private investment caused by government budget deficits. Finally, the trade deficit could increase by $100 billion. The increased trade deficit is the equivalent of foreign governments and individuals purchasing $100 billion in new government bonds. So, the international indebtedness of the government increases.

Crowding out A reduction in private investment caused by government budget deficits.

The Conventional View: Crowding Out Private Investment

The conventional view among economists is that persistent budget deficits lead to higher real interest rates and crowd out private investment. If the government borrows $100 billion, that is $100 billion that households and firms cannot borrow to finance private investment. In other words, national savings have decreased. Because there are now fewer funds available for the private sector to borrow, competition among borrowers causes the real interest rate to increase. The higher real interest rate increases the cost of borrowing to finance investment, so investment spending decreases.

With a lower level of spending on new capital goods such as factories and computers, the private capital stock grows more slowly. As a result, the private capital stock in the future is not as large as it otherwise would have been. Therefore, the conventional view suggests that persistent budget deficits lead to a higher real interest rate, a smaller capital stock, and a lower level of potential GDP in the long run. This analysis suggests that there are significant long-run costs to running persistent budget deficits. We have to bear in mind, however, that budget deficits may finance investments in roads, bridges, and education, all of which may help increase economic growth. In addition, budget deficits might help stimulate the economy and reduce unemployment in the short run if the economy is below potential GDP. Policymakers have to balance the costs and benefits of budget deficits.

Ricardian Equivalence

Most economists agree that if government expenditure increases, national saving will decrease. The effect of tax cuts on national saving is subject to more debate, however. Robert Barro of Harvard University began the modern debate over the effects of tax cuts by reviving an argument he attributed to David Ricardo, the great nineteenth-century British economist.

Following Barro's argument, **Ricardian equivalence** is the theory that forward-looking households fully anticipate the future taxes required to pay off government debt,

Ricardian equivalence
The theory that forward-looking households fully anticipate the future taxes required to pay off government debt, so that reductions in lump-sum taxes have no effect on the economy.

Macro Data: Do Government Deficits Increase Real Interest Rates?

The conventional view predicts that government budget deficits lead to higher real interest rates. What is the evidence to support this prediction? Economists William Gale of the Brookings Institution and Peter Orszag, former director of the U.S. Office of Management and Budget, conducted a study in which they found relatively large effects of fiscal policy on long-term real interest rates. Gale and Orszag found that each 1-percentage-point increase in the deficit relative to GDP raises long-term real interest rates by 0.25 to 0.35 percentage point. They also found that the increase is between 0.40 and 0.70 percentage point when the primary budget deficit increases by 1 percentage point of GDP.

Studies using the debt-to-GDP ratio as the measure of fiscal policy, rather than the deficit-to-GDP ratio, often find smaller effects of fiscal policy on real interest rates. Economists Eric Engen of the Board of Governors of the Federal Reserve System and Glenn Hubbard of Columbia University examined the effect of government debt on real interest rates and investment. They found that a 1-percentage-point increase in the debt-to-GDP ratio increases long-term real interest rates by about 0.03 percentage point, which is a relatively small amount. The CBO estimates that gross federal debt held by the public will rise from 68% of GDP during 2011 to 93% of GDP

by 2022. This is a 25% increase in the debt-to-GDP ratio in just 10 years. The study by Engen and Hubbard suggests that the forecasted increase in the debt-to-GDP ratio will increase long-term real interest rates 0.75 percentage points over what they otherwise would have been. The higher real interest rates should lead to lower investment.

Economists have found a variety of estimates of the effects of fiscal policy on long-term real interest rates. The differences arise because some studies focus on the federal debt, others focus on deficits, and the definitions of *debt* and *deficit* can vary from study to study. In addition, the statistical techniques that economists use can also vary from study to study. As a result, the estimated magnitude of the effect of fiscal policy on long-term real interest rates varies. However, most studies support the conventional view that fiscal policy affects these rates.

Sources: William Gale and Peter Orszag, "Budget Deficits, National Savings, and Interest Rates," *Brookings Panel on Economic Activity*, Vol. 2004, No. 2, September 2004, pp. 101–187; and Eric Engen and R. Glenn Hubbard, "Federal Government Debt and Interest Rates," in Mark Gertler and Kenneth Rogoff, eds., *National Bureau of Economic Research Macroeconomics Annual*, Cambridge, MA: MIT Press, 2004, pp. 83–160.

See related problem 3.8 at the end of the chapter.

so that reductions in lump-sum taxes have no effect on the economy.[3] Lump-sum taxes are independent of the level of income and so do not have the distortionary effects on the decisions to save, invest, and work that changes in marginal tax rates do. If households consider lifetime disposable income and not just current disposable income when making consumption decisions, they will increase consumption only when lifetime disposable income increases and reduce consumption only when lifetime disposable income decreases.

Consider the effects of a $100 billion tax cut. To keep the analysis simple, let's just consider the situation over two years where any debt the government issues the first year it must pay off in the second year. Also assume that the government can borrow at an interest rate of 0%. This year, the government announces that it will cut taxes by $100 billion. Because the government must pay off the debt next year, it must raise taxes by $100 billion next year. Therefore, the decision by the government to cut taxes today by $100 billion is also a decision to increase taxes next year by $100 billion.

If households are forward looking in their consumption decisions, they recognize that their disposable income increases this year by $100 billion but then decreases next year by $100 billion. There is no change in lifetime disposable income for households, so there is no change in consumption. If consumption does not change, how do households alter their behavior in response to the $100 billion tax cut? Private saving must have increased by $100 billion in response to the tax cut. Ricardian equivalence implies that households use the extra disposable income from the tax cut to purchase government bonds this year and use the revenues from the maturing bonds next year to pay for the higher taxes.

Many economists are skeptical that Ricardian equivalence accurately describes the behavior of households. First, Ricardian equivalence assumes that households are forward looking in an extreme sense. In the previous example, we assumed that the relevant time frame was just two years. In reality, the government could cut taxes today and then not raise taxes to pay for the debt for 10 or more years. When the tax increase is in the distant future, households may not realize that their taxes will increase, so they may think that their lifetime disposable income has increased. As a result, they may increase consumption. Possibly the tax increase is not even in the current household's lifetime but instead occurs during their children's or grandchildren's lifetimes. In this case, the tax cut increases lifetime disposable income for existing households, so current consumption will increase, unless current households take into account the future incomes of their children and grandchildren. Of course, the tax increase in the future reduces lifetime disposable income of future households, but those households do not yet exist, so they cannot reduce consumption in the present.

Second, for Ricardian equivalence to hold, financial markets must work well enough that households can borrow or save as much as they would like at current interest rates. Suppose the government announces a tax increase this year of $100 billion and a corresponding tax cut of $100 billion next year. Lifetime disposable income has not

---

[3]David Ricardo actually considered but rejected the idea of Ricardian equivalence. Harvard economist Robert Barro is the most famous modern proponent of Ricardian equivalence. When Barro formulated the argument, he credited Ricardo for first mentioning the idea, and so the view has become known as Ricardian equivalence. See Robert J. Barro, "Are Government Bonds Net Wealth?" *Journal of Political Economy*, Vol. 82, No. 6, November–December 1974, pp. 1095–1117.

changed, but current disposable income has decreased by $100 billion. According to Ricardian equivalence, consumption will not change because, households can borrow to compensate for the drop in disposable income this year. But if some households are not able to borrow enough to keep consumption constant—perhaps because they lack acceptable collateral to get a loan—the tax increase will cause consumption to decrease.

Third, Ricardian equivalence applies only to lump-sum taxes, while tax changes typically involve changes in tax rates. As Barro acknowledges, changes in tax rates may affect household behavior by, for example, affecting the decision of individuals to supply labor. As a result, a tax increase today may reduce the quantity of labor supplied and reduce real GDP today. Taxes on capital income will affect the accumulation of the capital stock, which will also affect real GDP. So, tax changes that affect the behavior of households and firms may affect real GDP and consumption.

The Fiscal Challenges Facing the United States

When we discussed the composition of federal government expenditure and revenue in Section 15.1, we saw that transfer programs such as Medicare, Medicaid, and Social Security have been growing in importance. Rising spending on these programs is the main challenge for fiscal policy in the future. The United States and most other industrialized countries will experience similar issues due to the aging of their populations, so our main points apply to many countries.

Projections of Federal Government Revenue and Expenditure

The Congressional Budget Office (CBO) is responsible for forecasting federal government revenue and expenditure in future years. Doing so also allows the CBO to forecast the federal budget deficit and the likely path of the debt-to-GDP ratio.[4] Figure 15.6

15.4

Learning Objective
Explain the fiscal challenges facing the United States.

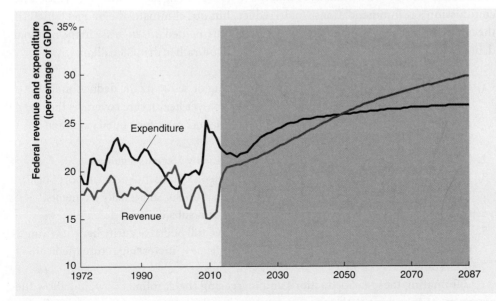

Figure 15.6

Federal Revenue and Expenditure as a Percentage of GDP, 1972–2087

The CBO projects that the federal budget will move from deficit to surplus beginning in 2049.

Note: The shaded area represents the CBO forecast.

Source: U.S. Congressional Budget Office.

---

[4]Congressional Budget Office, "The 2012 Long-Term Budget Outlook," June 5, 2012.

shows that revenue is expected to increase from 15.8% of GDP in 2012 to 29.8% of GDP in 2087. This change represents a significant increase in revenue above its historical average and by itself should lead to lower deficits and a lower debt-to-GDP ratio. Expenditure is expected to increase from 23.4% of GDP in 2012 to 26.8% of GDP in 2087. So, the CBO forecasts a substantial budget surplus of 3.0% of GDP for 2087, compared to a 2012 budget deficit of 7.6% of GDP. The CBO projects that the federal budget will move from deficit to surplus beginning in 2049. Given the uncertainties of economic projections that far in the future, the CBO's estimates need to be used with caution.

Making the Connection

Many Proposals but Not Much Progress on the Deficit

President Obama created the National Commission on Fiscal Responsibility and Reform to present ideas for reducing the federal budget deficit and putting the federal government's debt on a more sustainable path. The CBO projects that if current policies continue, the gross federal debt held by the public will eventually exceed 250% of U.S. GDP. The gap between projected expenditure and revenue is large enough that Dave Cote, CEO of Honeywell International and a member of the National Commission, asked, "What happens when the bank, in this case foreign countries like China, doesn't want to loan you any more money?" Senator Kent Conrad of North Dakota echoed these sentiments when he said: "If we fail to act now, our country could find itself in a circumstance in which we have to take draconian action at the worst possible time, in the midst of a crisis," which is what recently occurred in Europe with the debt crises in Greece, Ireland, Spain, and other countries.

To ensure that the United States does not experience Europe's problem, the commission recommended a number of changes to government expenditure and taxes. The commission's recommendations would reduce, but not eliminate, the budget deficit. If the commission's recommendations were fully implemented, *the increase* in the national debt between 2012 and 2020 would be only $4 trillion rather than $8 trillion.

The commission's recommendations were:

1. Raise $1.1 trillion in tax revenues by eliminating or reducing the deduction for home mortgage interest, the deduction for employer health care coverage, the tax exemption for municipal bonds, and preferential tax rates for capital gains and dividend income.
2. Increase the federal government's tax on gasoline by 15 cents a gallon.
3. Increase federal government taxes on higher-income households to support Social Security by raising or eliminating the income cap on Social Security payments.
4. Cap federal spending, including spending on farm subsidies and defense.
5. Eventually increase the retirement age to receive full Social Security benefits from 67 to 69. The commission also advocated significantly increasing future Medicare premiums.

Eliminating these tax deductions and increasing the gasoline tax would allow the government to reduce both corporate and personal income tax rates, potentially increasing aggregate supply (see Chapter 13). The bulk of the proposed benefit cuts would be borne by households that rely on government transfer programs, such as Medicare and Social Security. Most of the benefit cuts would be phased in over several decades and would not affect current retirees.

In December 2010, the commission's recommendations won the votes of 11 of 18 commission members, which was short of the 14 votes required to bring the recommendations to Congress for a vote.

Another panel, led by former Senator Pete Domenici and Alice Rivlin, budget director for President Bill Clinton, recommended measures that would reduce the debt by about $6 trillion between 2012 and 2020. The reductions would come from reform of the federal tax code; changes to Social Security, Medicare, and Medicaid; and a freeze on some domestic and defense spending.

Yet another attempt to address the federal government's deficit and debt problems was made in 2011 by the so-called "Gang of Six" consisting of three Democrats and three Republicans in the U.S. Senate. Although the Gang of Six failed to reach agreement on deficit-reducing measures in 2011, members of the "Gang" and other senators renewed attempts in 2012 to agree on a reform of federal tax code, control of entitlement spending, and limits on defense and discretionary spending.

By late 2012, the president and Congress had not adopted any of the recommendations of these commissions and panels. This failure demonstrates the difficulty of reaching bipartisan agreement to reduce the deficit. Ultimately, though, both supporters and opponents of the various reform recommendations believe it is critical to eventually reach a consensus on measures to reduce the nation's long-term deficit.

Sources: John Harwood, "In Presidential Race's Give-and-Take, Hope for a Fiscal Compromise," *New York Times*, April 22, 2012; and Jon Healey, "Fiscal Cliff Looming, the 'Gang of Six' Rides Again," *Los Angeles Times*, June 9, 2012; "Deficit Panel: In Members' Words," *Wall Street Journal*, December 1, 2010; Jackie Calmes, "Panel Seeks Cuts in Social Security and Higher Taxes," *New York Times*, November 11, 2010, p. A1; Damian Paletta and Jonathan Weisman, "Deficit Plan Wins Backers—Bipartisan Support Adds Momentum Despite Sharp Criticism from Left and Right," *Wall Street Journal*, December 2, 2010; and "National Commission on Fiscal Responsibility and Reform," *New York Times*, December 3, 2010.

See related problem 4.4 at the end of the chapter.

Will the United States Pay Off Its Debt?

The CBO's projections shown in Figure 15.6 indicate that the debt-to-GDP ratio will increase moderately over the next few years and then begin to decline. Because the federal budget is projected to be in surplus beginning in 2049, the debt-to-GDP ratio eventually falls to zero in 2069, which means that all of the publicly held national debt will have been paid off.

But the projections shown in Figure 15.6 are based on the assumption that spending and taxing laws as they were in June 2012 continue. Large tax increases and spending cuts were scheduled to occur in January 2013. The projections in Figure 15.6 assume that these tax increases and spending cuts occur and are maintained in future years. The CBO also prepares projections based on what it calls an "Extended Alternative Fiscal Scenario." This scenario assumes the continuation of current *policies* rather than current laws. So, with this scenario, the CBO assumes that tax and spending policies that were in effect in 2012 are continued in later years. Figure 15.7 shows that changing assumptions

Figure 15.7

Two Scenarios for Federal Debt as a Percentage of GDP, 2012–2087

The CBO prepares two projections of future federal revenue and expenditure. The projection that assumes that current laws will continue into the future results in the debt-to-GDP ratio falling beginning in 2014 and becoming zero by 2069. The projection which assumes that current policies continue into the future results in the debt-to-GDP ratio exploding to 250% by 2043.

Source: U.S. Congressional Budget Office.

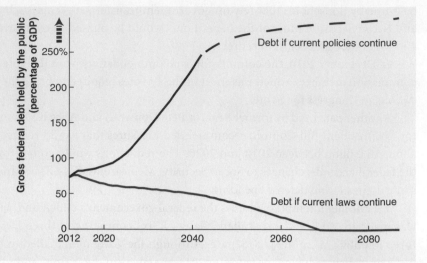

about future spending and taxes has a huge effect on projections of the debt-to-GDP ratio. While assuming that current *laws* continue causes the debt-to-GDP ratio to decline toward zero, as shown by the blue line, assuming that current *policies* continue results in the debt-to-GDP ratio exploding to 250% by 2043, as shown by the red line. In fact, the ratio increases even further from there, but the CBO doesn't calculate it, reasoning that in practice, the president and Congress would change polices to avoid further increases.

If current policies continue, the debt-to-GDP ratio explodes because government spending on transfer programs such as Medicare, Medicaid, and Social Security outpaces increases in revenue. In addition, the federal government has to pay interest on the new debt it issues, so net interest payments rise dramatically. Figure 15.8 shows the composition of federal government expenditure from 1972 to 2042. "Other expenditure" includes spending on defense, education, infrastructure, research and development, and all other federal spending apart from Social Security, Medicare and Medicaid, and net

Figure 15.8

Composition of Federal Government Expenditure, 1972–2042

The CBO forecasts that rising spending on Medicare, Medicaid, Social Security, and interest payments will cause federal expenditure to increase from 23.9% of GDP in 2011 to 38.6% of GDP in 2042.

Note: The shaded area represents the CBO forecast.

Source: U.S. Congressional Budget Office.

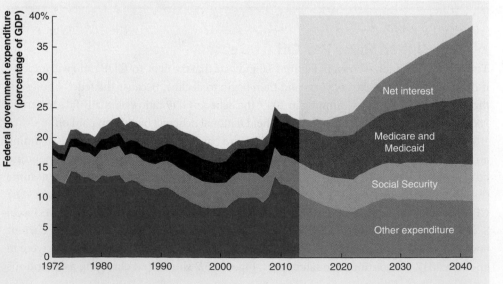

interest payments. This expenditure is projected to decrease from 11.6% of GDP in 2012 to 9.5% of GDP in 2042. In contrast, spending on Medicare, Medicaid, and Social Security is projected to rise from 10.4% of GDP in 2012 to 18.3% of GDP in 2042. Interest payments are also projected to increase from 1.4% of GDP in 2011 to 11.8% of GDP in 2042. In other words, in 2042 the federal government will be paying more in interest on the national debt than it will for all other spending, apart from Social Security, Medicare, and Medicaid. And it will be spending nearly twice as much on Social Security, Medicare, and Medicaid as on all other programs.

Total federal expenditure averaged 20.5% of GDP from 1972 to 2012. Figure 15.8 tells us that under current policies, federal expenditure may soar to 38.6% of GDP in 2042. The key driver of this increase will be spending on Social Security, Medicare, and Medicaid and interest payments on the national debt. Spending on Social Security, Medicare, and Medicaid will increase because the population is aging, and healthcare costs are expected to rise faster than inflation. So if these programs remain as they are, the federal government will consume a much larger share of GDP in the future.

Policy Options

Most economists believe that the expected future budget deficits and increasing debt-to-GDP ratio will crowd out private investment spending and reduce the size of the capital stock below what it would otherwise be. A smaller capital stock will reduce income per capita in future years.

If the federal government wants to avoid the decrease in income that results from a smaller capital stock, it has several options.

Could the Federal Government Rely on Seigniorage? The government can finance a budget deficit by issuing new Treasury bonds or through seigniorage. The CBO's forecasts of the costs of current fiscal policy assume that the federal government finances the budget deficits by issuing new bonds. Can the federal government reduce the costs of its fiscal policy by financing the deficits with seigniorage? No. Seigniorage would require increasing the growth rate of the money supply, which in the long run also increases nominal interest rates through the Fisher effect. So, financing budget deficits by increasing the money supply will cause interest payments to rise more rapidly. The new higher nominal interest rates will increase the budget deficit further, which will require even more seigniorage and an even faster growth rate of the money supply. As the growth rate of the money supply increases, the economy will eventually run the risk of hyperinflation. It is unlikely that the federal government could sustain the current fiscal policy using seigniorage. In effect, the government would be *monetizing* the budget deficit. Countries that rely on monetizing the deficit, such as Germany after World War I, run the risk of experiencing hyperinflation.

Could the Federal Government Rely on Increased Taxes on Wages and Capital Income? If the government increases taxes on wages, the opportunity cost of leisure will decrease, and households will supply less labor, which will decrease potential GDP. The government may consider raising payroll taxes, which are taxes levied on both workers and employers to support the Social Security and Medicare programs. The portion of the payroll tax used to fund Social Security has an income cap, although the portion used to fund Medicare does not. So, the federal government could raise a substantial amount of funds by increasing the amount of income subject to the Social Security payroll tax.

Although, once again, after-tax wages will decline, which may reduce potential GDP. If the government increases taxes on capital income by raising taxes on dividends and capital gains or by raising the corporate income tax, the after-tax return to capital will decline. As a result, households will save less, and investment and the capital stock will decline, which will decrease potential GDP. Whether the government increases individual income taxes, payroll taxes, or taxes on capital income, the result is likely to be a reduction in potential GDP. In particular, if the federal government were to attempt to eliminate future deficits *solely* through tax increases, the negative effects on potential GDP could be very large.

Could the Federal Government Rely on Reductions to Primary Expenditure? The federal government could reduce expenditure on programs such as education, science, and technology. Education expenditure allows individuals to accumulate human capital that makes them more productive and increases total factor productivity. Expenditure on science and technology increases knowledge, which also increases total factor productivity. As we saw when discussing long-run economic growth, when total factor productivity increases, potential GDP also increases. Therefore, cutting these programs may lead to a decrease in potential GDP similar to what would occur if the government increased taxes.

The federal government could also reduce expenditure on infrastructure projects such as roads and bridges. The private sector decides which and how many private capital goods to produce, while the government determines spending on capital goods such as roads and bridges. Economists call roads, bridges, and similar infrastructure *government capital*. Government capital is useful for producing goods and services. For example, many firms use highways for transportation, so infrastructure and other government capital are important factors of production.

Christophe Kamps, a senior economist at the European Central Bank, estimates that in OECD countries, a 1% increase in the government capital stock increases real GDP by about 0.22%. He finds that increasing the private capital stock by 1% increases real GDP by 0.26%, so government and private capital are about equally productive.[5] The findings of Kamps and other economists suggest that if the government reduces spending on government capital goods to make fiscal policy sustainable, it may reduce potential GDP.

The government could also reduce spending on national defense. Spending on national defense does not affect total factor productivity, but it does provide other important benefits, notably national security. Even if the federal government reduced defense spending to zero, there would still be a budget deficit because defense spending was 4.7% of GDP during 2011, while the federal primary budget deficit was 7.5%. Cutting defense spending can reduce, but not eliminate, the deficit. Just as relying solely on tax increases to eliminate the long-term deficit is not feasible, relying solely on cuts in government expenditure is also not feasible.

Could the Federal Government Rely on Reductions to Medicare, Medicaid, and Social Security? Regardless of how the federal government ultimately deals with the looming fiscal challenges, the adjustments are likely to be costly. To maintain the promised expenditure on Social Security, Medicare, and Medicaid, the federal government will have to take actions that are likely to reduce potential GDP and, therefore, average income. To

---

[5]Christophe Kamps, "New Estimates for Government Net Capital Stocks for 22 OECD Countries, 1960–2001," *International Monetary Fund Staff Papers*, Vol. 53, No. 1, 2006, pp. 120–150.

Table 15.1 The Effects of Potential Changes to Fiscal Policy

If the government tries to make the debt sustainable by . . .	then . . .	causing . . .	resulting in . . .
increasing seigniorage	the growth rate of the money supply will increase substantially	a rapid increase in inflation	an eventual collapse of the financial system and lower potential GDP.
increasing taxes on wages	the opportunity cost of leisure will decrease	households to supply less labor	lower potential GDP.
increasing taxes on capital income	the after-tax return to capital goods will decrease	firms and households to accumulate less capital	lower potential GDP.
decreasing expenditure on education, science, and technology	reductions in the accumulation of human capital and in research and development will occur	a slowdown in the growth of technology	lower potential GDP
decreasing expenditure on government capital goods	the government capital stock will decrease	private capital goods to become less productive	lower potential GDP.
decreasing expenditure on Social Security, Medicare, and Medicaid	the government will not support the elderly and poor as much as projected	some of the elderly and poor to bear the burden of reducing the deficit	lower income and standard of living for some of the elderly and poor.

the extent that the government reduces spending on these programs, it forces those who benefit from them to bear some of the cost of adjusting fiscal policy. Economic research does provide some guidance on the magnitude of the costs involved.

Using economic efficiency as the standard, most economic models imply that reducing government spending is preferable to increasing taxes. Economists Alberto Alesina of Harvard University, Silvia Ardagna of Harvard University, Roberto Perotti of Bocconi University, and Fabio Schiantarelli of Boston College have studied the effects of fiscal policy on investment in OECD countries.[6] They found that when spending on programs similar to Social Security, Medicare, and Medicaid increases by 1 percentage point of GDP, in equilibrium private investment decreases by 1.3 percentage points of GDP. Increasing taxes on labor by 1 percentage point of GDP to pay for these types of programs decreases investment by another 0.7 percentage points of GDP. The CBO projects that these programs may increase from 10.4% of GDP in 2012 to 18.3% of GDP in 2042.

Although economic research indicates that eliminating the long-run deficit mainly by reducing spending on Social Security, Medicare, and Medicaid would lead to smaller reductions in potential GDP, significant reductions in spending on these programs would seem inequitable to many people. Any policy changes to address the long-run fiscal challenges facing the United States are likely to take into account both equity and efficiency. Therefore, it seems probable that policymakers will ultimately enact some combination of expenditure reductions and tax increases. Table 15.1 summarizes the effects of potential changes to fiscal policy.

---

[6]Alberto Alesina, Silvia Ardagna, Roberto Perotti, and Fabio Schiantarelli, "Fiscal Policy, Profits, and Investment," *American Economic Review*, Vol. 92, No. 3, June 2002, pp. 571–589.

Answering the Key Question

Continued from page 543

At the beginning of this chapter, we asked:

"How can the United States solve its long-run fiscal problem?"

If current policies continue, the CBO forecasts that starting around 2020 there will be rapid increases in both federal government expenditure and revenue. Because revenue will lag well behind expenditure, large budget deficits will lead to a rising debt-to-GDP ratio. The CBO forecasts that the debt-to-GDP ratio will rise to such high levels that fiscal policy will become unsustainable. Policymakers will be faced with difficult choices regarding tax increases and expenditure cuts. Either raising taxes or cutting expenditure seems likely to reduce potential GDP. Balancing equity and efficiency will be part of the process of arriving at a sustainable fiscal policy. Cutting any one category of expenditure or raising any one type of tax will probably not be sufficient to eliminate the long-run budget deficit.

Key Terms and Problems

Key Terms

Budget deficit, p. 545
Crowding out, p. 556
Gross federal debt, p. 547

Gross federal debt held by the
   public, p. 544
Primary budget deficit (*PD*), p. 545

Ricardian equivalence, p. 557
Seigniorage, p. 545

15.1 ## Debt and Deficits in Historical Perspective
Discuss basic facts about the U.S. government's fiscal situation.

Review Questions

1.1 What is the difference between total federal debt and gross federal debt held by the public?

1.2 Why is debt usually measured using the debt-to-GDP ratio rather than the absolute amount of debt? How is the debt-to-GDP ratio used to determine whether a fiscal policy is sustainable?

1.3 What is the difference between the budget deficit and the primary budget deficit? Use the government's budget constraint to express the relationship between the budget deficit and the primary budget deficit algebraically.

Problems and Applications

1.4 Gross federal debt was greater than $16 trillion at the end of 2012. Historically, interest rates on Treasury bonds have been considerably higher than they were in 2012. Assume, for simplicity, that the government pays the same interest rate on all outstanding debt. What is the approximate annual interest payment if the debt is $16 trillion and the interest rate is:

a. 0.5%?

b. 3%?

c. 5%?

1.5 The CBO estimates that the federal budget deficit was $1.3 trillion in 2012. If gross federal debt were $16 trillion then for each of the interest rates given in problem 1.4, calculate the primary budget deficit and the difference between the deficit and the primary budget deficit.

1.6 Briefly explain whether you agree with the following statement: "Because the government can always print more money, the size of the budget deficit doesn't matter."

1.7 The dollar value of the U.S. public debt is the highest in U.S. history and the highest, in absolute terms, in the world. Is this fact a reason to be concerned about the debt? Briefly explain.

15.2 The Sustainability of Fiscal Policy
Explain when fiscal policy is sustainable and when it is not sustainable.

Review Questions

2.1 What does it mean to say that fiscal policy is either sustainable or unsustainable? What are the consequences for a country of having a fiscal policy that is unsustainable?

2.2 Identify each term in the following equation:

$$\Delta\left(\frac{B_t}{P_t Y_t}\right) = \frac{PD_t}{P_t Y_t} + (r_t - g_y)\frac{B_{t-1}}{P_{t-1} Y_{t-1}} - \frac{\Delta MB_t}{P_t Y_t}.$$

How can this equation be used to determine whether a country's debt is sustainable? In your analysis, assume that seigniorage and the government's primary deficit are both zero.

Problems and Applications

2.3 For each of the following scenarios, explain the effect on the debt-to-GDP ratio.

a. The growth rate of the labor force decreases.

b. The nominal interest rate on existing bonds increases.

c. The monetary base increases, which causes the rate of inflation to rise.

d. The monetary base decreases, but there is no change in the rate of inflation.

2.4 [Related to the Making the Connection **on page 552**] In July 2012, the Greek finance minister announced that the country's 2012 deficit would be 5.4% of GDP, down from 9% in 2011, and primary public expenditure would decline by more than €2.7 billion from the previous year. Aside from spending cuts, does Greece have any other alternatives for reducing its deficit? Briefly explain.
Source: "Greece Budget 2012," finance.mapsofworld.com/budget/greece/.

2.5 Briefly explain whether you agree with the following statement: "The only way for a country with a budget deficit to have sustainable fiscal policy in the long run is to cut government spending."

2.6 In 2012, interest rates in the United States remained at historically low levels, and the Fed indicated that it would not increase its target for the federal funds rate until at least mid-2015. A July 2012 article in the *New York Times* reported, "[Federal Reserve Chairman] Bernanke told Congress that . . . he and other Fed officials had concluded that the central bank needed to expand its stimulus campaign unless the nation's economy showed signs of improvement, including job growth." How is a monetary policy of maintaining low interest rates likely to affect the sustainability of fiscal policy?
Source: Binyamin Appelbaum, "Fed Leaning Closer to New Stimulus if No Growth Is Seen," *New York Times*, July 24, 2012.

2.7 [Related to Solved Problem 15.2 **on page 554**] The sustainability of fiscal policy is partly a function of the growth rate of GDP. Some economists have forecast that Japan's growth rate may decrease below the current 10-year average of 0.7%.

a. If the growth rate of GDP fell to −0.5%, how would this affect the sustainability of Japan's fiscal policy?

b. Based on the growth rate in part (a) and using the other values from Solved Problem 15.2, calculate the level of the primary deficit required to make Japan's fiscal policy sustainable.

MyEconLab Visit **www.myeconlab.com** to complete these exercises online and get instant feedback. Exercises that update with real-time data are marked with 🌐.

2.8 Suppose that a country has a debt-to-GDP ratio of 64%. Its growth rate of real GDP is 3%. Assume that seigniorage is zero and the real interest rate is 2%. What primary deficit as a percentage of GDP would be required to make fiscal policy sustainable?

15.3 The Effects of Budget Deficits in the Long Run
Understand how fiscal policy affects the economy in the long run.

Review Questions

3.1 Briefly describe the ways to finance a government budget deficit.

3.2 Explain what effects a government budget deficit and a surplus have on long-term real interest rates, the capital stock, labor productivity, and potential GDP.

3.3 Explain Ricardian equivalence. Why are some economists skeptical about the validity of Ricardian equivalence?

Problems and Applications

3.4 [Related to the Chapter Opener on page 543] The chapter opener suggests that deficits are generally a problem for countries. Based on the discussion in Section 15.3, are there circumstances in which it might be possible that deficits could increase productivity and long-run growth?

3.5 Use the following equation to demonstrate how an increase in the budget deficit must increase the trade deficit if neither consumption nor investment changes:

$$[(G + TR) - T] = S_{Household} - I - NX.$$

What must happen if there is an increase in the budget deficit in a closed economy?

3.6 In early 2011, Congress renewed the tax cuts first passed by the Bush administration in 2001 for a 2-year period. The original tax cuts were set to expire 10 years after they were first passed.

a. Assume that the tax cuts were lump-sum tax cuts. If Ricardian equivalence holds, what should have been the effect of the original tax cuts?

b. The original tax cuts changed income tax rates so that they were not lump-sum tax cuts. How does this fact change your answer to part (a)?

3.7 In March 2012, Spain announced budget cuts of €27 billion, in an effort to reduce its budget deficit. A *CNN* article quotes Treasury Minister Cristobal Montoro: "We are in a critical situation. This is the most austere budget in our democracy." The budget proposal included spending cuts for government agencies, infrastructure, defense, and education, as well as reduced aid for immigrants. The proposal also included increases in business taxes and a salary freeze and extended work hours for civil servants.

a. What is the likely effect of these actions on saving, investment, and the real interest rate?

b. In what ways are the short-run and long-run effects of this deficit reduction likely to differ?

Source: Al Goodman, "Spain Announces 27 Billion Euros in Budget Cuts," *CNN*, March 30, 2012.

3.8 [Related to the Macro Data feature on page 557] Studies have shown a link between rising debt-to-GDP ratios and real interest rates. Investment is not the only category of spending that might be sensitive to interest rates.

a. How might consumption be affected by rising interest rates due to a government deficit? Will all types of consumption be affected equally?

b. Do the data presented suggest that rising interest rates are currently a significant concern in the United States?

MyEconLab Visit **www.myeconlab.com** to complete these exercises online and get instant feedback. Exercises that update with real-time data are marked with (w).

15.4 The Fiscal Challenges Facing the United States
Explain the fiscal challenges facing the United States.

Review Questions

4.1 Explain the main reasons for the projected increases in the U.S. budget deficit in coming years. Based on these projected future budget deficits, explain why the current fiscal policy of the federal government is unsustainable.

4.2 List the policy options for making fiscal policy sustainable. What are the advantages and disadvantage of each of these options?

Problems and Applications

4.3 The budget deficit projections in this chapter include net interest payments on the debt, the size of which depends on interest rates. What is likely to happen to interest rates and interest payments if the size of the deficit continues to increase?

4.4 [Related to the Making the Connection on page 560] Evidence suggests that the method of deficit reduction that least reduces economic efficiency may be slower growth in transfer payments, such as Social Security and Medicare.

   a. If consumers believe that deficit reduction must occur in this way, how might they change their current behavior?

   b. How might consumer expectations of future Social Security cuts make the process of deficit reduction easier or more difficult?

4.5 According to an analysis conducted by *USA Today*: "The typical American household would have paid nearly all of its income in taxes last year to balance the budget if the government used standard accounting rules to compute the deficit." Under standard accounting rules, future retirement benefit commitments must be included in financial statements, but these commitments are not included in CBO calculations of U.S. federal debt. When including these retirement benefit figures, the official deficit of $1.3 trillion in 2011 would increase to $5 trillion. How would using standard accounting rules to measure the deficit change debt-to-GDP ratio estimates, and what does this analysis indicate about the fiscal challenges facing the United States?

Source: Dennis Cauchon, "Real Federal Deficit Dwarfs Official Tally," *USA Today*, May 24, 2012.

Data Exercises

D15.1: [Excel exercise] Countries in the euro zone, are required to place limits on the debt and budget deficits of the national government. Deficits are required to be less than 3% of GDP and government debt is required to be less than 60% of GDP. The International Monetary Funds' World Economic Outlook provides data on government deficits and debt that will allow you to determine how well governments meet both of these criteria. The data are available at http://www.imf.org/external/pubs/ft/weo/2012/01/weodata/index.aspx

   a. For France, Germany, Greece, Italy, and Spain, download annual data for the 2011 to 2017 period on "General government net lending/borrowing" as a percent of GDP to use as a measure of the budget deficit. Note that the values for later years are forecasted values and that negative values indicate a budget deficit. Calculate the average forecasted budget deficit from 2012 to 2017.

   b. Repeat part (a) for government debt using "General government gross debt."

MyEconLab Visit **www.myeconlab.com** to complete these exercises online and get instant feedback. Exercises that update with real-time data are marked with ⬤.

c. How will fiscal policy have to change for these countries to meet the requirements for remaining in the euro zone?

d. What would be the short-run effect of these policy changes on the euro zone economy? What would be the short-run effect on the U.S. economy?

D15.2: [Excel exercise] The International Monetary Funds' "World Economic Outlook" provides annual data on government debt and deficit for the United Kingdom from 1980 to the present. The data are available at http://www.imf.org/external/pubs/ft/weo/2012/01/weodata/index.aspx

a. Download the data for "General government net lending/borrowing" as a measure of the budget deficit. Note that a negative number indicates a budget deficit. In addition, download the data for "General government gross debt" as a percent of GDP as a measure of government debt.

b. Graph the data. How do the debt and deficit data compare to the values for the United States discussed in the chapter?

D15.3: [Excel exercise] Using data from the St. Louis Federal Reserve (FRED) (http://research.stlouisfed.org/fred2/), examine the change in foreign ownership of U.S. government debt.

a. Download quarterly data on Federal debt held by foreign and international investors (FDHBFIN) and nominal GDP (GDP) from 1970 to the present.

b. Calculate the foreign ownership of U.S. debt as a percentage of GDP. Plot the data on a graph.

c. What trends do you notice?

d. Suppose that the U.S. government suddenly lost the ability to borrow from abroad. What would be the immediate effect on the U.S. economy? Briefly explain.

D15.4: [Excel exercise] The International Monetary Fund's "World Economic Outlook "contains data on government debt for many of the countries in the world. The data are available at http://www.imf.org/external/pubs/ft/weo/2012/01/weodata/index.aspx.

a. Download data for "General government gross debt" as a percent of GDP as a measure of government debt for the current year.

b. Calculate the mean and standard deviation for government debt for all of the countries in the database. Is the U.S. government debt above or below the average? Is it above or below the median?

c. What does your answer to part (b) tell you about the U.S. government's fiscal situation compared to other countries? Explain.

d. The International Monetary Fund also provides forecasts of government debt in the future. Pick the year furthest into the future and repeat parts (b) and (c).

D15.5: [Excel exercise] The International Monetary Fund's "World Economic Outlook" contains data on government spending and taxes. The data are available at http://www.imf.org/external/pubs/ft/weo/2012/01/weodata/index.aspx. The United States is frequently described as having lower levels of government spending and taxes compared to countries in Western Europe.

a. For the sub-category of countries that the International Monetary Fund describes as "Major advanced economies (G7)" download annual data on "General government revenue" and "General government total expenditure" both measured as a percent of GDP from 2001 to the present.

b. Plot the revenue data on a graph. How does the United States compare to the countries from Western Europe?

c. Repeat part (b) for total expenditure.

Appendix A

Showing the Conditions for a Sustainable Fiscal Policy

To derive equations for the sustainability of fiscal policy, take the equation for the government's budget constraint on page 545, divide it by nominal GDP, and move the term representing seigniorage to the left side of the equation to obtain:

$$\frac{PD_t}{P_tY_t} + i_t\frac{B_{t-1}}{P_tY_t} - \frac{\Delta MB_t}{P_tY_t} = \frac{\Delta B_t}{P_tY_t}.$$

Because $\Delta B_t = B_t - B_{t-1}$, we can rewrite the above equation as:

$$\frac{PD_t}{P_tY_t} + i_t\frac{B_{t-1}}{P_tY_t} + \frac{B_{t-1}}{P_tY_t} - \frac{\Delta MB_t}{P_tY_t} = \frac{B_t}{P_tY_t}.$$

Grouping like terms, we obtain:

$$\frac{PD_t}{P_tY_t} + (1 + i_t)\frac{B_{t-1}}{P_tY_t} - \frac{\Delta MB_t}{P_tY_t} = \frac{B_t}{P_tY_t}.$$

We can multiply and divide by last period's nominal GDP and rearrange terms to obtain:

$$\frac{PD_t}{P_tY_t} + (1 + i_t)\frac{B_{t-1}}{P_{t-1}Y_{t-1}}\left(\frac{P_{t-1}Y_{t-1}}{P_tY_t}\right) - \frac{\Delta MB_t}{P_tY_t} = \frac{B_t}{P_tY_t}.$$

The new term in parentheses is the inverse of 1 plus the growth rate of nominal GDP. The growth rate of nominal GDP equals the inflation rate plus the growth rate of real GDP, so we can rewrite the equation as:

$$\frac{PD_t}{P_tY_t} + \left(\frac{1 + i_t}{1 + \pi_t + g_{Y_t}}\right)\frac{B_{t-1}}{P_{t-1}Y_{t-1}} - \frac{\Delta MB_t}{P_tY_t} = \frac{B_t}{P_tY_t}.$$

The ratio $\left(\dfrac{1 + i_t}{1 + \pi_t + g_{Y_t}}\right) \cong 1 + i_t - \pi_t - g_{Y_t}$, so the above equation becomes:

$$\frac{PD_t}{P_tY_t} + (1 + i_t - \pi_t - g_{y_t})\frac{B_{t-1}}{P_{t-1}Y_{t-1}} - \frac{\Delta MB_t}{P_tY_t} = \frac{B_t}{P_tY_t}.$$

This expression is just:

$$\frac{PD_t}{P_tY_t} + \frac{B_{t-1}}{P_{t-1}Y_{t-1}} + (i_t - \pi_t - g_{y_t})\frac{B_{t-1}}{P_{t-1}Y_{t-1}} - \frac{\Delta MB_t}{P_tY_t} = \frac{B_t}{P_tY_t}.$$

Now, move the $\dfrac{B_{t-1}}{P_{t-1}Y_{t-1}}$ term to the right side of the equation, and the result is:

$$\Delta\left(\frac{B_t}{P_tY_t}\right) = \frac{PD_t}{P_tY_t} + [i_t - (\pi_t + g_y)]\frac{B_{t-1}}{P_{t-1}Y_{t-1}} - \frac{\Delta MB_t}{P_tY_t}.$$

The Fisher effect tells us that the real interest rate is the nominal interest rate minus inflation, or:

$$r_t = i_t - \pi_t.$$

If we plug the Fisher effect into the previous equation, we get:

$$\Delta\left(\frac{B_t}{P_t Y_t}\right) = \frac{PD_t}{P_t Y_t} + [r_t - g_y]\frac{B_{t-1}}{P_{t-1} Y_{t-1}} - \frac{\Delta MB_t}{P_t Y_t}.$$

Appendix B

Showing the Relationship between Budget Deficits and Private Expenditure

15.B

Learning Objective:

Derive the equation showing the relationship between budget deficits and private expenditure.

To derive the relationship between budget deficits and private expenditure, we start with the basic national income identity:

$$Y = C + I + G + NX.$$

We add transfer payments to each side and subtract taxes from each side of the equation to obtain:

$$Y + TR - T = C + I + [G + TR - T] + NX.$$

Next, we move consumption to the left side of the equation to obtain:

$$Y + TR - T - C = I + [G + TR - T] + NX.$$

Recall that private savings is:

$$S_{\text{Household}} = Y + TR - T - C.$$

Private savings is therefore just the left side of the previous equation, so:

$$S_{\text{Household}} = I + [(G + TR) - T] + NX.$$

Finally, solve for the government's budget deficit, and the result is:

$$[(G + TR) - T] = S_{\text{Household}} - I - NX.$$

CHAPTER 16

Consumption and Investment

Learning Objectives

After studying this chapter, you should be able to:

16.1 Discuss the macroeconomic implications of microeconomic decision making by households and firms (pages 574–575)

16.2 Explain the determinants of personal consumption (pages 576–591)

16.3 Explain the determinants of private investment (pages 591–603)

Are All Tax Cuts Created Equal?

Suppose you read that to increase growth in real GDP and reduce unemployment, the president and Congress have enacted a tax cut. Your employer tells you to expect an extra $80 per month in your paycheck. What will you do with the money? Spend all of it? Save all of it? Spend some and save some? Will your decision depend on whether the tax cut will last just one year or is a permanent change in the tax laws?

How consumers respond to a tax cut clearly affects how much the tax cut will increase aggregate expenditure. In particular, most economists believe that whether a tax cut is *temporary* or *permanent* affects consumers' decisions about how much of a tax cut they will spend. If you are like most consumers, you will spend more of that $80 per month tax cut if it is permanent than if it is temporary.

So, we can conclude that policymakers should rely on permanent tax cuts rather than temporary tax cuts to stimulate the economy. But permanent tax cuts will result in continuing budget deficits unless the tax cuts are offset by spending decreases. Policymakers, then, are faced with a dilemma: Permanent tax cuts are more effective in stimulating the economy but can cause long-run fiscal problems.

President Barack Obama and Congress wrestled with this problem in 2010. In November 2010, the U.S. economy was recovering slowly from the 2007–2009 recession, and the unemployment rate was 9.8%, which

Continued on next page

Key Issue and Question

Issue: Households and firms make decisions about how much to consume and invest based on expectations about the future.

Question: How does government tax policy affect the decisions of households and firms?

Answered on page 603

was actually higher than the 9.5% rate in June 2009, when the recession had ended. Should policymakers further increase government spending or enact new tax cuts? To complicate matters, policymakers were facing a deadline of January 1, 2011, when tax cuts passed in 2001 and 2003, during the administration of President George W. Bush, were set to expire.

In December 2010, with the deadline looming, President Obama signed a law that extended for two years the tax cuts of 2001 and 2003, provided a one-year reduction of 2 percentage points in the payroll taxes used to fund the Social Security and Medicare programs, and enacted various tax incentives for businesses to invest in new capital goods. Supporters of the bill argued that the payroll and personal income tax cuts would encourage households to increase consumption, while the tax incentives to businesses would increase investment. Opponents of the act were skeptical that real

GDP and employment would rise significantly because the tax cuts were temporary. They also pointed out that the falling tax revenue would increase the federal government's budget deficit, which was already near record peacetime levels. A larger budget deficit would necessarily increase the national debt.

How much did these tax cuts increase aggregate expenditure? As of this writing, not enough time has passed for economists to have arrived at a consensus judgment. Early estimates, though, indicated that the tax cut package may have increased the growth rate of real GDP during 2011 by between 0.5% and 1.0%.

The response of households and firms to changes in taxes play an important role in formulating economic policy. In this chapter, we look more closely at how households and firms make their decisions about consumption and investment. Doing so will help us to better predict the effectiveness of different fiscal policy actions.

Sources: David Herszenhorn, "Congress Passes Tax Cut Package for $801 Billion," *New York Times*, December 17, 2010; Janet Hook and John McKinnon, "Congress Passes Tax Deal: Divided Legislature Adopts Sweeping Measure to Avert Increases, Add New Breaks," *Wall Street Journal*, December 17, 2010; and Sudeep Reddy, "The Tax Agreement: Package Would Give Obama a Stealthy Stimulus," *Wall Street Journal*, December 8, 2010.

The behavior of consumption and investment is important in explaining how the economy responds both to shocks—unexpected events that have an effect on an important sector of the economy or on the economy as a whole—and to macroeconomic policy. In this chapter, we look more closely at the determinants of consumption and investment to better understand how shocks and policy affect economic activity.

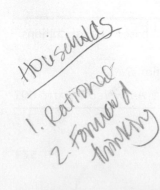

16.1

Learning Objective

Discuss the macroeconomic implications of microeconomic decision making by households and firms.

The Macroeconomic Implications of Microeconomic Decision Making: Intertemporal Choice

The key decisions that affect GDP are made at the microeconomic level—that is, by households and firms. For example, the decision of a household in California to save for retirement rather than purchase a car or the decision of the Ford Motor Company to begin building a new factory in Tennessee now rather than wait until next year will, by themselves, not have a large effect on GDP. However, the combined decisions of *all* households and firms are critically important for the economy. In this section, we discuss similarities and differences between spending by households and firms.

Households and Firms are Forward Thinking

Economists assume that households and firms share two important characteristics: First, they act rationally to meet their objectives. Economists assume that the objective of households is to maximize *utility*, or well-being, and that the objective of firms is to maximize profits. Second, they are *forward looking*—that is, they take into account the future when making decisions. The decision of a household to consume or save today is really a decision about when to consume because saving today makes it possible to consume in the future. Households save to accumulate the assets necessary to purchase a house, pay for college, or pay for consumption during retirement. To prepare for retirement, most households save part of their current income by purchasing stocks, shares of mutual funds, or other financial assets. What we expect to happen in the future affects our decisions today. For example, suppose you conclude that the value of your house will increase more rapidly than you had previously expected. As a result, you will need to save less out of your current income for retirement and can consume more today. We can conclude that: *Expectations about the future affect consumption decisions today.*

Expectations about the future are also critical for investment decisions by firms. Capital goods, such as factories, last many years, so a firm must consider the profits to be earned from a factory in the future when deciding whether to invest. If, for example, Ford thought that demand for cars was going to decrease in the future, it would be less likely to build a factory today. So, expectations about future profitability can affect the level of investment—and, therefore, GDP—today.

An Important Difference Between Consumption and Investment

Although households and firms are forward looking in their decisions, their behavior can be quite different. In particular, as Figure 16.1 shows, consumption and investment behave differently during recessions. The volatility in the growth rate of investment in the United States is much greater than the volatility in the growth rate of consumption. For example, during the first quarter of 2009, consumption decreased by 1.6% at an annual rate, but investment decreased by 43.0%! During a typical recession, investment usually decreases much more than consumption. In fact, during some recessions, such as the 2001 recession, consumption has actually risen. To understand how policy affects economic activity, it is important to understand why investment is more volatile than consumption. We focus on consumption in Section 16.2 and investment in Section 16.3.

investment volatility >

consumption growth rate volatility

MyEconLab Real-time data

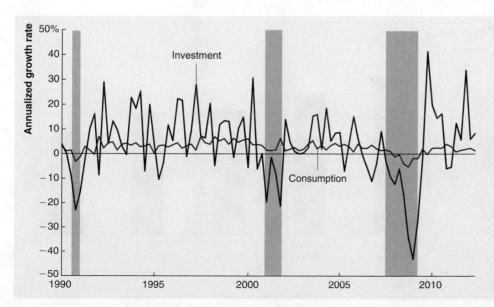

Figure 16.1

Growth Rates for Real Personal Consumption and Real Gross Private Investment, 1990–2012

The growth rate of gross private investment is much more volatile than the growth rate of personal consumption. Investment has always decreased during recessions (shaded areas), but consumption has actually increased during some recessions.

Note: The data are quarterly, and the growth rates are at an annual rate.

Sources: U.S. Bureau of Economic Analysis; and National Bureau of Economic Research.

16.2

Learning Objective

Explain the determinants of personal consumption.

Factors That Determine Consumption

Consumption is less volatile than investment because households tend to smooth consumption over time in response to fluctuations in disposable income. In this section, we discuss the determinants of consumption and explain why consumption is relatively smooth.

Consumption and GDP

Figure 16.2 shows that, while household consumption averages 61.5% of GDP for all countries for which the World Bank has data, this percentage varies significantly across countries. Household consumption averages nearly 80% of GDP in low-income countries but about 60% in high- and middle-income countries.

The relative importance of consumption can vary over time. For example, consumption in the United States rose from 61% of GDP in 1967 to over 71% of GDP in 2011, above that in most other high-income countries. Economists disagree about the reason for the increase, but developments in financial markets probably played a role, as many households experienced increases in wealth that led them to save less of their income and spend more of it. When the stock market boomed during the 1980s and 1990s, many households found that they did not need to save as much out of disposable income for retirement. Rising real estate wealth also contributed. Finally, financial innovations made it easier for households to borrow against the equity in their home and to obtain credit cards. As a result, consumption in the United States increased as a percentage of GDP.

Some types of consumption are more volatile than others. Figure 16.3 shows the growth rates of expenditure in the United States on durable consumption goods, nondurable consumption goods, and services. The figure shows that expenditure on durable consumption goods such as cars and furniture is quite volatile, but expenditure on nondurable goods such as food and clothing and on services such as health care is much less volatile. Expenditure on durable goods almost always decreases significantly during

Figure 16.2

Consumption Around the World

For most countries, consumption is the largest component of GDP. Consumption is a larger fraction of GDP in the United States than in most other high-income countries.

Source: The World Bank, *World Development Indicators*.

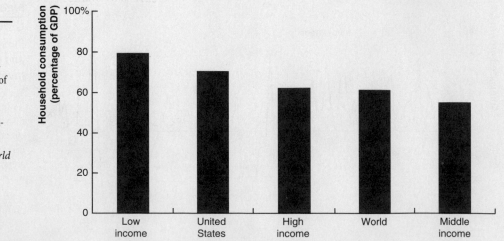

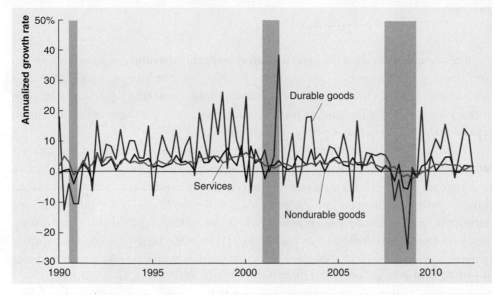

Figure 16.3

Growth Rates in Real Expenditure on Durable Goods, Nondurable Goods, and Services, 1990–2012

Expenditure on durable consumption goods is much more volatile than expenditure on nondurable goods and services. Shaded areas indicate recessions.

Note: The data are quarterly, and the growth rates are at an annual rate.

Sources: U.S. Bureau of Economic Analysis; and National Bureau of Economic Research.

recessions, while expenditure on services decreases by much less or even increases. For example, during the 2007–2009 recession, expenditure on durable goods decreased by 13.1%, expenditure on nondurable goods decreased by 3.7%, and expenditure on services decreased by only 1.5%. Why are households more willing to delay purchases of new cars and other durable goods than they are health care and other services? To answer this question, we first need to discuss an important constraint on household consumption.

The Intertemporal Budget Constraint and Consumption Smoothing

Consider a simple model of consumption in which there are just two time periods (the current year and next year) and there is no government, so we can ignore taxes and transfer payments. In this situation, the only reason you would save is to finance future consumption. We will initially assume that there is no limit on your ability to use financial markets to borrow or to save at the real interest rate, r.

We call the dollar amount that you consume this year (year 1) C_1, and the amount that you consume next year (year 2) C_2. You receive labor income this year, Y_1, and labor income next year, Y_2. During the first year, the part of your income that you save is S_1. So, for the first year:

labor income = consumption + saved income

$$Y_1 = C_1 + S_1.$$

The amount that you save this year earns you a return equal to the real interest rate, r. So, next year, you will have the initial amount you saved plus the interest earned, $(1 + r)S_1$, which you can use to add to your consumption during the second year. So, consumption during year 2 is:

$$C_2 = Y_2 + (1 + r)S_1.$$

We then have the following expression, which relates lifetime consumption to lifetime income:[1]

$$C_1 + \frac{C_2}{1 + r} = Y_1 + \frac{Y_2}{1 + r}.$$

Intertemporal budget constraint A budget constraint that applies to consumption and income in more than one time period; it shows how much a household can consume, given lifetime income.

This equation is called the **intertemporal budget constraint** because it applies to consumption and income in more than one time period. The budget constraint tells us that lifetime consumption (the left side) equals lifetime income (the right side). Although in our simple model, "lifetime" is just two years, we could use the same reasoning to expand the model to as many periods as we wanted to.

To understand the intertemporal budget constraint, assume that the real interest rate is zero. In that case, the sum of your consumption in both years equals the sum of your income from both years. If you prefer to perfectly smooth consumption—that is, equalize your consumption in both years—you will have $C_1 = C_2$. Suppose you work during the first year, so income is positive, $Y_1 = \$60,0000$, and then you retire during the second year, so income in that year is zero, $Y_2 = 0$. To be able to consume during retirement, you will save \$30,000 during the first year and purchase assets such as stocks or bonds, and then you will sell those assets during the second year to finance your consumption during the second period. If, instead, your income were zero during the first year while you were going to school, $Y_1 = 0$, and \$60,000 in the second year when you worked, $Y_2 = \$60,000$, then you would borrow \$30,000 in financial markets during the first year to finance consumption during that period and then repay the loan in the second period.

Two Theories of Consumption Smoothing

We can use this simple model to show the effect of changes in income on consumption. Nobel Laureate Milton Friedman developed the **permanent-income hypothesis** to explain consumption smoothing.[2] According to this hypothesis, household consumption depends on *permanent income*, and households use financial markets to save and borrow to smooth consumption in response to fluctuations in *transitory income*. Suppose you work for an accounting firm where you receive a salary and are eligible for a bonus for

Permanent-income hypothesis The hypothesis that household consumption depends on permanent income and that households use financial markets to save and borrow to smooth consumption in response to fluctuations in transitory income.

---

[1]Here is how we arrived at this equation: If we substitute the expression for saving in period 1, $S_1 = Y_1 - C_1$, into the expression for consumption in period 2, $C_2 = Y_2 + (1 + r)S_1$, we obtain:

$$C_2 = Y_2 + (1 + r)(Y_1 - C_1).$$

Dividing each side of the equation by $(1 + r)$ produces:

$$\frac{C_2}{(1 + r)} = \frac{Y_2}{(1 + r)} + (Y_1 - C_1).$$

Rearranging terms to put consumption on the left side and income on the right side yields the equation in the text:

$$C_1 + \frac{C_2}{1 + r} = Y_1 + \frac{Y_2}{1 + r},$$

which is the household's intertemporal budget constraint, which tells us that the present value of lifetime consumption equals the present value of lifetime income.

[2]Milton Friedman, *A Theory of the Consumption Function*, Princeton, NJ: Princeton University Press, 1957.

exceptional work. Your salary is your **permanent income** because you normally expect to receive it each year. Your bonus is **transitory income** because you do not expect to receive it each year. You can think of permanent income as average lifetime income and transitory income as a temporary deviation from the lifetime average. Household income is the sum of permanent income, $Y^{\text{Permanent}}$, and transitory income, $Y^{\text{Transitory}}$:

$$Y = Y^{\text{Permanent}} + Y^{\text{Transitory}}.$$

Milton Friedman argued that the level of consumption depends primarily on the level of permanent income:

$$C = aY^{\text{Permanent}},$$

where a is a constant and represents the fraction of permanent income that households consume. Friedman argued that if someone experienced an unexpected windfall, such as winning the lottery or receiving a temporary tax cut, the person would view most of that income as transitory. As a result, the person would save most of it and consume very little. Similarly, if someone experienced an unexpected job loss, the person's income would fall temporarily, meaning that transitory income would be negative. In this case, the person would borrow to keep consumption at the typical level. In contrast, if the person received a permanent increase in income due to unexpectedly obtaining a better job, consumption would increase significantly. Similarly, if a person accepted a job at a lower salary, the person's permanent income would fall, as would the person's consumption. We can conclude that: *Consumption responds more to changes in permanent income than to changes in transitory income.*

Nobel Laureate Franco Modigliani played an important role in developing the *life-cycle hypothesis* as an alternative explanation of consumption smoothing. According to the **life-cycle hypothesis**, households borrow and save to transfer funds from high-income periods, such as their working years, to low-income periods, such as their retirement years, periods of unemployment, or years as a student in college. For example, to maintain consumption during retirement, you have to save during your working years. When you retire and no longer receive a salary, you can use the income from your stocks, bonds, and other assets or sell your assets to finance consumption. You are saving during the part of your life cycle when income is high in order to transfer funds to the part of your life cycle when your income is low. In both the permanent-income hypothesis and the life-cycle hypothesis, people consume less in the present so that they have the resources to finance consumption in the future. In other words, *the goal of saving is to provide for future consumption.*

Figure 16.4 provides an example of the life-cycle hypothesis that shows how you can smooth your consumption so that it is constant each year. Initially, your income is less than your consumption, so you borrow to finance consumption. As income rises, you borrow less. After age 40, your income is greater than consumption, so you pay off the debts acquired during earlier years and begin to save for retirement. After retirement at age 67, your income falls below consumption, so you sell off assets accumulated during your working years to finance consumption.

If you completely smooth consumption so that it is the same during each year of life, then your consumption equals the sum of your initial wealth and your lifetime

Permanent income
Income that households normally expect to receive each year.

Transitory income
Income that households do not expect to receive each year.

Life-cycle hypothesis
The theory that households use financial markets to borrow and save to transfer funds from high-income periods, such as working years, to low-income periods, such as retirement years or periods of unemployment.

Figure 16.4

Consumption, Income, and Saving over the Life Cycle

If you plan to keep consumption constant over your life cycle, you will borrow when you are young and income is low, accumulate assets during peak earning years, and then sell off assets during retirement, when income is zero.

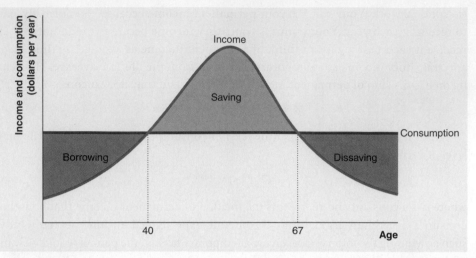

income divided by the number of years you expect to live. If you earn Y each year and expect to work for B years, then your lifetime income is BY. If you expect to live for N years, then your consumption is:

$$C = \frac{\text{Wealth} + BY}{N}.$$

This expression is equivalent to:

$$C = \left(\frac{1}{N}\right)\text{Wealth} + \left(\frac{B}{N}\right)Y,$$

where:

$\left(\frac{1}{N}\right)$ = how much spending increases when wealth increases by \$1, or the *marginal propensity to consume out of wealth*

and

$\left(\frac{B}{N}\right)$ = the *marginal propensity to consume* out of income.

Marginal propensity to consume (*MPC*) The amount by which consumption increases when disposable income increases by \$1.

The **marginal propensity to consume** (*MPC*) out of income is the amount by which consumption increases when disposable income increases by \$1. For example, if you expect to live for another 50 years ($N = 50$) and work for another 40 years ($B = 40$), then your marginal propensity to consume out of income is: $40 \div 50 = 0.80$. In other words, you will consume \$80 per year for each additional \$100 of income you earn. However, it is important to recognize that this is an example of the marginal propensity to consume out of *permanent* increases in income. If an increase in income is transitory, then consumption will increase much less. People also use wealth to finance consumption, and if you expect to live 50 more years, the marginal propensity to consume out of wealth equals $1 \div 50 = 0.02$, so you will consume \$2 per year for each additional \$100 in wealth.

Do households really smooth consumption? Our discussion indicates that households should smooth consumption if they are maximizing utility. And many economists have found strong evidence in favor of consumption smoothing for aggregate consumption.[3] We can conclude that consumption smoothing is a powerful force that affects a large portion of consumer expenditure in the United States.

Figure 16.3 on page 577 suggests that households more completely smooth expenditure on services and nondurable goods than on durable goods. Because durable goods, such as cars, last many years, households have flexibility about when to replace them. If you experience an unexpected decrease in income due to a job loss during a recession, you are likely to continue driving your current car rather than buy a new one. So, expenditures on durable goods decrease during a recession, as households respond to temporarily low income by delaying these purchases. In contrast, nondurable goods, such as food and clothing, are consumed or wear out and must be purchased more frequently. Services, such as health care, are consumed the moment they are purchased, so people have to purchase a service when they need it. Therefore, expenditure on nondurable goods and services tends not to decrease as much during recessions. For these reasons, expenditure on durable goods is more volatile than expenditure on nondurable goods and services.

Permanent Versus Transitory Changes in Income

The permanent-income hypothesis and the life-cycle hypothesis imply that households will smooth consumption over time. As a result, permanent changes in income will have much larger effects on consumption than will transitory or one-time changes in income. We can illustrate this point using the life-cycle hypothesis. Suppose that you are currently 20 years old, your wealth is zero, you will work for 40 years at a constant salary of $50,000, and you expect to live to age 70. Your lifetime income is $50,000 \times 40$ years $= \$2,000,000$, so your consumption is:

$$C = \left(\frac{1}{50}\right)0 + \left(\frac{40}{50}\right)\$50,000 = \frac{\$2,000,000}{50} = \$40,000.$$

Therefore, each year you will consume $40,000 and save $10,000. Now suppose that you experience a transitory increase in your income to $60,000 during your first year of work. Your lifetime income is now ($50,000 \times 39$ years) + ($60,000 \times 1$ year) = $2.01 million, and you still expect to live to age 70, so:

$$C = 0 + \frac{\$2,010,000}{50} = \$40,200.$$

If you completely smooth consumption, then you consume only $200 per year out of the $10,000 transitory income. Your marginal propensity to consume out of transitory income is just:

$$MPC^{\text{Transitory}} = \frac{\Delta C}{\Delta Y} = \frac{\$200}{\$10,000} = 0.02.$$

---

[3]A classic article is Robert E. Hall, "Intertemporal Substitution in Consumption," *Journal of Political Economy*, Vol. 96, No. 2, April 1988, pp. 339–357.

The *MPC* out of transitory changes in income is low because you smooth the $10,000 increase in income over the 50 additional years you expect to live. In fact, the *MPC* out of a one-time change in income is always:

$$MPC^{\text{Transitory}} = \frac{1}{N}.$$

The situation is quite different if your salary permanently increases to $60,000 per year, starting with your first year of work. In this case, your lifetime income is now $60,000 × 40 years = $2.4 million, so:

$$C = 0 + \frac{\$2,400,000}{50} = \$48,000.$$

Your consumption increases by $8,000 per year when the change in income is permanent. As a result, the *MPC* is:

$$MPC^{\text{Permanent}} = \frac{\Delta C}{\Delta Y} = \frac{\$8,000}{\$10,000} = 0.80.$$

The *MPC* is much larger for permanent changes in income. As we will see in the next section, policymakers who want to use changes in taxes to increase consumption should take into account that the *MPC* for permanent income changes is higher than the *MPC* for transitory income changes.

Consumption and the Real Interest Rate

Households use financial markets to smooth consumption by borrowing and saving, and the real interest rate plays an important role in these decisions. A change in the real interest rate changes not only the "price" of consumption today but also the incomes of households. As a result, a change in the real interest rate has both a *substitution effect* and an *income effect*.

The real interest rate is the "price" at which an individual trades off current consumption for future consumption. For example, if the real interest rate is 10% and you put $10,000 into your savings account, it will grow to (1 + 0.10) × $10,000 = $11,000 at the end of the year. To consume $10,000 this year, you must give up $11,000 of consumption next year. If the real interest rate is 20%, then your saving grows to (1 + 0.20) × $10,000 = $12,000 at the end of the year. To consume $10,000 this year, you must give up $12,000 of consumption next year. The higher the real interest rate, the more "expensive" consumption this year becomes. When the real interest rate increases, households reduce current consumption and increase future consumption. This mechanism is the substitution effect.

substitution effect:
i ↑ C ↓

There is also an income effect associated with a change in the real interest rate. The direction of the income effect depends on whether the individual is a net borrower or lender. If you are a lender, an increase in the real interest rate effectively increases your income. For example, if you have $1,000 in your savings account and the real interest rate is 10%, then you will have (1 + 0.10) × $1,000 = $1,100 at the end of the year. But if the real interest rate is 20%, then you will have (1 + 0.20) × $1,000 = $1,200 at the end of the year. The extra $100 acts as an increase in your income, which causes you to consume more in the current period. Therefore, the income and substitution effects move in opposite directions for lenders.

Table 16.1 The Effect of the Real Interest Rate on Consumption

	You are a lender	You are a borrower
Substitution effect	Negative	Negative
Income effect	Positive	Negative
Net effect	Unclear	Negative

The income and substitution effects work in the same direction when someone is a borrower. The increase in the real interest rate causes a decrease in income, so current consumption decreases. Suppose, for example, that instead of saving $1,000, you borrow $1,000. In this case, the increase in the real interest rate from 10% to 20% will cause your interest payments to increase, which decreases your wealth by $100. As a result, current consumption decreases. Table 16.1 summarizes the effect of an increase in the real interest rate on consumption.

The substitution effect is negative for all households because an increase in the real interest rate leads to a decrease in current consumption. The income effect is positive for lenders and negative for borrowers. An increase in the real interest rate will therefore definitely decrease current consumption for households that are borrowers because both the income and substitution effects are negative. The effect on lenders is unclear because the income and substitution effects move in opposite directions.

Whether an increase in the real interest rate increases or decreases current consumption depends partly on whether there are more net borrowers or more net lenders in the economy, and we cannot answer this question with theory alone. For our discussion, we will assume that the substitution effect is larger, so that an increase in the real interest rate will increase saving and decrease current consumption even for households who are lenders.

Housing Wealth and Consumption

Wealth, in addition to income and interest rates, is an important determinant of consumption. For many people, their home is their most valuable asset. But while the value of a person's home might be important for his or her consumption, it may not be important for aggregate consumption. A number of economists have estimated the effect of housing wealth on consumption. For example, the Congressional Budget Office (CBO) estimates that a $1 increase in housing wealth increases consumption by $0.07.[4] However, research by Charles Calomiris of Columbia University and Stanley Longhofer and William Miles of Wichita State University suggests that the CBO's estimate of the wealth effect is too large.[5] They argue that a decrease in housing wealth has little effect on aggregate consumption.

---

[4]Congressional Budget Office, "Housing Wealth and Consumer Spending," January 2007. The CBO considers two estimates—a high estimate of 0.07, which we use, and a low estimate of 0.02. Table 1 of the report discusses recent estimates for the effect which range from a low of 0.017 to a high of 0.21.

[5]Charles Calomiris, Stanley Longhofer, and William Miles, "The (Mythical?) Housing Wealth Effect," National Bureau of Economic Research working paper 15075, June 2009.

The research of some other economists supports the conclusions of Calomiris, Longhofer, and Miles. For example, Willem Buiter, chief economist of Citigroup, believes that a decrease in housing prices hurts some households but helps other households.[6] Buiter argues that a decrease in housing prices reduces the wealth of older households and of households planning to purchase and move into houses less expensive than their current house. The decrease in housing wealth should reduce the consumption of these households. But a decrease in housing prices increases the wealth of both younger households that are more likely to be renters and households planning to purchase and live in houses more expensive than their current house. The decrease in housing prices means these households have to save less from their current income to accumulate the funds necessary to purchase a house. So, wealth and consumption for these households increase. Whether aggregate consumption increases or decreases depends on the mix of households and the marginal propensity to consume out of wealth for each group of households.

The collapse in housing prices after 2006 contributed significantly to the 2007–2009 recession, but recent economic research suggests that the effect of the decrease in housing wealth on consumption was likely small. The effect that the decrease in housing prices had on financial markets and the residential construction industry was probably more important than the effect on consumption.

How Policy Affects Consumption

Government policy affects consumption by altering disposable income today and in the future. Recall that *disposable income* is total income plus transfer payments minus taxes:

$$Y^D = Y + TR - T.$$

To see how government policy can affect consumption, consider the earlier example in which you were 20 years old, planned to work for 40 years, earning $50,000 per year, and expected to live until age 70. We saw that you would consume $40,000 per year, but that conclusion was based on the assumption that you pay no taxes. If you pay $10,000 per year in taxes and receive no transfer payments, your disposable income is just $40,000 per year, and your lifetime disposable income is $1,600,000. Therefore, your consumption is:

$$C = \left(\frac{1}{N}\right)\text{Wealth} + \left(\frac{B}{N}\right)Y^D = \left(\frac{1}{N}\right)0 + \left(\frac{40}{50}\right)40 = \frac{\$1,600,000}{50} = \$32,000.$$

If your disposable income is $40,000 per year and you consume $32,000 per year, then you are saving $8,000 per year. When taxes were $0 in our previous example, you consumed $40,000 and saved $10,000 per year, so an increase in taxes causes both consumption and saving to decrease. A permanent increase in taxes from $0 to $10,000 reduced consumption by $8,000. In the language of the permanent-income hypothesis, the tax increase represents a decrease in permanent income, so consumption responds significantly. In Solved Problem 16.2, we ask you to determine the effect of a temporary decrease in taxes. Given what you already know about the permanent-income hypothesis, you should be able to predict that the effect of temporary tax cuts is relatively modest.

---

[6]Willem Buiter, "Housing Wealth Isn't Wealth," *Economics: The Open-Access, Open-Assessment E-Journal*, , Vol. 4, No. 22, August 5, 2010, pp. 1–29.

Table 16.2 summarizes the factors that affect consumption.

Table 16.2 Summary of Factors That Affect Household Consumption

If the following occurs . . .	consumption . . .	because . . .
a one-time increase in disposable income	increases	households smooth the one-time increase in income over their entire lifetimes.
a permanent increase in disposable income	increases	households experience a large increase in lifetime income.
a decrease in the real interest rate	increases	households borrow more and save less to increase their consumption.
an increase in household wealth	increases	households will consume part of the wealth during each time period (college age, working age, retirement age).

Solved Problem 16.2

Effects of a Temporary Tax Cut on Your Consumption

In the chapter opener, we saw that President Obama and Congress temporarily reduced the payroll tax, beginning in 2011. Should this temporary tax cut have had a large effect on consumption? We can gain some insight by continuing with our previous example in which you are 20 years old, you plan to work for 40 years at an after-tax salary of $40,000, and you expect to live to age 70. Assume that your initial wealth is zero. Now suppose the government gives you a one-time tax rebate of $1,000 during your first year of work. Predict the effect of the tax rebate on your consumption.

Solving the Problem

Step 1 **Review the chapter material.** The problem asks you to use the theory of consumption to determine the effect of a one-time tax rebate on consumption, so you may want to review the section "Factors That Determine Consumption," which begins on page 576.

Step 2 **Determine the effect on your lifetime disposable income**. Your lifetime disposable income is now:

$$\$40,000 \times 39 \text{ years} + \$41,000 \times 1 \text{ year} = \$1,601,000.$$

Step 3 **Show the effect of the tax cut if you smooth consumption.** If you smooth consumption completely, then you have the following:

$$C = \left(\frac{1}{N}\right)\text{Wealth} + \left(\frac{B}{N}\right)Y^D = \frac{\$1,601,000}{50} = \$32,020.$$

Step 4 **Compare your new level of consumption to your initial level of consumption.** Before the one-time tax rebate, you consumed $32,000 and saved $8,000 during the first year. Now you consume $32,020 and save $8,980 during the first year because you smooth the $1,000 tax rebate over the entire 50 years that you expect to live. A one-time tax rebate is a transitory increase in disposable income. Given our discussion of the permanent-income hypothesis and consumption smoothing, it should come as no surprise that a one-time tax rebate has a small effect on consumption.

See related problems 2.6 and 2.10 at the end of the chapter.

Credit Rationing of Households

So far, we have assumed that households can easily borrow and save as necessary to smooth consumption. If households can borrow against future income, then households that currently have low income but expect higher income in the future can borrow against future income to smooth consumption. For example, students can obtain student loans to finance their education or use credit cards to purchase goods and services even if they do not currently have jobs. As a result, current consumption can exceed current income. Because financial markets do not work perfectly, however, households face borrowing constraints because it is often difficult for banks and other lenders to distinguish between households that are likely to repay loans and those that are likely to default on loans. Borrowers have better information than a bank about their job security and other factors that may affect their ability to repay a loan. As a result, there is *asymmetric information* in financial markets, which makes it risky for banks to make loans to households.

Financial institutions can raise the real interest rate on loans to compensate for this risk, but increasing the real interest rate changes the mix of potential borrowers. Some households are safe borrowers because they seek loans only if they are sure they can repay them. Other households are risky borrowers because they are willing to take out loans even if they are not sure that they can repay them. The higher real interest rate means that fewer households can now afford to get loans, so safe borrowers drop out of the market for loans. But risky borrowers remain, so the pool of potential borrowers has more risky borrowers relative to safe borrowers than before. The riskiness of loans has increased, which may cause financial institutions to increase the real interest rate again. But this action makes the pool of potential borrowers even riskier, and so on.

Banks and other financial institutions know asymmetric information exists, so they often require that households have collateral for loans and that they make a down payment of, say, 20% of the purchase price. With a down payment, defaulting on a loan costs the borrower some of his or her own funds. Households are considered *credit rationed* if they cannot borrow against future income at the current interest rate.

The theory of consumption predicts that the *MPC* out of transitory income is relatively low. But if a household is credit rationed, the *MPC* out of transitory income may be high. A household that is credit rationed would like to consume more but cannot because it cannot borrow money. As a result, a credit-rationed household is consuming at a lower level than the household would prefer. When the credit-rationed household has an increase in transitory income, it may spend most of the increase in an attempt to reach the preferred level of consumption. If a large number of households face credit rationing, then changes in transitory income, such as the temporary decrease in payroll taxes passed in December 2010, can have a large effect on consumption.

Research by economists David Gross of Compass Lexecon and Nicholas Souleles of the University of Pennsylvania provides evidence of credit rationing.[7] The consumption-smoothing model assumes that households can borrow as much as they want to smooth consumption. With this assumption, a household should not increase its debt when a credit card company increases the household's credit limit. But if households are credit rationed, they may use the increase in the credit limit to increase consumption. In addition, the households most likely to experience credit rationing are those currently at their credit limits. Gross and Souleles showed that an increase in credit limits results in an immediate increase in credit card debt. The effect is large: A $1,000 increase in a credit limit is associated with an increase in credit card debt of $100 to $140. Gross and Souleles estimated that, if every household in the United States received a $2,000 increase in the credit limit on each of its credit cards, then consumption would increase by about $40 billion. This change would amount to about 10% of the typical yearly increase in consumption for the U.S. economy as a whole. Gross and Souleles also showed that the increase in credit card debt is much larger for households that are already near their credit limits. These results are consistent with the presence of credit rationing.

Other evidence about the effects of credit rationing on consumption is less definite. For example, Robert Hall of Stanford University and Frederic Mishkin of Columbia University examined the consumption behavior of households and found that consumption smoothing is more important than credit rationing.[8] They found that 80% of consumption spending is consistent with the consumption-smoothing model, while the remainder is consistent with the presence of credit rationing. Hall and Mishkin's results indicate that credit rationing may not be a critical determinant of aggregate consumption, although it may be important for individual households.

Credit rationing may have played an important role during the 2007–2009 recession. Atif Mian of the University of California, Berkeley, and Amir Sufi of the University of Chicago examined the relationship between consumption and consumer credit at the county level in the United States during the 2007–2009 recession.[9] They found that credit card companies continued to increase the credit available to U.S. households during the first part of the recession, so households could still smooth consumption. But when the financial crisis suddenly worsened in September and October 2008, credit card companies began to reduce borrowing limits. The limits were imposed at the same time

[7]David Gross and Nicholas Souleles, "Do Liquidity Constraints and Interest Rates Matter for Consumer Behavior? Evidence from Credit Card Data," *Quarterly Journal of Economics*, Vol. 117, No. 1, February 2002, pp. 149–185.

[8]Robert Hall and Frederic Mishkin, "The Sensitivity of Consumption to Transitory Income: Estimates from Panel Data on Households," *Econometrica*, Vol. 50, No. 2, March 1982, pp. 461–481.

[9]Atif Mian and Amir Sufi, "Household Leverage and the Recession of 2007 to 2009," *IMF Economic Review*, Vol. 58, No. 1, August 2010, pp. 74–117.

that home values were declining and banks were making it more difficult for households to borrow against the equity in their homes. The reduced availability of credit made it difficult for households to smooth consumption. Not surprisingly, the Bureau of Economic Analysis reports that spending on consumer durable goods decreased by 12% at an annual rate during the third quarter of 2008 and then by 22.3% during the fourth quarter of 2008. The work of Mian and Sufi indicates that credit rationing may have contributed to the large decrease in spending on consumer durables during the second half of 2008, so credit rationing may help explain why the 2007–2009 recession was so severe.

Making the Connection

The Temporary Cut in Payroll Taxes

The U.S. government levies Social Security payroll taxes in the amount of 12.4% on an individual's salary up to an income limit that increases each year. Half of the tax, 6.2%, is collected from the employee, and the other half is collected from the employer. As part of the tax cut package signed into law on December 17, 2010, the government reduced the employee portion of the payroll tax by 2 percentage points, to 4.2%, for one year. Congress extended the payroll tax cut an additional year, but not until February 2012, so in 2011 workers and employers were not able to anticipate having more than a one-year tax cut. For someone earning $70,000 in 2011, the payroll tax cut increased disposable income by $1,400, and for someone earning $106,800, which was the income limit in 2011, the payroll tax cut increased disposable income by $2,100. The total expected cost to the U.S. government of the payroll tax cut was $111 billion in 2011.

Supporters of the payroll tax cut believed that it was an efficient way to quickly provide an increase in disposable income for 155 million workers, leading to increased consumption and real GDP. Supporters argued that because it would be received disproportionately by low- and middle-income households, the tax cut would increase disposable income for households with higher marginal propensities to consume. In addition, the tax cut was thought likely to increase consumption by credit-rationed households. Households that are credit rationed consume less than they would prefer, so they are more likely than other households to use a tax cut to increase consumption when their current disposable incomes increase. Economists at Deutsche Bank predicted that the payroll tax cut would increase the growth rate of real GDP in the United States by 0.7% during 2011.

The actual growth rate of real GDP for 2011 was 1.8%, down from 2.4% in 2010. Although economists do not know how much of the growth in real GDP in 2011 was due to the payroll tax cut, the conclusions of the permanent-income hypothesis and the life-cycle hypothesis suggest that the effect of a temporary payroll tax cut is likely to be modest. The 2010 and 2011 payroll tax cuts were both supposed to last just one year, so they only temporarily increased disposable income. Therefore, they resulted in transitory increases in disposable income and, as Solved Problem 16.2 shows, transitory increases in disposable income should have relatively little effect on consumption. The research on the temporary tax rebates of 2001 and 2008 also suggests that transitory tax cuts have relatively small effects on consumption.

The experiences with the 2001 and 2008 tax rebates suggest that households save a large part of a payroll tax cut. Jimmy Lee, chief executive at Strategic Wealth Associates, recommended that households use a payroll tax cut to increase their retirement savings. If households followed the advice of wealth managers such as Lee, then a payroll tax cut has a relatively small effect on consumption.

In addition to their effect on consumption and real GDP, payroll tax cuts also reduce the revenue available to pay retirees who receive monthly Social Security checks. Robert Reischauer, former director of the Congressional Budget Office, worried that politicians will be tempted to extend the tax cuts again in future years, which would result in even less revenue to fund Social Security. "Imagine . . . next December the unemployment rate is 8 percent . . . We'll still be trying to stimulate employment and terminating the payroll tax holiday will be a big hit on most families, one that will hurt job growth." But former Social Security analyst Andrew Biggs claims that a payroll tax cut may actually increase tax revenue by reducing retirement rates among older workers. Research by Biggs found that payroll tax cuts could induce many workers to remain in the labor force longer by raising their after-tax wage and, in turn, increase non–Social Security tax revenues. In future years, economists will evaluate the effect of the payroll tax cuts of 2010 and 2011 on the growth of real GDP as well as on tax revenue.

Sources: Jackie Calmes, "Disagreement Over Payroll Tax Cut's Impact on Social Security," *New York Times*, December 15, 2011; Andrew Biggs, "A Payroll Tax Cut Could Help Social Security," *Wall Street Journal*, April 24, 2012; Sudeep Reddy, "The Tax Agreement: Package Would Give Obama a Stealthy Stimulus," *Wall Street Journal*, December 8, 2010; Stephen Ohlemacher, "Does Tax Cut Threaten Social Security? White House Says It Will Not Affect Solvency of Program, but Some Worry," *Houston Chronicle*, December 13, 2010; and U.S. Bureau of Economic Analysis.

See related problem 2.9 at the end of the chapter.

Precautionary Saving

So far, we have assumed that households know their future disposable income with certainty. In fact, of course, households do not know the future and may adjust consumption and saving to protect themselves from unexpected events. **Precautionary saving** is the extra saving by households to protect themselves from unexpected decreases in future income due to job loss, illness, or disability. In this case, saving acts as insurance against unexpected declines in income. For example, if the economy enters a recession and households believe that the probability of a job loss has increased, they are likely to increase precautionary saving and reduce consumption.

One way to think of precautionary saving is to view households as having a desired level of wealth. When wealth is above the desired level, households draw down their assets to finance consumption. In contrast, if wealth is below the desired level, households save to reach the target. For example, suppose that a household prefers to have six months of disposable income in the stock market to protect against a job loss or unexpected medical bills. If stock prices unexpectedly rise and the household's wealth becomes equal to seven months of disposable income, the household will increase spending until its wealth decreases to six months of disposable income. If an unexpected event decreases the household's wealth, then the household is likely to decrease consumption to rebuild its wealth.

Precautionary saving
Extra saving by households to protect themselves from unexpected decreases in future income due to job loss, illness, or disability.

The theory of consumption emphasizes the importance of future events in determining the level of consumption and saving. An increase in uncertainty about the future will increase the desired level of wealth and lead to lower consumption until households have attained the new level of wealth. A decrease in uncertainty about the future will lead to higher spending until households have attained the new lower level of wealth. In this way, uncertainty can affect aggregate consumption and help cause economic fluctuations.

Christopher Carroll of Johns Hopkins University and Andrew Samwick of Dartmouth College have estimated the relative importance of precautionary saving for U.S. households.[10] According to their estimates, households have accumulated nearly half their net worth to protect themselves from unexpected negative future events. If the estimates of Carroll and Samwick are accurate, then precautionary saving plays an important role in the economy.

Tax Incentives and Saving

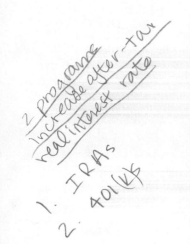

When households save, they are interested in the *after-tax real interest rate*. For any given real interest rate, taxes on income earned from saving reduce the after-tax real interest rate and so reduce the incentive to save.

Two important federal programs reduce taxes on saving, thereby increasing the after-tax real interest rate. First, individual retirement accounts (IRAs) reduce taxes and increase the after-tax real interest rate. A traditional IRA allows an individual to contribute funds to an account without paying taxes until he or she retires and withdraws funds from the account. Because an individual typically does not withdraw funds from the account until many years in the future, the IRA increases the after-tax real interest rate on saving for retirement. Second, many Americans save for retirement using employer-sponsored 401(k) plans that allow them to invest part of their salary in financial assets. Income contributed to a 401(k) account isn't taxed until the contributor withdraws the funds during retirement. So, the 401(k) also increases the after-tax real interest rate on saving.

Glenn Hubbard of Columbia University and Jonathan Skinner of Dartmouth College have surveyed studies of IRAs and 401(k) plans.[11] They note that part of the problem with assessing the effectiveness of these plans in increasing saving is determining whether they result in net new saving or just cause households to switch savings from financial assets without tax incentives, such as savings accounts in banks, to IRAs and 401(k) plans. In addition, if the tax incentives are financed through government budget deficits, then government saving decreases by $1 for every $1 of tax reduction on household saving. After weighing the evidence, Hubbard and Skinner conclude that the plans do increase national saving. They argue that in the long run, IRAs increase the

---

[10]Christopher Carroll and Andrew Samwick, "How Important Is Precautionary Savings?" *Review of Economics and Statistics*, Vol. 80, No. 3, August 1998, pp. 410–419.

[11]Glenn Hubbard and Jonathan Skinner, "Assessing the Effectiveness of Saving Incentives," *Journal of Economic Perspectives*, Vol. 10, No. 4, Fall 1996, pp. 73–90.

private capital stock by $5 for each $1 reduction in government tax revenue, and 401(k) plans increase the private capital stock by $17 for each $1 reduction in government tax revenue. These effects of tax incentives are large and suggest that government programs designed to increase saving lead to a significant increase in the capital stock. Growth models suggest that an increase in the capital stock will increase labor productivity and the standard of living.

Factors That Determine Private Investment

16.3

Learning Objective
Explain the determinants of private investment.

Now that we have reviewed the factors that determine consumption, we consider the factors that determine investment. In this section, we focus on the determinants of investment in new plant and equipment.

Figure 16.5 shows gross capital formation (a measure of investment) as a percentage of GDP. Investment in the United States has typically been a smaller component of GDP than in most other countries. For example, in 2010, the United States invested only 15% of GDP, while the average for other high-income countries was 18%. In fact, the average low-income country now invests more as a percentage of GDP than does the United States. Investment has been particularly important in many countries that have begun to experience rapid economic growth. For example, investment was 35% of GDP in India and 48% in China in 2010.

Although investment is a much smaller share of GDP than is consumption for nearly all countries, Figure 16.1 on page 575 shows that for the United States, investment is much more volatile than consumption, and it therefore may contribute significantly to the business cycle. Figure 16.6 shows that some categories of investment are more volatile than others. From the mid-1980s to 2007, economic fluctuations were relatively mild in the United States, prompting economists to call this period the *Great Moderation*. Before the Great Moderation, spending on residential investment was more volatile than either spending on nonresidential structures or spending on equipment

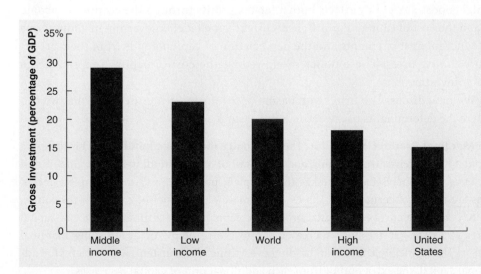

Figure 16.5

Gross Capital Formation Around the World

The United States has consistently invested a smaller share of GDP than most other countries.

Source: The World Bank, *World Development Indicators*.

Figure 16.6

Growth Rates for Types of Investment, 1975–2012

Prior to the Great Moderation, residential investment was the most volatile category of investment. However, since the Great Moderation, all three types of investment have experienced about the same level of volatility. Shaded areas indicate recessions.

Sources: U.S. Bureau of Economic Analysis and National Bureau of Economic Research.

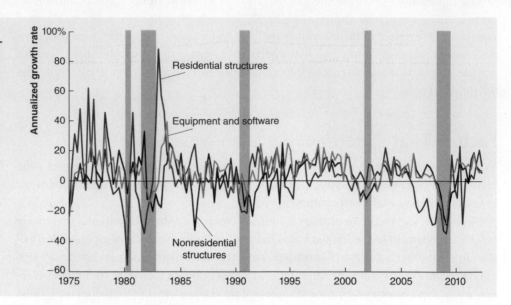

and software. Since the beginning of the Great Moderation, the three categories of investment have experienced about the same volatility.

The Investment Decisions of Firms

Desired capital stock
The level of the capital stock that maximizes a firm's profits.

The **desired capital stock** is the level of the capital stock that maximizes a firm's profits. Firms determine their desired capital stock by comparing the benefits and costs of purchasing additional capital goods. The benefit is the profit firms earn from selling the goods and services that the additional capital goods produce. There are three types of costs associated with purchasing capital: (1) the price of the capital goods, (2) the cost of depreciation, and (3) the interest payments to finance the purchase of the capital goods. Tax policy affects both after-tax profits through the corporate income tax and the cost of capital. For instance, currently the federal government allows firms to deduct interest payments and the depreciation of capital goods from their profits before paying taxes. These policies help reduce the cost of capital and encourage greater investment.

We now discuss the firm's purchasing decisions in greater detail so that we can analyze the determinants of the desired capital stock.

Marginal product of capital (*MPK*) The extra output a firm receives from adding one more unit of capital, holding all other inputs and efficiency constant.

The Marginal Product of Capital The **marginal product of capital (*MPK*)** is the extra output a firm receives from adding one more unit of capital, holding all other inputs and efficiency constant. Because it takes time to plan, purchase, and install capital goods, firms are more concerned with the expected marginal product of capital in the future, MPK^e, than the current marginal product of capital. The marginal product of capital decreases as the capital stock increases due to the principle of diminishing marginal returns. This principle states that, holding everything else constant, as firms employ additional capital, the extra output from each additional unit of capital decreases.

What matters to a firm is not the expected marginal product in any one year but the expected marginal product over the entire life of the capital goods. If the Ford Motor Company is considering building another automobile factory in the United States that will last 50 years, it must consider not only the marginal product of capital this year but also the marginal product of capital for the next 50 years. For example, Ford must consider what will happen to the demand for automobiles if the world price of crude oil increases. It must also try to anticipate the effects of government policies, such as those to limit carbon emissions, that might raise its production costs. Because Ford is interested in its after-tax profit, it also has to anticipate the taxes that it will have to pay in the future.

We have emphasized how firms respond rationally to changes in their expectations of future profits. Taking a different approach, John Maynard Keynes argued in *The General Theory of Employment, Interest, and Money* that firms are sometimes overtaken by periods of irrational pessimism and optimism known as **animal spirits** that affect their investment behavior. We can think of animal spirits as causing sudden changes in the expected marginal product of capital. When firms are overtaken by irrational optimism, they expect that the marginal product of capital will be higher in the future, and when they are overtaken by irrational pessimism, they expect that the marginal product of capital will be lower in the future. These fluctuations in optimism and pessimism are driven by hopes and fears and not by objective evidence. For example, during the late 1990s, many Internet firms were able to obtain funds in financial markets and undertake investments even though the firms were not yet profitable and had little chance of ever becoming profitable. Therefore, in Keynes's sense, it was likely that animal spirits drove investment by these firms.

Animal spirits Periods of irrational pessimism and optimism that affect the investment behavior of firms.

The User Cost of Capital The **user cost of capital (*uc*)** is the expected real cost to a firm of using an additional unit of capital during a period of time. This cost depends on the real price of the capital good, the real interest cost of borrowing to finance the purchase of the capital good, and the depreciation cost associated with actually using the capital good. Most firms are small relative to the market and do not affect the price of capital goods, p_k, or the real interest rate, r. In addition, the depreciation rate, d, is determined by the technology that a firm uses and not by the quantity of capital goods the firm purchases. Therefore, the real price of capital goods, the real interest rate, and the rate of depreciation are constants that a firm can take as given.

User cost of capital (*uc*) The expected real cost to a firm of using an additional unit of capital during a period of time.

The interest cost to a firm equals rp_k and represents the cost of borrowing funds to purchase a capital good. Even if a firm does not borrow to purchase the capital good, it still incurs this cost because the firm could have loaned the funds to other firms or households and received interest income. So, the interest cost is really an opportunity cost. Some capital wears out each period due to normal use, so firms incur a (non-cash) depreciation cost equal to dp_k. The user cost of capital is the sum of these two costs:

$$uc = rp_k + dp_k = (r + d)p_k.$$

Because a firm is small relative to the market, the user cost of capital does not change as its capital stock changes.

Figure 16.7

The Desired Capital Stock

The desired capital stock for an individual firm occurs at point A where the user cost of capital (uc) equals the expected marginal product of capital (MPK^e). The expected marginal product of capital curve slopes downward due to diminishing marginal returns.

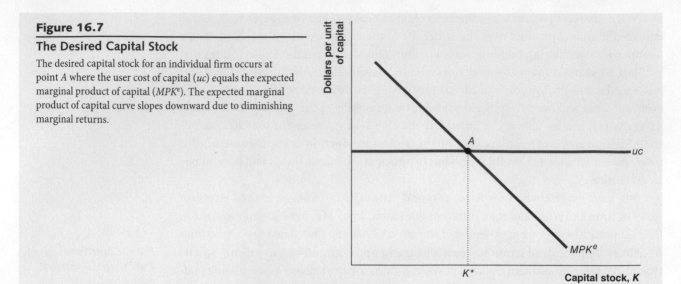

The Desired Capital Stock A firm maximizes profits when the expected marginal product of capital equals the user cost of capital:

$$MPK^e = (r + d)p_k.$$

The desired capital stock (K^*) is the level of the capital stock that maximizes profits. Figure 16.7 shows that the desired capital stock for an individual firm occurs at the intersection of the expected marginal product of capital curve and the user cost of capital curve. The user cost of capital curve is a horizontal line because it is independent of the level of the capital stock. The expected marginal product of capital curve slopes downward due to diminishing marginal returns.

Figure 16.8 shows the effect of a decrease in the expected marginal product of capital. If a firm expects that the demand for its product will decrease in the future, the

Figure 16.8

A Decrease in the Expected Marginal Product of Capital and the Desired Capital Stock

If a firm expects consumer demand for its product to decrease in the future, then expected output and the expected marginal product of capital will decrease. As a result, the MPK^e curve will shift to the left and the desired capital stock decreases from K_1^* to K_2^*.

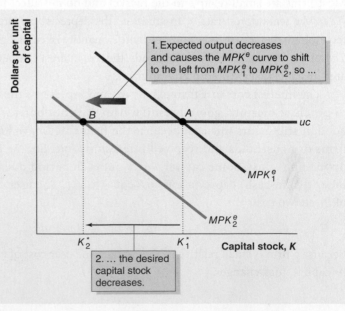

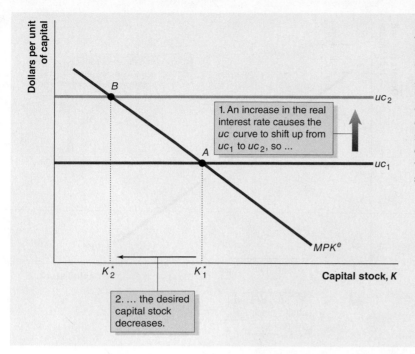

Figure 16.9

An Increase in the User Cost of Capital and the Desired Capital Stock

An increase in the real interest rate increases the user cost of capital, so the user cost of capital curve shifts up from uc_1 to uc_2 and the desired capital stock decreases from K_1^* to K_2^*. An increase in the user cost of capital due to an increase in either the price of capital or the depreciation rate would have the same effect on the desired capital stock.

expected marginal product of capital curve will shift to the left, and the desired capital stock will decrease from K_1^* to K_2^*.

Changes in the user cost of capital also cause the desired capital stock to change. Figure 16.9 shows that an increase in the real interest rate increases the user cost of capital, so the user cost of capital curve shifts up. As a result, the desired capital stock decreases. An increase in either the depreciation rate or the real price of capital would also increase the user cost of capital and reduce the desired capital stock.

Corporate Taxes and the Desired Capital Stock

After-tax profits, rather than before-tax profits, affect a firm's decision making. For example, if the corporate income tax rate is 30%, a firm retains 70% of its before-tax profits. We can think of corporate taxes as reducing the expected marginal product of capital. If the corporate income tax rate is t, then the firm gets to keep $(1 - t)$ of the output from each unit of capital. If $t = 0.30$, the firm gets to keep $(1 - 0.30) = 0.70$ of output. When accounting for taxes, the expected marginal product of capital is $(1 - t)MPK^e$. Incorporating taxes, the equation for the desired capital stock becomes:

$$(1 - t)MPK^e = (r + d)p_k.$$

Rearranging terms, this expression becomes:

$$MPK^e = \frac{(r + d)p_k}{(1 - t)},$$

where the term on the right side is the **tax-adjusted user cost of capital**, which is the after-tax real cost to a firm of purchasing and using an additional unit of capital during a period of time. If the government increases the corporate income tax rate, the tax-adjusted user cost of capital will increase, and the desired capital stock will decrease.

Tax-adjusted user cost of capital The after-tax expected real cost to a firm of purchasing and using an additional unit of capital during a period of time.

Figure 16.10

An Increase in the Tax-Adjusted User Cost of Capital and the Desired Capital Stock

An increase in the corporate income tax rate causes the after-tax user cost of capital to increase from uc_1 to uc_2, so the desired capital stock decreases from K_1^* to K_2^*.

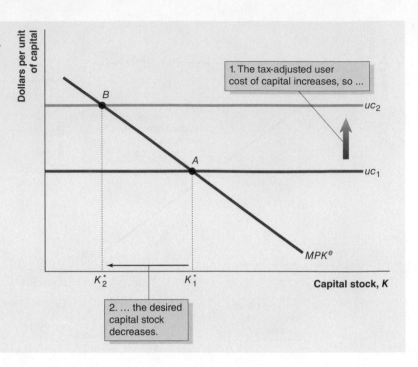

1. The tax-adjusted user cost of capital increases, so ...

2. ... the desired capital stock decreases.

Figure 16.10 shows that the increase in the corporate income tax rate causes the after-tax user cost of capital to increase from uc_1 to uc_2. As a result, the desired capital stock decreases from K_1^* to K_2^*.

Macro Data: How Important Are Corporate Taxes for Investment?

The model of investment indicates that corporate taxes may have an important effect on the desired capital stock and, therefore, on aggregate investment. Jason Cummins of Brevan Howard Asset Management LLP, Kevin Hassett of the American Enterprise Institute, and Glenn Hubbard of Columbia University estimated the effect of major tax reforms on investment by firms in 14 countries: Australia, Belgium, Canada, Denmark, France, Germany, Italy, Japan, the Netherlands, Norway, Spain, Sweden, the United Kingdom, and the United States. Cummins, Hassett, and Hubbard focused only on major tax reforms, such as the 1986 Tax Reform Act in the United States, which dramatically decreased the corporate income tax rate from 46% to 34%. They found that in 12 of the 14 countries, a reduction in corporate income taxes significantly increased the level of corporate investment activity.

Cummins, Hassett, and Hubbard also examined changes in corporate income taxes within the United States from 1962 to 1988. During this period, the federal government decreased the corporate income tax rate, in a series of steps, from 52% to 34%. Cummins, Hassett,

and Hubbard treated each of these changes as a "natural experiment" to examine the effect of tax changes on investment by firms. They found that after every major tax reform during this period, there was a significant change in investment. For example, the Revenue Act of 1964 reduced the corporate income tax rate from 52% in 1963 to 48% in 1965. As a result, the ratio of equipment investment to the existing stock of equipment increased by 7%. Because the Solow growth model (see Chapter 5) tells us that investment is an important determinant of labor productivity and the standard of living, we can conclude that reductions in the corporate income tax may raise the standard of living.

Sources: Jason Cummins, Kevin Hassett, and Glenn Hubbard, "Tax Reforms and Investment: A Cross-Country Comparison," *Journal of Public Economics*, Vol. 62, No. 1–2, October 1996, pp. 237–273; and Jason Cummins, Kevin Hassett, and Glenn Hubbard, "A Reconsideration of Investment Behavior Using Tax Reforms as Natural Experiments," *Brookings Papers on Economic Activity*, Vol. 25, No. 2, 1994, pp. 1–74.

See related problem 3.7 at the end of the chapter.

Table 16.3 summarizes the factors that affect the desired capital stock.

Table 16.3 Factors that Affect the Desired Capital Stock

If there is . . .	then . . .	so, the desired capital stock . . .	Graph of the effect on the capital stock . . .
a decrease in expected future profits	the marginal product of capital curve shifts to the left	decreases.	
an increase in the real interest rate	the user cost of capital curve shifts up	decreases.	
an increase in the depreciation rate	the user cost of capital curve shifts up	decreases.	
an increase in the real price of capital goods	the user cost of capital curve shifts up	decreases.	
an increase in the corporate income tax rate	the tax-adjusted user cost of capital curve shifts up	decreases.	

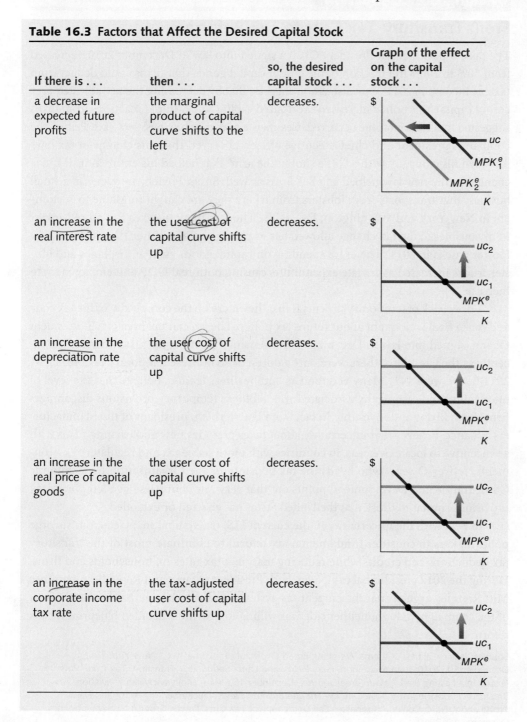

Making the Connection

From Transitory Tax Cuts to Tax Reform

The tax cut package that President Obama signed into law in December 2010, increased from 50% to 100% the fraction of the cost of capital goods that firms could deduct from taxable income in 2011. Our discussion suggests that by decreasing the tax-adjusted user cost of capital, this policy increased the desired capital stock. Initial reactions from firms suggested that this outcome occurred. Cessna is a maker of business jets. Jack Pelton, the company's president and chief executive officer, observed that this change in tax laws provided his company with a "little shot in the arm" that helped his entire industry. The changes in the new law helped smaller firms as well. Susan Povich, an owner of a small business that transports fresh lobsters from where they are caught in Maine to customers in New York and Washington, DC, said: "The less I pay in taxes the more I invest in my business"; the tax change allowed her to purchase three rather than just two new lobster trucks in 2011. The extra spending on capital goods such as airplanes and lobster trucks increased aggregate expenditure, causing both real GDP and employment to increase.

A drawback of temporary tax cuts is that they increase the complexity of the tax code and make firms uncertain about future tax policy. The special tax breaks that President Obama signed into law in December 2010 remained in effect for just two years. As recently as the late 1990s, there were only a dozen or so of these temporary tax breaks. By 2011, there were 141. Many economists and business leaders believe that the level of uncertainty and complexity associated with all these temporary provisions discourages firms from hiring and investing. In fact, Tom Duesterberg, president of the Manufacturers Alliance, believes that uncertainty about taxes provides new and existing firms with an incentive to locate overseas, in countries with more stable tax and regulatory environments. Jeffrey Owens, who heads the tax division for the Organisation for Economic Co-operation and Development, points out that very few countries have temporary tax provisions similar to those that the United States has enacted or extended.

To deal with the uncertainty in the current U.S. tax system, many economists urge policymakers to consider fundamental tax reform to eliminate most of the transitory tax deductions and credits while reducing marginal tax rates on households and firms. During the 2012 presidential campaign, both President Obama and Republican nominee Mitt Romney argued that the current tax system needed to be overhauled. In the heat of the campaign, though, neither side was willing to provide a detailed blueprint for tax reform.

Sources: Jackie Calmes, "Obama Weighing Broad Overhaul of Income Tax," *New York Times*, December 10, 2010; John McKinnon, Gary Fields, and Laura Saunders, "Transitory Tax Code Puts Nation in a Lasting Bind," *Wall Street Journal*, December 15, 2010; Molly McMillin, "Aviation: Tax Breaks Will Boost Industry," *McClatchy–Tribune Business News*, December 14, 2010; and Daniel Trotta and Kristina Cooke, "Businesses Say Demand, Not Tax Cuts, Drives Growth," www.cnbc.com, December 16, 2010.

See related problem 3.8 at the end of the chapter.

From the Desired Capital Stock to Investment

A firm that has too small a capital stock will not be able to produce enough goods and services to maximize its profits. A firm that has too large a capital stock has to spend too much to maintain it and therefore cannot maximize its profits.

Adjusting its capital stock requires a firm to purchase new capital or sell unwanted capital and to also spend time determining which capital goods to purchase or sell. Firms adjust their capital stock slowly in response to shocks to protect themselves from the negative consequences of building a factory that is too big or building too many factories or too many assembly lines.

Unexpected events that affect the desired capital stock occur frequently. Some events—such as the discovery of a new technology—indicate that future profits will increase, thereby increasing the desired capital stock. Other events—such as a large tax increase—indicate that future profits will decrease, thereby decreasing the desired capital stock. Because of this uncertainty, firms slowly adjust the capital stock as they acquire new information about changes in technology, taxes, and other relevant factors. We can capture the behavior of firms by assuming that when there is a gap between the desired and actual capital stock, $(K_t^* - K_{t-1})$, the firm eliminates a constant fraction, z, of that gap each period, through investment:

$$I_t = z(K_t^* - K_{t-1}) + dK_{t-1},$$

where $0 < z < 1$. If z is 0.10, then firms eliminate 10% of the gap between the actual and the desired capital stock each year; if z is 0.20, then firms eliminate 20% of the gap, and so on. This equation tells us that firms set gross investment, or investment before taking into account depreciation, equal to a level high enough to replace the depreciated capital stock, dK_{t-1}, plus a constant fraction of the gap between the desired capital stock next year and this year's capital stock. Any shock that causes the desired capital stock to increase also causes gross investment to increase. For example, an increase in expected profits in the future will increase the desired capital stock. As a result, firms will increase investment as they slowly try to accumulate more capital goods or a larger factory.

Solved Problem 16.3

Depreciation, Taxes, and Investment Spending

In December 2010, President Obama signed into law a bill that, among other things, increased the fraction of investment spending that firms are allowed to depreciate for tax purposes from 50% to 100%. For example, prior to the act, if Ford spent $100 million to build a new factory, then the company could deduct $50 million ($0.50 \times$ $100 million) from its taxable income for the year. After the act was passed,

Ford could deduct the full $100 million from its taxable income, thereby increasing its after-tax profit. This provision effectively reduces the tax rate on investment projects for the year 2011. What effect should this provision have had on the desired capital stock and the level of investment in 2011? Draw a graph to illustrate your answer. Should this provision have stimulated the economy in 2011?

Solving the Problem

Step 1 **Review the chapter material.** The problem asks you to use the theory of investment to determine the effect of a change in the tax treatment of depreciation, so you may want to review the section "Factors That Determine Private Investment," which begins on page 591.

Step 2 **Determine the effect on the desired capital stock and draw a graph to illustrate your answer.** Allowing firms to deduct 100% of investment spending from taxable income reduces the tax rate on investment projects for the year 2011 from t_1 to t_2. As a result, the tax-adjusted user cost of capital will decrease for 2011 from uc_1 to uc_2. Your graph should show that the tax-adjusted user cost of capital shifts down and that the desired capital stock increases:

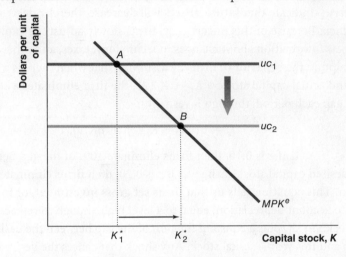

Step 3 **Explain whether this tax provision helped to stimulate the economy.** The equation for investment on page 599 tells us how investment spending is related to the desired capital stock:

$$I_t = z(K_t^* - K_{t-1}) + dK_{t-1}.$$

The increase in the desired capital stock means that the gap between the desired capital stock and the previous period's capital stock, $(K_t^* - K_{t-1})$, has increased. As a result, firms will increase investment spending today in order to increase the capital stock toward the desired level.

The model for investment spending tells us that increasing the amount of investment that firms can deduct from taxable income should lead to an increase in investment spending. Increased investment should have resulted in increased output and employment in 2011. But allowing firms to increase the amount of investment that is deductible from taxable income will also increase the government's budget deficit. Policymakers weigh any short-run benefits from a change in tax laws against the long-run costs.

See related problem 3.11 at the end of the chapter.

Tobin's *q*: Another Framework for Explaining Investment

Nobel Laureate James Tobin of Yale University developed a theory that linked the level of investment to the stock market.[12] **Tobin's *q*** is the ratio of the market value of a firm to the replacement cost of its capital:

$$q = \frac{\text{Market value of the firm}}{\text{Replacement cost of capital}}.$$

In this equation, the market value of the firm equals the price per share of the firm's stock multiplied by the number of shares of stock. For example, Apple Inc. had about 1 billion shares outstanding, and it traded for about $640 per share in mid-2012, so the market value of Apple was approximately $640 × 1 billion = $640 billion. The replacement cost of capital equals what it would cost to purchase the firm's current stock of capital goods. If Apple owns a building that would cost $100 million to rebuild, then the replacement cost for the building is $100 million. Apple's capital stock was worth about $80 billion, so calculating Tobin's *q*, we get $640 billion/$80 billion = 8. That is, the market valued Apple's capital as being eight times more than it would cost Apple to purchase the capital.

A firm's *q value* is a signal from participants in financial markets about whether it is profitable for the firm to acquire more capital goods and use them to expand production. If the value of Tobin's *q* is greater than 1, the market value of a firm is greater than the cost to the firm of acquiring capital. So, you would expect to see the firm increase its capital stock when Tobin's *q* is greater than 1. In our example, Tobin's *q* is 8 for Apple, so the market is sending a very strong signal to Apple to invest in more capital goods. Similarly, if Tobin's *q* is less than 1, the market value of the firm is less than its replacement cost, so the signal from financial markets is that the firm should decrease its capital stock. Therefore, you would expect investment to decrease at a firm with a Tobin's *q* of less than 1.

The Tobin's *q* model links investment to fluctuations in stock prices. If expected future profits increase, the price of a share of stock will increase, raising the market value of the firm and Tobin's *q*. As a result, the firm may increase investment. The emphasis that the Tobin's *q* model places on expected future profitability is very similar to the emphasis on the expected marginal product of capital in our earlier discussion.

Stock prices are volatile because expectations about future profitability of firms are also volatile. When expectations about future profits decrease substantially, there is a decrease in Tobin's *q*, which can cause firms to decrease investment. Similarly, when expectations about future profits increase, there is an increase in Tobin's *q*, and the level of investment. So, if investors' expectations of the future profitability of firms are volatile, investment will also be volatile, as Figure 16.1 on page 575 shows.

Credit Rationing and the Financial Accelerator

The model of investment assumes that firms undertake all profitable investment opportunities. If a firm has enough funds on hand, it pays for an investment project with

Tobin's *q* The ratio of the market value of a firm to the replacement cost of its capital.

[12]James Tobin, "A General Equilibrium Approach to Monetary Theory," *Journal of Money, Credit, and Banking*, Vol. 1, No. 1, February 1969, pp. 15–29.

those resources. Otherwise, the firm borrows the funds. But just as financial markets do not work perfectly for households, financial markets do not work perfectly for firms. Asymmetric information exists, so some firms may not be able to borrow the funds to finance all profitable investment projects. These firms are credit rationed. For example, a farmer-turned-developer in Pennsylvania named Mark Wagner wanted to convert his farmland into a housing development. But before he could build houses, he needed to put in sewer and water lines, construct roads, grade the land, and so on. To pay for these activities, Wagner needed a loan from a bank. Unfortunately, Wagner was unable to obtain a loan from any of the local banks and was quoted as saying "They're not loaning anyone money. They're all gun shy. Find me someone who'll give me $10 million, and I'll start building again."[13]

Credit rationing exists because banks and other lenders cannot perfectly observe the financial condition of firms or the willingness of firms to repay loans. To avoid themselves from making loans to firms that cannot repay them, banks require firms to post collateral. During recessions, the value of collateral and corporate profits decreases, so firms have more difficulty financing new investment projects. In addition, banks often tighten their lending requirements. As a result, firms such as Mark Wagner's development company lose access to loans. The presence of credit rationing suggests that investment depends on the state of the economy. Federal Reserve Chairman Ben Bernanke, Mark Gertler of New York University, and Simon Gilchrist of Boston University call the dependence of investment on the state of the economy the *financial accelerator*.[14]

Credit rationing and the financial accelerator are another reason gross private investment is so volatile. If a recession reduces firms' profits, credit-rationed firms are forced to cut back on investment. If, in addition, the recession leads to a decline in the price of financial assets, credit-rationed firms have less collateral to use for loans. These firms therefore get fewer loans and carry out less investment.

Steven Fazzari and Bruce Petersen of Washington University in St. Louis and Glenn Hubbard of Columbia University looked for evidence that firms face financing constraints.[15] They found that small manufacturing firms with less than $10 million in assets obtained 67% of their long-term debt from banks, while large manufacturing firms with $1 billion or more in assets obtained about 15% of their long-term debt from banks. Evidently, smaller firms face financing constraints that force them to rely on bank financing.

Because financing constraints become more binding during recessions, the financial accelerator can worsen economic downturns. As a result, the financial

---

[13]Matt Assad, "Arrested Development," *(Allentown, PA) Morning Call*, May 8, 2010.

[14]Ben Bernanke, Mark Gertler, and Simon Gilchrist, "The Financial Accelerator and the Flight to Quality," *Review of Economics and Statistics*, Vol. 78, No. 1, February 1996, pp. 1–15.

[15]Steven Fazzari, Glenn Hubbard, and Bruce Petersen, "Financing Constraints and Corporate Investment," *Brookings Paper on Economic Activity*, Vol. 1, December 1988, pp. 141–206; and Glenn Hubbard, "Capital Market Imperfections and Investment," *Journal of Economic Literature*, Vol. 36, No. 1, March 1998, pp. 193–225.

accelerator provides an additional explanation for why investment is as volatile as shown in Figure 16.1 on page 575.

Uncertainty and Irreversible Investment

Federal Reserve Chairman Ben Bernanke has argued that some of the volatility of investment comes from investment projects being irreversible.[16] That is, once an investment project is finished, it is hard for a firm to use the fixed capital for another activity. For example, if Ford builds an automobile factory in Tennessee, Ford or another firm would have difficultly using that factory to produce other goods. In addition to the irreversible nature of most investment projects, useful information about the profitability of an investment project arrives over time. If the market for automobiles collapses after Ford builds a factory, then the value of the factory will decline sharply.

Ford does not have to build the factory today; it has the option of waiting until it has acquired more useful information about the profitability of the factory. But the sooner Ford builds the factory, the sooner the factory will start producing automobiles and potentially start adding to the firm's profits. Firms trade off the benefit of receiving profits earlier by starting an investment project today against the benefit of waiting to acquire more information thereby potentially avoiding losses if the economy enters a recession.

Suppose there is an increase in uncertainty about the future price of output, the future price of inputs, future interest rates, or regulation. In that case, the value to firms of waiting to acquire additional information also increases and current investment is likely to decrease. When aggregate shocks such as oil price increases, changes in monetary policy, or changes in housing prices occur, the value of waiting to obtain more information increases. As a result, some firms may postpone investment projects, thereby magnifying the initial effect of the shock. The fact that investments are irreversible and can be delayed makes investment more volatile.

Answering the Key Question

Continued from page 573

At the beginning of this chapter, we asked:

"How does government tax policy affect the decisions of households and firms?"

Temporary tax cuts and tax rebates are likely to have smaller effects on consumption than are permanent changes in taxes. If a large number of households are credit rationed, however, even temporary tax cuts can have a significant effect on consumption.

Corporate taxes increase the tax-adjusted user cost of capital, which reduces the desired capital stock. Therefore, decreases in corporate taxes can help stimulate the economy during economic downturns because the decreases lead firms to increase their investment in order to increase their capital stock.

---

[16]Ben Bernanke, "Irreversibility, Uncertainty, and Cyclical Investment," *Quarterly Journal of Economics*, Vol. 98, No. 1, February 1983, pp. 85–106.

Key Terms and Problems

Key Terms

Animal spirits, p. 593

Desired capital stock, p. 592

Intertemporal budget constraint, p. 578

Life-cycle hypothesis, p. 579

Marginal product of capital (*MPK*), p. 592

Marginal propensity to consume (*MPC*), p. 580

Permanent income, p. 579

Permanent-income hypothesis, p. 578

Precautionary saving, p. 589

Tax-adjusted user cost of capital, p. 595

Tobin's *q*, p. 601

Transitory income, p. 579

User cost of capital (*uc*), p. 593

| **16.1** | **The Macroeconomic Implications of Microeconomic Decision Making: Intertemporal Choice** |

Discuss the macroeconomic implications of microeconomic decision making by households and firms.

Review Questions

1.1 Explain what economists mean when they characterize households and firms as forward looking.

1.2 Describe the relative volatility of investment and consumption.

Problems and Applications

1.3 Loose lending standards in the years before the financial crisis of 2007–2009 allowed some borrowers to falsify information about their income and creditworthiness when applying for loans. What would you expect to happen to lending standards in the wake of the financial crisis, and how might this affect consumers' ability to allocate spending over time?

1.4 Briefly explain whether you agree with the following statement: "A firm would never increase investment during a recession if its sales are currently very low."

| **16.2** | **Factors That Determine Consumption** |

Explain the determinants of personal consumption.

Review Questions

2.1 Write the equation for the intertemporal budget constraint. How does the intertemporal budget constraint change when there are taxes? Why might the intertemporal consumption choices of credit-rationed households be inefficient?

2.2 Explain Milton Friedman's permanent-income hypothesis and Franco Modigliani's life-cycle hypothesis. How are these hypotheses similar to one another, and how are they different?

2.3 Describe the income and substitution effects of a rise in the real interest rate.

2.4 Briefly explain why the marginal propensity to consume out of transitory income is different from the marginal propensity to consume out of permanent income.

Problems and Applications

2.5 For each of the following scenarios, explain the expected effect on consumption.

MyEconLab Visit **www.myeconlab.com** to complete these exercises online and get instant feedback. Exercises that update with real-time data are marked with 🔗.

a. Housing prices rise.

b. The government increases personal income taxes.

c. Uncertainty about the economy causes the desired level of saving to increase.

d. A tax cut that was expected to be temporary becomes permanent.

2.6 [Related to Solved Problem 16.2 **on page 585**] Suppose that you expect to work for another 50 years and then live 20 years in retirement. You have no wealth, and there are no taxes. You want to smooth consumption over your lifetime, and you will earn $75,000 per year.

a. Calculate consumption in each period.

b. Now assume that you unexpectedly receive an inheritance of $500,000. How will your consumption change?

c. The government decides to tax you $15,000 per year. What is your new level of consumption? [Assume that you still receive the inheritance in part (b).]

d. How would your consumption change if the government cut taxes this year from $15,000 to $10,000, but taxes next year and in the future return to $15,000 per year? [Assume that you still receive the inheritance in part (b).]

e. How would your consumption change if the government permanently decreased taxes from $15,000 to $10,000 per year? [Assume that you still receive the inheritance in part (b).]

2.7 Some economists advocate a change from an income tax to a consumption tax, such as a national sales tax. A sales tax makes consumption more expensive and so encourages households to save. How would such a change, all other things being equal, affect each of the following?

a. Current consumption

b. Current saving

c. Capital formation

d. Future GDP

2.8 [Related to the Chapter Opener **on page 573**] An article for *CNNMoney* reports that if the government cuts spending and raises taxes as expected on January 1, 2013 then economic growth will slow in 2013 and the U.S. may enter a recession.

a. Is it possible that expectations of a recession in 2013 affected consumption expenditures in 2012? Briefly explain.

b. The personal savings rate for U.S. households rose from 3.2% in November 2011 to 4.2% in July 2012. Is this increase consistent with your answer to part (a)? Briefly explain.

Source: Jeanne Sahadi, "Fiscal Cliff to Improve Debt Outlook, but Cause Recession," *CNNMoney*, August 22, 2012.

2.9 [Related to the Making the Connection **on page 588**] In 2010, President Obama and Congress agreed to temporarily extend tax cuts that were initially passed during the administration of George W. Bush. President Obama and Congress also agreed to temporary cuts in Social Security payroll taxes. Both sets of tax cuts were set to expire on January 1, 2013 and the decision to further extend these temporary tax cuts was widely debated during the fall of 2012.

a. At the time the tax cuts were enacted, most news coverage described them as temporary. Suppose that the public believed that the tax cuts were temporary. What would be the consequences for consumption of letting the tax cuts expire as scheduled?

b. Suppose that despite what they read in the news coverage, the public believed that the tax cuts would be permanent. In that case, what would be the consequences of letting the tax cuts expire as scheduled?

c. Briefly explain the differences in your answers to parts (a) and (b) of this question.

2.10 [Related to Solved Problem 16.2 **on page 585**] Suppose you are currently 25 years old, your wealth is zero, you will retire at age 55, after working at a constant salary of $150,000, and you expect to live to age 85. Use the life-cycle hypothesis to answer the following questions. Assume that you completely smooth consumption.

a. What is your lifetime income?

b. What is your yearly consumption?

Now assume that you receive a one-time signing bonus of $30,000 when you first accept your job.

c. What is your lifetime income?

d. What is your yearly consumption?

e. What is the *MPC* out of the transitory increase in your income?

Now assume that the signing bonus specified above is a yearly bonus that you will receive each year you are employed.

f. What is your lifetime income?

g. What is your yearly consumption?

h. What is the *MPC* out of the permanent yearly increase in your income?

16.3 Factors That Determine Private Investment
Explain the determinants of private investment.

Review Questions

3.1 How does a firm decide on its desired level of capital?

3.2 How do corporate taxes affect the desired level of the capital stock? Explain how the desired level of the capital stock determines the level of investment.

3.3 What is Tobin's *q*, and how does it link financial markets to investment?

3.4 Explain how credit rationing and the financial accelerator can account for the volatility of investment.

Problems and Applications

3.5 For each of the following scenarios, use a graph to show how the firm's desired capital stock is likely to change.

a. Technological change increases the productivity of capital.

b. The Fed decreases interest rates, while the inflation rate is unchanged.

c. The real price of capital goods decreases.

d. The economy is expected to remain in recession for several years.

3.6 Suppose that the real interest rate is 5%, the depreciation rate is 8%, the real price of capital is $10, and the tax rate is 10%.

a. Calculate the tax-adjusted user cost of capital.

b. Calculate the tax-adjusted user cost of capital if the depreciation rate increases to 10%.

c. Return to the original depreciation rate of 8% and calculate the tax-adjusted user cost of capital if the tax rate falls to 6%.

3.7 [Related to the Macro Data feature **on page 596**] During the 2012 presidential election, both President Obama and Governor Romney advocated reducing the tax rate on corporate profits. Suppose that corporate tax rates are reduced.

a. What is the effect on the desired capital stock and the level of investment? Briefly explain.

b. What effect will this tax reduction have on labor productivity and level of real GDP in the long run? Briefly explain.

3.8 [Related to the Making the Connection **on page 598**] In a CNBC interview in September 2012, James Bullard, president of the Federal Reserve Bank of Saint Louis, said that "The uncertainty around

---

the future of the U.S. economy is a serious damper on investment." He further said that uncertainty about taxes and other policies were deterring businesses from investing. He also noted that the Congressional Budget Office was predicting that tax increases and government spending cuts scheduled for January 1, 2013 were likely to cause a recession.

a. Explain how uncertainty about U.S. taxes might lead firms to reduce investment.

b. Suppose that firms believe that the U.S. will enter a recession in 2013 due to tax increases and government spending cuts. What effect would this belief have had on investment spending and real GDP in 2012? Briefly explain.

c. The growth rate of non-residential fixed investment was 19.0% during the third quarter of 2011, but just 3.6% during the second quarter of 2012. Is this decrease in the growth rate of investment consistent with President Bullard's concerns? Briefly explain.

Source: Jennifer Dauble, "CNBC Exclusive: CNBC Transcript: Federal Reserve Bank of St. Louis President and CEO James Bullard on CNBC Today," September 27, 2012. Available at: http://www.cnbc.com/id/49167408/CNBC_EXCLUSIVE_CNBC_TRANSCRIPT_FEDERAL_RESERVE_BANK_OF_ST_LOUIS_PRESIDENT_CEO_JAMES_BULLARD_ON_CNBC_TODAY.

3.9 The U.S. recovery from the 2007–2009 recession was relatively slow through 2012. While there are many reasons for the slow recovery, how might the high degree of uncertainty about future economic conditions have contributed?

3.10 In 2009, the stock market value of most firms was lower than it was in 2006.

a. Why would the market value of most firms have fallen?

b. The growth rate of non-residential investment steadily fell from 8.0% in 2006 to −18.1% in 2009. Is this decline consistent with Tobin's q model of investment? Briefly explain.

3.11 [**Related to** Solved Problem 16.3 **on page 599**] The following graph shows the marginal product of

capital and the user cost of capital. Assume that the economy is currently at point A, with the capital stock equal to K_1^*.

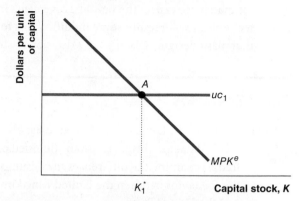

a. All other things being equal, how would you expect Federal Reserve policy that increases the money supply to change the user cost of capital? What effect would you expect this change in the user cost of capital to have on investment and the capital stock in the short run? Show your answer on the graph.

b. Now return to the original graph and suppose that there is an improvement in technology that makes capital more productive. How would the productivity increase change investment and the capital stock in the short run? Show your answer on the graph.

3.12 John Maynard Keynes described firms as having "animal spirits," meaning that they often make decisions based on emotion as much as on more objective factors.

a. How might animal spirits explain the volatility of investment relative to consumption?

b. Are consumers also sometimes motivated by emotion? If so, why isn't consumption more volatile?

3.13 Based on rapidly falling prices of competitors' photovoltaic modules used in the production of solar panels, General Electric (GE) announced in July 2012 that it was stopping production on what was supposed to be the largest solar factory in the United States. In a *Forbes* article, Danielle Merfeld, GE's general manager for solar technologies, is quoted as saying: "The good news is we are keeping our factory in place in the sense of the equipment and the tools that are there. But ultimately we expect the new improvements in technology will require some modifications to that plant design." Discuss GE's decision to stop production as it relates to uncertainty and irreversible investment. What trade-off did GE face in making its decision to halt production of this factory?

Source: Todd Woody, "GE Halts Work on the U.S.'s Biggest Solar Factory to Return to the Lab," *Forbes*, July 3, 2012.

Data Exercises

D16.1: Using the St. Louis Federal Reserve Bank's FRED database (http://research.stlouisfed.org/fred2/) examine the differences in consumption behavior between the United Kingdom and the United States.

a. Download annual data from 1955 to the present on nominal private final consumption expenditure in the United Kingdom (GBRPFCEADSMEI) and the United States (USAPFCEADSMEI). For the same time period, download annual data on nominal GDP for the United Kingdom (GBRGDPNADSMEI) and the United States (USAGDPNADSMEI).

b. Calculate consumption's share of GDP for both the United Kingdom and the United States. Plot the two series on a graph.

c. What differences and similarities do you see in the two data series?

D16.2: [Excel exercise] For the United States, the chapter showed that consumption is less volatile than GDP, but that investment is more volatile than GDP. Using the St. Louis Federal Reserve Bank's FRED database (http://research.stlouisfed.org/fred2/) examine the behavior of consumption and investment spending in Japan.

a. For 1994 to the present, download quarterly data on real private final consumption (JPNPFCEQDSNAQ), real gross fixed capital formation (JPNGFCFQDSNAQ), and real GDP (JPNRGDPQDSNAQ) for Japan.

b. Calculate the compound annual growth rate for each quarter for all three data series. Economists often use the standard deviation as a measure of volatility. Calculate the standard deviation for all three series of growth rates.

c. Is consumption more or less volatile than GDP? Is this result consistent with consumption smoothing? Explain. Is investment more or less volatile than GDP?

d. The growth rate of real GDP is one measure of the business cycle. Is the behavior of consumption and investment over the business cycle similar or different than in the United States. Briefly explain.

D16.3: Both the permanent-income hypothesis and the life-cycle hypothesis predict that consumption is less volatile than income. Using the St. Louis Federal Reserve Bank's FRED database (http://research.stlouisfed.org/fred2/) evaluate this prediction for the United States.

a. Download quarterly data for real consumption (PCECC96) and real GDP (GDPC1) from 1947 to the present and calculate the compound average annual growth rates for both data series.

b. Economists often measure the volatility of a data series using the standard deviation. Calculate the standard deviation of both consumption and GDP.

c. Are the results in part (b) consistent with the permanent-income hypothesis and the life-cycle hypothesis? Briefly explain.

Glossary

Adaptive expectations: The assumption that people make forecasts of future values of a variable using only past values of the variable. *(p. 387)*

Adverse selection: A situation in which one party to a transaction takes advantage of knowing more than the other party. *(p. 73)*

Aggregate demand (*AD*) curve: A curve that shows the relationship between aggregate expenditure on goods and services by households and firms and the inflation rate. *(p. 507)*

Aggregate demand and aggregate supply (*AD–AS*) model: A model that explains short-run fluctuations in the output gap and the inflation rate. *(p. 515)*

Aggregate production function: An equation that shows the relationship between the inputs employed by firms and the maximum output firms can produce with those inputs. *(p. 149)*

Aggregate supply (*AS*) curve: A curve that shows the total quantity of output, or real GDP, that firms are willing and able to supply at a given inflation rate. *(p. 512)*

Animal spirits: Periods of irrational pessimism and optimism that affect the investment behavior of firms. *(p. 593)*

Asset: Anything of value owned by a person or a firm. *(p. 66)*

Asymmetric information: A situation in which one party to an economic transaction has better information than does the other party. *(pp. 73 and 432)*

Automatic stabilizers: Taxes, transfer payments, or government expenditures that automatically increase or decrease along with the business cycle. *(p. 468)*

Balance of payments: A record of a country's trade with other countries in goods, services, and assets. *(p. 111)*

Balanced growth: A situation in which the capital–labor ratio and real GDP per worker grow at the same constant rate. *(p. 193)*

Bank panic: A situation in which many banks simultaneously experience runs. *(p. 78)*

Bank run: The process by which large numbers of depositors who have lost confidence in a bank simultaneously withdraw enough funds to force the bank to close. *(pp. 78 and 414)*

Board of Governors: The governing board of the Federal Reserve System, consisting of seven members appointed by the president of the United States. *(p. 416)*

Bond: A financial security issued by a corporation or government that represents a promise to repay a fixed amount of funds. *(p. 66)*

Bubble: The situation in which the price of an asset rises significantly above the asset's fundamental value; an unsustainable increase in the price of a class of assets. *(p. 81)*

Budget deficit: The situation in which the government's expenditure is greater than its tax revenue. *(pp. 469 and 545)*

Budget surplus: The situation in which the government's expenditure is less than its tax revenue. *(p. 469)*

Business cycle: Alternating periods of economic expansion and economic recession. *(pp. 2 and 296)*

Capital: Goods, such as machine tools, computers, factories, and office buildings, that are used to produce other goods and services. *(p. 29)*

Capital account: The part of the balance of payments that records (generally) minor transactions, such as migrants' transfers, and sales and purchases of non-produced, non-financial assets. *(p. 112)*

Capital–labor ratio: The dollar value of capital goods per unit of labor; measured as the dollar value of capital divided by the total number of workers. *(p. 162)*

Central bank credibility: The degree to which households and firms believe the central bank's announcements about future policy. *(p. 527)*

Central bank reaction function: A rule or formula that a central bank uses to set interest rates in response to changing economic conditions. *(p. 506)*

Classical dichotomy: The assertion that in the long run, nominal variables, such as the money supply or the price level, do not affect real variables, such as the levels of employment and real GDP. *(p. 217)*

Classical economics: The perspective that business cycles can be explained using equilibrium analysis. *(p. 296)*

Closed economy: An economy in which households, firms, and governments do not borrow, lend, or trade internationally. *(p. 110)*

Cobb–Douglas production function: A widely used macroeconomic production function that takes the form $Y = AK^{\alpha}L^{1-\alpha}$. *(p. 149)*

Coincident indicators: Economic variables that tend to rise and fall at the same time as real GDP. *(p. 314)*

Commodity money: A good used as money that has value independent of its use as money. *(p. 218)*

Constant returns to scale: A property of a production function such that if all inputs increase by the same percentage, real GDP increases by the same percentage. *(p. 150)*

Consumer price index (CPI): An average of the prices of the goods and services purchased by the typical urban family of four. *(p. 45)*

Consumption: The purchase of new goods and services by households. *(p. 32)*

Contagion: The process by which a run on one financial institution spreads to other financial institutions, resulting in a financial crisis. *(p. 78)*

Countercyclical variable: An economic variable that moves in the opposite direction as real GDP—decreasing during expansions and increasing during recessions. *(p. 313)*

Crowding out: A reduction in private investment caused by government budget deficits. *(pp. 134, 491, and 556)*

Currency appreciation: An increase in the market value of one country's currency relative to another country's currency. *(p. 117)*

Currency depreciation: A decrease in the market value of one country's currency relative to another country's currency. *(p. 117)*

Current account: The part of the balance of payments that records a country's net exports, net investment income, and net transfers. *(p. 112)*

Cyclical unemployment: Unemployment caused by a recession; measured as the difference between the actual level of unemployment and the level of unemployment when the unemployment rate equals the natural rate of unemployment. *(p. 271)*

Cyclical unemployment rate: The difference between the unemployment rate and the natural unemployment rate. *(p. 308)*

Cyclically adjusted budget deficit or surplus: The deficit or surplus in the federal government's budget if real GDP equaled potential GDP; also called the full-employment budget deficit or surplus. *(p. 472)*

Default risk: The risk that a borrower will fail to make payments of interest or principal. *(p. 348)*

Deflation: A sustained decrease in the price level. *(p. 10)*

Depreciation rate: The rate at which the capital stock declines due to either capital goods becoming worn out by use or becoming obsolete. *(p. 179)*

Desired capital stock: The level of the capital stock that maximizes a firm's profits. *(p. 591)*

Discount rate: The interest rate that the Federal Reserve charges on discount loans. *(p. 420)*

Discretionary fiscal policy: Government policy that involves deliberate changes in taxes, transfer payments, or government purchases to achieve macroeconomic policy objectives. *(p. 468)*

Disposable income: National income plus transfer payments minus personal tax payments. *(p. 465)*

Efficiency wage: A higher-than-market wage that a firm pays to motivate workers to be more productive and to increase profits. *(p. 285)*

Endogenous growth theory: A theory of economic growth that tries to explain the growth rate of technological change. *(p. 198)*

Endogenous variable: A variable that is explained by an economic model. *(p. 17)*

Exchange rate system: An agreement among countries about how exchange rates should be determined. *(p. 119)*

Exogenous variable: A variable that is taken as given and is not explained by an economic model. *(p. 17)*

Expansion: The period of a business cycle during which real GDP and employment are increasing. *(p. 296)*

Expected real interest rate: The nominal interest rate minus the expected inflation rate. *(p. 233)*

Factor of production: Any input used to produce goods and services. *(p. 29)*

Federal funds rate: The interest rate that banks charge each other on short-term loans. *(p. 416)*

Federal Open Market Committee (FOMC): The 12-member Federal Reserve committee that directs open market operations. *(p. 416)*

Federal Reserve: The central bank of the United States; usually referred to as "the Fed." *(p. 48)*

Federal Reserve System: The central bank of the United States; commonly referred to as "the Fed." *(p. 415)*

Fiat money: Money, such as paper currency, that has no value apart from its use as money. *(p. 220)*

Final good or service: A good or service purchased by a final user. *(p. 27)*

Financial account: The part of the balance of payments that records purchases of assets a country has made abroad and foreign purchases of assets in the country. *(p. 112)*

Financial asset: A financial claim. *(p. 66)*

Financial crisis: A significant disruption in the flow of funds from lenders to borrowers. *(pp. 12 and 75)*

Financial intermediary: A firm, such as a commercial bank, that borrows funds from savers and lends them to borrowers. *(p. 67)*

Financial market: A place or channel for buying or selling stocks, bonds, or other financial securities. *(p. 66)*

Financial system: The financial intermediaries and financial markets that together facilitate the flow of funds from lenders to borrowers. *(pp. 31 and 65)*

Fiscal policy: Changes in federal government taxes, purchases of goods and services, and transfer payments that are intended to achieve macroeconomic policy objectives. *(pp. 12 and 462)*

Fisher effect: The assertion by Irving Fisher that the nominal interest rate rises or falls point-for-point with changes in the expected inflation rate. *(p. 234)*

Fisher equation: The equation stating that the nominal interest rate is the sum of the expected real interest rate and the expected inflation rate. *(p. 234)*

Fixed exchange rate system: A system in which exchange rates are set at levels determined and maintained by governments. *(p. 119)*

Floating exchange rate system: A system in which the foreign-exchange value of currency is determined in the foreign exchange market. *(p. 120)*

Frictional unemployment: Short-term unemployment that arises from the process of matching the job skills of workers to the requirements of jobs. *(p. 269)*

GDP deflator: A measure of the price level, calculated by dividing nominal GDP by real GDP and multiplying by 100; also called the GDP implicit price deflator. *(p. 40)*

Government purchases: Spending by federal, state, and local governments on newly produced goods and services. *(p. 33)*

Gross domestic product (GDP): The market value of all final goods and services produced in a country during a period of time. *(p. 27)*

Gross federal debt: The total dollar value of Treasury bonds plus the dollar value of the small amount of bonds and other securities issued by other federal agencies. *(p. 547)*

Gross federal debt held by the public: Debt that includes the bonds and other securities issued by the U.S. Treasury (and a small amount of securities issued by federal agencies) not held by the federal government. *(pp. 474 and 544)*

Gross national product (GNP): The value of final goods and services produced by residents of a country, even if the production takes place outside that country. *(p. 35)*

Human capital: The accumulated knowledge and skills that workers acquire from education and training or from life experiences. *(pp. 166 and 198)*

Hyperinflation: Extremely high rates of inflation, exceeding 50% per month. *(p. 220)*

Impact lag: The period of time between a policy change and the effect of that policy change. *(p. 436)*

Implementation lag: The period of time between when policymakers recognize that a shock has occurred and when they adjust policy to the shock. *(p. 436)*

Inflation rate: The percentage increase in the price level from one year to the next. *(p. 9)*

Insolvent: The situation in which the value of the assets held by a bank or another firm declines to less than the value of its liabilities, leaving the bank with negative net worth. *(p. 78)*

Interest parity condition: The proposition that differences in interest rates on similar bonds in different countries reflect investors' expectations of future changes in exchange rates. *(p. 127)*

Interest rate: The cost of borrowing funds, usually expressed as a percentage of the amount borrowed. *(p. 49)*

Interest-rate risk: The risk that the price of a financial asset will fluctuate in response to changes in market interest rates. *(p. 98)*

Intermediate good or service: A good or service that is an input into another good or service, such as a tire on a truck. *(p. 27)*

Intertemporal budget constraint: A budget constraint that applies to consumption and income in more than one time period; it shows how much a household can consume, given lifetime income. *(p. 578)*

Investment: Spending by firms on new factories, office buildings, machinery, and additions to inventories, plus spending by households and firms on new houses. *(p. 33)*

IS curve: A curve in the *IS–MP* model that shows the combination of the real interest rate and aggregate output that represents equilibrium in the market for goods and services. *(p. 334)*

IS–LM model: A macroeconomic model which assumes that the central bank targets the money supply. *(p. 370)*

IS–MP model: A macroeconomic model consisting of an *IS* curve, which represents equilibrium in the goods market; an *MP* curve, which represents monetary policy; and a Phillips curve, which represents the short-run relationship between the output gap (which is the percentage difference between actual and potential real GDP) and the inflation rate. *(p. 334)*

Keynesian economics: The perspective that business cycles represent disequilibrium or nonmarket-clearing behavior. *(p. 296)*

Labor-augmenting technological change: Improvements in economic efficiency that increase the productivity of labor but that do not directly make capital goods more efficient. *(p. 190)*

Labor force: The sum of employed and unemployed workers in the economy. *(pp. 8 and 51)*

Labor productivity: The quantity of goods and services that can be produced by one worker or by one hour of work. *(p. 3)*

Lagging indicators: Economic variables that tend to rise and fall after real GDP. *(p. 314)*

Leading indicators: Economic variables that tend to rise and fall in advance of real GDP. *(p. 313)*

Leverage: A measure of how much debt an investor takes on in making an investment. *(p. 76)*

LM curve: A curve that shows the combinations of the real interest rate and output that result in equilibrium in the money market. *(p. 370)*

Life-cycle hypothesis: The theory that households use financial markets to borrow and save to transfer funds from high-income periods, such as working years, to low-income periods, such as retirement years or periods of unemployment. *(p. 579)*

Liquidity: The ease with which an asset can be exchanged for cash. *(p. 72)*

Long-run economic growth: The process by which increasing productivity raises the average standard of living. *(p. 3)*

M1: A narrow measure of the money supply: The sum of currency in circulation, checking account deposits, and holdings of traveler's checks. *(p. 222)*

M2: A broad measure of the money supply: All the assets that are included in M1, as well as time deposits with a value of less than $100,000, savings accounts, money market deposit accounts at banks, and noninstitutional money market mutual fund shares. *(p. 222)*

Macroeconomic shock: An unexpected exogenous event that has a significant effect on an important sector of the economy or on the economy as a whole. *(p. 297)*

Macroeconomics: The study of the economy as a whole, including topics such as inflation, unemployment, and economic growth. *(p. 2)*

Managed float exchange rate system: A system in which private buyers and sellers in the foreign exchange market determine the value of currencies most of the time, with occasional government intervention. *(p. 120)*

Marginal product of capital (MPK): The extra output a firm receives from adding one more unit of capital, holding all other inputs and efficiency constant. *(pp. 151 and 592)*

Marginal product of labor (MPL): The extra output a firm receives from adding one more unit of labor, holding all other inputs and efficiency constant. *(pp. 151 and 262)*

Marginal propensity to consume (MPC): The amount by which consumption spending changes when disposable income changes. *(pp. 336 and 580)*

Medium of exchange: Something that is generally accepted as payment for goods and services; a function of money. *(p. 219)*

Menu costs: The costs to firms of changing prices due to reprinting price lists, informing customers, and angering customers; costs related to expected inflation. *(pp. 238 and 299)*

Microeconomics: The study of how households and firms make choices, how they interact in markets, and how the government attempts to influence their choices. *(p. 2)*

Monetary base (or high-powered money): The sum of currency in circulation and bank reserves. *(p. 224)*

Monetary policy: The actions that central banks take to manage the money supply and interest rates to pursue macroeconomic policy objectives. *(pp. 12 and 414)*

Monetary rule: A commitment by the central bank to follow specific and publicly announced guidelines for monetary policy. *(p. 530)*

Money multiplier: A number that indicates how much the money supply increases when the monetary base increases by $1. *(p. 224)*

Moral hazard: Actions people take after they have entered into a transaction that make the other party to the transaction worse off. *(p. 74)*

MP curve: A curve in the *IS–MP* model that represents Federal Reserve monetary policy. *(p. 334)*

Multiplier: The change in equilibrium GDP divided by the change in autonomous expenditure. *(pp. 317 and 338)*

Multiplier effect: A series of induced increases (or decreases) in consumption spending that results from an initial increase (or decrease) in autonomous expenditure; this effect amplifies the effect of economic shocks on real GDP. *(pp. 316 and 338)*

National income accounting: The rules used in calculating GDP and related measures of total production and total income. *(p. 29)*

Natural rate of unemployment: The normal rate of unemployment, consisting of frictional unemployment plus structural unemployment. *(p. 271)*

Net capital outflows: Capital outflows minus capital inflows. *(p. 114)*

Net exports: The value of all exports minus the value of all imports. *(p. 34)*

Nominal exchange rate: The price of one country's currency in terms of another country's currency. *(p. 115)*

Nominal GDP: The value of final goods and services calculated using current-year prices. *(p. 38)*

Nominal interest rate: The stated interest rate on a loan. *(p. 49)*

Normative analysis: Analysis concerned with what ought to be. *(p. 18)*

Okun's law: A statistical relationship discovered by Arthur Okun between the cyclical unemployment rate and the output gap. *(p. 308)*

Open economy: An economy in which households, firms, and governments borrow, lend, and trade internationally. *(p. 110)*

Open market operations: The Federal Reserve's purchases and sales of securities, usually U.S. Treasury securities, in financial markets. *(pp. 224 and 416)*

Output gap: The percentage deviation of actual real GDP from potential GDP. *(p. 307)*

Permanent income: Income that households normally expect to receive each year. *(p. 579)*

Permanent-income hypothesis: The hypothesis that household consumption depends on permanent income and that households use financial markets to save and borrow to smooth consumption in response to fluctuations in transitory income. *(p. 578)*

Personal consumption expenditures price (PCE) index: A price index similar to the GDP deflator, except that it includes only the prices of goods from the consumption category of GDP. *(p. 48)*

Phillips curve: A curve that represents the short-run relationship between the output gap (or the unemployment rate) and the inflation rate. *(p. 334)*

Policy trilemma: The hypothesis that it is impossible for a country to have exchange rate stability, monetary policy independence, and free capital flows at the same time. *(p. 451)*

Positive analysis: Analysis concerned with what is. *(p. 18)*

Potential GDP: The level of real GDP attained when firms are producing at capacity and labor is fully employed. *(p. 296)*

Precautionary saving: Extra saving by households to protect themselves from unexpected decreases in future income due to job loss, illness, or disability. *(p. 589)*

Present value: The value today of funds that will be received in the future. *(p. 90)*

Primary budget deficit (PD): The difference between government purchases of goods and services plus transfer payments minus tax revenue. *(p. 545)*

Procyclical variable: An economic variable that moves in the same direction as real GDP—increasing during expansions and decreasing during recessions. *(p. 313)*

Profit: Total revenue minus total cost. *(p. 155)*

Purchasing power parity: The theory that, in the long run, nominal exchange rates adjust to equalize the purchasing power of different currencies. *(p. 124)*

Quantitative easing: A central bank policy that attempts to stimulate the economy by buying long-term securities. *(p. 433)*

Quantity equation (or equation of exchange): An identity that states that the money supply multiplied by the velocity of money equals the price level multiplied by real GDP. *(p. 228)*

Quantity theory of money: A theory about the connection between money and prices that assumes that the velocity of money is constant. *(p. 228)*

Rational expectations: The assumption that people make forecasts of future values of a variable using all available information; formally, the assumption that expectations equal optimal forecasts, using all available information. *(p. 527)*

Real exchange rate: The rate at which goods and services in one country can be exchanged for goods and services in another country. *(p. 117)*

Real gross domestic product (GDP): The value of final goods and services, adjusted for changes in the price level. *(pp. 4 and 38)*

Real interest rate: The nominal interest rate adjusted for the effects of inflation. *(p. 49)*

Recession: The period of a business cycle during which real GDP and employment are decreasing. *(p. 296)*

Recognition lag: The period of time between when a shock occurs and when policymakers recognize that the shock has affected the economy. *(p. 436)*

Reserve requirements: Regulations that require banks to hold a fraction of checking account deposits as vault cash or deposits with the Fed. *(p. 421)*

Reserves: A bank asset consisting of vault cash plus bank deposits with the Federal Reserve. *(p. 224)*

Ricardian equivalence: The theory that forward-looking households fully anticipate the future taxes required to pay off government debt, so that reductions in lump-sum taxes have no effect on the economy. *(p. 557)*

Risk: The chance that the value of a financial security will change relative to what you expect. *(p. 72)*

Risk structure of interest rates: The relationship among interest rates on bonds that have different characteristics but the same maturity. *(pp. 96 and 348)*

Securitization: The process of converting loans and other financial assets that are not tradable into securities. *(p. 73)*

Seigniorage: The government's profit from issuing fiat money; also called inflation tax. *(pp. 236 and 545)*

Shoe-leather costs: The costs of inflation to households and firms from holding less money and making more frequent trips to the bank; costs related to expected inflation. *(p. 237)*

Solow growth model: A model that explains how the long-run growth rate of the economy depends on saving, population growth, and technological change. *(p. 177)*

Stagflation: A combination of high inflation and recession, usually resulting from a supply shock such as an increase in the price of oil. *(pp. 386 and 516)*

Standard of deferred payment: An asset that facilitates transactions over time; a function of money. *(p. 219)*

Steady state: An equilibrium in the Solow growth model in which the capital–labor ratio and real GDP per worker are constant but capital, labor, and output are growing. *(p. 180)*

Stock: A financial security that represents a legal claim on a share in the profits and assets of a firm. *(p. 66)*

Store of value: The accumulation of wealth by holding dollars or other assets that can be used to buy goods and services in the future; a function of money. *(p. 219)*

Structural unemployment: Unemployment that arises from a persistent mismatch between the job skills or attributes of workers and the requirements of jobs. *(p. 270)*

Tax wedge: The difference between the before-tax and after-tax return to an economic activity. *(p. 486)*

Tax-adjusted user cost of capital: The after-tax expected real cost to a firm of purchasing and using an additional unit of capital during a period of time. *(p. 595)*

Taylor rule: A monetary policy guideline developed by economist John Taylor for determining the target for the federal funds rate. *(p. 531)*

Term premium: The additional interest investors require in order to be willing to buy a long-term bond rather than a comparable sequence of short-term bonds. *(pp. 99 and 347)*

Term structure of interest rates: The relationship among the interest rates on bonds that are otherwise similar but that have different maturities. *(pp. 96 and 346)*

Time value of money: The way the value of a payment changes depending on when the payment is received. *(p. 93)*

Time-inconsistency problem: The tendency of policymakers to announce one policy in advance in order to change the expectations of households and firms and then to follow another policy after households and firms have made economic decisions based on the announced policy. *(p. 534)*

Tobin's *q*: The ratio of the market value of a firm to the replacement cost of its capital. *(p. 601)*

Too-big-to-fail policy: A policy in which the federal government does not allow large financial firms to fail for fear of damaging the financial system. *(p. 443)*

Total factor productivity (*TFP*): An index of the overall level of efficiency of transforming capital and labor into real GDP. *(p. 153)*

Transfer payments: Payments by the government to individuals for which the government does not receive a good or service in return. *(p. 33)*

Transitory income: Income that households do not expect to receive each year. *(p. 579)*

Unemployment insurance: A government program that allows workers to receive benefits for a period of time after losing their jobs. *(p. 270)*

Unemployment rate: The percentage of the labor force that is unemployed. *(pp. 8 and 51)*

Unit of account: A way of measuring value in an economy in terms of money; a function of money. *(p. 219)*

User cost of capital (*uc*): The expected real cost to a firm of using an additional unit of capital during a period of time. *(p. 593)*

Velocity of money: For a given period, the average number of times that each dollar in the money supply is used to purchase a good or service that is included in GDP. *(p. 228)*

Index

Key Symbols and Abbreviations

π_t: Current inflation rate

π_t^e: Expected inflation rate

π_{Target}: Explicit inflation

α: Capital's share in national income

$1 - \alpha$: Labor's share in national income

A: Index of how efficiently the economy transforms capital and labor into real GDP; total factor productivity

AD: Aggregate demand curve

AE: Aggregate expenditure

AS: Aggregate supply curve

B: U.S. Treasury bonds

C: Personal consumption expenditures

C: Currency in circulation

CA: Current account balance

CPI: Consumer price index

D: Checking account deposits

d: Depreciation rate

DP: Default-risk premium

ER: Excess reserves

E_t = Nominal exchange rate today

E_{t+1}^e = Expected nominal exchange rate one year from now

f: Rate of job finding

G: Government purchases

g_y: Growth of real GDP

I: Investment or gross private domestic investment

i: Nominal interest rate

i: Investment per worker

i_D: Domestic interest rate

i_F: Foreign interest rate

i_{Target}: Target for the nominal federal funds rate

i_{LT}: Long-term nominal interest rate

IS curve: Equilibrium in the goods market; shows the equilibrium combinations of the real interest rate and real GDP (or the output gap)

K: Quantity of capital goods available to firms, or the capital stock

k: Capital per worker, or the capital–labor ratio

k^*: Steady-state capital–labor ratio

L: Quantity of labor

LM curve: Equilibrium in the money market; shows the equilibrium combinations of the real interest rate and the output gap

M: Money supply

MB: Monetary base

m: Money multiplier

$M1$: A narrow measure of the money supply

$M2$: A broad measure of the money supply

M: Sum of currency in circulation, C, and checking account deposits, D

MP curve: Monetary policy curve

MPC: Marginal propensity to consume

MPK: Marginal product of capital

MPL: Marginal product of labor

n: Labor force growth rate

NCF: Net capital outflows

NX: Net exports of goods and services

P: Price level

PCE: Personal consumption expenditures price index

PD: Primary budget deficit

r: Real interest rate

r: Real rental price of capital

r_{LT}: Long-term real interest rate

r^*: Long-run equilibrium real federal funds rate

rr_D: Required reserve ratio

R: Nominal rental cost of capital

R: Bank reserves

RR: Required bank reserves

s: Rate of job separation

s: Saving rate

S_{Foreign}: Saving from the foreign sector

$S_{\text{Government}}$: Saving from the government

$S_{\text{Household}}$: Saving from households

s_t: Effects of a supply shock

T: Taxes

TR: Transfer payments

TSE: Term structure effect

U: Natural rate of unemployment

U_t: Current rate of unemployment

W: Nominal wage

w: Real wage

Y: Real GDP; also national income and total income

y: Real GDP per worker

$\widetilde{Y}$: Output gap

Y^D: Disposable income

Y^P: Potential GDP

Equations